THE EPIC OF MAN TO 1500

THE EPIC

TO

PRENTICE-HALL, INC.   *Englewood Cliffs, New Jersey*

OF MAN

1500

a collection of readings edited by

L. S. STAVRIANOS

THE EPIC OF MAN TO 1500
A Collection of Readings

EDITED BY L. S. STAVRIANOS

P-13-283309-3
C-13-283317-4
Library of Congress Catalog Card Number: 79-127058
Printed in the United States of America

Current printing (last digit):

10 9 8 7 6 5 4 3 2 1

PRENTICE-HALL INTERNATIONAL, INC., *London*
PRENTICE-HALL OF AUSTRALIA, PTY., LTD., *Sydney*
PRENTICE-HALL OF CANADA, LTD., *Toronto*
PRENTICE-HALL OF INDIA PRIVATE LIMITED, *New Delhi*
PRENTICE-HALL OF JAPAN, INC., *Tokyo*

Preface

The distinctive feature of this volume of readings is that it is globally oriented rather than West oriented. It reflects the viewpoint of an observer perched on the moon, surveying our planet as a whole, rather than that of one who is ensconced in London or Paris, or, for that matter, in Peking or Delhi. The guiding principle of this book has been that no Western movement or institution be treated unless non-Western movements or institutions of similar magnitude or world significance also be treated. This rationale explains the equal treatment accorded to all the Eurasian civilizations, rather than a concentration on Greece and Rome and the medieval West. It also explains the separate treatment of the non-Eurasian regions, which, until the expansion of Europe, were in fact largely, though not completely, isolated from Eurasia and from each other.

One criterion was followed in choosing the readings: their effectiveness in illuminating the subject under consideration. Short readings are sometimes more forceful than long ones, and secondary sources often provide more insight than primary ones. Accordingly the following selections are of varied lengths and from diverse sources. The connective tissue of narrative introductions is designed to provide an integrated account of major trends and to relate the selections to those trends.

L. S. STAVRIANOS

OTHER BOOKS BY L. S. STAVRIANOS:

The Balkans, 1815–1914

*Balkan Federation: A History of the Movement Toward
        Balkan Unity in Modern Times*

The Balkans Since 1453

The Epic of Modern Man: A Collection of Readings, editor

A Global History of Man (with others)

Greece: American Dilemma and Opportunity

The Ottoman Empire: Was It the Sick Man of Europe?

Readings in World History, editor (with others)

The World Since 1500: A Global History

The World To 1500: A Global History

Contents

Chapter Eleven

End of classical civilizations 176

Part

IV

MEDIEVAL CIVILIZATIONS OF EURASIA

500-1500

Chapter Twelve

Eurasian ecumene 205

Chapter Thirteen

Rise of Islam 210

MAN BEFORE
CIVILIZATION

Introduction:
nature of
world history

WORLD HISTORY: ORIGINS AND NATURE

1

Despite its obvious relevance for our present age, world history remains con-spicuous by its absence, both in writing and in teaching. In the following selection, a distinguished British scholar provides the historical background of this situation. He presents a survey of the history *of world history and analyzes the nature and prospects for this field of study.**

Of all the approaches to history none has been less explored than that which we usually call world-history or universal or 'oecumenical' history. And yet there is probably no type of history which is closer to our present preoccupations or more nearly attuned to the world in which we live. The reasons why the history most needed today is universal history lie all around us. They are a reflection of the unification of the world by science and technology and by the revolutionary advance of mass communications, a consequence of the familiar fact that we can no longer isolate ourselves from events in any quarter of the globe. Taiwan and Indo-China today are as near, and what happens there as relevant for us, as Greece or Portugal a century ago. Furthermore, the processes of industrial so-ciety, which originated in western Europe and North America, are now world-wide, their impact universal. Because the peoples of the Soviet Union, of China and India, and the other nations in Asia and Africa and Latin America, are playing an integral part in the political development of our world, a history which is limited to a more or less fragmentary account of the evolution of western

* Geoffrey Barraclough, "Universal History," in *Approaches to History: A Symposium,* ed. H. P. R. Finberg (London: Routledge & Kegan Paul Ltd.; Toronto: University of Toronto Press, 1962), pp. 83-87, 102-9.

civilization is inevitably less than adequate for present needs. The civilizations of China and India and Islam—in interplay, of course, with impulses coming from Europe—are just as much a part of the historical background of our times as is the civilization of the west. The emergence of the greater part of mankind from political subjection to political independence and political influence necessitates a shift in historical perspective. In short, the very forces which have transformed our view of the present compel us to widen our view of the past. It is this new situation which makes the need for universal history—by which we mean a history that looks beyond Europe and the west to humanity in all lands and ages—a matter of immediate practical urgency.

Nevertheless it would be a mistake to suppose that preoccupation with universal history is simply a consequence of the vast political changes which the world has undergone since 1939. In returning to world-history today we are returning to an older tradition which reaches back beyond the nineteenth century to the origins of modern critical historical study and which held its own until the close of the eighteenth century. For the men of the Enlightenment the idea of world-history was particularly congenial. It fitted in with their notion of progress, their view of mankind advancing steadily from primitive barbarism to reason and virtue and civilization. It fitted in also with their secular and rationalist spirit. So long as the authority of the Bible remained unchallenged, and all known historical events had to be fitted into a rigid biblical context, there could be no universal history as we know it; and since the Reformation affirmed rather than weakened the authority of the Bible, the concept of world-history was slow to take shape. Earlier historical interpretation, ever since the time of St. Augustine and Orosius, had followed the pattern of Christian revelation—creation, crucifixion, last judgement—or had divided the past into periods corresponding to the four world-empires presaged in the book of Daniel: the Assyrian, the Persian, the Greek, the Roman. Both schemes gave rise to insoluble difficulties, particularly when the attempt was made to relate them to peoples whose history fell outside the realm of Judaeo-Christian experience. The last great historical work written in the spirit of Christian eschatology was Bossuet's *Discours sur l'histoire universelle* (1681). But Bossuet's position was incompatible with the new spirit of scientific enquiry stirring in the late seventeenth century; and from around 1655 we can perceive how the irreconcilability of biblical tradition with the facts brought to light by the great discoveries was preparing the ground for a new, secular view of world-history. The French Calvinist Isaac de la Peyrère, who was unable to reconcile what he knew of Chinese history with the story of Adam and Eve, and the Dutch historian George Hornius, paved the way for Voltaire, whose *Essai sur les Moeurs et l'Esprit des Nations* (1752) is commonly regarded as "the first real world-history," and for the vast co-operative universal history—the first of its kind—which was published in England in thirty-eight volumes from 1736 onwards. Voltaire expressly accused his predecessor, Bossuet, of doing less than justice to the Arabs and the Babylonians and the Persians, and of ignoring the Chinese and Indians altogether; his history, in short, was unacceptable because his point of view was less than oecumenical.

The first great historical achievement of the eighteenth century was to bring the extra-European world into the field of enquiry and thus to make universal history possible. Its second achievement, associated from about 1760 with the rising Göttingen school led by J. C. Gatterer and A. L. Schlözer, was to ventilate and debate the problems of method and practice involved in the writing of world-history. But this early interest in universal history, so characteristic of the Age of Reason, began to falter at the time of the French Revolution, and from the close of the eighteenth century until the First World War—in many respects, indeed, until the Second World War—it was in eclipse. The causes were many One was the sense, as historical knowledge deepened and widened, of the insufficiency of the earlier attempts to view the history of the world as a whole. The eighteenth-century approach to world-history was more successful in conception than in execution. It expressed a vision of the general progress of society and culture, instead of a mere calendar of battles and political events; but too often it resulted in a series of facile generalizations or patterns of a philosophical nature imposed on history from outside without criticism or detailed study of the records. And even those, such as Herder and Hegel, who sought to do justice to the oriental peoples, wrote without an adequate foundation of concrete historical knowledge. It was therefore not surprising, as a more scientific attitude to history developed, that the superficiality of eighteenth-century historical writing was more deeply felt, and also that the very feasibility of universal history was called into question. In the first place, it was argued, the foundation of critical knowledge for anything so ambitious was totally insufficient; as Schlözer pointed out, the whole history of the ancient world would require re-writing if the Egyptian and Persian sources ever became as readily available as those of Greece and Rome. In the second place, it seemed that the writing of universal history made demands on human knowledge greater than the human intellect could ever hope to encompass; the field it covered was so immense that inevitably the knowledge which any single individual could bring to bear was too limited to carry the burden. Co-operative histories, on the other hand, amounted to little more than compendia or encyclopaedias; their result was not world-history, which treated mankind as a unity, but an aggregate of national histories with little, if any, cohesion or connection.

These were among the technical reasons why, from the beginning of the nineteenth century, world-history passed into the shadows. But fundamentally more important was a change in the climate of ideas. From the time of the French Revolution cosmopolitan gave way to national thinking; the nation-state asserted its place as the focus of human endeavour, the natural centre of all activity, and increasingly it was doubted whether there was any wider unity than the sovereign nation. But if the nation was the supreme expression of human striving, it followed that national history was the only type of history that ultimately mattered. There were, it is true, a few dissenting voices, such as that of the Swiss historian Jakob Burckhardt; but by the second half of the nineteenth century this was the prevailing view, borne out, it seemed, by the progress of national unification in Germany and Italy. Its victory was aided by the adaptation to historical study of vulgarized Darwinian concepts and by biological analogies, particularly the concepts of the struggle for existence and the survival of the fittest. If, in fact, there were such a thing as universal history in a world in which the ultimate realities were the nation-states, then its subject-matter could only be their rivalries and conflicts, the clash of empires, the attempts of particular powers to establish a position of hegemony and bring the world (or as much of the world as they could encompass) under their rule and influence. But in any case the nation remained the focal point of historical study, for it was here, in the heart of the people and in the minds of its leaders, that the driving forces originated.

It needed the catastrophe of two world wars to shake the foundations of this historical attitude, and even today it is still so engrained that it frequently determines the unconscious assumptions of historians who would not consciously subscribe to such a view. We do not need to consider the problematical character, in the world today, of the concept of sovereignty, which looms so large yet means so little, to realize that the era of the national state, as understood in the nineteenth century, was circumscribed in time and is now in the throes of a process of attrition. Its predominance was a historically conditioned phenomenon which lasted approximately a hundred and fifty years. By every test of national theory—language, racial unity, and the like—the political groups which count in the world of the second half of the twentieth century are supra-national in dimension, and the process of economic and technological change has cast serious doubt on the viability of the national state under modern conditions. If it is to keep pace with these developments history must break through the national framework in which the nineteenth century imprisoned it. . . . .

. . . . .

What differences may we expect, in practice, from history conceived and written from a universal point of view? What does the shift in perspective from a parochial or national to a global perspective imply? The question is best answered by practical examples; and it will suffice if we take one from the thirteenth, one from the sixteenth, and one from the nineteenth centuries.

For English historians the dominant feature of the early thirteenth century was the constitutional struggle under John and Henry III; for French historians it was the consolidation of French unity and the strengthening of the monarchy by Philip Augustus and Louis IX; for German historians, it was Frederick II's restoration of imperial fortunes, the conflict of empire and papacy, and the collapse of Germany's position in Europe after Frederick's death in 1250. If, however, we sidestep these national positions, each with its own peculiar emphasis, and try instead to pick out the events which were important from a global point of view, the result is totally different. The most arresting event of the period from the point of view of world-history was undoubtedly the great conquering movement of the Mongol people under Genghis Khan and his son Ogdai, who extended their dominion over China and vast tracts of Asia and swept west across the steppes of Russia into Hungary, Poland, and Silesia. Neither king John nor king Philip nor even the emperor Frederick II was a world-figure (though Frederick came nearer to that rank); Genghis Khan indubitably was. Hence the historian with a global vision will place the great Mongol ruler, whose achievements were far more momentous for mankind than anything which happened in England in his lifetime, at the centre of his picture; and he will redesign the rest to fit the altered perspective. Even European history, looked at from this point of view, will be seen in different proportions: that is to say, the familiar story of the rise of the western national monarchies will loom less large, and the emphasis will shift to Russia and the borderlands of eastern Europe, which felt the brunt of the Mongol incursions, while the historian of the church will be less preoccupied with the quarrels of empire and papacy and more concerned with papal efforts to cope with the situation confronting Christianity in the east.

When we pass to the sixteenth and early seventeenth centuries, the situation is different; but once again a global point of view—or an effort to put those things first which have a more than national or continental bearing—results in a far-reaching change of emphasis. For European historians the main threads in this period are dynastic conflicts—particularly the conflict of France and Spain in Italy, the Netherlands, and Germany—the rise of absolute monarchies, the Protestant revolt and the wars of religion, the Thirty Years' War, the struggle for mastery of the seas, and the beginnings of overseas expansion. From a global point of view much of this is of subordinate interest, if not irrelevant. Nevertheless, this time Europe remains in the centre of the picture, because even in universal terms there is no doubt that the outstanding development of world-wide significance was the emergence of Europe from a peripheral to a central position. At the close of the fifteenth century Europe was only one of four Eurasian centres of civilization, and by no means the most prominent. By the end of the eighteenth century it had gained control of the ocean routes, organized an immensely profitable worldwide commerce, and conquered vast territories in the Americas and India and Siberia. Thus in the perspective of world-history the period stands out as a period of transition from the regional isolation of the pre-1492 era to the European global hegemony of the nineteenth century; and for this reason, not because of a narrowly 'Europacentric' view of the past, Europe as the main centre of innovation and decision remains prominent. But the aspects of European history which receive emphasis are inevitably different. In terms of their global significance, the battles that stand out will not be those, such as Pavia (1525), which loom so large in the common run of history books, but Mohacs (1526), Lepanto (1571), Itamarca (1640); and it is significant that two of the three were naval battles. The defeat of the Turks at Lepanto, in particular, marked the shift of the axis of European history away from the Mediterranean to the Atlantic seaboard in the west and thus a significant stage in the history of European expansion. This expansion, as the distinguishing feature of the period— in the medieval centuries Europe had been hemmed in by the expanding civilizations of the Near East—is from a universal point of view the central theme. The first question it raises—a question which has not hitherto been systematically studied, though it takes us deep into European history—is what the roots of expansion were, or why it started from Europe and not from one of the other Eurasian centres of civilization. The second question is the manner in which the nature and course of European expansion was affected by the Chinese, Moslem, American, and Eurasian civilizations with which it came into contact. Thirdly, it raises the question of the impact of overseas expansion on European life and culture; and finally it is important to see the fluctuations in Europe's attitude to the non-European world—the rise and decline of respect for the Ottoman Empire, India, and China, the different attitudes of Christian missionaries to the American peoples, and the like. These are some of the questions, largely neglected, which an attempt to review and reinterpret what we call the 'early modern period' from a global point of view brings into new prominence.

When we come to the nineteenth century, we reach a period when the predominance of Europe is as marked in the economic and technological as in the political field, and when the expansion of Europe had carried European ideas and values to every quarter of the globe. Never at any moment in history, it would seem, was there more ample justification for setting Europe at the centre of world affairs; never can we more confidently say that what went on in Europe, the rivalries and conflicts of the European powers, determined the course of events in Asia and Africa and the new world. But here again, if we look at the situation from a global rather than a European standpoint, the familiar dimensions change and new factors come into view. The traditional story, with its concentration on the rise of German and Italian nationalism, the European balance of power, the question of the Straits and of the Narrow Seas, is not wrong, but for a world-wide perspective it is inadequate. Down to 1914, it seemed as though the relations of the European powers would settle the future of the world, and that European expansion was simply carrying the principle of balance of power, on which the relations of the European nations were based, into the other continents. In reality, as the transformation of the war of 1914–18 from a European into a world war was soon to demonstrate, that was only half the story. When the tottering Ottoman Empire was admitted to the concert of European powers in 1856, and when, a generation later, the United States and Japan were recognized as 'great powers', in addition to the six nations which happened at the time to be the strongest in Europe, it was clear that world-leadership was no longer a European prerogative. Hence the detailed studies of European diplomacy and of the conflicts of the European powers to which historians have given so much attention need to be balanced by an analysis of the contacts of the expanding imperialisms of Great Britain and Russia and the United States, on the northwest frontier of India, in Persia, in China, and on the Pacific seaboard of the North American continent, in California and Oregon and Alaska. These contacts, and the conflicts which arose from them, marked the rise, in place of the European balance of power, of the world-wide international system under which we live; they are of fundamental importance because—unlike the international politics of Bismarckian Europe—they were the beginning of a new era in world-history. . . .

. . . . .

It should also be clear from the examples which have been given that there are no insuperable obstacles on a practical level to the study of world-history. It is no more difficult to teach and to learn world-history, at all levels from school to university, than it is to teach and learn European history; indeed, the basic method is exactly the same—that is to say, just as no one in a one-year survey of modern or medieval European history at the university would set out to cover the separate histories of England, France, Germany, Italy, Spain, Russia, the Balkans, and Scandinavia, so no one would attempt to deal, one by one, with all the world's civilizations. But it is no more impossible to convey a basic understanding of the characteristics and experiences of the major civilizations of the world, and of world-wide movements such as the diffusion of the great religions, the invasions of the central Eurasian nomads, or the expansion of Europe, than it is for the historian of Europe to describe the development of the states which were important at any given period, and European movements such as the Reformation, the Industrial Revolution, or Nationalism. The amount of knowledge to be absorbed is no larger nor is it basically more diversified; it is simply chosen on a different principle. . . . Every present indication is that the central problems with which we shall have to cope in the next generation will not be European problems but the relationship between the west and the peoples of Asia and Africa.

. . . . .

In the world as constituted today, not to teach world-history is to court disaster. If history is falling into disrepute, if for many people it seems to be lost in unessentials instead of guiding us to the threshold of the world we know, the reason is not far to seek: what it needs is a larger vision, a breakthrough to new dimensions. It is this breakthrough to new dimensions that world-history offers— and a vision of historical reality which measures up to our experience and to the perspectives opening out before us in the second half of the twentieth century.

From earliest times man has been self-centered. This self-centeredness is characteristic of primitive peoples living today. The tribal names of some of these peoples, such as the Zuni, the Dene, and the Kiowa, are native terms for "human beings," that is, themselves. Those outside the tribal group are beyond their mental horizon. They cannot perceive mankind as a unit; they feel no common cause with their species. Thus man traditionally has been locally-minded, raising high the barriers between "we" and "they." This provincialism persisted even after man developed high civilizations, though it was now more sophisticated and disguised. Yet basically all peoples still saw themselves, and persist in seeing themselves, as the hub of history. This is especially true of the "Westerners" who have been dazzled and misled by the fact that their civilization has affected the entire globe in recent centuries. The nature and extent of this self-centeredness of mankind is made clear in the following selection by an American authority on world history.*

In the sixteenth century the Italian missionary, Matteo Ricci, brought to China a European map of the world showing the new discoveries in America. The Chinese were glad to learn about America, but one point in the map offended them. Since it split the earth's surface down the Pacific, China appeared off at the right-hand edge; whereas the Chinese thought of themselves as literally the "Middle Kingdom," which should be in the centre of the map. Ricci pacified them by drawing another map, splitting the Atlantic instead, so that China appeared more central; and maps are still commonly drawn that way in that part of the world.

Europeans of course have clung to the first type of map, showing Europe in the upper centre; while the commonest maps in North America show the U.S.A. in that post of honour, even at the cost of splitting a continent in two. The temptation not only to put one's own land in the centre of the map, but one's own people in the centre of history, seems to be universal.

The most famous case of this is indeed that of the "Middle Kingdom." Many Chinese used to suppose that the temple of Heaven at the Emperor's capital, Peking, marked the exact centre of the earth's surface. To be sure, Chinese scholars even in the Middle Ages were aware that China could not be said to be mathematically central; they knew the general lay of Europe and Africa and the Indian Ocean, and a writer could remark that the "centre" of the earth was along the equator. Nevertheless, even for sober historians the pivotal fact of human history was the condition of the great Chinese empire, in which was concentrated all the splendour of polished civilization.

At times the empire was strong. Then (as they told it) the Emperor was able to command peace among the fair lands stretching out around his capital; the choicest products of the mountains on the one hand and the sea on the other poured in to enrich the vast fertile plains of the empire; and the barbarians of the less favoured lands beyond—deserts, mountains, and remote islands—divided and weakened by the Emperor's wise policies, came to bring humble tribute and to learn what they could of the arts of civilization.

Thus came the Koreans, the Japanese, the Tibetans; thus came also the English

* M. G. S. Hodgson, "In the Centre of the Map," *The UNESCO Courier*, VIII (May 1956), 16-18.

from their distant islands, seeking Chinese luxuries and offering little in return the Emperor could approve—such as opium. Even the English envoys were graciously received, but when they showed want of proper respect for the Emperor they were dismissed with contempt.

At other times the imperial power grew feeble, local rulers seized power and tyrannized the people, prosperity faded. It was then (as they told it) the barbarians came as insulting conquerors, and civilization was eclipsed in the world. Thus came the Central Asian Turks, thus came the Mongols under Kublai Khan; and thus came the English when the Manchu dynasty was declining, invading the Middle Kingdom (whose wealth attracted every barbarous nation) and forcing their crude ways upon the people.

It could in fact be claimed that for a time China was the wealthiest and most populous, the most aesthetically cultivated and even the most powerful state on the earth; but when this fact was made the basis for the Chinese picture of the world, the result was tragic miscalculation.

For the medieval Hindu the world was a place for the purification of souls. Kings and their empires came and went, the gods themselves arose and perished —time was infinite, space immense, with unlimited opportunity for every soul to reap in birth after rebirth what it had sown. In much of the universe, indeed, souls dwelt in untroubled bliss; it was the distinction of our own toiling, earthy regions that here men could choose responsibility between good and evil and their consequences. Here life was arranged for the exercise of virtue, each caste of men having its own function in society; if a man fulfilled one role well, in another life he would have a higher role to play, and might eventually rise beyond the transient vicissitudes of existence altogether.

Accordingly, so far as history was significant, it was as ages varied in the degree to which society was well enough ordered to give virtue its due place. As a given cosmic cycle wore on, disorder increased and justice faded. Our own age (they explained) was in the latter part of such a cycle; only in the central parts of the earthy regions—in India, that is—was society still well ordered: there Brahmins still offered sacrifices and the other castes ruled or served according to their status.

In the benighted lands to the east and west—so tainted already with decline that pious Brahmins dared not set foot there—souls were doomed to be born as barbarous Mlecchas; there they lived unhallowed lives till they should earn the right to be born in India. As our degenerate age drew on, even in India itself the social order was upset, rulers rose from the basest castes, and finally even Mlecchas entered as conquerors—Muslims from the west, and even the remotest Europeans. Through all this outward humiliation, however, the Hindu could know that there in the central lands where the sacred Ganges flowed he could still live the way of truth and holiness—inaccessible to lesser breeds of men—and aspire to the highest degrees of rebirth.

To the medieval Muslim the world looked very different from what it did to his Chinese or to his Hindu contemporaries. History was not a matter of the varying strength and weakness of an imperial centre of authority and civilization, nor was it a passing incident in an infinite succession of worlds. Rather it was the story of a single species created just some 5,000 years ago by God to do His will once for all. From Adam on, God had sent thousands of prophets to the various peoples, bringing to each its laws and sciences; at last he sent Mohammed, proclaiming the final law in which all earlier truth was perfected and which was gradually to prevail over the whole world, replacing all former laws.

Many Muslims believed that Mohammed's birthplace, Mecca, was the centre of the earth's surface. To Mecca, men pilgrimaged yearly from the farthest parts of the earth, and it was supposed that in the heavens above it the angels themselves performed worship; here was the very throne of God, where heaven and earth were nearest. To be sure, scholars knew that the earth was a sphere, and God equally present everywhere in the hearts of the believers. But their more sober picture of the world was equally effective in supporting the eminence of Islam. They thought of the inhabited quarter of the globe as a land mass lying between the equator and the North Pole, and between the oceans to the west and to the east—roughly Eurasia and northern Africa.

This was divided into seven "climes" from south to north, and from extreme heat to cold. Muslims writing in the latitude of Syria or Iran explained that in the hot south men grew lazy and so remained backward in civilization; and likewise in the far north where it was cold—in northern Europe, for instance—men's skins were pallid and their minds sluggish. Hence it was that only in the central, moderate climes, like the Mediterranean lands or Iran, were minds most active and civilization most advanced; from there the blessings of Islam were gradually being brought even to the remotest areas, among the Negroes in the hot south and the white men in the cold north.

World histories written by medieval Muslims, might therefore, have a preliminary section on the older Persians, Hebrews, and Romans; but, from the time of Mohammed, the modern part of the history dealt almost exclusively with the Islamic peoples. Other peoples might be curious in their quaint ways; the Chinese might be clever at gadgets, and the Greeks at philosophy; but now the only peoples whose story really counted were those who had abandoned their old local creeds with their many idols or their many saints' images and joined in the imageless worship of the One God, in the international brotherhood of Islam which, advancing farther every year, already stretched from the straits of Gibraltar to those of Malacca.

The West-Europeans of the same age had many of the same ideas of history and geography as the Muslims, getting them from the same Greek and Hebrew sources; but their interpretation was very different. For them history was the story of God's progressive dispensations of law or of grace to his favoured people. Out of the descendants of Adam, God had first chosen the Hebrews, but with the coming of Christ it was a "new Israel," the Christians, that received His favours.

Even among the Christians God had made a further selection—casting aside those of the Levant and Greece as heretics or schismatics, in favour of the West-Europeans under the Pope at Rome. The favoured people of each age lived under a succession of great monarchies: in earlier times Chaldean, Persian, and Greek, which all conquered the Hebrews; but last and greatest, under which Christ Himself was born, the empire of Rome in the west, which should endure till Judgement Day.

The West-Europeans allowed that the centre of the world's surface was Jerusalem (by exaggerating the length of the Mediterranean, their maps could show Spain and China as equally distant from it); but they assured themselves that, just as at the beginning of history Paradise was in the east where the sun rises, so in these latter days the centre of God's vicarship on earth was in the west, where the sun sets; henceforth Rome was the centre of all authority, spiritual and temporal.

In modern times all these medieval pictures of the world have vanished, or been modified. With the discovery of America and the circumnavigation of the globe, the discovery that Earth is a tiny planet in an immensity of space, that mankind has been upon it hundreds of thousands of years and is still a newcomer, we have had to rethink our situation. The great ideals of faith and of culture have to be seen in spiritual terms rather than as reflected in the very map of the universe.

The West-Europeans were the first to be really faced with the new discoveries and have consequently led the way toward creating a new picture of the world. But they have not yet escaped the temptation to make geography and history centre upon themselves. One need only examine the table of contents of any proper Western "world history." Civilization began in Mesopotamia and Egypt (with perhaps some local variants in India and China); but (it would seem) soon history was almost a monopoly of the Greeks; and though other peoples might still be curious, in their quaint ways, hereafter it was really only Europe that counted—and after the rise of Rome only Western Europe; here was the home of truth and liberty.

If during long centuries it was hard to find either truth or liberty in Western Europe, this period was regretfully labelled the Dark Ages of mankind; but in modern times the West-Europeans have duly gone forth to enlighten (and subdue) the world—so that the history of a henceforth "Westernized" world may be safely reduced almost to that of the West itself.

The map of the world is constructed accordingly. Westerners distinguish five or six "continents": Africa, Asia, North and South America—and Europe. It is sometimes ingenuously remarked how much smaller Europe is than the "other continents"—yet in political discussions, in grouping statistics, or in historical comparisons these divisions repeatedly recur as if fixed by nature.

In European "world atlases" each European country has its own map, with the rest of the world in a few pages at the end. The map ordinarily selected to show the world as a whole is ideally suited to reinforce this way of seeing mankind. On the Mercator world map not only is Europe in the upper centre it is represented as a good deal larger than the other great culture areas. Most of these lie south of the fortieth parallel, while Europe is almost wholly north of it, where Mercator's projection begins to exaggerate the size of things enormously.

Accordingly even on the world map, which ought to provide a sense of proportion, there is space to name a great many places in Europe, while in other populous centres like India or China, shown on a much smaller scale, only a few chief places need be indicated. Although equal-area projections of the world have long been available, in which shapes as well as sizes are much less distorted, Westerners understandably cling to a projection which so markedly flatters them. They explain (as if they were engaged in nothing but sailing) that the true angles given on the Mercator map are of convenience to navigators; and in atlases and wall-maps, in books of reference and in newspapers, when Westerners turn to see what the world looks like as a whole their preconceptions are authoritatively gratified.

The story is often told of a small tribe whose word for "mankind" was the name of the tribe itself. Other tribes were merely incidental in their picture of the world—perhaps not even fully human. Chinese, Hindus, Muslims, and Westerners alike have smiled perhaps too quickly at the rather perilous naiveté of that small tribe.

Chapter Two

Man the food gatherer

MEN ARE MORE ALIKE   3

*The fundamental basis of world history is the biological unity of mankind. Indeed the two are completely interactive and interdependent. Yet the emphasis customarily is placed on the differences among men rather than on their far more numerous and basic similarities. This common distortion is corrected here by an American historian who draws upon the resources of several disciplines to show that "Men are More Alike." ***

. . . *Homo sapiens* is a species! Within the species varieties occur. But as with the trees and forests the varieties ought not obscure the view. It is upon certain aspects of the common nature and common cultural development of the species that this essay is focused. . . .

The outward likenesses, often overlooked because they are commonplace, are easy to see. All men walk upright, and, unlike most other vertebrates, normally use stairs instead of branches. Nine tenths of the mature members of the species measure four-feet-ten to six-feet-two in height, a relatively small difference if all vertical dimensions are considered. Nearly all men as adults weigh from 90 to 220 pounds, a small range compared to the variations in animal life. All of them require daily, though they may not get them, from 2500 to 4000 calories and a certain variety of vitamins to be gained from meat, grains, green and leafy vegetables, and fruit. With few exceptions all of them have facility for manipulating their thumbs, and for conceptual thought and speech as no other animals do. More than any other living thing they can store up knowledge, establish traditions. They are not forced to start

* Boyd C. Shafer, "Men Are More Alike," *American Historical Review*, LVII, No. 3 (April 1952), 593-612. Reprinted with permission.

from scratch but can, though this is rare enough, begin with the accumulated experience and wisdom of the species. Unlike the dog and the ape, men may use (though they rarely do) the spoken word and books to avoid the mistakes of their ancestors and thus determine the direction of human evolution. Though the opposite seems most often true, man is, to a greater degree than any other form of life, teachable. He is at times, potentially at least, rational and the ranges of his comprehension and adaptability are wider. Men, it also seems, are singular in that they can modify what were once termed their "instincts," and may, without artificial conditioning, acquire neuroses. At the same time only they find escape in laughter and tears. . . .

Men are all vertebrates and mammals. They are all multicellular animals with the same kinds of nervous, blood, respiratory, and reproductive systems. The same approximate percentages of chemical elements make up their bodies. So long as there are males and females reproduction between all varieties is possible, even probable. Their females all carry their young nine months and usually produce only one offspring at a time. Maturation for all offspring is comparatively slow. Unlike all other animals the desire of their adults for sexual activity is continuous: the adult male is normally capable of reproducing at any time and the adult female of about fifteen to forty-five years of age twelve times a year. Probably none of them, Lysenko notwithstanding, can inherit acquired characteristics. All of them, regardless of race or nationality, have the same few O, A, B, and AB blood types. Though learned studies use terms like brachiocephalic and dolichocephalic their head shapes vary little, all being somewhat oblong. While their hair is round or oblong and straight or kinky, it is hair, and all usually have it in slightly varying intensities at the same points on their bodies. Their coloration runs from white to black but all gradations exist, while microscopic examination shows but slight differences in pigmentation and even these differences seem rapidly to be fading.

Where differences occur, little is known of what they signify. On the basis of fact no one can say whether color, hair, head shape, or blood type have any relationship to the quality of a man, to his character, philosophy, and intelligence, or to how he will react in any circumstance. Observable differences like these may be easily classified and the classifications statistically presented in impressive, encyclopedic volumes. That is all. These particular differences occur. Nothing more can be added, no more meaning can be attached to them. . . .

Since Darwin men's differences have been transformed into a sliding scale for moral evaluation, a scale which somehow indicates inferiority and superiority. During the latter half of the nineteenth century men calling themselves scientists, though their interpretation of "survival of the fittest" was certainly erroneous, first erected complex classifications of human characteristics with the clear purpose of showing how much fitter and therefore better were some groups of men than others. Their reasoning (read Houston Stewart Chamberlain or Madison Grant for the popular versions) went something like this: (1) men are naturally different as is proved by their observable physical and mental traits; (2) some are naturally fitter, hence superior; (3) some races and nations are naturally fittest and therefore superior; and (4) nature and evolution made men this way and hence some races and nations should be masters and others servants. With this structure of illogic, differences became the ideological basis of social action. And further to prove superiority, the significance of the obvious differences has been deepened and new distinctions are fanatically sought.

No intelligent man who knows anything of science and methods of scientific research need be told of the absurdity of this unreason. . . .

Who are the "fittest," the little, wiry men who formed the bulk of Rommel's North African army, the giants who play American football and basketball, the pale, bespectacled, physical scientists in the laboratories, the emaciated saints of the Middle Ages who surely went to Heaven soonest, or that "cream" of contemporary Western nations, the steel-nerved navigators and pilots of the long-range bombing planes? If it be agreed that the last are today's fittest, does it follow that their respective races or nations are? Are races and nations fittest just because they can destroy other races and nations most efficiently? Does, finally, fitness indicate anything about superiority unless certain prejudices are accepted as absolute values? Does, indeed, survival indicate anything but luck? The survivors in the next war, as in those of the past, will very likely be those who survive—nothing more. . . .

Systematic theories of racial differences are of recent origin, dating back for the most part only to the eighteenth century when it was becoming more important to be superior and powerful than to go to Heaven. The theories (they are only that by the grace of inaccurate terminology) have varied widely in time and often with the race or nationality of the investigator. Moreover, racial characters, if they exist, seem to have changed quite unbelievably through the years. Once ("Nordic") England was called "merry" but that was not the England of Attlee and Cripps. Once a Venetian ambassador spoke of the "low morals and excellent cooking" of the English but that was in the sixteenth not the nineteenth century. In praising folly, Erasmus spoke of the martial reputation of the ("Mediterranean") Spaniards, a characteristic few would accuse them of possessing in our times. Once what we call the northern European ("Nordics?") were supposed to be "full of spirit" but unintelligent (Aristotle); the modern version is quite different. None of this proves that theories based upon race are completely untrue. It shows only that there is nothing scientific or God-given about them and that they are for the most part merely *a priori* guesses of men about other men.

The fallacies based upon racial interpretation of human societies may be slowly crumbling. Those pertaining to nationalism still cling as tenaciously as only prejudices can. The human race seems united on a common desire to destroy itself and nationalism happens to be one of the most popular, contemporary methods.

For the present purposes nationalism may be defined as a sentiment of unity held by a social group, a sentiment based upon an apparent common cultural heritage and upon a desire to live separately and independently as a group in the future. This sentiment of unity at the same time is a sentiment of exclusiveness, and members of nations generally feel indifferent or hostile to members of other like nations. Both the unity and the exclusiveness are founded upon real or imagined differences between national groups. If the people of a group has a common past (and historians may give them one if they do not) of language, race, religion, if it has its own historically claimed rocks and rills and "natural" boundaries, in short, if its members have a common culture and a common geographic location, then its language, race, religion, and rocks and rills are held to be different from, and by a long jump in logic better and more beautiful than, those of other like groups. The well-developed nationalist asserts, "My country, right or wrong," or *Deutschland über Alles.* "A true nationalist," declared the *Action francaise,* which in the French Third Republic was no minor authority, is one who "places the fatherland above everything. . . ."

Of course, there is no more natural basis for the nationalistic interpretation of man and his relationships than there is for prejudices concerning race. . . . Every nationality is a mixture of many peoples, races, tribes, families. The modern French are in origin of the Mediterranean, Alpine, Nordic, and a good many other "races."

The modern Italians are compounded of Etruscans, Ligurians, Romans, Iberians, Greeks, Gauls, Teutons, and in recent times almost every nationality in Europe and some in Africa. Nor are the Germans, Russians, or Americans any purer.

All modern history is a document attesting to national intermixture: migrations, invasions, wars, conquests, marriages. In various degrees every nationality is a conglomeration of the short and tall, the round and the long headed, the dumb and the smart, the virtuous and the sinful. Any one of these characteristics is endlessly duplicated. In fact the attempt to classify nations according to any biological or inherent mental characteristic is only a naive error inherited from early propagandist historians like Tacitus and pseudo-anthropologists like Gobineau. Defoe could have been speaking of any nationality with his

> Thus from a mixture of all kinds began
> That heterogeneous thing, an Englishman.

. . . Men are physiologically, racially, nationally at least as much alike as they are different. That is not surprising. *Homo sapiens* is a species. The individuals of the species are not only much alike but so are their problems and their institutions. This is not so strange either. They have inhabited one globe in a comparatively short period of whatever is universal time. They all have had to provide for sustenance and protection against the elements. They have all had to seek the best circumstances for reproduction and the rearing of their children. They all have had a common desire for some kind of creative activity, for a "noble employment of their leisure" if not an "instinct for workmanship." Now they have the common problem of controlling science so that they may survive. . . .

Schiller sang, "What is the greatest of nations but a fragment?"—A fragment of humanity, one might add, which the Jew Jesus, the Frenchman Montesquieu, the German Goethe held to be above the arbitrary divisions into which petty patriots, narrow scholars, sadistic dictators, cheap journalists, and popular novelists have divided mankind.

4   CULTURE DIFFUSION

As fundamental as the concept of man's biological unity, emphasized in the above reading, is the concept of his cultural unity. Man is man, and is fundamentally different from the animals about him, because he is a cultural creature—because he creates his own culture, which has become an increasingly significant component of his environment. This raises the basic question of culture diffusion, for the history of man is fundamentally the history of cultural interaction and exchange. In the following selection, a distinguished British archaeologist analyzes the nature, the antiquity, and the extent of culture diffusion in man's past.*

* V. Gordon Childe, "A Prehistorian's Interpretation of Diffusion." Reprinted by permission of the publishers from Harvard Tercentenary Conference of Arts & Sciences, *Independence, Convergence, and Borrowing,* pp. 3, 4, 7-11, 14. Cambridge, Mass.: Harvard University Press, Copyright 1937, 1965, by the President and Fellows of Harvard College.

. . . Prehistoric archaeology has effected a revolution in man's knowledge of his own past, comparable in scale to the revolutions achieved by modern physics and astronomy. Instead of the beggarly five thousand years patchily and fitfully illumined by written records, archaeology now offers the historian a vista of two hundred and fifty thousand years; like a new optical instrument it has already extended our range of backward vision fiftyfold and is every year expanding the field surveyed with the new perspective. With the field of historical vision thus deepened and enlarged the sociologist should be able better to gauge both the antiquity of diffusion and its significance as a factor in promoting progress.

Of course, the archaeologist's attention is focused primarily on man's material culture—the equipment, the extracorporeal organs, that enable human groups to survive and multiply. But within the human species improvement in that equipment takes the place of the hereditary bodily modifications that demarcate genera in the biologists's evolutionary hierarchy. And so such improvement may be taken as a proof of progress in the sense that organic evolution attests a survival of the fittest. But the speed of progress, thus defined, so extraordinarily rapid as compared with organic evolution, seems to be due to the distinctively human capacity of learning from one's neighbor; inventions and devices, created by one society as adjustments to its special environment, can be adopted by another and adapted to its rather different requirements. But that is exactly what I mean by diffusion. To me diffusion means essentially the pooling of ideas, building up from many sides the cultural capital of humanity, or, to use the late Professor Dixon's happy metaphor, diffusion is the process "whereby the achievements of all peoples are distilled into the vessel of Culture."

Now the rigorous proof of diffusion as just defined is essentially a task for archaeology. . . .

. . . Archaeology traces with more or less confidence migrations whereby human groups, or at least the "cultures" symbolizing such, were brought into different environments or into immediate contact with other human groups. The demonstration of folk-migrations is so familiar from European archaeology that it suffices here to recall that such mass movements almost invariably involve intercourse between differently adjusted communities. Whatever the ultimate fate of either party, invaders inevitably learn something from those whose former territory they traverse or occupy; the older inhabitants, for their part, cannot fail to borrow some items from the newcomers' equipment.

But archaeology can also demonstrate intercourse between groups that severally remain fixed in their proper territories. It may be well to indicate briefly the methods of the demonstration. This consists of course in tracing interchange of products between the communities concerned. The most unequivocal of such indications of intercourse is afforded by the transportation of substances far from places where they occur in nature. Even in the Old Stone Age during the last European ice age, marine shells and fish-bones have been found far from the sea in the caves of the Dordogne; indeed, Breuil has suggested a regular commerce between the familiar reindeer hunters of the interior and coastal tribes not as yet directly known to archaeology. And, of course, by the New Stone Age the transportation of materials over long distances is established by many cases: to the familiar examples like the flint from Grande Pressigny (in west-central France) used in Switzerland, Belgium, and the Channel Islands, or the Mediterranean shells from Danubian graves in Bohemia, Central Germany, and the Rhineland new instances are constantly being added. For example, axes made of Preselite (blue stone) from Pembrokeshire in southwestern Wales have recently been identified in North Ireland and in Wiltshire, while axes from stone occurring only at Graig Lwydd on the slopes of Penmaen Mawr, North Wales, were carried as far afield as Wiltshire.

And sometimes this transportation of substances not only reveals the possibility of a commerce in ideas too, but also explicitly attests actual diffusion. The emmer wheat grown by the earliest neolithic inhabitants of Denmark and the sheep they bred are not descendants of any wild species native to northern or western Europe. The wild ancestors of emmer must be sought in the east Mediterranean region, and the Stone Age sheep of Europe are believed to be of Asiatic stock. Thus in Denmark, and indeed throughout northwestern Europe, the very traits, which on the economic interpretation of prehistory define the New Stone Age, are themselves incontrovertible evidences of diffusion. Here the food-producing economy based on the cultivation of exotic cereals and the breeding of foreign animals cannot have been evolved locally, but must have been introduced from without.

But it is the archaeological exploration of the Near East and the co-operation therein of geology that are providing the most striking and also the earliest proofs of frequent communication over really substantial distances. In the neolithic settlements around the Fayum Lake, perhaps the oldest yet known and dating from 5000 B.C., Caton-Thompson collected shells brought from the Mediterranean and others from the Red Sea, as well as various exotic stones of still uncertain provenance. A little later obsidian was being used for the manufacture of tools by the earliest inhabitants of the Tigris-Euphrates delta and of Assyria as well as by the predynastic Egyptians. Yet supplies of the volcanic glass are geographically very restricted; the Armenian massif or the island of Melos are the most likely sources. The only recorded sources of lapis lazuli are on the Iranian plateau. Yet this stone was being imported into Egypt and Sumer by 4000 B.C. and during the first half of the third millennium was reaching the Indus valley, Baluchistan, Russian Turkestan, and Troy, on the Asiatic shore of the Hellespont. It would be tedious to continue this catalogue, to which each well-conducted expedition adds new items. The transportation of exotic materials over long distances thus attested in prehistoric times only foreshadows that intensive importation of raw materials into Egypt and Sumer to which written records also bear witness as soon as they begin.

Scarcely less conclusive proofs of intercourse are afforded by the distributions of manufactured articles. Of course *ex hypothesi* its "country of origin" is not stamped upon a prehistoric commodity, but it can generally be determined with a high degree of probability. Sometimes the actual factories can be located. At Graig Lwydd, for instance, was found not only the sole deposit of the rock used but also the workshop where the axes, exported to Wiltshire, were fashioned.

But generally the place of origin is determined mainly by statistical and cartographic methods. For instance, we scrutinize closely and compare a large sample of seals from various regions in the Near East. Among several hundred from Mesopotamian sites we notice six or seven differing from the rest in form, technique, material, and style. Only from the Indus valley can we find many seals exhibiting the same peculiarities, but there they constitute the bulk of the collection. It is therefore a fairly safe inference that the seals in question were manufactured in the Indus cities. The stray specimens from Sumer can only be exports thence or just possibly products of an Indian seal-cutter plying his native craft in Sumer. Or again thousands of sherds of fine knob-ornamented wheel-made pottery from Harappa and Mohenjo-daro define both the distinctive character and the Indian origin of the fabric; the stray fragments picked up at Eshnuna in Babylonia are as clearly imports as is an English beer-bottle, stamped with the makers' name, picked up in an East African kraal, and their origin is no more doubtful. In practice of course archaeologists abbreviate the demonstration. They are sufficiently familiar with their material to recognize whether a type is "distinctive" without setting out mathematically its frequency in a random sample; and they prefer to establish the origin of the type by plotting its distribution on a map rather than by tabulating figures. Such abbreviation in no wise detracts from the statistical accuracy of the argument. But of course in prehistory statistics may be just as misleading as in any other science. Certain metal types happen to turn up most frequently in Northern Europe although neither the raw materials nor the technical presuppositions for their production were available there. Still, using his statistics judiciously and armed with sufficient knowledge to discount freaks of distribution, the prehistorian can with reasonable confidence recognize a South Russian pin in a neolithic tomb in Denmark, British spear-heads in graves or hoards of the Bronze Age in Holstein, the Rhineland, and the Paris basin, Syrian vases in First Dynasty tombs in Egypt, and Egyptian slate palettes in Byblos before 3000 B.C.

Data of the kind just described are submitted as affording rigorous proofs of intercourse between scattered human groups. Considering the limitations of the archaeologist's material—furs, feathers, textiles, basketry, and wooden objects that bulk so large in the commerce of contemporary "primitives" have been irrevocably lost—the paucity of likely articles submitted to petrographic or chemical analysis, and the still restricted range of scientific exploration, they establish a remarkable amount of intercourse at surprisingly early periods. . . .

. . . Archaeology can offer concrete and tangible proofs of intercourse beginning already during the Ice Age and growing ever more intensive and extensive. As fast as excavation advances into hitherto unexplored regions or unplumbed depths of the Old World tangible proofs come to light of intercourse with more familiar regions. Already archaeology can demonstrate beyond cavil a web of communications extending from the Atlantic to the Oxus and the Indus by the third millennium before our era as surely as can history from the tenth century thereafter. Systematic excavations in Siberia and China, in North Africa and Arabia, will surely reveal further extensions of the web. And deeper diggings may well demonstrate an enhanced antiquity for the nexus in all directions. . . .

CULTURE OF THE FOOD GATHERERS   5

*The culture of contemporary food gatherers cannot be assumed to be identical to that of early man in Paleolithic times. Nevertheless the manner of earning a livelihood was the same, and this doubtless determined a basic similarity of cultures in fundamentals if not in details. Hence the significance of the following classic account of the Arunta tribe of Australia for shedding light on the presumed general nature of Paleolithic society. One of the authors of this study was a trained scientist, and the other an Australian official who worked with the aborigines for twenty years. Both men were fully initiated members of the Arunta tribe.**

The native tribes with which we are dealing occupy an area in the centre of the Australian continent which, roughly speaking, is not less than 700 miles in length

***** B. S. Spencer and F. J. Gillen, *The Native Tribes of Central Australia* (London: Macmillan & Co., Ltd., 1899), pp. 1-54.

from north to south, and stretches out east and west of the transcontinental telegraph line, covering an unknown extent of country in either direction. . . .

Each of the various tribes speaks a distinct dialect, and regards itself as the possessor of the country in which it lives. In the more southern parts, where they have been long in contact with the white man, not only have their numbers diminished rapidly, but the natives who still remain are but poor representatives of their race, having lost all or nearly all of their old customs and traditions. With the spread of the white man it can only be a matter of comparatively a few years before the same fate will befall the remaining tribes, which are as yet fortunately too far removed from white settlements of any size to have become degraded. However kindly disposed the white settler may be, his advent at once and of necessity introduces a disturbing element into the environment of the native, and from that moment degeneration sets in, no matter how friendly may be the relations between the Aborigine and the new-comers. The chance of securing cast-off clothing, food, tobacco, and perhaps also knives and tomahawks, in return for services rendered to the settler, at once attracts the native into the vicinity of any settlement however small. The young men, under the new influence, become freed from the wholesome restraint of the older men, who are all-powerful in the normal condition of the tribe. The strict moral code, which is certainly enforced in their natural state, is set on one side, and nothing is adopted in place of it. The old men see with sorrow that the younger ones do not care for the time-honoured traditions of their fathers, and refuse to hand them on to successors who, according to their ideas, are not worthy to be trusted with them; vice, disease, and difficulty in securing the natural food, which is driven away by the settlers, rapidly diminish their numbers, and when the remnant of the tribe is gathered into some mission station, under conditions as far removed as they can well be from their natural ones, it is too late to learn anything of the customs which once governed tribal life.

Fortunately from this point of view the interior of the continent is not easily accessible, or rather its climate is too dry and the water supply too meagre and untrustworthy, to admit as yet of rapid settlement, and therefore the natives, in many parts, are practically still left to wander over the land which the white man does not venture to inhabit, and amongst them may still be found tribes holding firmly to the beliefs and customs of their ancestors.

If now we take the Arunta tribe as an example, we find that the natives are distributed in a large number of small local groups, each of which occupies, and is supposed to possess, a given area of country, the boundaries of which are well known to the natives. In speaking of themselves, the natives will refer to these local groups by the name of the locality which each of them inhabits. . . .

Still further examination of each local group reveals the fact that it is composed largely, but not entirely, of individuals who describe themselves by the name of some one animal or plant. Thus there will be one area which belongs to a group of men who call themselves kangaroo men, another belonging to emu men, another to Hakea flower men, and so on, almost every animal and plant which is found in the country having its representative amongst the human inhabitants. The area of country which is occupied by each of these, which will be spoken of as local Totemic groups, varies to a considerable extent, but is never very large, the most extensive one with which we are acquainted being that of the witchetty grub people of the Alice Springs district. This group at the present time is represented by exactly forty individuals (men, women, and children), and the area of which they are recognized as the proprietors extends over about 100 square miles. In contrast to this, one particular group of "plum-tree" people is only, at the present day, represented by one solitary individual, and he is the proprietor of only a few square miles. . . .

As amongst all savage tribes the Australian native is bound hand and foot by custom. What his fathers did before him that he must do. If during the performance of a ceremony his ancestors painted a white line across the forehead, that line he must paint. Any infringement of custom, within certain limitations, is visited with sure and often severe punishment. At the same time, rigidly conservative as the native is, it is yet possible for changes to be introduced. We have already pointed out that there are certain men who are especially respected for their ability, and, after watching large numbers of the tribe, at a time when they were assembled together for months to perform certain of their most sacred ceremonies, we have come to the conclusion that at a time such as this, when the older and more powerful men from various groups are met together, and when day by day and night by night around their camp fires they discuss matters of tribal interest, it is quite possible for changes of custom to be introduced. . . . The only thing that we can say is that, after carefully watching the natives during the performance of their ceremonies and endeavouring as best we could to enter into their feelings, to think as they did, and to become for the time being one of themselves, we came to the conclusion that if one or two of the most powerful men settled upon the advisability of introducing some change, even an important one, it would be quite possible for this to be agreed upon and carried out. That changes have been introduced, in fact, are still being introduced, is a matter of certainty. . . .

Turning again to the group, we find that the members of this wander, perhaps in small parties of one or two families, often, for example, two or more brothers with their wives and children, over the land which they own, camping at favourite spots where the presence of waterholes, with their accompaniment of vegetable and animal food, enables them to supply their wants.

In their ordinary condition the natives are almost completely naked, which is all the more strange as kangaroo and wallaby are not by any means scarce, and one would think that their fur would be of no little use and comfort in the winter time, when, under the perfectly clear sky, which often remains cloudless for weeks together, the radiation is so great that at nighttime the temperature falls several degrees below freezing point. The idea of making any kind of clothing as a protection against cold does not appear to have entered the native mind, though he is keen enough upon securing the Government blanket when he can get one, or, in fact, any stray cast-off clothing of the white man. The latter is however worn as much from motives of vanity as from a desire for warmth; a lubra with nothing on except an ancient straw hat and an old pair of boots is perfectly happy. . . .

If, now, the reader can imagine himself transported to the side of some waterhole in the centre of Australia, he would probably find amongst the scrub and gum-trees surrounding it a small camp of natives. Each family, consisting of a man and one or more wives and children, accompanied always by dogs, occupies a *mia-mia,* which is merely a lean-to of shrubs so placed as to shield the occupants from the prevailing wind, which, if it be during the winter months, is sure to be from the south-east. In front of this, or inside if the weather be cold, will be a small fire of twigs, for the black fellow never makes a large fire as the white man does. In this respect he certainly regards the latter as a strange being, who makes a big fire and then finds it so hot that he cannot go anywhere near to it. The black fellow's idea is to make a small fire such that he can lie coiled round it and, during the night, supply it with small twigs so that he can keep it alight without making it so hot that he must go further away.

Early in the morning, if it be summer, and not until the sun be well up if it be winter, the occupants of the camp are astir. Time is no object to them, and, if there be no lack of food, the men and women all lounge about while the children laugh and play. If food be required, then the women will go out accompanied by the children and armed with digging sticks and *pitchis,* and the day will be spent out in the bush in search of small burrowing animals such as lizards and small marsupials. The men will perhaps set off armed with spears, spear-throwers, boomerangs and shields in search of larger game such as emus and kangaroos. The latter are secured by stalking, when the native gradually approaches his prey with perfectly noiseless footsteps. Keeping a sharp watch on the animal, he remains absolutely still, if it should turn its head, until once more it resumes its feeding. Gradually, availing himself of the shelter of any bush or large tussock of grass, he approaches near enough to throw his spear. The end is fixed into the point of the spear thrower, and, aided by the leverage thus gained, he throws it forward with all his strength. Different men vary much in their skill in spear-throwing, but it takes an exceptionally good man to kill or disable at more than twenty yards. Sometimes two or three men will hunt in company, and then, while one remains in ambush, the others combine to drive the animals as close as possible to him. Euros are more easily caught than kangaroos, owing to the fact that they inhabit hilly and scrub country, across which they make "pads," by the side of which men will lie in ambush while parties of women go out and drive the animals towards them. On the ranges the rock-wallabies have definite runs, and close by one of these a native will sit patiently, waiting hour by hour, until some unfortunate beast comes by.

In some parts the leaves of the pituri plant are used to stupify the emu. The plan adopted is to make a decoction in some small waterhole at which the animal is accustomed to drink. There, hidden by some bush, the native lies quietly in wait. After drinking the water the bird becomes stupefied, and easily falls a prey to the black fellow's spear. Sometimes a bush shelter is made, so as to look as natural as possible, close by a waterhole, and from behind this animals are speared as they come down to drink. It must be remembered that during the long dry seasons of Central Australia waterholes are few and far between, so that in this way the native is aided in his work of killing animals. In some parts advantage is taken of the inquisitive nature of the emu. A native will carry something which resembles the long neck and small head of the bird and will gradually approach his prey, stopping every now and then, and moving about in the aimless way of the bird itself. The emu, anxious to know what the thing really is, will often wait and watch it until the native has the chance of throwing his spear at close quarters. Sometimes a deep pit will be dug in a part which is known to be a feeding ground of the bird. In the bottom of this a short, sharply-pointed spear will be fixed upright, and then, on the top, bushes will be spread and earth scattered upon them. The inquisitive bird comes up to investigate the matter, and sooner or later ventures on the bushes, and, falling through, is transfixed by the spear. Smaller birds such as the rock pigeons, which assemble in flocks at any waterhole, are caught by throwing the boomerang amongst them, and larger birds, such as the eagle-hawk, the down of which is much valued for decorating the body during the performance of sacred ceremonies, are procured by the same weapon.

It may be said that with certain restrictions which apply partly to groups of individuals and partly to individuals at certain times of their lives, everything which is edible is used for food. . . .

When a euro or kangaroo is killed, the first thing that is always done is to dislocate the hind-legs so as to make the animal what is called *atnuta* or limp. A small hole is cut with a flint in one side of the abdomen, and after the intestines have been pulled out, it is closed up with a wooden skewer. The intestines are usually cooked by rolling them about in hot sand and ashes, any fat which may be present being carefully removed, as it is esteemed a great delicacy. One of the first things to be done is to extract the tendons from the hind limbs. To do this the skin is cut through close to the foot with the sharp bit of flint which is attached to the end of the spear-thrower. A hitch is next taken round the tendon with a stick, and then, with one foot against the animal's rump, the man pulls until the upper end gives way. Then the loose end is held in the teeth, and, when tightly stretched, the lower end is cut through with the flint and the tendon thus extracted is twisted up and put for safe keeping beneath the waist girdle, or in the hair of the head just behind the ear. These tendons are of great service to the natives in various ways, such as for attaching the barbed points on to the ends of the spears, or for splicing spears or mending broken spear-throwers. Meanwhile a shallow pit, perhaps one or two feet deep, has been dug with sticks, and in this a large fire is made. When this burns up, the body is usually held in the flames to singe off the fur, after which it is scraped with a flint. Sometimes this part of the performance is omitted. The hind legs are cut off at the middle joint and the tail either divided in the middle or cut off close to the stump. When the fire has burnt down the animal is laid in the pit on its back with its legs protruding through the hot ashes, which are heaped up over it. After about an hour it is supposed to be cooked, and is taken off, laid on green boughs so as to prevent it from coming in contact with the earth, and then cut up, the hind legs being usually removed first. In some parts where the fur is not singed off, the first thing that is done after removing the body from the fire is to take off the burnt skin. The carver assists himself, during the process of cutting the body up into joints, to such dainty morsels as the heart and kidneys, while any juice which accumulates in the internal cavities of the body is greedily drunk. . . .

The tracking powers of the native are well-known, but it is difficult to realize the skill which they display unless one has seen them at work. Not only does the native know the track of every beast and bird, but after examining any burrow he will at once, from the direction in which the last track runs, tell you whether the animal is at home or not. From earliest childhood boys and girls alike are trained to take note of every track made by every living thing. With the women especially it is a frequent amusement to imitate on the sandy ground the tracks of various animals, which they make with wonderful accuracy with their hands. Not only do they know the varied tracks of the latter, but they will distinguish those of particular men and women. In this respect the men vary greatly, a fact which is well-known to, and appreciated by, those in charge of the native police in various parts of the interior of the continent. Whilst they can all follow tracks which would be indistinguishable to the average white man, there is a great difference in their ability to track when the tracks become obscure. The difference is so marked that while an ordinary good tracker will have difficulty in following them while he is on foot, and so can see them close to, a really good one will unerringly follow them up on horse or camel back. Not only this, but, strange as it may sound to the average white man whose meals are not dependent upon his ability to track an animal to its burrow or hiding place, the native will recognise the footprint of every individual of his acquaintance.

Whilst in matters such as tracking, which are concerned with their everyday life, and upon efficiency in which they actually depend for their livelihood, the natives show conspicuous ability, there are other directions in which they are as conspicuously deficient. This is perhaps shown most clearly in the matter of counting. At Alice Springs they occasionally count, sometimes using their fingers in doing so, up to five, but frequently anything beyond four is indicated by the word *oknira,* meaning much or great. One is *nintha,* two *thrama* or *thera,* three *urapitcha,* four *therankathera,* five *theranka-theranintha.* Time is counted by "sleeps" or "moons," or phases of the moon, for which they have definite terms: longer periods they reckon by means of seasons, having names for summer and winter. They have further definite words expressing particular times, such as morning before sunrise (*ingwunthagwuntha*), evening (*ungwūrila*), yesterday (*abmirka*), day before yesterday (*abmirkairpina*), to-morrow (*ingwuntha*), day after to-morrow (*ingwunthairpina*), in some days (*ingwunthalkura*), in a short time (*ingwunthaunma*), in a long time (*ingwuntha arbarmaninja*). It may also be said that for every animal and plant which is of any service to them, and for numberless others, such as various forms of mice, insects, birds, etc., amongst animals, and various kinds of shrubs and grasses amongst plants, they have distinctive names; and, further still, they distinguish the sexes, *marla* indicating the female sex, and *uria* the male. In many respects their memory is phenomenal. Their mental powers are simply developed along the lines which are of service to them in their daily life.

However, to return to the native camp once more. If we examine their weapons and implements of various kinds, that is those usually carried about, they will be found to be comparatively few in number and simple. A woman has always a *pitchi,* that is a wooden trough varying in length from one to three feet, which has been hollowed out of the soft wood of the bean tree, or it may be out of hard wood such as mulga or eucalypt. In this she carries food material, either balancing it on her head or holding it slung on to one hip by means of a strand of human hair or ordinary fur string across one shoulder. Not infrequently a small baby will be carried about in a *pitchi.* The only other implement possessed by a woman is what is popularly called a "yam stick," which is simply a digging stick or, to speak more correctly, a pick. The commonest form consists merely of a straight staff of wood with one or both ends bluntly pointed, and of such a size that it can easily be carried in the hand and used for digging in the ground. When at work, a woman will hold the pick in the right hand close to the lower end, and, alternately digging this into the ground with one hand, while with the other she scoops out the loosened earth, will dig down with surprising speed. In parts of the scrub, where live the honey ants, which form a very favourite food of the natives, acre after acre of hard sandy soil is seen to have been dug out, simply by the picks of the women in search of the insect, until the place has just the appearance of a deserted field where diggers have, for long, been at work "prospecting." Very often a small *pitchi* will be used as a shovel or scoop, to clear the earth out with, when it gets too deep to be merely thrown up with the hand, as the woman goes on digging deeper and deeper until at last she may reach a depth of some six feet or even more. Of course the children go out with the women, and from the moment that they can toddle about they begin to imitate the actions of their mother. In the scrub a woman will be digging up lizards or honey ants while close by her small child will be at work, with its diminutive pick, taking its first lessons in what, if it be a girl, will be the main employment of her life. . . .

The men's weapons consist of shield, spears, boomerang and spear-thrower, all of which are constantly carried about when on the march. The shields, though they vary in size, are of similar design over practically the whole Central area. They are uniformly made of the light wood of the bean tree, so that their actual manufacture is limited to the more northern parts where this tree grows. The

Warramunga tribe are especially noted for their shields, which are traded far and wide over the Centre. . . .

The spear-thrower is perhaps the most useful single thing which the native has. It is in the form of a hollowed out piece of mulga front two feet to two feet six inches in length, with one end tapering gradually to a narrow handle, and the other, more suddenly, to a blunt point, to which is attached, by means of tendon, a short, sharp bit of hard wood which fits into a hole in the end of a spear. At the handle end is a lump of resin into which is usually fixed a piece of sharp-edged flint or quartzite, which forms the most important cutting weapon of the native. . . .

Each local group has certain favourite camping grounds by the side of water-holes, where food is more or less easily attainable, and in spots such as these there will always be found clusters of *mia-mias,* made of boughs, which are simply replaced as the old ones wither up, or when perhaps in the hot weather they are burnt down. . . .

During the day-time the women are sure to be out in search of food, while the men either go out in search of larger game, or else, if lazy and food be abundant, they will simply sleep all day, or perhaps employ their time in making or trimming up their weapons. When conditions are favourable every one is cheerful and light-hearted, though every now and then a quarrel will arise, followed perhaps by a fight, which is usually accompanied by much noise and little blood-shed. On such occasions, if it be the women who are concerned, fighting clubs will be freely used and blows given and taken which would soon render *hors de combat* an ordinary white woman, but which have comparatively little effect upon the black women; the men usually look on with apparent complete indifference, but may sometimes interfere and stop the fight. If, however, two men are fighting, the mother and sisters of each will cluster round him, shouting at the top of their voices and dancing about with a peculiar and ludicrous high knee action, as they attempt to shelter him from the blows of his adversary's boomerang or fighting club, with the result that they frequently receive upon their bodies the blows meant for the man whom they are attempting to shield.

As a general rule the natives are kindly disposed to one another, that is of course within the limits of their own tribe, and, where two tribes come into contact with one another on the border land of their respective territories, there the same amicable feelings are maintained between the members of the two. There is no such thing as one tribe being in a constant state of enmity with another so far as these Central tribes are concerned. Now and again of course fights do occur between the members of different local groups who may or may not belong to the same or to different tribes. . . .

We may, in general terms, describe the Arunta native as being somewhat under the average height of an Englishman. His skin is of a dark chocolate colour, his nose is distinctly platyrhinic with the root deep set, his hair is abundant and wavy, and his beard, whiskers and moustache well-developed and usually frizzled and jet black. His supra-orbital ridges are well-developed, and above them the forehead slopes back with the hair removed so as to artificially increase its size. His body is well formed and very lithe, and he carries himself gracefully and remarkably erect with his head thrown well back.

Naturally, in the case of the women, everything depends upon their age, the younger ones, that is those between fourteen and perhaps twenty, have decidedly well-formed figures, and, from their habit of carrying on the head *pitchis* containing food and water, they carry themselves often with remarkable grace. As is usual, however, in the case of savage tribes the drudgery of food-collecting and child-bearing tells upon them at an early age, and between twenty and twenty-five they begin to lose their graceful carriage; the face wrinkles, the breasts hang pendulous, and, as a general rule, the whole body begins to shrivel up, until, at about the age of thirty, all traces of an earlier well-formed figure and graceful carriage are lost, and the woman develops into what can only be called an old and wrinkled hag. . . .

When times are favourable the black fellow is as light-hearted as possible. He has not the slightest thought of, or care for, what the morrow may bring forth, and lives entirely in the present. At night time men, women and children gather round the common camp fires talking and singing their monotonous chants hour after hour, until one after the other they drop out of the circle, going off to their different camps, and then at length all will be quiet, except for the occasional cry of a child who, as not seldom happens, rolls over into the fire and has to be comforted or scolded into quietness.

There is, however, in these, as in other savage tribes, an undercurrent of anxious feeling which, though it may be stilled and, indeed, forgotten for a time, is yet always present. In his natural state the native is often thinking that some enemy is attempting to harm him by means of evil magic, and, on the other hand, he never knows when a medicine man in some distant group may not point him out as guilty of killing someone else by magic. It is, however, easy to lay too much stress upon this, for here again we have to put ourselves into the mental attitude of the savage, and must not imagine simply what would be our own feelings under such circumstances. It is not right, by any means, to say that the Australian native lives in constant dread of the evil magic of an enemy. The feeling is always, as it were, lying dormant and ready to be at once called up by any strange or suspicious sound if he be alone, especially at night time, in the bush; but on the other hand, just like a child, he can with ease forget anything unpleasant and enter perfectly into the enjoyment of the present moment. Granted always that his food supply is abundant, it may be said that the life of the Australian native is, for the most part, a pleasant one.

In common with all other Australian tribes, those of the Centre have been shut off from contact with other peoples, and have therefore developed for long ages without the stimulus derived from external sources. . . .

Chapter Three

Man the food producer

Early Agriculture in Southeast Europe   6

The agricultural revolution by which man made the fateful transition from food gathering to food producing seems to have occurred first about 7000 B.C. in the Middle East. From there agriculture spread in all directions, including across the Aegean to Southeast Europe. The following description of excavations in northern Greece reveals that agriculture was practiced there about 6000 B.C., along lines basically similar to those in the Middle East, though with local variations. This selection also gives some notion of the manner in which archeologists proceed to reconstruct the past.*

The Macedonian plain of northern Greece is covered today with orchards and fields of cotton and sugar beets. The aspect of the plain was quite different 8,000 years ago: its central portion was flooded either by an arm of the Aegean Sea or by a shallow lake. Along the shore lived farmer-herdsmen who raised wheat, barley and lentils, tended sheep and goats and may also have herded cattle and pigs. These facts are known because one of the many low-lying mounds on the Macedonian plain has recently been excavated. Called Nea Nikomedeia after a nearby modern village, the mound marks the site of the oldest dated Neolithic community yet found in Europe.

Perhaps even more important than the antiquity of the site is the fact that the patterns of living it reveals, although they are basically similar to the patterns of village life in early Neolithic sites as far east as Iraq and Iran, have their own exclusively European characteristics. The evidence for the existence of a thriving

* Robert J. Rodden, "An Early Neolithic Village in Greece," *Scientific American* (April 1965), pp. 83-92. Reprinted with permission. Copyright © 1965 by Scientific American, Inc. All rights reserved.

village in northern Greece near the end of the seventh millennium B.C. makes it necessary to reconsider the accepted view that the agricultural revolution of the Neolithic period was relatively late in reaching Europe from its area of origin in the Middle East. In southeastern Europe, at least, the transition from hunting, fishing and food-gathering in scattered bands to farming, herding and permanent village life must have taken place far earlier than has generally been thought.

· · · · ·

The Nea Nikomedeia mound had come to the attention of Photios Petsas of the Greek Archaeological Service in 1958, when local road builders bulldozed away three-quarters of an acre of it to use as highway fill. Petsas put a stop to this and, when we consulted him in 1960, directed us to the site. On the bulldozed surface, level with the surrounding plain, we found fragments of pottery and other artifacts that closely resembled the finds from the lowest excavated levels at Neolithic sites in central Greece.

. . . Excavation quickly demonstrated that there was a rich layer of early Neolithic material at Nea Nikomedeia; pottery and other artifacts from this layer showed affinities with material from the earliest pottery-using Neolithic settlements in central Greece and, as we had hoped, with artifacts from the first well-established farming communities to the north.

Impressions of cereal grains, preserved on pottery surfaces, and more than 400 fragments of animal bones demonstrated that the first settlers at Nea Nikomedeia practiced an economy of mixed farming and herding. The 1961 excavations also established the fact that the first houses at the site were rectangular structures with mud walls supported by a framework of wooden poles. Samples of organic material from the site were sent for analysis to the Radiocarbon Dating Laboratory at the University of Cambridge; the analysis yielded a figure of 6220 B.C. ± 150 years. This is the earliest date as yet assigned to Neolithic material from Europe.

· · · · ·

The whole of the mound was not opened during the 1963 season, and some house outlines that continued into the unexcavated portions of the site are not completely revealed. What has been exposed, however, makes it evident that the settlement consisted of individual buildings situated two to five yards apart on a slight knoll at the edge of what was then a marshy lake or inlet. There were two periods of early Neolithic building at Nea Nikomedeia. They are separated in places by a deposit of what appears to be the beginning of a humus soil, so that the second building period evidently represents a reoccupation of the site after a period of abandonment. In any case, the earlier settlement was the smaller of the two, and it was surrounded by a pair of concentric walls on the landward side of the knoll. At the time of the second building period the settlement expanded up to the limit of these walls, which were then replaced by a deep ditch. The ditch shows evidence of having been filled with water; perhaps it served as a moat.

Seven major structures of the earlier building period were uncovered in 1963; six of them are most likely dwellings. Carbonized remains of wood indicate that the frames of the houses were made of oak. The mud walls of the buildings were constructed in the following manner: Sapling uprights were set in place three to four feet apart and the space between them was filled in with bundles of reeds standing on end. The reeds were then plastered on the inside surface with mud mixed with chaff and on the outside with white clay. Many of the footings both for the walls and for the roof supports were made a yard or so deep, evidently to ensure that the buildings would not be affected by frost heave or by the wetness of the waterfront subsoil. Because the mud-plastered walls would have been subject to damage by rain, it is assumed that the houses of Nea Nikomedeia had peaked and thatched roofs with overhanging eaves that would carry off rainwater.

Although the six house plans are different, they have several features in common. The basic unit was evidently a square about 25 feet to a side. Two one-room houses show exactly these dimensions. A third building, consisting of a large main room and a narrow room along one side, was 25 feet wide; its full length could not be determined. The same plan—a large main room with a narrow room attached—is also found in the best-preserved dwelling uncovered at Nea Nikomedeia. At one end of the narrow room in this house stood a raised platform of plaster into which were sunk a hearth basin and a storage bin; on the opposite side of the house was a fenced-off porch area.

A considerably larger structure, some 40 feet square and divided into three parts by parallel rows of heavy timbers, is also attributable to the first building period at Nea Nikomedeia. It was uncovered in the part of the excavation closest to the center of the mound. Five figurines of women were found within the bounds of its walls. Both its size and its contents suggest that the building served some ritual purpose.

Although much analytical work still remains to be done, preliminary findings by the botanists and zoologists who are working with the expedition provide a good outline of the economy of this early Neolithic community. The fact that the farmers of the first settlement grew wheat, barley and lentils is indicated by carbonized material; the particular varieties of these plants have not yet been identified. A study of the animal bones recovered in 1961, together with a preliminary analysis of some 25,000 additional specimens recovered in 1963, suggest that sheep and goats played the primary role in animal husbandry. The bones of pigs and cattle were also present, but in far fewer numbers. In addition to tending their flocks the people of Nea Nikomedeia engaged in hunting, fowling and fishing. Deer, hare and wild pig were among the game animals; the presence of fish bones and the shells of both saltwater cockles and freshwater mussels shows that the early settlers also exploited the resources of their coastal environment.

. . . . .

. . . it is evident that the economy of Nea Nikomedeia rested on a fourfold base, with wheat and barley as the major cereal crops, and sheep and goats as sources of meat and presumably of hides and milk. There is no reason to doubt that the first inspiration for the cultivation of these cereals and the husbanding of these animals came to Europe from the Middle East, although as yet the earliest links connecting the two regions have not been discovered. The essentials of the economy at Nea Nikomedeia, then, were foreign in origin; what about the other elements of village life? In reflecting on the settlement's tools, pottery, articles of personal adornment and ritual objects, one seeks similarities to material from other sites in Europe and abroad. In this way what was unique at Nea Nikomedeia can be distinguished from what was derived from—or perhaps contributed to—other areas.

The tool kit of the first settlers included both the classic artifacts of polished stone—axes, adzes and chisels—that originally gave the Neolithic, or New Stone, age its name, and a variety of chipped blades of flint and chert from which the farmers made scrapers, arrowheads and the cutting edges of rude sickles. The bow and arrow and the sling were among the hunters' weapons; hundreds of clay slingstones have been unearthed. The settlers also made bone needles (possibly including net-making needles), awls and fishhooks. Such a list, with a few exceptions or additions, would be typical of any other nearly contemporary community in southeastern Europe, Asia Minor or the Middle East. Nonetheless, there are consistent local traditions; as an example, the chipped stone artifacts from Nea Nikomedeia resemble those from sites in central Greece, eastern Yugoslavia and central Bulgaria and differ from those found in southern Greece, Asia Minor and the Middle East.

The earliest pottery at the site shows great technical competence in manufacture, in the range of vessel shapes and in decoration. The settlers made open bowls, large narrow-mouthed storage jars, small ladles, miniature vessels and peculiar shoe-shaped pots that may have been put into a bed of coals to heat their contents. Many of the smaller bowls were provided with lugs, which are perforated vertically or horizontally, so that they could be suspended by cords. Almost all the pots have thin walls and bases that are ring-shaped or disk-shaped. The potters decorated some of their wares by painting and some with finger impressions on the outside surface.

The earliest-known phases of Neolithic settlement in central Bulgaria and eastern Yugoslavia are characterized by pottery that bears finger-impressed decorations or designs in white paint; examples of both can be found at Nea Nikomedeia, but neither is common. That they are found at all, however, lends weight to the conclusion that connecting links of some kind existed between these early Macedonian farmers and those to the north. The pottery evidence indicates even closer ties between Nea Nikomedeia and the earliest pottery-using settlements in central Greece. Both there and at Nea Nikomedeia wares decorated with block designs, triangles and patterns of wavy lines—all painted in red on a cream-colored background—are commonplace.

These pottery motifs provide an example of the ways in which Nea Nikomedeia may have contributed culturally to areas outside Europe. The tradition of painting pottery with red designs on a cream-colored background appears several hundred years later in southern Asia Minor with the beginnings of the Hacilar culture [see "Hacilar: A Neolithic Village Site," by James Mellaart; *Scientific American,* August, 1961]. By the same token, some of the pots of Nea Nikomedeia are decorated with human faces made by pinching up a "nose" and adding ovals of clay as "eyes." Similarly decorated pots have been found in post-Neolithic levels at Hacilar and also at the earlier sites of Hassuna and Matarrah in Iraq. In the absence of well-defined intermediate steps, it must remain a matter of conjecture whether or not the presence of pots with human faces at these widely separated sites represents the diffusion of an idea or an independent invention.

Both European and Asiatic characteristics can be found among the articles of personal adornment at Nea Nikomedeia. A bone belt-fastener with a hook-and-eye clasp was uncovered during the 1963 season; a number of such fasteners have been found in the early Neolithic levels at Çatal Hüyük. A bone hook from Soufli Magoula, an early Neolithic site in central Greece, may be another European example of the same kind of object. Clay stamps, each exhibiting a different geometric pattern, are relatively common at Nea Nikomedeia; similar stamps are known from central Greece and elsewhere in southeastern and central Europe. Some of the stamps found at Nea Nikomedeia, however, have designs similar to those on stamps from Çatal Hüyük.

Some Neolithic sites in the Middle East—Tell Judeideh in Syria, Jarmo and Hassuna in Iraq and Tepe Siyalk in Iran—contain curious stone objects that look somewhat like primitive nails. The excavations at Nea Nikomedeia have yielded a great number of these objects, neatly wrought out of white marble, and a lesser number of tiny studs made of green serpentine. It is probable that the nails were headdress decorations and that the studs were earplugs. Such carefully shaped and polished articles of marble and serpentine represent a high level of technical achievement.

Of particular interest is the fact that the settlers made clay figurines of men and women; these stylized sculptures reflect a high level of artistic sensibility. The more sophisticated figurines were made in sections and then pegged together before they hardened; the component parts are the head, the torso (including the arms) and two separate legs. The head usually consists of a slightly flattened cylinder from which a prominent pointed nose is pinched up; as with the faces on the pots, the eyes are often represented by applied lumps of clay. Figurines of women outnumber those of men; in the commonest type of female figurine the thighs are modeled to an exaggerated roundness. The breasts are mere knobs, supported by the hands.

Other clay figurines include rather less elegant models of sheep and goats. It is puzzling that these economically important animals are rendered with such relative crudity whereas three effigies of frogs found at Nea Nikomedeia were beautifully carved in green and blue serpentine and then polished. The site's marshy locale makes it reasonable to suppose that its inhabitants were well acquainted with these amphibians, but what significance the frog may have possessed that inspired the execution of its portrait in stone is unknown.

It is commonly assumed that early societies engaged in the newly discovered art of food production soon developed beliefs about the supernatural in which human, animal and plant fertility were emphasized. The exaggerated forms of the figurines of women uncovered at Nea Nikomedeia, together with the fact that five of them were found together within the confines of the site's largest structure, seem to indicate that fertility beliefs played a part in the life of this particular Neolithic community. The excavations have provided a further insight into the community's spiritual views: There was evidently little or no regard for the dead. Burial pits were located outside the house walls and sometimes in the debris of buildings that had fallen into disuse; the inhabitants appear to have taken little trouble to prepare the graves. In some instances one gains the impression that the dead were crammed into a barely adequate depression. No personal adornment, food offerings or grave goods have been found with the skeletons. In one enigmatic instance, however, a skeleton was found with a large pebble thrust between its jaws.

In summary, the characteristics of early Neolithic village life as it was practiced by the farmers of Nea Nikomedeia show basic parallels with life in similar Neolithic villages in Asia Minor and the Middle East. The most telling of these parallels are the very roots of the Neolithic revolution itself: the cultivation of wheat and barley and the domestication of sheep and goats. This village in the Macedonian marshes, however, was no mere foothold established in Europe by pioneers from the Middle East. Village plans, house plans and building methods comparable to those used at Nea Nikomedeia are known from two nearby regions. The first of these regions includes the early Neolithic sites of Karanovo and Azmak in central Bulgaria; parts of plans of similar houses have also been exposed at several of the early sites in central Greece. It seems probable, therefore, that a Neolithic pattern of life characterized by a well-established architectural tradition adapted to the European environment and locally available materials stands behind the finds both at Nea Nikomedeia and at the sites of these other early settlements in southeastern Europe.

The precise origins of this architectural tradition remain unknown, but it is one that contrasts strongly with the custom of building houses one against another around the nucleus of a courtyard, which dominates village construction in Asia Minor and the Middle East during the late seventh millennium and early sixth millennium B.C. In the last analysis, such evidence may mean that southeastern Europe will have to be considered a part of that zone—heretofore generally deemed to lie exclusively in Asia Minor and the Middle East—in which were made the primary discoveries that led to the development of Old World civilization.

7 Low Productivity of the Neolithic Tribesman

Despite the technological progress made during Neolithic times, productivity was low compared to that following the advent of civilization. The reason, paradoxically, was the egalitarianism of Neolithic society. Land was available to everyone, and there were no landlords or tax collectors to force production above bare family needs. This is made clear in the following calendar of the work of the Bemba tribe of Northern Rhodesia during the month of September 1933.* Admittedly this is a slack time of the year, and a time when more beer is drunk than normally. Nevertheless it is apparent that the "daily grind," the hallmark of modern society, was conspicuous by its absence under tribal conditions comparable to those of Neolithic times. This is evident also in Reading 15, "Tribesmen and Peasants."

September 1st, 1933. Two gourds of beer ready, one drunk by old men, one by young men. A new baby born. Women gather from other villages to congratulate, and spend two or three days in the village. Women's garden work postponed during this time.

2nd. Old men go out to clear the bush. Young men sit at home finishing the sour dregs of the beer. More visits of neighbouring women to see the new baby. Few women go out to do garden work.

3rd (Sunday). Young men and women go to a church service conducted in a neighbouring village by a visiting Mission doctor. No garden work.

4th. Visit of the Mission doctor to Kasaka. Protestants and Catholics both attend the services. No garden work.

5th. Old men cut trees. Young men sit at home and shape axe-handles. Some women working again.

6th. Old and young men working by 6:30 a.m. and hard at it till 2 p.m. Two gourds of beer divided between old and young in the evening. Women working in their gardens normally.

7th. A buck shot by observer's party. Young men go out to fetch the meat. Women grind extra flour to eat with it. Two gourds of beer also made ready and drinking begins at 2 p.m. By 4 o'clock young men swaggering around the village, ready to quarrel, which they finally do. Dancing at night. Old women

---

* A. I. Richards, *Land, Labour and Diet in Northern Rhodesia* (London: Oxford University Press and International African Institute, 1939), pp. 162-164.

hilarious, and rebuked by their daughters for charging into a rough dance on the village square. Not enough beer for the younger women. They remain sober and express disapproval of the rest. No garden work done, except by old men.

8th. Every one off to their gardens in high spirits at 8 a.m. Back at 12 a.m. Young men sit in shelter and drink beer dregs for two hours, singing Scotch Mission hymns in sol-fa. Young girls go out on a miniature fish-poisoning expedition, but catch nothing.

9th and 10th. Observers away. D10, son of D11 born.* A crowd of relatives from neighbouring villages come to congratulate. No garden work said to have been done.

11th. The baby born on September 1st (daugthter of a visiting relative) dies. Mourners arrive from surrounding villages. Eight young women go to do their tribute labour for chief. All garden work postponed.

12th. Mourning party leaves with bereaved mother, accompanied by women of Kasaka wailing up the road. Young women still away at capital. Little garden work done by women. Men tree-cutting half the day.

13th. Heads of A, B, C, D go visiting relatives twenty-two miles away, with their wives, to mourn. Clearing bush by two men. Garden work done by two women. Meat distributed.

14th. A1, B1, C1, D1 and wives still away. One man clears bush. Meat still available. Young women still away doing tribute labour.

15th. Three men begin digging dry-weather gardens by the river. Little boys go bird-snaring. Young women still away at the capital. Nobody to get relish. No proper meal cooked.

16th. Eight men clear bush. One away hunting. Three young men home for week-end from work at Shiwa Dandu. Young women return from doing tribute labour in the evening, greeted by shouts from the whole community. Old women all remain in village.

17th (Sunday). Great heat. Young men sit about in shelter all day, comb each other's hair, shave, and delouse each other. No relish available. Women too tired to cook.

18th. Seven men work again clearing bush. Five women piling branches.

19th. Nine men clear bush. One woman hoeing. Three women piling branches. Young women go fish-poisoning and catch one fish (about 2 lb.).

20th. Six men clear bush. One house-building.

21st. Five men clear bush. Five women pile branches.

22nd. Three men clear bush. One man hoes. Four young men go fishing with three of the wives. Three piling branches.

23rd. Five men clear bush. One goes on digging a dry-weather garden. Five women pile branches. One hoes.

24th (Sunday). Four gourds of beer divided between whole village. Sufficient for women as well as men. Beer-drinking lasts two days off and on.

25th. Two old men only able to tree-cut. Young men afraid to climb trees because of 'beer before the eyes'. They sit in their shelter and make baskets. B4 hunts with his own gun. One woman only does garden work. Young boys snare birds. Remains of beer drunk.

26th. Old men work. Young men 'too cold'. B4 still away hunting.

27th. Five men clear bush. One man and four women carry meat sixteen miles to Shiwa. . . .

* Editor's Note: Code numbers and letters refer to persons identified on kinship charts.

28th. Every one (men and women) off at 6 a.m. Work till 2 p.m., declaring they are strong with meat. A little beer in the evening.

29th. Rain at night. First net-hunt possible. All men and children join in. Nothing killed. Six women pile branches.

30th. More beer. Four men clear bush. E3 digs dry-weather garden.

October 1st (Sunday). Young women whitewash houses.

2nd. Headman provides beer for a working bee. All men join to clear bush for him and drink afterwards.

This calendar makes no attempt to give a complete record of the activities of the people, as unfortunately the data are not sufficiently full. It brings out certain interesting points, however. The first is the irregularity of the work done and the greater industry of the old as compared with the young, especially among the men. By noting the chart letters of those who went to clear the bush or to pile branches each day, it will be seen that the only natives who went consecutively to work were the old men of the village, those reckoned by the Government as too feeble to pay tax. . . . This was admittedly a slack time of the year, but it will be noted that the arrival of visitors, such as relatives or the local missionaries, births and deaths in the village or neighbourhood, the absence of the young women doing tribute labour, or beer parties, disrupted the work of the village or brought it to a standstill. On no single day did every man and woman go off to work.

8   ACHIEVEMENTS OF MAN BEFORE CIVILIZATION

The contemporary world is in large part the product of the great civilizations of Eurasia that followed the agricultural revolution. Yet preliterate man did possess a vast amount of naturalistic knowledge that is taken for granted and thus overlooked, but which nevertheless provided the solid foundation upon which the succeeding civilizations were based. This survey, by an American anthropologist, of the knowledge and techniques attained before civilization makes clear the debt owed by contemporary man to his preliterate ancestors.*

During the course of cultural evolution up to the Agricultural Revolution a very considerable amount of genuine, matter-of-fact knowledge was acquired and accumulated. Some of this knowledge was very widespread, much of it was locally restricted, depending upon the uniformity or diversity of local circumstances of habitat. The totality of these local knowledges is impressive and forms the foundation for the naturalistic philosophies of more advanced cultures and for the science of our culture. It will be interesting and instructive to pass in review these traditions of genuine knowledge in primitive cultures.

Primitive peoples knew their habitats intimately. They knew what useful resources it contained, where red ocher, clay, or flint might be found. They knew

* From *The Evolution of Culture: The Development of Civilization to the Fall of Rome,* by L. A. White, pp. 268-72. Copyright © 1959 by McGraw Hill, Inc. Used with permission of McGraw-Hill Book Company.

the distribution of flora and fauna and which species were useful or edible and which were useless or injurious. They knew the habits of local birds, animals, fish, and insects and how to take them for food and other uses. Eskimos were able to make topographic sketches of the territory within which they lived and traveled so accurately that they could be used to good advantage by arctic explorers.

Preliterate peoples possessed knowledge concerning the heavenly bodies and temporal and seasonal sequences. Constellations of stars were distinguished and named. Polaris was spotted, and the movements of planets followed. Even such a primitive tribe as the Ona of Tierra del Fuego distinguished Sirius, Procyon, and Betelgeuse. Morning and evening stars received particular attention. They knew that there are twelve to thirteen lunations in a complete solar cycle; these "moons" were frequently named according to the time of the year—"new-leaves moon," or "first-snowflurries moon." Seasons were distinguished according to latitude. Among some tribes systematic observations were made upon the sun. The Pueblo Indians of the Southwest, for example, had a special priest to observe the risings of the sun in order to determine the times of the solstices.

Virtually all kinds of tools were invented and developed by primitive peoples, such as knives, axes, scrapers, hammers, awls, needles, and so on. Machines, i.e., mechanical devices composed of moving and interrelated parts, such as the bow drill and pump drill, were occasionally developed. Tubular drill bits and abrasives were used. In the field of weapons, spears, harpoons, clubs, shields, and armor were developed. The atlatl, or spear thrower, the blowgun, and the bow and arrow are particularly ingenious devices. Hammocks were invented and used by the Indians of the Amazon. All techniques for producing fire known to man prior to the invention of matches in the early nineteenth century were developed by primitive peoples: percussion (flint and iron pyrites), friction (the fire drill and fire saw), and compression (the fire piston). The fire piston is an especially ingenious device. Tinder is placed in the bottom of a cylinder and is ignited by being raised to the kindling temperature by air compression. The principle involved here was later incorporated in the Diesel engine, where fuel is ignited in the cylinder by compression rather than by an electric spark. Rubber was manufactured by the American Indians and used as balls in games in Meso-America and to make enema syringes in Amazonia.

A great many techniques involving considerable knowledge were developed by primitive peoples in one culture or another. The manufacture of good pottery, the proper admixture of tempering material with clay and the subsequent firing, requires a great deal of knowledge and skill. Similarly the art of making buckskin requires an extensive knowledge of materials and techniques. The textile arts—carding, spinning, twinning, twilling, weaving—require knowledge, skill, and apparatus. Bark cloth, made from the inner bark of mulberry or fig trees, beaten to almost paper thinness with corrugated mallets, was made in Polynesia and west Africa. Felt was made by various peoples of central Asia. The nonsubmersible kayak and the sealskin float used to retard the escape of harpooned sea mammals among the Eskimos demonstrate an understanding of physical principles. The snowhouse in the same cultures is also a remarkable exhibition of realistic knowledge and understanding, not to mention the utilization of the thermos-bottle principle in some of these houses. Some Eskimo groups sewed caribou skins together and suspended them from the walls and ceilings of their snowhouses, separating the two by a few inches. A layer of non-heat-conducting air is thus interposed between the skins and the snow wall, which is of course an example of the principle utilized in thermos bottles in our culture. The Eskimos also made and used goggles, with narrow slits instead of lenses, to protect them from the glare of sunlight reflected from the snow. Outrigger canoes are ingenious contrivances which utilize a number of mechanical principles.

In the field of chemistry, primitive peoples by and large amassed a considerable store of knowledge of materials and processes. They knew how to make paints and pigments, some of which had a quality and durability that have never been surpassed. They discovered the use of mordants, substances for fixing colors. One of the most remarkable chemical processes on primitive cultural levels is to be found in northeastern South America. There, some tribes have learned to remove a deadly poison, hydrocyanic acid, from a species of manioc, which then becomes a staple article of diet. They have done this by a complicated process of grinding, drying, and leaching, which incidentally uses a most ingenious mechanical basketry device known as a cassava squeezer. How these primitive Indians ever discovered that they could separate a deadly poison from a plant otherwise nutritious is something to wonder at.

A great many poisons were known and used on preliterate cultural levels. The primitive Semang, and other peoples of Southeast Asia, used the lethal sap of the upas tree (*Antiaris*) to tip darts and arrows. Curare, made from the sap of *Strychnos toxifera,* was widely used in northeastern South America. It paralyzes the respiratory muscles, causing death but leaving the carcass quite edible. Some peoples tipped arrows with a mixture of snake venom and liver. Hemlock and the Calabar bean among other poisons were also used to kill members of one's own society.

Many plant materials have been used to kill or stupefy fish so that they might be easily taken for food. The active, or significant, ingredient of some of these plants is saponin, a soaplike material that smothers the fish. Tannic acid or an alkaloid of some kind is the active agent in others. The aborigines of Australia drugged pools with pituri, an alkaloid, in order to stupefy and catch emu.

Chemical knowledge of many primitive tribes is expressed in other ways also. Tribes of the Northwest Coast of America chewed tobacco with lime, made by burning shells. In the Andean region coca leaves, and in Melanesia and Southeast Asia betel nuts, were chewed with lime in order to produce an effect the nature of which is not too well understood. According to one authority, lime helps to liberate "the arecoline alkaloid from the areca [betel] nut." Also, lime acts as a gastric sedative and is an antidote for mineral and oxalic poisoning.

The Indians of the Andean highlands prepared corn for the manufacture of beer (*chicha*) by chewing it in order to institute a chemical process by the action of saliva upon the grain. Starch must be transformed into sugar before it can be fermented. Saliva contains an enzyme called ptyalin, which breaks down starches, first to simple dextrins, then to maltose, a crystalline sugar. In Polynesia, the kava root was chewed, no doubt for a similar reason, in the preparation of kava, a slightly intoxicating drink.

Agriculture and animal husbandry are the achievements of preliterate peoples. No new plant or animal has been brought under domestication by modern civilized peoples. On the other hand, a number of useful plants, cultivated by primitive peoples, have been virtually ignored by modern civilization: *Chenopodium* (quinoa) and oca, for example. Primitive peoples discovered the most suitable plants to domesticate and cultivate and devised effective techniques for their cultivation. They developed and improved cultivated plants by selective breeding and learned to increase yields by fertilization and irrigation.

All the kinds of foods known to modern civilization—starches, sugars, fats or oils, proteins, "greens," etc.—were known and used on preliterate cultural levels. This does not mean, of course, that the diet of every tribe was varied and well balanced; it merely means that modern civilization uses no kind of food that was not known to some primitive tribe somewhere.

In the preparation and preservation of foods, too, primitive peoples acquired a vast amount of knowledge and skill. Stone boiling and earth ovens exemplify their ingenuity and resourcefulness. Foods were preserved in a variety of ways. In arctic regions they were frozen. In other regions certain foods—fruits, vegetables, and meats—were preserved by drying. Sometimes they were sealed up airtight with tallow. In short, preliterate peoples devised virtually all the techniques known to us today for preserving food except the tin can and the airtight glass jar.

Medical diagnosis and practice among primitive peoples were not wholly magical by any means. They took a rational view of many ailments and attempted to treat them realistically in matter-of-fact ways. In certain cultures, broken bones were set with splints, tourniquets were used, poultices and bandages employed. Steam baths were used and massage practiced by many peoples. Bloodletting was a widespread therapeutic practice, as it was in European culture until quite recent times. Some tribes of South America administered enemas, using a rubber syringe for this purpose. In surgery, the Melanesians and Peruvians developed great skill in cutting out broken bones of the skull to relieve pressure on the brain. "In this delicate operation known as 'trephining,' " says Lowie, "they were more successful than European physicians of the Eighteenth Century." The Peruvian surgeons also amputated feet with success; pictures on pottery bowls show men with an artificial foot, taking part, however, in a ceremony or dance. Doctors among the Ganda are said to have been able "to cure men partially disembowelled from spear wounds by washing the portruding intestines, forcing them gently back into the abdomen, and keeping them in place with a piece of gourd."

The human heads, shrunk by the Jivaro Indians, might be mentioned in this connection, also, since they involve knowledge and skill in anatomical surgery and mummification. The Jivaro remove the bones of the head and reduce it to the size of a fist, retaining at the same time the original facial features. They are preserved by smoking—and perhaps other techniques—and kept as trophies.

Many plant materials were used by primitive peoples in nonmagical or only partially magical, contexts in the treatment of ailments of many kinds. It is now known that many plants used by aborigines for medicinal purposes such as cascara, sweet flag (Acorus), Angelica, seneca snakeroot, sassafras, licorice, eucalyptus, etc., do have therapeutic value. It is exceedingly difficult, however, to determine what effect certain medicinal plants will have on patients because of the complexity of the chemical content of the plants, on the one hand, and the personal idiosyncrasies of individuals, on the other. In the use of plants for medicinal purposes, however, primitive peoples have discovered and recognized many important drugs, such as tobacco, cocaine, quinine, ipecac, hashish, peyote, datura, and fly agaric.

The roster of beverages among preliterate peoples demonstrates a very considerable knowledge of the properties of materials and of techniques of preparation. Many peoples have brewed leaves of plants to make "teas." The Pueblo Indians made a tasty and nutritious drink of corn which had been soaked and allowed to sprout, then dried, parched, ground, and used as we would use coffee.

Coffee is indigenous in Abyssinia, but the origin of coffee drinking is not definitely known. It appears to have been introduced to Western culture by the Arabs about the sixteenth century. Whether coffee drinking was invented by a preliterate people or not is unknown, but it is interesting to note, in this connection, that the Ganda of Uganda did not drink coffee, but carried the beans—boiled, dried, and sometimes roasted—on their persons for occasional chewing. The Aztecs drank chocolate, made from the cacao bean, flavored with vanilla, honey, or pepper. Some tribes drink milk, fresh or fermented, from mares as well as from cows.

The saps of various trees, e.g., maple and palm, are drunk, fresh or fermented. A great variety of "wines," made from sap or fruit juices, are drunk by many peoples. The Hottentots drank an alcoholic beverage made by diluting wild honey with water and adding certain roots to promote fermentation. The Ganda made a mildly intoxicating beer of ripe bananas and millet flour. The Aztecs drank pulque, an alcoholic beverage made from the sap of the agave. We have already spoken of the kava drink of Polynesia and the maize beer, or *chicha,* of Peru. About the only advance made by modern civilization in the art of making liquors is the distillation process.

In the realm of music, primitive peoples have much to their credit. They developed musical systems and styles and advanced the vocal art as far as part singing. Their musical systems were often exceedingly complicated rhythmically —much more so than our own—but were relatively simple harmonically. Virtually all kinds of musical instruments known to the modern world today were invented and developed by primitive peoples: stringed instruments of all kinds, which incidentally may have originated in the musical bow; percussion instruments—drums, clackers, rattles; wind instruments—flutes, trumpets, pan pipes (our great pipe organs today are simply pan pipes enormously magnified).

Primitive peoples have some noteworthy achievements to their credit in ocean travel and navigation. Prior to the voyages of Columbus, the most extensive overseas voyages, as distinguished from coastwise travel, were made by the Polynesians. It is 2,500 miles from Rapa to Easter Island. Regular voyages between Hawaii and Tahiti, a distance of about 2,350 miles, were made. Their seacraft sometimes exceeded 100 feet in length. War canoes of Fiji could accommodate 200 men, warriors, and crew, and some Tahitian canoes are said to have seated as many as 300. Coastwise commercial craft of New Guinea, consisting of as many as seven to fourteen dugouts lashed together side by side, and measuring up to 59 feet long by 51 feet wide, could carry as much as 34 tons of cargo.

The Marshall Islanders devised and used some very ingenious navigational charts. They were frameworks made of the midribs of cocoanut leaves arranged in such a way as to indicate the location of reefs, ocean swells, and currents. The position of islands was indicated by cowrie shells tied to the frame.

The accumulated knowledge, skills, tools, machines, and techniques developed by primitive, preliterate peoples laid the basis for civilization and all the higher cultures. They invented and developed all the basic tools, weapons, and utensils. They developed the major arts and crafts, such as the ceramic and textile arts, and initiated the art of metallurgy. Food and fiber plants were brought under domestication by them, and they developed the techniques for their culture. They originated the domestication of animals.

Thus during the first hundreds of thousands of years of culture history, primitive peoples were acquiring realistic and matter-of-fact knowledge and originating and perfecting rational and effective techniques. This age-old process of accumulation and development culminated in the Agricultural Revolution, which, as we have seen, profoundly transformed the whole cultural tradition. It is indeed remarkable to see how close to the present day primitive peoples have come at many points on the technological level. Western civilization surpassed primitive techniques of making fire by mechanical friction or percussion only within the last 150 years. And the principle underlying artificial illumination—burning fuel with or without a container and with or without a wick—has been outgrown only within the last 75 years. As recently as 1850 in the United States, white frontiersmen as well as Indians were using the bow and arrow in buffalo hunting in preference to the best of firearms then available to them. And Tylor tells us that Russian troops armed with bow and arrow marched down the boulevards of Paris in 1815 in celebration of the defeat of Napoleon. Thus the bow and arrow, a mechanical triumph of preliterate cultures, has been rendered obsolete as a practical device only within recent years—almost within the memory of persons now living.

ANCIENT CIVILIZATIONS
OF EURASIA,
3500–1000 B.C.

Chapter Four

Origins of ancient civilizations

NATURE OF CIVILIZATION

9

In learning to grow his food, man prepared the way for the next step in his historical evolution—the step to civilization, or the urban revolution. Not all peoples who became agriculturists also became civilized. But none who failed to realize the agricultural revolution were able to go on to the urban. In this selection a distinguished British archaeologist presents ten criteria that distinguish a civilization from the preceding Neolithic society.*

The concept of 'city' is notoriously hard to define. The aim of the present essay is to present the city historically—or rather prehistorically—as the resultant and symbol of a 'revolution' that initiated a new economic stage in the evolution of society. The word 'revolution' must not of course be taken as denoting a sudden violent catastrophe; it is here used for the culmination of a progressive change in the economic structure and social organization of communities that caused, or was accompanied by, a dramatic increase in the population affected—an increase that would appear as an obvious bend in the population graph were vital statistics available. Just such a bend is observable at the time of the Industrial Revolution in England. Though not demonstrable statistically, comparable changes of direction must have occurred at two earlier points in the demographic history of Britain and other regions. Though perhaps less sharp and less durable, these too should indicate equally revolutionary changes in economy. They may then be regarded likewise as marking transitions between stages in economic and social development.

Sociologists and ethnographers last century classified existing pre-industrial

* V. Gordon Childe, "The Urban Revolution," *Town Planning Review*, XXI (April 1950), 3-17.

societies in a hierarchy of three evolutionary stages, denominated respectively 'savagery,' 'barbarism' and 'civilization.' If they be defined by suitably selected criteria, the logical hierarchy of stages can be transformed into a temporal sequence of ages, proved archaeologically to follow one another in the same order wherever they occur. Savagery and barbarism are conveniently recognized and appropriately defined by the methods adopted for procuring food. Savages live exclusively on wild food obtained by collecting, hunting or fishing. Barbarians on the contrary at least supplement these natural resources by cultivating edible plants and—in the Old World north of the Tropics—also by breeding animals for food.

Throughout the Pleistocene Period—the Palaeolithic Age of archaeologists—all known human societies were savage in the foregoing sense, and a few savage tribes have survived in out of the way parts to the present day. In the archaeological record barbarism began less than ten thousand years ago with the Neolithic Age of archaeologists. It thus represents a later, as well as a higher stage, than savagery. Civilization cannot be defined in quite such simple terms. Etymologically the word is connected with 'city,' and sure enough life in cities begins with this stage. But 'city' is itself ambiguous so archaeologists like to use 'writing' as a criterion of civilization; it should be easily recognizable and proves to be a reliable index to more profound characters. Note, however, that, because a people is said to be civilized or literate, it does not follow that all its members can read and write, nor that they all lived in cities. Now there is no recorded instance of a community of savages civilizing themselves, adopting urban life or inventing a script. Wherever cities have been built, villages of preliterate farmers existed previously (save perhaps where an already civilized people have colonized uninhabited tracts). So civilization, wherever and whenever it arose, succeeded barbarism.

We have seen that a revolution as here defined should be reflected in the population statistics. In the case of the Urban Revolution the increase was mainly accounted for by the multiplication of the numbers of persons living together, i.e., in a single built-up area. The first cities represented settlement units of hitherto unprecedented size. Of course it was not just their size that constituted their distinctive character. We shall find that by modern standards they appeared ridiculously small and we might meet agglomerations of population today to which the name city would have to be refused. Yet a certain size of settlement and density of population, is an essential feature of civilization.

Now the density of population is determined by the food supply which in turn is limited by natural resources, the techniques for their exploitation and the means of transport and food-preservation available. The last factors have proved to be variables in the course of human history, and the technique of obtaining food has already been used to distinguish the consecutive stages termed savagery and barbarism. Under the gathering economy of savagery population was always exceedingly sparse. In aboriginal America the carrying capacity of normal unimproved land seems to have been from .05 to .10 per square mile. Only under exceptionally favourable conditions did the fishing tribes of the Northwest Pacific coast attain densities of over one human to the square mile. As far as we can guess from the extant remains, population densities in palaeolithic and pre-neolithic Europe were less than the normal American. Moreover such hunters and collectors usually live in small roving bands. At best several bands may come together for quite brief periods on ceremonial occasions such as the Australian corroborrees. Only in exceptionally favoured regions can fishing tribes establish anything like villages. Some settlements on the Pacific coasts comprised thirty or so substantial and durable houses, accommodating groups of several hundred persons. But even these villages were only occupied during the winter; for the rest of the year their inhabitants dispersed in smaller groups. Nothing comparable has been found in pre-neolithic times in the Old World.

The Neolithic Revolution certainly allowed an expansion of population and enormously increased the carrying capacity of suitable land. On the Pacific Islands neolithic societies today attain a density of 30 or more persons to the square mile. In pre-Columbian North America, however, where the land is not obviously restricted by surrounding seas, the maximum density recorded is just under 2 to the square mile.

Neolithic farmers could of course, and certainly did, live together in permanent villages, though, owing to the extravagant rural economy generally practised, unless the crops were watered by irrigation, the villages had to be shifted at least every twenty years. But on the whole the growth of population was not reflected so much in the enlargement of the settlement unit as in a multiplication of settlements. In ethnography neolithic villages can boast only a few hundred inhabitants (a couple of 'pueblos' in New Mexico house over a thousand, but perhaps they cannot be regarded as neolithic). In prehistoric Europe the largest neolithic village yet known, Barkaer in Jutland, comprised 52 small, one-roomed dwellings, but 16 to 30 houses was a more normal figure; so the average local group in neolithic times would average 200 to 400 members.

These low figures are of course the result of technical limitations. In the absence of wheeled vehicles and roads for the transport of bulky crops men had to live within easy walking distance of their cultivations. At the same time the normal rural economy of the Neolithic Age, what is now termed slash-and-burnt or jhumming, condemns much more than half the arable land to lie fallow so that large areas were required. As soon as the population of a settlement rose above the numbers that could be supported from the accessible land, the excess had to hive off and found a new settlement.

The Neolithic Revolution had other consequences beside increasing the population, and their exploitation might in the end help to provide for the surplus increase. The new economy allowed, and indeed required, the farmer to produce every year more food than was needed to keep him and his family alive. In other words it made possible the regular production of a social surplus. Owing to the low efficiency of neolithic technique, the surplus produced was insignificant at first, but it could be increased till it demanded a reorganization of society.

Now in any Stone Age society, palaeolithic or neolithic, savage or barbarian, everybody can at least in theory make at home the few indispensable tools, the modest cloths and the simple ornaments everyone requires. But every member of the local community, not disqualified by age, must contribute actively to the communal food supply by personally collecting, hunting, fishing, gardening or herding. As long as this holds good, there can be no full-time specialists, no persons nor class of persons who depend for their livelihood on food produced by others and secured in exchange for material or immaterial goods or services.

We find indeed today among Stone Age barbarians and even savages expert craftsmen (for instance flint-knappers among the Ona of Tierra del Fuego), men who claim to be experts in magic, and even chiefs. In palaeolithic Europe too there is some evidence for magicians and indications of chieftainship in pre-neolithic times. But on closer observation we discover that today these experts are not full-time specialists. The Ona flintworker must spend most of his time hunting; he only adds to his diet and his prestige by making arrowheads for clients who reward him with presents. Similarly a pre-Columbian chief, though entitled to customary gifts and services from his followers, must still personally lead hunting and fishing expeditions and indeed could only maintain his authority by his industry and prowess in these pursuits. The same holds good of barbarian societies that are still in the neolithic stage, like the Polynesians where industry in gardening takes the place of prowess in hunting. The reason is that there simply will not be enough food to go round unless every member of the group contributes to the supply. The social surplus is not big enough to feed idle mouths.

Social division of labour, save those rudiments imposed by age and sex, is thus impossible. On the contrary community of employment, the common absorption in obtaining food by similar devices guarantees a certain solidarity to the group. For co-operation is essential to secure food and shelter and for defence against foes, human and subhuman. This identity of economic interests and pursuits is echoed and magnified by identity of language, custom and belief; rigid conformity is enforced as effectively as industry in the common quest for food. But conformity and industrious co-operation need no State organization to maintain them. The local group usually consists either of a single clan (persons who believe themselves descended from a common ancestor or who have earned a mystical claim to such descent by ceremonial adoption) or a group of clans related by habitual intermarriage. And the sentiment of kinship is reinforced or supplemented by common rites focussed on some ancestral shrine or sacred place. Archaeology can provide no evidence for kinship organization, but shrines occupied the central place in preliterate villages in Mesopotamia, and the long barrow, a collective tomb that overlooks the presumed site of most neolithic villages in Britain, may well have been also the ancestral shrine on which converged the emotions and ceremonial activities of the villagers below. However, the solidarity thus idealized and concretely symbolized, is really based on the same principles as that of a pack of wolves or a herd of sheep; Durkheim has called it 'mechanical.'

Now among some advanced barbarians (for instance tattooers or wood-carvers among the Maori) still technologically neolithic we find expert craftsmen tending towards the status of full-time professionals, but only at the cost of breaking away from the local community. If no single village can produce a surplus large enough to feed a full-time specialist all the year round, each should produce enough to keep him a week or so. By going round from village to village an expert might thus live entirely from his craft. Such itinerants will lose their membership of the sedentary kinship group. They may in the end form an analogous organization of their own— a craft clan, which, if it remain hereditary, may become a caste, or, if it recruit its members mainly by adoption (apprenticeship throughout Antiquity and the Middle Age was just temporary adoption), may turn into a guild. But such specialists, by emancipation from kinship ties, have also forfeited the protection of the kinship organization which alone under barbarism, guaranteed to its members security of person and property. Society must be reorganized to accommodate and protect them.

In pre-history specialization of labour presumably began with similar itinerant experts. Archaeological proof is hardly to be expected, but in ethnography metalworkers are nearly always full time specialists. And in Europe at the beginning of the Bronze Age metal seems to have been worked and purveyed by perambulating smiths who seem to have functioned like tinkers and other itinerants of much more recent times. Though there is no such positive evidence, the same probably happened in Asia at the beginning of metallurgy. There must of course have been in addition other specialist craftsmen whom, as the Polynesian example warns us, archaeologists could not recognize because they worked in perishable materials.

One result of the Urban Revolution will be to rescue such specialists from nomadism and to guarantee them security in a new social organization.

About 5,000 years ago irrigation cultivation (combined with stock-breeding and fishing) in the valleys of the Nile, the Tigris-Euphrates and the Indus had begun to yield a social surplus, large enough to support a number of resident specialists who were themselves released from food-production. Water-transport, supplemented in Mesopotamia and the Indus valley by wheeled vehicles and even in Egypt by pack animals, made it easy to gather food stuffs at a few centres. At the same time dependence on river water for the irrigation of the crops restricted the cultivable areas while the necessity of canalizing the waters and protecting habitations against annual floods encouraged the aggregation of population. Thus arose the first cities— units of settlement ten times as great as any known neolithic village. It can be argued that all cities in the old world are offshoots of those of Egypt, Mesopotamia and the Indus basin. So the latter need not be taken into account if a minimum definition of civilization is to be inferred from a comparison of its independent manifestations.

But some three millennia later cities arose in Central America, and it is impossible to prove that the Mayas owed anything directly to the urban civilizations of the Old World. Their achievements must therefore be taken into account in our comparison, and their inclusion seriously complicates the task of defining the essential preconditions for the Urban Revolution. In the Old World the rural economy which yielded the surplus was based on the cultivation of cereals combined with stock-breeding. But this economy had been made more efficient as a result of the adoption of irrigation (allowing cultivation without prolonged fallow periods) and of important inventions and discoveries—metallurgy, the plough, the sailing boat and the wheel. None of these devices was known to the Mayas; they bred no animals for milk or meat; though they cultivated the cereal maize, they used the same sort of slash-and-burn method as neolithic farmers in prehistoric Europe or in the Pacific Islands today. Hence the minimum definition of a city, the greatest factor common to the Old World and the New will be substantially reduced and impoverished by the inclusion of the Maya. Nevertheless ten rather abstract criteria, all deducible from archaeological data, serve to distinguish even the earliest cities from any older or contemporary village.

(1) In point of size the first cities must have been more extensive and more densely populated than any previous settlements, although considerably smaller than many villages today. It is indeed only in Mesopotamia and India that the first urban populations can be estimated with any confidence or precision. There excavation has been sufficiently extensive and intensive to reveal both the total area and the density of building in sample quarters and in both respects has disclosed significant agreement with the less industrialized Oriental cities today. The population of Sumerian cities, thus calculated, ranged between 7,000 and 20,000; Harappa and Mohenjo-daro in the Indus valley must have approximated to the higher figure. We can only infer that Egyptian and Maya cities were of comparable magnitude from the scale of public works, presumably executed by urban populations.

(2) In composition and function the urban population already differed from that of any village. Very likely indeed most citizens were still also peasants, harvesting the lands and waters adjacent to the city. But all cities must have accommodated in addition classes who did not themselves procure their own food by agriculture, stock-breeding, fishing or collecting—full-time specialist craftsmen, transport workers, merchants, officials and priests. All these were of course supported by the surplus produced by the peasants living in the city and in dependent

villages, but they did not secure their share directly by exchanging their products or services for grains or fish with individual peasants.

(3) Each primary producer paid over the tiny surplus he could wring from the soil with his still very limited technical equipment as tithe or tax to an imaginary deity or a divine king who thus concentrated the surplus. Without this concentration, owing to the low productivity of the rural economy, no effective capital would have been available.

(4) Truly monumental public buildings not only distinguish each known city from any village but also symbolize the concentration of the social surplus. Every Sumerian city was from the first dominated by one or more stately temples, centrally situated on a brick platform raised above the surrounding dwellings and usually connected with an artificial mountain, the staged tower or ziggurat. But attached to the temples, were workshops and magazines, and an important appurtenance of each principal temple was a great granary. Harappa, in the Indus basin, was dominated by an artificial citadel, gird with a massive rampart of kiln-baked bricks, containing presumably a palace and immediately overlooking an enormous granary and the barracks of artizans. No early temples nor palaces have been excavated in Egypt, but the whole Nile valley was dominated by the gigantic tombs of the divine pharaohs while royal granaries are attested from the literary record. Finally the Maya cities are known almost exclusively from the temples and pyramids of sculptured stone round which they grew up.

Hence in Sumer the social surplus was first effectively concentrated in the hands of a god and stored in his granary. That was probably true in Central America while in Egypt the pharaoh (king) was himself a god. But of course the imaginary deities were served by quite real priests who, besides celebrating elaborate and often sanguinary rites in their honour, administered their divine masters' earthly estates. In Sumer indeed the god very soon, if not even before the revolution, shared his wealth and power with a mortal viceregent, the 'City-King,' who acted as civil ruler and leader in war. The divine pharaoh was naturally assisted by a whole hierarchy of officials.

(5) All those not engaged in food-production were of course supported in the first instance by the surplus accumulated in temple or royal granaries and were thus dependent on temple or court. But naturally priests, civil and military leaders and officials absorbed a major share of the concentrated surplus and thus formed a 'ruling class.' Unlike a palaeolithic magician or a neolithic chief, they were, as an Egyptian scribe actually put it, 'exempt from all manual tasks.' On the other hand, the lower classes were not only guaranteed peace and security, but were relieved from intellectual tasks which many find more irksome than any physical labour. Besides reassuring the masses that the sun was going to rise next day and the river would flood again next year (people who have not five thousand years of recorded experience of natural uniformities behind them are really worried about such matters!), the ruling classes did confer substantial benefits upon their subjects in the way of planning and organization.

(6) They were in fact compelled to invent systems of recording and exact, but practically useful, sciences. The mere administration of the vast revenues of a Sumerian temple or an Egyptian pharaoh by a perpetual corporation of priests or officials obliged its members to devise conventional methods of recording that should be intelligible to all their colleagues and successors, that is, to invent systems of writing and numeral notation. Writing is thus a significant, as well as a convenient, mark of civilization. But while writing is a trait common to Egypt, Mesopotamia, the Indus valley and Central America, the characters themselves were different in

each region and so were the normal writing materials—papyrus in Egypt, clay in Mesopotamia. The engraved seals or stelae that provide the sole extant evidence for early Indus and Maya writing, no more represent the normal vehicles for the scripts than do the comparable documents from Egypt and Sumer.

(7) The invention of writing—or shall we say the inventions of scripts—enabled the leisured clerks to proceed to the elaboration of exact and predictive sciences— arithmetic, geometry and astronomy. Obviously beneficial and explicitly attested by the Egyptian and Maya documents was the correct determination of the tropic year and the creation of a calendar. For it enabled the ruler to regulate successfully the cycle of agricultural operations. But once more the Egyptian, Maya and Babylonian calendars were as different as any systems based on a single natural unit could be. Calendrical and mathematical sciences are common features of the earliest civilizations and they too are corollaries of the archaeologists' criterion, writing.

(8) Other specialists, supported by the concentrated social surplus, gave a new direction to artistic expression. Savages even in palaeolithic times had tried, sometimes with astonishing success, to depict animals and even men as they saw them— concretely and naturalistically. Neolithic peasants never did that; they hardly ever tried to represent natural objects, but preferred to symbolize them by abstract geometrical patterns which at most may suggest by a few traits a fantastical man or beast or plant. But Egyptian, Sumerian, Indus and Maya artist-craftsmen—full-time sculptors, painters, or seal-engravers—began once more to carve, model or draw likenesses of persons or things, but no longer with the naive naturalism of the hunter, but according to conceptualized and sophisticated styles which differ in each of the four urban centres.

(9) A further part of the concentrated social surplus was used to pay for the importation of raw materials, needed for industry or cult and not available locally. Regular 'foreign' trade over quite long distances was a feature of all early civilizations and, though common enough among barbarians later, is not certainly attested in the Old World before 3,000 B.C. nor in the New before the Maya 'empire.' Thereafter regular trade extended from Egypt at least as far as Byblos on the Syrian coast while Mesopotamia was related by commerce with the Indus valley. While the objects of international trade were at first mainly 'luxuries,' they already included industrial materials, in the Old World notably metal the place of which in the New was perhaps taken by obsidian. To this extent the first cities were dependent for vital materials on long distance trade as no neolithic village ever was.

(10) So in the city, specialist craftsmen were both provided with raw materials needed for the employment of their skill and also guaranteed security in a State organization based now on residence rather than kinship. Itinerancy was no longer obligatory. The city was a community to which a craftsman could belong politically as well as economically.

Yet in return for security they became dependent on temple or court and were relegated to the lower classes. The peasant masses gained even less material advantages; in Egypt for instance metal did not replace the old stone and wood tools for agricultural work. Yet, however imperfectly, even the earliest urban communities must have been held together by a sort of solidarity missing from any neolithic village. Peasants, craftsmen, priests and rulers form a community, not only by reason of identity of language and belief, but also because each performs mutually complementary functions, needed for the well-being (as redefined under civilization) of the whole. In fact the earliest cities illustrate a first approximation to an organic solidarity based upon a functional complementarity and interdependence between all its members such as subsist between the constituent cells of an organism. Of course this was only a very distant approximation. However necessary the concentration of the surplus really were with the existing forces of production, there seemed a glaring conflict on economic interests between the tiny ruling class, who annexed the bulk of the social surplus, and the vast majority who were left with a bare subsistence and effectively excluded from the spiritual benefits of civilization. So solidarity had still to be maintained by the ideological devices appropriate to the mechanical solidarity of barbarism as expressed in the pre-eminence of the temple or the sepulchral shrine, and now supplemented by the force of the new State organization. There could be no room for sceptics or sectaries in the oldest cities.

These ten traits exhaust the factors common to the oldest cities that archaeology, at best helped out with fragmentary and often ambiguous written sources, can detect. No specific elements of town planning for example can be proved characteristic of all such cities; for on the one hand the Egyptian and Maya cities have not yet been excavated; on the other neolithic villages were often walled, an elaborate system of sewers drained the Orcadian hamlet of Skara Brae; two-storeyed houses were built in pre-Columbian *pueblos,* and so on.

The common factors are quite abstract. Concretely Egyptian, Sumerian, Indus and Maya civilizations were as different as the plans of their temples, the signs of their scripts and their artistic conventions. In view of this divergence and because there is so far no evidence for a temporal priority of one Old World centre (for instance, Egypt) over the rest nor yet for contact between Central America and any other urban centre, the four revolutions just considered may be regarded as mutually independent. On the contrary, all later civilizations in the Old World may in a sense be regarded as lineal descendants of those of Egypt, Mesopotamia or the Indus.

But this was not a case of like producing like. The maritime civilizations of Bronze Age Crete or classical Greece for example, to say nothing of our own, differ more from their reputed ancestors than those did among themselves. But the urban revolutions that gave them birth did not start from scratch. They could and probably did draw upon the capital accumulated in the three allegedly primary centres. That is most obvious in the case of cultural capital. Even today we use the Egyptians' calendar and the Sumerians' divisions of the day and the hour. Our European ancestors did not have to invent for themselves these divisions of time nor repeat the observations on which they are based; they took over—and very slightly improved systems elaborated 5,000 years ago! But the same is in a sense true of material capital as well. The Egyptians, the Sumerians and the Indus people had accumulated vast reserves of surplus food. At the same time they had to import from abroad necessary raw materials like metals and building timber as well as 'luxuries.' Communities controlling these natural resources could in exchange claim a slice of the urban surplus. They could use it as capital to support full-time specialists—craftsmen or rulers—until the latters' achievement in technique and organization had so enriched barbarian economies that they too could produce a substantial surplus in their turn.

Chapter Five

Styles of ancient civilizations

MAN'S EARLIEST CIVILIZATION   **10**

The first civilization of mankind took form on the arid and forbidding plains of the Tigris-Euphrates Valley. In the lower part of the valley, at the head of the Persian Gulf, were founded the cities of Sumer, the Old Testament's "land of Shinar." In developing these cities the Sumerians made certain technological and institutional innovations that comprise the transition from Neolithic culture to civilization. The following account by a distinguished Sumerologist describes the nature and significance of these innovations.*

The Tigris-Euphrates plain is a hot, arid land. Six thousand years ago it was a wind-swept barren. It had no minerals, almost no stone, no trees, practically no building material of any kind. It has been described as a land with "the hand of God against it." Yet it was in this desolate region that man built what was probably the first high civilization. Here were born the inventions of writing, farming technology, architecture, the first codes of law, the first cities. Perhaps the very poverty of the land provided the stimulus that mothered these inventions. But the main credit must go to the people who created them—a most remarkable people called the Sumerians.

These Sumerians, as now revealed by long archaeological research, were a surprisingly modern folk. In many ways they were like the pioneers who built the U. S.—practical, ambitious, enterprising, jealous of their personal rights, technologically inventive. Having no stone or timber, they built with marsh reeds and river mud, invented the brick mold and erected cities of baked clay. They canalled the waters of the Tigris and Euphrates rivers into the arid fields and turned Sumer into

* S. N. Kramer, "The Sumerians," *Scientific American* (October 1957), pp. 71-81. Reprinted with permission.

a veritable Garden of Eden. To manage their irrigation systems they originated regional government, thus emerging from the petty social order of the family and village to the city-state. They created a written language and committed it to permanent clay tablets. They traded their grain surpluses to distant peoples for metals and other materials they lacked. By the third millennium B.C. the culture and civilization of Sumer, a country about the size of the state of Massachusetts, had spread its influence over the whole Middle East, from India to the Mediterranean. And there is hardly an area of our culture today—in mathematics or philosophy, literature or architecture, finance or education, law or politics, religion or folklore—that does not owe some of its origins to the Sumerians.

One might suppose that the story of the Sumerians and their accomplishments would be one of the most celebrated in history. But the astonishing fact is that until about a century ago the modern world had no idea that Sumer or its people had ever existed. For more than 2,000 years they had simply vanished from the human record. Babylonia and ancient Egypt were known to every history student, but the earlier Sumerians were buried and forgotten. Now, thanks to a century of archaeological labor and to the Sumerians' own cuneiform tablets, we have come to know them intimately—as well as or better than any other people of the early history of mankind. The story of how the lost Sumerian civilization was discovered is itself a remarkable chapter. This article will review briefly how the history of the Sumerians was resurrected and what we have learned about them.

THE CUNEIFORM TABLETS.   Modern archaeologists began to dig in Mesopotamia for its ancient civilizations around a century ago. They were looking for the cities of the Assyrians and Babylonians, who of course were well known from Biblical and Greek literature. As the world knows, the diggers soon came upon incredibly rich finds. At the sites of Nineveh and other ancient Assyrian cities they unearthed many clay tablets inscribed with the wedge-shaped writing called cuneiform. This script was taken to be the invention of the Assyrians. Since the Assyrians were apparently a Semitic people, the language was assumed to be Semitic. But few clues were available for decipherment of the strange cuneiform script.

Then came a development which was to be as important a key to discovery in Mesopotamia as the famous Rosetta Stone in Egypt. In western Persia, notably on the Rock of Behistun, European scholars found some cuneiform inscriptions in three languages. They identified one of the languages as Old Persian, another as Elamite, and the third as the language of the Assyrian tablets. The way was now open to decipher the cuneiform writing—first the Old Persian, then the Assyrian, of which it was apparently a translation.

When scholars finally deciphered the "Assyrian" script, they discovered that the cuneiform writing could not have been originated by the Assyrian Semites. Its symbols, which were not alphabetic but syllabic and ideographic, apparently were derived from non-Semitic rather than Semitic words. And many of the cuneiform tablets turned out to be written in a language without any Semitic characteristics whatever. The archaeologists had to conclude, therefore, that the Assyrians had taken over the cuneiform script from a people who had lived in the region before them.

Who were this people? Jules Oppert, a leading 19th-century investigator of ancient Mesopotamia, found a clue to their name in certain inscriptions which referred to the "King of Sumer and Akkad." He concluded that Akkad was the northern part of the country (indeed, the Assyrians and Babylonians are now called Akkadians), and that Sumer was the southern part, inhabited by the people who spoke the non-Semitic language and had invented cuneiform writing.

So it was that the Sumerians were rediscovered after 2,000 years of oblivion. Oppert resurrected their name in 1869. In the following decades French, American, Anglo-American and German expeditions uncovered the buried Sumerian cities—Lagash, Nippur, Shuruppak, Kish, Ur (Ur of the Chaldees in the Bible), Erech, Asmar and so on. The excavation of ancient Sumer has proceeded almost continuously for three quarters of a century; even during World War II the Iraqi went on digging at a few sites. These historic explorations have recovered hundreds of thousands of Sumerian tablets, great temples, monuments, tombs, sculptures, paintings, tools, irrigation systems and remnants of almost every aspect of the Sumerian culture. As a result we have a fairly complete picture of what life in Sumer was like 5,000 years ago. We know something about how the Sumerians looked (from their statues); we know a good deal about their houses and palaces, their tools and weapons, their art and musical instruments, their jewels and ornaments, their skills and crafts, their industry and commerce, their *belles lettres* and government, their schools and temples, their loves and hates, their kings and history.

THE PEOPLES OF SUMER. Let us run quickly over the history. The area where the Sumerians lived is lower Mesopotamia, from Baghdad down to the Persian Gulf. It is reasonably certain that the Sumerians themselves were not the first settlers in this region. Just as the Indian names Mississippi, Massachusetts, etc., show that North America was inhabited before the English-speaking settlers came, so we know that the Sumerians were preceded in Mesopotamia by another people because the ancient names of the Tigris and Euphrates rivers (*Indigna* and *Buranun*), and even the names of the Sumerian cities (Nippur, Ur, Kish, etc.), are not Sumerian words. The city names must be derived from villages inhabited by the earlier people.

The same kind of clue—words that turn up in the Sumerian writing but are plainly not Sumerian in origin—tells us something about those first settlers in Sumer. As Benno Landsberger of the University of Chicago, one of the keenest minds in cuneiform research, has shown, among these pre-Sumerian words are those for farmer, herdsman, fishermen, plow, metal smith, carpenter, weaver, potter, mason and perhaps even merchant. It follows that the predecessors of the Sumerians must already have developed a fairly advanced civilization. This is confirmed by excavations of their stone implements and pottery.

The dates of Sumer's early history have always been surrounded with uncertainty, and they have not been satisfactorily settled by tests with the new method of radiocarbon dating. According to the best present estimates, the first settlers occupied the area some time before 4000 B.C.; new geological evidence indicates that the lower Tigris-Euphrates Valley, once covered by the Persian Gulf, became an inhabitable land well before that date. Be that as it may, it seems that the people called Sumerians did not arrive in the region until nearly 3000 B.C. Just where they came from is in doubt, but there is some reason to believe that their original home had been in the neighborhood of a city called Aratta, which may have been near the Caspian Sea: Sumerian epic poets sang glowingly of Aratta, and its people were said to speak the Sumerian language.

Wherever the Sumerians came from, they brought a creative spirit and an extraordinary surge of progress to the land of Sumer. Uniting with the people who already inhabited it, they developed a rich and powerful civilization. Not long after they arrived, a king called Etana became the ruler of all Sumer: he is described in Sumerian literature as "the man who stabilized all the lands," and he may therefore be the first empire builder in human history. Sumer reached its fullest flowering around 2500 B.C., when its people had developed the cuneiform symbols and thereby originated their finest gift to civilization—the gift of written communication and history. Their own history came to an end some 800 years later: about 1720 B.C. In that year Hammurabi of Babylon won control of the country, and Sumer disappeared in a Babylonian kingdom.

LIFE IN SUMER. The Sumerians' writings and disinterred cities, as I have said, make it possible to reconstruct their life in great detail. Their civilization rested on agriculture and fishing. Among their inventions were the wagon wheel, the plow and the sailboat, but their science and engineering went far beyond these elementary tools. For irrigation the Sumerians built intricate systems of canals, dikes, weirs and reservoirs. They developed measuring and surveying instruments, and a sexagesimal number system (*i.e.,* based on the number 60) with a place notation device not unlike our decimal system. Their farming was highly sophisticated: among their tablets is a veritable farmer's almanac of instructions in agriculture.

In the crafts, the Sumerians' inventions included the potter's wheel, metal casting (of copper and bronze), riveting, soldering, engraving, cloth fulling, bleaching and dyeing. They manufactured paints, leather, cosmetics, perfumes and drugs. Prescriptions recorded on some of their tablets show that the Sumerian physician had command of a large assortment of *materia medica,* prepared from plants, animals and inorganic sources.

Although the Sumerians' economy was primarily agricultural, their life was centered mainly in the cities. Here lived many of the farmers, herdsmen and fishermen, as well as merchants, craftsmen, architects, doctors, scribes, soldiers and priests. Artisans and traveling merchants sold their products in the central town market, and were paid in kind or in money—usually silver coin in the form of a disk or ring. The dozen or so cities in Sumer probably ranged from 10,000 to 50,000 in population. Each was enclosed by a wall and surrounded with suburban villages and hamlets.

The dominant feature of every Sumerian city was a massive temple mounted on a high terrace. It usually had the form of a ziggurat, Sumer's most distinctive contribution to religious architecture. This is a pyramidal tower with a series of ascending terraces winding around the outside. To break the unattractive blankness of the temple's mud-brick walls, the Sumerian architects introduced buttresses and recesses, and they also beautified the building with columns decorated in colored mosaics. Inside the temple were rooms for the priests and a central shrine with a niche for the statue of the god. Each city in Sumer had a different tutelary god, and the Sumerians considered the city the god's property. Thus the city of Nippur, for example, belonged to Enlil, the god of the air. Nippur became Sumer's chief religious and cultural center, and Enlil was elevated to the highest rank as father of all the gods.

Originally the cities were governed by the citizens themselves, presided over by a governor of their selection. On all important decisions the citizens met in an assembly divided into two chambers—the "elders" and the "men." But for military reasons they gradually relinquished this democratic system. Each city acquired a ruler—at first elected, later hereditary—who organized its defense against the other cities and against foreign invaders. In the course of time the king rivaled the city's religious leaders in wealth and influence. The rulers of Sumer's dozen or so city-states also contended with one another for control of the whole country, and the history of Sumer is largely a record of bitter conflicts among its cities, which eventually led to its downfall.

The life of the individual citizen in a Sumerian city was remarkably free and prosperous. The poorest citizen managed to own a farm and cattle or a house and garden. To be sure, slavery was permitted, and a man could sell his children or his entire family to pay off his debts. But even slaves had certain legal rights: they could engage in business, borrow money and buy their freedom. (The average price for an adult slave was 10 shekels—less than the price of an ass.) The great majority of Sumerians were free citizens, going about their business and the pursuit of happiness with a minimum of restrictions. This did not, however, apply to children, who were under the absolute authority of their parents, could be disinherited or sold into slavery, and had to marry mates chosen by the parents. But in the normal course of events Sumerian families cherished their children and were knit closely together by love and mutual obligations. Women had many legal rights, including the right to hold property and engage in business. A man could divorce his wife on comparatively slender grounds, or, if they had no children, he was allowed to take a second wife.

Most Sumerian families lived in a one-story, mud-brick house consisting of several rooms grouped around an open court. The well-to-do had two-story houses of about a dozen rooms, plastered and whitewashed inside and out; these houses boasted servants' rooms and sometimes even a private chapel. Often the house had a mausoleum in the basement where the family buried its dead. The Sumerians believed that the souls of the dead traveled to a nether world where existence continued more or less as on earth. They therefore buried pots, tools, weapons and jewels with the dead. When a king died, the palace sometimes buried with him some of his courtiers and servants and even his chariot and animals.

Sumerian men were often clean-shaven, but many of them wore a long beard and had long hair parted in the middle. In early times their usual dress was a flounced skirt and felt cloak; later these were replaced by a long shirt and a big fringed shawl draped over the left shoulder, leaving the right arm bare. The common dress for women was a long shawl covering the body from head to foot, except for the right shoulder. Women usually braided their hair into a heavy pigtail and wound it around the head, but on important occasions they wore elaborate headdresses consisting of ribbons, beads and pendants.

Music apparently occupied a large place in the life of the Sumerians—at home, in school and in the temple. Beautifully constructed harps and lyres were found in the royal tombs at Ur. Research has also turned up references to drums, tambourines, reed and metal pipes, and hymns written on tablets. Some of the important personages in the palaces and temples of the Sumerian cities were musicians.

The Sumerians cannot be said to have produced any great art, but they did show considerable skill in carving and sculpture. Perhaps their most original contribution to the graphic arts was the cylinder seal—a stone cylinder with a carved design which was impressed in clay by rolling the cylinder over it. These designs, or seals, appear on clay tablets, jar covers and so on. They depict scenes such as a king on the battlefield, a shepherd defending his flock from wild beasts, heraldic arrangements of animals. Eventually the Sumerians settled on one favorite seal design which became almost their trademark—a scene showing a worshipper being presented to a god by his personal good angel.

RELIGION.   The Sumerians lived by a simple, fatalistic theology. They believed that the universe and their personal lives were ruled by living gods, invisible to mortal eyes. The chief gods were those of water, earth, air and heaven, named respectively Enki, Ki, Enlil and An. From a primeval sea were created the earth, the atmosphere, the gods and sky, the sun, moon, planets and stars, and finally life.

There were gods in charge of the sun, moon and planets, of winds and storms, of rivers and mountains, of cities and states, of farms and irrigation ditches, of the pickax, brick mold and plow. The major gods established a set of unchangeable laws which must be obeyed willy-nilly by everything and everybody. Thus the Sumerians were untroubled by any question of free will. Man existed to please and serve the gods, and his life followed their divine orders. Because the great gods were far away in the distant sky and had more important matters to attend to, each person appealed to a particular personal god, a "good angel," through whom he sought salvation. Not that the people neglected regular public devotions to the gods. In the Sumerian temples a court of professionals, including priests, priestesses, musicians and eunuchs, offered daily libations and sacrifices of animal and vegetable fats. There were also periodic feasts and celebrations of which the most important was a royal ceremony ushering in each new year.

This ceremony is traceable to the cycle of nature in Mesopotamia. Every summer, in the hot, parched months, all vegetation died and animal life languished. In the autumn the land began to revive and bloom again. The Sumerian theology explained these events by supposing that the god of vegetation retired to the nether world in the summer and returned to the earth around the time of the new year; his sexual reunion with his wife Inanna, the goddess of love and procreation, then restored fertility to the land. To celebrate this revival and ensure fecundity, the Sumerians each year staged a marriage ceremony between their king, as the risen god, and a priestess representing the goddess Inanna. The marriage was made an occasion of prolonged festival, ritual, music and rejoicing.

The Sumerians considered themselves to be a chosen people, in more intimate contact with the gods than was the rest of mankind. Nevertheless they had a moving vision of all mankind living in peace and security, united by a universal faith and perhaps even by a universal language. Curiously, they projected this vision into the past, into a long-gone golden age, rather than into the future. As a Sumerian poet put it:

> Once upon a time there was no snake, there was no scorpion,
> There was no hyena, there was no lion,
> There was no wild dog, no wolf
> There was no fear, no terror,
> Man had no rival.
>
> Once upon a time . . .
> The whole universe, the people in unison,
> To Enlil in one tongue gave praise.

To students of the ancient religions of the Near East, much of the Sumerian cosmology and theology is easily recognizable. The order of the universe's creation, the Job-like resignation of sinful and mortal man to the will of the gods, the mystic tale of the dying god and his triumphant resurrection, the Aphrodite-like goddess Inanna, the ideals of "humaneness"—these and many other features of the Sumerian creed survive without much change in the later religions of the ancient world. Indeed, the very name of the Sumerian dying god, Dumuzi, endures as Biblical Tammuz, whose descent to the nether regions was still mourned by the women of Jerusalem in the days of the prophet Ezekiel. It is not too much to say that, with the decipherment of the Sumerian tablets, we can now trace many of the roots of man's major religious creeds back to Sumer.

CUNEIFORM. But the Sumerians' chief contribution to civilization was their invention of writing. Their cuneiform script is the earliest known system of writing in man's history. The cuneiform system served as the main tool of written communication throughout western Asia for some 2,000 years—long after the Sumerians themselves had disappeared. Without it, mankind's cultural progress would certainly have been much delayed.

The Sumerian script began as a set of pictographic signs devised by temple administrators and priests to keep track of the temple's resources and activities. They inscribed the signs in clay with a reed stylus, and this accounts for the curious wedge-shaped characters. In the course of the centuries Sumarian scholars developed the signs into purely phonetic symbols representing words or syllables.

More than 90 per cent of the tablets that have been excavated in Sumer are economic, legal and administrative documents, not unlike the commercial and governmental records of our own day. But some 5,000 of the finds are literary works; myths and epic tales, hymns and lamentations, proverbs, fables, essays. They qualify as man's oldest known literature—nearly 1,000 years older than the *Iliad* and the Hebrew Bible. In addition the tablets include a number of Sumerian "textbooks," listing the names of trees, birds, insects, minerals, cities, countries and so forth. There are even commemorative narratives which constitute mankind's first writing of history.

From the Sumerians' invention of writing grew the first formal system of education—another milestone in human intellectual progress. They set up "professional" schools to train scribes, secretaries and administrators; in time these vocational schools became also centers of culture where scholars, scientists and poets devoted their lives to learning and teaching.

The head of the school was called "the school father"; the pupils, "school sons." Among the faculty members were "the man in charge of drawing," "the man in charge of Sumerian," "the man in charge of the whip." There was no sparing of the rod. The curriculum consisted in copying and memorizing the lists of words and names on the textbook tablets, in studying and composing poetic narratives, hymns and essays and in mastering mathematical tables and problems, including tables of square and cube roots.

Teachers in ancient Sumer seem to have been treated not unlike their counterparts in the U. S. today: their salaries were low and they were looked upon with a mixture of respect and contempt. The Sumerians were an aggressive people, prizing wealth, renown and social prestige. As their tablets suggest, they were far more concerned with accounts than with academic learning.

Their restless ambition and aggressive spirit are reflected in the bitter rivalry among their cities and kings. The history of Sumer is a story of wars in which one city after another rose to ascendancy over the country. Although there are many gaps in our information, we can reconstruct the main outlines of that history from references in the tablets. The first recorded ruler of Sumer, as I have mentioned, was Etana, king of Kish. Probably not long afterward a king of Erech by the name of Meskiaggasher founded a dynasty which ruled the whole region from the Mediterranean to the Zagros Mountains northeast of Sumer. The city of Kish then rose to dominance again, only to be supplanted by the city of Ur, whose first king, Mesannepadda, is said to have ruled for 80 years and made Ur the capital of Sumer. After Mesannepadda's death, Sumer again came under the rule of the city of Erech, under a king named Gilgamesh who became the supreme hero of Sumerian history—a brave, adventurous figure whose deeds were celebrated throughout the ancient world of western Asia. The next great ruler who appears in the record was

Lugalannemundu of the city of Adab; he is reported to have ruled 90 years and to have controlled an empire extending far beyond Sumer. But his empire also fell apart, and a king of Kish named Mesilim became the dominant figure in Sumer. Later rule over the country was won by the city of Lagash. The last ruler of the Lagash dynasty, a king named Urukagina, has the distinction of being the first recorded social reformer. He suppressed the city's harsh bureaucracy, reduced taxes, and brought relief to widows, orphans and the poor. One of King Urukagina's inscriptions contains the word "freedom"—the first appearance of this word in man's history. But within less than 10 years a king of the neighboring city of Umma overthrew Urukagina and put the city of Lagash to the torch.

THE FALL OF SUMER.   The cities' incessant struggle for power exhausted Sumer. A Semitic people from the west, under the famous warrior Sargon the Great, marched into the country and established a new dynasty. Sargon founded a capital called Agade (from which came the name Akkadian) and made it the richest and most powerful city in the Middle Eastern world. He conquered almost all of western Asia and perhaps also parts of Egypt and Ethiopia. Sargon's sons held on to the empire, but his grandson, Naramsin, brought Sumer to disaster. For reasons unknown, he destroyed the holy city of Nippur, and soon afterward he was defeated by semibarbaric invaders from the mountains of Iran who overran Sumer and completely wiped out the city of Agade.

It took the Sumerians several generations to recover. But their civilization did come to life again, under a governor of Lagash named Gudea, whose face is the best known to us of all the Sumerians because a score of statues of him have been found in the ancient temples of Lagash. Gudea re-established contacts and trade with the rest of the known world and put Sumer on the path to prosperity. After Gudea, however, the rivalry among its cities broke out again and became Sumer's final undoing. The city of Ur, under a king named Ur-Nammu, defeated Lagash; Ur-Nammu founded a new rule called the Third Dynasty of Ur. It was to be Sumer's last dynasty.

Ur-Nammu was a strong and benevolent ruler. According to inscriptions that have recently come to light, he removed "chiselers" and grafters and established a law code which insured honest weights and measures and took care that the poor should not "fall a prey to the wealthy." Ur-Nammu's code is especially significant for the fact that instead of the barbarous rule of "an eye for an eye and a tooth for a tooth" common among early societies it established a money fine as punishment for assaults.

In spite of Sumer's civilized kings and prosperity, time was running out for the Sumerians. Their internal rivalries and the growing pressure of surrounding peoples soon overwhelmed them. Semitic nomads from the Arabian desert to the west (the Amorites of the Bible) took over the Sumerian cities of Isin, Larsa and Babylon. Ur itself was conquered by the Elamites to the east, who carried off its last king, Ibbi-Sin. In the following two and a half centuries the Semitic rulers of Isin and Larsa, and then Larsa and Babylon, struggled for control of the country. Finally, in about the year 1720 B.C., Hammurabi defeated Rim-Sin, the last king of Larsa, and Babylon emerged as the dominant city of southern Mesopotamia. The Sumerians were submerged by the Semites and lost their identity as a people. In time their name was erased from the memory of man; the Sumerian language disappeared as a living, spoken tongue, though for centuries it continued to be the written language studied in schools.

The Sumerians firmly believed that when man died, his emasculated spirit descended to a dark, dreary nether world. The spirit and fame of this proud, vigorous people certainly suffered a remarkable eclipse after their empire fell. But what their minds created survives throughout the living corpus of present-day civilization: it appears in the form of a Biblical proverb, a statutory law, a heroic folktale, an Aesopic fable, a zodiacal sign, a Euclidean theorem, the weight of a coin, the degree of an angle. And in the cuneiform tablets which were the Sumerians' pre-eminent gift we have found the earliest intellectual record of man's strivings toward civilization.

THE EPIC OF GILGAMESH 11

A great body of literature, which first took form under the Sumerians, flourished with many changes among the succeeding Babylonians, Assyrians, and other peoples. Outstanding among these literary creations is the Epic of Gilgamesh. *Apart from its exceptional literary merits, it is noteworthy as the earliest example of epic composition and also as the first attempt to discuss the profound mystery of life and death. The following essay by a British scholar analyzes the epic as a distinctive expression of the Mesopotamian philosophy of life in contrast to the Egyptian.**

I

To move from the rooms devoted to ancient Egyptian civilization in one of our great museums to those in which the relics of ancient Mesopotamian life are displayed is to experience a sudden change of ethos. Although these two earliest civilizations of the Near East were contemporaneous and in their material achievement equal, each was characterized by a distinctive spirit that can still be clearly felt, even through the media of the broken monuments that modern archaeology has recovered. To the museum visitor this difference is perhaps most manifest as he passes from viewing the specimens of Egyptian linear and plastic art to those of Mesopotamia. Although in the Egyptian scenes strange and repellent deities often appear in solemn ritual acts, there are numerous representations of the ordinary events of social life that clearly reveal a real *joie de vie* and appreciation of both the beautiful and the homely. Where scenes of violence are depicted, as in the many monuments of royal victories, the representation usually has a kind of symbolic character, so that the grim physical realities are not intruded on the viewer. Very different is the impression given by the remains of Mesopotamian art, whether of Sumerian, Babylonian or Assyrian origin. There is a notable absence of representation of the events of everyday life; warfare and its consequences form the subject of the bulk of the surviving monuments, and in its depiction a grim satisfaction seems to show itself by rendering with the utmost realism the grisly details of the fate of those who were conquered. Even when the Assyrian monarchs chose to alternate such monuments of their triumphs with accounts of their prowess in hunting, the artists not only gloried in their great ability to represent in stone the lithesome strength of the lions that were hunted, but they were equally concerned to portray the reality of the beasts' dying agony when transfixed with arrows and lances.

* Reprinted with the permission of Charles Scribner's Sons from *Religion in Ancient History,* by S. G. F. Brandon, pp. 149-64. Copyright © 1969 by S. G. F. Brandon.

The grim spirit that pervades Mesopotamian art is the more remarkable when it is recalled that, to continue the comparison, so much of our evidence of Egyptian art comes from the tombs and might consequently be expected to have been sombre in both subject and spirit. That Egyptian art is not so, despite its mortuary connexions, has its explanation in a fact that affords a clue to the difference of ethos between Egyptian and Mesopotamian culture. The immense preoccupation of the Egyptians with death, which is so strikingly attested by their mummies, tombs, mortuary equipment and funerary papyri, was fundamentally inspired by optimism. . . . the ancient Egyptian believed that, through ritual assimilation to the resurrected god Osiris, he could attain to a new and blessed life after death. Hence, although he naturally feared the awful experience of death, he could view his destiny optimistically, believing that by divine grace and his own effort he could continue his personal existence into the next world and in a happy condition. The inhabitant of ancient Mesopotamia, be he Sumerian, Babylonian or Assyrian, had no such hope. His religion taught a dismal eschatology. He was instructed to believe that the gods had created mankind to serve them by building temples and offering regular sacrifices. But that was mankind's only *raison d'être;* beyond that there was nothing for which its members could strive or hope. To their human servants the gods were generally thought to be benevolent and to prosper their undertakings, provided that men in their turn were loyal and diligent in their service. Disobedience would result in the withdrawal of divine providence, and the disobedient would thereby be exposed to the assault of maleficent demons who brought disease and other misfortunes. But divine providence extended only to this life; for the gods had withheld immortality from their creatures. Thus, even a life of pious service to the gods was of no avail; man's destiny, as man, was limited to the years of his life in this world.

But the ancient Mesopotamian did not believe that death brought annihilation. Indeed, he might have been happier if he could have believed so. The concept of personal annihilation required a greater degree of sophistication than Mesopotamian thought was then capable of, and it would seem that the primitive instinct to envisage the continuance of personal identity led to a belief in a form of *post-mortem* survival. Death was thought to effect an awful change in the individual, who became an *edim* or *edimmu*. It is not certain how this change was envisaged. Some texts seem to imply that there was a transformation of being into something hideous and repulsive; other evidence appears to indicate that the dead preserved consciousness of their personal identity and could be affected by the provision or the lack of mortuary offerings. But, whatever the form of their existence, their condition was most wretched. At death they departed to the realm of the infernal god Nergal, which was grimly named *kur-nu-gi-a,* "the land of no-return." It was thought to lie deep beneath the earth on which mankind dwelt. It is graphically described in a curious text known as the *Descent of Ishtar into the Underworld* as "the house in which there is no light, and those who dwell therein have earth for their sustenance and clay for their food, and are in profound darkness; they are clothed like birds with wings; dust is both door and bolt of that place." The Hebrew conception of *Sheol,* as it is found in *Job* x. 21-2, derives from the same eschatological tradition. Moreover, in *kur-nu-gi-a* there was no distinction between the dead, high or low, good or bad—all were in the same condition of hopeless misery. Hence this life had not that moral significance for the Mesopotamian that it had for the Egyptian, who believed that his condition in the next world would be determined by his conduct in this, for after death his heart would be weighed against the symbol of truth in the presence of Osiris.

Taught to see his destiny in terms of this grim eschatology, it was inevitable that the inhabitant of ancient Mesopotamia should adopt a pessimistic view of life. This did not mean that life in Mesopotamia was more unhappy than it was elsewhere in the ancient world. There is, indeed, an abundance of evidence that the good things of life were sought after and enjoyed as much as they ever were in Egypt. And, strangely perhaps to our thinking, there is evidence too of genuine devotion to the gods and apparent joy in their service, although it was by their decree that men were mortal. Despite this testimony to the general tenor of social life, however, the logic of the traditional eschatology was inescapable, and, beneath the surface of ordinary life, it is evident that many were deeply concerned with the inevitable problem of coming to terms with their dismal end. Of this quest the literature of ancient Mesopotamia has left us a supreme memorial in the *Epic of Gilgamesh,* which is not only our earliest example of epic composition, but also the first attempt to discuss the problem of man's destiny.

II

The *Epic of Gilgamesh* in its most complete form survives on twelve large clay tablets, which were recovered from the remains of the library in the temple of Nabu and from the palace library of King Assurbanipal at Nineveh. These versions of the *Epic* date from the seventh century B.C.; but it is evident that work in some form is far older, for fragments of it have been found in Sumerian and early Akkadian. From the fact that some of these older pieces contain variants from the Assyrian version, there is reason for thinking that the *Epic* in its most complete form is a composition made up of a number of earlier independent legends. One particularly interesting indication of this, to which attention will be more closely drawn below, is the interpolation into the narrative of the story of the Flood, which was evidently of quite independent origin and purpose and wholly unconnected with the Gilgamesh theme. It has been suggested by some scholars that the *Epic* in its more complete form is the product of philosophical reflection that manifested itself at Babylon about 2000 B.C. Certainly, in the form in which we have it from the Assyrian libraries, it is a carefully conceived literary composition, intended to present a definite philosophy of life through the recitation of the tragic career of a hero well known to contemporary folklore.

For Gilgamesh was evidently one of the great figures of Mesopotamian tradition. He is represented on early Sumerian seal-stones engaged in heroic labours, his name appears in the Sumerian king-list inscribed on the Weld-Blundell prism, now in the Ashmolean Museum at Oxford, and it is frequently found in the formulae of omens and oaths. Gilgamesh thus appears to have been a kind of semi-divine hero in Mesopotamian folklore; but, although he is described as partly human and partly divine, the pathos of his tragedy as it is presented in the *Epic* resides in the fact that he knows himself to be mortal as other men are.

A recent editor of the *Epic* has said, "The Gilgamesh Epic is a meditation on death, in the form of a tragedy." It is truly such; but it is also much more. Its author—if indeed one man alone was responsible for its completed form—has made his narrative the vehicle for the only viable philosophy of life that the accepted eschatology allowed, and he has, moreover, taken the opportunity therein to give expression to current thought on a number of minor issues. An interesting instance of this occurs in what might fairly be called the first act of the drama.

When the curtain rises on the first scene, we are given a vivid picture of what tyrannical rule meant in an ancient Sumerian city-state. Gilgamesh is the prince of Uruk; he is a man of dynamic character, handsome in appearance, and mighty in his strength. To him Uruk owes its great walls and temples; but from his lust and rapacity its citizens suffered—no boy or maiden was safe from him. To save the people of Uruk from their ordeal the gods take a hand, and a mighty wild man named Enkidu is created to contend with Gilgamesh and control his daemonic energy. The presentation of Enkidu, who is one of the key-characters of the *Epic,* is skilfully managed and utilized to show what were believed to be the effects of civilized living on mankind. When we first see Enkidu he is a wild hairy creature, who lives with the animals, and eats grass and drinks water as they do. To tame Enkidu a courtesan, who probably served in the temple of Ishtar, the tutelary goddess of the city, is sent out to him. She teaches him to eat bread, to drink wine and to wear clothes, and she seduces him with her sophisticated arts. And so Enkidu is civilized. The consequences of his change of life are described with a subtle insight. The former savage finds that the bond of sympathy that had existed between himself and the animals is broken, and they now flee from his sight and he has lost his former swiftness of foot and cannot follow them.

A civilized man, mighty in stature and strength, Enkidu now enters into Uruk and meets Gilgamesh. A tremendous struggle ensues between them. Gilgamesh finally conquers, but he respects the strength and spirit of his adversary, and the two become fast friends. Together they then set out on some heroic exploits, which includes the slaying of a terrible ogre. With considerable dramatic skill, in view of the sequel, the occasion is used to depict Gilgamesh as making light of the danger of death in his thirst for glory.

On their victorious return to Uruk the heroes are led to insult the great goddess Ishtar and to kill a sacred bull. The gods decide that one of them must be punished by death, and Enkidu is chosen.

His fate is made known to Enkidu in a dream, and, as in the legend of the *Descent of Ishtar into the Underworld,* the process of death and the "land of no-return" are described with that grim realism that must be regarded as typical of the ancient Mesopotamian mind. Enkidu dreams that he is seized by the death-god and carried off:

> . . . to the House of Darkness, the dwelling of Irkalla,
> To the House, from which there is no return for those who enter,
> By the way, whose course turns not back,
> To the House, whose dwellers are bereft of light,
> Where dust is their sustenance, clay their food,
> Clothed are they as a bird with garment of wings,
> The light they see not, in darkness dwelling.
> In the House of Dust which I entered,
> The sceptres were abased, the crowns deposited:
> There dwelt the mighty ones, who had borne rule in early time . . .
> In the House of Dust which I entered,
> There dwelt the high-priest and he who led the lamentation,
> There dwelt the master of incantations and the ecstatic,
> There dwelt the chief ministers of the great gods (Tablet VII, 33-42, 45-48).

Enkidu falls sick, and as his end approaches he bitterly laments his fate, and he curses the courtesan who had lured him from his rustic life to live in the sophisticated city. He dies, and Gilgamesh mourns his loss with a poignancy of expression that can still be felt, even through the medium of translation into a modern language:

> "He who with me underwent all hard[ships]—
> Enkidu, whom I loved dearly,
> Who with me underwent all hardships—
> Has now gone to the fate of mankind!
> Day and night I have wept over him.
> I would not give him up for burial—
> In case my friend should rise at my plaint—
> Seven days and seven nights,
> Until a worm fell out of his nose.
> Since his passing I have found not life,
> I have roamed like a hunter in the midst of the steppe."

But Enkidu's death robs Gilgamesh not only of the presence of his friend; it comes to him as an awful revelation of the common fate of man. Although he shrugged off its threat in the days of their high-hearted companionship, now that he had seen death at close range in his friend, he was terrified. For in Enkidu's death he saw the presage of his own:

> "I also shall die: will it not be with me as it is with Enkidu?
> Woe has entered my heart,
> The fear of death has seized me."

Confronted now with the chill fact of his own mortality, Gilgamesh's instinct is to flee. But where can he go to escape the common lot of man? In his agony of mind, he recalls that two human beings alone had escaped that fate. Away beyond the world's end dwelt the legendary Utanapishtim and his wife, the sole survivors of an earlier race of men whom the gods had destroyed in a mighty flood. To Utanapishtim, therefore, Gilgamesh determines to go to learn the secret of his immortality.

The way to the dwelling place of Utanapishtim is long and difficult and beset by many dangers. But Gilgamesh struggles on, and in the course of his journey he meets Siduri, whose title has been variously translated as the "wine-maiden," the "divine barmaid," and the "ale-wife." Whatever the original meaning of the epithet, Siduri is meant to play an important rôle in the *Epic*. She inquires of the weary, travelled-stained Gilgamesh the purpose of his journey. When she learns of his quest, she replies:

> "Gilgamesh, whither runnest thou?
> The life which thou seekest thou wilt not find;
> (For) when the gods created mankind,
> They allotted death to mankind,
> (But) life they retained in their keeping.
> Thou, O Gilgamesh, let thy belly be full;
> Day and night be thou merry;
> Make every day a day of rejoicing.
> Day and night do thou dance and play.
> Let thy raiment be clean,

Thy head be washed, (and) thyself bathed in water.
Cherish the little one holding thy hand,
(And) let the wife rejoice in thy bosom.
This is the lot of [mankind]."

Here is set forth the quintessence of the Mesopotamian philosophy of life—a practical guide to living that was necessitated and coloured by the accepted eschatology. And the fact that the author of the *Epic* has put its statement in the mouth of Siduri is surely significant. In the ancient legend that the Yahwist writer utilized in the story of Noah in the Hebrew book of *Genesis* (v. 28-9, ix. 20), Noah is represented as mitigating the hard lot, to which mankind had been condemned, by the discovery of the use of wine "that maketh glad the heart of man." In the *Epic of Gilgamesh,* which also draws on the common treasury of Semitic folklore, Siduri, the personification of wine, counsels the labouring Gilgamesh to solace himself to the fullest with those joys that are available to man and not to waste himself in the pursuit of a hopeless quest.

But Gilgamesh will not heed this *carpe diem* philosophy, and he presses on against the terrors and miseries that continue to beset his path. At length his patience and fortitude are rewarded, and he wins his way to the remote abode of Utanapishtim and his wife. But this achievement avails him nothing, but rather serves to emphasize the hopelessness of his quest. For, when he enquires of Utanapishtim the secret of his immortality, the latter in reply tells him the story of the great Flood that had destroyed all mankind, and from which he and his wife alone of human beings had escaped in a great ship that they had built. It was in consequence of their marvellous escape that the god Enlil had decreed that they should never die and had placed them in their remote abode far beyond the habitations of other men. Their case then was unique, and the explanation of it served but to emphasize to Gilgamesh the hopelessness of his quest, for he could not win immortality in that way.

The interpolation of the legend of the Flood at this point of the *Epic* shows great literary skill. Although it does in fact interrupt the theme of the narrative by introducing a different topic of great intrinsic interest, the Flood story is cleverly made to reinforce the argument that mortality is the natural state of man. We may rejoice that the author of the *Epic* in its completed form did thus interpolate the Flood story, because it has preserved to us a celebrated legend of ancient Mesopotamia, of which only fragments have survived in other contexts. It is, indeed, exciting still to read the account of George Smith who first identified the story, when sorting and arranging the broken tablets of the Ninevite libraries: "Commencing a steady search among these fragments, I soon found half of a curious tablet which had evidently contained originally six columns. . . . On looking down the third column, my eye caught the statement that the ship rested on the mountains of Nizir, followed by the account of the sending forth of the dove, and its finding no resting-place and returning. I saw at once that I had here discovered a portion at least of the Chaldean account of the Deluge." When Smith announced his discovery to the Society of Biblical Archaeology on December 3rd, 1872, a great sensation was caused. The importance of the discovery for the study of the Old Testament was at once understood, and the *Daily Telegraph* of London reflected the public interest by providing £1,000 to send Smith to Nineveh to search for further fragments of the precious tablets.

That the author of the *Gilgamesh Epic* chose thus to incorporate the legend of the Flood into his narrative affords an instructive parallel, and possibly the precedent, to the action of the Yahwist writer whose work is preserved in our present version of the book of *Genesis*. As the Mesopotamian seems to have felt that he must incorporate this wondrous story of the ancient past into his composition and did so with commendable skill, the Hebrew in his generation appears also to have been similarly desirous of working it into his narrative; but his literary ability was not so great and its introduction badly interrupts his theme of Noah as the *Heilbringer* of mankind by his invention of viniculture (*Genesis* v. 28-9, vi. 9-ix. 17, ix. 20).

But to return to the main theme of the *Gilgamesh Epic:* what follows after Utanapishtim tells his story seems perhaps to the modern mind of a kind of anti-climax. The logic of Utanapishtim's story would appear a fitting *dénouement* to the account of Gilgamesh's quest, and the disconsolate hero's return to his native city the proper ending to his tragedy. But the ancient author thought otherwise. He goes on to tell how Utanapishtim's wife took pity on the forlorn Gilgamesh and persuaded her husband to reveal to him the secret location of a marvellous plant that has the properties of an elixir of eternal youth: it is appropriately called "The old man becomes young as the man (in his prime)." The plant grows in the depths of the sea, and Gilgamesh dives for it by attaching heavy stones to his feet as the modern pearldivers of Bahrein used to do. Having obtained the means of prolonging his life, Gilgamesh is now presented in another guise. Instead of availing himself at once of its wondrous virtue, he determines to take the plant back to Uruk, apparently to share boon with his people. But fate prevents him. While bathing at a waterhole, the plant is seized by a serpent which appropriates its virtue. The episode is of considerable interest for the comparative study of folklore. The snake's ability to slough its skin has obviously fascinated many primitive peoples. They have concluded that the snake has the secret of renewing its youth, a secret that mankind covets. Possibly the ancient Mesopo-tamian writer thought that his theme required that he should explain the serpent's apparent possession of the secret that man so dearly sought. Again it is instruc-tive to compare Hebrew traditional lore on this point. In the *Genesis* story of the Temptation and Fall of Adam (iii. 1-19), the serpent is the agent whereby man loses his original immortality, although the serpent does not, as in the *Gilgamesh Epic,* obtain immortality for itself.

With empty hands, his quest in vain, Gilgamesh finally returns to Uruk. The moral of his failure needs no underlining. Man is by nature mortal and he must learn to accept his fate and adjust his view of life accordingly. The *Epic* ends rather strangely with Gilgamesh exulting in the excellence of the construction of his city. Perhaps here lies its final point—a man should find contentment in the work that he can do for the community of which he is a member.

The Assyrian recension of the *Epic* contains a twelfth tablet that records an incident that has no place in the narrative of Gilgamesh's quest, but that un-doubtedly has been added because of a certain similarity of subject matter. It depicts Gilgamesh desiring to see Enkidu, who is held in the underworld, owing to his violation of certain taboos. Nergal, the lord of the underworld, permits the shade of Enkidu to ascend to the world above. The two heroes meet and embrace each other. Then Gilgamesh asks his dead friend to tell him about the under-world. At first Enkidu refuses to tell him, because the truth is too horrible to hear. Gradually, however, he reveals the conditions there, beginning with a grim account of the decomposition of the physical body. This description of the underworld seems designed for some special purpose, for it becomes an account of the differing conditions in which various categories of the dead dwell. Although the general state of all is grim, those whose heirs are diligent in their mortuary service and those who have fallen in battle have a better lot than certain others, especially those who have died in remote places and whose bodies lie unburied. Clearly the text of this tablet has no part in the impressive theme of the *Epic* contained on the other tablets. Its purpose probably was to promote the regular observation of the prescribed mortuary service.

III

Man's attempt at different ages and in various cultural environments to make sense of his experience of life and to understand his own nature and destiny is a subject of deep and abiding interest, and one of basic concern to the historian. Thus the *Epic of Gilgamesh* is a document of unrivalled value for the insight that it affords into the *Weltanschauung* of the ancient Mesopotamians. For the comparative study of religions its value is also immense. We have already touched upon the differences of the Egyptian and Mesopotamian views of life; interesting comparisons can also be made with other contemporary cultures of the ancient world. Although the subject is too vast and too complicated to be entered upon at this juncture, it is worth noting that in ancient Israel the cult of Yahweh also had an eschatology as dismal as that of Mesopotamia. The inadequacy of this eschatology to a faith aspiring to a conception of deity as the embodiment of both supreme power and absolute justice is the cause of Job's agony as he questions his fate in the noble book that bears his name. To more mundane spirits among the Jews, who were prepared to see life in terms of the traditional faith, the logic of the old eschatology induced a philosophy of life remarkably reminiscent of the hedonism of Siduri in her counsel of Gilgamesh: "Go thy way, eat thy bread with joy, and drink thy wine with a merry heart. . . . Let thy garments be always white; and let not thy head lack ointment. Live joyfully with the wife whom thou lovest all the days of thy vanity: for that is thy portion in life, and in thy labour wherein thou labourest under the sun . . . for there is no work, nor device, nor knowledge, nor wisdom in the grave (Hebrew, 'Sheol'), whither thou goest" (*Ecclesiastes* ix. 7-10). The history of Hebrew religion, in a very true sense, is the record of the struggle of the individual for the assurance of ultimate personal significance against the eschatology of an ethnic faith that accorded him only a temporary significance.

The basic importance of eschatology in the evaluation of the individual and his destiny, thus so eloquently attested in the literatures of Mesopotamia and Israel, receives abundant confirmation in the writings of ancient Greece, where the traditional Homeric eschatology was equally pessimistic. It will suffice here to cite one most notable instance. It occurs in the celebrated account of the living Odysseus' descent into Hades to learn the cause of his misfortunes (*Odyssey,* XI, 487–491). Odysseus meets there the shade of the great Achilles, who had been the champion *par excellence* of the Greek military aristocracy, fighting before the walls of Troy until his death in the battle. Odysseus salutes him and dilates on the great reputation that his prowess had won, ending with the trite assurance: "Wherefore grieve not at all that thou art dead, Achilles." The reply of Achilles is devastating in its exposure of the hollowness of fame among the living when seen from the other side of the grave. "Nay, seek not to speak soothingly to me of death, glorious Odysseus. I should choose, so I might live on earth, to serve as the hireling of another, of some portionless man whose livelihood was but small, rather than be lord over all the dead that have perished."

In ancient Greece the inadequacy of the Homeric eschatology to meet the individual's need for the assurance of some tolerable destiny was partly met by the mystery cults of Eleusis and of Orphism. But Mesopotamian religion was never able to provide the comfort of some *post-mortem* hope. Significantly the dying-rising god of vegetation, Tammuz, though having certain traits in common with Osiris, never became the supreme saviour-god and judge of the dead that Osiris was in Egypt. Possibly some innate realism prevented the Mesopotamians from seeing death other than objectively. But the *Epic of Gilgamesh* remains an eloquent witness to the poignancy of their interrogation of the meaning of human life and destiny.

HAMMURABI'S CODE 12

Early in the second millennium B.C. the land of Sumer was invaded by the Semitic Amorites who established a number of kingdoms. One of these was Babylonia, which under the rule of Hammurabi (ca. 1704–1662 B.C.), expanded to encompass the entire valley. In the light of retrospect, however, Hammurabi's greatest achievement was not his conquests but rather the promulgation of the code that bears his name. This was not the first collection of laws issued by Mesopotamian kings, but it was by far the most comprehensive and sophisticated. In fact this code is the best available mirror of Mesopotamian society, and this is its chief significance for us today. The code was in- scribed on a stela, or stone pillar, that was unearthed in fragments by French archae- ologists in 1901. On rejoining the stela, they discovered that several columns had been erased and the stone repolished, presumably by order of a later monarch who meant to substitute his own name and titles. Hence the absence of sections 66 to 99 in the following text transcribed from the stela.*

Witchcraft and the ordeal by water

§ 1. If a man has accused another of laying a *nêrtu* (death spell?) upon him, but has not proved it, he shall be put to death.

§ 2. If a man has accused another of laying a *kišpu* (spell) upon him, but has not proved it, the accused shall go to the sacred river, he shall plunge into the sacred river, and if the sacred river shall conquer him, he that accused him shall take possession of his house. If the sacred river shall show his innocence and he is saved, his ac- cuser shall be put to death. He that plunged into the sacred river shall appropriate the house of him that accused him.

False witness in capital suit

§ 3. If a man has borne false witness in a trial, or has not estab- lished the statement that he has made, if that case be a capital trial, that man shall be put to death.

In civil case

§ 4. If he has borne false witness in a civil law case, he shall pay the damages in that suit.

Judgment once given not to be altered

§ 5. If a judge has given a verdict, rendered a decision, granted a written judgment, and afterward has altered his judgment, that judge shall be prosecuted for altering the judgment he gave and shall

* C. H. W. Johns, *Babylonian and Assyrian Laws, Contracts and Letters* [Library of Ancient Inscriptions] (New York: Charles Scribner's Sons, 1904), pp. 44-67.

pay twelvefold the penalty laid down in that judgment. Further, he shall be publicly expelled from his judgment-seat and shall not return nor take his seat with the judges at a trial.

Burglary and acceptance of stolen goods

§ 6. If a man has stolen goods from a temple, or house, he shall be put to death; and he that has received the stolen property from him shall be put to death.

Dealings with irresponsible persons

§ 7. If a man has bought or received on deposit from a minor or a slave, either silver, gold, male or female slave, ox, ass, or sheep, or anything else, except by consent of elders, or power of attorney, he shall be put to death for theft.

Theft

§ 8. If a patrician has stolen ox, sheep, ass, pig, or ship, whether from a temple, or a house, he shall pay thirtyfold. If he be a plebeian, he shall return tenfold. If the thief cannot pay, he shall be put to death.

Procedure in case of the discovery of lost property

§ 9. If a man has lost property and some of it be detected in the possession of another, and the holder has said, "A man sold it to me, I bought it in the presence of witnesses"; and if the claimant has said, "I can bring witnesses who know it to be property lost my me"; then the alleged buyer on his part shall produce the man who sold it to him and the witnesses before whom he bought it; the claimant shall on his part produce the witnesses who know it to be his lost property. The judge shall examine their pleas. The witnesses to the sale and the witnesses who identify the lost property shall state on oath what they know. Such a seller is the thief and shall be put to death. The owner of the lost property shall recover his lost property. The buyer shall recoup himself from the seller's estate.

§ 10. If the alleged buyer on his part has not produced the seller or the witnesses before whom the sale took place, but the owner of the lost property on his part has produced the witnesses who identify it as his, then the [pretended] buyer is the thief; he shall be put to death. The owner of the lost property shall take his lost property.

§ 11. If, on the other hand, the claimant of the lost property has not brought the witnesses that know his lost property, he has been guilty of slander, he has stirred up strife, he shall be put to death.

§ 12. If the seller has in the meantime died, the buyer shall take from his estate fivefold the value sued for.

Judgment by default

§ 13. If a man has not his witnesses at hand, the judge shall set him a fixed time not exceeding six months, and if within six months he has not produced his witnesses, the man has lied; he shall bear the penalty of the suit.

Kidnapping

§ 14. If a man has stolen a child, he shall be put to death.

Abduction of slave

§ 15. If a man has induced either a male or female slave from the house of a patrician, or plebeian, to leave the city, he shall be put to death.

Harboring a fugitive slave

§ 16. If a man has harbored in his house a male or female slave from a patrician's or plebeian's house, and has not caused the fugitive to leave on the demand of the officer over the slaves condemned to public forced labor, that householder shall be put to death.

The capture of a fugitive slave

§ 17. If a man has caught either a male or female runaway slave in the open field and has brought him back to his owner, the owner of the slave shall give him two shekels of silver.

§ 18. If such a slave will not name his owner, his captor shall bring him to the palace, where he shall be examined as to his past and returned to his owner.

§ 19. If the captor has secreted that slave in his house and afterward that slave has been caught in his possession, he shall be put to death.

§ 20. If the slave has fled from the hands of his captor, the latter shall swear to the owner of the slave and he shall be free from blame.

Burglary

§ 21. If a man has broken into a house he shall be killed before the breach and buried there.

Highway robbery

§ 22. If a man has committed highway robbery and has been caught, that man shall be put to death.

§ 23. If the highwayman has not been caught, the man that has been robbed shall state on oath what he has lost and the city or district governor in whose territory or district the robbery took place shall restore to him what he has lost.

§ 24. If a life [has been lost], the city or district governor shall pay one mina of silver to the deceased's relatives.

Theft at a fire

§ 25. If a fire has broken out in a man's house and one who has come to put it out has coveted the property of the householder and appropriated any of it, that man shall be cast into the self-same fire.

Duties and privileges of an officer over the levy

§ 26. If a levy-master, or warrant-officer, who has been detailed on the king's service, has not gone, or has hired a substitute in his place, that levy-master, or warrant-officer, shall be put to death and the hired substitute shall take his office.

§ 27. If a levy-master, or warrant-officer, has been assigned to garrison duty, and in his absence his field and garden have been given to another who has carried on his duty, when the absentee has returned and regained his city, his field and garden shall be given back to him and he shall resume his duty.

Rights and duties of his son

§ 28. If a levy-master, or warrant-officer, has been assigned to garrison duty, and has a son able to carry on his official duty, the field and garden shall be given to him and he shall carry on his father's duty.

§ 29. If the son be a child and is not able to carry on his father's duty, one-third of the field and garden shall be given to his mother to educate him.

Penalty for neglect of his benefice

§ 30. If such an official has neglected the care of his field, garden, or house, and let them go to waste, and if another has taken his field, garden, or house, in his absence, and carried on the duty for three years, if the absentee has returned and would cultivate his field, garden, or house, it shall not be given him; he who has taken it and carried on the duty connected with it shall continue to do so.

§ 31. If for one year only he has let things go to waste and he has returned, his field, garden, and house shall be given him, and he himself shall carry on his duty.

His ransom, if captured

§ 32. If such an official has been assigned to the king's service (and captured by the enemy) and has been ransomed by a merchant and helped to regain his city, if he has had means in his house to pay his ransom, he himself shall do so. If he has not had means of his own, he shall be ransomed by the temple treasury. If there has not been means in the temple treasury of his city, the state will ransom him. His field, garden, or house shall not be given for his ransom.

§ 33. If either a governor or a prefect has appropriated to his own use the corvée, or has accepted and sent on the king's service a hired substitute in his place, that governor, or prefect, shall be put to death.

§ 34. If either a governor, or a prefect, has appropriated the property of a levy-master, has hired him out, has robbed him by high-handedness at a trial, has taken the salary which the king gave to him, that governor, or prefect, shall be put to death.

§ 35. If a man has bought from a levy-master the sheep, or oxen, which the king gave him, he shall lose his money.

§ 36. The field, garden, or house, of a levy-master, warrant-officer, or tributary shall not be sold.

§ 37. If a man has bought field, garden, or house, of a levy-master, a warrant-officer, or tributary, his title-deed shall be destroyed and he shall lose his money. He shall return the field, garden, or house to its owner.

§ 38. A levy-master, warrant-officer, or tributary, shall not bequeath anything from the field, garden, or house of his benefice to his wife or daughter, nor shall he give it for his debt.

§ 39. From the field, garden, or house which he has bought and acquired, he shall make bequests to his wife, or daughter, or shall assign for his debt.

§ 40. A votary, merchant, or resident alien may sell his field, garden, or house, and the buyer shall discharge the public service connected with the field, garden, or house that he has bought.

§ 41. If a man has given property in exchange for the field, garden, or house, of a levy-master, warrant-officer, or tributary, such an official shall return to his field, garden, or house, and he shall appropriate the property given in exchange.

§ 42. If a man has hired a field to cultivate and has caused no corn to grow on the field, he shall be held responsible for not doing the work on the field and shall pay an average rent.

§ 43. If he has not cultivated the field and has left it alone, he shall give to the owner of the field an average rent, and the field which he has neglected he shall break up with mattocks and plough it, and shall return it to the owner of the field.

§ 44. If a man has taken a piece of virgin soil to open up, on a three years' lease, but has left it alone, has not opened up the land, in the fourth year he shall break it up, hoe it, and plough it, and shall return it to the owner of the field, and shall measure out ten GUR of corn for each GAN of land.

§ 45. If a man has let his field to a farmer and has received his rent for the field but afterward the field has been flooded by rain, or a storm has carried off the crop, the loss shall be the farmer's.

§ 46. If he has not received the rent of his field, whether he let it for a half, or for a third, of the crop, the farmer and the owner of the field shall share the corn that is left in the field, according to their agreement.

Landlord
cannot
restrain a
satisfactory
tenant from
subletting

§ 47. If a tenant farmer, because he did not start farming in the early part of the year, has sublet the field, the owner of the field shall not object; his field has been cultivated; at harvest-time he shall take rent, according to his agreement.

§ 48. If a man has incurred a debt and a storm has flooded his field or carried away the crop, or the corn has not grown because of drought, in that year he shall not pay his creditor. Further, he shall post-date his bond and shall not pay interest for that year.

Rights in a crop pledged for debt

§ 49. If a man has received money from a merchant and has given to the merchant a field, planted with corn, or sesame, and has said to him, "Cultivate the field and reap and take the corn, or sesame, that shall be grown"; if the bailiff has reared corn, or sesame, in the field, at harvest-time the owner of the field shall take what corn, or sesame, has been grown in the field and shall pay corn to the merchant for his money that he took of him and its interest, and for the maintenance of the bailiff.

§ 50. If the field he gave was [already] cultivated, or the sesame was grown up, the owner of the field shall take the corn, or sesame, that has been grown in the field, and shall return the money and its interest to the merchant.

§ 51. If he has not money enough, he shall give to the merchant sesame, or corn, according to its market price, for the money which he took from the merchant and its interest, according to the king's standard.

§ 52. If the bailiff has not reared corn or sesame in the field the debtor's obligation shall not be lessened.

Riparian responsibilities

§§ 53, 54. If a man has neglected to strengthen his dike and has not kept his dike strong, and a breach has broken out in his dike, and the waters have flooded the meadow, the man in whose dike the breach has broken out shall restore the corn he has caused to be lost. [54]. If he be not able to restore the corn, he and his goods shall be sold, and the owners of the meadow whose corn the water has carried away shall share the money.

Penalty for neglect to shut off water

§ 55. If a man has opened his runnel for watering and has left it open, and the water has flooded his neighbor's field, he shall pay him an average crop.

§ 56. If a man has let out the waters and they flood the young plants in his neighbor's field, he shall measure out ten GUR of corn for each GAN of land.

Damage done to growing crop by sheep

§ 57. If a shepherd has not agreed with the owner of the field to allow his sheep to eat off the green crop and without consent of the owner has let his sheep feed off it, the owner of the field shall harvest his crop, but the shepherd who without consent of the owner of the field caused his sheep to eat it shall give to the owner of the field, over and above his crop, twenty GUR of corn for each GAN of land.

§ 58. If, after the sheep have come up out of the meadows and have passed into the common fold at the city gate, a shepherd has placed his sheep in a field and caused his sheep to feed in the field, the shepherd shall keep the field he has grazed, and, at harvest-time, he shall measure out to the owner sixty GUR of corn for each GAN of land.

§ 59. If a man without the consent of the owner has cut down a tree in an orchard, he shall weigh out half a mina of silver.

§§ 60, 61. If a man has given a field to a gardener to plant a garden and the gardener has planted the garden, he shall train the garden four years; in the fifth year the owner of the garden and the gardener shall share the garden equally, the owner of the garden shall gather his share and take it. [61]. If the gardener, in planting the garden, has not planted all, but has left a bare patch, he shall reckon the bare patch in his share.

§ 62. If he has not planted the field which was given him as a garden; then, if it was arable land, the gardener shall measure out to the owner of the field an average rent for the years that were neglected, and shall perform the stipulated work on the field (*i.e.,* make it into a garden), and return it to the owner of the field.

§ 63. If the land was uncultivated, he shall do the stipulated work on the field, and return to the owner of the field and shall measure out for each year ten GUR of corn for each GAN.

§ 64. If a man has given his garden to a gardener to farm, the gardener, as long as he holds the garden, shall give the owner of the garden two-thirds of the produce of the garden and shall take one-third himself.

§ 65. If the gardener has not tilled the garden and has diminished the yield, the gardener shall pay an average rent.

Here came the five erased columns, of which the three following sections are restored from copies in Ashurbânipal's library:

§ X. [If a man has borrowed money of a merchant and has given a date grove] to the merchant and has said to him, "Take the dates that are in my grove for your money"; that merchant shall not consent, the owner of the grove shall take the dates that are in the grove and shall answer to the merchant for the money and its interest, according to the tenor of his agreement, and the owner of the grove shall take the surplus of the dates that are in the grove.

§ Y. [If a man has let a house] and the tenant has paid to the owner of the house the full rent for a term of years, and if the owner of the house has ordered the tenant to leave before his time is up, the owner of the house, because he has ordered his tenant to leave before his time is up, [shall repay a proportionate amount] from what the tenant has paid him.

Acceptance of
goods in
payment
of debt, in
default of
money or corn

§ Z. [If a man has borrowed money of a merchant] and has not corn or money wherewith [to pay], but has goods; whatever is in his hands, he shall give to the merchant, before the elders. The merchant shall not object; he shall receive it.

After the loss of about thirty-five sections the Code resumes:

§ 100. [If an agent has received money of a merchant, he shall write down the amount] and [what is to be] the interest of the money, and when his time is up, he shall settle with his merchant.

§ 101. If he has not had success on his travels, he shall return double what he received to the merchant.

§§ 102, 103. If the merchant has given money, as a speculation, to the agent, who during his travels has met with misfortune, he shall return the full sum to the merchant. [103]. If, on his travels, an enemy has forced him to give up some of the goods he was carrying, the agent shall specify the amount on oath and shall be acquitted.

§ 104. If a merchant has given to an agent corn, wool, oil, or any sort of goods, to traffic with, the agent shall write down the money value, and shall return that to the merchant. The agent shall then take a sealed receipt for the money that he has given to the merchant.

§ 105. If the agent forgets and has not taken a sealed receipt for the money he gave to the merchant, money that has not been acknowledged by receipts shall not be put down in the accounts.

§ 106. If an agent has taken money of a merchant, and his principal suspects him, that principal shall prosecute his agent, put him on oath before the elders, as to the money taken; the agent shall pay to the merchant threefold what he misappropriated.

§ 107. If the principal has overcharged the agent and the agent has [really] returned to his principal whatever his principal gave him, and if the principal has disputed what the agent has given him, that agent shall put his principal on oath before the elders, and the merchant, because he has defrauded the agent, shall pay to the agent sixfold what he misappropriated.

§ 108. If the mistress of a beer-shop has not received corn as the price of beer or has demanded silver on an excessive scale, and has made the measure of beer less than the measure of corn, that beer-seller shall be prosecuted and drowned.

§ 109. If the mistress of a beer-shop has assembled seditious slanderers in her house and those seditious persons have not been captured and have not been haled to the palace, that beer-seller shall be put to death.

§ 110. If a votary, who is not living in the convent, open a beer-shop, or enter a beer-shop for drink, that woman shall be put to death.

§ 111. If the mistress of a beer-shop has given sixty KA of *sakani* beer in the time of thirst, at harvest, she shall take fifty KA of corn.

§ 112. If a man staying abroad has given silver, gold, precious stones, or portable goods to another man to transport, and if that man has not delivered the consignment, where he has carried it, but has appropriated it, the owner of the consignment shall prosecute him, and the carrier shall give to the owner of the consignment fivefold whatever was intrusted to him.

§ 113. If a man has a debt of corn, or money, due from another and without the consent of the owner of the corn has taken corn from the granary, or barn, the owner of the corn shall prosecute him for taking the corn from the granary, or barn, without his consent, and the man shall return all the corn he took, and further lose whatever it was that he had lent.

§ 114. If a man has no debt of corn or money due from a man on whom he has levied a distraint, for each such distraint he shall pay one-third of a mina of silver.

§ 115. If a man has corn or money due from another man and

has levied a distraint and the hostage has died a natural death in the house of the creditor, he cannot be held responsible.

§ 116. If the hostage has died of blows or want in the house of the creditor, the owner of the hostage shall prosecute his creditor, and if the deceased were free born, the creditor's son shall be put to death; if a slave, the creditor shall pay one-third of a mina of silver, Further, he shall lose whatever it was that he lent.

Limitations on the holding of such hostages

§ 117. If a man owes a debt, and he has given his wife, his son, or his daughter [as hostage] for the money, or has handed someone over to work it off, the hostage shall do the work of the creditor's house; but in the fourth year he shall set them free.

§ 118. If a debtor has handed over a male or female slave to work off a debt, and the creditor proceeds to sell same, no one can complain.

§ 119. If a man owes a debt, and he has assigned a maid who has borne him children for the money, the owner of the maid shall repay the money which the merchant gave him and shall ransom his maid.

Responsibility of owners of warehouses

§ 120. If a man has deposited his corn for safe keeping in another's house and it has suffered damage in the granary, or if the owner of the house has opened the store and taken the corn, or has disputed the amount of the corn that was stored in his house, the owner of the corn shall declare on oath the amount of his corn, and the owner of the house shall return him double.

Rate of payment for storage of corn

§ 121. If a man has stored corn in another man's house he shall give, on each GUR of corn, five KA of corn, yearly, as the rent for storage.

Receipt for deposit of valuables

§ 122. If a man has given another gold, silver, or any goods whatever, on deposit, all that he gives shall he show to witnesses, and take a bond and so give on deposit.

§ 123. If he has given on deposit without witnesses and bonds, and has been defrauded where he made his deposit, he has no claim to prosecute.

Responsibility of bankers

§ 124. If a man has given on deposit to another, before witnesses, gold, silver, or any goods whatever, and his claim has been contested, he shall prosecute that man, and [the man] shall return double what he disputed.

Their own losses no excuse

§ 125. If a man has given anything whatever on deposit, and, where he has made his deposit, something of his has been lost together with something belonging to the owner of the house, either by house-breaking or a rebellion, the owner of the house who is in default shall make good all that has been given him on deposit, which he has lost, and shall return it to the owner of the goods. The owner of the house shall look after what he has lost and recover it from the thief.

Depreciation of property

§ 126. If a man has said that something of his is lost, which is not lost, or has alleged a depreciation, though nothing of his is lost, he shall estimate the depreciation on oath, and he shall pay double whatever he has claimed.

Slander of votary or married woman

§ 127. If a man has caused the finger to be pointed at a votary, or a man's wife, and has not justified himself, that man shall be brought before the judges, and have his forehead branded.

§ 128. If a man has taken a wife and has not executed a marriage-contract, that woman is not a wife.

§ 129. If a man's wife be caught lying with another, they shall be strangled and cast into the water. If the wife's husband would save his wife, the king can save his servant.

§ 130. If a man has ravished another's betrothed wife, who is a virgin, while still living in her father's house, and has been caught in the act, that man shall be put to death; the woman shall go free.

§ 131. If a man's wife has been accused by her husband, and has not been caught lying with another, she shall swear her innocence, and return to her house.

§ 132. If a man's wife has the finger pointed at her on account of another, but has not been caught lying with him, for her husband's sake she shall plunge into the sacred river.

§ 133. If a man has been taken captive, and there was maintenance in his house, but his wife has left her house and entered into another man's house; because that woman has not preserved her body, and has entered into the house of another, that woman shall be prosecuted and shall be drowned.

§ 134. If a man has been taken captive, but there was not maintenance in his house, and his wife has entered into the house of another, that woman has no blame.

§ 135. If a man has been taken captive, but there was no maintenance in his house for his wife, and she has entered into the house of another, and has borne him children, if in the future her [first] husband shall return and regain his city, that woman shall return to her first husband, but the children shall follow their own father.

§ 136. If a man has left his city and fled, and, after he has gone, his wife has entered into the house of another; if the man return and seize his wife, the wife of the fugitive shall not return to her husband, because he hated his city and fled.

§ 137. If a man has determined to divorce a concubine who has borne him children, or a votary who has granted him children, he shall return to that woman her marriage-portion, and shall give her the usufruct of field, garden, and goods, to bring up her children. After her children have grown up, out of whatever is given to her children, they shall give her one son's share, and the husband of her choice shall marry her.

§ 138. If a man has divorced his wife, who has not borne him children, he shall pay over to her as much money as was given for her bride-price and the marriage-portion which she brought from her father's house, and so shall divorce her.

§ 139. If there was no bride-price, he shall give her one mina of silver, as a price of divorce.

§ 140. If he be a plebeian, he shall give her one-third of a mina of silver.

§ 141. If a man's wife, living in her husband's house, has persisted in going out, has acted the fool, has wasted her house, has belittled her husband, he shall prosecute her. If her husband has said, "I divorce her," she shall go her way; he shall give her nothing as her price of divorce. If her husband has said, "I will not divorce her," he may take another woman to wife; the wife shall live as a slave in her husband's house.

Status of a wife who repudiates her husband

§ 142. If a woman has hated her husband and has said, "You shall not possess me," her past shall be inquired into, as to what she lacks. If she has been discreet, and has no vice, and her husband has gone out, and has greatly belittled her, that woman has no blame, she shall take her marriage-portion and go off to her father's house.

§ 143. If she has not been discreet, has gone out, ruined her house, belittled her husband, she shall be drowned.

Marriage with a votary

§ 144. If a man has married a votary, and that votary has given a maid to her husband, and so caused him to have children, and, if that man is inclined to marry a concubine, that man shall not be allowed to do so, he shall not marry a concubine.

§ 145. If a man has married a votary, and she has not granted him children, and he is determined to marry a concubine, that man shall marry the concubine, and bring her into his house, but the concubine shall not place herself on an equality with the votary.

A votary's rights against a maid assigned to her husband

§ 146. If a man has married a votary, and she has given a maid to her husband, and the maid has borne children, and if afterward that maid has placed herself on an equality with her mistress, because she has borne children, her mistress shall not sell her, she shall place a slave-mark upon her, and reckon her with the slave-girls.

§ 147. If she has not borne children, her mistress shall sell her.

Status of a wife afflicted with a disease

§ 148. If a man has married a wife and a disease has seized her, if he is determined to marry a second wife, he shall marry her. He shall not divorce the wife whom the disease has seized. In the home they made together she shall dwell, and he shall maintain her as long as she lives.

§ 149. If that woman was not pleased to stay in her husband's house, he shall pay over to her the marriage-portion which she brought from her father's house, and she shall go away.

Wife's right to property deeded to her by her husband

§ 150. If a man has presented field, garden, house, or goods to his wife, has granted her a deed of gift, her children, after her husband's death, shall not dispute her right; the mother shall leave it after her death to that one of her children whom she loves best. She shall not leave it to her kindred.

Marital responsibility for anti-nuptial debts

§ 151. If a woman, who is living in a man's house, has persuaded her husband to bind himself, and grant her a deed to the effect that she shall not be held for debt by a creditor of her husband's; if that man had a debt upon him before he married that woman, his creditor shall not take his wife for it. Also, if that woman had a debt upon her before she entered that man's house, her creditor shall not take her husband for it.

§ 152. From the time that that woman entered into the man's house they together shall be liable for all debts subsequently incurred.

Connivance at husband's murder by a wife

§ 153. If a man's wife, for the sake of another, has caused her husband to be killed, that woman shall be impaled.

§ 154. If a man has committed incest with his daughter, that man shall be banished from the city.

§ 155. If a man has betrothed a maiden to his son and his son has known her, and afterward the man has lain in her bosom, and been caught, that man shall be strangled and she shall be cast into the water.

§ 156. If a man has betrothed a maiden to his son, and his son has not known her, and that man has lain in her bosom, he shall pay her half a mina of silver, and shall pay over to her whatever she brought from her father's house, and the husband of her choice shall marry her.

§ 157. If a man, after his father's death, has lain in the bosom of his mother, they shall both of them be burnt together.

§ 158. If a man, after his father's death, be caught in the bosom of his step-mother, who has borne children, that man shall be cut off from his father's house.

§ 159. If a man, who has presented a gift to the house of his prospective father-in-law and has given the bride-price, has afterward looked upon another woman and has said to his father-in-law, "I will not marry your daughter"; the father of the girl shall keep whatever he has brought as a present.

§ 160. If a man has presented a gift to the house of his prospective father-in-law, and has given the bride-price, but the father of the girl has said, "I will not give you my daughter," the father shall return double all that was presented him.

§ 161. If a man has brought a gift to the house of his prospective father-in-law, and has given the bride-price, but his comrade has slandered him and his father-in-law has said to the suitor, "You shall not marry my daughter," [the father] shall return double all that was presented him. Further, the comrade shall not marry the girl.

§ 162. If a man has married a wife, and she has borne him children, and that woman has gone to her fate, her father shall lay no claim to her marriage-portion. Her marriage-portion is her children's only.

§ 163. If a man has married a wife, and she has not borne him children, and that woman has gone to her fate; if his father-in-law has returned to him the bride-price, which that man brought into the house of his father-in-law, her husband shall have no claim on the marriage-portion of that woman. Her marriage-portion indeed belongs to her father's house.

§ 164. If the father-in-law has not returned the bride-price, the husband shall deduct the amount of her bride-price from her marriage-portion, and shall return her marriage-portion to her father's house.

§ 165. If a man has presented field, garden, or house to his son, the first in his eyes, and has written him a deed of gift; after the father has gone to his fate, when the brothers share, he shall keep the present his father gave him, and over and above shall share equally with them in the goods of his father's estate.

§ 166. If a man has taken wives for the other sons he had, but has not taken a wife for his young son, after the father has gone to his fate, when the brothers share, they shall set aside from the goods of their father's estate money, as a bride-price, for their young brother, who has not married a wife, over and above his share, and they shall cause him to take a wife.

Inheritance of children in case of two fruitful marriages

§ 167. If a man has taken a wife, and she has borne him children and that woman has gone to her fate, and he has taken a second wife, and she also has borne children; after the father has gone to his fate, the sons shall not share according to mothers, but each family shall take the marriage-portion of its mother, and all shall share the goods of their father's estate equally.

Disinheritance of a son

§ 168. If a man has determined to disinherit his son and has declared before the judge, "I cut off my son," the judge shall inquire into the son's past, and, if the son has not committed a grave misdemeanor such as should cut him off from sonship, the father shall not disinherit his son.

§ 169. If he has committed a grave crime against his father, which cuts off from sonship, for the first offence he shall pardon him. If he has committed a grave crime a second time, the father shall cut off his son from sonship.

Status of children by a slave-woman

§ 170. If a man has had children borne to him by his wife, and also by a maid, if the father in his lifetime has said, "My sons," to the children whom his maid bore him, and has reckoned them with the sons of his wife; then after the father has gone to his fate, the children of the wife and of the maid should share equally. The children of the wife shall apportion the shares and make their own selections.

§ 171. And if the father, in his lifetime, has not said, "My sons," to the children whom the maid bore him, after the father has gone to his fate, the children of the maid shall not share with the children of the wife in the goods of their father's house. The maid and her children, however, shall obtain their freedom. The children of the wife have no claim for service on the children of the maid.

The rights of a widow in personal property

The wife shall take her marriage-portion, and any gift that her husband has given her and for which he has written a deed of gift and she shall dwell in her husband's house; as long as she lives, she shall enjoy it, she shall not sell it. After her death it is indeed her children's.

§ 172. If her husband has not given her a gift, her marriage-portion shall be given her in full, and, from the goods of her husband's estate, she shall take a share equal to that of one son.

Her rights in the home

If her children have persecuted her in order to have her leave the house, and the judge has inquired into her past, and laid the blame on the children, that woman shall not leave her husband's house. If that woman has determined to leave, she shall relinquish to her children the gift her husband gave her, she shall take the marriage-portion of her father's estate, and the husband of her choice may marry her.

Dower rights of her children by second marriage

§ 173. If that woman, where she has gone, has borne children to her later husband, after that woman has died, the children of both marriages shall share her marriage-portion.

§ 174. If she has not borne children to her later husband, the children of her first husband shall take her marriage-portion.

§ 175. If either a slave of a patrician, or of a plebeian, has married the daughter of a free man, and she has borne children, the owner of the slave shall have no claim for service on the children of a free woman. And if a slave, either of a patrician or of a plebeian, has married a free woman and when he married her she entered the slave's house with a marriage-portion from her father's estate, be he slave of a patrician or of a plebeian, and from the time that they started to keep house, they have acquired property; after the slave, whether of a patrician or of a plebeian, has gone to his fate, the free woman shall take her marriage-portion, and whatever her husband and she acquired, since they started house-keeping. She shall divide it into two portions. The master of the slave shall take one half, the other half the free woman shall take for her children.

§ 176. If the free woman had no marriage-portion, whatever her husband and she acquired since they started house-keeping he shall divide into two portions. The owner of the slave shall take one half, the other half the free woman shall take for her children.

§ 177. If a widow, whose children are young, has determined to marry again, she shall not marry without consent of the judge. When she is allowed to remarry, the judge shall inquire as to what remains of the property of her former husband, and shall intrust the property of her former husband to that woman and her second husband. He shall give them an inventory. They shall watch over the property, and bring up the children. Not a utensil shall they sell. A buyer of any utensil belonging to the widow's children shall lose his money and shall return the article to its owners.

§ 178. If a female votary, or vowed woman, has had given her by her father a portion, as for marriage, and he has written her a deed, and in the deed which he has written her he has not written that she may leave it as she pleases, and has not granted her all her desire; after her father has gone to his fate, her brothers shall take her field, or garden, and, according to the value of her share, shall give her corn, oil, and wool, and shall content her heart. If they do not give her corn, oil, and wool, according to the value of her share, and do not satisfy her, she shall let her field and garden to a farmer, whom she chooses, and the farmer shall support her. The field, garden, or whatever her father gave her, she shall enjoy, as long as she lives. She shall not sell it, nor mortgage it. The reversion of her inheritance indeed belongs to her brothers.

§ 179. If a female votary, or vowed woman, has had a portion given her by her father, and he has written her a deed, and in the deed that he has written her has [declared] that she may give it as she pleases, and has granted her all her desire; after her father has gone to his fate, she shall leave it as she pleases; her brothers shall make no claim against her.

§ 180. If the father has not given a portion to his daughter, who is a female votary, or vowed woman; after her father has gone to his fate, she shall share in the property of her father's house, like any other child. As long as she lives, she shall enjoy her share; after her, it indeed belongs to her brothers.

§ 181. If a father has vowed his daughter to a god, as a temple maid, or a virgin, and has given her no portion; after the father has gone to his fate, she shall share in the property of her father's estate, taking one-third of a child's share. She shall enjoy her share, as long as she lives. After her, it belongs to her brothers.

§ 182. If a father has not given a portion, as for marriage, to his daughter, a votary of Marduk of Babylon, and has not written her a deed; after her father has gone to his fate, she shall share with her brothers from the goods of her father's estate, taking one-third of a child's share. She shall not be subject to duty. The votary of Marduk shall leave it after her to whom she pleases.

§ 183. If a father has given a portion, as for marriage, to his daughter by a concubine, and has given her to a husband, and has written her a deed; after her father has gone to his fate, she shall not share in the goods of her father's house.

§ 184. If a man has not given a portion, as for marriage, to his daughter by a concubine, and has not given her to a husband; after her father has gone to his fate, her brothers shall present her with a marriage-portion, according to the wealth of her father's estate, and shall give her to a husband.

§ 185. If a man has taken a young child, a natural son of his, to be his son, and has brought him up, no one shall make a claim against that foster child.

§ 186. If a man has taken a young child to be his son, and after he has taken him, the child discover his own parents, he shall return to his father's house.

§ 187. The son of a royal favorite, of one that stands in the palace, or the son of a votary shall not be reclaimed.

§§ 188, 189. If a craftsman has taken a child to bring up and has taught him his handicraft, he shall not be reclaimed. If he has not taught him his handicraft that foster child shall return to his father's house.

§ 190. If a man has brought up the child, whom he has taken to be his son, but has not reckoned him with his sons, that foster child shall return to his father's house.

§ 191. If a man has brought up the child, whom he took to be his son, and then sets up a home, and after he has acquired children, decides to disinherit the foster child, that son shall not go his way [penniless]; the father that brought him up shall give him one-third of a son's share in his goods and he shall depart. He shall not give him field, garden, or house.

§ 192. If the son of a palace favorite or the son of a vowed woman has said to the father that brought him up, "You are not my father," or to the mother that brought him up, "You are not my mother," his tongue shall be cut out.

§ 193. If the son of a palace favorite or the son of a vowed woman has come to know his father's house and has hated his father that brought him up, or his mother that brought him up, and shall go off to his father's house, his eyes shall be torn out.

§ 194. If a man has given his son to a wet-nurse to suckle, and that son has died in the hands of the nurse, and the nurse, without consent of the child's father or mother, has nursed another child, they shall prosecute her; because she has nursed another child, without consent of the father or mother, her breasts shall be cut off.

Assault
on a father

§ 195. If a son has struck his father, his hands shall be cut off.

§ 196. If a man has knocked out the eye of a patrician, his eye shall be knocked out.

§ 197. If he has broken the limb of a patrician, his limb shall be broken.

§ 198. If he has knocked out the eye of a plebeian or has broken the limb of a plebeian, he shall pay one mina of silver.

§ 199. If he has knocked out the eye of a patrician's servant, or broken the limb of a patrician's servant, he shall pay half his value.

§ 200. If a patrician has knocked out the tooth of a man that is his equal, his tooth shall be knocked out.

§ 201. If he has knocked out the tooth of a plebeian, he shall pay one-third of a mina of silver.

Brutal assault

§ 202. If a man has smitten the privates of a man, higher in rank than he, he shall be scourged with sixty blows of an ox-hide scourge, in the assembly.

§ 203. If a man has smitten the privates of a patrician of his own rank, he shall pay one mina of silver.

§ 204. If a plebeian has smitten the privates of a plebeian, he shall pay ten shekels of silver.

§ 205. If the slave of anyone has smitten the privates of a free-born man, his ear shall be cut off.

Fatal assault

§ 206. If a man has struck another in a quarrel, and caused him a permanent injury, that man shall swear, "I struck him without malice," and shall pay the doctor.

§ 207. If he has died of his blows, [the man] shall swear [similarly], and pay one-half a mina of silver; or,

§ 208. If [the deceased] was a plebeian, he shall pay one-third of a mina of silver.

Assaults upon
pregnant
women

§ 209. If a man has struck a free woman with child, and has caused her to miscarry, he shall pay ten shekels for her miscarriage.

§ 210. If that woman die, his daughter shall be killed.

§ 211. If it be the daughter of a plebeian, that has miscarried through his blows, he shall pay five shekels of silver.

§ 212. If that woman die, he shall pay a half a mina of silver.

§ 213. If he has struck a man's maid and caused her to miscarry, he shall pay two shekels of silver.

§ 214. If that woman die, he shall pay one-third of a mina of silver.

Gradation of
surgeon's fees

§ 215. If a surgeon has operated with the bronze lancet on a patrician for a serious injury, and has cured him, or has removed with a bronze lancet a cataract for a patrician, and has cured his eye, he shall take ten shekels of silver.

§ 216. If it be plebeian, he shall take five shekels of silver.

§ 217. If it be a man's slave, the owner of the slave shall give two shekels of silver to the surgeon.

Penalties for
unskilful
operations

§ 218. If a surgeon has operated with the bronze lancet on a patrician for a serious injury, and has caused his death, or has removed a cataract for a patrician, with the bronze lancet, and has made him lose his eye, his hands shall be cut off.

§ 219. If the surgeon has treated a serious injury of a plebeian's slave, with the bronze lancet, and has caused his death, he shall render slave for slave.

§ 220. If he has removed a cataract with the bronze lancet, and made the slave lose his eye, he shall pay half his value.

§ 221. If a surgeon has cured the limb of a patrician, or has doctored a diseased bowel, the patient shall pay five shekels of silver to the surgeon.

§ 222. If he be a plebeian, he shall pay three shekels of silver.

§ 223. If he be a man's slave, the owner of the slave shall give two shekels of silver to the doctor.

§ 224. If a veterinary surgeon has treated an ox, or an ass, for a severe injury, and cured it, the owner of the ox, or the ass, shall pay the surgeon one-sixth of a shekel of silver, as his fee.

§ 225. If he has treated an ox, or an ass, for a severe injury, and caused it to die, he shall pay one-quarter of its value to the owner of the ox, or the ass.

§ 226. If a brander has cut out a mark on a slave, without the consent of his owner, that brander shall have his hands cut off.

§ 227. If someone has deceived the brander, and induced him to cut out a mark on a slave, that man shall be put to death and buried in his house; the brander shall swear, "I did not mark him knowingly," and shall go free.

§ 228. If a builder has built a house for a man, and finished it, he shall pay him a fee of two shekels of silver, for each SAR built on.

§ 229. If a builder has built a house for a man, and has not made his work sound, and the house he built has fallen, and caused the death of its owner, that builder shall be put to death.

§ 230. If it is the owner's son that is killed, the builder's son shall be put to death.

§ 231. If it is the slave of the owner that is killed, the builder shall give slave for slave to the owner of the house.

§ 232. If he has caused the loss of goods, he shall render back whatever he has destroyed. Moreover, because he did not make sound the house he built, and it fell, at his own cost he shall rebuild the house that fell.

§ 233. If a builder has built a house for a man, and has not keyed his work, and the wall has fallen, that builder shall make that wall firm at his own expense.

§ 234. If a boatman has built a boat of sixty GUR for a man, he shall pay him a fee of two shekels of silver.

§ 235. If a boatman has built a boat for a man, and has not made his work sound, and in that same year that boat is sent on a voyage and suffers damage, the boatman shall rebuild that boat, and, at his own expense, shall make it strong, or shall give a strong boat to the owner.

§ 236. If a man has let his boat to a boatman, and the boatman has been careless and the boat has been sunk or lost, the boatman shall restore a boat to the owner.

Responsibility
of boatmen
carrying
goods

§ 237. If a man has hired a boat and boatman, and loaded it with corn, wool, oil, or dates, or whatever it be, and the boatman has been careless, and sunk the boat, or lost what is in it, the boatman shall restore the boat which he sank, and whatever he lost that was in it.

§ 238. If a boatman has sunk a man's boat, and has floated it again, he shall pay half its value in silver.

§ 239. If a man has hired a boatman, he shall pay him six GUR of corn yearly.

Law of
collision

§ 240. If a boat, on its course, has run into a boat at anchor, and sunk it, the owner of the boat that was sunk shall estimate on oath whatever was lost in his boat, and the owner of the moving vessel, which sank the boat at anchor, shall make good his boat and what was lost in it.

Working
ox not to be
distrained

§ 241. If a man has levied a distraint on a working ox, he shall pay one-third of a mina of silver.

§ 242. If a man has hired a working ox for one year, its hire is four GUR of corn.

§ 243. As the hire of a milch cow one shall give three GUR of corn to its owner.

Liability for
loss of ox or
ass by accident

§ 244. If a man has hired an ox, or an ass, and a lion has killed it in the open field, the loss falls on its owner.

§ 245. If a man has hired an ox and has caused its death, by carelessness, or blows, he shall restore ox for ox, to the owner of the ox.

§ 246. If a man has hired an ox, and has broken its leg, or cut its neck (?), he shall restore ox for ox, to the owner of the ox.

§ 247. If a man has hired an ox, and knocked out its eye, he shall pay to the owner of the ox half its value.

Responsibility
for unavoid-
able accidents
to a hired ox

§ 248. If a man has hired an ox, and has broken its horn, cut off its tail, or torn its muzzle, he shall pay one-quarter of its value.

§ 249. If a man has hired an ox, and God has struck it, and it has died, the man that hired the ox shall make affidavit and go free.

Death by
goring,
accidental

§ 250. If a bull has gone wild and gored a man, and caused his death, there can be no suit against the owner.

§ 251. If a man's ox be a gorer, and has revealed its evil propensity as a gorer, and he has not blunted its horn, or shut up the ox, and then that ox has gored a free man, and caused his death, the owner shall pay half a mina of silver.

§ 252. If it be a slave that has been killed, he shall pay one-third of a mina of silver.

Responsibility
of a tenant
farmer

§ 253. If a man has set another over his field, hired him, allotted him tools, and intrusted him with oxen for cultivating the field and provided harnesses for them, and if that man has appropriated the seed or provender, and they have been found in his possession, his hands shall be cut off.

§ 254. If he has taken the provender or rations and has enfeebled the oxen, he shall make it good from the corn he has hoed.

§ 255. If he has let out the man's oxen for hire, or stolen the seed-corn, or has not produced a crop, that man shall be prosecuted, and he shall pay sixty GUR of corn for each GAN.

§ 256. If he is not able to pay his compensation, he shall be torn in pieces on that field by the oxen.

§ 257. If a man has hired a field-laborer, he shall pay him eight GUR of corn yearly.

§ 258. If anyone has hired an ox-herd he shall pay him six GUR of corn yearly.

§ 259. If a man has stolen a watering-machine from the meadow, he shall pay five shekels of silver to the owner of the watering-machine.

§ 260. If a man has stolen a *shadduf,* or a plough, he shall pay three shekels of silver.

§ 261. If a man has hired a herdsman, to pasture oxen, or sheep, he shall pay him eight GUR of corn yearly.

§ 262. If a man has intrusted ox or ass to . . . [Passage mutilated.]

§ 263. If he has lost the ox, or ass, given to him, he shall restore ox for ox, and ass for ass to its owner.

§ 264. If a herdsman, who has had oxen or sheep given to him to pasture, has received his wages for the business, and been satisfied, then diminish the herd or lessen the offspring, he shall give increase and produce according to the nature of his agreements.

§ 265. If a herdsman, to whom oxen or sheep have been given, has defaulted, has altered the price, or sold them, he shall be prosecuted, and shall restore oxen, or sheep, tenfold, to their owner.

§ 266. If lightning has struck a fold, or a lion has made a slaughter, the herdsman shall purge himself by oath, and the owner of the fold shall bear the loss of the fold.

§ 267. If the herdsman has been careless, and a loss has occurred in the fold, the herdsman shall make good the loss in the fold; he shall repay the oxen, or sheep, to their owner.

§ 268. If a man has hired an ox, for threshing, its hire is twenty KA of corn.

§ 269. If he has hired an ass, for threshing, its hire is ten ḲA of corn.

§ 270. If he has hired a young animal, for threshing, its hire is one KA of corn.

§ 271. If a man has hired oxen, a wagon, and its driver, he shall pay one hundred and sixty ḲA of corn daily.

§ 272. If a man has hired the wagon alone, he shall pay forty KA of corn daily.

§ 273. If a man has hired a laborer from the beginning of the year to the fifth month, he shall pay six ŠE of silver daily; from the sixth month to the close of the year, he shall pay five ŠE of silver daily.

§ 274. If a man has hired an artisan, he shall pay as his daily wages, to a . . . five ŠE of silver, to a potter five ŠE of silver, to a tailor five ŠE of silver, to a stone-cutter . . . ŠE of silver, to a . . . ŠE of silver, to a . . . ŠE of silver, to a carpenter four ŠE of silver, to a rope-maker four ŠE of silver, to a . . . ŠE of silver, to a builder . . . ŠE of silver.

§ 275. If a man has hired a boat, its hire is three ŠE of silver daily.

§ 276. If he has hired a fast boat he shall pay two and a half ŠE daily.

§ 277. If a man has hired a ship of sixty GUR he shall pay one-sixth of a shekel of silver daily for its hire.

§ 278. If a man has bought a male or female slave and the slave has not fulfilled his month, but the *bennu* disease has fallen upon him, he shall return the slave to the seller and the buyer shall take back the money he paid.

§ 279. If a man has bought a male or female slave and a claim has been raised, the seller shall answer the claim.

§ 280. If a man, in a foreign land, has bought a male, or female, slave of another, and if when he has come home the owner of the male or female slave has recognized his slave, and if the slave be a native of the land, he shall grant him his liberty without money.

§ 281. If the slave was a native of another country, the buyer shall declare on oath the amount of money he paid, and the owner of the slave shall repay the merchant what he paid and keep his slave.

§ 282. If a slave has said to his master, "You are not my master," he shall be brought to account as his slave, and his master shall cut off his ear.

CONSTRUCTING THE PYRAMIDS 13

Twenty-five centuries ago when the Greek historian Herodotus visited the pyramids in Egypt, these enormous monuments already were regarded with reverence and awe as ancient relics. Today tourists still go to Egypt to see these pyramids and are still impressed by their simplicity and massiveness, their durability and grandeur. The pyramids also symbolize well the divine kingship of ancient Egypt, with its concentration of power and wealth resting on the broad base of the population. This description of the techniques used by a people with the simplest tools to construct the pyramids is by an archaeologist at the American University of Beirut.*

. . . The ancient Egyptians possessed only the simplest hand tools and lacked what today would be considered the most elementary machinery. They didn't use the wheel until the Great Pyramid had stood a thousand years and never used the pulley at all. Yet the monuments they left stagger the imagination. The Step Pyramid complex at Saqqara, built nearly 4,800 years ago, is enclosed by a dressed stone wall one mile in circumference. At Karnak visitors can walk for hours through forests of columns and gateways without seeing the whole temple. How were they constructed?

In ancient Egypt the quarrying, transport and erection of obelisks—symbolic stone shafts representing the sun—were common problems. And in their solution can be found answers to many questions on how ancient Egyptians achieved what appear to be miracles of construction. From records left by the Egyptians it appears that the huge obelisks—single shafts of granite up to 100 feet high and weighing 500 tons—were usually quarried at Aswan. When an obelisk was needed, stone cutters

---

* William A. Ward, "They Built for Eternity," *Aramco World* (March-April 1966), pp. 28-33.

at Aswan would search the quarry for a mass of rock free of faults and large enough to permit a segment of stone the size of an obelisk to be cut out in one piece. They would mark off the general outline of the obelisk on the smoothed flat surface and undertake to separate the monolith from the parent mass, sometimes cutting it free with ball-hammers of a hard stone such as dolerite, other times employing a more complex method. In a shallow slit chiseled into the rock and outlining the shape the stonecutters bored holes at regular intervals, drove in wooden wedges and soaked them. As the water seeped into them the wedges expanded slowly, splitting the rock along the chiseled lines until the whole monolith came free. After rough shaping and dressing it was transported to the building site.

Moving a block of stone this size was an exercise in brute strength. From Aswan —where an unfinished obelisk of enormous proportions lies to this day—they were usually floated along the Nile. But that meant that first the volume—and hence the weight—of the stone had to be calculated. This was done, according to data found on mathematical papyri, with exactly the same formula used today to calculate the volume of a truncated pyramid, a figure of the same geometric type as an obelisk.

Having established the weight of the obelisk the engineers could go ahead with the rest of the planning: estimating the number of laborers who would be needed, making arrangements for the laborers to be found and brought to the quarry, calculating the size of the log raft needed to float the obelisk, finding timber and transporting it to the quarry and getting construction started. It was a complicated task and even after the raft had been built and the obelisk rolled over onto it there was still considerable work ahead. A canal had to be dug in which at the time of the annual Nile flood, when the river waters spread out over the whole valley, the raft could be floated to the river proper with little difficulty. Such canals were dug by hand, first from a point near the quarry to the river, and then from the river to the building site. After the stonecutters had polished the obelisk to a smooth finish and cut inscriptions into its surface, the engineers launched the final operation: raising the great shaft to a standing position, one of the most fascinating feats achieved in the ancient world.

Prior to the arrival of the obelisk an incline of earth or sand, held in place by brick retaining walls, was built at the point where the obelisk was to stand. The incline covered the obelisk base. After the obelisk was unloaded from its raft at the site, teams of men dragged it up the incline with ropes, the lower end first. More laborers then went to work excavating the sand beneath the lower end so that gradually the end of the obelisk began to tilt downward into a near vertical position. Eventually one edge could be guided into a groove in the base. At that point hundreds of laborers in teams—hauling on guide lines—pulled it into an upright position. The rest of the incline and the retaining walls were then removed and the obelisk was left standing free and firm, and able, as has proven true, to stand for thousands of years.

That, anyway, is the theory and although the supporting evidence is sound, there are still a few points which remain hypothetical and other points which are still being disputed. For example, according to the records obelisks were transported on log rafts. But there is pictorial evidence from Queen Hatsheput's mortuary temple at Deir el-Bahri that obelisks were carried down the Nile in boats. A large relief shows two obelisks on the deck of a barge in the traditional shape of a sailing-boat hull being towed by 30 rowing boats. In one of the inscriptions from this temple, the word for "boat" is carved in hieroglyphs using a picture of such a barge carrying an obelisk. On the other hand, from what is known of Egyptian ship construction, a heavy load like that would have capsized any ship built along normal lines. There are some who tend to believe that the Egyptians possessed adequate knowledge to build boats capable of hauling obelisks in this fashion, but real boats found in excavations certainly do not bear this out. The theories are still theories.

The single most ambitious enterprise undertaken in ancient Egypt was of course the largest—and today the best known—of the pyramids of Gizeh. This monument covers 13 acres at the base and in its original condition stood 481 feet high and was constructed of about 2,300,000 blocks of stone, each weighing about 2½ tons. Yet although it is the most famous and the most familiar, the question "How did they do it?" still can't be answered fully. It is known that it was built without the use of either wheels or pulleys, but conjecture still plays and always has played a large part in the answers. Herodotus, for example, recording stories he heard from Egyptian priests, describes wooden machines which, he says, were used to lift the heavy stones from one level to another. Through the years the idea developed and spread that the Egyptians had discovered and hidden away secret methods and machinery. Actually the pyramid, even in the time of Herodotus, was already 2,000 years old and the truth had long since been swallowed up in legend and superstition.

But even though hypothetical, even the most reasonable theories explaining the pyramids are no less interesting than the fantastic theories produced by imaginative amateurs. Each of the 2,300,000 blocks, for example, had to be measured, cut, dressed, polished, moved, floated, moved again and put in place in almost precisely the same way that the obelisks were. To put it another way, the problems involved in constructing the pyramid were exactly the same as those of erecting obelisks but multiplied two million times!

As in any building project, the first problem that confronted those ancient engineers was how to obtain raw materials. It was a problem of unprecedented magnitude. They needed granite slabs for the inner chambers. They needed huge blocks of yellow limestone for the main courses. They needed white limestone for facing, tons of copper to make the tens of thousands of tools, enormous supplies of palm, flax and papyrus fibers with which to make rope to haul and pull and lift, and great quantities of wood to build rafts, sledges, levers and rollers. To meet these needs expeditions set forth in all directions. For granite they went to Aswan. For yellow limestone they went into the local hills. For white limestone they went to Turah, a few miles from Gizeh. They went to Sinai, too, for copper, and to the mountains of Lebanon for timber. In short, they ranged throughout the Middle East, simultaneously setting in motion mining, quarrying, lumbering and transportation projects of a scope that would be impressive even today.

The personnel problems were of similar proportions. Although, as inscriptions indicate, laborers made up the bulk of these expeditions, there were hosts of specialists too: masons, transport crews, military contingents, interpreters, a small army of scribes and—a typically Egyptian detail—scorpion charmers to deal with these vicious creatures. Physicians were also included since, contrary to the myths about cruel Egyptian taskmasters, workmen were much too valuable to be either whipped to death or left to die under the desert sun.

At the building site itself another army of workmen was required—laborers, masons, overseers, architects and thousands of service personnel. The total number involved in building the Great Pyramid was estimated in Herodotus' day as 100,000 men and a more recent estimate, made by a qualified archeologist, puts the figure at 250,000. In either case, the problems of organization, of housing and feeding them—for a period of 20 years—would have been staggering since these workers (again contrary to popular notions) were *not* slaves, but the free population of Egypt, most of whom worked for and were paid by the state. This was during the months when there was no farming. In the growing seasons they returned to the fields, leaving a skeleton crew of artisans behind to quarry stone, manufacture tools, dress the building blocks and make other preparations for the next season of construction.

The core of the pyramid was built in horizontal courses, rising like steps, each level a bit smaller than the step below. Since several courses make a truncated pyramid, the mathematical formula noted earlier in reference to obelisks played a vital role. With it the Chief Architect could calculate the total volume of several courses of stone, determine well in advance the materials, workmen and tools which would be needed for the coming season's construction and order the requisite amounts from the far-flung sources of supply.

As the courses of the pyramid rose higher, inclines of sand and rubble were constructed along each side. These slopes were fitted crossways with logs to facilitate the movement of wooden sledges on which the building-stones were dragged up to the ever rising surface. Once the core of the pyramid was finished, the outer casing of triangular stones—which, in effect, filled in the steps—was laid on. Since the inclines rose all the way to the top, the casing stones were added beginning at the peak. As the work on the casing proceeded downward, the inclines were gradually removed until the lowest course was finished and the monument stood free as a true pyramid, with its smooth sides sloping down in an unbroken white surface from peak to base. Unhappily, over the centuries these limestone casing blocks have been removed for other buildings, except for a few at the base. As a result, only the stepped core of the pyramid remains today.

The pyramid itself is little more than a tombstone marking a royal burial. In most pyramids the burial chamber is at or below ground level, reached through a passageway leading from a hidden entrance on the north side. In the Great Pyramid, changes in plan during construction created two chambers in the pyramid itself and one below ground level, all with the appropriate passageways. (A change in plan while building was in progress was frequent in Egyptian architecture.) The chambers in the Great Pyramid proper are mostly of granite and show certain unique characteristics. The Grand Gallery, part of the passage ascending to the burial chamber, is 153 feet long and 28 feet high. The upper three-fourths of the walls form a huge corbel vault the entire length of the gallery. The burial chamber at the upper end of the gallery is of granite and is topped by five low chambers and a peaked roof, also of granite slabs which average 50 tons each. This construction prevented the ponderous weight of the pyramid from crushing the burial chamber and is found in simpler form in several other pyramids.

The pyramid proper was only part of the total burial monument. A temple was built on the east side and a long stone causeway led from this temple down to the riverbank where a second temple stood. Each pyramid complex originally contained all these elements, though much has been destroyed. The causeway foundation was one of the first parts to be constructed, as this afforded a convenient path for dragging the building-stones up from the rafts at the river's edge.

The construction of rock-cut tombs demanded many of the same techniques as those used in the stone quarries. Excavating a rock-cut tomb simply meant quarrying passages and chambers out of living rock. Depending on the kind of stone, ball-hammers or metal hand tools were used to cut into the face of the cliff. Softer stone was chipped out in small pieces, harder stone was removed in blocks to be used later in other structures. Natural pillars were left in the larger galleries to support the mass above. The entire surface of such a man-made cave was then smoothed and covered with sculptured reliefs and inscriptions. If the stone was of poor quality, the walls were either painted or covered with a thick plaster surface in which the reliefs and inscriptions were cut.

This kind of structure presented less of a problem than a monument constructed of stone blocks. There was no massive transport of building materials involved and the labor force was certainly less. The total bulk of stone moved was, of course, proportionately smaller. The rock-cut tomb of King Merneptah (1223–1211 B.C.), for example, has a volume of approximately 6,000 cubic yards, almost negligible when compared to about 2,500,000 cubic yards for the Great Pyramid. Still, it is difficult to descend into one of the rock-cut tombs, particularly those of the Valley of the Kings, without admiring the often spectacular results. No less than the pyramids, the rock-cut tombs were engineering feats of considerable skill, considering that they were carved out of solid mountains entirely by hand.

By contrast, the construction of great temples, which would seemingly have presented great engineering difficulties, was relatively easy. Even a large temple hall with rows of tall columns, high walls and a massive stone roof required only adaptations of the same methods as those employed for obelisks, such as filling the entire area of a hall or temple or palace with earth and rubble as columns were put up. The columns were built of separate drums placed one upon another much as walls were built of separate layers of blocks. Thus the walls, gateways and columns all rose at the same rate and height, and the level, packed sand rose with each course of stone. By the time the stone roofing was laid on the building was completely filled with sand with huge inclines sloping off to ground level. After the building was completed, the earth filling and inclines were patiently removed in small reed baskets carried on the hips and shoulders of the workers—exactly as it is done today on many construction projects in the Middle East. At last, sometimes decades later, the temple would emerge, a testament to the skill and resourcefulness of builders and craftsmen who will forever remain unknown.

It should be added, perhaps, that the hypotheses concerning such construction are based largely on what the Egyptians themselves have said, in the form of completed and unfinished monuments as well as many types of inscriptions. Scenes on the walls of tomb chapels show that teams of men or oxen were used to drag stones weighing several tons. Names of individual work crews appear on blocks of stone they moved. Texts record the construction of their boats or barges for the transport of stones. There is even a written record of the erection of a huge royal statue which describes an earthen incline up which the statue was dragged, base first, to be lowered into position in the manner used to erect an obelisk. Another papyrus preserves the specifications for a brick-enclosed incline more than 1,200 feet long and 100 feet high at the upper end and the actual remains of such inclines have been discovered at many sites in association with several types of structures.

There is also ample evidence that hand tools were the basic means of cutting even the largest blocks and excavating tombs. Egyptian reliefs show workmen using them; many of these tools have been discovered in the course of modern excavation; and the markings left by chisels, adzes—small axes with arched blades—and ball-hammers are visible everywhere in tombs and quarries. (Even today in the Middle East workmen can be seen using identical tools, squatting in identical positions patiently chipping away at blocks of stone intended for the most modern buildings.)

The slits, cut in stone to receive wooden wedges for splitting large blocks from the parent mass, can be seen by the thousands in the Aswan quarries. There is debris in the quarries, suggesting that rough dressing and shaping were carried on in the quarry. And, finally, there are architectural drawings so accurate that the actual monuments they represent can sometimes be identified. The architect's plan for the tomb of Ramses IV includes measurements for the various corridors and galleries. One plan for a private estate even shows the trees in the garden, and on a fragment of pottery of the 21st century B.C. a landscape architect plotted the grove of trees that once stood before the earlier temple at Deir el-Bahri.

14 INDIA'S FORGOTTEN CIVILIZATION

Archaeologists have unearthed a great civilization in northwest India that was contemporary to, though far more extensive than, those of Mesopotamia and Egypt. It flourished in relative isolation for approximately a thousand years (2500–1500 B.C.) before distintegrating under circumstances that are not altogether clear. This civilization was then completely forgotten until the 1920's, when archaeologists began to dig in certain mysterious mounds in a desolate area called by the local people Mohenjo-Daro, or Place of the Dead. The excavations here, and in other localities along the Indus River valley, revealed the existence of this long-dead civilization. Much remains obscure, however, awaiting further excavations and the decipherment of the few remaining examples of the local script. The current state of knowledge is set forth in this account by a well-known British archaeologist.*

When we think of the birthplace of civilization, we are apt to think only of Babylonia and Egypt. It was in the valleys of the Tigris-Euphrates and of the Nile, the archaeologists say, that agriculture began and mankind built the first villages, the first cities and the first kingdoms—Sumer and· Egypt. Few people realize that there was a third great kingdom which rose and flourished side by side with them at the same time. This nameless and forgotten empire of antiquity, occupying the Indus Valley in western India, was far larger and more tightly ruled than Sumer or Egypt. It is nameless, and much less known than the other two, only because its language has not yet been deciphered and the remains of its writings cannot be read. Archaeologists hope that the code may some day be broken, as the hieroglyphics of ancient Egypt were deciphered, by discovery of a bilingual inscription— a Rosetta Stone of the Indus Valley. Until that momentous event, the story of this ancient Indian civilization must remain as incomplete as a silent picture. But the archaeological evidence tells enough to enable us to compare this culture with the more fully documented civilizations of Sumer and Egypt.

The study is a vital and exciting one, for it concerns the history of human ideas. Here in western Asia there rose three parallel but separate civilizations. In all three, technology followed much the same sequence: the invention of writing (that "incidental by-product of a strong sense of private property," as the U. S. archaeologist Ephraim Speiser so pleasantly put it), the development of skill in working bronze and precious metals, the evolution of architecture from mud huts to palaces, the growth of transport and trade and the rise of centralized government. Yet while the technological development of the three empires was nearly identical, their intellectual concepts and forms of society were very different. With respect to the peoples

* S. Piggott, "A Forgotten Empire of Antiquity," *Scientific American* (November 1953), pp. 43-48. Reprinted with permission. Copyright © 1953 by Scientific American, Inc. All rights reserved.

90

of Sumer and Egypt, we can read their differences of thought in their literature, and in the Indus Valley we can read it in the archaeological record of the people's way of life. For the Indus civilization had a unique individuality of its own, already marked with some of the features of what was to become the characteristic Hindu culture of historic India. The comparative study of these three earliest civilizations shows how varied were the intellectual means whereby mankind found ways to create and maintain a stable society.

Archaeologists have named the Indus kingdom the Harappa Civilization, after a modern village which stands on the site of one of the great ancient towns. The Harappa Civilization had developed from a peasant to an urban culture by about 2500 B.C., and it endured for at least a thousand years before it was destroyed by invaders. It was a nation based on cities, towns and villages, with a Bronze Age technology and a central government strong enough to keep the peace and organize the economy for the common welfare.

Like the other ancient civilizations, it was centered on a river system—that of the Indus and its tributaries. But it was enormously larger, at least seven times bigger in area than the kingdom of Sumer. Two great cities and some 60 to 70 towns, villages and trading posts have already been unearthed, and more are likely to reward diggers in the future. The Harappa empire apparently covered a triangle stretching from a 600-mile seaboard at the base to an apex in the Himalayan foothills nearly 1,000 miles away. Its two cities stood like twin capitals 400 miles apart on the river system; they were at the sites now occupied by Mohenjo-Daro (the Mounds of the Dead) on the Indus and Harappa on the Ravi tributary. The cities were roughly square, and probably each about one square mile in area. We can only guess at their population: probably the cities had some 20,000 inhabitants each and the empire as a whole a population of at least 70,000 to 100,000.

The cities and towns show every evidence of a culture at least as far advanced as that of the neighboring civilizations to the west. Though they had no stone palaces, their buildings were of brick, which, in response to the climate of monsoon rains, was baked hard in the modern manner, instead of being sundried as elsewhere in the ancient East. The Harappa people did metalwork in copper and bronze, created jewelry of gold and semiprecious stones, wove cotton cloth, made pottery, used wheeled vehicles and were widely literate.

Even a superficial survey of the material culture of the Harappa Civilization shows that we are not dealing with a loose confederacy of city-states, each with its local customs, but with a highly organized kingdom directed by a strong central government according to a carefully planned scheme. The two major cities are very much alike and appear to have spoken with a single voice. Throughout the area there was a remarkable uniformity of products: pottery was mass-produced and the baked bricks were of standard sizes. Indeed, the weights and measures of the Harappa empire seem to have been regulated to a degree of accuracy unknown elsewhere in the ancient world.

There is little archaeological evidence as to the origins of the Harappa Civilization; we know it only as a fully developed empire. Probably its beginnings stemmed from the region to the northwest some time in the Fourth Millennium B.C. But its development was entirely independent, and even at its height the Harappa kingdom had only sporadic and small-scale trading contacts with Sumer and none at all with the Egyptian empire.

The most remarkable fact about the known history of the Harappa Civilization is its stability and conservatism. For a thousand years, from its arrival at a state of maturity about 2500 B.C., there was almost no significant change, as far as the archaeological record shows. Through all those centuries the culture stood still in an arrested state of development: its script, its pottery, its architecture, its sculpture and seal-engraving, is curiously primitive metal tools—all these remained the same. There are no signs of disturbance by dynastic change or warfare. From time to time the town at Mohenjo-Daro was destroyed by floods, and after each inundation the city was rebuilt exactly as before, even to the same line for the house fronts along the streets. Such immemorial conservatism, such unwavering continuity of tradition, is unparalleled elsewhere in the ancient world, even in Egypt.

When the end did come, it came quickly, and to a people unprepared to defend their long-established civilization against attack from outside. Though the two great cities boasted walled citadels, we find there no sign of weapons such as might equip an army and no evidence of military battles or resistance. Somewhere around 1500 B.C. warrior bands from the west simply overran the kingdom. The urban civilization of the Harappa world ended and was replaced by scattered barbarian farmsteads.

What were the distinctive qualities of this enduring but fragile civilization? For one thing, their writing was unusual for the ancient world. It consisted of a stiff hieroglyphic script with a total of about 400 characters, nearly half of which were variants on a basic 250 or so. This relatively small number of signs in a non-alphabetic language implies an advanced stage in the craft of writing—the earliest writing in Sumer, for instance, had 2,000 signs. The samples of Harappa writing that have been found are mainly engraved stone seals which, as elsewhere in the ancient world, seem to have been used to identify personal property. The Harappa script was pictographic (apparently there was no cursive form), and the longest inscriptions discovered do not exceed 20 characters. Thus even when the Harappa writings are deciphered, they will not give us a lost literature. But to know to what language group they can be assigned will be of great importance.

The Harappa scale of weights was curious and without parallel. The unit was equivalent to 13.64 grams (a little less than half an ounce). But the scale defining multiples of the unit was calculated in a peculiar way: the unit itself was the ratio 16, and at the lower end of the scale the multiples were binary (doubling each time), while the heavier weights were reckoned in decimal multiples. Thus the weights ran in the ratio 1, 2, 8/3, 4, 8, 16, 32, 64, 160, 200, 320, 640 and so on. Fractions of a unit were expressed in thirds. This sequence has been deduced from a number of cubical stone weights found at sites in the Harappa kingdom. Unlike other peoples of antiquity, the Harappans seem to have stuck to their weight system with considerable precision, and the enforcement of the standard over so wide an area suggests careful control and inspection.

The Harappa people also used exact linear measurements. They had two units—a foot of 13.2 inches and a cubit of 20.62 inches. Investigators have found actual Harappa rules, engraved on shell and on bronze, and by check measurements on buildings have ascertained that the units were accurately followed. The Harappa foot and cubit units were the same as those used in other empires of the ancient Orient, which suggests that they came from a common source.

The centralization of authority which the uniformity of weights and measures and of mass-produced products in the Harappa empire bespeaks is even more insistently expressed in the cities themselves. At Mohenjo-Daro enough has been recovered of the town plan to show that it was conceived and laid out as a conscious civic creation from the start; the city was not the rabbit warren typical of the ancient (and much of the modern) Orient. A grid of streets, some of them 30 feet wide, divided the square city into 12 major blocks. Each measured some 1,200 by 800 feet (roughly six times the size of a typical block in New York City). The houses were set closely together, and on the street side they presented blank walls without any architectural embellishment except their doorways. In back they faced interior courtyards and were separated by lanes and alleyways. The dwellings were extremely well built of fired brick, and their walls seem to have been plastered and painted inside and out. They had bathrooms with paved floors, and drains leading to a main sewer system beneath the streets, where manholes covered by large tiles gave access for cleaning. In the walls were rubbish chutes opening into brick bins. The whole system shows a concern for sanitation and cleanliness, and a civic organization to that end, unique in oriental antiquity.

The houses generally did not vary greatly in size, suggesting no more inequalities in wealth than one would expect to find in a middle-class population of shopkeepers, craftsmen and merchants. But in both major cities there were separate blocks of two-room cottages which apparently were the quarters of manual workers—a supposition which is reinforced by the fact that at Harappa this housing stood hard by a group of circular corn-grinding platforms and a great communal granary.

The dominant feature of each city was its citadel, a massive rectangular platform at least 50 feet high. At Mohenjo-Daro this structure appears to have occupied one of the central blocks on the western side of the grid. The citadel at Harappa seems to have been similarly placed, but its position is less certain because the city is much less well preserved than its twin and has been badly plundered for its brick. The citadel platforms were built of mud brick with walls of burnt brick. Terraced ways led up to their gates, and the citadels were topped by rectangular bastions and angle-towers.

At Mohenjo-Daro the granary was within the citadel walls; there are still remnants of the loading platforms built to handle the grain. Of the buildings that stood on the citadel platform the most remarkable was an open bath about 8 feet deep and 40 feet long by 24 feet wide. The bath was surrounded by a veranda and changing-rooms and had steps leading down into it. Near it was a large building with a cloistered court and a pillared hall some 80 feet square. There was also a building, possibly a temple, which unfortunately is now almost obliterated by a Buddhist monastery later built on the site. And there were buildings similar in plan to the dwellings of the town. But none of the structures in the citadel could be interpreted as a palace.

These citadels, with their monumental walls, gateways, approach ramps and special buildings, must have been the seats of the centralized power of the Harappa Civilization. What was the source of the rulers' extraordinary authority? Clearly it was not primarily the force of arms, for no sign of any distinctively military equipment has been found in the kingdom. One can guess that their authority was spiritual. The conservative uniformity of the culture and the peaceful coexistence of the two major cities suggest that the kingdom was ruled by men who were priests before they were kings. The art and architecture of the Harappa Civilization look very much like precursors of the Hindu culture: nothing could be more characteristic of a Hindu sacred site than the great bath or "tank" at Mohenjo-Daro. On an engraved seal found in the same city is a figure which is easily recognizable as the prototype of Siva, one of the Hindu divinities. There are a hundred similar indications. All the archaeological evidence suggests that the Harappa polity was a theocracy ruled by priest-kings from sacred citadels, as Tibet is ruled today from the Potala at Lhasa and from Shigatse.

With ancient Egypt and Babylonia, the Harappa Civilization in India takes its place as the third area where urban civilization was born in the Old World. Like the others, it was based on a common stock of peasant skills acquired in little corn-growing, cattle-breeding communities, such as had grown up during the fifth and fourth millennia B.C. in many regions between the Nile and the Indus. But the Harappa people, like those of Egypt and Sumer, worked out their own distinctive and arresting variant of an urban civilization.

The very qualities that enabled the Harappa Civilization to endure unchanged for a thousand years apparently were responsible for its quick collapse at the end. Its peaceful, delicately adjusted economy could not survive an invasion. The invaders probably were the Indo-European tribes (the originators of the languages which were to become Sanskrit and Iranian) who began to migrate eastward from the western rim of Asia soon after 2000 B.C. These horse-driving squires and cattle drovers trampled out the Harappa culture, and a Dark Age of comparative barbarism ensued. But the Harappa Civilization was not completely extinguished, and from the new mixture of peoples and ideas came the traditions which molded historic Hinduism.

Chapter Six

End of ancient civilizations

Tᴀɪʙᴇsᴍᴇɴ ᴀɴᴅ Pᴇᴀsᴀɴᴛs   15

From the long-run historical viewpoint, the advent of civilization represented a step forward for mankind. Natural resources were exploited more efficiently, productivity increased, population rose correspondingly, and knowledge accumulated from generation to generation thanks to the new art of writing and to new professions. But from the short-run viewpoint, civilization meant class differentiation and exploitation, which contrasted starkly with the egalitarianism of Neolithic society. The first of the following selections, a description of the Siang tribal rice growers of Central Borneo, brings out the communal spirit that pervades economic and social relationships. This spirit is evident also in Reading 7, "Low Productivity of the Neolithic Tribesman."

The second selection demonstrates how different was the position of a peasant with the rise of civilization in ancient Egypt. This is a typical exhortation to schoolboys, depicting the trials and exploitation of the hapless peasant in contrast to the privileged position of the scribe. The third selection, by a French physician who lived in India for several years in the mid-seventeenth century, is a description of the position of the peasants and urban dwellers under the Mogul dynasty. The final selection, by two American missionaries in India in the 1920's, demonstrates that the position of the Indian peasants has remained basically unchanged and still contrasts strikingly with that of Neolithic tribesmen.

Siang Tribal Rice Growers *

. . . Almost the entire life of these people is concerned with wresting a living from the jungle, hunting the birds and animals, collecting fruits and vegetables, or

---

* J. H. Provine, "Cooperative Ricefield Cultivation among the Siang Dyaks of Central Borneo," *American Anthropologist,* Vol. 39, No. 1 (1937), 80-91. Reproduced by permission of the American Anthropological Association.

95

clearing the land to provide space and sunshine for the cultivation of their main crop, rice. The hardest and most important of these activities from the point of view of the effort expended, though not from the amount of time each year devoted to it, is the clearing of the jungle land for cultivation.

The amount of land available for cultivation is practically unlimited, though the people of each village rather definitely regard the land surrounding it as belonging to the men of that village for purposes of cultivation. Individually, however, they do not regard themselves as having anything more than a temporary claim to use the land. As long as a man wishes to use land which is being cleared or has been cleared by him, no one can take it from him. If a man abandons a used plot after its first year, and moves to another without manifesting in some way his intention to retain his use of the first plot, such as by planting *javau*, vegetables, or perhaps rubber, or by simple announcement of his retention of an interest in the plot, someone else may come in and cultivate the old field. There is a well recognized feeling, however, that if an abandoned field is wanted for use by another within one or two or even three years, permission must first be obtained from the user. After two or three years usually anyone may clear and cultivate it.

. . . . .

The site having been chosen, the first work is the clearing of the underbrush, creepers, grass, and small trees. After these have been cut, the debris is allowed to dry out thoroughly—a few days being sufficient—before the larger trees are felled upon it. Then the larger trees are attacked with the small axes, partially cut through until the top or the edge of the clearing is reached, when the peripheral trees are completely felled. . . . Of course, such method of felling does not perfectly nor completely clear a plot, and a good bit of hard work still must be done felling those trees which have withstood the avalanche of the first felling.

After the trees are down many of the larger branches still extend high into the air, and these must be cut off in order to allow for more complete burning. This leveling process, known as *mehera,* is almost as strenuous work as felling the trees originally. After the leveling the trees are allowed to dry out and the plot is burned, on a windy day if possible. A second burning may or may not be necessary. The fields are usually ready for planting by the middle of October.

Each family, that is, a man, his wife, and their unmarried children, has its own ricefield. The fields are not necessarily located in the same general region, nor in the same direction from the village, though in former years when head-hunting and raiding parties had constantly to be taken into consideration, it was usual for all the fields to be very close together if not actually adjoining. At present, two or more families, sometimes as many as ten or twelve, often go together in the preparation of the same area, cooperating through all the different stages of felling the trees, burning, planting, watching, and harvesting. If sufficient good land is available in one location, it is desirable to join together in cultivating it; for though head-hunting and raids no longer give the people much concern, joint cultivation supplies a companionship and economic advantage that is very desirable. During the growing season, when the animal pests are bad, watching of the fields can be done turn and turn about if several families are involved. Further, as one man at Nono Kliwon expressed it, if there are several fields together, it is not likely that the animal pests will ruin any particular crop completely, but rather will injure all partially, whereas if a man is alone the pests may clear out his entire field.

. . . . .

The man is considered as the head of the household, the room in the long house where he and his family reside is referred to as his, and it is expected of him that he will provide to the best of his ability the rice, wild game, and jungle produce, while the women will take care of the children, husk the rice, make mats, and do the cooking. It is unseemly for a woman to do the hardest kinds of work, to fell large trees, to hunt wild pig, or even to bring in a load of firewood; and a man who spends his entire time around the house to the neglect of his jungle work is guilty of a breach of responsibility.

. . . . .

Women who have lost their husbands through death, desertion, or other cause, and who have not been successful in procuring another are oftentimes forced to cultivate their own plots by themselves. Of course, some of them are fortunate enough to have parents or brothers or other relatives to whom they can look for help, but when such is not the case they must engage in the hard work of clearing their own ground, usually confining themselves, however, to those areas which have been previously used and on which the growth has not yet attained any great size. On the whole, the women can swing an axe as effectively as the men. When they do cultivate their own plots, they may enter into *hando* arrangements with their friends and neighbors, and may, if not too poor, which they usually are, secure feast labor. If a woman is left with several small children and has no relatives upon whom she can call, she is usually assisted by the others in the village, through gifts of rice and wild pig or by help in the clearing of her field; at least until such time as the children have become old enough to help her.

With the exception of the children, who until they are married are cared for in their father's house, and the old people who no longer are able to do hard work in the field, everyone must cultivate a field of some sort. The old men and women are cared for by their relatives, or these lacking, by friends and neighbors, and though no definite reciprocal obligations arise from the help extended to them, the old men ordinarily contribute a helpful share to the family existence by gathering and stripping rattan, sharpening tools, carving out boards and troughs, tending the children; the old women by weaving, cooking, tending the children, or such other small duties as devolve upon the stay-at-homes. With these exceptions no one is exempt from the necessity of making a ricefield, not even the medicine man or the chief.

. . . The Siangs, as other Dyaks, are notorious for their hospitality and visitors from other villages are readily accepted and provided for, sometimes for considerable periods of time. But if a man after considerable time makes no attempt or offer to reciprocate in some way for the hospitality afforded him, he is asked to move on. The Siang territory is a small one, communication between the villages is frequent, so that a man's shiftless ways quite soon spread to all the long houses and that man's reception becomes gradually less and less hearty. No really deserving person who through sickness or other misfortune has come to difficulty will be permitted to suffer or starve among the Siangs, but an undeserving person is seldom tolerated longer than is necessary to find out what he is.

Peasants of Ancient Egypt *

I am told, thou dost forsake writing, thou givest thyself up to pleasures; thou settest thy mind on work in the field, and turnest thy back on the God's Words. Dost

* A. Erman, *The Literature of the Ancient Egyptians* (London: Methuen & Co., Ltd., 1927), p. 193.

thou not bethink thee how it fareth with the husbandman, when the harvest is registered? The worm hath taken half of the corn, the hippopotamus hath devoured the rest. The mice abound in the field, and the locust hath descended. The cattle devour, and the sparrows steal. Woe to the husbandman!

The remainder, that lieth upon the threshing floor, the thieves make an end of that. The . . . of copper is destroyed; the pair of horses dieth at the threshing and ploughing.

And now the scribe landeth on the embankment and will register the harvest. The porters carry sticks, and the negroes palm-ribs. They say: "Give corn." "There is none there." He is stretched out and beaten; he is bound and thrown into the canal —— ——. His wife is bound in his presence, his children are put in fetters. His neighbours leave them, they take to flight, and look after their corn.

But the scribe, he directeth the work of all people. For him there are no taxes, for he payeth tribute in writing, and there are no dues for him. Prithee, know that.

Peasants of Seventeenth-Century India *

Of the vast tracts of country constituting the empire of Hindostan, many are little more than sand, or barren mountains, badly cultivated, and thinly peopled; and even a considerable portion of the good land remains untilled from want of labourers; many of whom perish in consequence of the bad treatment they experience from the governors. These poor people, when incapable of discharging the demands of their rapacious lords, are not only often deprived of the means of subsistence, but are bereft of their children, who are carried away as slaves. Thus it happens that many of the peasantry, driven to despair by so execrable a tyranny, abandon the country, and seek a more tolerable mode of existence, either in the towns, or camps; as porters, carriers of water, or cavalry servants. Sometimes they fly to the territories of a rajah, because there they find less oppression, and are allowed a greater degree of comfort.

. . . . .

The king [of India], as proprietor of the land, makes over a certain quantity to military men [or timariots], as an equivalent for their pay; and this grant is called jagieer, or, as in Turkey, timar; the word jagieer signifying the spot from which to draw, or the place of salary. Similar grants are made to governors, in lieu of their salary, and also for the support of their troops, on condition that they pay a certain sum annually to the king out of any surplus revenue that the land may yield. The lands not so granted are retained by the king as the peculiar domains of his house and are seldom, if ever, given in the way of jagieer; and upon these domains he keeps farmers, who are also bound to pay him an annual rent.

The persons thus put in possession of the land, whether as timariots, governors or farmers, have an authority almost absolute over the peasantry, and nearly as much over the artisans and merchants of the towns and villages within their district; and nothing can be imagined more cruel and oppressive than the manner in which it is exercised. There is no one before whom the injured peasant, artisan or tradesman, can pour out his just complaints; no great lords, parliaments or judges of presidial courts exist, as in France, to restrain the wickedness of those merciless oppressors, and the cadis, or judges, are not invested with sufficient power to redress the wrongs of these unhappy people. This sad abuse of the royal authority may not be felt in

* F. Bernier, *Travels in the Mogul Empire* (London, 1826), pp. 229-30, 252-54, 256-57.

the same degree near capital cities, such as Delhi and Agra, or in the vicinity of large towns and seaports, because in those places acts of gross injustice cannot easily be concealed from the court.

This debasing state of slavery obstructs the progress of trade and influences the manners and mode of life of every individual. There can be little encouragement to engage in commercial pursuits, when the success with which they may be attended, instead of adding to the enjoyments of life, provokes the cupidity of a neighbouring tyrant possessing both power and inclination to deprive any man of the fruits of his industry. When wealth is acquired, as must sometimes be the case, the possessor, so far from living with increased comfort and assuming an air of independence, studies the means by which he may appear indigent: his dress, lodging and furniture, continue to be mean, and he is careful, above all things, never to indulge in the pleasures of the table. In the mean time, his gold and silver remain buried at a great depth in the ground; . . .

. . . The peasant cannot avoid asking himself this question: "Why should I toil for a tyrant who may come tomorrow and lay his rapacious hands upon all I possess and value, without leaving me, if such should be his humour, the means to drag on my miserable existence?"—The timariots, governors and farmers, on their part reason in this manner "Why should the neglected state of this land create uneasiness in our minds? and why should we expend our own money and time to render it fruitful? we may be deprived of it in a single moment, and our exertions would benefit neither ourselves nor our children. Let us draw from the soil all the money we can, though the peasant should starve or abscond, and we should leave it, when commanded to quit, a dreary wilderness."

The facts I have mentioned are sufficient to account for the rapid declension of the Asiatic states. It is owing to this miserable system of government that most towns in Hindostan are made up of earth, mud, and other wretched materials; that there is no city or town which, if it be not already ruined and deserted, does not bear evident marks of approaching decay.

Peasants of Twentieth-Century India *

"To a newcomer we may seem suspicious, obstinate, intolerant, backward—everything that goes with refusal to change. We did not choose these characteristics for ourselves. Experience forced them upon our fathers. And the warnings of our fathers, added to our own experiences, have drilled them into us. Refusal to change is the armor with which we have learned to protect ourselves. If we and our fathers had accepted the new ideas and customs commended to us, we might have made greater progress. But greater progress would have drawn the eyes of a covetous world toward us. And then our lot would have been worse than before. Where are the cities that flourished for a time? In ruins. While they climbed to great heights and fell to the depths of destruction, we kept to the old reliable level. And we have survived. We are not blind to the advantages of the new, but unless we know just where it will lead us, we prefer to let it pass us by.

"At times you cannot hide your impatience with our caution. There was the plow which you urged us to accept. You saw only the advantages it offered in turning our soil during the months when it has always lain packed and hard. We saw beyond

* W. H. and C. V. Wiser, *Behind Mud Walls 1930-1960* (Berkeley and Los Angeles: University of California Press, 1964), pp. 117-20, 122-25, 128. The material in this reading consists entirely of statements by Indian villagers cited by W. H. and C. V. Wiser.

that. We felt the added perspiration of working in the killing sun of June, and saw the risk of exposing our bullocks to the cruelty of heat and sun, especially when they are hardly strong enough to pull such a plow. You know how we dread the sickness or loss of an animal. We knew the weight of the plow and foresaw the difficulties of carrying it on our shoulders from one small plot to another far away. And we saw the eyes of rent collectors, greedily watching the results of our added toil. We were sorry to disappoint you, but we could not risk such an expensive and doubtful experiment, when the benefits would most likely not stay with us. The plow that Bala's brother won at your exhibition last spring is better. It is light, like our plows, and good for ordinary plowing. But Bala's brother has not dared to use it. He is so prosperous that he is afraid of anything that makes a show of still greater prosperity. In that he may seem foolish to you. But we do not blame him for his caution.

"When you insisted upon entering your *bhangi* pastor's boy in school, we set up all the defenses our intolerance could supply. All our lives we have watched *bhangis* at their defiling work. No matter how much you clean them up and change their names, they are repulsive to us. From the time when our earliest impressions were formed we have despised them. You can let yourself forget the work which they do, and the flesh of swine which they eat. We cannot. Much more important than this is the change which might come from their new way of living and thinking. *Bhangis* might prove troublesome if not kept *bhangis*. They must stay where they have always been, and remain content with the work which is theirs to do. If they want to rise to something better, who then will keep our village clean? Each of us has been born to his appointed task. Perhaps we are what we are because of former lives. We do not know. Everything is in the hands of the gods. But this we do know: The old order has served us well for centuries. It has provided a task for everyone who is born into it. And it has provided for the carrying out of every task needed for village self-sufficiency, by men trained from childhood. If change once begins, how far will it go? What if *bhangis* should try to be farmers, and farmers try to be carpenters, and carpenters try to be teachers? There would be confusion and wrangling, and work badly done. No, the old order with its unalterable allotments is much more satisfactory.

"If we can assure ourselves that the better implement or the more generous custom will lead to no harmful consequences to ourselves, we may try to make it ours. We have replaced many of our charms with treatments which you or your doctors have advised. We have made changes in our houses, because we have seen that they are good and that they involve no risks. We are sowing new seed because we have been shown the better crops on the demonstration farm. You must be patient with our slowness and caution. An arm that has long been held stiff cannot be bent without effort and complainings. Our sons with their reading and their larger world may insist upon more changes. If so, we pray that they may have means of self-protection to cover their progress. For us who are not wise in the ways of the new world, the old, well-measured ways are safest.

"Our walls which conceal all that we treasure, are a necessary part of our defense. Our forefathers hid themselves from a covetous world behind mud walls. We do the same. Barriers are no longer needed as protection against cruel raiders. But they are needed against those ruthless ones who come to extort. For the old purpose, our fathers built their walls strong enough to shut out the enemy, and made them of earth so that they might be inconspicuous. For the present purpose they must remain inconspicuous and yet be high enough to conceal us and our possessions from the greedy ones. But now they are better protection if instead of being kept strong they are allowed to become dilapidated. Dilapidation makes it harder for the covetous visitor to tell who is actually poor and who simulates poverty. When men become so strong that the agents of authority work with them for their mutual benefit, they dare to expose their prosperity in walls of better materials and workmanship. But if the ordinary man suddenly makes his will conspicuous, the extortioner is on his trail. You remember what a short time it was after Puri put up his imposing new veranda with a good grass roof, that the police watchman threatened to bring a false charge against him. He paid well for his show of progress. Old walls tell no tales.

"Neither do old clothes. When we are to deal with strangers we choose our dress to the occasion, not to our means. And most occasions call for poor clothes. You have heard them complain in the hospital that they are at a loss to know who should be charity patients and who should pay. We would be foolish to bring upon ourselves big bills, when the simple matter of dress will give us charity rates.

.　.　.　.　.　.

"In all of our self-protective activities, each of us is not thinking of his own self. No villager thinks of himself apart from his family. He rises or falls with it. In the cities families are scattering. But we need the strength of the family to support us. We do not trust the outside world, and we are suspicious of each other. Our lives are oppressed by mean fears. We fear the rent collector, we fear the police watchman, we fear everyone who looks as though he might claim some authority over us; we fear our creditors, we fear our patrons, we fear too much rain, we fear locusts, we fear thieves, we fear the evil spirits which threaten our children and our animals, and we fear the strength of our neighbor. Do you wonder that we unite the strength of brothers and sons? That man is to be pitied who must stand alone against the dangers, seen and unseen, which beset him. Our families are our insurance. When a man falls ill, he knows that his family will care for him and his children until he is able to earn again. And he will be cared for without a word of reproach. If a man dies, his widow and children are sure of the protection of a home. To make certain of meeting the needs of our families in times of stress, we want hidden silver and we want land. These will preserve us from starvation through all trials. The village has survived the coming and going of many landlords and many rulers by remaining inconspicuous and providing its own sustenance.

"You and others have told us that with newer methods we would be spared much labor. Perhaps, but we do not fear work. You have seen us go out to our irrigation wells at dawn and return at dusk, day after day through chilly winter months. You have watched us driving our bullocks slowly round and round over the threshing floors through the sun and wind of scorching April days. During suffocating June weather you have watched us repairing our roofs and our house walls. Then with the coming of the rains you have seen us back in the fields with our plows. And you know that those of us who care for the crafts, do not idle when trade is slack, but work long hours in the fields. We are well acquainted with toil. It has always been with us. But these new ideas of more results from less labor are untried and confusing. How do we know that they will not leave some of us without employment? You must give us time to weigh them and their consequences.

. . . In the cities they devise ways of exploiting us. We know how to drive bargains when we sell our wheat or our sugar cane. We are at home in the wholesale market. But when we get our money and want to take home some cloth, the shopkeepers get out the pieces which they have been unable to dispose of, and persuade us to buy them at exorbitant prices. We know they are laughing at us. But we want cloth, and the next shopkeeper will cheat us as badly as the last. Wherever we go in the town, sharp eyes are watching to tempt our precious rupees from us. There is no one to advise us honestly or to help us escape from fraudulent men. When we go to town to attend the courts, there are men everywhere waiting to take advantage of our ignorance and fear. Our lawyers charge fees which they know are beyond our means to pay. And then if we win a case they think they deserve an extra large gift. Sometimes there is a sincere helper among them, but we are never sure who is what.

"There are the politicians who come to us and declare themselves champions of the village. They must think us very gullible. Do they suppose we are blind to the fact that it is only during the days before election that they take a passionate interest in us? . . .

"And what of the priests who should be our comforters and guides? Those among us who have priestly duties to perform, go through them punctiliously, just as the ceremonies require. At night our village head sometimes reads aloud from the *Ramayana*. In religion, as in all things, we have learned to depend on whatever we can provide for ourselves, when free from work. The men who devote their lives to priestly duties visit us, to be sure. But they come with a conch or a bell, the sound of which sends our womenfolk scuttling to the grain jar. At our doors they stop just long enough to have the donations poured into their bags. When the bags are full they move on. They tell us that the grain is for the temple on the edge of town, or for one on the Ganges. We do not stop to inquire further. They are priests, and we have always given. Sometimes a priest comes to recite verses. But he does it only in the house where the feast is prepared and his pay is promised. . . .

"There are our landlords, to whom we might look for interest and help, if we dared. But we have learned not to dare. One landlord is on a committee which administers the estate on behalf of a trust fund which is used for various charitable purposes. But the charity evidently limits itself to the city. We see no evidences of it in the men who come to collect rents from us. The other landlord has grown rich from his many villages. But we do not begrudge him his riches, because he proclaims his desire to be just toward his tenants. But he is too busy with his many properties to take time for any one village. We have never seen him. All we know about him are the reports which our headman brings from the big *durbars* to which he is invited once a year. . . ."

16   Indian and Greek Epics

Both Greece and India were invaded in the second millennium B.C. *by Indo-European peoples—the Achaeans and the Dorians in the one case, and the Aryans in the other. These newcomers disrupted the indigenous Minoan and Indus Valley civilizations, substituting new agricultural, tribal, and comparatively primitive societies. These new societies are depicted in their respective epics—Homer's* Iliad *and* Odyssey, *and the* Vedas. *The following comparative study of these epics by a professor of Sanskrit literature at Xavier College, Calcutta, points out their similarities, reflecting their common social background, as well as their differences, arising from contrasting temperaments and perspectives.**

* R. Antoine, "Indian and Greek Epics" in *Approaches to the Oriental Classics,* ed. W. T. de Bary (New York: Columbia University Press, 1959), pp. 96-112.

THE GENERAL PATTERN OF HEROIC SOCIETY.   All the great heroic traditions owe their existence to tribal culture. The basis on which tribal society rests is the principle of kinship and its social unit is the family group. Whereas the higher culture of the territorial state is founded on the idea of individual citizenship and gives rise to urban civilization, the tribal organization ignores national feeling and finds its social expression in feudalism. Feudalism is essentially an exchange of services between defenseless peasants and the military lord. In return for the protection which the lord gives them, the peasants offer him their land and promise to man his armies. When, to the economic necessity of finding a protector, is added the element of personal devotion to the leader, the cult of the hero is born.

On the other hand, epic poetry is usually retrospective. It develops at a time when tribal society enters into contact with a higher civilization and tends to project into the past certain elements of urban culture which give to the old capitals an anachronic aspect of modernity. It is this marginal character of epic poetry which explains how tribal heroes can gradually be transformed into national heroes.

It is interesting to note how epic poetry, in three different historical contexts, blossomed at an intermediary period, a kind of "Middle Ages" between two urban civilizations. In India, after the disappearance of the Indus civilization and before the rise of the Mauriyas; in Greece, after the decline of Aegean culture and before the emergence of Athenian dominance; in Europe, after the fall of the Roman Empire and of the short-lived Carolingian renaissance and before the urban civilization of the fourteenth century.

1. *The aristocrats at war.*   Heroic society is an aristocratic society. In the Greek epic, the heroes are called the *"'aristoi,"* i.e., the best among men. Stereotyped adjectives are used, referring probably to some well-known quality of some ancestor, and the name of the father or a patronymic *"taddhitānta"* continually reminds us that nobility is hereditary. The feuds which result in bloody battles have never the character of national wars in which the common people play the prominent part. In fact, the common people do not appear at all except as a necessary background against which the valor and prowess of the heroes stand out in greater splendor. Most of the fights are single fights, extraordinary duels witnessed by a crowd of spellbound soldiers and retainers.

The origin of the great battles is, in all cases, the personal offense of a hero's honor. And it is generally a woman who supplies the occasion. In the *Iliad,* it is self-evident. The Greek tribes, personified in their leaders, agree to avenge the honor of Menelaus whose wanton wife has eloped with the Trojan Paris. There is not the slightest hint of a national campaign, and the leadership of Agamemnon has no other reason than the necessity of a concerted attack. Again, it is the wounded pride of Achilles which proves fatal to the Greek armies and brings the Trojans within an ace of victory. The young lady whom Achilles had received as a prize for his bravery is arbitrarily taken away from him by Agamemnon. Finally, if Achilles decided to enter the fray, it is not out of a sense of solidarity with the routed Greeks, but of the purely personal desire to avenge his friend's death. National feeling, if it exists at all in the *Iliad,* is to be found among the Trojans. For them, everything is at stake, as it will be for the Greeks at the time of Marathon and Salamis. Yet, in spite of the simple solution of returning to her lawful husband the woman who is the cause of their extreme misfortune, they choose to fight because the Greeks have challenged them. It is a question of *panache* and it overrides the security of the city.

The tragedy of the *Rāmāyana* begins with the foolish claim of a vain woman,

Kaikeyi. King Dasaratha who knows her claim to be unreasonable considers himself bound by the sacred duty of keeping his word. The welfare of his subjects and their undisguised disapproval count for nothing before his misconceived obligation toward Bharata's mother. And thus Rāma, Sītā, and Lakshmana leave for the forest. Bharata is the only one whose attitude must have made sense to the more enlightened. But his efforts are all in vain. The capture of Sītā by Rāvana constitutes a lesser national problem than Helen's elopement, for the people of Ayodhyā have nothing to do in rescuing her. It is a personal injury to Rāma who, instead of calling on his own people to fight with him for their beloved princess, gets involved in the family dispute of a monkey tribe and gains the allegiance of the winning side. After Rāvana's defeat and recovery of Sītā, it may be argued that Rāma gives up the arbitrary rule of feudal lord and rates very high the feelings and opinions of his subjects. The fire ordeal and the second banishment of Sītā are undeniable proofs of his new policy. Yet, one wonders if that new policy heralds the dawn of a new era. It is so much in keeping with Rāma's submissiveness at the time of his banishment. Rightly has Rāma been given as the ideal of the "shānta" hero and one aspect of his love for peace seems to be that trouble should be avoided at any cost: neither his right to the throne, nor his absolute conviction that Sītā is innocent can arouse in him the passion necessary to resist the trouble-makers.

The destinies of the Pāndavas and the Kauravas are decided in a game of dice. This is typical of a feudal setting where the rulers dispose of their kingdoms as they would of their private fortunes. The overbearing pride of the winners and the spiteful humiliation of the losers reaches its climax in the Draupadī incident. It is around the ill-used Draupadī that the personal antagonism of the feudal lords crystallizes. The terrible imprecation of Bhīma against Duhshāsana, "I shall split his breast and drink his blood" (Mahābhārata, Sabhaparva, 90.57), is the real declaration of war and the long exile will be unable to delete its memory. Its gruesome realization can easily bear comparison with the savage profanation of Hector's body at the hands of Achilles.

After the exile, when the Pāndavas delegate Krishna to Duryodhana in order to reach a compromise, it is Draupadī, with her untied hair as a perpetual reminder of her humiliation, who passionately opposes all kinds of peaceful settlement. The way in which Krishna conducts the interview with the leader of the Kauravas is strongly influenced by the bellicose attitude of Pāncālī.

2. *The aristocrats in peace time.* Success in war being at the same time the condition of survival and the highest glory to which the heroes aspire, it is quite natural to see the young aristocrats apply themselves enthusiastically to their military training. Under the wise guidance of Drona, the young Pāndavas and Kauravas vie with one another in the display of their skill, while the elders and a crowd of simple admirers look on with immense delight. Their loud acclamation fills the air (Hahābhārata, Adi-parva, 144.39).

In the *Rāmāyana*, young Rāma receives his training from Vishvāmitra. The expedition against the demons is not just a game but is meant to give Rāma an idea of the evil forces with which he will have to grapple in his maturity. Homer has not depicted the early training of his heroes. Old Phoenix, however, gives us a glimpse of Achilles' education. Pleading with the sulking hero, Phoenix tells him: "My noble Lord Achilles, if you really think of sailing home and are so obsessed by anger that you refuse to save the gallant ships from going up in flames, what is to become of me without you, my dear child? How could I possibly stay there alone? Did not the old charioteer Peleus make me your guardian when he sent you off from Phthia to join Agamemnon? You were a mere lad, with no experience of the hazards of war, nor of debate, where people make their mark. It was to teach you all these things, to make a speaker of you, and a man of action, that he sent me with you; and I could not bring myself to let you go, dear child, and to stay behind, not if God himself undertook to strip me of my years and turn me into the sturdy youngster I was when I first left Hellas, the land of lovely women." (*Iliad*, Rieu trans. [Penguin], Book X, p. 172.)

Skill and strength are the necessary qualities of warriors. But these qualities have also a social importance which cannot be ignored. They are rated so high that a king is ready to give his daughter in marriage to the strongest, irrespective of the caste to which he belongs. Dhrishtadyumna, brother of Draupadī solemnly declares: "Be he a brahmin or a king or a merchant or a shūdra, he who will string this excellent bow will get my sister in marriage." (*Mahābhārata*, Adi-parva, 203.19–20.)

Sītā is won by Rāma because he alone can bend the bow. Draupadī is won by Arjuna for the same reason. Arjuna, to avoid detection, had come in the guise of a brahmin. The amusing scene describing the misgivings of the brahmins as one of them rises to perform a feat which the well-trained princes were unable to accomplish makes us guess the pride and joy they felt when Arjuna defeated the kings at their own game. At the end of the *Odyssey,* Ulysses, having reached Ithaca after his long peregrinations, finds his place occupied by the suitors. Penelope, prompted by Athena, decides to put them to the test: "Listen, my lords, you have fastened on this house in the long absence of its master, as the scene of your perpetual feasts, and you could offer no better pretext for your conduct than your wish to win my hand in marriage. That being the prize, come forward now, my gallant lords; for I challenge you to try your skill on the great bow of King Ulysses. And whichever man among you proves the handiest at stringing the bow and shoots an arrow through everyone of these twelve axes, with that man I will go, bidding goodbye to this house which welcomed me as a bride." The suitors fail. No doubt, they are grieved at the loss of Penelope, but, as Eurymachus puts it, "What does grieve me more is the thought that our failure with his bow proves us such weaklings compared with the godlike Ulysses. The disgrace will stick to our names for ever." Like Arjuna, Ulysses appears unrecognized and humbly asks to be allowed to test the strength of his hands. The suitors are annoyed: "We don't want the common folk to be saying things like this, 'A poor lot, these; not up to the fine gentleman whose wife they want to marry! *They* can't string his bow. But in comes some casual tramp, strings the bow with the greatest ease and shoots through all the marks!' That is the kind of thing they will say; and our reputation might suffer." (*Odyssey,* Rieu trans. [Penguin], Book XXII, pp. 317–18, 324.) We live here in the same world and breathe the same atmosphere as in Drupada's palace and Janaka's capital.

3. *The aristocrats facing the mystery of life.* Life in the Epic Age was essentially active. Games, gambling, conquests, and military campaigns kept the heroes occupied, while the recital by bards of the glorious deeds of their ancestors gave an ever new luster to the flame of chivalry. Before the compilation of the main epic narratives as we have them today, there must have existed a great number of independent lays celebrating different families or dynasties. The *Mahābhārata* contains a great wealth of such stories quoted as examples to the heroes. The *Iliad* and the *Odyssey,* though less rich than the *Mahābhārata,* use the same device and the Greek tragedy testifies to the existence of numerous epic cycles not incorporated in the works of Homer. The teaching which appealed to

the knights of old was a concrete teaching which left out abstruse speculations. It may be reasonably surmised that Arjuna and the Krishna of the *Bhagavad Gītā* belong to a later age when speculation had taken precedence over action.

In fact, a life of action has its own problems. Man realizes that his plans are often thwarted and that he is not the sovereign master of his destiny. There are mysterious forces at work which must be reckoned with. Above all, the great mystery of death is ever present in the precarious life of warriors. The heroic mentality acknowledges the presence of the mystery, is deeply impressed by it, but does not attempt to give it an abstract solution.

In the face of the mystery of life with its passions, its failures, its cruelty, the hero, while feeling responsible for his actions, knows that the divine power ordains and guides everything. To our rationalistic minds, his position may seem to be illogical: either one is a fatalist and denies human freedom and responsibility, or one believes in freedom and denies the supreme power of fate. But our argument would not disturb the hero's belief. It is reality which interests him and reality is complex. The human and divine words are not juxtaposed, they intermingle so intimately that to consider one apart from the other destroys the very texture of reality. It is the divine world which gives to human existence its third dimension and makes of it a living and full-blooded tragedy. Who would be so devoid of sensitivity as to affirm that the epic heroes are mere marionettes activated by the mechanical device of a hidden magician?

Naturalism which has cut off human life from its mysterious roots and claims to explain everything by an analysis of superficial psychology would have made our heroes smile. They knew better and the modern tendency to reaffirm the mystery is much closer to the heroic mentality than the so-called realism of the last century. It is not without significance that depth psychology borrows from the epic some of its most important symbolism. The inner mystery it tries to penetrate may not be without connection with the transcendent mystery which the heroes of old acknowledged with awe and trembling.

Death, the lurking and inevitable menace, is a constant reminder of life's precarious stability. Sadly recalling the forebodings of defeat in a long and beautiful threnody, old King Dhritarāshtra, in a crescendo of despair punctuated by the recurring refrain "tadā nashamse vijayāya Sanjaya," concludes by expressing his desire to leave this fruitless existence: "O Sanjaya, since life is such my desire is to die without delay, for I do not see the slightest advantage in keeping alive." (*Mahābhārata,* Adi-parva, i. 245.)

In true epic fashion, Sanjaya replies by quoting the examples of hundreds of kings and warriors, far superior to the Kaurava princes, who have lived, fought, and died. Their death takes nothing away from their fame and valor, and life is worth living as long as fate does not snatch it away. Sanjaya does not speculate about future life or rebirth, he states the mystery of life and death and accepts it as a matter of fact: "There is no reason to lament over what is to be. Who can, through endeavor, change the course of fate? Time is the root of everything, of life and death, of happiness and adversity." (*Mahābhārata,* Adi-parva, i. 271–72.)

In the *Iliad,* the scene between Hector and Andromache has the same message to convey. Andromache is frightened by the bellicose enthusiasm of her husband: "Hector, you are possessed. This bravery of yours will be your end. You do not think of your little boy and of your unhappy wife, whom you will make a widow soon. Some day the Achaeans are bound to kill you in a massed attack. And when I lose you I might as well be dead. There will be no comfort left, when you have met your doom—nothing but grief." Hector is not indifferent to his wife's appeal. He loves his son and his wife dearly. Yet, he is a warrior and fate calls him to battle. "My dear, I beg you not to be too much distressed. No one is going to send me down to Hades before my proper time. But Fate is a thing that no man born of woman, coward or hero, can escape. Go home now, and attend to your own work, the loom and the spindle, and see that the maidservants go on with theirs. War is men's business; and this war is the business of every man in Ilium, myself above all." (*Iliad,* Book VI, pp. 128–29.)

INDIAN AND GREEK PERSPECTIVES.   Although much more might be said about the similarity between the Indian and· the Greek epic, we must now turn our attention to what makes them different. For they are different. There is an atmosphere, a spiritual climate proper to the Indian epic, as there is an outlook and a perspective which characterize the Homeric world. Why is it, for instance, that not a single Greek hero decides, after a life full of activity, to end his days in the peaceful retirement of the forest? Or how is it that the *Rāmāyana* and the *Mahābhārata* have been and still are religious books from which millions draw spiritual comfort and guidance, whereas the *Iliad* and the *Odyssey,* which have shaped the Greek temperament, have never been sacred books?

The mystery of death is ever present in the life of epic heroes. But the Indian temperament, so well depicted in the boy Nachiketas of the *Katha-Upanishad,* seeks to penetrate the mystery which the Greek temperament is rather inclined to accept. Hence, a fundamental difference between the two outlooks. The more deeply the Indian soul meditates and reflects on the transitoriness of life, the less importance it gives to purely human achievement. The more forcibly death appears as inevitable to the Greek hero, the more urgent also the necessity to live fully the short time which destiny allots to man. The similarity which we have pointed out in the first part of this essay is the similarity of a spontaneous and prospective tendency which precedes all metaphysical reflection. The Greek epic remains all through spontaneous and prospective. The Indian epic shows a gradual evolution toward a more reflexive and meditative attitude. In Greece, epic poetry and the metaphysical quest have remained two separate achievements. In India, both have met and blended, and that blending has conferred on the epic itself a character of its own. It has been the work of long centuries, especially for the *Mahābhārata.* Each generation had its contribution to make, and the whole work was not written under guidance of a logical mind anxious to safeguard the logical consistency of the various portions, but under the inspiration of the vital unity of a living people whose growth and development are reflected in its numerous verses as the changing landscape in the waters of a powerful river. What we are looking for in our study of the epic is not an abstract system which could be neatly summarized in a few clear and definite propositions, but human and concrete attitudes which reveal not the vision of a few philosophers but the temperament of living peoples. Our aim is not to pass a verdict or to decide that one temperament is better than the other, but to vibrate in unison with both temperaments since both are able to reveal to us hidden depths of the human soul.

1. *The Indian and the Greek temperament as revealed in the composition of the epic.*   When we read the Greek epic, we are forced to concentrate on the story and on the heroes. Without preamble, the *Iliad* begins with the narrative of Achilles' wrath. In spite of lengthy speeches and inconsistencies in the narrative, the story of the Achaeans' gradual discomfiture proceeds apace, and we are never allowed to forget the central theme. The sulking Achilles remains ever present, and we are anxiously waiting for the relenting of his stubborn resentment. The

death of Patroclus arouses Achilles from his inaction and the doom of Ilium is sealed. The *Odyssey* is perhaps the first novel ever written. Ulysses drifting on the high seas, among unspeakable dangers, pursued by the vindictiveness of the god Poseidon, relates his adventures and finally reaches his dear Ithaca, while his son Telemachus, unable to solve the difficulties which he faces at home, undertakes a long and vain quest for his father. Both finally meet at Ithaca and defeat the suitors.

The *Mahābhārata* has been called "a vast repository of Hindu traditional lore, philosophy and legend." Its bulk is eight times as great as that of the *Iliad* and *Odyssey* put together. It would be ridiculous to look for a well-focused narrative without digressions. It is not meant to be a simple story, and its greatness lies in the fact that, around the main story which occupies about one fifth of the whole work, the folklore, the wisdom, and the religious aspirations of long centuries have clustered into an immense florilegium of Indian life. The Ādi-parvan, after announcing the great tale, keeps us waiting for sixty chapters (i.e., over 2,000 verses) before beginning the story of the Pāndavas and Kauravas. Then, like a majestic river, the story follows its slow development, with many interruptions. The Sabhā-parvan with its 2,500 verses brings us to the exile of the Pāndavas. The Vana-parvan is a real storehouse of legends and beautiful tales and spreads over more than 17,000 verses. It is a real forest of myths, legends, and instructions of all kinds. The Virāta-parvan is like a short interlude of more than 2,000 verses. After the failure of a peaceful solution and the preparation of the armies (Udyoga-parvan with nearly 8,000 verses), Sanjaya's account of the great battle begins. The Bhīma-parvan (close to 6,000 verses) ends with the pathetic sight of Bhīma dying on a bed of arrows. The Drona-parvan (about 9,500 verses) relates the fall of Jayadratha and the end of Drona. Bhīma's revenge over Duhshāsana and Karna's death at the hands of Arjuna are related in the Karna-parvan (about 5,000 verses). After a long interruption devoted to the relation of Balarāma's pilgrimage to the Sarasvatī, the battle comes to an end with the unfair victory of Bhīma over Duryodhana. That is the Shālya-parvan (about 4,000 verses). The remaining Kauravas attack the Pāndavas at night and massacre their armies. The five brothers and Krishna escape death (Sauptika-parvan with 800 verses). In the Strī-parvan (800 verses), the Kaurava ladies, headed by Gāndhārī, visit the battlefield. The story is ended. But the great poem goes on with the Shānti-parvan (14,000 verses) and the Anushāsana-parvan (8,000 verses) embodying the teachings of Bhīma. They are the richest portions of the *Mahābhārata* as a treasure-house of Indian tradition: artha-shāstra, dharma-shāstra, civil law, strategy, popular wisdom, cosmogony, theology, yoga, psychology—all the branches of knowledge are represented in that immense discourse which must have taken centuries to be written. The story is resumed with Yudishthira's Ashvameda. Dhritarāshtra, accompanied by Gāndhārī, Kuntī, and Vidura, retires to the forest and is granted a vision of the deceased warriors. After the death of Balarāma and Krishna, the Pāndavas renounce the world.

Although the *Rāmāyana* is much more similar to the Greek epic than the *Mahābhārata,* there are elements in its composition which differentiate it sharply from Homer's poems. Like Homer, Vālmīki is a historical poet who has composed a great epic of startling literary qualities. There is even a great similarity between the general theme of the poems: the great war brought about by the abduction of a princess, the siege of the abductor's capital, the victory of the lawful husband, and the return of the princess to her conjugal home. There is little doubt that the origin of the *Rāmāyana,* like that of the *Iliad* and the *Odyssey,* is to be found in the heroic traditions of warring tribes. Yet, like the *Mahābhārata,* although to a lesser extent, the *Rāmāyana* incorporates an imposing collection of interpolated legends and myths which have no direct connection with the central theme. More explicitly than in the *Mahābhārata,* the hero of the *Rāmāyana* has become a divine incarnation, and the human interest of the story, without being destroyed, is sublimated into a divine episode.

2. *Humanism, Greek and Indian.* From a purely literary point of view, we might be tempted to conclude that the Greek epic avoids many of the defects of the Indian epic by a greater fidelity to the objective it has in view. Yet, we may wonder if the lengthy digressions of the Indian epic and the tendency to divinize its heroes have nothing else to reveal than bad literary workmanship. Is there not a fundamental difference between the Greek and the Indian conception of humanism? "Conception" is perhaps the wrong word, for we are not comparing two systems of philosophy, but two literary testimonies. It would be better, perhaps, to speak of two tendencies, two innate visions which try to find an expression without ever succeeding in reducing it to a clear-cut system. Have you ever heard the same story told by two persons of different temperaments? An extrovert will tell the story with passion, but a passion for the story itself, and he will leave out his personal reflections and subjective impressions, because he obscurely knows that the story can speak for itself. An introvert will allow his mind to wander and try to find in the incidents of the story props for his personal considerations regarding life and destiny. His passion is more interior, and the story itself will gradually lose something of its importance, without, however, disappearing completely. The thread of the narrative will be loose yet continuous. Am I far off the mark when I qualify the Greek epic temperament as extrovert, and the Indian as introvert?

The extrovert humanism of Greece. Spengler's remark that the soul of European antiquity is "pure present" is certainly very true of the Greek epic. We have already remarked on the hero's attitude toward death and what follows. It is a mystery which he recoils from investigating and which he accepts without question. Similarly, the mystery of human suffering and human wickedness is solved summarily. "Are not the gods responsible for that, weaving catastrophe into the pattern of events to make a song for future generations?" That is how King Alcinous consoles Ulysses for the loss of many of his dear friends. What the king is interested in is the story which Ulysses has to tell: "Explain to us what secret sorrow makes you weep as you listen to the tragic story of the Argives and the fall of Troy." (*Odyssey,* Book VIII, p. 138.)

What matters for the Greek hero is to make the most of the time allotted to him. Too much speculation is of no avail; it will not postpone the fatal day foreseen by the gods. To fight, to enjoy the pleasures of love and of congenial company, to make a name for himself, "to listen to a minstrel, while the tables are laden with bread and meat, and a steward carries round the wine and fills the cups," that is life, and the rest does not count. The transitoriness of human existence never prompts the Greek hero to give up the world to retire to the forest. Death is the great retirement and it will come in its appointed time.

There are no demons in the Greek epic. The Cyclops himself is just a savage of immense physical strength who does not represent in any way the dark power which resists the ruling of the gods. Both evil and good in human behavior have a divine origin. They remain human and we witness in them that strange blending of fatalism and responsibility which are the two facets of all human activities. Listen to Helen after her return to her husband's palace. She is fully conscious of her sin when she declares: "The Achaeans boldly declared war and took the field against Troy for my sake, shameless creature that I was." Yet, she also knows that it was not her independent doing: "Aphrodite blinded me when she lured me to Troy from my own dear country and made me forsake my daughter, my bridal chamber, and a husband who had all one could wish in the way of brains and good looks." (*Odyssey*, Book IV, pp. 68, 71.)

But the gods themselves are so very close to man. Except for the blind submission which they command regarding their arbitrary decisions and partialities, they behave exactly like the heroes of the poem, more recklessly even, for they have nobody to fear. Those humanized gods of the Homeric pantheon will remain "a fit inspiration for an athletic contest, a statue, or an ode, but [they are] of little use to the philosopher, and entirely unsympathetic to the simple everyday sorrows of mankind." Although they rule everything, they never rob the heroes of their humanity. Their quarrels are reflected in the conflicts that oppose man to man, they positively help their protégés and are personally engaged in the battles of men. But the human warriors do not rise above their human status. We may compare, in this connection, the decisive fight between Achilles and Hector, and the final struggle between Rāma and Rāvana. We are in two different worlds, the Greek world in which man would be what he is without divine interference, the Indian world in which man, a mere instrument raised to a divine efficiency, breaks his human limits. The Greek heroes are so human that they make one forget the divine operation which sustains them. The Indian gods are so prominent that they blur the human outlines of the heroes.

The introvert humanism of India. This last remark of mine should not lead one to conclude that I have failed to respond to the deep human appeal of innumerable passages of the Indian epic. I shall try to explain my meaning by a concrete example. I, who am not a Vedāntin, have great friends who are Vedāntins. In our usual human relations I fully appreciate their humane qualities. But I know that, deep down in their soul, they have a vision which is incompatible with that human distinction between "I" and "Thou" which is the very foundation of friendship. And that makes me feel uneasy. My attitude towards the Indian epic is something of that kind. I love Rāma and Sītā. Yudhishthira arouses my admiration. The Strī-parvan brings tears to my eyes. Arjuna's grief at the news of his son's death moves me deeply. As long as I forget the pattern to which they belong I feel one with them. But there is a pattern. Before trying to describe it, let us first understand how the Indian epic completes and deepens the Greek vision of life.

The simple fact that the *Mahābhārata* and the *Rāmāyana* are accepted, even today, as the divine answer to the religious aspirations of millions is a clear indication of the depth of their message. They have given an answer to the eternal questions of the "why," the "whence," and the "whither" of human existence. The epic story has become an occasion to reflect on the instability of things mundane and to seek for stability. The great heroes who survive the heroic struggle for power realize that power is an empty shell which must be discarded. Evil is a reality which is at work in the world, and the demons are bent on checking the divine control of the universe. They represent a terrible force, both external and internal to man, against which it is the duty of all, according to each one's situation, to fight. Human destiny is not to find its fulfillment in this world. Wisdom more than bravery has the key to the mystery of life. The heroes are continually invited to make the decisive struggle an internal struggle towards final emancipation, while the external struggle is nothing but a passing phase of the world of appearances. With the Indian epic, we enter into a vast pattern in which human life, human emotions, human values are assumed and transformed.

In the *Rāmāyana,* that pattern is outlined in the first book which is certainly a later addition revealing to a nicety the Indian temperament. The gods are much troubled by the demon Rāvana who cannot be destroyed except by man. But, in order to kill him, one would need divine power. Hence, Vishnu agrees to be born as a man. The divine struggle weaves itself into a human fabric. Dasharatha begets four sons. Rāma is the full incarnation of Vishnu, his three brothers are partial incarnations. We may forget about that divine prelude when we read the story of the exile, of the siege of Lankā, and of Rāvana's defeat. But what we discuss here is not whether or not the addition of the first book fulfills its purpose, but the fact that the first book has been added. In the perspective of that first book, the whole human story of Rāma and Sītā, the abduction of Sītā by Rāvana, and the battle between Rāma and Rāvana, become a kind of camouflage of the real story. A camouflage, as we have pointed out, which is not always successful, since the heroes often lose their human dimensions.

For the *Mahābhārata,* the pattern is much more complex. Toward the end, we come to know that all the heroes are divine incarnations. But let us consider one instance, the *Bhagavad Gītā.* There is Arjuna, deeply moved at the prospect that he has to fight against his relatives, and his gurus. Krishna encourages him to do his duty as a worthy Kshatriya, and that remains within the boundaries of the Greek epic. But when Krishna teaches Arjuna about the eternity of the Self and the illusion of the bodily individuality, the whole struggle, viewed from that perspective, vanishes into something unreal. The whole thing is a big puppet show in which the actors are moved by supernatural agencies.

The Indian pattern, as distinguished from the Greek outlook, is characterized by the fact that there is no strict division between the divine, the demonic, and the human. The Law of Rebirth allows the spirit to move across the three worlds in its pilgrimage toward liberation. How many demons do we not see released from their bondage once the heroes, under divine guidance, act as the unconscious instruments of a superior power? That fluidity of the Indian universe dissolves, as it were, all that is specifically divine, demonic or human, into an immense current of mysterious and predetermined events which follow their course under the appearance of spontaneity.

Appearance or reality? That is the question which the confrontation of the Greek and the Indian epic brings to our minds, but which it does not solve. Both the Indian and the Greek heroes have a keen perception of "that void, that nothingness at the bottom of things," but are inclined to react differently to it. While the Greek hero feels that human existence is a gift which must be enjoyed, the Indian hero tends to see in it a bondage from which one should escape. The greatest passages of both epics are those where the gift-aspect and the bondage-aspect are blended into that energizing humility which is man's closest realization of what he is.

CLASSICAL
CIVILIZATIONS
OF EURASIA,
1000 B.C.–A.D. 500

Chapter Seven

Incipient Eurasian ecumene

EXPANDING HORIZONS OF THE CLASSICAL WORLD 17

One of the fundamental differences between the ancient and classical civilizations was in their range. The ancient civilizations were all confined to their respective river valleys and largely isolated from each other by the surrounding sea of barbarism. The classical civilizations, by contrast, stretched across entire regions and had direct contact with each other. During the first century after Christ, for example, the Roman, Parthian, Kushan and Han empires spanned without any break the entire breadth of Eurasia from the Scottish Highlands to the China Seas. Thus during the Classical Age there existed for the first time a Eurasian entity or ecumene.

This ecumene was still at the incipient stage. The interaction and mutual knowledge of the various regions was rudimentary. The Homeric Greeks, for example, knew only the Middle East; Alexander knew also of India but not of China; the Chinese had heard vaguely of Rome as the place of origin of exotic products such as glass, "stone wool" (asbestos), and "night-shining jewel" (fluorspar). The Classical Age, then, was a period of expanding horizons, but the resulting ecumenism remained at the incipient stage; it did not reach fruition until medieval times.

Examples of the expanding horizons of these centuries are to be found in Reading 23, "A Greek View of India, Fourth Century B.C.," *and Reading 24, "A Chinese View of India, Seventh Century* A.D." *The following selection is from the* Histories *of Polybius, a Greek writer who, in describing the course of events from 220 to 145* B.C., *was impressed by the fact that the Romans had conquered "nearly the whole inhabited world," and hence concluded that "from this time forth History becomes a connected whole: the affairs of Italy and Libya are involved with those of Asia and Greece, and the tendency of all is to unity."* *

* E. S. Shuckburgh, trans., *The Histories of Polybius* (Bloomington: Indiana University Press, 1962), pp. 1-5.

Had the praise of History been passed over by former Chroniclers it would perhaps have been incumbent upon me to urge the choice and special study of records of this sort, as the readiest means men can have of correcting their knowledge of the past. But my predecessors have not been sparing in this respect. They have all begun and ended, so to speak, by enlarging on this theme: asserting again and again that the study of History is in the truest sense an education, and a training for political life; and that the most instructive, or rather the only, method of learning to bear with dignity the vicissitudes of fortune is to recall the catastrophes of others. It is evident, therefore, that no one need think it his duty to repeat what has been said by many, and said well. Least of all myself: for the surprising nature of the events which I have undertaken to relate is in itself sufficient to challenge and stimulate the attention of every one, old or young, to the study of my work. Can any one be so indifferent or idle as not to care to know by what means, and under what kind of polity, almost the whole inhabited world was conquered and brought under the dominion of the single city of Rome, and that too within a period of not quite fifty-three years? Or who again can be so completely absorbed in other subjects of contemplation or study, as to think any of them superior in importance to the accurate understanding of an event for which the past affords no precedent.

We shall best show how marvellous and vast our subject is by comparing the most famous Empires which preceded, and which have been the favourite themes of historians, and measuring them with the superior greatness of Rome. There are but three that deserve even to be so compared and measured: and they are these. The Persians for a certain length of time were possessed of a great empire and dominion. But every time they ventured beyond the limits of Asia, they found not only their empire, but their own existence also in danger. The Lacedaemonians, after contending for supremacy in Greece for many generations, when they did get it, held it without dispute for barely twelve years. The Macedonians obtained dominion in Europe from the lands bordering on the Adriatic to the Danube,—which after all is but a small fraction of this continent,—and, by the destruction of the Persian Empire, they afterwards added to that the dominion of Asia. And yet, though they had the credit of having made themselves masters of a larger number of countries and states than any people had ever done, they still left the greater half of the inhabited world in the hands of others. They never so much as thought of attempting Sicily, Sardinia, or Libya: and as to Europe, to speak the plain truth, they never even knew of the most warlike tribes of the West. The Roman conquest, on the other hand, was not partial. Nearly the whole inhabited world was reduced by them to obedience: and they left behind them an empire not to be paralleled in the past or rivalled in the future. Students will gain from my narrative a clearer view of the whole story, and of the numerous and important advantages which such exact record of events offers.

My History begins in the 140th Olympiad. The events from which it starts are these. In Greece, what is called the Social war: the first waged by Philip, son of Demetrius and father of Perseus, in league with the Achaeans against the Aetolians. In Asia, the war for the possession of Coele-Syria which Antiochus and Ptolemy Philopator carried on against each other. In Italy, Libya, and their neighbourhood, the conflict between Rome and Carthage, generally called the Hannibalian war. My work thus begins where that of Aratus of Sicyon leaves off. Now up to this time the world's history had been, so to speak, a series of disconnected transactions, as widely separated in their origin and results as in their localities. But from this time forth History becomes a connected whole: the affairs of Italy and Libya are involved with those of Asia and Greece, and the tendency of all is to unity. This is why I have fixed upon this era as the starting-point of my work. For it was their victory over the Carthaginians in this war, and their conviction that thereby the most difficult and most essential step towards universal empire had been taken, which encouraged the Romans for the first time to stretch out their hands upon the rest, and to cross with an army into Greece and Asia.

Now, had the states that were rivals for universal empire been familiarly known to us, no reference perhaps to their previous history would have been necessary, to show the purpose and the forces with which they approached an undertaking of this nature and magnitude. But the fact is that the majority of the Greeks have no knowledge of the previous constitution, power, or achievements either of Rome or Carthage. I therefore concluded that it was necessary to prefix this and the next book to my History. I was anxious that no one, when fairly embarked upon my actual narrative, should feel at a loss, and have to ask what were the designs entertained by the Romans, or the forces and means at their disposal, that they entered upon those undertakings, which did in fact lead to their becoming masters of land and sea everywhere in our part of the world. I wished, on the contrary, that these books of mine, and the prefatory sketch which they contained, might make it clear that the resources they started with justified their original idea, and sufficiently explained their final success in grasping universal empire and dominion.

There is this analogy between the plan of my History and the marvellous spirit of the age with which I have to deal. Just as Fortune made almost all the affairs of the world incline in one direction, and forced them to converge upon one and the same point; so it is my task as an historian to put before my readers a compendious view of the part played by Fortune in bringing about the general catastrophe. It was this peculiarity which originally challenged my attention, and determined me on undertaking this work. And combined with this was the fact that no writer of our time has undertaken a general history. Had any one done so my ambition in this direction would have been much diminished. But, in point of fact, I notice that by far the greater number of historians concern themselves with isolated wars and the incidents that accompany them: while as to a general and comprehensive scheme of events, their date, origin, and catastrophe, no one as far as I know has undertaken to examine it. I thought it, therefore, distinctly my duty neither to pass by myself, nor allow any one else to pass by, without full study, a characteristic specimen of the dealings of Fortune at once brilliant and instructive in the highest degree. For fruitful as Fortune is in change, and constantly as she is producing dramas in the life of men, yet never assuredly before this did she work such a marvel, or act such a drama, as that which we have witnessed. And of this we cannot obtain a comprehensive view from writers of mere episodes. It would be as absurd to expect to do so as for a man to imagine that he has learnt the shape of the whole world, its entire arrangement and order, because he has visited one after the other the most famous cities in it; or perhaps merely examined them in separate pictures. That would be indeed absurd: and it has always seemed to me that men, who are persuaded that they get a competent view of universal from episodical history, are very like persons who should see the limbs of some body, which had once been living and beautiful, scattered and remote; and should imagine that to be quite as good as actually beholding the activity and beauty of the living creature itself. But if some one could there and then reconstruct the animal once more, in the perfection of its beauty and the charm of its vitality, and could display it to the same people, they would beyond doubt confess that they had been far from conceiving the truth, and had been little better than dreamers. For indeed some idea of a whole may be got from a part, but an accurate knowledge and clear comprehension cannot. Wherefore we must conclude that episodical history contributes exceedingly little to the familiar knowledge and secure grasp of universal history. While it is only by the combination and comparison of the separate parts of the whole,—by observing their likeness and their difference,—that a man can attain his object: can obtain a view at once clear and complete; and thus secure both the profit and the delight of History.

Chapter Eight

Greco-Roman civilization

The classical age of Greece is generally recognized as one of the great golden ages of human history. Fundamental contributions were made in art, literature, philosophy, and science. Also democracy, both in theory and in practice, blossomed for the first time in the Athens of the fifth century B.C. *The classic definition of this democracy was given at the time by its illustrious practitioner Pericles, in the form of his funeral oration commemorating the Athenian soldiers who had fallen in battle against Sparta in 431* B.C. *On the other hand there is another contemporary account by the mysterious "Old Oligarch," whose identity still remains unknown. In contrast to Pericles' panegyric, the writing of the "Old Oligarch" is strongly critical of, and sarcastic towards, Athenian democracy, though respectful of its efficiency. Finally the account by a distinguished historian, Professor A. H. M. Jones of Cambridge University, provides a reasoned appraisal of fifth-century* B.C. *Athens in the light of modern scholarship.*

Pericles' Funeral Oration *

Most of those who have spoken here before me have commended the lawgiver who added this oration to our other funeral customs; it seemed to them a worthy thing that such an honour should be given at their burial to the dead who have fallen on the field of battle. But I should have preferred that, when men's deeds have been brave, they should be honoured in deed only, and with such an honour as this public funeral, which you are now witnessing. Then the reputation of many would not have been imperilled on the eloquence or want of eloquence of one, and their

* Benjamin Jowett, trans., *The History of Thucydides* (New York: Tandy-Thomas, 1909), Book II, 35-46.

virtues believed or not as he spoke well or ill. For it is difficult to say neither too little nor too much; and even moderation is apt not to give the impression of truthfulness. The friend of the dead who knows the facts is likely to think that the words of the speaker fall short of his knowledge and of his wishes; another who is not so well informed, when he hears of anything which surpasses his own powers, will be envious and will suspect exaggeration. Mankind are tolerant of the praises of others so long as each hearer thinks that he can do as well or nearly as well himself, but, when the speaker rises above him, jealousy is aroused and he begins to be incredulous. However, since our ancestors have set the seal of their approval upon the practice, I must obey, and to the utmost of my power shall endeavour to satisfy the wishes and beliefs of all who hear me.

I will speak first of our ancestors, for it is right and seemly that now, when we are lamenting the dead, a tribute should be paid to their memory. There has never been a time when they did not inhabit this land, which by their valour they have handed down from generation to generation, and we have received from them a free state. But if they were worthy of praise, still more were our fathers, who added to their inheritance, and after many a struggle transmitted to us their sons this great empire. And we ourselves assembled here to-day, who are still most of us in the vigour of life, have carried the work of improvement further, and have richly endowed our city with all things, so that she is sufficient for herself both in peace and war. Of the military exploits by which our various possessions were acquired, or of the energy with which we or our fathers drove back the tide of war, Hellenic or Barbarian, I will not speak; for the tale would be long and is familiar to you. But before I praise the dead, I should like to point out by what principles of action we rose to power, and under what institutions and through what manner of life our empire became great. For I conceive that such thoughts are not unsuited to the occasion, and that this numerous assembly of citizens and strangers may profitably listen to them.

Our form of government does not enter into rivalry with the institutions of others. We do not copy our neighbours, but are an example to them. It is true that we are called a democracy, for the administration is in the hands of the many and not of the few. But while the law secures equal justice to all alike in their private disputes, the claim of excellence is also recognised; and when a citizen is in any way distinguished, he is preferred to the public service, not as a matter of privilege, but as the reward of merit. Neither is poverty a bar, but a man may benefit his country whatever be the obscurity of his condition. There is no exclusiveness in our public life, and in our private intercourse we are not suspicious of one another, nor angry with our neighbour if he does what he likes; we do not put on sour looks at him which, though harmless, are not pleasant. While we are thus unconstrained in our private intercourse, a spirit of reverence pervades our public acts; we are prevented from doing wrong by respect for the authorities and for the laws, having an especial regard to those which are ordained for the protection of the injured as well as to those unwritten laws which bring upon the transgressor of them the reprobation of the general sentiment.

And we have not forgotten to provide for our weary spirits many relaxations from toil; we have regular games and sacrifices throughout the year; our homes are beautiful and elegant; and the delight which we daily feel in all these things helps to banish melancholy. Because of the greatness of our city the fruits of the whole earth flow in upon us; so that we enjoy the goods of other countries as freely as of our own.

Then, again, our military training is in many respects superior to that of our adversaries. Our city is thrown open to the world, and we never expel a foreigner or prevent him from seeing or learning anything of which the secret if revealed to an enemy might profit him. We rely not upon management or trickery, but upon our own hearts and hands. And in the matter of education, whereas they from early youth are always undergoing laborious exercises which are to make them brave, we live at ease, and yet are equally ready to face the perils which they face. And here is the proof. The Lacedæmonians come into Attica not by themselves, but with their whole confederacy following; we go alone into a neighbour's country; and although our opponents are fighting for their homes and we on a foreign soil, we have seldom any difficulty in overcoming them. Our enemies have never yet felt our united strength; the care of a navy divides our attention, and on land we are obliged to send our own citizens everywhere. But they, if they meet and defeat a part of our army, are as proud as if they had routed us all, and when defeated they pretend to have been vanquished by us all.

If then we prefer to meet danger with a light heart but without laborious training, and with a courage which is gained by habit and not enforced by law, are we not greatly the gainers? Since we do not anticipate the pain, although, when the hour comes, we can be as brave as those who never allow themselves to rest; and thus too our city is equally admirable in peace and in war. For we are lovers of the beautiful, yet simple in our tastes, and we cultivate the mind without loss of manliness. Wealth we employ, not for talk and ostentation, but when there is a real use for it. To avow poverty with us is no disgrace; the true disgrace is in doing nothing to avoid it. An Athenian citizen does not neglect the state because he takes care of his own household; and even those of us who are engaged in business have a very fair idea of politics. We alone regard a man who takes no interest in public affairs, not as a harmless, but as a useless character; and if few of us are originators, we are all sound judges of policy. The great impediment to action is, in our opinion, not discussion, but the want of that knowledge which is gained by discussion preparatory to action. For we have a peculiar power of thinking before we act and of acting too, whereas other men are courageous from ignorance but hesitate upon reflection. And they are surely to be esteemed the bravest spirits who, having the clearest sense both of the pains and pleasures of life, do not on that account shrink from danger. In doing good, again, we are unlike others; we make our friends by conferring, not by receiving favours. Now he who confers a favour is the firmer friend, because he would fain by kindness keep alive the memory of an obligation; but the recipient is colder in his feelings, because he knows that in requiting another's generosity he will not be winning gratitude but only paying a debt. We alone do good to our neighbours, not upon a calculation of interest, but in the confidence of freedom and in a frank and fearless spirit.

To sum up: I say that Athens is the school of Hellas, and that the individual Athenian in his own person seems to have the power of adapting himself to the most varied forms of action with the utmost versatility and grace. This is no passing and idle word, but truth and fact; and the assertion is verified by the position to which these qualities have raised the state. For in the hour of trial Athens alone among her contemporaries is superior to the report of her. No enemy who comes against her is indignant at the reverses which he sustains at the hands of such a city; no subject complains that his masters are unworthy of him. And we shall assuredly not be without witnesses; there are mighty monuments of our power which will make us the wonder of this and of succeeding ages; we shall not need the praises of Homer or of any other panegyrist whose poetry may please for the moment, although his representation of the facts will not bear the light of day. For we have compelled every land and every sea to open a path for our valour, and have everywhere planted eternal memorials of our friendship and of our enmity. Such is the city for whose sake these men nobly fought and died; they could not bear the thought that she might be taken from them; and every one of us who survive should gladly toil on her behalf.

I have dwelt upon the greatness of Athens because I want to show you that we are contending for a higher prize than those who enjoy none of these privileges, and to establish by manifest proof the merit of these men whom I am now commemorating. Their loftiest praise has been already spoken. For in magnifying the city I have magnified them, and men like them whose virtues made her glorious. And of how few Hellenes can it be said as of them, that their deeds when weighed in the balance have been found equal to their fame! Methinks that a death such as theirs has been given the true measure of a man's worth; it may be the first revelation of his virtues, but is at any rate their final seal. For even those who come short in other ways may justly plead the valour with which they have fought for their country; they have blotted out the evil with the good, and have benefited the state more by their public services than they have injured her by their private actions. None of these men were enervated by wealth or hesitated to resign for pleasures of life; none of them put off the evil day in the hope, natural to poverty, that a man, though poor, may one day become rich. But, deeming that the punishment of their enemies was sweeter than any of these things, and that they could fall in no nobler cause, they determined at the hazard of their lives to be honourably avenged, and to leave the rest. They resigned to hope their unknown chance of happiness; but in the face of death they resolved to rely upon themselves alone. And when the moment came they were minded to resist and suffer, rather than to fly and save their lives; they ran away from the word of dishonour, but on the battlefield their feet stood fast, and in an instant, at the height of their fortune, they passed away from the scene, not of their fear, but of their glory.

Such was the end of these men; they were worthy of Athens, and the living need not desire to have a more heroic spirit, although they may pray for a less fatal issue. The value of such a spirit is not to be expressed in words. Any one can discourse to you for ever about the advantages of a brave defence, which you know already. But instead of listening to him I would have you day by day fix your eyes upon the greatness of Athens, until you become filled with the love of her; and when you are impressed by the spectacle of her glory, reflect that this empire has been acquired by men who knew their duty and had the courage to do it, who in the hour of conflict had the fear of dishonour always present to them, and who, if ever they failed in an enterprise, would not allow their virtues to be lost to their country, but freely gave their lives to her as the fairest offering which they could present at her feast. The sacrifice which they collectively made was individually repaid to them; for they received again each one for himself a praise which grows not old, and the noblest of all sepulchres—I speak not of that in which their remains are laid, but of that in which their glory survives, and is proclaimed always and on every fitting occasion both in word and deed. For the whole earth is the sepulchre of famous men; not only are they commemorated by columns and inscriptions in their own country, but in foreign lands there dwells also an unwritten memorial of them, graven not on stone but in the hearts of men. Make them your examples, and, esteeming courage to be freedom and freedom to be happiness, do not weigh too nicely the perils of war. The unfortunate who has no hope of a change for the better has less reason to throw away his life than the prosperous who, if he survive, is always liable to a change for the worse, and to whom any accidental fall makes the most serious difference. To a man of spirit, cowardice and disaster coming together are far more bitter than death striking him unperceived at a time when he is full of courage and animated by the general hope.

Wherefore I do not now commiserate the parents of the dead who stand here; I would rather comfort them. You know that your life has been passed amid manifold vicissitudes; and that they may be deemed fortunate who have gained most honour, whether an honourable death like theirs, or an honourable sorrow like yours, and whose days have been so ordered that the term of their happiness is likewise the term of their life. I know how hard it is to make you feel this, when the good fortune of others will too often remind you of the gladness which once lightened your hearts. And sorrow is felt at the want of those blessings, not which a man never knew, but which were a part of his life before they were taken from him. Some of you are of an age at which they may hope to have other children, and they ought to bear their sorrow better; not only will the children who may hereafter be born make them forget their own lost ones, but the city will be doubly a gainer. She will not be left desolate, and she will be safer. For a man's counsel cannot have equal weight or worth, when he alone has no children to risk in the general danger. To those of you who have passed their prime, I say: Congratulate yourselves that you have been happy during the greater part of your days; remember that your life of sorrow will not last long, and be comforted by the glory of those who are gone. For the love of honour alone is ever young, and not riches, as some say, but honour is the delight of men when they are old and useless.

To you who are the sons and brothers of the departed, I see that the struggle to emulate them will be an arduous one. For all men praise the dead, and, however pre-eminent your virtue may be, hardly will you be thought, I do not say to equal, but even to approach them. The living have their rivals and detractors, but when a man is out of the way, the honour and good-will which he receives is unalloyed. And, if I am to speak of womanly virtues to those of you who will henceforth be widows, let me sum them up in one short admonition: To a woman not to show more weakness than is natural to her sex is a great glory, and not to be talked about for good or for evil among men.

I have paid the required tribute, in obedience to the law, making use of such fitting words as I had. The tribute of deeds has been paid in part; for the dead have been honourably interred, and it remains only that their children should be maintained at the public charge until they are grown up: this is the solid prize with which, as with a garland, Athens crowns her sons living and dead, after a struggle like theirs. For where the rewards of virtue are greatest, there the noblest citizens are enlisted in the service of the state. And now, when you have duly lamented, every one his own dead, you may depart.

"Old Oligarch's" Critique *

The Athenians, in my opinion, are entitled to little commendation for having originally adopted their present political institutions, because they are calculated to give an undue ascendancy to the poor and the bad over the rich and the good: I cannot therefore commend them. These institutions, however, as they have been adopted, can be demonstrated by abundant proofs to be admirably adapted to support the spirit of their constitution, and to enable them to transact public business, though among the rest of the Greeks a contrary opinion is prevalent.

* "On the Athenian Republic," in *The Whole Works of Xenophon,* trans. A. Cooper *et al.* (Philadelphia: T. Wardle, 1845), pp. 695-702.

First then, at Athens, the poor and the plebeians are wisely rendered more influential than the nobles and the rich; because the lower orders man the ships, and extend the power of the republic: for pilots, and pursers, and commanders of fifties, and boatswains, and shipbuilders, acquire much more real influence to a republic than the nobility and richer citizens. This being the state of their affairs, it seems a matter of justice that all the citizens should participate in the offices of state, whether they be filled by lot or by open suffrage, and that every citizen who chooses should be allowed to speak publicly at their deliberations.

The people never require a participation in those offices, whether superior or inferior, in which are centred the safety or danger of the whole nation: nor do they expect to be eligible to the offices of generals or masters of horse, as the people know that it is much more advantageous for them not to engage in such offices, but allow them to be possessed by the rich; but the people lay claim to all those offices to which salaries are attached, and which better the circumstances of their families.

The Athenians invariably give greater advantages to the bad, the poor, and the plebeians, than to the good; and this circumstance, though it has excited the wonder of many, still proves incontestably their desire to preserve the spirit of a democratical government. For the poor, the plebeians, and the lower orders, when held in consideration, and when their numbers increase, extend the democracy: but when the rich and good are prosperous, then the plebeians are exerting themselves to strengthen a party opposed to them in interest.

In every country the better portion of the people is hostile to a democratical government: for among that class the least petulance and injustice exist, and the most ardent desire of reputation and probity; but among the plebeians the greatest ignorance, insubordination, and wickedness are to be found: for their poverty leads them to crimes, and unskilfulness and ignorance, through want of money to some men. . . .

It might be remarked that they should not have allowed every person without distinction to speak publicly and attend the senate, but should have restricted this right to men of the greatest genius and virtue: yet in this respect they have consulted excellently, by permitting even the bad to speak. For if the higher orders alone had harangued and deliberated, it might be of advantage to men like themselves, but not so to the plebeians: and at present when every one may speak, a bad man is enabled to rise and propose what may be advantageous to himself and his equals.

The question may be asked, What proposal can such a man make, likely to be profitable either to himself or the people? But they know well that his ignorance and wickedness, coupled with good will towards them, are more likely to be beneficial to them than the virtue and wisdom of the good man conjoined with malice.

Such institutions will not produce the best system of government, but they are admirably calculated to preserve the democracy. The people by no means desire a well constituted republic which would inevitably subject them to slavery; they prefer to be free and to govern. A bad constitution gives them little uneasiness; for what you consider a bad political condition, enlarges their power and preserves their freedom.

If you desire a well constituted republic, you must first procure men of the greatest talents to make the laws; then the good will punish the bad; and consult on what is most beneficial to the commonwealth, and not allow persons like madmen to consult, harangue, and address public assemblies. These advantages would speedily reduce the plebeians to a state of slavery.

The licentiousness of slaves and of aliens at Athens is excessive; none are allowed to strike them; nor will the slave yield to the freeman. I will explain the cause of this practice being indigenous. If it were customary for the slave, or alien, or freedman to be struck by the freeman, the citizen of Athens would frequently be beaten under the supposition of his being a slave; for neither in dress nor personal appearance are the people superior to slaves or aliens.

It may be reckoned a subject of wonder that slaves are there allowed to live luxuriously, some of them even magnificently; yet even in this they appear to have acted with judgment. For where a naval power exists, it is necessary, for pecuniary considerations, to humour the slaves, and allow them a more liberal mode of living, that their masters may receive from them their hire for labour performed in the fleet; for where the slaves are rich, it is no longer expedient that my slave should dread you; but in Lacedæmon my slave dreads you; and where my slave is afraid of you, there is danger lest he should surrender his property to get rid of personal fear.

This consideration urges us to grant an equality of rights to slaves and freemen; and also to aliens and citizens, because the republic requires the aid of aliens on account of the multiplicity of her arts and the exigencies of the naval service. This is the reason that we have justly admitted the aliens to an equality of rights.

. . . . . .

It might be observed that the strength of the Athenians lies in their allies being able to contribute money. But to the plebeians it seems to be a greater advantage that each individual Athenian should possess the property of their allies, and that the allies should have only so much as to enable them to supply themselves with food and to till the fields without being able to conspire against their masters.

The Athenian people, at first sight, appear to have enacted a bad law, in obliging their allies to resort to Athens for the decision of their lawsuits. The Athenian people, on the other hand, only consider what advantage is likely to accrue to themselves from this practice. First of all, they receive the court dues throughout the year; besides, remaining at ease at home, without sailing to foreign lands, they administer the government of the allied states; preserve their lower orders, and ruin their enemies in the courts of justice: but if each of the allies had the administration of justice at home, as they bear a deadly hatred to the Athenians, they would ruin those among themselves who were most friendly to the Athenian people.

In addition to these, the Athenian people gain these advantages from justice being administered to the allies at Athens; for first, the city receives the hundredth part of what is landed at the Piræus, and the keepers of lodging-houses gain profit, and those who possess cattle and slaves for hire: heralds, too, are benefitted by the arrival of the allies.

Besides, if the allies did not come for decision in law-suits to Athens, they would only pay their respects to those of the Athenians who were delegated to visit them, such as generals and trierarchs and ambassadors; but at present each individual of the allies is obliged to flatter the Athenian plebeians, knowing that when he comes to Athens, the decision of his lawsuit depends solely and entirely on the people, who are the law at Athens. He is obliged, in courts of justice, to supplicate the people, and even when one enters the court to seize him by the hand. By these means the allies are rendered much more the slaves of the Athenian people.

. . . . . .

The Athenians seem also not to have consulted well, in always supporting the worst party in revolted cities. Yet, in this respect, they act with judgment; for if they chose the best, they would support a party entertaining notions on political points different from themselves: for in no state are the better class of citizens friendly to the plebeians, though the worst class are friendly to the plebeians; for equals entertain friendly notions of their equals. These reasons induce the Athenians to prefer what is advantageous to themselves.

A. H. M. Jones's Appraisal *

Prima facie the Athenian democracy would seem to have been a perfectly designed machine for expressing and putting into effect the will of the people. The majority of the magistrates were annually chosen by lot from all qualified candidates who put in their names, so that every citizen had a chance to take his turn in the administration. In the fifth-century only the military officers, of whom the most important were the ten generals, were elected by the assembly. In the fourth, when finance became a difficult problem, a few high financial officers were also elected. This was an inevitable concession to aristocratic principles: for the Greeks considered popular election to be aristocratic rather than democratic, since the ordinary voter will prefer a known to an unknown name—and in point of fact the generals usually tended to be men of wealth and family, though a professional soldier or two were usually members of the board in the fourth-century. But the assembly, of which all adult male citizens were members, kept a strict control over the generals, who received precise instructions and departed from them at their peril. The assembly was in a very real sense a sovereign body, holding forty regular meetings a year and extraordinary sessions as required, and not merely settling general questions of policy, but making detailed decisions in every sphere of government—foreign affairs, military operations, finance.

The administrative lynch-pin of the constitution was the council of five-hundred, annually chosen by lot from all the demes (wards or parishes) of Athens and Attica in proportion to their size, and thus forming a fair sample of the people as a whole. It had two main functions, to supervise and co-ordinate the activities of the magistrates, and to prepare the agenda of the assembly. No motion might be put to the assembly unless the question had been placed on the order paper by the council and duly advertised; snap divisions were thus precluded. On uncontroversial issues the council usually produced a draft motion, which could however be freely debated and amended in the assembly by any citizen; in this way much formal business was cleared away. On controversial issues the council normally—and naturally in view of its composition—forebore to express an opinion, and merely put the question before the people, leaving it to any citizen to draft the motion during the actual debate. The presidents of the council and the assembly were chosen daily by lot from the council to preclude any undue influence from the chair.

Finally, as ultimate guardians of the constitution, there were the popular law courts. Juries were empanelled by lot for each case from a body of six-thousand citizens annually chosen by lot, and decided not only private cases but political issues. These juries as a regular routine judged any charges of peculation or malfeasance brought against magistrates on laying down their office; they decided the fate of any citizen accused of treason or of "deceiving the people" by his speeches in the assembly; they could quash any motion voted in the assembly as being contrary to the laws, and punish its author. Political trials were frequent in Athens, and in the fourth-century in particular the indictment for an illegal motion was constantly employed for political purposes, often on very technical grounds. The

* A. H. M. Jones, "The Economic Basis of the Athenian Democracy," *Past & Present*, I (February 1952), 13-25.

126

result was that the popular juries—in such cases sometimes thousands strong—tended to become a Supreme Court.

In general all citizens who were not expressly disqualified for some offence, such as unpaid debt to the treasury, had equal political rights: in particular all could speak and vote in the assembly. For membership of the council and of the juries and probably for all magistracies there was an age qualification of thirty years. For offices, or at any rate some of them, there were also qualifications of property: but these were mostly moderate and, by the late fourth-century, at any rate, and probably by the fifth, were in practice ignored. To make the system work truly democratically it was further necessary that every citizen, however poor, should be able to afford the time for exercising his political rights, and from the time of Pericles pay was provided for this purpose. Magistrates were paid at varying rates according to the nature of their duties; members of the council received five obols a day by the fourth-century—the rate may have been lower in the fifth; and members of the juries were given a subsistence allowance of two obols, raised in 425 B.C. to three. Finally from the beginning of the fourth-century citizens who attended the assembly—or rather the quorum who arrived first, for a limited sum of money was allocated to each assembly—were paid a subsistence allowance of one, then two, then three obols. Later the rate was more liberal, one drachma for ordinary days, one and a half for the ten standing meetings when the agenda was heavier.

Two charges have been brought against the Athenian democracy, one both by ancient and by modern critics, the other in recent times only. The first is that the pay, which was an essential part of the system, was provided by the tribute paid by Athens' allies in the Delian League, and that the democracy was therefore parasitic on the empire: the second, that Athenians only had the leisure to perform their political functions because they were supported by slaves—the democracy was in fact parasitic on slavery.

To the first charge there is a very simple answer, that the democracy continued to function in the fourth-century when Athens had lost her empire; the Second Athenian League, which lasted effectively only from 377 to 357, was never a paying proposition, the contributions of the allies by no means covering the cost of military and naval operations. And not only did the democracy continue to function, but a new and important form of pay, that for attendance in the assembly, was introduced early in the century. This being so it is hardly worth while to go into the financial figures, particularly as there must be many gaps in our calculations. The magistrates numbered about 350 in the later fourth-century, and, if they received on an average one drachma a day, the annual bill would be 21 talents. The council, if all the members were paid for every day of the year, would have cost rather under 26 talents a year, but if councillors, like jurors, were paid for actual attendance, the bill would be considerably less, since sessions were not held every day and many members did not attend regularly. Assembly pay cannot be calculated as we do not know how large the quorum was. The major item was the 6,000 jurors, for whom Aristophanes budgets 150 talents a year, presumably by the simple method of multiplying 3 obols by 6,000 jurors by 300 court days (the courts did not sit on the forty or more assembly days nor on the numerous festivals). This is a theoretical maximum, for the whole 6,000 were not empanelled in juries on every court day—Aristophanes' jurors rise at dead of night to queue for their tickets. As against this, the internal revenue of Athens, apart from imperial receipts, can be inferred to have been in the range of 400 talents a year in the fifth-century. Since other peacetime expenditure was minimal pay was thus amply covered by internal income at this period. In the fourth-century the revenue dropped considerably;

Demosthenes indeed states that earlier in the century it amounted to only 130 talents. He is perhaps thinking of the regular income from taxes and rents, excluding receipts from fines, confiscations, and court fees, which were a considerable proportion of the whole. Even so, we know that in the first half of the fourth-century it was at times a tight squeeze. By 340, however, the regular revenue had risen to 400 talents again, and things were easy.

That Athens profited financially from her empire is of course true. But these profits were not necessary to keep the democracy working. They enabled Athens to be a great power, and to support a much larger citizen population at higher standards of living. One oligarchic critic emphasises the casual profits incidental on Athens' position as an imperial city; the imperial litigation which brought in more court fees, the increased customs revenue, the demand for lodgings, cabs and slaves to hire. Advocates and politicians made money by pleading the legal cases of the allies, and promoting measures in their favour. But these were chicken-feed compared with the solid benefits of empire, the tribute amounting to 400 talents a year and other imperial income raising the annual total to 600 talents, and the acquisition of land overseas, mainly by confiscation from rebellious allied communities or individuals.

The land was utilized either for colonies, which were technically separate states, but being composed of former Athenian citizens were virtually overseas extensions of the Athenian state, or for cleruchies, that is settlements of Athenians who remained full citizens, liable to Athenian taxation and military service, though in practice they naturally would rarely exercise their citizen rights at Athens. Both types of settlement were normally manned from the poorer citizens. Most will have come from the lowest property class, *thetes,* who possessed property rated under 2,000 drachmae and were liable only for naval service or as light-armed troops on land. The allotments were (in the one case where figures are given) of sufficient value to qualify the owner to rank as a *zeugites* liable to military service as a heavy-armed infantryman or hoplite. By her colonies and cleruchies Athens raised more than ten thousand of her citizens from poverty to modest affluence, and at the same time increased her hoplite force by an even larger number, the cleruchs with their adult sons serving in the ranks of the Athenian army and the colonists as allied contingents.

The tribute was partly spent on the upkeep of a standing navy, partly put to reserve. Pericles is stated to have kept sixty triremes in commission for eight months in the year, and he maintained a fleet of three hundred in the dockyards. The dockyards must have given employment to an army of craftsmen, as well as to 500 guards, and the crews of the cruising triremes would have numbered 12,000 men, paid a drachma a day for 240 days in the year. Not all the dockyard workers will have been citizens, nor all the naval ratings, but many thousands of Athenian *thetes* enjoyed regular well-paid employment thanks to the empire. Of the money put to reserve a part, probably 2,000 talents, was spent on public works, notably the Parthenon and the Propylaea, which again, as Plutarch explains, gave employment to the poorer classes. The remainder formed a war fund of 6,000 talents, which was ultimately spent during the Peloponnesian war on pay to hoplites and sailors.

In response to the favourable economic conditions provided by the empire the population of Athens seems to have risen by leaps and bounds during the half-century between the Persian war (480–479) and the opening of the Peloponnesian war (431). The figures are unfortunately very incomplete and not altogether certain, but the general picture is clear enough; they refer to citizens liable to military and naval service, that is males between 20 and 60. At Salamis (480) the Athenians manned 180 triremes, which required 36,000 men. As Attica had been evacuated and no army was mustered this figure probably represents the whole able-bodied population including resident aliens, so that the citizens may be reckoned at about 30,000. At Artemisium, earlier in the same year, the Athenians, supplemented by the population of the little city of Plataea, had manned 127 triremes (25,400 men, perhaps 20,000 Athenians). As an invasion of Attica was expected the hoplites were probably held in reserve and only *thetes* served in the fleet. At Plataea (479) 8,000 Athenian hoplites fought, but a large fleet was simultaneously in commission, which will have carried perhaps 2,000 marines of hoplite status: for Marathan (490) Athens had mustered 9,000 hoplites. These figures suggest a total population of 30,000 citizens, a figure given elsewhere by Herodotus, divided 1 : 2 between hoplites and *thetes*. At the opening of the Peloponnesian war there were well over 20,000 citizen hoplites on the muster rolls. The rise will have been due partly to the general rise in prosperity which enabled many *thetes,* who owned little or no land, to acquire sufficient house-property, slaves, or cash capital to qualify as hoplites; but mainly to the grant of allotments of land to *thetes* in the cleruchies. For the thetic class we have no reliable figures, for the large fleets which Athens commissioned at this period were certainly manned not only by citizens but by resident aliens and by foreigners drawn from the cities of the empire. But if, as Plutarch suggests, the sixty ships kept regularly in commission during peace time were largely manned by citizens, the crews of these, together with sundry standing land forces (1,600 archers and 500 shipyard guards, for instance) and the 6,000 jurors, of whom a large proportion were probably *thetes,* would account for 20,000 men, and in addition there were the workers employed in the shipyards, on public works and in private industry. Despite the rise of many thousands into the hoplite class, the *thetes* must have certainly maintained and probably considerably increased their numbers. It is worthy of note that a fair proportion of the new hoplites resided abroad in cleruchies, whereas the *thetes* mostly lived in Athens and Piraeus. This helps to account for the radical tone of the fifth-century democracy, and the predominance, noted with disfavour by oligarchic critics, of the "naval masses" in its councils.

The Peloponnesian war caused great losses both by battle casualties and by the plague: 1,000 hoplites fell at Delium and 600 at Amphipolis, and 2,700 hoplites and 130 triremes carrying perhaps 13,000 citizen sailors, if half the crews were Athenians, were sent to Sicily, of whom only a remnant ever saw Athens again, while in the plague 4,700 men of hopliate status and an uncounted number of *thetes* perished. Towards the end of the war (411) there seem to have been only 9,000 hoplites resident in Attica, and after the war the cleruchs were all dispossessed. In 322 the hoplite class still numbered only 9,000 despite a revival of prosperity. By that date the *thetes* numbered only 12,000. Other evidence suggests that both figures were about the same earlier in the century. The loss of the empire and the fall of Athens in 404 must have compelled many thousands of citizens, dispossessed cleruchs and unemployed sailors and dockyard workers, to emigrate or take service as mercenaries abroad. A general decrease in prosperity caused the population to sink to a level well below that of the Persian wars, and in particular reduced the thetic class. Hence the increasingly bourgeois tone of the fourth-century democracy.

The second charge against the Athenian democracy, that it was parasitic on slavery, is more difficult to answer with any certainty. It will be as well first to make plain the elements of the problem. The Athenians, like all Greek peoples, regarded themselves as a kinship group, and citizenship depended strictly on descent (always on the father's side and, by a law passed in 451 and re-enacted in 403, on the mother's side also) and not on residence, however long. The population of Attica therefore consisted not only of citizens, but of free aliens, mainly immigrants who had settled permanently and often lived at Athens for generations, but also including freed slaves and persons of mixed descent; and of slaves, mainly imported but some home-bred. It is unhistorical to condemn the Athenian democracy because it did not give political rights to all residents of Attica; it was the democracy of the Athenian people. It is however relevant to enquire whether the Athenian people was a privileged group depending on the labour of others. Sparta might be called technically a democracy (though the hereditary kings and the council of elders balanced the power of the people) inasmuch as the whole body of Spartiates chose the ephors, in whose hands the government effectively lay, but the Spartiates were a body of *rentiers* supported by ten or twenty times the number of native serfs, the helots. Was the Athenian democracy of this order? The resident aliens (metics) do not concern us here. They made a great contribution to Athenian prosperity, particularly in the fields of industry, commerce and banking—indeed they seem to have dominated the two latter. They were voluntary immigrants and could leave when they wished (except in time of war). That so many domiciled themselves permanently in Attica—a census taken at the end of the fourth-century showed 10,000 metics as against 21,000 citizens—is a testimony to their liberal treatment. They enjoyed full civil (as opposed to political) rights, except that they could not own land—hence their concentration on industry and commerce—and were subject to all the duties of citizens, including military and naval service and taxation at a slightly higher scale. They were a contented class, and many demonstrated their loyalty to their adoptive city by generous gifts at times of crisis.

What of slaves? Here it will be as well to clear up another misconception. It is often stated, mainly on the authority of Plato and Aristotle, that "the Greeks" considered manual work degrading. Now it is true that gentlemen like Plato and Aristotle despised workers and justified their contempt by asserting that manual work deformed the body and the soul. But that this was the attitude of the average poor Greek there is no evidence. An anecdote recorded by Xenophon probably gives a better insight into his point of view. Eutherus, a dispossessed cleruch, has been reduced to earning his living by manual labour. Socrates asks what he will do when his bodily strength fails and suggests that he find a job as a rich man's bailiff. Eutherus is horrified at the suggestion—"I could not endure to be a slave . . . I absolutely refuse to be at any man's beck and call." What the Athenian *thes* objected to was not hard work—incidentally his main military duty in the fifth-century was rowing in the galleys, a task in most later civilisations considered fit only for infidel slaves or convicts—but being another man's servant. He would work as an independent craftsman or at a pinch as a casual labourer, but he would not take even a black-coated job as a regular employee; we find that such highly responsible posts as the manager of a bank or the foreman overseer of a mine are filled by slaves or freedmen of the owner.

Is it true, as we are still too often told, that the average Athenian, in the intervals between listening to a play of Sophocles and serving as a magistrate, councillor or juror, lounged in the market place, discussing politics and philosophy, while slaves toiled to support him? Contemporary critics of the democracy did not think so. Plato's Socrates, analysing the people in a democracy, divides them into the drones, that is the active politicians and their cliques of supporters, and the mass of the people "who support themselves by their labour and do not care about politics, owning very little property; this is the largest and most powerful element in a democracy when it is assembled." Xenophon's Socrates, rebuking

Charmides for his shyness at addressing the assembly, asks if he is afraid "of the fullers among them or the shoemakers or the carpenters or the smiths or the peasants or the merchants or the shopkeepers: for the assembly is composed of all of them." Aristotle, analysing the people (that is the mass of poor citizens) in different cities, classifies them as craftsmen, shopkeepers, seamen of various kinds —fishermen, ferrymen, sailors on merchantmen or warships—and casual day labourers and those who have little property so that they can enjoy no leisure.

Slaves were employed in many capacities—as domestic servants, as clerks and agents in commerce and banking, in agriculture, and in industry and mining. All well-to-do Athenian families had several servants, and no doubt wealthy men kept large households of a dozen or more—precise figures are lacking—but the domestic servant probably did not go very far down the social scale. A man for whom Lysias wrote a little speech does indeed roundly assert that everyone has slaves; but he is trying to convince the jury that it is contrary to public policy to encourage slaves to inform against their masters. In comedy domestic slaves appear when dramatically convenient, even in the poorest households, but this evidence is suspect: comedy was written after all by well-to-do authors, and slaves provided a variety of stock comic turns. It has been argued that because in the fifth-century every hoplite took with him an attendant to carry his food and kit, and was allowed a drachma a day by the state on his account (in addition to his own drachma) that every hoplite must have owned an able bodied male slave. Those hoplites who owned suitable slaves certainly used them for this purpose, but there is no evidence that every hoplite's attendant was his own slave. The high rate of the state allowance, on the contrary, is only explicable on the assumption that many hoplites would have to hire a man for the purpose, and Thucydides' inclusion of the baggage carriers with the light armed among the Athenian casualties at Delium implies that they were citizens. More significant than these uncertain inferences is a remark by Demosthenes, who, castigating the harshness with which Androtion and Timocrates collected the arrears of war-tax, pictures them "removing doors and seizing blankets and distraining on a servant girl, if anyone employed one." Now the payers of war tax can be estimated to have numbered only about 6,000 out of a population of 21,000. If not all of them had a domestic servant, one may hazard that under a quarter of the population enjoyed that luxury.

Commerce and banking need not detain us, as the numbers were small. In agriculture, too, we hear little of slaves. The property of large landowners did not normally consist of a single great estate, but of several farms scattered over Attica. Some of these farms were let to free tenants, Athenian or metic; one at least—the home farm—would be worked by a minimum staff of slaves, supplemented by hired labour; for it was uneconomic in a seasonal trade like agriculture to maintain all the year round enough slaves to cope with peak demands. The hired labour was sometimes supplied by slave gangs, leased from a contractor to do a particular job, such as to get in the harvest or the vintage; but it often consisted of free persons—in one of his private speeches Demosthenes remarks that many citizen women were driven by poverty to work in the harvest. Shepherds seem normally to have been slaves, but the politician Phrynichus is alleged to have been one in his poverty-stricken youth. How far down the scale of wealth the use of agricultural slaves went it is difficult to say, but the greater part of Attica was probably occupied by peasant farmers too poor to afford them. Of the six thousand citizens who paid war tax, a large number were, as Demosthenes puts it, "farmers who stinted themselves, but owing to the maintenance of their children and domestic expenses and other public demands fell into arrears with their war tax." These were the men who often could not afford a single domestic servant, and certainly did not maintain a farm hand; they would fall into the class which Aristotle described as using the labour of their wives and children through lack of slaves. Below them were the remaining three thousand of the hoplite class who did not qualify for war tax, and will have owned property to the value of between 25 and 20 minae. These were quite poor men; Demosthenes introducing a poor hoplite witness apologies to the jury—"he is poor, it is true, but not a rascal"— and the wealthy Mantitheus, when his deme mustered for a call-up, found that many of his fellow-demesmen were embarrassed for journey-money, and distributed 30 drachmae to each. A farm worth 20 minae would, on the basis of the single land price recorded, comprise about five acres, and would bring in if let only about 160 drachmae a year in rent, not enough to feed, let alone clothe, a single man; it can only have supported a family if worked by family labour.

In industry, and particularly mining, slaves were employed on a larger scale. The wealthy Nicias in the fifth-century is said to have owned 1,000 slaves, whom he let out to a mining contractor at one obol a day, the contractor feeding and clothing them and replacing casualties; two rich contemporaries are said to have owned 600 and 300 respectively whom they exploited in a similar way. In the fourth-century another mine concessionaire owned 30 slaves, which was probably a more usual number. Well-to-do Athenians also normally invested a small proportion of their wealth in slave craftsmen, who either worked together in a factory, or independently, paying their owner a fixed sum and keeping for themselves whatever they earned beyond it. The largest factory of which we hear, the shield factory of the brothers Lysias and Polemarchus, numbered nearly 120 men; but this is quite exceptional, and is due to the fact that the owners were metics, who could not invest in land, and that the thirty years of the Peloponnesian War had naturally led to a boom in armaments. In the fourth-century Pasion the banker also ran a shield factory as a side-line; it brought in a net revenue of a talent a year, and must have contained over 60 men; Pasion again was a metic, until he was rewarded with the citizenship for his public services, and he was the richest man in Athens of the time—he had before he died acquired land to the value of 20 talents besides his bank and factory. Demosthenes' father was also exceptional in owning two factories, 32 knife makers and 20 bed makers, with a capital value of nearly 6½ talents (4 talents in slaves and 2½ talents in raw materials in stock) out of a total fortune of 14 talents, the rest of which was in cash and investments with the exception of his house and furniture. We hear of some others in the fifth-century whose wealth was entirely invested in slaves; Isocrates' father rose to affluence from the profits of a group of flute-makers, and Xenophon makes Socrates cite five contemporaries, including a miller, a baker and cloakmaker, who lived comfortably on the earnings of their slaves. More usually rich Athenians seem to have distributed their capital between land, house-property, some cash investments and a dozen or so slave craftsmen. Socrates, asking a high-class prostitute where her money came from, suggests (ironically) land, house-property or craftsmen as typical sources of income. Timocrates inherited, besides land and houses, nine or ten shoemakers, who paid two obols a day each as rent: Leostratus owned bronzesmiths to the value of 35 minae (about a dozen, that is): Ciron, besides an estate worth a talent, and two houses, owned a few rent-paying slaves, valued with three domestic slaves and the furniture at 13 minae: Euctaeus possessed a farm, a house, a baths, and a brothel and wine-shop and some craftsmen.

These facts and figures concern the well-to-do families who could afford to pay a professional speech-writer to compose a plea in their mutual litigation about their inheritances, and who normally belonged to the 1,200 richest families enrolled on the trierarchic register. How far humbler folk owned industrial slaves it is very difficult to say. Xenophon in one passage speaks of those who could, buying slaves as fellow-workers, which might suggest that a craftsman sometimes bought a man and trained him as an apprentice; and a poor cripple, pleading for his public assistance of 1 obol a day, complains that he is getting old and his children are too young to support him (a rather unlikely conjunction of pleas) and that he is too poor to buy a slave to carry on his work. This may suggest that a craftsman who bought a slave and trained him was looking forward to retiring on his earnings. But, as Aristophanes recognised, the greater part of the work in industry as in agriculture was done by poor citizens. Addressing them Poverty declared in the *Plutus:* "If wealth should gain his sight again and distribute himself equally, no one would practice a craft or skill. And when you have lost both of these, who will work as a smith or a shipwright or a tailor or a wheelwright or a shoemaker or a bricklayer or a launderer or a tanner or plough the land or harvest the crops, if you can live in idleness and neglect all this work?"

We have no reliable evidence for the total number of slaves in Attica at any time. For the late fourth-century we have two figures, which, if we could rely on them, would be startling. The Byzantine lexicon of Suidas cites Hypereides (probably in connection with his proposal to free the slaves after the battle of Chaeronea in 338 B.C.) as speaking of "more than 150,000 from the silver mines and over the rest of the country." Athenaeus, who wrote at the end of the second century A.D., quotes Ctesicles, a chronicler of unknown date, as stating that at the census held by Demetrius of Phaleron (317–07) 400,000 slaves were registered. These are, as Beloch has convincingly demonstrated, quite impossible figures, and must have been corrupted in the course of their transmission to the late sources in which we read them. To turn to more reliable, if less explicit evidence, according to Thucydides more than twenty thousand slaves, mainly industrial, escaped during the ten years' occupation of Deceleia by the Spartans; these would probably be in the main miners and agricultural slaves, but would include many city workers, since the seventeen miles of city walls cannot have been so completely patrolled as to prevent escapes. Xenophon declares that the mines could provide employment for many more than ten thousand, as those—if any—who remembered what the slave tax used to fetch before the Deceleian war could testify (he was writing sixty years later). But whatever their numbers their distribution is fairly clear. They were owned in the main by the 1,200 richest families and in decreasing numbers by the next 3,000 or so. It is unlikely that any slaves were owned by two-thirds to three-quarters of the citizen population. The great majority of the citizens earned their living by the work of their hands, as peasant farmers, craftsmen, shopkeepers, seamen and labourers; so contemporary witnesses state, and so the detailed evidence, so far as it goes, suggests. In only one occupation was slave labour predominant, in mining, and even here, contrary to common belief, some citizens worked. Xenophon, advocating that the state acquire a large body of slaves to be leased to the citizens for use in the mines, suggests that not only will existing contractors add to their manpower but that "there are many of those who are themselves in the mines who are growing old, and many others, both Athenians and aliens, who would not or could not work with their hands, but would gladly make their living by supervising." In one of the Demosthenic speeches we meet a man who boasts "In earlier times I made a lot of money from the silver mines, working and toiling myself with my own hands": he had struck lucky and was now one of the three hundred richest men in Athens.

That the poorer citizens lived on state pay for political services is, even for the fourth-century, when the system was most fully developed, demonstrably false. A man could only be a councillor two years in his life, and could hold none of the magistracies chosen by lot for more than one annual tenure. He could by attending the assembly—and getting there in time to qualify for pay—earn a drachma on thirty days and one and a half drachmae on ten days in the year. On some festivals—the number varied according to the state of the exchequer—he could draw his theoric payment of 2 obols. On other days, if lucky enough to be successful in the annual ballot for the 6,000 jurors, he could queue in hopes of being empanelled on a jury and earning 3 obols, just enough to feed himself. At this rate a bachelor without dependants could barely with consistent good luck scrape a living; for a man with a family it was quite impossible.

The majority of the citizens were then workers who earned their own living and whose political pay served only to compensate them in some measure for loss of working time. Agricultural and industrial slaves in the main merely added to the wealth of a relatively small rentier class, whose principal source of income was land; this same class employed most of the domestic slaves. It only remains to ask how far the Athenian state drew its revenue, directly or indirectly, from slaves. The state owned a certain number of slaves. Most famous are the 1,200 Scythian archers who policed the assembly and the law courts and enforced the orders of the magistrates. There were a number of others ranging from the workers in the mint to the city gaoler and the public slave par excellence who had custody of the public records and accounts. Athens thus ran her police force and her rudimentary civil service in part by slave labour—the clerks of the magistrates were mostly salaried citizens. There was apparently a tax on slaves, known only from the mention in Xenophon cited above, but it can hardly have been an important item in the revenue to receive so little notice. The mines, which were mainly exploited by slave labour, also brought in revenue to the state, but less than might have been expected seeing that concessionaries sometimes made large fortunes. The mines flourished in the fifth-century, from their first serious exploitation in 483 till the Spartan occupation of Deceleia in 413. They then went through a prolonged bad period till the 330s, when they were again in full swing. We have no figures for the fifth-century. In the fourth we have a full record of one year's concessions (367–6), when the sums paid totalled 3,690 drachmae, and a partial record of a later year—probably 342–1—when the revenue came to about 3 talents. There may have been a royalty payment of 1/24th in addition to the prices paid for concessions, but, as there is no contemporary record of this payment, which is mentioned only by a Byzantine lexicographer, this is doubtful. It is somewhat mysterious where the 400 talents of Athenian revenue came from, but a negligible proportion of it arose even indirectly from slave labour.

The charge brought by fifth-century oligarchic critics (and thoughtlessly repeated by many modern writers), that the Athenian democracy depended for its political pay on the tribute of the subject allies, was brought to the test of fact when Athens lost her empire in 403 B.C., and was proved to be a calumny when the democracy continued to pay the citizens for their political functions out of domestic revenues. The modern charge that the Athenian democracy was dependent on slave labour was never brought to the test, since the Athenians never freed all their slaves. This is not surprising, for slavery was an established institution, which most people accepted without question as "according to nature," and to abolish it would have meant a wholesale disregard of the rights of property, which the Athenians throughout their history were careful to respect. It is more surprising that on some occasions of crisis motions for a partial or wholesale freeing of slaves were carried. In 406 all male slaves of military age were freed and granted the citizenship to man the ships which won the battle of Arginusae. After the expulsion of the Thirty in 403 Thrasybulus, the left wing leader of the restored democracy, carried a measure, later quashed as illegal by the moderate leader Archinus, to free and enfranchise all slaves who had fought for the democracy. In 338, after the defeat of Chaeronea, the left wing politician Hypereides proposed and carried a motion to free all (able bodied male) slaves to resist the Macedonians; this motion was again quashed as illegal by a conservative politician.

These facts suggest that there was no bitterness between the mass of the citizens and the slaves, but rather a sense of fellow-feeling. This was a point which shocked contemporary Athenian oligarchs. The "old oligarch" speaks bitterly of the insolence of slaves at Athens, and complains that it is illegal to strike them—the reason, he explains, is that the people are indistinguishable in dress and general appearance from slaves, and it would be easy to strike a citizen by mistake. The moderate oligarch Theramenes is careful to assure his colleagues among the Thirty that he is not one of "those who think there would not be a good democracy until slaves and those who through poverty would sell the city for a drachma participate in it." Plato mocks at the excess of freedom in the democracy, in which "men and women who have been sold are no less free than their purchasers."

Though the Athenians treated their slaves with a humanity which was exceptional according to the standards of the time, they never abolished slavery, and the charge that Athenian democracy was dependent on their labour was never brought to the test of fact. But had Hypereides' motion been allowed to stand, and extended to slaves of all ages and both sexes, it would not seem, on the basis of the evidence cited earlier in this article, that its effects would have been catastrophic. All wealthy and well to do citizens (or rather their wives and unmarried daughters) would have been incommoded by having to do their own housework. A very small number of wealthy or comfortably off men who had invested all their money in mining and industrial slaves would have been reduced to penury. And a larger number, but still a small minority, would have lost the proportion of their income which derived from industrial slaves, and would have had to let their farms instead of cultivating them by slave labour. A number of craftsmen would have lost their apprentices and journeymen. But the great majority of Athenians who owned no slaves but cultivated their own little farms or worked on their own as craftsmen, shopkeepers or labourers, would have been unaffected.

FRUITS OF ROMAN IMPERIALISM   19

During the third century B.C. *Rome defeated Carthage, its great rival in the western Mediterranean. In the following century Rome expanded eastward, overrunning the Balkans and the eastern Mediterranean, and becoming the ruler of the entire Mediterranean basin. The initial results of this empire building proved disastrous, for Rome as well as for the conquered provinces. The yeomanry of Italy, which had provided the manpower for the triumphant legions, was decimated by the years of overseas service and by the subsequent influx of slaves and cheap grain from the provinces. The peasants were forced to sell their holdings to the new class of ultrarich and to drift to the cities where they became a rootless and restless proletariat. A land reform effort in the second century B.C. by Tiberius Gracchus and his brother Gaius was aborted by the bitter opposition of the Senate. The following description of the social disorders in Italy and the fruitless struggle of the Gracchi brothers is taken from the* Roman History *written about A.D. 150 by a civil servant, Appian of Alexandria.*

As for the conquered provinces, it was said that their governors operated on the following timetable: in the first year they recovered their election expenses; in the second they accumulated funds to appease the judges before whom they would stand trial for extortion; and in the third year they made their personal fortune. What this meant in actual practice is evident in the following indictment by Cicero of the administration of Governor Gaius Verres in Sicily (73–71 B.C.).

The Gracchi *

The Romans, as they subdued the Italian nations successively in war, seized a part of their lands and built towns there, or established their own colonies in those already existing, and used them in place of garrisons. Of the land acquired by war they assigned the cultivated part forthwith to settlers, or leased or sold it. Since they had no leisure as yet to allot the part which then lay desolated by war (this was generally the greater part), they made proclamation that in the meantime those who were willing to work it might do so for a share of the yearly crops—a tenth of the grain and a fifth of the fruit. From those who kept flocks was required a share of the animals, both oxen and small cattle. They did these things in order to multiply the Italian race, which they considered the most laborious of peoples, so that they might have plenty of allies at home. But the very opposite thing happened; for the rich, getting possession of the greater part of the undistributed lands, and being emboldened by the lapse of time to believe that they would never be dispossessed, and adding to their holdings the small farms of their poor neighbors, partly by purchase and partly by force, came to cultivate vast tracts instead of single estates, using for this purpose slaves as laborers and herdsmen, lest free laborers should be drawn from agriculture into the army. The ownership of slaves itself brought them great gain from the multitude of their progeny, who increased because they were exempt from military service. Thus the powerful ones became enormously rich and the race of slaves multiplied throughout the country, while the Italian people dwindled in numbers and strength, being oppressed by penury, taxes, and military service. If they had any respite from these evils they passed their time in idleness, because the land was held by the rich, who employed slaves instead of freemen as cultivators.

For these reasons the people became troubled lest they should no longer have sufficient allies of the Italian stock, and lest the government itself should be endangered by such a vast number of slaves. Not perceiving any remedy, as it was not easy, nor exactly just, to deprive men of so many possessions they had held so long, including their own trees, buildings, and fixtures, a law was once passed with difficulty at the instance of the tribunes, that nobody should hold more than

* Horace White, trans., *The Roman History of Appian of Alexandria* (London: George Bell & Sons, 1899), pp. 5-21.

500 jugera of this land, or pasture on it more than 100 cattle or 500 sheep. To ensure the observance of this law it was provided also that there should be a certain number of freemen employed on the farms, whose business it should be to watch and report what was going on. Those who held possession of lands under the law were required to take an oath to obey the law, and penalties were fixed for violating it, and it was supposed that the remaining land would soon be divided among the poor in small parcels. But there was not the smallest consideration shown for the law or the oaths. The few who seemed to pay some respect to them conveyed their lands to their relations fraudulently, but the greater part disregarded it altogether.

At length Tiberius Sempronius Gracchus, an illustrious man, eager for glory, a most powerful speaker, and for these reasons well known to all, delivered an eloquent discourse, while serving as tribune, concerning the Italian race, lamenting that a people so valiant in war, and blood relations to the Romans, were declining little by little in the pauperism and paucity of numbers without any hope of remedy. He inveighed against the multitude of slaves as useless in war and never faithful to their masters, and adduced the recent calamity brought upon the masters by their slaves in Sicily, where the demands of agriculture had greatly increased the number of the latter; recalling also the war waged against them by the Romans, which was neither easy nor short, but long-protracted and full of vicissitudes and dangers. After speaking thus he again brought forward the law, providing that nobody should hold more than 500 jugera of the public domain. But he added a provision to the former law, that the sons of the present occupiers might each hold one-half of that amount, and that the remainder should be divided among the poor by triumvirs, who should be changed annually.

This was extremely disturbing to the rich because, on account of the triumvirs, they could no longer disregard the law as they had done before; nor could they buy the allotments of others, because Gracchus had provided against this by forbidding sales. They collected together in groups, and made lamentation, and accused the poor of appropriating the results of their tillage, their vineyards, and their dwellings. Some said that they had paid the price of the land to their neighbors. Were they to lose the money with the land? Others said that the graves of their ancestors were in the ground, which had been allotted to them in the division of their fathers' estates. Others said that their wives' dowries had been expended on the estates, or that the land had been given to their own daughters as dowry. Money-lenders could show loans made on this security. All kinds of wailing and expressions of indignation were heard at once. On the other side were heard the lamentations of the poor—that they had been reduced from competence to extreme penury, and from that to childlessness, because they were unable to rear their offspring. They recounted the military services they had rendered, by which this very land had been acquired, and were angry that they should be robbed of their share of the common property. They reproached the rich for employing slaves, who were always faithless and ill-tempered and for that reason unserviceable in war, instead of freemen, citizens, and soldiers. While these classes were lamenting and indulging in mutual accusations, a great number of others, composed of colonists, or inhabitants of the free towns, or persons otherwise interested in the lands and who were under like apprehensions, flocked in and took sides with their respective factions. Emboldened by numbers and exasperated against each other they attached themselves to turbulent crowds, and waited for the voting on the new law, some trying to prevent its enactment by all means, and others supporting it in every possible way. In addition to personal interest the spirit of rivalry spurred both sides in the preparations they were making against each other for the day of the comitia.

What Gracchus had in his mind in proposing the measure was not wealth, but an increase of efficient population. Inspired greatly by the usefulness of the work, and believing that nothing more advantageous or admirable could ever happen to Italy, he took no account of the difficulties surrounding it. When the time for voting came he advanced many other arguments at considerable length and also asked them whether it was not just to divide among the common people what belonged to them in common; whether a citizen was not worthy of more consideration at all times than a slave; whether a man who served in the army was not more useful than one who did not; and whether one who had a share in the country was not more likely to be devoted to the public interests. He did not dwell long on this comparison between freemen and slaves, which he considered degrading, but proceeded at once to a review of their hopes and fears for the country, saying that the Romans had acquired most of their territory by conquest, and that they had hopes of occupying the rest of the habitable world, but now the question of greatest hazard was, whether they should gain the rest by having plenty of brave men, or whether, through their weakness and mutual jealousy, their enemies should take away what they already possessed. After exaggerating the glory and riches on the one side and the danger and fear on the other, he admonished the rich to take heed, and said that for the realization of these hopes they ought to bestow this very land as a free gift, if necessary, on men who would rear children, and not, by contending about small things, overlook larger ones; especially since they were receiving an ample compensation for labor expended in the undisputed title to 500 jugera each of free land, in a high state of cultivation, without cost, and half as much more for each son of those who had sons. After saying much more to the same purport and exciting the poor, as well as others who were moved by reason rather than by the desire for gain, he ordered the scribe to read the proposed law.

Marcus Octavius, another tribune, who had been induced by those in possession of the lands to interpose his veto (for among the Romans the tribune's veto always prevailed), ordered the scribe to keep silence. Thereupon Gracchus reproached him severely and adjourned the comitia to the following day. Then he stationed a sufficient guard, as if to force Octavius against his will, and ordered the scribe with threats to read the proposed law to the multitude. He began to read, but when Octavius again vetoed he stopped. Then the tribunes fell to wrangling with each other, and a considerable tumult arose among the people. The leading citizens besought the tribunes to submit their controversy to the Senate for decision. Gracchus seized on the suggestion, believing that the law was acceptable to all well-disposed persons, and hastened to the senate-house. There, as he had only a few followers and was upbraided by the rich, he ran back to the forum and said that he would take the vote at the comitia of the following day, both on the law and on the magistracy of Octavius, to determine whether a tribune who was acting contrary to the people's interest could continue to hold his office. And so he did, for when Octavius, nothing daunted, again interposed, Gracchus distributed the pebbles to take a vote on him first. When the first tribe voted to abrogate the magistracy of Octavius, Gracchus turned to him and begged him to desist from this veto. As he would not yield, the votes of the other tribes were taken. There were thirty-five tribes at that time. The seventeen that voted first angrily sustained this motion. If the eighteenth should do the same it would make a majority. Again did Gracchus, in the sight of the people, urgently importune Octavius in his present extreme danger not to prevent this most pious work, so useful to all Italy, and not to frustrate the wishes so earnestly entertained by the people, whose desires he ought rather to share in his character of tribune, and not to risk the loss of his office by public condemnation. After speaking thus he called the gods to witness that he did not willingly do any despite to his colleague. As Octavius was still unyielding he went on taking the vote. Octavius was forthwith reduced to the rank of a private citizen and slunk away unobserved.

Quintus Mummius was chosen tribune in his place, and the agrarian law was enacted. The first triumvirs appointed to divide the land were Gracchus himself, the proposer of the law, his brother of the same name, and his father-in-law, Appius Claudius, since the people still feared that the law might fail of execution unless Gracchus should be put in the lead with his whole family. Gracchus became immensely popular by reason of the law and was escorted home by the multitude as though he were the founder, not of a single city or race, but of all the nations of Italy. After this the victorious party returned to the fields from which they had come to attend to this business. The defeated ones remained in the city and talked the matter over, feeling bitterly, and saying that as soon as Gracchus should become a private citizen he would be sorry that he had done despite to the sacred and inviolable office of tribune, and had opened such a fountain of discord in Italy.

At the advent of summer the notices for the election of tribunes were given, and as the day for voting approached it was very evident that the rich were earnestly promoting the election of those most inimical to Gracchus. The latter, fearing that evil would befall if he should not be reelected for the following year, summoned his friends from the fields to attend the comitia, but as they were occupied with their harvest he was obliged, when the day fixed for the voting drew near, to have recourse to the plebeians of the city. So he went around asking each one separately to elect him tribune for the ensuing year, on account of the danger he had incurred for them. When the voting took place the first two tribes pronounced for Gracchus. The rich objected that it was not lawful for the same man to hold the office twice in succession. The tribune Rubrius, who had been chosen by lot to preside over the comitia, was in doubt about it, and Mummius, who had been chosen in place of Octavius, urged him to turn over the comitia to his charge. This he did, but the remaining tribunes contended that the presidency should be decided by lot, saying that when Rubrius, who had been chosen in that way, resigned, the casting of lots ought to be done over again for all. As there was much strife over this question, Gracchus, who was getting the worst of it, adjourned the voting to the following day. In utter despair he clothed himself in black, while still in office, and led his son around the forum and introduced him to each man and committed him to their charge, as if he were about to perish at the hands of his enemies.

The poor were moved with deep sorrow, and rightly so, both on their own account (for they believed that they were no longer to live in a free state under equal laws, but were reduced to servitude by the rich), and on account of Gracchus himself, who had incurred such danger and suffering in their behalf. So they all accompanied him with tears to his house in the evening, and bade him be of good courage for the morrow. Gracchus cheered up, assembled his partisans before daybreak, and communicated to them a signal to be displayed in case of a fight. He then took possession of the temple on the Capitoline hill, where the voting was to take place, and occupied the middle of the assembly. As he was obstructed by the other tribunes and by the rich, who would not allow the votes to be taken on this question, he gave the signal. There was a sudden shout from those who saw it, and a resort to violence in consequence. Some of the partisans of Gracchus took position around him like body-guards. Others, having girded themselves, seized the fasces and staves in the hands of the lictors and broke them in pieces. They drove the rich out of the assembly with such disorder and wounds that the tribunes fled from their places in terror, and the priests closed the doors of the temple. Many ran away pell-mell and scattered wild rumors. Some said that Gracchus had deposed all the other tribunes, and this was believed because none of them could be seen. Others said that he had declared himself tribune for the ensuing year without an election.

Under these circumstances the Senate assembled at the temple of Fides. It is astonishing to me that they never thought of appointing a dictator in this emergency, although they had often been protected by the government of a single ruler in such times of peril. Although this resource had been found most useful in former times few people remembered it, either then or later. After reaching the decision that they did reach, they marched up to the Capitol, Cornelius Scipio Nasica, the pontifex maximus, leading the way and calling out with a loud voice, "Let those who would save the country follow me." He wound the border of his toga about his head either to induce a greater number to go with him by the singularity of his appearance, or to make for himself, as it were, a helmet as a sign of battle for those who looked on, or in order to conceal from the gods what he was about to do. When he arrived at the temple and advanced against the partisans of Gracchus they yielded to the reputation of a foremost citizen, for they saw the Senate following with him. The latter wrested clubs out of the hands of the Gracchans themselves, or with fragments of broken benches or other apparatus that had been brought for the use of the assembly, began beating them, and pursued them, and drove them over the precipice. In the tumult many of the Gracchans perished, and Gracchus himself was caught near the temple, and was slain at the door close by the statues of the kings. All the bodies were thrown by night into the Tiber.

So perished on the Capitol, and while still tribune, Gracchus, the son of the Gracchus who was twice consul, and of Cornelia, daughter of that Scipio who subjugated Carthage. He lost his life in consequence of a most excellent design, which, however, he pursued in too violent a manner. This shocking affair, the first that was perpetrated in the public assembly, was seldom without parallels thereafter from time to time. On the subject of the murder of Gracchus the city was divided between sorrow and joy. Some mourned for themselves and for him, and deplored the present condition of things, believing that the commonwealth no longer existed, but had been supplanted by force and violence. Others considered that everything had turned out for them exactly as they wished.

.   .   .   .   .

. . . Gaius Gracchus, who had made himself agreeable to them as a triumvir, offered himself for the tribuneship. He was the younger brother of Tiberius Gracchus, the promotor of the law, and had been silent for some time on the subject of the fate of his brother, but since many of the senators treated him scornfully he announced himself as a candidate for the office of tribune. As soon as he was elected to this distinguished position he began to lay plots against the Senate, and proposed that a monthly distribution of corn should be made to each citizen at the public expense, which had not been customary before. Thus he got the leadership of the people quickly by one measure of policy, in which he had the coöperation of Fulvius Flaccus. Directly after that he was chosen tribune for the following year, for in cases where there was not a sufficient number of candidates the law authorized the people to choose from the whole number then in office.

Thus Gaius Gracchus became tribune a second time. Having bought the plebeians, as it were, he began, by another like political manœuvre, to court the equestrian order, who hold the middle place between the Senate and the plebeians. He transferred the courts of justice, which had become discredited by reason of bribery, from the senators to the knights, reproaching the former especially with the recent examples of Aurelius Cotta, Salinator, and, third in the list, Manius Equilius (the one who subdued Asia), all notorious bribe-takers, who had been acquitted by the judges, although ambassadors sent to complain against them were still present, going around uttering hateful accusations against them. The Senate was extremely ashamed of these things and yielded to the law, and the people ratified it. In this way were the courts of justice transferred from the Senate to the knights. It is said that soon after the passage of this law Gracchus remarked that he had broken the power of the Senate once for all. This saying of Gracchus has been even more confirmed by experience in the course of events. This power of sitting in judgment on all Romans and Italians, including the senators themselves, in all matters as to property, civil rights, and banishment, exalted the knights like rulers over them and put senators on the same level with subjects. Moreover, as the knights voted in the election to sustain the power of the tribunes, and obtained from them whatever they wanted in return, they became more and more formidable to the senators. So it shortly came about that the political mastery was turned upside down, the power being in the hands of the knights, and the honor only remaining with the Senate. The knights went so far that they not only held power over the senators, but they openly flouted them beyond their right. They also became addicted to bribe-taking, and having once tasted these enormous gains, they indulged in them even more basely and immoderately than the senators had done. They suborned accusers against the rich and did away with prosecutions for bribe-taking altogether, partly by concert of action and partly by force and violence, so that the practice of this kind of investigation became entirely obsolete. Thus the judiciary law gave rise to another struggle of factions, which lasted a long time and was not less baneful than the former ones.

Gracchus made long roads throughout Italy and thus put a multitude of contractors and artisans under obligations to him and made them ready to do whatever he wished. He proposed the founding of numerous colonies. He also called on the Latin allies to demand the full rights of Roman citizenship, since the Senate could not with decency refuse this privilege to their blood relations. To the other allies, who were not allowed to vote in Roman elections, he sought to give the right of suffrage, in order to have their help in the enactment of laws which he had in contemplation. The Senate was very much alarmed at this, and it ordered the consuls to give the following public notice, "Nobody who does not possess the right of suffrage shall stay in the city or approach within forty stades of it while voting is going on concerning these laws." The Senate also persuaded Livius Drusus, another tribune, to interpose his veto against the laws proposed by Gracchus, but not to tell the people his reasons for doing so; for a tribune was not required to give reasons for his veto. In order to conciliate the people they gave Drusus the privilege of founding twelve colonies, and the plebeians were so much pleased with this that they began to scoff at the laws proposed by Gracchus.

Having lost the favor of the rabble, Gracchus sailed for Africa in company with Fulvius Flaccus, who, after his consulship, had been chosen tribune for the same reasons as Gracchus himself. A colony had been voted to Africa on account of its reputed fertility, and these men had been expressly chosen the founders of it in order to get them out of the way for a while, so that the Senate might have a respite from demagogism. They marked out a town for the colony on the place where Carthage had formerly stood, disregarding the fact that Scipio, when he destroyed it, had devoted it with curses to sheep-pasturage forever. They assigned 6000 colonists to this place, instead of the smaller number fixed by law, in order further to curry favor with the people thereby. When they returned to Rome they invited the 6000 from the whole of Italy. The functionaries who were still in Africa laying out the city wrote home that wolves had pulled up and scattered the boundary marks made by Gracchus and Fulvius, and the soothsayers considered this an ill omen for the colony. So the Senate summoned the comitia, in which it was proposed to repeal the law concerning this colony. When Gracchus and Fulvius saw their failure in this matter they were furious, and declared that the Senate had lied about the wolves. The boldest of the plebeians joined them, carrying daggers, and proceeded to the Capitol, where the assembly was to be held in reference to the colony.

Now the people were assembled, and Fulvius had begun speaking about the business in hand, when Gracchus arrived at the Capitol attended by a body-guard of his partisans. Disturbed by what he knew about the extraordinary plans on foot he turned aside from the meeting-place of the assembly, passed into the portico, and walked about waiting to see what would happen. Just then a plebeian named Antyllus, who was sacrificing in the portico, saw him in this disturbed state, seized him by the hand, either because he had heard something or suspected something, or was moved to speak to him for some other reason, and asked him to spare his country. Gracchus, still more disturbed, and startled like one detected in a crime, gave the man a piercing look. Then one of his party, although no signal had been displayed or order given, inferred merely from the very sharp glance that Gracchus cast upon Antyllus that the time for action had come, and thought that he should do a favor to Gracchus by striking the first blow. So he drew his dagger and slew Antyllus. A cry was raised, the dead body was seen in the midst of the crowd, and all who were outside fled from the temple in fear of a like fate. Gracchus went into the assembly desiring to exculpate himself of the deed. Nobody would so much as listen to him. All turned away from him as from one stained with blood. Gracchus and Flaccus were nonplused and, having lost the chance of accomplishing what they wished, they hastened home, and their partisans with them. The rest of the crowd occupied the forum throughout the night as though some calamity were impending. Opimius, one of the consuls, who was staying in the city, ordered an armed force to be stationed at the Capitol at daybreak, and sent heralds to convoke the Senate. He took his own station in the temple of Castor and Pollux in the centre of the city and there awaited events.

When these arrangements had been made the Senate summoned Gracchus and Flaccus from their homes to the senate-house to defend themselves. But they ran out armed toward the Aventine hill, hoping that if they could seize it first the Senate would agree to some terms with them. They ran through the city offering freedom to the slaves, but none listened to them. With such forces as they had, however, they occupied and fortified the temple of Diana, and sent Quintus, the son of Flaccus, to the Senate seeking to come to an arrangement and to live in peace. The Senate replied that they should lay down their arms, come to the senate-house, tell what they wanted, or else send no more messengers. When they sent Quintus a second time the consul Opimius arrested him, as being no longer an ambassador after he had been warned, and at the same time sent an armed force against the Gracchans. Gracchus fled across the river by the Sublician bridge, with one slave, to a grove where he presented his throat to the slave, as he was on the point of being arrested. Flaccus took refuge in the workshop of an acquaintance. As his pursuers did not know which house he was in they threatened to burn the whole row. The man who had given shelter to the suppliant hesitated to point him out, but directed another man to do so. Flaccus was seized and put to death. The heads of Gracchus and Flaccus were carried to Opimius, and he gave their weight in gold to those who brought them. The people plundered their houses. Opimius arrested their fellow-conspirators, cast them into prison, and ordered that they should be strangled. He allowed Quintus, the son of Flaccus, to choose his own mode of death. After this a lustration was performed in behalf of the city for the bloodshed, and the Senate ordered the building of a temple to Concord in the forum.

So the sedition of the younger Gracchus came to an end. Not long afterward a law was enacted to permit the holders to sell the land about which they had quarrelled; for even this had been forbidden by the law of the elder Gracchus. Presently the rich bought the allotments of the poor, or found pretexts for seizing them by force. So the condition of the poor became even worse than it was before. . . .

Cicero on Verres *

Gentlemen of the Court: At this great political crisis, there seems to have been offered to you, not through man's wisdom but almost as the direct gift of heaven, the very thing that was most to be desired; a thing that will help, more than anything else, to mitigate the unpopularity of your Order and the discredit attaching to these Courts of Law. A belief has by this time established itself, as harmful to the whole nation as it is perilous to yourselves, and everywhere expressed not merely by our own people but by foreigners as well: the belief that these Courts, constituted as they now are, will never convict any man, however guilty, if only he has money. And now, at the moment of supreme danger for your Order and your judicial privileges, when preparations have been made for an attempt, by means of public meetings and proposals for legislation, to fan the flames of senatorial unpopularity, Gaius Verres appears, to stand his trial before you: a man already condemned, in the world's opinion, by his life and deeds; already acquitted, according to his own confident assertions, by his vast fortune. . . . The character of the man I am prosecuting is such, that you may use him to restore the lost good name of these Courts, to regain favour at home, and to give satisfaction abroad: he has robbed the Treasury, and plundered Asia and Pamphylia; he has behaved like a pirate in his city praetorship, and like a destroying pestilence in his province of Sicily.

. . . . .

. . . nowhere did he multiply and magnify the memorials and the proofs of all his evil qualities so thoroughly as in his governorship of Sicily; which island for the space of three years he devastated and ruined so effectually that nothing can restore it to its former condition, and it hardly seems possible that a long lapse of years and a succession of upright governors can in time bring it a partial revival of prosperity. So long as Verres was governing it, its people were protected neither by their own laws, nor by the decrees of the Roman Senate, nor by the rights that

* Reprinted by permission of the publishers and The Loeb Classical Library from Cicero, *The Verrine Orations,* trans. L. H. G. Greenwood (Cambridge, Mass.: Harvard University Press), excerpts from vols. I and II.

belong to all nations alike. None of them has anything left to-day, except what either escaped the notice of this avaricious and intemperate ruffian, or remained over when his greed was glutted. For the space of three years, the law awarded nothing to anybody unless Verres chose to agree; and nothing was so undoubtedly inherited from a man's father or grandfather that the courts would not cancel his right to it, if Verres bade them do so. Countless sums of money, under a new and unprincipled regulation, were wrung from the purses of the farmers; our most loyal allies were treated as if they were national enemies; Roman citizens were tortured and executed like slaves; the guiltiest criminals bought their legal acquittal, while the most honourable and honest men would be prosecuted in absence, and condemned and banished unheard; strongly fortified harbours, mighty and well-defended cities, were left open to the assaults of pirates and buccaneers; Sicilian soldiers and sailors, our allies and our friends, were starved to death; fine fleets, splendidly equipped, were to the great disgrace of our nation destroyed and lost to us. Famous and ancient works of art, some of them the gifts of wealthy kings, who intended them to adorn the cities where they stood, others the gifts of Roman generals, who gave or restored them to the communities of Sicily in the hour of victory—this same governor stripped and despoiled every one of them. Nor was it only the civic statues and works of art that he treated thus; he also pillaged the holiest and most venerated sanctuaries; in fact, he has not left the people of Sicily a single god whose workmanship he thought at all above the average of antiquity or artistic merit. As to his adulteries and the like vile offences, a sense of decency makes me afraid to repeat the tale of his acts of wanton wickedness: and besides, I would not wish, by repeating it, to add to the calamities of those who have not been suffered to save their children and their wives from outrage at the hands of this lecherous scoundrel.

. . . . .

Now I do not suppose that Verres will at this point deny that he has numerous statues, and more pictures than he can count, in his possession. But I understand it to be his habit now and then to assert that these objects, which he has stolen by force or fraud, have really been bought. It would appear that he was sent out to Achaia and Asia and Pamphylia, at the national expense and with the title of assistant governor, in order to engage in the statue and picture trade. . . . You cannot deny that you brought away a large number of beautiful statues and a large number of fine paintings. I only wish you would deny it! Show me the record, either in your own accounts or your father's, of your buying a single one of these things, and I surrender.

. . . . .

And now it is worth our while to observe how censors were appointed in Sicily during his praetorship. For the censorship is, of all offices, the one which in Sicily the citizens take most care to entrust to the right man, because all Sicilians pay their annual tribute in proportion to their assessed wealth, and in making the assessment the censor is entrusted with complete power to value each property and fix the amount due. Consequently the community exercises the greatest care in selecting the person who is to be trusted so largely with its property, and on the other hand the competition for the office is especially keen in the community because of the great power conferred by it. Verres decided that his dealings with this matter should be quite open; he would resort to no dishonest drawing of lots or cutting days out of the calendar. He certainly tried to do nothing underhand or fraudulent here; with the purpose of banishing from all his cities those eager and covetous desires for office that are the ruin of so many states, he announced that he would himself appoint the censors in every city. Upon the praetor's declaring his great market open, there was a general rush to see him at Syracuse; his official residence was a seething mass of excited human cupidity; nor was this surprising, when the polling-stations of all those cities were concentrated in a single house, and the fierce ambitions of an entire province shut up in a single room. Prices were openly ascertained and offers openly made, after which the two censors for each state were assigned by Timarchides. This person, by doing the work and interviewing the candidates himself, and bearing the unpleasantness of so laborious a piece of business, achieved the conveyance of all the profits to Verres without troubling him at all. How large the profits made by this man Timarchides were you have not so far had the opportunity of learning exactly; but still you did learn, at the first hearing, from the evidence of many witnesses, in how many rascally ways he plundered his victims.

Now you may wonder how this freedman gained so much control of Verres' affairs; and therefore I will tell you briefly the sort of man he is, that you may appreciate both the iniquity of Verres in giving him a place on his staff, a place, moreover, of high rank and consideration, and also the disastrous consequences for the province. In the seduction of women, and all such licentious wickedness, I learnt that this fellow Timarchides was remarkably well constituted and adapted to further the evil debauches of this prince of scoundrels, to track out and visit and accost and pervert, and do anything else that such affairs demand, with un-limited cunning, boldness, and effrontery. . . . You must know, therefore, that for these three years it was . . . Timarchides who was the real slave king over all the towns of Sicily; that the wives and the children, the goods and the money of Rome's oldest and closest allies were at the mercy of Timarchides. Well, it was this Timarchides who, as I have said, received the bribes and distributed censors to the various cities: so long as Verres was praetor there was not even a pretence made of appointing censors by election.

. . . . .

Naturally, the behaviour of these censors was like that of those members of our own government who have acquired their offices by bribery; they took care to dis-charge their functions so as to fill up the hole made in their finances. The assessment made during your praetorship was made in a way that brought the financial adminis-tration in every city to a standstill. For all the wealthiest men had their assessments reduced, while the poorest had theirs increased. . . .

The man of whom I speak, Gavius of Consa, was one of those Roman citizens whom Verres threw into prison. Somehow or other he escaped from the Stone Quarries, and made his way to Messana. Italy was now visible only a few miles away, and the walls of Regium with its population of Roman citizens; he had come forth from the awful shadow of death, revived and strengthened by the light of freedom and the fresh air of justice; and so he began to talk indignantly to people in Messana of how he, a Roman citizen, had been thrown into prison, and how he was going straight to Rome and would be ready for Verres on his arrival there. The poor fellow was not aware that to say such things in Messana was equivalent to saying them to the governor in his own house; for Verres, as I have already ex-plained, had chosen this town to assist him in his crimes, to receive his stolen goods, and to share the secret of all his abominable deeds. The result was that Gavius was at once seized and taken before the chief magistrate of Messana. Verres chanced to arrive there that same day, and it was reported to him that there was a Roman citizen with an angry story about having been in the Stone Quarries at Syracuse, who was already going aboard a ship, uttering unpleasantly savage threats against Verres, when they had dragged him ashore again and kept him in custody for Verres to deal with as he thought best. Verres thanked these people, commending warmly their kind and careful attention to his interests. Then he made for the market-place, on fire with mad and wicked rage, his eyes blazing, and cruelty showing clearly in every feature of his face. Everyone was wondering how far he would go and what he was meaning to do, when he suddenly ordered the man to be flung down, stripped naked and tied up in the open market-place, and rods to be got ready. The unhappy man cried out that he was a Roman citizen, a burgess of Consa; that he had served in the army under the distinguished Roman knight Lucius Raecius, who was in business at Panhormus and could assure Verres of the truth of his story. To this Verres replied that he had discovered that Gavius had been sent to Sicily as a spy by the leaders of the fugitive army, a charge which was brought by no informer, for which there was no evidence, and which nobody saw any reason to believe. He then ordered the man to be flogged severely all over his body. There in the open market-place of Messana a Roman citizen, gentlemen, was beaten with rods; and all the while, amid the crack of the falling blows, no groan was heard from the unhappy man, no words came from his lips in his agony except "I am a Roman citizen." By thus proclaiming his citizenship he had been hoping to avert all those blows and shield his body from torture; yet not only did he fail to secure escape from those cruel rods, but when he persisted in his entreaties and his appeals to his citizen rights, a cross was made ready—yes, a cross, for that hapless and broken sufferer, who had never seen such an accursed thing till then.

. . . . .

. . . To bind a Roman citizen is a crime, to flog him is an abomination, to slay him is almost an act of murder: to crucify him is—what? There is no fitting word that can possibly describe so horrible a deed. . . . It was not Gavius, not one obscure man, whom you nailed upon that cross of agony: it was the universal principle that Romans are free men. . . .

20   Pax Romana

The social ailments and disorders of the late Republican period were finally resolved with the firm but enlightened rule of Julius Caesar and of his adopted son and heir, Octavius, or as he is known in history, Augustus (31 B.C.–A.D. 14). It was their strong measures and their sweeping reforms that laid the foundation for the Pax Romana *that was to prevail for two centuries. The following panegyric by Aelius Aristides of Smyrna, delivered in 143, stresses the positive aspects of the Roman Empire at its height. Unlike Tacitus, Aristides reflects the contentment of at least the middle and upper classes with the security and prosperity of imperial rule.**

* J. H. Oliver, "The Ruling Power: A Study of the Roman Empire in the Second Century after Christ through the Roman Oration of Aelius Aristides," *Transactions,* American Philosophical Society, Vol. 43 (Philadelphia, 1953), Part 4, pp. 895-99, 901-02, 906-07.

It is a time-honored custom of travellers setting forth by land or sea to make a prayer pledging the performance of some vow—whatever they have in mind—on safe arrival at their destination. I recall a poet who playfully parodied the custom by pledging "a grain of incense—with gilded horns!" As for me the vow that I made as I journeyed hither was not of the usual stupid and irrelevant kind, nor one unrelated to the art of my profession: merely that if I came through safely I would salute your city with a public address.

But since it was quite impossible to pledge words commensurate with your city, it became evident that I had need of a second prayer. It is perhaps really presumptuous to dare undertake an oration to equal such majesty in a city. However, I have promised to address you, and I can speak only as I can.

·   ·   ·   ·   ·

Some chronicler, speaking of Asia, asserted that one man ruled as much land as the sun passed, and his statement was not true because he placed all Africa and Europe outside the limits where the sun rises in the East and sets in the West. It has now however turned out to be true. Your possession is equal to what the sun can pass, and the sun passes over your land. Neither the Chelidonean nor the Cyanean promontories limit your empire, nor does the distance from which a horseman can reach the sea in one day, nor do you reign within fixed boundaries, nor does another dictate to what point your control reaches; but the sea like a girdle lies extended, at once in the middle of the civilized world and of your hegemony.

Around it lie the great continents greatly sloping, ever offering to you in full measure something of their own. Whatever the seasons make grow and whatever countries and rivers and lakes and arts of Hellenes and non-Hellenes produce are brought from every land and sea, so that if one would look at all these things, he must needs behold them either by visiting the entire civilized world or by coming to this city. For whatever is grown and made among each people cannot fail to be here at all times and in abundance. And here the merchant vessels come carrying these many products from all regions in every season and even at every equinox, so that the city appears a kind of common emporium of the world.

Cargoes from India and, if you will, even from Arabia the Blest one can see in such numbers as to surmise that in those lands the trees will have been stripped bare and that the inhabitants of these lands, if they need anything, must come here and beg for a share of their own. Again one can see Babylonian garments and ornaments from the barbarian country beyond arriving in greater quantity and with more ease than of shippers from Naxos or from Cythnos, bearing something from those islands, had but to enter the port of Athens. Your farms are Egypt, Sicily and the civilized part of Africa.

Arrivals and departures by sea never cease, so that the wonder is, not that the harbor has insufficient space for merchant vessels, but that even the sea has enough, [if] it really does.

And just as Hesiod said about the ends of the Ocean that there is a common channel where all waters have one source and destination, so there is a common channel to Rome and all meet here, trade, shipping, agriculture, metallurgy, all the arts and crafts that are or ever have been, all the things that are engendered or grow from the earth. And whatever one does not see here neither did nor does exist. And so it is not easy to decide which is greater, the superiority of this city in respect to the cities that now are or the superiority of this empire in respect to the empires that ever were.

·   ·   ·   ·   ·

Now, however, the present empire has been extended to boundaries of no mean distance, to such, in fact, that one cannot even measure the area within them. On the contrary, for one who begins a journey westward from the point where at that period the empire of the Persian found its limit, the rest is far more than the entirety of his domain, and there are no sections which you have omitted, neither city nor tribe nor harbor nor district, except possibly some that you condemned as worthless. The Red Sea and the Cataracts of the Nile and Lake Maeotis, which formerly were said to lie on the boundaries of the earth, are like the courtyard walls to the house which is this city of yours. On the other hand, you have explored Ocean. Some writers did not believe that Ocean existed at all, or did not believe that it flowed around the earth; they thought that poets had invented the name and had introduced it into literature for the sake of entertainment. But you have explored it so thoroughly that not even the island therein has escaped you.

. . . . .

All directions are carried out by the chorus of the civilized world at a word or gesture of guidance more easily than at some plucking of a chord; and if anything need be done, it suffices to decide and there it is already done.

The governors sent out to the city-states and ethnic groups are each of them rulers of those under them, but in what concerns themselves and their relations to each other they are all equally among the ruled, and in particular they differ from those under their rule in that it is they—one might assert—who first show how to be the right kind of subject. So much respect has been instilled in all men for him who is the great governor, who obtains for them their all.

. . . . .

For of all who have ever gained empire you alone rule over men who are free. Caria has not been given to Tissaphernes, nor Phrygia to Pharnabazus, nor Egypt to someone else; nor is the country said to be enslaved, as household of so-and-so, to whomsoever it has been turned over, a man himself not free. But just as those in states of one city appoint the magistrates to protect and care for the governed, so you, who conduct public business in the whole civilized world exactly as if it were one city state, appoint the governors, as is natural after elections, to protect and care for the governed, not to be slave masters over them. Therefore governor makes way for governor unobtrusively, when his time is up, and far from staying too long and disputing the land with his successor, he might easily not stay long enough even to meet him.

Appeals to a higher court are made with the ease of an appeal from deme to dicastery, with no greater menace for those who make them than for those who have accepted the local verdict. Therefore one might say that the men of today are ruled by the governors who are sent out, only in so far as they are content to be ruled.

. . . There is an abundant and beautiful equality of the humble with the great and of the obscure with the illustrious, and, above all, of the poor man with the rich and of the commoner with the noble, and the word of Hesiod comes to pass, "For he easily exalts, and the exalted he easily checks," namely this judge and princeps as the justice of the claim may lead, like a breeze in the sails of a ship, favoring and accompanying, not the rich man more, the poor man less, but benefiting equally whomsoever it meets.

. . . . .

But there is that which very decidedly deserves as much attention and admiration now as all the rest together. I mean your magnificent citizenship with its grand conception, because there is nothing like it in the records of all mankind. Dividing into two groups all those in your empire—and with this word I have indicated the entire civilized world—you have everywhere appointed to your citizenship, or even to kinship with you, the better part of the world's talent, courage, and leadership, while the rest you recognized as a league under your hegemony.

Neither sea nor intervening continent are bars to citizenship, nor are Asia and Europe divided in their treatment here. In your empire all paths are open to all. No one worthy of rule or trust remains an alien, but a civil community of the World has been established as a Free Republic under one, the best, ruler and teacher of order; and all come together as into a common civic center, in order to receive each man his due.

. . . . .

Wars, even if they once occurred, no longer seem to have been real; on the contrary, stories about them are interpreted more as myths by the many who hear them. If anywhere an actual clash occurs along the border, as is only natural in the immensity of a great empire, because of the madness of Getae or the misfortune of Libyans or the wickedness of those around the Red Sea, who are unable to enjoy the blessings they have, then simply like myths they themselves quickly pass and the stories about them.

. . . . .

Homer said, "Earth common of all," and you have made it come true. You have measured and recorded the land of the entire civilized world; you have spanned the rivers with all kinds of bridges and hewn highways through the mountains and filled the barren stretches with posting stations; you have accustomed all areas to a settled and orderly way of life. Therefore, I see on reflection that what is held to be the life before Triptolemus is really the life before your time,—a hard and boorish life, not far removed from that of the wild mountains. Though the citizens of Athens began the civilized life of today, this life in its turn has been firmly established by you, who came later but who, men say, are better.

. . . . .

But the trial which we undertook at the beginning of our speech is beyond any man's power, namely to compose the oration which would equal the majesty of your empire, for it would require just about as much time as time allotted to the empire, and that would be all eternity. Therefore it is best to do like those poets who compose dithyrambs and paeans, namely to add a prayer and so close the oration.

Let all the gods and the children of the gods be invoked to grant that this empire and this city flourish forever and never cease until stones [float] upon the sea and trees cease to put forth shoots in spring, and that the great governor and his sons be preserved and obtain blessings for all.

My bold attempt is finished. Now is the time to register your decision whether for better or for worse.

CHRISTIANITY AND THE ROMAN EMPIRE   21

In its later years the Roman Empire was wracked by internal ailments and external invasions. During this dreary time of troubles the Christian church was the only vital and vigorous organization. Despite repeated persecutions it continued to gain ad-

herents until it won toleration, and eventually, in the late fourth century, became the state religion. One of the outstanding champions of the Church during its difficult early years was Tertullian of Carthage (ca. 150–220). In his best known work, Apology, *written in 197, he passionately defends his faith against typical accusations such as cannibalism, incest, adultery, and subversion.**

. . . This then is the first proof that we lay before you of the injustice of your hatred towards the name of Christian. This unfairness is at once exaggerated and refuted by the same plea that seems to excuse it, namely ignorance. For what could be more unfair than that men should hate that of which they know nothing, even if the fact deserve this hatred? For then only does the fact deserve hatred, when it is already ascertained whether it deserves it. In default of the knowledge of its deserts, whence can the justice of hatred be defended, seeing that it is to be tested not by the verdict passed but by a good conscience? When therefore men hate because they do not know the character of what they hate, what is to hinder the thing hated from being of the sort they ought not to hate? . . . No (Christian) feels shame, or regret, except of course that he was so late in becoming one. If he is defamed, he rejoices; if he is prosecuted, he does not defend himself; if he is questioned, he at once confesses, if he is condemned, he returns thanks. What evil can there be in this which has none of the characters of evil? . . .

Again, supposing it to be true that we are criminals of deepest dye, why are we treated differently by you from our fellows, I mean all other criminals, since the same guilt ought to meet with the same treatment? When others are called by whatever name is applied to us, they employ both their own voices and the services of a paid pleader to set forth their innocence. They have every opportunity of answering and cross-questioning, since it is not even legal that persons should be condemned entirely undefended and unheard. But the Christians alone are not permitted to say anything to clear themselves of the charge, to uphold the truth, to prevent injustice in the judge. The one thing looked for is that which is demanded by the popular hatred, the confession of the name, not the weighing of a charge. Whereas, if you were inquiring into the case of some criminal, you would not be satisfied to give a verdict, immediately on his confession of the crime of homicide or sacrilege or incest or treason, to speak of the charges levelled against us, unless you also demanded an account of the accessory facts, the character of the act, the frequency of its repetition, the place, the manner, the time, who were privy to it, who were accomplices in it. In our case no such procedure is followed, although there was an equal necessity to sift by investigation the false charges that are bandied about, how many slaughtered babes each had already tasted, how many times he had committed incest in the dark, what cooks, what dogs had been present (on the occasion). Oh what fame would that governor have acquired, if he had ferreted out some one, who had already eaten up a hundred infants! But we find that in our case even such inquiry is forbidden. For Plinius Secundus, when he was in command of a province, after condemning some Christians, and having dislodged others from the stand they had taken up, was nevertheless greatly troubled by their very numbers, and then consulted the Emperor Trajan as to what he should do in future, stating that, apart from the obstinate refusal to sacrifice, he had found out nothing else about their mysteries, save meetings before dawn to sing to Christ and to God, and to establish one common rule of life, forbidding murder, adultery, fraud, treachery and other crimes. Then Trajan replied that such people were not indeed to be sought out, but that if they were brought before the court they ought to be punished. O self-contradictory verdict which says they are not to be sought out, because they are innocent, and yet orders them to be punished as criminals; . . .

Again, many people are so blinded with prejudice that even when they are bearing witness to a man's excellence, they mingle with it a taunt against the name of Christian. 'So-and-so is a good fellow, were it not that he is a Christian.' So another says 'I marvel that a philosopher like So-and-so should have so suddenly turned Christian.' No one reflects whether the fact that So-and-so is good or wise is due to his Christianity, or the fact that So-and-so is a Christian results from his being wise and good. They praise what they know, and blame what they do not know, and that which they know they spoil because they are really ignorant of it. . . .

Having then made this sort of preface by way of hammering into men's heads the unfairness of the popular hatred towards us, I will now join issue as to the question of innocence, and will not only rebut the charges against us, but will even cause them to recoil on the very men who make them; . . .

We are called abominable from the sacrament of infanticide and the feeding thereon, as well as the incestuous intercourse, following the banquet, because the dogs, that overturn the lamps, (our pimps forsooth of the darkness) bring about the shamelessness engendered by our impious lusts. Yet we are but called so on each occasion, and you take no pains to bring to light what we have been so long charged with. Therefore either prove the fact, if you believe it, or refuse to believe it, you who have not proved it. . . .

You accuse us of refusing to worship the gods, and to spend money on sacrificing for the emperors. It follows that we refuse to sacrifice for others on the same principle that we refuse even to sacrifice for ourselves, viz. by refusing once for all to worship the gods. Consequently we are charged with sacrilege and treason. This is the main point in the case, nay it is the whole case, and certainly worthy of investigation, if neither prejudice nor unfairness is to be the judge, the one despairing of the truth, the other objecting to it. We cease to worship your gods, from the moment we learn that they are no gods. This therefore is what you ought to demand, that we should prove that they are no gods, and therefore not to be worshipped, because then only would it have been our duty to worship them, if they had been gods. . . .

'But to us they are gods,' you say. If that be so, how is it that you on the contrary are found impious, sacrilegious, and irreligious towards your gods? you who neglect those whose existence you take for granted, who destroy those whom you fear, who mock even those whom you avenge? . . .

. . . when I turn to your literature, whence you derive instruction in practical wisdom, and the duties of gentlemen, what ridiculous situations do I find! gods engaged like pairs of gladiators and fighting desperately together on account of the Trojans and the Achaeans, Venus wounded by an arrow from a human hand, because she wished to snatch her son Aeneas, when almost killed, from the same Diomede (who had wounded herself); Mars reduced almost to a shadow by thirteen months in chains, Jupiter rescued by the agency of some monster from meeting the same violence at the hands of the other divinities, and at one time weeping the misfortune of Sarpedon, at another burning with shameful lust for his sister, and telling her the while of the mistresses in the long past, none of them so much loved as she. . . . There is also the great lyric poet (I mean Pindar), who sings that Aesculapius was deservedly punished with a thunderbolt by reason of his greed, which made him practise the healing art injuriously. Jupiter is evil, if the thunderbolt is his, devoid of natural feeling for his grandson, and jealous of the skilled practitioner. Such stories ought never to have been revealed if true; if false, ought never to have been invented, among really religious people. Nor do the writers of tragedies or comedies refrain from publishing in their prologues the sorrows or wanderings of the family of some god. I say nothing of the philosophers, being quite content with Socrates, who, in mockery of the gods, swore by the oak and the goat and the dog. . . .

I think I have now given sufficient proof about true and false divinity, since I have shown how the proof holds together, not only by discussions or reasonings, but also by the evidence of those very beings whom you believe to be gods, so that nothing now needs to be revised for the present purpose. Since, however, a special reference has been made to the Roman name, I will not pass over the controversy, provoked by the prejudiced assertion that the Romans owing to their scrupulous piety have been raised to such a height of glory, as to have gained dominion over the world, and to have proved the existence of their gods by the fact that those flourish beyond all others who beyond all others are mindful of their duty to them. This reward was paid, forsooth, by the Roman gods in gratitude. The extension of the empire was due to Sterculus and Mutunus and Larentina! For I could not suppose that foreign gods wished more favour shown to a foreign race than to their own, and gave the land of their fathers, in which they were born, grew up, were ennobled and were buried, to those from across the sea. Let Cybele see to it, if she learned to love the city of Rome as the memorial of the Trojan race, her own native race forsooth, which she had guarded against the arms of the Greeks, if she had the forethought to desert to the avengers, who, she knew, would subdue Greece, the vanquisher of Phrygia. Therefore even in our time she has exhibited a signal proof of honour conferred on Rome, when on the removal of Marcus Aurelius from the conduct of public affairs, by death, at Sirmium on the seventeenth of March, that most holy high-priest (of Cybele) on the twenty-fourth of that same March, on which he made a libation of impure blood, mutilating his arms also, none the less issued the usual orders for the safety of the emperor Marcus, though his life was already ended. Oh slothful messengers! Oh sleepy despatches! whose fault it was that Cybele had no earlier news of the emperor's demise, so as to prevent the ridicule of such a goddess by the Christians. But even Jupiter would not immediately have allowed his own Crete to be upset by the Roman fasces, forgetting the Idaean cave and the Corybantic cymbals and the pleasing odour of his nurse there. Would he not have preferred his own grave there to any Capitol, so that the land which covered the ashes of Jupiter should rather rule over the world? Would Juno have wished that the Carthaginian city, 'which she loved next to Samos,' should be destroyed by the race of the sons of Aeneas (above all others)? To the best of my knowledge:

> 'Here stood her chariot: here, if Heav'n were kind,
> The seat of awful empire she design'd.'

The unhappy wife and sister of Jupiter could not prevail against the fates! It is evident 'Jupiter himself depends on destiny.' Yet the Romans have not offered so much honour to the fates which gave up Carthage to them against the will and prayer of Juno, as they have to the common whore Larentina. . . .

This meets the charge of injury to your gods, since we cannot be supposed to injure that which we have shown to be non-existent. Therefore when we are challenged to sacrifice, we make a stand against it on the strength of our conscience, whereby we are assured who those are to whom these services extend under the profanation of images and the deification of human names. But some think it madness that, when we might both sacrifice at the time and depart uninjured, while retaining our own private opinions, we should prefer stubbornness to safety. Forsooth you are giving us advice how to take advantage of you; but we recognise the source of such hints, who it is that prompts all this, and how at one time by cunning advice, at another by harsh cruelty, he is working towards the overthrow of our firmness.

. . . . .

. . . Therefore it is that we offend against the majesty of the emperors, because we do not subject them to their own creatures, because we do not make sport of the duty of (praying for) their safety, since we do not think that it lies in hands soldered with lead. But you are the irreligious people, who seek it where it is not, ask it of those who cannot give it, passing over him in whose power it is. Furthermore you persecute those who know how to ask it, who can also obtain it, since they know how to ask.

For we invoke on behalf of the safety of the emperors a God who is everlasting, a God who is real, a God who is living, whom even the emperors themselves prefer should be propitious to them beyond all others. They know who gave them empire, they know, as human beings, who gave them life also, they feel that he is the only God, in whose power alone they are, to whom they are second, after whom they are first, before all and above all gods. . . . But why should I say more about the religious attitude and the loyalty of the Christians towards the emperor? We are bound to look up to him as the one whom our Lord has chosen. I should be justified in saying: the Caesar is more ours (than yours), as having been appointed by our God. Accordingly, as he is mine, I work more for his safety, since I not only ask it from Him who is able to grant it, or because I who ask it am such an one as deserves to obtain it, but also because by lowering the greatness of the Caesar as compared with that of God, I commend him the more to God, to whom alone I subject him. . . . Augustus, the creator of the empire, refused even to be called Lord: for this too is a surname of God. Of course I shall call the emperor lord, but with the usual spelling, and only when I am not forced to call him Lord with a capital, in place of God. But I am free so far as he is concerned; for I have but one Master, the almighty and eternal God, the same who is also his God. . . .

Chapter Nine

Indian civilization

22   Traditional Civilization of India

In the perspective of world history, India is the home of one of the most ancient, distinctive, and significant civilizations of mankind. Its roots go back to the original civilization of the Indus Valley (see Reading 14, "India's Forgotten Civilization") and to the innovations introduced by the Aryan invaders (see Reading 16, "Indian and Greek Epics"). The following selection analyzes the basic concepts underlying this traditional civilization, which, to a considerable degree, endures to the present day. The author is a well-known Indian educator who has served as Secretary of the Indian Ministry of Education and Vice-President of the Unesco Executive Board.*

What is culture? I shall not try to define this term. If, however, I was asked this question in India I would reply simply: culture is the soul of a people, the basic beliefs, attitudes and spiritual values of the Indian people which have become their way of life.

The culture of India or the Indian way of life is the product of a long and continuous history, parts of which are unknown and unwritten. From the third millennium before Christ, when a great civilization flourished on the banks of the Indus, to the present day, there has been basically one, unbroken stream of culture which found its course very early, flowing sometimes in rocky country and under rough weather, but always broadening and assimilating. Some time before the Vedic hymns were written, the Indian seers discovered the two great virtues of contemplation and compassion, and passed these on into the making of a civilization; from this all else followed. In the growth of a civilization, material

* P. Kirpal, "Indian Culture Today: I—The Heritage of the Past," *Unesco Features,* June 1969, pp. 6-10.

development precedes and largely determines abstract ideas in the early stages of history. In India it seems that from the earliest times ideas played a dominant rôle in creating a civilized way of life; from the very beginning the poet seer was more important to society than the warlord who led the tribe.

To synthesize different races, languages, creeds, beliefs and customs into a comprehensive whole and to attempt always to create increasing unity out of growing diversity became the main occupation of leaders of thought and action through the long centuries of India's history. We have, therefore, the most diverse racial, social, religious, artistic and cultural elements of the various regions of a vast sub-continent, developed within or received from outside, all welded into an unmistakable cultural pattern. This pattern has different forms and symbols built around the same spirit and essence of things, always attempting to express a broad unity of thought and outlook in the midst of a rich and free diversity of the patterns of living.

What is the essence of Indian culture which is shared by all our people?

There are, I think, three big ideas underlying all the external variety and complex manifestations of Indian culture: (i) an overriding belief in the reality of the life of the spirit and its superiority over temporal phenomena and passing experiences; (ii) conformity to the principle of Ahimsa or non-violence and tolerance as a guide to practical conduct; and (iii) an implicit belief in a sense of order and method governing the life and nature of the individual, of society, of the universe and even of the Divinity.

LIFE OF THE SPIRIT. The most essential feature of Hindu culture is the belief that the essence of man is in reality the same spirit which pervades the whole universe and in which a direct consciousness of God can be experienced. The *Upanishads* proclaim this truth beyond any shadow of doubt: "Thou art that" (Tat Twam asi); "This self is the Absolute Reality" (Ayam Atma Brahma); "The spirit that is in man and the spirit that is in the sun are one and identical" (Sa yascha ayam purusho yasha asan Aditya sa eka). The knowledge of this spiritual reality can be gained by practising various forms of Yoga or discipline. In yoga the processes of introspection, intuition and Samadhi (mystic experience) are refined and perfected, and by these methods incomplete and imperfect man can become aware of the vast unconscious and the limitless conscious strata of being within himself. The Absolute Reality, which is spiritual in essence, cannot be grasped by the mind alone nor can it be described in any language or terms invented by the mind. The seers who have experienced this spiritual Reality say that it is infinite (ananta) awareness (juanam) characterized by bliss (ananda). According to the *Yogavasistha,* "the nature of the Absolute Reality cannot be satisfactorily talked about or discussed; it can only be experienced within the depth of one's own being" (VI b 31.37). "It is neither a being, nor a non-being, nor anything between the two. It is nothing, yet everything. It cannot be grasped by mind and expressed in words. It is empty of all possible contents, yet is the deepest of all enjoyments." (*Yogavasistha,* III, 119–23). The search for the nature of the Absolute or Brahman and the efforts to experience it within ourselves are the main pursuits of Indian philosophy and Religion.

The spiritual identity or interconnectedness of all beings follows from the concept of Brahman. This truth was revealed to Rama by his teacher Vasistha in these words: "How can the thought that some one is one's brother and another is not, hold good when there is one and the same all-pervading self present in all of us? Oh, Ram, beings of all species are your brothers, as there is no being who is unconnected with you." (*Yogavasistha* V 20.4 - V 18.46). The oldest of the *Upanishads,* the *Isha Upanishad,* expressed the same truth in the following words: "Whosoever beholds all beings in the same self and the same self in all beings does not hate anybody. When a man knows that all beings are ultimately the self and realizes this unity in experience, then there remains no delusion or grief for him." Many teachers and seers of ancient India have elaborated this idea and derived from it their ethics of universal brotherhood and benevolence.

Thus the main feature of Hinduism is a deep faith in an unseen reality of which all life is a manifestation, a profound belief in the primacy of spiritual experience which cannot be grasped by the mind alone.

On the authority of Aristoxenus, a writer on musical theory and a pupil of Aristotle, the Greek philosopher Eusebios narrates an interview between Socrates and an Indian philosopher some time in the 5th century B.C. Aristoxenus, the musician, tells the following story about the Indians: one of these men met Socrates at Athens and asked him what was the scope of his philosophy. 'An enquiry into the human phenomena,' Socrates answered. At this the Indian burst out laughing: 'How can a man inquire into human phenomena,' he exclaimed, 'when he is ignorant of divine ones?'

Perhaps this anecdote signifies a profound difference of outlook and approach between East and West. According to the Hindus we cannot understand man, much less plan for his happiness, without being aware of the divine spirit of which he is a part. Only spiritual reality is real; all else is to be transcended and related to this reality in which we experience complete knowledge and absolute truth.

THE PRINCIPLE OF AHIMSA OR NON-VIOLENCE AND TOLERANCE. From this follows the second great principle underlying Indian culture, the principle of Ahimsa or non-violence and tolerance. Mahatma Gandhi once wrote: "Hinduism insists on the brotherhood not only of all mankind but of all that lives. It is a conception which makes one giddy, but we have to work up to it. The moment we have restored real living equality between man and man, we shall be able to establish equality between man and the whole creation. When that day comes we shall have peace on earth and good will to all men." Ahimsa means more than freedom from ill-will against all beings at all times and in all ways, much more than mere non-violence. It is a positive attitude to life, a practical rule of conduct requiring the observance of good will, tolerance and reverence. Mahatma Gandhi used Ahimsa not only as a political weapon in overcoming by moral force the physical force of a mightly empire; he used it equally effectively in awakening the masses of people from sloth and slavery and in rousing their moral fervour and their dormant faith in the greatness of man and his destiny.

SENSE OF ORDER IN THE UNIVERSE. The destiny of man is not governed by blind fate or incomprehensible forces entirely outside our knowledge and control. There is a sense of order in the universe which we can discover—and this brings us to the third great idea permeating the life and thought of the Indians. Most of our religious and philosophical speculation is a search for order and system; all Indian art is the creation and expression of order out of complexity, system out of chaos. Originally the Caste system was a workable ordering of society which was not so irrational in its right observance; later on it degenerated into undeserved privilege and stupid exclusiveness. The life of the individual was regulated by the Ashrama system or the division of life into four distinct periods called the Brahmachavya Ashrama (student life), Grishasta Ashrama (householder's life) Vanaprastha Ashrama (life of social service), and Sanyasa Ashrama (life of meditation). The moral order of society is laid down in the ethical principles and duties according to Dharma.

There is a great emphasis on the performance of duties and on a disciplined way of life in Indian culture. The Indian word for culture is "sanskriti" which comes from a root meaning to purify, to sublimate, to mould and perfect. The concept of "right" is significantly absent from Indian literature. In the *Bhagavadgita,* Lord Krishna teaches his friend Arjuna to perform the duties that are demanded by his station in life, without any expectation of gain or reward from any quarter; the performance of one's duties without any hope of gain or reward is the best worship of God. Duty well done in a spirit of sacrifice is the condition of Rights. In a brief and terse message to Unesco on the subject of Human Rights, Gandhi summed up the Indian view: "I learnt from my illiterate but wise mother that all rights to be deserved and preserved came from duty well done. Thus the very right to live accrues to us only when we do the duty of citizenship of the world. From this one fundamental statement, perhaps it is easy to define the duties of Man and Woman and correlate every right to some corresponding duty to be first performed. Every other right can be shown to be usurpation hardly worth fighting for."

The belief in Reincarnation and the law of Karma is part of the cosmic order. According to the law of Karma everyone must bear the consequences of his deeds. No one can escape Karma. "Even the gods have to undergo the good and evil consequences of their acts" says the author of the *Mahabharata.* It is stated in the *Yogavasistha:* "There is no place in the universe—no mountain, no sky, no ocean, no heaven—where one does not undergo the good or evil consequences of the deeds done by one." (Ill. 95.33) Physical death does not stop the operation of the law of Karma. The soul passes from one body to another and the law of Karma operates relentlessly until enlightenment and good actions lead to Nirvana or emancipation from the cycle of births and deaths.

Spiritual freedom and merit are attained after long discipline and continuous performance of good deeds by the individual. The *Yogavasistha* describes a Jivanmukta or a liberated man who has attained such merit in these words: "Pleasures do not delight him; pains do not distress. Although externally engaged in wordly actions, he has no attachment in his mind to any object whatsoever. His conduct does not annoy anybody; he behaves like an ideal citizen and is a friend of all. Outwardly he is very busy, but at heart very calm and quiet. He is free from the restrictions of Caste, creed, stage of life (Ashrama), custom and scriptures. He rests unagitated in the Supreme Bliss. He does not work to get anything for himself. He is always happy and his face is never without the lustre of cheerfulness. In spite of being occupied with actions appropriate to time, place and circumstance, he is not touched by pleasure or pain arising from them. He never feels despondent, proud, agitated, cast down, troubled or elated. He is full of energy and magnanimity, even when surrounded by enemies. He works without any anxiety, egoistic feeling, pride or impurity of heart. He finds equal pleasure in old age, death, misery, poverty and in ruling over an empire. He keeps his body healthy and does not starve it of its appropriate requirements. The life of a liberated sage is really the noblest and happiest life. From him goodness is scattered all around. Having seen him, having heard about him, having met him and having remembered him, all creatures feel delighted."

23 A Greek View of India, Fourth Century B.C.

Few Indian sources are available for the study of Indian history. Because of the Hindu conviction that human destiny is not to find its fulfillment in this world, history traditionally was regarded as subordinate to philosophy, and of interest only insofar as it could illumine eternal verities. Hence the paucity and amorphousness of Indian historical sources and the need to depend on the accounts left by more secular-minded foreign visitors. One of these was the Greek Megasthenes, ambassador for Seleucus I to the court of Chandragupta at Pataliputra about 302 B.C. His account survives only in the form of quotations in the works of later writers such as the geographer Strabo. In view of the absence of indigenous literature, this remains a prime source for the Indian society of the period.*

According to him (Megasthenês) the population of India is divided into seven parts. The philosophers are first in rank, but form the smallest class in point of number. Their services are employed privately by persons who wish to offer sacrifices or perform other sacred rites, and also publicly by the kings at what is called the Great Synod, wherein at the beginning of the new year all the philosophers are gathered together before the king at the gates, when any philosopher who may have committed any useful suggestion to writing, or observed any means for improving the crops and the cattle, or for promoting the public interests, declares it publicly. If any one is detected giving false information thrice, the law condemns him to be silent for the rest of his life, but he who gives sound advice is exempted from paying any taxes or contributions.

The *second* caste consists of the husbandmen, who form the bulk of the population, and are in disposition most mild and gentle. They are exempted from military service, and cultivate their lands undisturbed by fear. They never go to town, either to take part in its tumults, or for any other purpose. It therefore not unfrequently happens that at the same time, and in the same part of the country, men may be seen drawn up in array of battle, and fighting at risk of their lives, while other men *close at hand* are ploughing and digging in *perfect* security, having these soldiers to protect them. The whole of the land is the property of the king, and the husbandmen till it on condition of receiving one-fourth of the produce.

The *third* caste consists of herdsmen and hunters, who alone are allowed to hunt, and to keep cattle, and to sell draught animals or let them out on hire. In return for clearing the land of wild beasts and fowls which devour the seeds sown in the fields, they receive an allowance of grain from the king. They lead a wandering life and live under tents.

The *fourth* class, after herdsmen and hunters, consists of those who work at trades, of those who vend wares, and of those who are employed in bodily labour. Some of these pay tribute, and render to the state certain prescribed services. But the armour-makers and shipbuilders receive wages and their victuals from the king, for whom alone they work. The general in command of the army supplies

* *Ancient India as Described by Megasthenes and Arrian,* tr. by J. W. McCrindle, reprinted from the "Indian Antiquary" 1876-77 (Calcutta: Chuckervertty, Chatterjee & Co., Ltd., 1926), pp. 83-89.

the soldiers with weapons, and the admiral of the fleet lets out ships on hire for the transport both of passengers and merchandize.

The *fifth* class consists of fighting-men, who, when not engaged in active service, pass their time in idleness and drinking. They are maintained at the king's expense, and hence they are always ready, when occasion calls, to take the field, for they carry nothing of their own with them but their own bodies.

The *sixth* class consists of the overseers, to whom is assigned the duty of watching all that goes on, and making reports secretly to the king. Some are entrusted with the inspection of the city, and others with that of the army. The former employ as their coadjutors the courtezans of the city, and the latter the courtezans of the camp. The ablest and most trustworthy men are appointed to fill these offices.

The *seventh* class consists of the councillors and assessors of the king. To them belong the highest posts of government, the tribunals of justice, and the general administration of public affairs. No one is allowed to marry out of his own caste, or to exchange one profession or trade for another, or to follow more than one business. An exception is made in favour of the philosopher, who for his virtue is allowed this privilege.

Of the great officers of state, some have charge of the market, others of the city, others of the soldiers. Some superintend the rivers, measure the land, as is done in Egypt, and inspect the sluices by which water is let out from the main canals into their branches, so that every one may have an equal supply of it. The same persons have charge also of the huntsmen, and are entrusted with the power of rewarding or punishing them according to their deserts. They collect the taxes, and superintend the occupations connected with land, as those of the woodcutters, the carpenters, the blacksmiths, and the miners. They construct roads, and at every ten stadia set up a pillar to show the by-roads and distances. Those who have charge of the city are divided into six bodies of five each. The members of the first look after everything relating to the industrial arts. Those of the second attend to the entertainment of foreigners. To these they assign lodgings, and they keep watch over their modes of life by means of those persons whom they give to them for assistants. They escort them on the way when they leave the country, or, in the event of their dying, forward their property to their relatives. They take care of them when they are sick, and if they die bury them. The third body consists of those who inquire when and how births and deaths occur, with the view not only of levying a tax, but also in order that births and deaths among both high and low may not escape the cognizance of Government. The fourth class superintends trade and commerce. Its members have charge of weights and measures, and see that the products in their season are sold by public notice. No one is allowed to deal in more than one kind of commodity unless he pays a double tax. The fifth class supervises manufactured articles, which they sell by public notice. What is new is sold separately from what is old, and there is a fine for mixing the two together. The sixth and last class consists of those who collect the tenths of the prices of the articles sold. Fraud in the payment of this tax is punished with death.

Such are the functions which these bodies separately discharge. In their collective capacity they have charge both of their special departments, and also of matters affecting the general interest, as the keeping of public buildings in proper repair, the regulation of prices, the care of markets, harbours, and temples. Next to the city magistrates there is a third governing body, which directs military affairs. This also consists of six divisions, with five members to each.

One division is appointed to coöperate with the admiral of the fleet, another with the superintendent of the bullock-trains which are used for transporting engines of war, food for the soldiers, provender for the cattle, and other military requisites. They supply servants who beat the drum, and others who carry gongs; grooms also for the horses, and mechanists and their assistants. To the sound of the gong they send out foragers to bring in grass, and by a system of rewards and punishments ensure the work being done with despatch and safety. The third division has charge of the foot-soldiers, the fourth of the horses, the fifth of the war-chariots, and the sixth of the elephants. There are royal stables for the horses and elephants, and also a royal magazine for the arms, because the soldier has to return his arms to the magazine, and his horse and his elephant to the stables. They use the elephants without bridles. The chariots are drawn on the march by oxen, but the horses are led along by a halter, that their legs may not be galled and inflamed, nor their spirits damped by drawing chariots. In addition to the charioteer, there are two fighting men who sit up in the chariot beside him. The war-elephant carries four men—three who shoot arrows, and the driver.

24 A Chinese View of India, Seventh Century a.d.

Chinese visitors, as well as Greek, have left valuable descriptions of India. Close to two hundred Chinese Buddhist pilgrims are known to have made the long and perilous journey to India to imbibe Buddhist teachings at their source. The most famous was Hsüan-tsang who went to India by way of Central Asia and visited all parts of the country between 635 and 643. Being more observant of secular life than most of his fellow pilgrims, Hsüan-tsang has left an invaluable account, which imparts flesh and blood to the bare bones of dates and dynastic names.*

The countries embraced under this term of India are generally spoken of as the five Indies. In circuit this country is about 90,000 *li;* on three sides it is bordered by the great sea; on the north it is backed by the Snowy Mountains. The north part is broad, the southern part is narrow. Its shape is like the half-moon. The entire land is divided into seventy countries or so. The seasons are particularly hot; the land is well watered and humid. The north is a continuation of mountains and hills, the ground being dry and salt. On the east there are valleys and plains, which being well watered and cultivated, are fruitful and productive. The southern district is wooded and herbaceous; the western parts are stony and barren. Such is the general account of this country.

· · · · ·

The towns and villages have inner gates; the walls are wide and high; the streets and lanes are tortuous, and the roads winding. The thoroughfares are dirty and the stalls arranged on both sides of the road with appropriate signs. Butchers, fishers, dancers, executioners, and scavengers, and so on, have their abodes without the city. In coming and going these persons are bound to keep on the left

---

* Si-Yu-Ki, *Buddhist Records of the Western World,* trans. Samuel Beal (London: Kegan Paul, 1884), I, 70-89. Reprinted by Paragon Book Reprint Corp., New York (1968).

side of the road till they arrive at their homes. Their houses are surrounded by low walls, and form the suburbs. The earth being soft and muddy, the walls of the towns are mostly built of brick or tiles. The towers on the walls are constructed of wood or bamboo; the houses have balconies and belvederes, which are made of wood, with a coating of lime or mortar, and covered with tiles. The different buildings have the same form as those in China: rushes, or dry branches, or tiles, or boards are used for covering them. The walls are covered with lime and mud, mixed with cow's dung for purity. At different seasons they scatter flowers about. Such are some of their different customs.

. . . . .

Their clothing is not cut or fashioned; they mostly affect fresh-white garments; they esteem little those of mixed colour or ornamented. The men wind their garments round their middle, then gather them under the armpits, and let them fall down across the body, hanging to the right. The robes of the women fall down to the ground; they completely cover their shoulders. They wear a little knot of hair on their crowns, and let the rest of their hair fall loose. Some of the men cut off their moustaches, and have other odd customs. On their heads the people wear caps (*crowns*), with flower-wreaths and jewelled necklets.

. . . . .

They are very particular in their personal cleanliness, and allow no remissness in this particular. All wash themselves before eating; they never use that which has been left over (*from a former meal*); they do not pass the dishes. Wooden and stone vessels, when used, must be destroyed; vessels of gold, silver, copper, or iron after each meal must be rubbed and polished. After eating they cleanse their teeth with a willow stick, and wash their hands and mouth.

Until these ablutions are finished they do not touch one another. Every time they perform the functions of nature they wash their bodies and use perfumes of sandal-wood or turmeric.

When the king washes they strike the drums and sing hymns to the sound of musical instruments. Before offering their religious services and petitions, they wash and bathe themselves.

. . . . .

With respect to the division of families, there are four classifications. The first is called the Brâhman (*Po-lo-men*), men of pure conduct. They guard themselves in religion, live purely, and observe the most correct principles. The second is called Kshattriya (*T'sa-ti-li*), the royal caste. For ages they have been the governing class: they apply themselves to virtue (*humanity*) and kindness. The third is called Vaiśyas (*feï-she-li*), the merchant class: they engage in commercial exchange, and they follow profit at home and abroad. The fourth is called Sûdra (*Shu-t'o-lo*), the agricultural class: they labour in ploughing and tillage. In these four classes purity or impurity of caste assigns to every one his place. When they marry they rise or fall in position according to their new relationship. They do not allow promiscuous marriages between relations. A woman once married can never take another husband. Besides these there are other classes of many kinds that intermarry according to their several callings. It would be difficult to speak of these in detail.

. . . . .

The chief soldiers of the country are selected from the bravest of the people, and as the sons follow the profession of their fathers, they soon acquire a knowledge of the art of war. These dwell in garrison around the palace (*during peace*), but when on an expedition they march in front as an advanced guard. There are four divisions of the army, viz.—(1) the infantry, (2) the cavalry, (3) the chariots, (4) the elephants. The elephants are covered with strong armour, and their tusks are provided with sharp spurs. A leader in a car gives the command, whilst two attendants on the right and left drive his chariot, which is drawn by four horses abreast. The general of the soldiers remains in his chariot; he is surrounded by a file of guards, who keep close to his chariot wheels.

The cavalry spread themselves in front to resist an attack, and in case of defeat they carry orders hither and thither. The infantry by their quick movements contribute to the defence. These men are chosen for their courage and strength. They carry a long spear and a great shield; sometimes they hold a sword or sabre, and advance to the front with impetuosity. All their weapons of war are sharp and pointed. Some of them are these—spears, shields, bows, arrows, swords, sabres, battle-axes, lances, halberds, long javelins, and various kinds of slings. All these they have used for ages.

. . . In the investigation of criminal cases there is no use of rod or staff to obtain proofs (*of guilt*). In questioning an accused person, if he replies with frankness the punishment is proportioned accordingly; but if the accused obstinately denies his fault, or in despite of it attempts to excuse himself, then in searching out the truth to the bottom, when it is necessary to pass sentence, there are four kinds of ordeal used—(1) by water, (2) by force, (3) by weighing, (4) by poison.

When the ordeal is by water, then the accused is placed in a sack connected with a stone vessel and thrown into deep water. They then judge of his innocence (*truth*) or guilt in this way—if the man sinks and the stone floats he is guilty; but if the man floats and the stone sinks then he is pronounced innocent.

Secondly, by fire. They heat a plate of iron and make the accused sit on it, and again place his feet on it, and apply it to the palms of his hands; moreover, he is made to pass his tongue over it; if no scars result, he is innocent; if there are scars, his guilt is proved. In case of weak and timid persons who cannot endure such ordeal, they take a flower-bud and cast it towards the fire; if it opens, he is innocent; if the flower is burnt, he is guilty.

Ordeal by weight is this: A man and a stone are placed in a balance evenly, then they judge according to lightness or weight. If the accused is innocent, then the man weighs down the stone, which rises in the balance; if he is guilty, the man rises and the stone falls.

Ordeal by poison is this: They take a ram and make an incision in its right thigh, then mixing all sorts of poison with a portion of the food of the accused men, they place it in the incision made in the thigh (*of the animal*); if the man is guilty, then the poison takes effect and the creature dies; if he is innocent, then the poison has no effect, and he survives.

By these four methods of trial the way of crime is stopped.

. . . . .

As the administration of the government is founded on benign principles, the executive is simple. The families are not entered on registers, and the people are not subject to forced labour (*conscription*). The private demesnes of the crown are divided into four principal parts; the first is for carrying out the affairs of state and providing sacrificial offerings; the second is for providing subsidies for the ministers and chief officers of state; the third is for rewarding men of distinguished ability; and the fourth is for charity to religious bodies, whereby the field of merit is cultivated (*planted*). In this way the taxes on the people are light, and the personal service required of them is moderate. Each one keeps his own worldly goods in peace, and all till the ground for their subsistence. These who cultivate the royal estates pay a sixth part of the produce as tribute. The merchants who engage in commerce come and go in carrying out their transactions. The river-passages and the road-barriers are open on payment of a small toll. When the public works require it, labour is exacted but paid for. The payment is in strict proportion to the work done.

· · · · ·

In cultivating the land, those whose duty it is sow and reap, plough and harrow (*weed*), and plant according to the season; and after their labour they rest awhile. Among the products of the ground, rice and corn are most plentiful. With respect to edible herbs and plants, we may name ginger and mustard, melons and pumpkins, the *Heun-to* (*Kandu?*) plant, and others. Onions and garlic are little grown; and a few persons eat them; if any one uses them for food, they are expelled beyond the walls of the town. The most usual food is milk, butter, cream, soft sugar, sugar-candy, the oil of the mustard-seed, and all sorts of cakes made of corn are used as food. Fish, mutton, gazelle, and deer they eat generally fresh, sometimes salted; they are forbidden to eat the flesh of the ox, the ass, the elephant, the horse, the pig, the dog, the fox, the wolf, the lion, the monkey, and all the hairy kind. Those who eat them are despised and scorned, and are universally reprobated; they live outside the walls, and are seldom seen among men.

· · · · ·

. . . There is no lack of suitable things for household use. Although they have saucepans and stewpans, yet they do not know the steamer used for cooking rice. They have many vessels made of dried clay; they seldom use red copper vessels: they eat from one vessel, mixing all sorts of condiments together, which they take up with their fingers. They have no spoons or cups, and in short no sort of chopstick.

KAUTILYA'S ARTHASHASTRA 25

One of the few Indian treatises on statecraft is the Arthashastra *by the Brahman Kautilya. He was the guide and mentor of Chandragupta Maurya, helping him to seize the throne in 321 B.C. and to retain it thereafter. The treatise appears to have been recorded in its present form several centuries after the death of its author. Much of its contents, however, relates to Indian institutions of Mauryan times, with Machiavellian-type advice on all aspects of statecraft—protection of the king, recruiting ministers, organization of espionage, conduct of foreign affairs, collection of revenues, formation of villages, and so forth.**

* R. Shamasastry, trans., *Kautilya's Arthashastra*, 7th ed. (Mysore: Mysore Printing and Publishing House, 1961), pp. 14, 17-19, 26, 28, 32, 34, 41-43, 45-47.

THE CREATION OF COUNCILLORS AND PRIESTS. Native, born of high family, influential, well trained in arts, possessed of foresight, wise, of strong memory, bold, eloquent, skilful, intelligent, possessed of enthusiasm, dignity and endurance, pure in character, affable, firm in loyal devotion, endowed with excellent conduct, strength, health and bravery, free from procrastination and ficklemindedness, affectionate, and free from such qualities as excite hatred and enmity—these are the qualifications of a ministerial officer (amātyasampat).

Such as are possessed of one-half or one-quarter of the above qualifications come under middle and low ranks.

Of these qualifications, native birth and influential position shall be ascertained from reliable persons; educational qualifications (śilpa) from professors of equal learning; theoretical and practical knowledge, foresight, retentive memory, and affability shall be tested from successful application in works; eloquence, skilfulness and flashing intelligence from power shown in narrating stories (kathāyōgēshu, i.e. in conversation); endurance, enthusiasm, and bravery in troubles; purity of life, friendly disposition, and loyal devotion by frequent association; conduct, strength, health, dignity, and freedom from indolence and ficklemindedness shall be ascertained from their intimate friends; and affectionate and philanthropic nature by personal experience.

. . . . .

THE INSTITUTION OF SPIES. Assisted by the council of his ministers tried under espionage, the king shall proceed to create spies: Spies under the guise of a fraudulent disciple (kāpatika-chhātra), a recluse (udāsthita), a householder (grihapatika), a merchant (vaidehaka), an ascetic practising austerities (tāpasa), a classmate or a colleague (satri), a fire-brand (tīksha), a poisoner (rasada), and a mendicant woman (bhikshuki).

A skilful person capable of guessing the mind of others is a fraudulent disciple. Having encouraged such a spy with honour and money rewards, the minister shall tell him, "Sworn to the king and myself, thou shalt inform us of whatever wickedness thou findest in others."

One who is initiated in asceticism and is possessed of foresight and pure character is a recluse. This spy, provided with much money and many disciples, shall carry on agriculture, cattle-rearing, and trade (vārtākarma) on the lands allotted to him for the purpose. Out of the produce and profits thus acquired, he shall provide all ascetics with subsistence, clothing and lodging, and send on espionage such among those under his protection as are desirous to earn a livelihood (vrittikāma), ordering each of them to detect a particular kind of crime committed in connection with the king's wealth, and to report of it when they come to receive their subsistence and wages. All the ascetics (under the recluse) shall severally send their followers on similar errands.

A cultivator, fallen from his profession, but possessed of foresight and pure character, is termed a householder spy. This spy shall carry on the cultivation of lands allotted to him for the purpose, and maintain cultivators, etc.—as before.

A trader, fallen from his profession, but possessed of foresight and pure character, is a merchant spy. This spy shall carry on the manufacture of merchandise on the lands allotted to him for purpose, etc.—as before.

A man with shaved head (munda) or braided hair (jatila) and desirous to earn livelihood as a spy under the guise of an ascetic practising austerities. Such a spy surrounded by a host of disciples with shaved head or braided hair may take his abode in the suburbs of a city, and pretend as a person barely living on a handful of vegetables or meadow grass (yavasamushti) taken once in the interval of a month or two, but he may take in secret his favourite foodstuffs (gūdhamishtamāhāram).

Merchant spies pretending to be his disciples may worship him as one possessed of preternatural powers. His other disciples may widely proclaim that "This ascetic is an accomplished expert of preternatural powers."

Regarding those persons who, desirous of knowing their future, throng to him, he may, through palmistry, foretell such future events as he can ascertain by the nods and signs of his disciples (angavidyayā śishyasamjnābhiścha) concerning the works of high-born people of the country—viz. small profits, destruction by fire, fear from robbers, the execution of the seditious, rewards for the good, forecast of foreign affairs (videśa pravrittivijñānam), saying, "This will happen to-day, that to-morrow, and that this king will do." Such assertions of the ascetic his disciples shall corroborate (by adducing facts and figures).

He shall also foretell not only the rewards which persons possessed of foresight, eloquence, and bravery are likely to receive at the hands of the king, but also probable changes in the appointments of ministers.

The king's minister shall direct his affairs in conformity to the forecast made by the ascetic. He shall appease with offer of wealth and honour those who have had some well-known cause to be disaffected, and impose punishments in secret on those who are for no reason disaffected or who are plotting against the king.

Honoured by the king with awards of money and titles, these five institutes of espionage (samsthāh) shall ascertain the purity of character of the king's servants.

* * * * *

THE BUSINESS OF COUNCIL MEETING.   Having gained a firm hold on the affection of both local and foreign parties, both in his own and enemy's state, the king shall proceed to think of administrative measures.

All kinds of administrative measures are preceded by deliberations in a well-formed council. The subject matter of a council shall be entirely secret, and deliberations in it shall be so carried that even birds cannot see them; for it is said that the secrecy of counsels was divulged by parrots, minas, dogs and other low creatures of mean birth. Hence without providing himself with sufficient safeguard against disclosure, he shall never enter into deliberations in a council.

Whoever discloses counsels shall be torn to pieces.

The disclosure of counsels may be detected by observing changes in the attitude and countenance of envoys, ministers, and masters. Change in conduct is change in attitude (ingitamanyathāvrittih); and observation of physical appearance is countenance (ākritigrahanamākārah).

Maintenance of the secrecy of a council matter, and keeping guard over officers that have taken part in the deliberation over it (shall be strictly observed) till the time of starting the work so considered approaches.

Carelessness, intoxication, talking in sleep, love, and other evil habits of councillors, are the causes of the betrayal of counsels.

* * * * *

The king may ask his ministers for their opinion, either individually or collectively, and ascertain their ability by judging over the reasons they assign for their opinions.

* * * * *

Those ministers shall have to consider all that concerns the parties of both the king and his enemy. They shall also set themselves to start the work that is not yet begun, to complete what has been begun, to improve what has been accomplished, and to enforce strict obedience to orders (niyōgasampadam).

. . . . .

PROTECTION OF PRINCES. Having secured his own personal safety first from his wives and sons, the king can be in a position to maintain the security of his kingdom against immediate enemies as well as foreign kings.

We shall treat of "Protection of Wives" in connection with "Duties towards the Harem."

Ever since the birth of princes, the king shall take special care of them.

"For," says Bhāradvāja, "princes, like crabs have a notorious tendency of eating up their begetter."

. . . . .

Sons are of three kinds: those of sharp intelligence; those of stagnant intelligence; and those of perverted mind.

Whoever carries into practice whatever he is taught concerning righteousness and wealth is one of sharp intelligence; whoever never carries into practice the good instructions he has imbibed is one of stagnant intelligence; and whoever entangles himself in dangers and hates righteousness and wealth is one of perverted mind.

If a king has an only son (of the last type), attempts shall be made to procreating a son to him; or sons may be begotten on his daughters.

When a king is too old or diseased (to beget sons), he may appoint a maternal relation or a blood relation (kulya) of his or any one of his neighbouring kings possessed of good and amicable qualities to sow the seed in his own field (kshētre-bījam i.e., to beget a son on his wife).

. . . . .

PERSONAL SAFETY. On getting up from the bed, the king shall be received by troops of women armed with bows. In the second compartment, he shall be received by the Kanchuki (presenter of the king's coat), the Ushnīshi (presenter of the king's head-dress), aged persons, and other harem attendants.

In the third compartment, he shall be received by crooked and dwarfish persons; in the fourth, by prime ministers, kinsmen and door-keepers with barbed missiles in their hand.

The king shall employ as his personal attendants those whose fathers and grandfathers had been royal servants, those who bear close relationship to the king, those who are well-trained and loyal, and those who have rendered good service.

Neither foreigners, nor those who have earned neither rewards nor honour by rendering good service, nor even natives found engaged in inimical works shall form the bodyguard of the king or the troops of the officers in charge of the harem.

In a well-guarded locality, the head-cook (māhānasika) shall supervise the preparation of varieties of relishing dishes. The king shall partake of such fresh dishes after making an oblation out of them first to the fire and then to birds.

When the flame and the smoke turn blue and crackle, and when birds (that eat the oblation) die, presence of poison (in the dish) shall be inferred. When the vapour arising from cooked rice possesses the colour of the neck of a peacock, and appears chill as if suddenly cooled, when vegetables possess an unnatural colour, and are watery and hardened, and appear to have suddenly turned dry, being possessed of broken layers of blackish foam, and being devoid of smell, touch and taste natural to them; when utensils reflect light either more or less than usual, and are covered with a layer of foam at their edges; when any liquid preparation possesses streaks on its surface; when milk bears a bluish streak in the centre of its surface; when liquor and water possess reddish streaks; when curd is marked with black and dark streaks, and honey with white streaks; when watery things appear parched as if over-cooked and look blue and swollen; when dry things have shrinked and changed in their colour; when hard things appear soft, and soft things hard; when minute animalculæ die in the vicinity of the dishes; when carpets and curtains possess blackish circular spots, with their threads and hair fallen off; when metallic vessels set with gems appear tarnished as though by roasting, and have lost their polish, colour, shine, and softness of touch, presence of poison shall be inferred.

As to the person who has administered poison, the marks are parched and dry mouth; hesitation in speaking; heavy perspiration; yawning; too much bodily tremour; frequent tumbling; evasion of speech; carelessness in work; and unwillingness to keep to the place assigned to him.

Hence physicians and experts capable of detecting poison shall ever attend upon the king.

.   .   .   .   .

Musicians shall entertain the king with those kinds of amusements in which weapons, fire, and poison are not made use of. Musical instruments as well as the ornaments of horses, chariots, and elephants shall invariably be kept inside (the harem).

The king shall mount over chariots or beasts of burden only when they are first mounted over by his hereditary driver or rider.

He shall get into a boat only when it is piloted by a trustworthy sailor and is conjoined to a second boat. He shall never sail on any ship which had once been weather-beaten; and (while boating on a good ship) his army shall all the while stand on the bank or the shore.

He shall get into such water as is free from large fishes (matsya) and crocodiles. He shall ramble only in such forests as are freed from snakes and crocodiles (grāha).

With a view of acquiring efficiency in the skill of shooting arrows at moving objects, he shall engage himself in sports only in such forests as are cleared by hunters and hound-keepers from the fear of highway-robbers, snakes, and enemies.

Attended by trustworthy bodyguard armed with weapons, he shall give interview to saints and ascetics. Surrounded by his assembly of ministers, he shall receive the envoys of foreign states.

.   .   .   .   .

FORMATION OF VILLAGES.   Either by inducing foreigners to immigrate (paradeśāpavāhanena) or by causing the thickly-populated centres of his own kingdom to send forth the excessive population (svadeśābhishyandavamanēna vā), the king may construct villages either on new sites or on old ruins (bhūtapūrvamabhūtapūrvam vā.)

Villages consisting each of not less than a hundred families and of not more than five hundred families of agricultural people of Sūdra caste, with boundaries extending as far as a krōśa (2,250 yds.) or two, and capable of protecting each other, shall be formed. Boundaries shall be denoted by a river, a mountain, forests, bulbous plants (grshti), caves, artificial buildings (sētubandha), or by trees such as śālmali (silk cotton tree), śamī (Acacia Suma), and kshīravrksha (milky trees).

There shall be set up a sthānīya (a fortress of that name) in the centre of eight hundred villages, a drōnemukha in the centre of four hundred villages, a khārvāṭika in the centre of two hundred villages, and a sangrahana in the midst of a collection of ten villages.

There shall be constructed in the extremities of the kingdom forts manned by boundary-guards (antapāla), whose duty shall be to guard the entrance into the kingdom. The interior of the kingdom shall be watched by trap-keepers (vāgurika), archers (śābara), hunters (pulinda), chandālas, and wild tribes (aranyachara).

Those who perform sacrifices (ṛtvik), spiritual guides, priests, and those learned in the Vēdas shall be granted Brahmadeya lands yielding sufficient produce and exempted from taxes and fines (adandkarāni).

Superintendents, accountants, gopas, sthānikas, veterinary surgeons (anīkastha), physicians, horse-trainers, and messengers shall also be endowed with lands, which they shall have no right to alienate by sale or mortgage.

Lands prepared for cultivation shall be given to taxpayers (karada) only for life (ekapurushikāni). Unprepared lands shall not be taken away from those who are preparing them for cultivation.

Lands may be confiscated from those who do not cultivate them and given to others; or they may be cultivated by village labourers (grāmabhṛtaka) and traders (vaidehaka), lest those owners who do not properly cultivate them might pay less (to the government). If cultivators pay their taxes easily, they may be. favourably supplied with grains, cattle, and money.

The king shall bestow on cultivators only such favour and remission (anugrahaparihārau) as will tend to swell the treasury, and shall avoid such as deplete it.

A king with depleted treasury will eat into the very vitality of both citizens and country people. Either on the occasion of opening new settlements or on any other emergent occasions, remission of taxes shall be made.

He shall regard with fatherly kindness those who have passed the period of remission of taxes.

He shall carry on mining operations and manufactures, exploit timber and elephant forests, offer facilities for cattle-breeding and commerce, construct roads fot traffic both by land and water, and set up market towns (panyapattana).

He shall also construct reservoirs (sētu), filled with water either perennial or drawn from some other source. Or he may provide with sites, roads, timber, and other necessary things those who construct reservoirs of their own accord. Likewise in the construction of places of pilgrimage (punyasthāna) and of groves.

. . . . .

The king shall provide the orphans (bāla), the aged, the infirm, the afflicted, and the helpless with maintenance. He shall also provide subsistence to helpless women when they are carrying and also to the children they give birth to.

Elders among the villagers shall improve the property of bereaved minors till the latter attain their age; so also the property of gods.

Chapter Ten

Chinese civilization

CONFUCIANISM   26

The Chinese civilization, like the Indian, is one of the major civilizations of man-kind. But unlike the Indian, its outstanding characteristic is its secularism. It is the only major civilization that did not produce a priestly hierarchy. Its principal thinkers were interested more in man's problems in this world than in his salvation and afterlife. This is quite clear in the teachings of Confucius, China's great culture hero and one of the most influential figures in world history. In contrast to the otherworldly interests of most Indian thinkers, the main concern of Confucius was the formulation of moral principles to guide human relations within a family and between a king and his subjects. The most important of these principles are set forth in the following selections from the Analects, *the record of Confucius' activities and conversations as compiled by his disciples.**

GOVERNMENT AND PUBLIC AFFAIRS. People despotically governed and kept in order by punishments may avoid infraction of the law, but they will lose their moral sense. People virtuously governed and kept in order by the inner law of self-control will retain their moral sense, and moreover become good.

Ching, Duke of the Ch'i State, questioned Confucius on the art of government. Confucius replied: Let the sovereign do his duty as a sovereign, the subject his duty as a subject, the father his duty as a father, and the son his duty as a son.—A good answer! said the Duke; for unless sovereign and subject, father and son do

---

* Lionel Giles, trans., *The Sayings of Confucius,* Wisdom of the East Series (London: John Murray Publishers Ltd., 1907), pp. 39ff.

their respective duties, however much grain there may be in the land, I could obtain none to eat.

The Master said: If the ruler is personally upright, his subjects will do their duty unbidden; if he is not personally upright, they will not obey, whatever his bidding.

The Master said: Government is good when it makes happy those who live under it and attracts those who live far away.

INDIVIDUAL VIRTUE. Tzu Yu put a question on the subject of filial piety. The Master said: The filial piety of today reduces itself to the mere question of maintenance. Yet this is something in which even our dogs and horses have a share. Without the feeling of reverence, what is there to distinguish the two cases?

The nobler sort of man in his progress through the world has neither narrow predilections nor obstinate antipathies. What he follows is the line of duty.

The nobler sort of man is proficient in the knowledge of his duty; the inferior man is proficient only in money-making.

To be able to do to others as we would be done by—this is the true domain of moral virtue.

The Master said: The nobler sort of man emphasises the good qualities in others, and does not accentuate the bad. The inferior sort does the reverse.

The nobler sort of man is dignified but not proud; the inferior man is proud but not dignified.

The higher type of man seeks all that he wants in himself; the inferior man seeks all that he wants from others.

RELIGION. To sacrifice to a spirit with which you have nothing to do, is mere servility.

Chi Lu inquired concerning men's duty to spirits. The Master replied: Before we are able to do our duty by the living, how can we do it by the spirits of the dead?—Chi Lu went on to inquire about death. The Master said: Before we know what life is, how can we know what death is?

27 TAOISM

The chief rival of Confucianism for the allegiance of the Chinese people was Taoism, an escapist and nature-loving creed that opposed any form of interference with the natural course of the universe. In contrast to Confucianism's emphasis on morality and social responsibility, Taoism urged individual freedom and a mystical union with nature. The ideal society for the Taoists was that which remained the most primitive and least governed, as indicated in the following selections.*

* Lionel Giles, trans., *The Sayings of Lao Tzu,* Wisdom of the East Series (London: John Murray Publishers Ltd., 1905), pp. 30ff.

The Sage occupies himself with inaction, and conveys instruction without words.

. . . . .

Purge yourself of your profound intelligence, and you can still be free from blemish. Cherish the people and order the kingdom, and you can still do without meddlesome action.

Who is there that can make muddy water clear? But if allowed to remain still, it will gradually become clear of itself. Who is there that can secure a state of absolute repose? But let time go on, and the state of repose will gradually arise.

Be sparing of speech, and things will come right of themselves.

A violent wind does not outlast the morning; a squall of rain does not outlast the day. Such is the course of Nature. And if Nature herself cannot sustain her efforts long, how much less can man!

Attain complete vacuity, and sedulously preserve a state of repose.

Tao is eternally inactive, and yet it leaves nothing undone. If kings and princes could but hold fast to this principle, all things would work out their own reformation. If, having reformed, they still desired to act, I would have them restrained by the simplicity of the Nameless Tao. The simplicity of the Nameless Tao brings about an absence of desire. The absence of desire gives tranquillity. And thus the Empire will rectify itself.

. . . . .

The Empire has ever been won by letting things take their course. He who must always be doing is unfit to obtain the Empire.

Keep the mouth shut, close the gateways of sense, and as long as you live you will have no trouble. Open your lips and push your affairs, and you will not be safe to the end of your days.

Practise inaction, occupy yourself with doing nothing.

Desire not to desire, and you will not value things difficult to obtain. Learn not to learn, and you will revert to a condition which mankind in general has lost.

Leave all things to take their natural course, and do not interfere.

. . . . .

Were I ruler of a little State with a small population, and only ten or a hundred men available as soldiers, I would not use them. I would have the people look on death as a grievous thing, and they should not travel to distant countries. Though they might possess boats and carriages, they should have no occasion to ride in them. Though they might own weapons and armour, they should have no need to use them. I would make the people return to the use of knotted cords. They should find their plain food sweet, their rough garments fine. They should be content with their homes, and happy in their simple ways. If a neighbouring State was within sight of mine—nay, if we were close enough to hear the crowing of each other's cocks and the barking of each other's dogs—the two peoples should grow old and die without there ever having been any mutual intercourse.

. . . . .

Those who know do not speak; those who speak do not know.

Abandon learning, and you will be free from trouble and distress.

. . . . .

There is nothing in the world more soft and weak than water, yet for attacking things that are hard and strong there is nothing that surpasses it, nothing that can take its place.

The soft overcomes the hard; the weak overcomes the strong. There is no one in the world but knows this truth, and no one who can put it into practice.

28   LEGALISM

Very different from both Confucianism and Taoism were the doctrines of Legalism. This was not a philosophy but a set of realistic, Machiavellian tenets designed to strengthen the state for the waging of war. Because China was torn by constant strife amongst rival feudal states during the fourth century B.C. *when Legalism was propounded, the aim of the Legalists was the unification of the country by superior military and economic power. How this power was to be attained is outlined in the following selection from the writings of one of the Legalist theoreticians, Han Fei Tzu.**

When the sage rules the state, he does not count on people doing good of themselves, but employs such measures as will keep them from doing any evil. If he counts on people doing good of themselves, there will not be enough such people to be numbered by the tens in the whole country. But if he employs such measures as will keep them from doing evil, then the entire state can be brought up to a uniform standard. Inasmuch as the administrator has to consider the many but disregard the few, he does not busy himself with morals but with laws.

. . . . .

Now, when witches and priests pray for people, they say: "May you live as long as one thousand and ten thousand years!" Even as the sounds, "one thousand and ten thousand years," are dinning upon one's ears, there is no sign that even a single day has been added to the age of any man. That is the reason why people despise witches and priests. Likewise, when the Confucianists of the present day counsel the rulers they do not discuss the way to bring about order now, but exalt the achievement of good order in the past. They neither study affairs pertaining to law and government nor observe the realities of vice and wickedness, but all exalt the reputed glories of remote antiquity and the achievements of the ancient kings. Sugar-coating their speech, the Confucianists say: "If you listen to our words, you will be able to become the leader of all feudal lords." Such people are but witches and priests among the itinerant counselors, and are not to be accepted by rulers with principles. Therefore, the intelligent ruler upholds solid facts and discards useless frills. He does not speak about deeds of humanity and righteousness, and he does not listen to the words of learned men.

Those who are ignorant about government insistently say: "Win the hearts of the people." If order could be procured by winning the hearts of the people, then even the wise ministers Yi Yin and Kuan Chung would be of no use. For all that the ruler would need to do would be just to listen to the people. Actually, the intelligence of the people is not to be relied upon any more than the mind of a baby. If the baby does not have his head shaved, his sores will recur; if he does not have his boil cut open, his illness will go from bad to worse. However, in

---

* W. T. de Bary et al., *Sources of Chinese Tradition* (New York: Columbia University Press, 1960), pp. 141-43, 146-50.

order to shave his head or open the boil someone has to hold the baby while the affectionate mother is performing the work, and yet he keeps crying and yelling incessantly. The baby does not understand that suffering a small pain is the way to obtain a great benefit.

Now, the sovereign urges the tillage of land and the cultivation of pastures for the purpose of increasing production for the people, but they think the sovereign is cruel. The sovereign regulates penalties and increases punishments for the purpose of repressing the wicked, but the people think the sovereign is severe. Again, he levies taxes in cash and in grain to fill up the granaries and treasuries in order to relieve famine and provide for the army, but they think the sovereign is greedy. Finally, he insists upon universal military training without personal favoritism, and urges his forces to fight hard in order to take the enemy captive, but the people think the sovereign is violent. These four measures are methods for attaining order and maintaining peace, but the people are too ignorant to appreciate them.

．　．　．　．　．

Now take a young fellow who is a bad character. His parents may get angry at him, but he never makes any change. The villagers may reprove him, but he is not moved. His teachers and elders may admonish him, but he never reforms. The love of his parents, the efforts of the villagers, and the wisdom of his teachers and elders—all the three excellent disciplines are applied to him, and yet not even a hair on his shins is altered. It is only after the district magistrate sends out his soldiers and in the name of the law searches for wicked individuals that the young man becomes afraid and changes his ways and alters his deeds. So while the love of parents is not sufficient to discipline the children, the severe penalties of the district magistrate are. This is because men became naturally spoiled by love, but are submissive to authority. . . .

That being so, rewards should be rich and certain so that the people will be attracted by them; punishments should be severe and definite so that the people will fear them; and laws should be uniform and steadfast so that the people will be familiar with them. Consequently, the sovereign should show no wavering in bestowing rewards and grant no pardon in administering punishments, and he should add honor to rewards and disgrace to punishments—when this is done, then both the worthy and the unworthy will want to exert themselves. . . .

The literati by means of letters upset laws; the cavaliers by means of their prowess transgress prohibitions. Yet the ruler treats them both with decorum. This is actually the cause of all the disorder. Every departure from the law ought to be apprehended, and yet scholars are nevertheless taken into office on account of their literary learning. Again, the transgression of every prohibition ought to be censured, and yet cavaliers are patronized because of their readiness to draw the sword. Thus, those whom the law reproves turn out to be those whom the ruler employs, and those whom the magistrates suppress are those whom the sovereign patronizes. Thus legal standard and personal inclination as well as ruler and ministers are sharply opposed to each other and all fixed standards are lost. Then, even if there were ten Yellow Emperors, they would not be able to establish any order. Therefore, those who practice humanity and righteousness should not be upheld, for if upheld, they would hinder concrete accomplishments. Again, those who specialize in refinement and learning should not be employed, for if employed, they would disturb the laws. There was in Ch'u an upright man named Kung, who, when his father stole a sheep, reported it to the authorities. The magistrate said: "Put him to death," as he thought the man was faithful to the ruler but disloyal to his father. So the man was apprehended and convicted. From this we can see that the faithful subject of the ruler was an outrageous son to his father. Again, there was a man of Lu who followed his ruler to war, fought three battles, and ran away three times. Confucius interrogated him. The man replied: "I have an old father. Should I die, nobody would take care of him." Confucius regarded him as virtuous in filial piety, commended and exalted him. From this we can see that the dutiful son of the father was a rebellious subject to the ruler. Naturally, following the censure of the honest man by the magistrate, no more culprits in Ch'u were reported to the authorities; and following the reward of the runaway by Confucius, the people of Lu were prone to surrender and run away. The interests of superior and subordinate being so different, it would be hopeless for any ruler to try to exalt the deeds of private individuals and, at the same time, to promote the public welfare of the state.

. . . . .

Now the people in the state all talk about proper government. Practically every family keeps copies of the Laws of Shang Yang and Kuan Chung, and yet the state is becoming poorer and poorer. This is because many talk about farming but few follow the plow. Again, people in the state all talk about warfare. Practically every family keeps copies of the books of Sun Wu and Wu Ch'i on the art of war, and yet the army is becoming weaker and weaker. This is because many talk about warfare but few put on armor.

The enlightened sovereign therefore employs a man's energies but does not heed his words, rewards men with meritorious services but without fail bans the useless. Accordingly, the people exert themselves to the utmost in obeying their superiors. Farming is hard toil indeed. Yet people attend to it because they think this is the way to riches. Similarly, warfare is a risky business. Yet people carry it on because they think this is the road to honor. Now if one could just cultivate refinement and learning and practise persuasion and speech, and thereby obtain the fruits of wealth without the toil of farming and receive ranks of honor without the risk of warfare, then who would not do the same? Naturally a hundred men will be attending to learning where one will apply his physical energies. When many attend to learning, the law will come to naught; when few apply their physical energies, the state will fall into poverty. That is the reason why the world is in chaos.

In the state ruled by an enlightened sovereign, one would find no recorded literature and the law would supply the only instruction; one would find no injunctions from the early kings and the magistrates would serve as the only instructors; one would find no [esteem for] bravery in achieving private vengeance, and killing of the enemy would be regarded as the only courageous deed. As a result, the people in the state would all conform to the law in their discourse, would aim at meritorious achievement in their actions, and would offer their services to the army out of bravery. Therefore, in time of peace the state would be rich; in time of war the army would be strong. These might be called the "kingly resources." When the "kingly resources" were stored up, the sovereign could avail himself of any situation that might arise in the state of the enemy. . . .

This then is the customary experience of a disorderly state: the learned men will exalt the ways of the early kings and make a show of humanity and righteousness. They will adorn their manners and clothes and embroider their arguments and speeches so as to scatter doubts on the law of the age and beguile the mind of the sovereign. The itinerant speakers will advocate deceptive theories and utilize foreign influence to accomplish their selfish purposes, being unmindful of the benefit of the state. The free-lance fighters will gather pupils and followers and set up standards of fidelity and discipline, hoping thereby to spread their reputation, but violating the prohibitions of the Five Ministries in the process. The courtiers will congregate in the powerful houses, use all kinds of bribes, and exploit their contacts with influential men in order to escape the burden of military service. The tradesmen and craftsmen will produce inferior wares and collect cheap articles, and wait for good opportunities to exploit the farmers. These five types of men are the vermin of the state. Should the ruler fail to eliminate such people as the five vermin and should he not uphold men of firm integrity and strong character, then he can hardly be surprised if within the seas there should be states that decline and fall, and dynasties that wane and perish.

Chapter Eleven

End of classical civilizations

29   THE HAN EMPIRE AND THE HSIUNG-NU

Between the third and the sixth centuries A.D. *the classical civilizations of Eurasia, weakened by internal dissension and deterioration, succumbed to the onslaught of barbarian invaders. This was true not only of the Roman Empire, whose "fall" has elicited much contemporary and modern commentary, but also of the Han Empire in China and of the Gupta in India. The following selections from the works of Pan Ku, a historian, and Ch'ao Ts'o, a statesman, describe the Hsiung-nu, the nomads who eventually overwhelmed the Han Empire.**

Pan Ku

The Hsiung-nu live in the north and are a nomadic people. They raise a variety of animals, most of which are horses, cattle, and sheep. Other animals such as camels and donkeys are comparatively small in number. They move constantly to seek water and grass; they have no cities, houses, or crop fields. Land, however, is divided among different tribal groups.

The Hsiung-nu do not have any written language; consequently all agreements or promises are made in oral form. Small children are taught to ride sheep and shoot birds and squirrels. When they grow older, they begin to shoot foxes and rabbits. Meat, instead of grain, is their staple food. All able-bodied men are expert archers and are members of the cavalry in their respective tribes.

Under normal circumstances when life is comparatively easy, the Hsiung-nu

---

* Pan Ku, "The Hsiung-nu," and Ch'ao Ts'o, "The Defense of Our Northern Frontier." As translated in *The Essence of Chinese Civilization,* by Dun J. Li. Copyright © 1967, by Litton Educational Publishing, Inc., by permission of Van Nostrand Reinhold Company.

earn their livelihood by tending their herds and augment it by hunting. When life becomes difficult, all men are taught the art of warfare, preparing ardently for the launching of attacks. This, you might say, is the nature of the Hsiung-nu. They rely on bows and arrows if the enemy is at a distance and switch to knives and spears in close combat. They attack when they are certain of victory, but are not ashamed to run away from the battlefield if they think that the odds are heavily against them. They go wherever there are profits to be realized; they do not know of such things as righteousness and propriety.

From the king down, all the Hsiung-nu people eat animals' meat, wear their skins, and convert their furs into garments. The young and the strong have priority to the best food; the elderly have to be satisfied with the leftovers. They highly value youth and strength, and look down upon the old and the weak. After the death of his father, a man will marry his step-mother. Likewise he takes his brother's wife as his own when and if his brother dies. . . .

In the first month of each year the khan holds court with all people in his tribe. In the fifth month he gathers all tribal members at Lung where he offers sacrifices to Heaven, Earth, gods, and spirits. Again in the fall when horses are strong and alert, he calls into session another assembly in a forest region, offering sacrifices to gods and spirits and counting the numbers of men and animals.

According to the Hsiung-nu law, he who kills another man will be punished by death. A robber will be condemned to slavery together with all members of his family. Small offenders will be lashed with a stick; serious offenders, on the other hand, will be thrown into jail where they usually die within a period of ten days. Thus throughout the Hsiung-nu empire there are fewer than ten people in jail at any time.

The khan worships the rising sun early in the morning and the moon in the evening. In seating arrangement the person who sits on the left and faces the north is the most honored among the group. The dead are buried in coffins, accompanied with gold, silver, and clothing. But the graves are not marked with trees, nor do the mourners wear mourning clothes. Upon the death of a khan approximately one hundred of his favorite ministers and concubines will be put to death so that their spirits will be able to follow his.

During a military campaign the Hsiung-nu watch closely the size of the moon. They attack when the moon is large and bright and withdraw when it becomes small and dim. A Hsiung-nu soldier who kills an enemy will be awarded one goblet of wine plus whatever material goods he has taken from his victim. If he captures a man or woman alive, the latter becomes his slave. Thus on the battlefield all Hsiung-nu soldiers fight valiantly for their own material ends, upon which they converge like hungry vultures. Upon a setback, however, they disintegrate quickly and disperse like flying clouds. Their favorite strategy is to entice their enemy to a pre-arranged place and then encircle him. After a battle, the warrior who brings home the body of a dead comrade will inherit all of the latter's worldly possessions.

Ch'ao Ts'o

Despite the fact that their territories are barren and unproductive, the northern barbarians have no difficulty in mustering enough strength to invade our border areas repeatedly. Why?

The northern barbarians eat meat, drink milk, and wear animal furs and skins. They have no fields, houses, or cities. Like birds and beasts, they move from place to place and stop only when they find water and good grass. When water or grass is exhausted, they move again until they find the same in some other place. There is no way of telling from where they have come or to which place they will go; nor do we know when they will come or go. This constant migration is the way they make their livelihood, to the same extent as we derive our livelihood from tilling the fields.

During their constant migration they often venture as far as our border provinces. Sometimes they set foot on Yen and Tai, and other times they penetrate as deep as Shangchün. Consequently garrisons have to be maintained throughout the northern frontier and also in the Lunghsi area.

The defense of the frontier by garrison soldiers poses a number of problems. If their number is small, the imperial government will have two choices when encountering a barbarian invasion. It can abstain from sending reinforcements, and in such case the people in the border areas, losing all hope of defending their territories, may decide to surrender themselves to the enemy. Suppose, say, that the imperial government makes the other choice and decides to send reinforcements. If the reinforcements are small, they may not be able to cope with the situation. If they are large, they will have to be dispatched from places far from the border areas; by the time they reach the frontier, the invaders may have already fled. Moreover, once a large force has been gathered on the frontier, the government will have a difficult time to decide what to do with it. If it is not sent back to the districts from where it came, the cost of maintaining it will be exhorbitant. If it is, the barbarians will certainly invade again. . . .

30   THE FALL OF LO-YANG

The previous reading reflects the apprehension of Chinese leaders concerning the ever-present sword of Damocles hanging over their heads in the form of the nomads of Central Asia. On many occasions the sword descended, as these nomads overran parts of China, and two of these nomad peoples—the Mongols and the Manchus—conquered the entire country. The following account by a British sinologist describes the capture of Lo-yang, the great capital city in North China, in terms reminiscent of the corresponding fall of Rome in the West a century later.*

In A.D. 311 Lo-yang, the capital of China and the greatest city of the whole eastern world, was captured and sacked by the Huns. For several centuries northern China was under foreign rule, and when at the end of the sixth century the north passed once more into Chinese hands the culture of the great native dynasties that ruled a powerful and united China (such, for example, as that of the T'ang) was in many ways a synthesis of nomad Turkic and traditional Chinese elements. The year 311, then (like the year 410, when the Goths sacked Rome), marks a turning-point in history. Gibbon, before describing the sack of Rome, pauses to give a

* A. Waley, "The Fall of Lo-yang," *History Today,* April, 1951, pp. 7-10.

general account of the city and the people who lived in it. We may well follow his example. What, then, materially and spiritually, was Lo-yang at the beginning of the fourth century? . . . It lies in the north-west corner of the province of Honan, some twenty miles south of the Yellow River. The population at the beginning of the fourth century was about 600,000. That of Rome may have been somewhat larger; otherwise there was probably no city in the world of that size. It measured about two miles from north to south and was about one and a half miles wide. The main streets were divided into three parts. In the middle, the Imperial Road ran between walls about three and a half feet high. Only the Emperor and his family and the highest officials (Presidents of Boards, and the like) could use this central road. Ordinary people used the tracks that ran on each side of it, and these tracks were "One Way"; traffic going from one of the city gates to the centre used the left-hand track; traffic going in the reverse direction used the track on the right. These main roads were flanked by avenues of elm and sophora.

The public buildings were of the utmost magnificence. The Indian monk Jivaka who came to Lo-yang about 305 declared that the great cluster of Palace buildings corresponded exactly with the Thirty-three Palaces of the paramount god Indra, as seen by the religious in ecstatic vision, "allowing (he added) for the fact that they are human work, not divine". The blinds of these Palace buildings were of mother-of-pearl, and at sunset flashed with a dazzling radiance. The great boulevard that led up to the Palace buildings was called Bronze Camel Street, after the huge bronze figure of a camel that stood at its head, in the square outside the Palace gates. The Government offices were in the Palace precincts; the city offices of the provincial administrations lay near the eastern city gates. There were three markets: the Metal Market in the centre of the town, the Horse Market in the east and a general market outside the southern walls. It would be possible to give a much more detailed picture of Lo-yang at other periods, both earlier and later. For Lo-yang *c.* 311 our sources are limited.

When we turn from the city to the people that lived in it we naturally find ourselves provided with ample information about the educated, governing class, but are left completely in the dark about the lives and thoughts of the ordinary people who formed the bulk of the population. This is inevitable; for all the records come from members of the ruling class (which was at this period almost completely hereditary), and this class was interested in the common people mainly in regard to their corporate utility as soldiers and tax-payers, though always with an eye to the menace that they constituted as possible insurgents.

The prevailing faction in this ruling class was strongly Taoist. They justified conservative *laissez-faire* of a familiar kind by the argument that Being must have sprung from Non-being. Thus Everything is the product of Nothing, and this Nothing (which had the power to produce a whole universe) must be a prodigious force. They identified this force with Tao, the Absolute of the early Taoists, and believed that by conforming to it one can share in its magic; that one has only to do nothing, and everything gets done. This led to (or was the excuse for) a contempt for administrative duties and social obligations. The basis of this as of most philosophies was an irrelevant analogy. Traditional Chinese thinking was concerned with the family, viewed as a tree. The founder of the family was the stock (*pên*) of the tree and its "ramifications" were of course the branches. Transferring this metaphor from the origin of families to the origin of Everything, the Taoists naturally regarded the manifold forms of Being as branches that had sprung from a single ancestral "stock", anterior to Being. This "stock" could only be Non-being, that is to say

"Nothing". "Nothing" thus becomes an Ancestor, a "stock", and it was a maxim of traditional religion that "every man must reverence the stock from which he springs". This same word "reverence", *ch'ung,* which means also "exalt", "worship", was applied by the Taoists to their cult of Nothing. They were not merely people who had reached a speculative conclusion about the priority of non-Being. They had transferred traditional ideas about the Ancestor to what M. Sartre calls *le néant,* and believed that by behaving in a way conformable to the character of their new Ancestor they could share in his *tê,* his magic power. In doing so they overlooked the fact that they had turned Nothing into Something—albeit Something very insubstantial and mysterious; which, if I remember rightly, is just what Professor Ayer once accused Heidegger and Sartre of doing.

As representative of these aristocratic Nihilists let us take Wang Yen (A.D. 266–311), Prime Minister at the time of the fall of Lo-yang. He belonged to one of the most distinguished families in China, the Wangs of Lang-yeh, and was descended from a long line of high officials. He was famous for his great beauty and in particular for the jade-like whiteness of his hands. He subscribed to the theory that though exceptional people can acquire transcendant powers through the cult of *le néant* (to use M. Sartre's convenient term), inferior people (among whom he modestly ranked himself) must be content if through their cult of the *néant* they manage (in a dangerous world) to save their own skins. He did his best to take a negative line towards everything, merely to drift with the tide of events; and as he belonged to the privileged class, had great ability, and, despite his principles, a considerable capacity for decisive action, he "drifted" into high post after high post, until (as we have seen) he became Prime Minister, though still protesting that he had "never had any such ambition" and had only reached his present eminence "by a series of routine promotions".

The favourite distraction of Wang Yen and his friends was "pure conversation", that is to say, talk for talk's sake, as opposed to talking with a view to action. "Mysteries" (*hsüan*), such as how the universe came into existence, were discussed, and problems about the relation of words to facts. For example, is a white horse a horse? And interwoven with these high themes were endless discussions about the characters of absent friends. The conversation, in fact, was very like that of clever undergraduates at our own Universities. Of the endless anecdotes about Wang Yen the one that I like best has also the convenience of introducing us to P'ei Wei, Wang Yen's chief philosophical opponent. At the height of his reputation as an expounder of Taoism Wang Yen was besieged by students who came to ask difficult questions. Once when he had been talking continuously for two days he said wearily to a young enquirer, "I am not feeling well to-day. P'ei Wei lives close by; you had better go and ask him". It was as though Dr. McTaggart, the great Idealist, had said to an importunate visitor, "You had better go and ask Bertrand Russell". For P'ei Wei's attitude was this: An absolute Negation could not possibly produce anything. "Being" must have produced itself. Only what "is", what "exists", can affect what exists. To talk of a society being ruled by Inactivity (*wu-wei*) is absurd. How can the Void, the Non-existent, do any good to us human creatures who, unlike it, *do* exist?

P'ei Wei's doctrine was called "exalting Being", as opposed to "exalting Nothing". According to him the ancestor whom we should reverence is not Nothing, but that mysterious thing "Being", which performed the prodigious feat of producing itself out of nothing.

Essentially, then, what P'ei Wei preached was ordinary common sense; but such a view was far from being common at Lo-yang, where the cult of Nothing was being continually reinforced by the arrival from India and Central Asia of eminent Buddhists whose doctrine of the Void (*sūnya*) was interpreted by the Chinese as an exotic version of their own Nihilism.

Such were the representatives of the two opposing schools of thought at Lo-yang.

Now let us turn to the Huns. They were remote cousins of the Western Huns who invaded Europe in the fifth century. Hard-pressed by another Turkic people, the Hsien-pi, they had been given permission by the Chinese at various times in the third century to settle in north-eastern China, where they were intended to act as a buffer against attacks by other nomads. Shih Lo, whom I am taking as the representative of the Hun side, was born in 274. His father was leader of one of the Hun tribes that had been settled by the Chinese on the north-east frontier. About A.D. 302 the Governor of this part of China who, like most provincial governors at that period, was a member of the Chinese Imperial family, found himself short of funds for military expenses and raised the necessary amount by kidnapping a number of Huns and selling them as slaves. Among those that were marched off "chained in pairs" was Shih Lo. He was purchased by a man who lived at P'ing-yüan, in north-western Shantung, close to the Imperial horse-breeding pastures. Here he got into touch with one of the grooms, and with money obtained by petty brigandage bribed him to join a band of adventurers whom Shih Lo had collected, and mount them on horses from the Imperial paddocks. They were joined by a number of Chinese malcontents, and under the leadership of the groom, who had now become their General with Shih Lo as his second-in-command, they began to plunder north-eastern China. In 307 they sacked the great city of Yeh, about 115 miles north-east of Lo-yang, and slaughtered its commander who was, in fact, the Governor who had sold Shih Lo into slavery. Shortly after this the groom General was heavily defeated by Government troops and Shih Lo, retiring to the north, put himself at the disposition of the main Hun ruler. He had by that time made himself a reputation as a soldier and at once became one of the most important Hun generals. The Huns had now determined to get even with the Chinese, who for so long had treated them as chattels. In 308 they reached the gates of Lo-yang, but were driven off under the energetic leadership of our Nihilist philosopher Wang Yen, who apparently had only a limited faith in the magic of Inactivity. There were more Hun reverses in 309. These were thought by the Huns to be due to the fact that the spirit of Mt. Sung, the guardian mountain of Lo-yang, had not been properly placated. After sacrifice to the spirit the Hun leaders were anxious to continue the attack; but their astrologer discovered that 311 not 309 would be the propitious year, and the Hun armies withdrew. In 310 the Hun chief died and there was a brief war of succession, which gave Lo-yang a breathing-space. In the winter of that year, however, the attack was renewed. Much of the country round Lo-yang was occupied by the Huns; food-supplies in the city ran out and a terrible famine began. In the early summer of 311 the main Chinese armies, under the command of Wang Yen, were completely routed at Hu-hsien, about 150 miles to the east of Lo-yang. Hu-hsien, strangely enough, was the place where Lao Tzu, the legendary founder of Taoism, was supposed to have been born and where sacrifices were made to his spirit. Did Wang Yen, one wonders, pause at his shrine?

A number of high-ranking prisoners were brought to Shih Lo's tent and questioned about the state of affairs in Lo-yang. Among the prisoners was Wang Yen himself. He gave "a full account of the reasons for the defeat". What he considered these to be we are not told. He mentioned, presumably, the chaos produced by a long period of dissension between the various royal princes, and the refusal of the provinces to come to the aid of the Capital. Shih Lo was much interested and sent for him again next day. In the course of the conversation Wang Yen spoke of his own career and once more protested, as he had done when he was made Prime Minister, that he was not interested in politics. It was Wang Yen's maxim (as we have seen above) that whereas the full-fledged Taoist saint can perform miracles by his detachment from concrete realities, the most that the common man can do is to "save his own skin", undeterred by conventional non-Taoist ideas of dignity and morality. True to this principle and hoping (or so we are told) to curry favour with Shih Lo, he suggested that the Hun should proclaim himself Emperor of China. "You took office when you were quite young," said Shih Lo, ignoring Wang Yen's suggestion, "made a name for yourself everywhere within the Four Seas, and now hold the highest office. How can you say that you have never had political ambitions? If any one man is responsible for the ruin of the Empire it is you." And he ordered him to be removed. Then turning to his lieutenant, K'ung Ch'ang, he said, "I have travelled about a good deal in my time, but nowhere have I met such a man as this. Oughtn't we to make use of him?" "He is one of the Three Grandees of the Chinese Empire," said K'ung Ch'ang. "He would never work whole-heartedly in the interest of the Huns. Moreover, he has certainly done nothing on this occasion to make us respect him." "We can at least not put him to the sword", said Shih Lo, and that night he sent men to push over the wall of the room in which Wang Yen was sleeping and suffocate him. Death by suffocation was more honourable than decapitation.

The Hun armies entered Lo-yang from the south and east. The destruction of the city began with the burning of the offices of the provincial administrations which lay, as we have seen, just inside the eastern gates. Fierce street-fighting ensued and it was not till a fortnight later that the Palace, in the northern part of the city, was reached. It was ransacked by the Huns who carried off everything of value, including the ladies of the Emperor's harem. The Emperor himself had made a previous attempt to escape by river to the east; but the Huns burnt his boats before the expedition was ready to start. He now slipped out by a back gate and attempted to escape westwards, in the direction of Ch'ang-an; but he was overtaken and captured. After being held captive for a short time he was sent to the Hun Capital in the north-east where, stripped of all his grandeurs, he was made to carry round the wine at Hun banquets. After sacking the Palace the Huns pillaged and burned the Imperial Tombs, the Ancestral Shrines and the various Ministries. There had been at one moment a plan to spare Lo-yang and make it the Hun Capital. But it was still almost surrounded by unsubdued Chinese territory and the leaders decided that it might prove difficult to hold. The whole city was therefore burnt to the ground and no considerable town stood there till the Wei Tartars made Lo-yang their Capital in 493.

News of the fall of Lo-yang, which was the terminus of a great Asiatic trade route, must have spread far beyond China. The one non-Chinese comment upon it that has come down to us occurs in a fragmentary letter (written probably in the summer of 313) by the Sogdian merchant Nanai-vandak to his colleague Nanai-dvār in Samarkand. It was found in the ruins of a watch-tower to the west of Tun-huang, on the western frontiers of China. The letter which is in Sogdian, an eastern dialect of early Persian, expresses astonishment that "those Huns who yesterday were the Emperor's vassals" should now have overthrown the empire. "And, Sir," Nanai-vandak writes, "the last Emperor—so they say—fled from Saragh (i.e., Lo-yang) because of the famine, and his Palace and walled city were set on fire . . . So Saragh is no more, Ngap (i.e., Yeh) no more!"

The German barbarians that were encamped on the eastern frontiers of the Roman Empire were the counterpart of the Hsiung-nu on the northwestern frontiers of the Han Empire. The historian Tacitus spent some time among the Germans, apparently as an official of the imperial government. In the following account, written about A.D. 100, he describes the customs and manners of the Germans, stressing their virtues as an example for his luxury-loving fellow countrymen.*

I myself subscribe to the opinion of those who hold that the German tribes have never been contaminated by intermarriage with other nations, but have remained peculiar and unmixed and wholly unl'ike other people. Hence the bodily type is the same among them all, notwithstanding the extent of their population. They all have fierce blue eyes, reddish hair and large bodies fit only for sudden exertion; they do not submit patiently to work and effort and cannot endure thirst and heat at all, though cold and hunger they are accustomed to because of their climate.

In general the country, though varying here and there in appearance, is covered over with wild forests or filthy swamps, . . . It is suitable enough for grain but does not permit the cultivation of fruit trees; and, though rich in flocks and herds, these are for the most part small, the cattle not even possessing their natural beauty nor spreading horns. The people take pride in possessing a large number of animals, these being their sole and most cherished wealth. Whether it was in mercy or wrath that the gods denied them silver and gold, I know not. Yet I would not affirm that no vein of German soil produces silver or gold; for who has examined? They do not care for their possession and use as much as might be expected. There are to be seen among them vessels of silver that have been presented as gifts to their ambassadors and chiefs, but they are held in no more esteem than vessels of earthenware; however, those nearest to us prize gold and silver because of its use in trade, and they recognize certain of our coins as valuable and choose those. The people of the interior practice barter and exchange of commodities in accordance with the simple and ancient custom. They like the old and well-known coins, those with milled edges bearing the stamp of a two-horse chariot. They are more anxious also for silver coins than for gold, not because of any special liking, but because a number of silver coins is more convenient in purchasing cheap and common articles.

Not even iron is abundant, as is shown by the character of their weapons. Some few use swords or long spears, but usually they carry javelins, called in their language *framea,* tipped with a short narrow piece of iron but so sharp and so easy to handle that as occasion demands they employ the same weapon for fighting at close range or at a distance. A horseman is content with a shield or a javelin, but the footmen, either nude or lightly clad in a small cloak, rain missiles, each man having many and hurling them to a great distance. There is no particular adornment to their weapons except that their shields are distinguished by the most carefully chosen colors. A few wear cuirasses, but hardly any have helmets of metal or leather. Their horses are noted neither for their beauty nor their speed, nor are they trained

---

* A. C. Howland, *Translations and Reprints from the Original Sources of European History,* VI, No. 3, "The Early Germans" (Philadelphia: University of Pennsylvania Press, n.d.), pp. 4-16.

to perform evolutions, as with us. They move straight ahead or make a single turn to the right, the wheel being executed with such perfect alignment that no man drops behind the one next to him. One would say that on the whole their chief strength lies in their infantry. A picked body of these are chosen from among all the youth and placed in advance of the line where they fight mixed with the horsemen, since their swiftness makes them fully equal to engaging in a cavalry contest. Their number is fixed; there are a hundred from each canton, and from this circumstance they take their name among their own people, so that what was at first a number is now become an appellation of honor. The main body of troops is drawn up in wedge-shaped formation. To yield ground, provided you press forward subsequently, is considered a mark of prudence rather than a sign of cowardice. They carry off the bodies of the fallen even where they are not victorious. It is the greatest ignominy to have left one's shield on the field, and it is unlawful for a man so disgraced to be present at the sacred rites or to enter the assembly; so that many after escaping from battle have ended their shame with the halter.

They choose their kings on account of their ancestry, their generals for their valor. The kings do not have free and unlimited power and the generals lead by example rather than command, winning great admiration if they are energetic and fight in plain sight in front of the line.

. . . . .

Concerning minor matters the chiefs deliberate, but in important affairs all the people are consulted, although the subjects referred to the common people for judgment are discussed beforehand by the chiefs. Unless some sudden and unexpected event calls them together, they assemble on fixed days either at the new moon or the full moon, for they think these the most auspicious times to begin their undertakings. They do not reckon time by the number of days, as we do, but by the number of nights. So run their appointments, their contracts; the night introduces the day, so to speak. A disadvantage arises from their regard for liberty in that they do not come together at once as if commanded to attend, but two or three days are wasted by their delay in assembling. When the crowd is sufficient they take their places fully armed. Silence is proclaimed by the priests, who have on these occasions the right to keep order. Then the king or a chief addresses them, each being heard according to his age, noble blood, reputation in warfare and eloquence, though more because he has the power to persuade than the right to command. If an opinion is displeasing they reject it by shouting; if they agree to it they clash with their spears. The most complimentary form of assent is that which is expressed by means of their weapons.

. . . . .

When they go into battle it is a disgrace for the chief to be outdone in deeds of valor and for the following not to match the courage of their chief; furthermore, for any one of the followers to have survived his chief and come unharmed out of a battle is life-long infamy and reproach. It is in accordance with their most sacred oath of allegiance to defend and protect him and to ascribe their bravest deeds to his renown. The chief fights for victory; the men of his following, for their chief. If the tribe to which they belong sinks into the lethargy of long peace and quiet, many of the noble youths voluntarily seek other tribes that are still carrying on war, because a quiet life is irksome to the Germans and they gain renown more readily in the midst of perils, while a large following is not to be provided for except by violence and war. For they look to the liberality of their chief for their war-horse and their deadly and victorious spear; the feasts and entertainments, however, furnished them on a homely but liberal scale, fall to their lot as mere pay. The means for this bounty are acquired through war and plunder. Nor could you persuade them to till the soil and await the yearly produce so easily as you could induce them to stir up an enemy and earn glorious wounds. Nay, even they think it tame and stupid to acquire by their sweat what they can purchase by their blood.

In the intervals of peace they spend little time in hunting, but much in idleness, given over to sleep and eating; all the bravest and most warlike doing nothing, while the hearth and home and the care of the fields is given over to the women, the old men, and the various infirm members of the family. . . .

It is well known that none of the German tribes live in cities, nor even permit their dwellings to be closely joined to each other. They live separated and in various places, as a spring or a meadow or a grove strikes their fancy. They lay out their villages, not as with us in connected or closely-joined houses, but each one surrounds his dwelling with an open space, either as a protection against conflagration or because of their ignorance of the art of building. They do not even make use of rough stones or tiles. They use for all purposes undressed timber, giving no beauty or comfort. Some parts they plaster carefully with earth of such purity and brilliancy as to form a substitute for painting and designs in color. They are accustomed also to dig out subterranean caves which they cover over with great heaps of manure as a refuge against the cold and a place for storing grain, for retreats of this sort render the extreme cold of their winters bearable and, whenever an enemy has come upon them, though he lays waste the open country, he is either ignorant of what is hidden underground or else it escapes him for the very reason that it has to be searched for.

Generally their only clothing is a cloak fastened with a clasp, or if they haven't that, with a thorn; this being their only garment, they pass whole days about the hearth or near a fire. The richest of them are distinguished by wearing a tunic, not flowing as is the case among the Sarmatians and Parthians, but close-fitting and showing the shape of their limbs. There are those, also, who wear the skins of wild beasts, those nearest the Roman border in a careless manner, but those further back more elegantly, as those do who have no better clothing obtained by commerce. They select certain animals, and stripping off their hides sew on them patches of spotted skins taken from those strange beasts that the distant ocean and the unknown sea bring forth. The women wear the same sort of dress as the men except that they wrap themselves in linen garments which they adorn with purple stripes and do not lengthen out the upper part of the tunic into sleeves, but leave the arms bare the whole length. The upper part of their breasts is also exposed. However, their marriage code is strict, and in no other part of their manners are they to be praised more than in this. For almost alone among barbarian peoples they are content with one wife each, excepting those few who because of their high position rather than out of lust enter into more than one marriage engagement.

· · · · ·

No other race indulges more freely in entertainments and hospitality. It is considered a crime to turn any mortal man away from one's door. According to his means, each one receives those who come with a well-furnished table. When his food has been all eaten up, he who had lately been the host becomes the guide and companion of his guest to the next house, which they enter uninvited. There is no distinction between guests; they are all received with like consideration. No one makes any difference between friend and stranger so far as concerns the rights of hospitality. If the guest on going away asks for any gift, it is customary to grant it to him, and the host on his side feels the same freedom from constraint in making a request. They take great pleasure in presents, but they do not reckon them as favors nor do they put themselves under obligations in accepting them.

As soon as they awake from sleep, which they prolong till late in the day, they bathe, usually in warm water as their winter lasts a great part of the year. After the bath they take food, each sitting in a separate seat and having a table to himself. Then they proceed to their business, or not less often to feasts, fully armed. It is no disgrace to spend the whole day and night in drinking. Quarreling is frequent enough as is natural among drunken men, though their disputes are rarely settled by mere wrangling but oftener by bloodshed and wounds. Yet it is at their feasts that they consult about reconciling enemies, forming family alliances, electing chiefs, and even regarding war and peace, as they think that at no other time is the mind more open to fair judgment or more inflamed to mighty deeds.

.   .   .   .   .

But they do not employ slaves as we do with distinct functions prescribed throughout the establishment. Each has his own domicile and rules his own house. The Lord exacts a certain amount of grain or cloth or a certain number of cattle as in the case of a tenant and this is the extent of his servitude. Other duties, those of the household, are performed by the lord's wife and children. To beat a slave or to punish him with chains and task work is rare. They occasionally kill one, not in the severity of discipline, but impetuously and in sudden wrath as they would kill an enemy, except that the deed goes without punishment. Freedmen do not rank much above slaves; they are not of much account in the household and never in the state, except only in those tribes that are ruled by kings. For there they are elevated above the free born and the nobles. The inferior position of the freedman elsewhere is the mark of the free state.

To trade with capital and to let it out at interest is unknown, and so it is ignorance rather than legal prohibition that protects them. Land is held by the villages as communities according to the number of the cultivators, and is then divided among the freedmen according to their rank. The extent of their territories renders this partition easy. They cultivate fresh fields every year and there is still land to spare. They do not plant orchards nor lay off meadow-lands nor irrigate gardens so as to require of the soil more than it would naturally bring forth of its own richness and extent. Grain is the only tribute exacted from their land, whence they do not divide the year into as many seasons as we do. The terms winter, spring and summer have a meaning with them, but the name and blessings of autumn are unknown.

There is no pomp in the celebration of their funerals. The only custom they observe is that the bodies of illustrious men should be burned with certain kinds of wood. They do not heap garments and perfumes upon the funeral pile. In every case a man's arms are burned with him, and sometimes his horse also. They believe that stately monuments and sculptured columns oppress the dead with their weight; the green sod alone covers their graves. Their tears and lamentations are quickly laid aside; sadness and grief linger long. It is fitting for women to mourn, for men to remember.

Such are the facts I have obtained in general concerning the origin and customs of the Germans as a whole. . . .

32

By the fifth century A.D. *the Germans, whom Tacitus had depicted as a model to emulate, had become conquerors to fear. This is evident in the following selection from the letters of St. Jerome, one of the great doctors of the Church. He was in Jerusalem when Rome was sacked in 410, and his observations on that disaster reflect the shock that it caused throughout the empire.**

For twenty years and more the blood of Romans has every day been shed between Constantinople and the Julian Alps. Scythia, Thrace, Macedonia, Thessaly, Dardania, Dacia, Epirus, Dalmatia, and all the provinces of Pannonia, have been sacked, pillaged and plundered by Goths and Sarmatians, Quadians and Alans, Huns and Vandals and Marcomanni. How many matrons, how many of God's virgins, ladies of gentle birth and high position, have been made the sport of these beasts! Bishops have been taken prisoners, presbyters and other clergymen of different orders murdered. Churches have been overthrown, horses stabled at Christ's altar, the relics of martyrs dug up.

> 'Sorrow and grief on every side we see
> And death in many a shape.'

The Roman world is falling, . . . The East seemed to be immune from these dangers and was only dismayed by the news that reached her. But lo! last year the wolves—not of Arabia, but from the far north—were let loose upon us from the distant crags of Caucasus, and in a short time overran whole provinces. How many monasteries did they capture, how many rivers were reddened with men's blood! They besieged Antioch and all the other cities on the Halys, Cydnus, Orontes, and Euphrates. They carried off troops of captives. Arabia, Phoenicia, Palestine and Egypt in their terror felt themselves already enslaved.

> 'Had I a hundred tongues, a hundred mouths,
> A voice of brass, I could not tell the names
> Of all those punishments.'

. . . . .

. . . The soldiers of Rome, who once subdued and ruled the world, now tremble and shrink in fear . . .

. . . a dreadful rumour reached us from the West. We heard that Rome was besieged, that the citizens were buying their safety with gold, and that when they had been thus despoiled they were again beleaguered, so as to lose not only their substance but their lives. The city which had taken the whole world was itself taken; nay, it fell by famine before it fell by the sword, and there were but a few found to be made prisoners. The rage of hunger had recourse to impious food; men tore one another's limbs, and the mother did not spare the baby at her breast,

---

* Reprinted by permission of the publishers and The Loeb Classical Library from St. Jerome, *Select Letters,* trans. F. A. Wright (Cambridge, Mass.: Harvard University Press), pp. 301-5, 463.

taking again within her body that which her body had just brought forth. 'In the night was Moab taken, in the night did her wall fall down.' 'O God, the heathen have come into thine inheritance; thy holy temple have they defiled; they have made Jerusalem an orchard. The dead bodies of thy servants have they given to be meat unto the fowls of the heaven, the flesh of thy saints unto the beasts of the earth. Their blood have they shed like water round about Jerusalem; and there was none to bury them.'

33   THE LIFE AND TIMES OF CHARLEMAGNE

After a period of disunity and discord, the Han dynasty of China was followed by the Sui and T'ang dynasties, which revived the traditional civilization and imperial structure. A similar course appeared to be developing in the West with the emergence of the Frankish Kingdom in Gaul. Under Karl, or Charles the Great (Charlemagne), this kingdom reached such proportions that it was regarded as the successor of the original Roman Empire. A vivid picture of the character and policies of Charlemagne has been left by the monk Eginhard, who served the emperor as private secretary and chaplain.*

I pass by the birth, infancy, and childhood of Karl, because there is no written record concerning them, nor is any one now known to survive who can speak from personal knowledge. I have therefore thought it foolish to write about them, and have given my attention to relating and explaining those actions, habits, and other portions of his life which are not matters of uncertainty; first narrating his military exploits at home and abroad, then his domestic habits and occupations, then his administration of the kingdom, and lastly, about his death, omitting nothing that is worthy and necessary to be narrated.

Karl was engaged in many wars.

· · · · ·

The greatest of all the wars waged by the King, except the Saxon, was that which now followed, against the Avars or Huns. He set about it with far more ardour and preparation that was bestowed upon any of the others. The King himself only made one expedition into Pannonia—it was that province which the Avar race then inhabited; the others he entrusted to the direction of his son Pippin, and to the prefects of the provinces, and to the counts and lieutenants. Although these commanders used the greatest exertions, it was not until the eighth year that the war was finished.

How many battles were fought, and how much blood shed, is fully attested by the complete depopulation of Pannonia; even the situation of the royal palace of the Kagan is so obliterated that no trace remains of a human habitation.

In this war the whole nobility of the Avars perished, and the glory of their nation was destroyed. All their riches and treasures, which they had long been accumulating, were carried away, nor can memory recall any war of the Franks

* Eginhard, *Life of the Emperor Karl the Great,* trans. William Glaister (London: George Bell & Sons, 1877), pp. 26ff.

in which they have gained greater booty or by which they have been more enriched. Indeed, we may confess that, up to this time, the Franks appeared to be a poor nation; but so much gold and silver was found in the palace, and such a quantity of valuable spoil was taken in the battles, as can scarcely be believed.

The Franks justly spoiled the Huns (Avars) of this booty, for the Huns themselves had no right to it, it being the plunder they had carried off from other nations.

. . . . .

The last war undertaken was against the Northmen who are called Danes, who, at first as pirates, and afterwards with a larger fleet, were ravaging the coasts of Gaul and Germany. Their King, Godfrey, was puffed up with the delusive hope of making himself master of all Germany, and persisted in regarding Frisia and Saxony as his own provinces. He had already brought the Abodriti under his power and had made them tributary to him.

He even used to boast that he would shortly appear with all his forces at Aachen, where the King's court was held. Foolish as his talk was, there were some who did not altogether discredit him. It was rather thought that he would have attempted something of the kind had not his sudden death prevented him. He was slain by one of his own servants, and thus his own life and the war he had begun were brought to an abrupt conclusion.

Such were the wars waged by the most potent prince with the greatest skill and success in different countries during the forty-seven years of his reign. Great and powerful as was the realm of the Franks, which Karl had received from his father Pippin, he nevertheless so splendidly enlarged it by these wars that he almost doubled it.

. . . . .

The renown of his Kingdom was also much increased by the friendly alliances he cultivated with different kings and nations. Alfonso, King of Galicia and Asturias, was so bound to him by the ties of friendship that, when he sent him letters or messengers, he used to command that he should be spoken of as being Karl's man. The Kings of the Scots, too, were by his munificence so devoted to his will, that they ever spoke of him as their Lord, and of themselves as his lieges and servants. Letters are still extant from them to him which show that this sort of relationship existed between them.

Haroun, king of the Persians, who, with the exception of India, ruled over nearly all the East, was held by the King in such hearty friendship, that he valued Karl's esteem above that of all other Kings and princes of the world, and thought that he alone was worthy to be honoured by his regard and munificence. When the officers sent by King Karl with offerings to the most sacred sepulchre and place of the resurrection of our Lord and Saviour came to Haroun and announced the pleasure of their master, he not only gave them permission to do as they desired, but granted that that revered and sacred spot should be considered as belonging to King Karl. When the ambassadors set out on their return, he sent with them his own envoys, who conveyed to the King strange and curious gifts, with garments and spices and other rich products of the East, just as he had sent him a few years before, upon his request, the only elephant he then possessed.

The Constantinopolitan Emperors, Nicephorus, Michael, and Leo, of their own accord, also sought his friendship and alliance, and sent to him several embassies; and since by assuming the Imperial title he had laid himself open to the grave suspicion of wishing to deprive them of Empire, he made with them the most binding treaty possible, that there might be no occasion of offence between them. But the Romans and Greeks always viewed with distrust the power of the Franks; hence arose the Greek proverb, "Have a Frank for a friend but not for a neighbour."

Illustrious as the King was in the work of enlarging his Kingdom and in conquering foreign nations, and though so constantly occupied with such affairs, he nevertheless began in several places very many works for the advantage and beautifying of his Kingdom. Some of these he was able to finish. Chief among them may be mentioned, as deserving of notice, the Basilica of the Holy Mother of God, built at Aachen, a marvel of workmanship; and the bridge over the Rhine at Mainz, five hundred paces in length, so broad is the river at that place. This bridge, however, was destroyed by fire the year before the King died, nor could it be restored on account of his approaching death, although it was in the King's mind to replace the wooden structure by a bridge of stone.

He also began some magnificent palaces, one not far from Mainz, near the village of Ingelheim, and another at Nymeguen, on the river Waal, which flows past the island of the Batavians on the southern side. He was more especially particular in giving orders to the priests and fathers to see to the restoration of those churches under their care, which in any part of his Kingdom he found had fallen into decay, taking care by his officers that his commands were obeyed. He also constructed a fleet for the war against the Northmen. For this purpose ships were built on the rivers of Gaul and Germany which flow into the North Sea. As the Northmen were making a practice of ravaging the coasts of Gaul and Germany with constant harryings, he posted towers and outlooks in all the harbours, and at the mouths of those rivers which ships could navigate. By these defences he prevented any enemy from being able to pass. He did the same thing in the south, on the coast of the provinces of Narbonne and Septimania, and all along the coast of Italy as far as Rome, for in those parts the Moors had lately taken to piracy. Thus Italy suffered no great damage from the Moors, nor Gaul or Germany from the Northmen, during the reign of Karl, except that Civita Vecchia, a city of Etruria, was betrayed to the Moors, who took it and destroyed it, and in Frisia some islands off the German coast were plundered by the Northmen.

Such does it appear was the character of the King, in defending, enlarging, and beautifying his Kingdom, and one must be permitted to admire his mental gifts and his great firmness of purpose in all circumstances, whether of prosperity or adversity.

. . . . .

The person of Karl was large and robust, and of commanding stature, though not exceeding good proportions, for it appears that he measured seven feet in height. The top of his head was round, his eyes large and animated, his nose somewhat long, his hair white, and his face bright and pleasant; so that, whether standing or sitting, he showed very great presence and dignity. Although his neck was thick and rather short, and his belly too prominent, still the fair proportions of his limbs concealed these defects. His walk was firm, and the whole carriage of his body was manly. His voice was clear, but not so strong as his frame would have led one to expect. His health was good until the last four years of his life, when he was attacked with frequent fevers, and latterly walked lame on one foot. Even in illness he leaned more on his own judgment than on the advice of physicians, whom he greatly disliked, because they used to recommend him to leave off roasted meats, which he preferred, and to accustom himself to boiled.

. . . . .

In his eating and drinking he was temperate; more particularly so in his drinking, since he had the greatest abhorrence of drunkenness in anybody, but more especially in himself and his companions. He was unable to abstain from food for any length of time, and often complained that fasting was injurious to him. . . .

While he was dining he listened to music or reading. History and the deeds of men of old used to be read. He derived much pleasure from the works of St. Augustine, especially from his book called "Civitas Dei." ("The City of God.")

. . . . .

He was ready and fluent in speaking, and able to express himself with great clearness. He did not confine himself to his native tongue, but took pains to learn foreign languages, acquiring such knowledge of Latin that he used to repeat his prayers in that language as well as in his own. Greek he could better understand than pronounce. In speaking he was so voluble that he almost gave one the impression of a chatterer. He was an ardent admirer of the liberal arts, and greatly revered their professors, whom he promoted to high honours. In order to learn grammar, he attended the lectures of the aged Peter of Pisa, a deacon; and for other instruction he chose as his preceptor Albinus, otherwise called Alcuin, also a deacon—a Saxon by race, from Britain, the most learned man of the day, with whom the King spent much time in learning rhetoric and logic, and more especially astronomy. He learned the art of computation, and with deep thought and skill very carefully calculated the courses of the planets.

Karl also tried to write, and used to keep his tablets and writing-book under the pillow of his couch, that when he had leisure he might practise his hand in forming letters; but he made little progress in a task too long deferred, and begun too late in life.

The Christian religion, in which he had been brought up from infancy, was held by Karl as most sacred, and he worshipped in it with the greatest piety. For this reason he built at Aachen a most beautiful church, which he enriched with gold and silver, and candle-sticks, and also with lattices and doors of solid brass. When columns and marbles for the building could not be obtained from elsewhere, he had them brought from Rome and Ravenna.

As long as his health permitted, he was most regular in attending the church at matins and evensong, and also during the night, and at the time of the Sacrifice; and he took especial care that all the services of the church should be performed in the most fitting manner possible, frequently cautioning the sacristans not to allow anything improper or unseemly to be brought into, or left in, the building.

. . . . .

To the Pope he made many and rich presents; and nothing lay nearer his heart during his whole reign than that the city of Rome should attain to its ancient importance by his zeal and patronage, and that the church of St. Peter should, through him, not only be in safe keeping and protection, but should also by his wealth be ennobled and enriched beyond all other churches. Although he thought so much of this, it was only four times, during the forty-seven years of his reign, that he had leisure to go to Rome for prayer and supplication.

The last visit he paid to Rome was not only for the above reasons, but also because the Romans had driven Pope Leo to ask his assistance—for they had grievously ill-treated him; indeed, his eyes had been plucked out and his tongue cut off.

Karl therefore went to Rome, and stayed there the whole winter in order to reform and quiet the Church, which was in a most disturbed state. It was at this time that he received the title of Emperor and Augustus, . . .

After he had taken the Imperial title, he turned his attention to the laws of his people, which seemed greatly to need it, since the Franks have two laws, which differ much in many places.

. . . He also wrote out and committed to memory the rude and very ancient songs which told of the exploits and wars of the kings of old. He also began a grammar of the speech of his country. He also gave names in the national tongue to the months of the year, for up to this time the Franks had distinguished them partly by Latin and partly by barbarian names. He likewise gave the proper names to the twelve winds, for previously names were known for hardly four. . . .

. . . During the winter, in the month of January, he was confined to his bed by a sharp attack of fever. He at once prescribed for himself a lowering diet, which was his usual treatment of fever, thinking that by this means he could throw off the disease, or at least control it; but inflammation of the side, which the Greeks call pleurisy, supervened. He still continued to starve himself, only keeping himself up by occasionally taking liquids; and on the seventh day after he had been confined to his bed he received the Holy Communion, and died soon after, at nine o'clock, on the 28th January, in the seventy-third year of his age and forty-seventh of his reign.

His body was reverently washed and tended, and then carried into the church and buried, to the great grief of all his poeple. . . . Above his tomb was erected a gilded monument, with his effigy and title upon it. His dignity was thus described—

UNDER THIS TOMB IS PLACED THE BODY OF KARL, THE GREAT AND ORTHODOX EMPEROR, WHO GLORIOUSLY ENLARGED THE REALM OF THE FRANKS, AND SUCCESSFULLY REIGNED DURING FORTY-SEVEN YEARS. HE DIED IN THE SEVENTY-THIRD YEAR OF HIS AGE,

JANY. XXVIII., ANNO DOMINI DCCCXIIII.

34   THE VIKINGS

In contrast to the course of events in China, Charlemagne's empire did not mark the restoration of classical civilization in the West. Instead, a new wave of invasions smashed the fragile Carolingian imperial structure. Moslem pirates attacked from the south across the Mediterranean, Magyar horsemen raided from the eastern steppes, and Norsemen, or Vikings, attacked in their "dragon ships" from the north. These invasions are of primary historical significance as they ended the possibility of a return to the classical pattern, thereby clearing the way for the eventual emergence of a new and unique civilization in the West. The following selection describes the nature and the impact of the wide-ranging operations of the Vikings.*

* E. Oxenstierna, "The Vikings," *Scientific American* (May 1967), pp. 67-78. Copyright © 1967 by Scientific American, Inc. All rights reserved.

To most Americans, I would venture to say, the Vikings are known as re-doubtable seafarers who raided England and France, colonized Iceland and Greenland and even landed in North America centuries before Columbus. Much less known are the Scandinavian traders and settlers who colonized parts of England and France and the whole of Sicily, established the first Russian state, traveled by inland waterways to the Black Sea and the Caspian, manned the Byzantine fleet and traded slaves and furs in the bazaars of Bagdad for Arab silver and Chinese silks.

In this article I shall emphasize these less familiar aspects of Viking history. A review of the subject is timely because much new archaeological evidence concerning these Scandinavian peoples has recently been uncovered, illuminating a period of history that is poorly represented in written records.

The Vikings emerged as a recognizable group at the end of a restless period, lasting almost 1,000 years, during which many peoples of northern Europe had migrated to almost every corner of the continent. For example, the Burgundians had moved to France from the island of Burgundarholm (now Bornholm) in the Baltic Sea. The Vandals had gone from Vandilsyssel in what is now Denmark all the way to Andalusia in southern Spain; the Lombards from the mouth of the Elbe on the Baltic to Lombardy in Italy, and the Angles and the Saxons from what is now northern Germany to England.

Not all these movements were to the south. A number of grave sites recently excavated on the Scandinavian peninsula indicate that early in the seventh century A.D. a farming population moved into mountain valleys and deep forests where no one had ever lived before. Even the poorest of these immigrant farmers had enough iron at his disposal—in terms of hoes, spades, plows, axes, knives and, not least, a good sword—to enable him to clear the forest and cultivate his fields. Within a few generations, however, the newly cleared forest soil was exhausted, and there was hunger all over Scandinavia.

During this same period a significant technological change took place: the oared galleys that had provided water transportation in Scandinavia were replaced by ships with sails. An excavation at Kvalsund in Norway shows that by about A.D. 600 sizable sailing vessels were being built. They were shallow-draft vessels with a planked deck but no keel.

It is no accident that, at a time when a new mobility at sea coincided with hunger at home, history should record the first Viking raid. It occurred on June 8, 793. The action took place on the island of Lindisfarne, in the North Sea near the border of Scotland and England. The number of ships that came up over the horizon that day is not recorded, but the actions of their crews were noted in detail by the English monks who where their victims. The Vikings slaughtered the monastery's herd of cattle and loaded the carcasses into their ships. They killed anyone who resisted. After removing everything in the monastery that was made of silver and gold they set fire to all the buildings. From the Christian viewpoint the episode was an atrocity. For the pagan Vikings it had been a routine *strandhugg* (victualing raid) in which the unexpected haul of precious metal and the absence of armed resistance must have been agreeable surprises.

The word of the raiders' easy success evidently spread through Scandinavia like wildfire. The next summer "dragon ships" (named for their dragon-shaped figurehead) attacked two monasteries along the same North Sea coast of Britain. The summer after that monasteries on three islands off the western coast of Scotland—Rechru, Iona and Skye—were plundered. By A.D. 799 raids on the

British Isles were common, and similar attacks on the Continent compelled the Emperor Charlemagne to organize a coast-watching force.

Thus began the activities that gained the Vikings a reputation as pirates. As I have indicated, however, these peoples had other interests. Let us turn from the North Sea to the Baltic, particularly to the Svea people of the area around the modern Swedish city of Uppsala, to the inhabitants of the island of Gotland and to the petty kings who controlled the base of the peninsula of Jutland. Both the Svea and the Gotlanders had established coastal settlements in Latvia and elsewhere across the Baltic before the middle of the seventh century. Indeed, the excavation of a large seventh-century cemetery at Grobin in Latvia has uncovered ornaments typical of both Gotlander men and women—proof that their trans-Baltic enclave was a genuine colony inhabited by married couples and not a mere outpost.

From the trans-Baltic settlements trade goods (the most important were furs) flowed back to Gotland and the main Svea centers of commerce: the island towns of Helgö and Birka in Lake Mälar, near modern Stockholm. Excavations at Helgö have revealed trade goods manufactured far to the south (for example glassware made in Cologne on the Rhine) that had no doubt been received in exchange for pelts or for the iron that also was an export of the Svea.

Items of even more distant origin have been uncovered by the digging at Helgö, which began in 1953. The bronze head of a crosier—the ornate shepherd's crook carried by abbots, bishops and other church officials as a symbol of their pastoral duties—is among the finds. It is of Irish manufacture; we can assume that it reached the Norwegian coast as part of some raider's loot and was then traded eastward to Helgö. A greater surprise was the discovery in 1955 of a small bronze figure of Buddha, complete with a golden caste mark on the forehead.

One of the way stations along this trade route between the north and Charlemagne's Europe was a Danish town at the base of the Jutland peninsula. Founded by King Godfred in A.D. 808, it stood near the present Kiel Canal at a point where only eight miles of land separate the Treene River and the North Sea from the Schlei River and the Baltic. Not only could goods moving north and south be easily transshipped here; the light dragon ships could themselves be hauled from one sea to the other on log rollers or mattresses of brushwood.

On all this traffic the Danes levied a profitable tariff. The town was Haithabu (modern Hedeby) and by A.D. 1000 it had grown as large as Cologne. Some of this area, which today lies in West Germany, was excavated before World War II; the work was resumed in 1960. Haithabu's cosmopolitan character during the last centuries of the first millennium can be judged by the kinds of objects that have been uncovered there. The excavators found, for example, a gold coin from Byzantium minted during the rule of the joint emperors Theophilus and Constantine (A.D. 829 to 842) in association with a gold-plated bronze buckle acquired in a raid on Ireland.

In 829 Charlemagne's son Louis the Pious received an embassy from the king of the Svea at a conclave that assembled at Worms on the Rhine. A regularization of trade was probably in the minds of both parties. In any case, Louis took advantage of the Svea delegation's return to Uppsala to send with them a missionary, a Benedictine monk. Accounts of the monk's mission indicate that he built a church but was not very successful in winning converts among the Vikings.

OVERLAND TO BYZANTIUM. Meanwhile in their colonies across the Baltic the Svea were doing more than farming and trading. They advanced in their light ships across eastern Europe as if its meadows and forests were the open sea. Sailing up the Düna and Memel rivers, they beached their shallow-draft vessels and carried them overland to launch them again in rivers flowing south—the Dnieper and the Volga. Scarcely 10 years after the Svea embassy had visited the Emperor of the West at Worms, Vikings who had sailed the inland waterways to the Black Sea paid their respects to the Emperor of the East at Byzantium. Indeed, one such Svea group traveled back to its own land not the way it had come but by way of the Mediterranean and Italy, traveling with the Eastern emperor's embassy to the new ruler of the West (Lothar, who succeeded Louis the Pious in 840). A contemporary chronicle introduces us to a new word: the returning Svea are referred to as "some men calling themselves and their people Rus."

It is worth a digression to consider this word. The coastal district east of Uppsala in Sweden is Roslagen, and to this day its inhabitants are called Rospiggar. (The word *rus* itself means "oarsman.") The Svea kings certainly raised levies in this district, each locality traditionally furnishing a ship and crew. It is at least plausible to suggest that the trans-Baltic Viking settlements included many such complements of *rus* from Roslagen. Further weight is lent to this suggestion by the fact that the Finnish name for Sweden is Ruotsi. It is not surprising, therefore, that the oldest political entity in eastern Europe, the city of Kiev and its surrounding lands on the Dnieper, should have come to be known as Rusland and eventually as Russia.

In czarist times, and even today, some Russian scholars have challenged this derivation of "Russia." In my view the archaeological record strongly supports the Viking origin of "Rusland." As in the Gotland graves in Latvia, graves in Russia have yielded a large number of women's ornaments that show typical Svea workmanship. Nearly 100 oval Svea clasps have been unearthed, for example. I take this to be clear proof that the same Viking warrior-merchants who traveled the inland waterways also settled, with their wives, the fertile Russian countryside. Moreover, an excavation in Kiev has uncovered a chamber tomb of typical Svea design, and on the chest of the entombed man was found a Svea "Thor's hammer." It takes little imagination to reach the conclusion that the man was a worshiper of the Norse gods and in all probability a Viking colonist.

At least at first, however, the inland voyagers must have considered trade more important than colonization. Soon many of the Svea knew all the details of the journey southward from Kiev. They knew the names of the seven rapids of the Dnieper where travelers had to portage, and had chosen an island (Berezany) in the Dnieper delta as a place to stop before sailing on across the Black Sea. Soon treaties were written between the Byzantine authorities and the Svea, mainly to restrict the voyagers' freedom of action. The Vikings were not allowed to spend the winter in Byzantium. No more than 50 Vikings at a time could enter the city, and then only unarmed. Purchases of silk, a highly prized commodity, were not to exceed 50 aurei in value. The traders may not have spent long periods at the island of Berezany, but one of them found time to leave a memorial stone there. Its runic inscription reads: "Grane raised this arch for his comrade Karl."

CONTACT WITH ISLAM. The route to Byzantium down the Dnieper was only one of the inland waterways used by the Viking traders. They also reached the Volga by way of the Gulf of Finland and Lake Ladoga, and descended to the Caspian Sea, a gateway to the world of the Turks and the Arabs. It was not even necessary to go all the way to the Caspian; at a half-way point on the Volga stood the rich trading city of Bolgar. The 10th-century Arab geographer Muq-qadasi names some of the goods sold in the market there: "Sable, squirrel, ermine, corsac, martin, foxes, beaver pelts, colorful hare, goatskin, wax, arrows, birch-bark, caps, fish-lime, fish teeth, beaver-gall, amber, horny leather, honey, hazel nuts, hawks, swords, armor, acorns, Slavonic slaves, small cattle and oxen—all this from Bolgar."

Another market town, at the mouth of the Volga, was equally colorful. There, near present-day Astrakhan, a 10th-century representative of the Bagdad caliph-ate named ibn Fadlan met a Viking trading party. "I have never seen humans more nobly built," he wrote. "They are tall as palm trees, red blond, with light skins. The man wears a cape slung over one shoulder, so that one hand is free. Every man carries an axe, a dirk and a sword. Each one has a bench on which he sits with his beautiful slaves who are for sale. [To worship] a man goes up to [a wooden] pillar and throws himself down on the ground and says, 'O my god, I come from far off and bring with me so and so many women and so and so many skins of martin. . . . Grant me a purchaser who has many gold and silver coins and buys everything from me. . . .' When a man possesses 10,000 silver coins he has a [necklace] made for his wife. If he has 20,000 she gets a second neck-lace. . . . Many chains therefore hang around the neck of a Rus woman."

There is no reason to doubt the importance of slaves as articles of trade. Who the slaves were is suggested by the fact that the Svea word for such human chattels, *trälar,* was soon abandoned in favor of the word *slavar.* Evidently most of the slaves were Slavs. Yet the Vikings' slaves would not have been exclusively Slavs; one wonders how many Franks, Irish and Anglo-Saxons served as invol-untary oarsmen on the dragon ships' homeward voyages and then moved on to the slave markets of the Scandinavian peninsula. Not all the slave markets were strictly in Viking country. Recent studies have shown that three of them were on the European mainland: Haithabu on the Baltic, Magdeburg on the Elbe and Regensburg on the Danube. One Viking merchant, called "Gille the Russian" because he always wore a Russian cap, was a common sight in the slave market of Göteborg, in what is now Sweden. His specialty was Irish girls; it is recorded that he sold one of them for three times the usual price, in spite of the fact that the girl was deaf. She must have been very beautiful.

The total number of Arab silver coins so far discovered in Scandinavia is about 57,000. The way in which these coins are distributed brings out an important fact about the various Viking groups and their separate areas of operations. It is apparent that the hoards were not a normal place of storage but a temporary refuge for treasure. Probably only when the possessors of precious metal believed they were about to be raided would they hastily dig a hole and hide their treasure, always in the expectation of reclaiming it when the trouble was past. This helps to explain why Gotland, which was a favorite target of raiders, has yielded not only the two largest hoards in Scandinavia but also the largest number of Arab coins—some 40,000 in all. Doubtless the hoards remained buried when their owners were victims of the very raids that caused them to hide their wealth.

In any case, only 17,000 additional Arab coins have been recovered from the Swedish mainland and modern Denmark, and Norway has yielded a mere 400. The geography of Scandinavia explains why this is so. For the Gotlanders and the peoples of the Swedish mainland the Baltic was virtually a private lake. They usually left it only to take to the inland waterways of Russia. The Danish peoples, on the other hand, faced both the North Sea and the Baltic. When they raided, England and the coast of Germany and France were their primary targets. When they traded, it was into the Baltic. It is not surprising that much Arab coinage should have come into Danish hands. As for the peoples of what is now Norway, their harbors on the North Sea were best suited to island-hopping operations that led them by way of the Shetland and the Orkney islands to the Irish Sea and the rich prizes along both its eastern and its western shore. It is therefore not surprising that they possesed very little Arab silver.

No one of these three main Viking spheres of influence was held exclusively. Consider the example of Harald Haadraade (Hard-Ruler), who commanded the Byzantine fleet under the Empress Zoë and even fought a naval engagement (off Monopoli, near Naples, in 1042) against fellow Vikings who had entered the Mediterranean from the west. Although a dominant figure among the eastern Vikings, Harald himself was a Norwegian who had spent his boyhood in Russia and had thus gravitated toward Byzantium. When he eventually returned home to occupy the Norwegian throne, he was no less active in western affairs. It was fighting off his raid on England in 1066 that wore out the English king Harold's troops and assured the Norman Conquest. Another example is provided by the Danish Vikings who moved into the normally Norwegian preserve of Ireland in the middle of the ninth century. The Danes fought beside the Irish to repulse the next Norwegian raiders to appear. On the whole, however, the Swedish Vikings stayed in the Baltic and the East, leaving the North Sea, the Atlantic and the parts of the Mediterranean that were unclaimed by Byzantium to the Norwegians and the Danes.

THE NORWEGIAN AND DANISH VIKINGS. In describing the activities of the Norwegians and the Danes during the ninth century one can draw a legitimate distinction between the occasions when they were raiding and those in which they were colonizing. The Norwegians certainly settled the northern islands they used as stepping-stones to the Irish Sea. Once established in western waters, they founded settlements in the Hebrides and on the islands nearer the western coast of Scotland and also made the Isle of Man a base of operations. Although the Norwegians began raiding Ireland as early as 820, their intentions were more ambitious than mere piracy. By the middle of the century they had established a royal line in Dublin and held extensive Irish lands.

Nor were the Danes—who, as we shall see, were second to none as raiders—exclusively piratical. Ragnar Lodbrok (Hairy-Breeches) was clearly a man of large plans. One of the first Danish Vikings to take advantage of the civil strife that had divided Europe into three quarrelsome kingdoms after the death of Charlemagne, he gave the king of France, Charles the Bald, a bad scare in 845 by sailing a 120-ship force up the Seine and capturing Paris. Charles's army was divided by the river. Ragnar routed the French troops on one bank while their comrades-in-arms on the other bank did nothing. Whatever aggressiveness may have remained in the French ebbed away when Ragnar hanged more than 100 of his prisoners as a sacrifice to Odin. Shortly thereafter Charles the Bald sent Ragnar a gift of 7,000 pounds of silver and asked him to desist.

Yet Ragnar's three sons, with a minimum of bloodshed in 876, successfully seized and colonized the eastern part of England—a region called the Five Boroughs after the five strongholds (Lincoln, Stamford, Leicester, Derby and Nottingham) from which the Danes administered it. The district remained populous and prosperous until William the Conqueror—himself of Viking descent—found that a "harrying of the north" was necessary if his new kingdom was to be free from Scandinavian interference.

Ragnar was not the first Viking to raid mainland Europe. Four years earlier, in May of 841, a Danish force under one Asgeir sailed up the Seine toward Paris. It sacked Rouen and advanced as far as St. Denis before turning back. Two years later another Viking force with 67 ships sailed up the Loire, ravaged Nantes and sailed downstream again to pass the winter in Noirmontier at the river's mouth.

The Vikings remained active on the North Sea coast. The Frisian city of Dorestad was looted almost yearly. In 845, the same year in which Ragnar attacked Paris, another Viking force burned Hamburg. The chronicles of the unsuccessful defense of Hamburg state that the assault was mounted by 600 dragon ships. If we give each vessel a complement of 40 men, we must assume a Viking force of 24,000! It seems more likely that the Viking fleet numbered perhaps 60, rather than 600, vessels.

The year 845 also saw the customary Viking raids on Ireland and, far more significant, the dispatch of a fleet (said to number 100 ships) that sailed south past France and Spain into the Mediterranean to trade or raid along the coast of Arab North Africa. The record of this first entry into the Mediterranean by the western Vikings is obscure. More information is available on these activities four years later, in 859. In that year Ragnar's son Björn Ironsides, together with a Viking named Hastings, sailed 62 dragon ships into the Mediterranean for a raid that lasted 36 months. Using an island at the mouth of the Rhone as their base, they plundered Nîmes, Arles and Valence. Then, pushing eastward into Italy, they sacked Pisa, Fiesole and Luna (a harbor town that no longer exists). On the way home Björn's Vikings stopped at Pamplona in Spain. There they happened to find the Prince of Navarre, for whom they were given a large ransom. The Vikings counted it a successful voyage, even though they lost 40 of their ships in a storm off Gibraltar. Among other things, their peaceable visit to Morocco during the voyage resulted in the Maghreb caliphate's dispatching an ambassador to Denmark. It is reported that he did not enjoy his visit.

In the winter of 878, two years after Ragnar's three sons had established the Five Boroughs in England, other Viking raiders gathered to see what could be accomplished elsewhere in the British Isles. Fortunately for England, but unfortunately for the continent of Europe, Alfred, a young English ruler in Wessex, defeated the invading force at Ethandun. The following spring the defeated Vikings landed en masse at the mouth of the Schelde River, gradually assembled a "Great Army" that finally numbered 700 ships and 40,000 men, and proceeded to ravage the Continent for the next 13 years.

At last, having gathered all the loot it could and finding little prospect for more in a famine year, the Great Army withdrew. The Viking force then sailed for England once again, but Alfred (now known as "the Great") was more than ready for them, this time with his own fleet. By 896, in the final years of Alfred's reign, the remnants of the Great Army sailed back to the Continent, reduced to little more than a band of mercenaries.

In the opening years of the 10th century European towns were no longer regularly sacked by major Viking forces, but the Viking influence on the Continent remained considerable. Fresh Viking forces continued to leave Denmark and Norway, seeking lands to occupy. One such emigré—Rollo—eventually became leader of all western Europe's Vikings.

The king of France, Charles the Simple, saw a solution to the Viking problem. In exchange for Rollo's baptism and an oath of fealty in 911, Charles granted the Viking leader all Normandy. It was from this Viking enclave that a century and a half later emerged both the leader and the troops who conquered England and reshaped its history.

THE DRAGON SHIPS. What single element in Viking history can be deemed most responsible for these northerners' success in battle, trade and emigration? It must surely by the dragon ship. The tallies of the Viking fleets of the ninth and 10th centuries make it clear that these ships were built in large numbers, but the fact remains that only a few of the vessels uncovered by the archaeologist's spade are typical dragon ships. From the remains we have and from literary descriptions, however, it is possible to reconstruct the Vikings' seafaring warships with reasonable accuracy.

The earliest-known Scandinavian ship, uncovered on a moor near Nydan in Denmark, dates back to about A.D. 300. Built of oak planks, it had a rounded bottom and a comparatively deep draft; it had no keel or mast. There were positions for 30 oars—15 on each side—and therefore 15 oarsmen's benches. The second-known Scandinavian ship, built some 300 years later and unearthed at Kvalsund, I have already mentioned. It shows considerable evolution, being wider in beam and shallower in draft than the Nydam ship. Although it lacks a true keel, it has a deck and provision for a mast.

The finest Viking ships discovered so far are all from sites near Oslo in Norway: Gokstad and Oseberg on the western shore of Oslofjord and Tune on the eastern shore. The Gokstad ship, uncovered in 1880, is 78 feet long, has a mast and also a keel consisting of a single oak timber. Its carrying capacity is estimated at 20 tons. It has 16 rowing benches, 32 oars in all. The Norwegian notable whose grave it marks appears to be one Olaf, a king who lived from about 810 to 880.

The Oseberg ship, which was discovered in 1904, is shorter by some six feet, has one less rowing bench and a mast that gives the impression of being small and weak. This ship is the burial place of Olaf's stepmother, Queen Asa, whose husband ruled from about 780 to 820. Both the ship and its contents are decorated with carvings of remarkable beauty and intricacy. Nonetheless, the Oseberg ship appears not to have been an oceangoing craft but a coastwise one. The third vessel, found near Tune in 1867, is the least well preserved of the three. It is estimated to have been some 66 feet long and to have had 11 or 12 rowing benches. All three vessels are preserved today in a special museum at Bygdöy, outside Oslo.

How closely do these Norwegian vessels resemble the Viking dragon ships? The Gokstad ship has passed an impressive empirical test: a faithful replica of it was sailed across the Atlantic in 1893 to be exhibited at the Chicago World's Fair. Not only was the voyage successful but also the crew found they could make a speed of as much as 10 to 11 knots in a brisk wind. It is therefore possible that some dragon ships were as small as the Gokstad ship. On the basis of literary descriptions, however, it appears that most dragon ships were larger.

The ships built for royalty at the turn of the millennium, although known only through oral tradition, were apparently larger still. At the Battle of Svolder in A.D. 1000 King Olaf of Norway appeared aboard the *Ormen Lange* (*Long Snake*), which was some 164 feet long and had 34 rowing benches. The last of the royal Norwegian ships, built by the shipwrights of Trondheim in 1263, had three more rowing benches than the *Ormen Lange*. Sang a skald: "[It] shall carry thee, majestic friend, like a keen hawk on the quarterdeck. Never did more beautiful ship sail with more magnificent king."

Not all Viking vessels were dragon ships. Viking freighters, called *knarr,* were known only from literary references, however, until 1962. In that year Danish archaeologists recovered several incomplete Viking ships from Roskilde Fjord on the Danish island of Seeland. For reasons at which we can only guess, the people of Roskilde had blocked their harbor by filling several ships with stones and sinking them in the mouth of the fjord. One of them, 53 feet long, was apparently a fast cargo vessel. Another vessel is almost 65 feet long and is notable for its breadth of beam and the stoutness of its timbers. It was evidently a carrier of heavy freight. To judge by the low railing and the number of oar holes of the third ship, it may have been a fast passenger vessel. A fourth appears to be a onetime dragon ship that was converted into a freighter late in its career. The remains of the other Roskilde ships are too fragmentary to tell us much about them.

Meanwhile other ships that may belong to the Viking period have been found in northern Germany. In 1953 a volunteer diver working with the director of the Schleswig Museum located one large vessel and parts of a smaller one in the harbor of Haithabu. All of us who are particularly interested in such matters look forward to what will be learned from these remains when the funds necessary for their recovery become available.

When and why did Viking fortunes—in trade if not in war—decline? To the first of these questions Scandinavian archaeology provides a remarkably detailed answer. The silver hoards recovered in Denmark, for example, contained no coins but Arab ones until 950. The hoards of the next 30 years contain both Arab coins and a few German ones. A century later exactly the opposite is true: of some 3,000 silver coins found in hoards that were buried between 1050 and 1070 only four are Arab. Evidently Viking contacts with the Moslem world dwindled to nothing within the span of a century.

As to the question of why, it is probably pertinent to note three historical developments that fall within the same period. First, the silver mines of central Asia (on which the Moslem rulers of the East depended for their metal) seem to have become exhausted at about this time. Second, a general advance of Turkish tribes in the Middle East and Near East denied the Russian waterways to the Swedish Vikings and severed their connections with Byzantium. Finally, the European powers on the Mediterranean halted the advance of Islam during this period and soon no longer needed the hardy Viking merchant-warriors to act as middlemen.

THE VIKINGS IN NORTH AMERICA. Our knowledge of one other important series of events in Viking history—the voyages west from Iceland—has also been increased as a result of recent archaeological research. The story of Eric the Red and his son Leif is too well known to need retelling here. Less well known, perhaps, is the tradition that another Greenlander, Thorfinn Karlsefni, took three ships and 160 men and in 1020 established a colony in what they called Vinland on the coast of North America. When Thorfinn's house in Greenland was excavated in 1930, the diggers came on a lump of anthracite coal that has been identified as having originated in the vicinity of Rhode Island.

At Brattalid, in Greenland's "eastern settlement," archaeologists have uncovered Leif Ericson's homestead. In 1965 these workers came on the remains of Leif's mother's chapel, a few hundred yards from the foundation of his house. Beside the chapel are 150 graves, from which 96 skeletons have been disinterred. It seems more than likely that one of them is Leif's.

For some centuries the New World settlement established by Leif—called Leifsbodarna in the Viking sagas—had been sought, without success. During the 1950's, however, a Norwegian investigator, Helge Ingstad, began to reconnoiter the coasts of Labrador and Newfoundland with a fresh idea in mind. Could the "vin" in Vinland mean something other than "wine," as had been generally supposed? Ingstad preferred to think that it meant "grass" or "pasturage." In 1961, near the isolated fishing village of L'Anse au Meadow in northern Newfoundland, an expedition under Ingstad uncovered traces of several buildings, including the foundation of a "great hall" identical with the one Leif had built for himself in Greenland. Charcoal associated with iron and slag at the site—evidently the remains of a smithy—has yielded a carbon-14 date of A.D. 1060 ± 70, which agrees reasonably well with the dates that are given in the sagas.

Three years' work at the Newfoundland site has yielded Ingstad a number of architectural details but very few artifacts. Perhaps the most significant one is a spindle whorl—the weight that acts as a flywheel when a spindle is used to twist yarn from raw wool—made of soapstone. Soapstone spindle whorls are common at Norse sites in Greenland and Iceland, as well as in Scandinavia.

GREENLAND'S DECLINE. The Greenland colonies from which the Viking visitors to North America came numbered some 300 homesteads at their height. They were cut off from contact with Iceland and Europe sometime during the 15th century, but before that they had had a bishop, two cloisters and 16 churches. They had even sent a tithe of walrus tusks to the Vatican (the record shows that 250 tusks were received in 1327). The only vessel regularly in the Greenland trade was wrecked in 1367 and not replaced, but archaeological evidence shows that contacts continued after that date. In Greenland graves are found woolen caps, peaked in a manner that became fashionable in Burgundy during the latter half of the 15th century.

Less than a century later, in 1540, a voyaging Icelander happened to sail past one of Greenland's settled fjords. He saw people, including a man lying dead on the ground, and decided not to land. A few years later a ship out of Hamburg called at Greenland but its captain was unable to find any signs of life.

MEDIEVAL CIVILIZATIONS OF EURASIA, 500–1500

Chapter Twelve

Eurasian ecumene

EXPANDING HORIZONS OF THE MEDIEVAL WORLD **35**

The Classical Age, as noted in Reading 17, "Expanding Horizons of the Classical World," was characterized by the emergence for the first time of an incipient Eurasian ecumene. During the Medieval Age the unifying process developed a step further with the evolution of a full-fledged Eurasian ecumene. This was partly the result of continued technological advance, especially in shipbuilding and navigation, and partly of the establishment of great empires such as the Islamic and the Mongol, which spanned not merely entire regions but a large part of all Eurasia. The classic manifestation of the new ecumene is the career of the Venetian merchant Marco Polo, who entered the service of Kublai Khan and travelled back and forth across the breadth of Eurasia. The following selections from Marco Polo's great travel account make clear how spectacularly the horizons of the medieval world were opening up, thanks to the existence of the Mongol Empire and to the advances in naval technology that made possible the far-flung voyages of Chinese as well as Western navigators. Marco Polo's concluding remarks point up the upsurge of maritime activity that was bringing together to an unprecedented degree the various parts of the Eurasian landmass.*

Great Princes, Emperors, and Kings, Dukes and Marquises, Counts, Knights, and Burgesses! and People of all degrees who desire to get knowledge of the various races of mankind and of the diversities of the sundry regions of the World, take this Book and cause it to be read to you. For ye shall find therein all kinds of

---

* Sir Henry Yule, ed. and trans., *The Book of Ser Marco Polo*, 3rd ed. (New York: Charles Scribner's Sons, 1903), I, 1, 2, 27, 30, 31, 374, 375, 423-26, II, 249-50, 253-54, 272, 331, 338, 341, 343, 411, 500.

wonderful things, and the divers histories of the Great Hermenia, and of Persia, and of the Land of the Tartars, and of India, and of many another country of which our Book doth speak, particularly and in regular succession, according to the description of Messer Marco Polo, a wise and noble citizen of Venice, as he saw them with his own eyes. Some things indeed there be therein which he beheld not; but these he heard from men of credit and veracity. And we shall set down things seen as seen, and things heard as heard only, so that no jot of falsehood may mar the truth of our Book, and that all who shall read it or hear it read may put full faith in the truth of all its contents.

For let me tell you that since our Lord God did mould with his hands our first Father Adam, even until this day, never hath there been Christian, or Pagan, or Tartar, or Indian, or any man of any nation, who in his own person hath had so much knowledge and experience of the divers parts of the World and its Wonders as hath had this Messer Marco!

. . . . .

Now it came to pass that Marco, the son of Messer Nicolo, sped wondrously in learning the customs of the Tartars, as well as their language, their manner of writing, and their practice of war; in fact he came in brief space to know several languages, and four sundry written characters. And he was discreet and prudent in every way, insomuch that the Emperor held him in great esteem. And so when he discerned Mark to have so much sense, and to conduct himself so well and beseemingly, he sent him on an ambassage of his, to a country which was a good six months' journey distant. The young gallant executed his commission well and with discretion.

. . . . .

When Mark returned from his ambassage he presented himself before the Emperor, and after making his report of the business with which he was charged, and its successful accomplishment, he went on to give an account in a pleasant and intelligent manner of all the novelties and strange things that he had seen and heard; . . .

Thereafter Messer Marco abode in the Kaan's employment some seventeen years, continually going and coming, hither and thither, on the missions that were entrusted to him by the Lord [and sometimes, with the permission and authority of the Great Kaan, on his own private affairs.] . . . And thus it came about that Messer Marco Polo had knowledge of, or had actually visited, a greater number of the different countries of the World than any other man; the more that he was always giving his mind to get knowledge, and to spy out and enquire into everything in order to have matter to relate to the Lord.

. . . . .

Now there was on that spot in old times a great and noble city called Cambaluc, which is as much as to say in our tongue "The city of the Emperor." But the Great Kaan was informed by his Astrologers that this city would prove rebellious, and raise great disorders against his imperial authority. So he caused the present city to be built close beside the old one, with only a river between them. And he caused the people of the old city to be removed to the new town that he had founded; and this is called Taidu. [However, he allowed a portion of the people which he did not suspect to remain in the old city, because the new one could not hold the whole of them, big as it is.]

As regards the size of this (new) city you must know that it has a compass of

24 miles, for each side of it hath a length of 6 miles, and it is four-square. And it is all walled round with walls of earth which have a thickness of full ten paces at bottom, and a height of more than 10 paces; but they are not so thick at top, for they diminish in thickness as they rise, so that at top they are only about 3 paces thick. And they are provided throughout with loop-holed battlements, which are all whitewashed.

There are 12 gates, and over each gate there is a great and handsome palace, so that there are on each side of the square three gates and five palaces; for (I ought to mention) there is at each angle also a great and handsome palace. In those palaces are vast halls in which are kept the arms of the city garrison.

The streets are so straight and wide that you can see right along them from end to end and from one gate to the other. And up and down the city there are beautiful palaces, and many great and fine hostelries, and fine houses in great numbers. [All the plots of ground on which the houses of the city are built are four-square, and laid out with straight lines; all the plots being occupied by great and spacious palaces, with courts and gardens of proportionate size. All these plots were assigned to different heads of families. Each square plot is encompassed by handsome streets for traffic; and thus the whole city is arranged in squares just like a chess-board, and disposed in a manner so perfect and masterly that it is impossible to give a description that should do it justice.]

. . . . . .

Now that I have told you in detail of the splendour of this City of the Emperor's, I shall proceed to tell you of the Mint which he hath in the same city. . . .

. . . and the way it is wrought is such that you might say he hath the Secret of Alchemy in perfection, and you would be right! For he makes his money after this fashion.

He makes them take of the bark of a certain tree, in fact of the Mulberry Tree, the leaves of which are the food of the silkworms,—these trees being so numerous that whole districts are full of them. What they take is a certain fine white bast or skin which lies between the wood of the tree and the thick outer bark, and this they make into something resembling sheets of paper, but black. . . .

With these pieces of paper, made as I have described, he causes all payments on his own account to be made; and he makes them to pass current universally over all his kingdoms and provinces and territories, and whithersoever his power and sovereignty extends. And nobody, however important he may think himself, dares to refuse them on pain of death. . . .

Furthermore all merchants arriving from India or other countries, and bringing with them gold or silver or gems and pearls, are prohibited from selling to any one but the Emperor. . . .

When any of those pieces of paper are spoilt—not that they are so very flimsy neither—the owner carries them to the Mint, and by paying three per cent. on the value he gets new pieces in exchange. . . .

Now you have heard the ways and means whereby the Great Kaan may have, and in fact *has,* more treasure than all the Kings in the World; and you know all about it and the reason why.

. . . . . .

Having finished our discourse concerning those countries wherewith our Book hath been occupied thus far, we are now about to enter on the subject of India, and to tell you of all the wonders thereof.

And first let us speak of the [Chinese] ships in which merchants go to and fro amongst the Isles of India.

These ships, you must know, are of fir timber. They have but one deck, though each of them contains some 50 or 60 cabins, wherein the merchants abide greatly at their ease, every man having one to himself. The ship hath but one rudder, but it hath four masts; and sometimes they have two additional masts, which they ship and unship at pleasure.

. . . . .

The fastenings are all of good iron nails and the sides are double, one plank laid over the other, and caulked outside and in. The planks are not pitched, for those people do not have any pitch, but they daub the sides with another matter, deemed by them far better than pitch; it is this. You see they take some lime and some chopped hemp, and these they knead together with a certain wood-oil; and when the three are thoroughly amalgamated, they hold like any glue. And with this mixture they do paint their ships.

Each of their great ships requires at least 200 mariners [some of them 300]. They are indeed of great size, for one ship shall carry 5000 or 6000 baskets of pepper [and they used formerly to be larger than they are now].

. . . . .

Chipangu [Japan] is an Island towards the east in the high seas, 1500 miles distant from the Continent; and a very great Island it is.

The people are white, civilized, and well-favoured. They are Idolaters, and are dependent on nobody. And I can tell you the quantity of gold they have is endless; for they find it in their own Islands, [and the King does not allow it to be exported. Moreover] few merchants visit the country because it is so far from the main land, and thus it comes to pass that their gold is abundant beyond all measure.

I will tell you a wonderful thing about the Palace of the Lord of that Island. You must know that he hath a great Palace which is entirely roofed with fine gold, just as our churches are roofed with lead, insomuch that it would scarcely be possible to estimate its value. Moreover, all the pavement of the Palace, and the floors of its chambers, are entirely of gold, in plates like slabs of stone, a good two fingers thick; and the windows also are of gold, so that altogether the richness of this Palace is past all bounds and all belief.

. . . . .

When you sail from Chamba [Indochina], 1500 miles in a course between south and south-east, you come to a great Island called Java. And the experienced mariners of those Islands who know the matter well, say that it is the greatest Island in the world, and has a compass of more than 3000 miles. It is subject to a great King and tributary to no one else in the world. The people are Idolaters. The Island is of surpassing wealth, producing black pepper, nutmegs, spikenard, galingale, cubebs, cloves, and all other kinds of spices.

This Island is also frequented by a vast amount of shipping, and by merchants who buy and sell costly goods from which they reap great profit. Indeed the treasure of this Island is so great as to be past telling.

. . . . .

When you leave the Island of Seilan [Ceylon] and sail westward about 60 miles, you come to the great province of Maabar which is styled India the Greater; it is best of all the Indies and is on the mainland.

. . . . .

You must know that in all this Province of Maabar there is never a Tailor to cut a coat or stitch it, seeing that everybody goes naked! For decency only do they wear a scrap of cloth; and so 'tis with men and women, with rich and poor, . . .

. . . . . .

The people are Idolaters, and many of them worship the ox, because (say they) it is a creature of such excellence. They would not eat beef for anything in the world, nor would they on any account kill an ox.

. . . . .

You must know that the heat here is sometimes so great that 'tis something wonderful. And rain falls only for three months in the year, viz. in June, July, and August. Indeed but for the rain that falls in these three months, refreshing the earth and cooling the air, the drought would be so great that no one could exist.

. . . . .

Madeigascar is an Island towards the south, about a thousand miles from Scotra. The people are all Saracens, adoring Mahommet. They have four *Esheks*, *i.e.* four Elders, who are said to govern the whole Island. And you must know that it is a most noble and beautiful Island, and one of the greatest in the world, for it is about 4000 miles in compass. The people live by trade and handicrafts.

In this Island, and in another beyond it called Zanghibar, about which we shall tell you afterwards, there are more elephants than in any country in the world. The amount of traffic in elephants' teeth in these two Islands is something astonishing.

In this Island they eat no flesh but that of camels; and of these they kill an incredible number daily. They say it is the best and wholesomest of all flesh; and so they eat of it all the year round.

. . . . . .

And now ye have heard all that we can tell you about the Tartars and the Saracens and their customs, and likewise about the other countries of the world as far as our researches and information extend. Only we have said nothing whatever about the Greater Sea and the provinces that lie round it, although we know it thoroughly. But it seems to me a needless and useless task to speak about places which are visited by people every day. For there are so many who sail all about that sea constantly, Venetians, and Genoese, and Pisans, and many others, that everybody knows all about it, and that is the reason that I pass it over and say nothing of it.

Chapter Thirteen

36   THE KORAN

The Koran, or "recitation," is the Sacred Book of Islam, regarded by Moslems as the word of Allah. Its 114 suras, or chapters, were revealed to Mohammed and written down after his death by his followers. Except for the opening prayer, the chapters were arranged in order of length, with the longest first, so that many of Mohammed's earliest statements appear towards the end of the book. Consequently it cannot be read with any expectation of logical exposition, though it is universally agreed that it is written with utmost elegance and purity of style in the original Arabic. The following passages from the Koran elucidate some of its more basic doctrines.*

The Koran

Chapter II., Verse 1. In the name of the Merciful and Compassionate God.
That is the Book! there is no doubt therein; a guide to the pious, who believe in the unseen, and are steadfast in prayer, and of what we have given them expend in alms; who believe in what is revealed to thee, and what was revealed before thee, and of the hereafter they are sure. These are in guidance from their Lord, and these are the prosperous.
Chapter VI., Verse 109. They swore by God with their most strenuous oath, that if there come to them a sign they will indeed believe therein. Say, "Signs are only in God's hands: but what will make you understand that, even when one has come, they will not believe?"
Chapter XLI., Verse 1. In the name of the Merciful and Compassionate God.

* Arthur N. Wollaston, *The Religion of the Koran* (London: John Murray Publishers Ltd., 1908), pp. 27-68, excerpts.

A revelation from the Merciful, the Compassionate; a book whose signs are detailed; an Arabic Koran for a people who do know; a herald of glad tidings and a warning.

Unity of God

Chapter II., Verse 256.   God, there is no god but He, the living, the self-subsistent. Slumber takes Him not, nor sleep. His is what is in the heavens and what is in the earth. Who is it that intercedes with Him save by His permission? He knows what is before them and what behind them, and they comprehend not aught of His knowledge but of what He pleases. His throne extends over the heavens and the earth, and it tires Him not to guard them both, for He is high and grand.

Chapter XIII., Verse 15.   On Him is the call of truth, and those who call on others than Him shall not be answered at all, save as one who stretches out his hand to the water that it may reach his mouth, but it reaches it not! The call of the misbelievers is only in error. . . .

Say, "Who is Lord of the heavens and the earth?" Say "God." Say, "Do ye take beside God patrons who cannot control profit or harm for themselves?" Say, "Shall the blind and the seeing be held equal? or shall the darkness and the light be held equal? or have they made associates with God who can create as He creates, so that the creation seem familiar to them?" Say, "God is the creator of everything, and He is the one, the dominant."

Chapter CXII., Verse 1.   In the name of the Merciful and Compassionate God.
Say, "He is God alone!
"God the Eternal!
"He begets not and is not begotten!
"Nor is there like unto Him any one!"

Muhammad the Apostle of God

Chapter III., Verse 136.   Muhammad is but an apostle; apostles have passed away before his time; what if he die or is killed, will ye retreat upon your heels? He who retreats upon his heels does no harm to God at all; but God will recompense the thankful. It is not for any soul to die, save by God's permission written down for an appointed time; but he who wishes for the reward of this world we will give him of it, and he who wishes for the reward of the future we will give him of it, and we will recompense the grateful.

Chapter IV., Verse 164.   But God bears witness to what He has revealed to thee; He revealed it in His knowledge, and the angels bear witness too, though God is witness enough.

(165).   Verily, those who misbelieve and obstruct the way of God, have erred a wide error.

Verily, those who misbelieve and are unjust, God will not pardon them, nor will He guide them on the road—save the road to Hell, to dwell therein for aye; that is easy enough to God! . . .

Chapter XXXIII., Verse 40.   Muhammad is not the father of any of your men, but the Apostle of God, and the Seal of the Prophets; for God all things doth know!

Resurrection

Chapter III., Verse 182. Every soul must taste of death; and ye shall only be paid your hire upon the resurrection day.

Chapter IV., Verse 89. God, there is no God but He! He will surely assemble you on the resurrection day, there is no doubt therein; who is truer than God in His discourse?

Chapter XI., Verse 19. Whosoever shall wish for the life of this world and its ornaments, we will pay them their works therein, and they shall not be cheated. These are those for whom there is nothing in the hereafter save the Fire; and void is what they made therein, and vain what they were doing!

Chapter XVII., Verse 52. They say, "What! when we have become bones and rubbish are we to be raised up a new creature?" Say, "Be ye stones or iron, or a creature, the greatest your breasts can conceive!" Then they shall say, "Who is to restore us?" Say, "He who originated you at first;" and they will wag their heads and say, "When will that be?" Say, "It may perhaps be nigh."

Chapter LXXV., Verse 35. Is not He able to quicken the dead?

Hell

Chapter IV., Verse 18. But whoso rebels against God and His Apostle, and transgresses His bounds, He will make him enter into fire, and dwell therein for aye; and for him is shameful woe.

Chapter IX., Verse 69. God has promised unto the hypocrites, men and women, and unto the misbelievers, hell-fire, to dwell therein for aye; it is enough for them! God shall curse them, and theirs shall be enduring woe.

Chapter LXXVIII., Verse 24. Verily, Hell is an ambuscade, a reward for the outrageous, to tarry therein for ages. They shall not taste therein cool nor drink, (25) but only boiling water and pus—a fit reward!

Paradise

Chapter III., Verse 14. Say, "But shall we tell you of a better thing than this?" For those who fear are gardens with their Lord, beneath which rivers flow; they shall dwell therein for aye, and pure wives and grace from God.

Chapter IV., Verse 123. But he who doeth good works—be it male or female— and believes, they shall enter into Paradise, and they shall not be wronged a jot.

Chapter XVIII., Verse 30. These, for them are gardens of Eden; beneath them rivers flow; they shall be adorned therein with bracelets of gold, and shall wear green robes of silk, and of brocade; reclining therein on thrones; pleasant is the reward, and goodly the couch!

Chapter XXXVI., Verse 55. Verily, the Fellows of Paradise upon that day shall be employed in enjoyment; they and their wives, in shade upon thrones, reclining; therein shall they have fruits, and they shall have what they may call for. . . .

Chapter LXXVIII., Verse 31. Verily, for the pious is a blissful place—gardens and vineyards, and girls with swelling breasts of the same age as themselves, and a brimming cup; (35) they shall hear therein no folly and no lie—a reward from thy Lord, a sufficient gift!

Predestination

Chapter VII., Verse 33. Every nation has its appointed time, and when their appointed time comes they cannot keep it back an hour, nor can they bring it on.

Chapter XVI., Verse 63. If God were to punish men for their wrongdoing, He would not leave upon the earth a single beast, but He respites them until a stated time; and when their time comes they cannot put it off an hour, nor can they bring it on.

Chapter LXII., Verse 8. Say, "Verily, the death from which ye flee will surely meet you, then shall ye be sent back to Him who knows the unseen and the visible, and He will inform you of that which ye have done!"

Almsgiving

Chapter II., Verse 211. They will ask thee what they are to expend in alms: say, "Whatsoever good ye expend it should be for parents and kinsmen, and the orphan and the poor, and the son of the road; and whatsoever good ye do, verily, of it God knows!"

. . . Verse 263. The likeness of those who expend their wealth in God's way is as the likeness of a grain that grows to seven ears, in every ear a hundred grains; for God will double unto whom he pleases; for God both embraces and knows.

(265). Kind speech and pardon are better than almsgiving, followed by annoyance, and God is rich and clement.

Chapter LXIV., Verse 16. Then fear God as much as ye can! and hear, and obey, and expend in alms, it is better for yourselves. But whosoever is saved from his own covetousness—these are the prosperous!

If ye lend to God a goodly loan, He will double it for you, and will forgive you; for God is grateful, clement!

He knows the unseen and the visible; the mighty, the wise!

Wine, Gaming, Foods and Usury, Infanticide, Ill-Treatment of Orphans

Chapter II., Verse 216. They will ask thee about wine and games of chance; say, "In them both is sin and profit to men; but the sin of both is greater than the profit of the same."

Chapter V., Verse 92. O ye who believe! verily, wine, and games of chance, and statues, and divining (arrows) are only an abomination of Satan's work; avoid them then that haply ye may prosper. Satan only desires to place enmity and hatred between you by wine and games of chance, and to turn you from the remembrance of God and from prayer; but will ye not desist, and obey God, and obey the Apostles, and beware, for if ye turn back, then know that our Apostle has only his message to preach.

Chapter V., Verse 4. Forbidden to you is that which dies of itself, and blood, and the flesh of swine, and that which is devoted to other than God, and the strangled, and the knocked down, and that which falls down, and the gored, and what wild beasts have eaten—except what ye slaughter in time—and what is sacrificed to idols and dividing carcases by arrows.

Chapter II., Verse 276. Those who devour usury shall not rise again, save as he riseth whom Satan hath paralysed with a touch; and that is because they say, "Selling is only like usury," but God has made selling lawful and usury unlawful; and he to whom the admonition from his Lord has come, if he desists, what has gone before is his; his matter is in God's hands. But whosoever returns (to usury) these are the Fellows of the Fire, and they shall dwell therein for aye. God shall blot out our usury, but shall make almsgiving profitable, for God loves not any sinful misbeliever.

Chapter VI., Verse 142. Losers are they who kill their children foolishly, without knowledge, and who prohibit what God has bestowed upon them, forging a lie against God, they have erred and are not guided.

Chapter XVII., Verse 33. And slay not your children for fear of poverty; we will provide for them; beware! for to slay them is ever a great sin!

Chapter IV., Verse 10. Verily, those who devour the property of orphans unjustly, only devour into their bellies fire, and they shall broil in flames.

Chapter VI., Verse 153. And draw not nigh unto the wealth of the orphan, save so as to better it, until he reaches full age, and give weight and measure with justice.

37   Moslems and Crusaders

Following Mohammed's death in A.D. 632, Islam expanded rapidly over North Africa and the Middle East, so that within little more than a century its sway extended from Morocco and the Pyrenees to India and Central Asia. By the eleventh century the West had become sufficiently strong to counterattack in a series of campaigns known as the Crusades. For two hundred years Christianity and Islam were engaged in the Holy Land in warfare interspersed with precarious truces. This was a clash of cultures as well as of religions, each side regarding the other as outlandish and uncivilized. This is apparent in the memoirs of Usāmah, Arab warrior, gentleman, and man of letters. Born in Syria in 1095, he was brought up in the tradition of Syrian chivalry, fighting constantly against the Crusaders. In his old age he wrote numerous books, the most outstanding being his memoirs. In addition to rich detail on methods of warfare and on the day to day battles, the reminiscences reflect the Moslem reaction to the Western intruders and their culture. The following selections deal with Western medical practice, sexual customs, and judicial procedures as seen through Moslem eyes.*

The lord of al-Munaytirah wrote to my uncle asking him to dispatch a physician to treat certain sick persons among his people. My uncle sent him a Christian physician named Thābit. Thābit was absent but ten days when he returned. So we said to him, "How quickly hast thou healed thy patients!" He said:

> They brought before me a knight in whose leg an abscess had grown; and a woman afflicted with imbecility. To the knight I applied a small poultice

---

* Philip K. Hitti, trans., *An Arab-Syrian Gentleman and Warrior in the Period of the Crusades: Memoirs of Usāmah ibn-Munqidh* (Beirut: Khayats, 1964), pp. 162-63, 164-66, 167-69.

until the abscess opened and became well; and the woman I put on diet and made her humor wet. Then a Frankish physician came to them and said, "This man knows nothing about treating them." He then said to the knight, "Which wouldst thou prefer, living with one leg or dying with two?" The latter replied, "Living with one leg." The physician said, "Bring me a strong knight and a sharp ax." A knight came with the ax. And I was standing by. Then the physician laid the leg of the patient on a block of wood and bade the knight strike his leg with the ax and chop it off at one blow. Accordingly he struck it—while I was looking on—one blow, but the leg was not severed. He dealt another blow, upon which the marrow of the leg flowed out and the patient died on the spot. He then examined the woman and said, "This is a woman in whose head there is a devil which has possessed her. Shave off her hair." Accordingly they shaved it off and the woman began once more to eat their ordinary diet—garlic and mustard. Her imbecility took a turn for the worse. The physician then said, "The devil has penetrated through her head." He therefore took a razor, made a deep cruciform incision on it, peeled off the skin at the middle of the incision until the bone of the skull was exposed and rubbed it with salt. The woman also expired instantly. Thereupon I asked them whether my services were needed any longer, and when they replied in the negative I returned home, having learned of their medicine what I knew not before.

I have, however, witnessed a case of their medicine which was quite different from that.

The king of the Franks had for treasurer a knight named Bernard [barnād], who (may Allah's curse be upon him!) was one of the most accursed and wicked among the Franks. A horse kicked him in the leg, which was subsequently infected and which opened in fourteen different places. Every time one of these cuts would close in one place, another would open in another place. All this happened while I was praying for his perdition. Then came to him a Frankish physician and removed from the leg all the ointments which were on it and began to wash it with very strong vinegar. By this treatment all the cuts were healed and the man became well again. He was up again like a devil.

Another case illustrating their curious medicine is the following:

In Shayzar we had an artisan named abu-al-Fath, who had a boy whose neck was afflicted with scrofula. Every time a part of it would close, another part would open. This man happened to go to Antioch on business of his, accompanied by his son. A Frank noticed the boy and asked his father about him. Abu-al-Fath replied, "This is my son." The Frank said to him, "Wilt thou swear by thy religion that if I prescribe to thee a medicine which will cure thy boy, thou wilt charge nobody fees for prescribing it thyself? In that case, I shall prescribe to thee a medicine which will cure the boy." The man took the oath and the Frank said:

Take uncrushed leaves of glasswort, burn them, then soak the ashes in olive oil and sharp vinegar. Treat the scrofula with them until the spot on which it is growing is eaten up. Then take burnt lead, soak it in ghee butter [samn] and treat him with it. That will cure him.

The father treated the boy accordingly, and the boy was cured. The sores closed and the boy returned to his normal condition of health.

I have myself treated with this medicine many who were afflicted with such disease, and the treatment was successful in removing the cause of the complaint.

. . . . .

Franks lack jealousy in sex affairs. The Franks are void of all zeal and jealousy. One of them may be walking along with his wife. He meets another man who takes the wife by the hand and steps aside to converse with her while the husband is standing on one side waiting for his wife to conclude the conversation. If she lingers too long for him, he leaves her alone with the conversant and goes away.

Here is an illustration which I myself witnessed:

When I used to visit Nāblus, I always took lodging with a man named Muʻizz, whose home was a lodging house for the Moslems. The house had windows which opened to the road, and there stood opposite to it on the other side of the road a house belonging to a Frank who sold wine for the merchants. He would take some wine in a bottle and go around announcing it by shouting, "So and so, the merchant, has just opened a cask full of this wine. He who wants to buy some of it will find it in such and such a place." The Frank's pay for the announcement made would be the wine in that bottle. One day this Frank went home and found a man with his wife in the same bed. He asked him, "What could have made thee enter into my wife's room?" The man replied, "I was tired, so I went in to rest." "But how," asked he, "didst thou get into my bed?" The other replied, "I found a bed that was spread, so I slept in it." "But," said he, "my wife was sleeping together with thee!" The other replied, "Well, the bed is hers. How could I therefore have prevented her from using her own bed?" "By the truth of my religion," said the husband, "if thou shouldst do it again, thou and I would have a quarrel." Such was for the Frank the entire expression of his disapproval and the limit of his jealousy.

Another illustration:

We had with us a bath-keeper named Sālim, originally an inhabitant of al-Maʻarrah, who had charge of the bath of my father (may Allah's mercy rest upon his soul!). This man related the following story:

I once opened a bath in al-Maʻarrah in order to earn my living. To this bath there came a Frankish knight. The Franks disapprove of girding a cover around one's waist while in the bath. So this Frank stretched out his arm and pulled off my cover from my waist and threw it away. He looked and saw that I had recently shaved off my pubes. So he shouted, "Sālim!" As I drew near him he stretched his hand over my pubes and said, "Sālim, good! By the truth of my religion, do the same for me." Saying this, he lay on his back and I found that in that place the hair was like his beard. So I shaved it off. Then he passed his hand over the place and, finding it smooth, he said, "Sālim, by the truth of my religion, do the same to madame [al-dāma]" (al-dāma in their language means the lady), referring to his wife. He then said to a servant of his, "Tell madame to come here." Accordingly the servant went and brought her and made her enter the bath. She also lay on her back. The knight repeated, "Do what thou hast done to me." So I shaved all that hair while her husband was sitting looking at me. At last he thanked me and handed me the pay for my service.

Consider now this great contradiction! They have neither jealousy nor zeal but they have great courage, although courage is nothing but the product of zeal and of ambition to be above ill repute.

216

····

Their judicial trials: A duel. I attended one day a duel in Nāblus between two Franks. The reason for this was that certain Moslem thieves took by surprise one of the villages of Nāblus. One of the peasants of that village was charged with having acted as guide for the thieves when they fell upon the village. So he fled away. The king sent and arrested his children. The peasant thereupon came back to the king and said, "Let justice be done in my case. I challenge to a duel the man who claimed that I guided the thieves to the village." The king then said to the tenant who held the village in fief, "Bring forth someone to fight the duel with him." The tenant went to his village, where a blacksmith lived, took hold of him and ordered him to fight the duel. The tenant became thus sure of the safety of his own peasants, none of whom would be killed and his estate ruined.

I saw this blacksmith. He was a physically strong young man, but his heart failed him. He would walk a few steps and then sit down and ask for a drink. The one who had made the challenge was an old man, but he was strong in spirit and he would rub the nail of his thumb against that of the forefinger in defiance, as if he was not worrying over the duel. Then came the viscount [*al-biskund*], i.e., the seignior of the town, and gave each one of the two contestants a cudgel and a shield and arranged the people in a circle around them.

The two met. The old man would press the blacksmith backward until he would get him as far as the circle, then he would come back to the middle of the arena. They went on exchanging blows until they looked like pillars smeared with blood. The contest was prolonged and the viscount began to urge them to hurry, saying, "Hurry on." The fact that the smith was given to the use of the hammer proved now of great advantage to him. The old man was worn out and the smith gave him a blow which made him fall. His cudgel fell under his back. The smith knelt down over him and tried to stick his fingers into the eyes of his adversary, but could not do it because of the great quantity of blood flowing out. Then he rose up and hit his head with the cudgel until he killed him. They then fastened a rope around the neck of the dead person, dragged him away and hanged him. The lord who brought the smith now came, gave the smith his own mantle, made him mount the horse behind him and rode off with him. This case illustrates the kind of jurisprudence and legal decisions the Franks have—may Allah's curse be upon them!

Ordeal by water. I once went in the company of al-Amīr Mu'īn-al-Dīn (may Allah's mercy rest upon his soul!) to Jerusalem. We stopped at Nāblus. There a blind man, a Moslem, who was still young and was well dressed, presented himself before al-amīr carrying fruits for him and asked permission to be admitted into his service in Damascus. The amīr consented. I inquired about this man and was informed that his mother had been married to a Frank whom she had killed. Her son used to practice ruses against the Frankish pilgrims and coöperate with his mother in assassinating them. They finally brought charges against him and tried his case according to the Frankish way of procedure.

They installed a huge cask and filled it with water. Across it they set a board of wood. They then bound the arms of the man charged with the act, tied a rope around his shoulders and dropped him into the cask, their idea being that in case he was innocent, he would sink in the water and they would then lift him up with the rope so that he might not die in the water; and in case he was guilty, he would not sink in the water. This man did his best to sink when they dropped him into the water, but he could not do it. So he had to submit to their sentence against him— may Allah's curse be upon them! They pierced his eyeballs with red-hot awls.

38

AVICENNA

The far-flung conquests of the Arabs brought them under the influence of Greek thought, particularly the science and philosophy of Aristotle. This is evident in the case of one of the greatest and most original thinkers of Islam, Abu Ali al-Husain ibn Abd Allah, called Ibn Sina, and known to the West as Avicenna. Born in Bukhara in A.D. *980, he describes in his* Autobiography *how he early mastered all fields of knowledge, and especially the writings of Aristotle. His essay* On the Nature of God, *in which he sought to demonstrate the existence of God, reflected Aristotle's influence in its emphasis on reason, while at the same time it accepted the authority and prophetic inspiration of Mohammed.**

Autobiography

My father was a man of Balkh, and he moved from there to Bukhara during the days of Nūh ibn Mansūr; in his reign he was employed in the administration, being governor of a village-centre in the outlying district of Bukhara called Kharmaithan. Near by is a village named Afshana, and there my father married my mother and took up his residence; I was also born there, and after me my brother. Later we moved to Bukhara, where I was put under teachers of the Koran and of letters. By the time I was ten I had mastered the Koran and a great deal of literature, so that I was marvelled at for my aptitude.

Now my father was one of those who had responded to the Egyptian propagandist (who was an Ismaili); he, and my brother too, had listened to what they had to say about the Spirit and the Intellect, after the fashion in which they preach and understand the matter. They would therefore discuss these things together, while I listened and comprehended all that they said; but my spirit would not assent to their argument. Presently they began to invite me to join the movement, rolling on their tongues talk about philosophy, geometry, Indian arithmetic; and my father sent me to a certain vegetable-seller who used the Indian arithmetic, so that I might learn it from him. Then there came to Bukhara a man called Abū 'Abd Allāh al-Nātilī who claimed to be a philosopher; my father invited him to stay in our house, hoping that I would learn from him also. Before his advent I had already occupied myself with Muslim jurisprudence, attending Ismā'īl the Ascetic; so I was an excellent enquirer, having become familiar with the methods of postulation and the techniques of rebuttal according to the usages of the canon lawyers. I now commenced reading the *Isagoge* (of Porphyry) with al-Nātilī: when he mentioned to me the definition of *genus* as a term applied to a number of things of different species in answer to the question "What is it?" I set about verifying this definition in a manner such as he had never heard. He marvelled at me exceedingly, and warned my father that I should not engage in any other occupation but learning; whatever problem he stated to me, I showed a better mental conception of it than he. So I continued until I had read all the straightforward parts of Logic with him; as for the subtler points, he had no acquaintance with them.

From then onward I took to reading texts by myself; I studied the commentaries, until I had completely mastered the science of Logic. Similarly with Euclid I read

* A. J. Arberry, trans., *Avicenna on Theology,* Wisdom of the East Series (London: John Murray Publishers Ltd., 1951), pp. 9-13, 25-37.

the first five or six figures with him, and thereafter undertook on my own account to solve the entire remainder of the book. Next I moved on to the *Almagest* (of Ptolemy); when I had finished the prolegomena and reached the geometrical figures, al-Nātilī told me to go on reading and to solve the problems by myself; I should merely revise what I read with him, so that he might indicate to me what was right and what was wrong. The truth is that he did not really teach this book; I began to solve the work, and many were the complicated figures of which he had no knowledge until I presented them to him, and made him understand them. Then al-Nātilī took leave of me, setting out for Gurganj.

I now occupied myself with mastering the various texts and commentaries on natural science and metaphysics, until all the gates of knowledge were open to me. Next I desired to study medicine, and proceeded to read all the books that have been written on this subject. Medicine is not a difficult science, and naturally I excelled in it in a very short time, so that qualified physicians began to read medicine with me. I also undertook to treat the sick, and methods of treatment derived from practical experience revealed themselves to me such as baffle description. At the same time I continued between whiles to study and dispute on law, being now sixteen years of age.

The next eighteen months I devoted entirely to reading; I studied Logic once again, and all the parts of philosophy. During all this time I did not sleep one night through, nor devoted my attention to any other matter by day. I prepared a set of files; with each proof I examined, I set down the syllogistic premises and put them in order in the files, then I examined what deductions might be drawn from them. I observed methodically the conditions of the premises, and proceeded until the truth of each particular problem was confirmed for me. Whenever I found myself perplexed by a problem, or could not find the middle term in any syllogism, I would repair to the mosque and pray, adoring the All-Creator, until my puzzle was resolved and my difficulty made easy. At night I would return home, set the lamp before me, and busy myself with reading and writing; whenever sleep overcame me or I was conscious of some weakness, I turned aside to drink a glass of wine until my strength returned to me; then I went back to my reading. If ever the least slumber overtook me, I would dream of the precise problem which I was considering as I fell asleep; in that way many problems revealed themselves to me while sleeping. So I continued until I had made myself master of all the sciences; I now comprehended them to the limits of human possibility. All that I learned during that time is exactly as I know it now; I have added nothing more to my knowledge to this day.

I was now a master of Logic, natural sciences and mathematics. I therefore returned to metaphysics; I read the *Metaphysica* (of Aristotle), but did not understand its contents and was baffled by the author's intention; I read it over forty times, until I had the text by heart. Even then I did not understand it or what the author meant, and I despaired within myself, saying, "This is a book which there is no way of understanding." But one day at noon I chanced to be in the booksellers' quarter, and a broker was there with a volume in his hand which he was calling for sale. He offered it to me, but I returned it to him impatiently, believing that there was no use in this particular science. However he said to me, "Buy this book from me: it is cheap, and I will sell it to you for four dirhams. The owner is in need of the money." So I bought it, and found that it was a book by Abū Nasr al-Fārābī *On the Objects of the Metaphysica*. I returned home and hastened to read it; and at once the objects of that book became clear to me, for I had it all by heart. I rejoiced at this, and upon the next day distributed much in alms to the poor in gratitude to Almighty God.

Now the Sultan of Bukhara at that time was Nūh ibn Mansūr, and it happened that he fell sick of a malady which baffled all the physicians. My name was famous among them because of the breadth of my reading; they therefore mentioned me in his presence, and begged him to summon me. I attended the sick-room, and collaborated with them in treating the royal patient. So I came to be enrolled in his service. One day I asked his leave to enter their library, to examine the contents and read the books on medicine; he granted my request, and I entered a mansion with many chambers, each chamber having chests of books piled one upon another. In one apartment were books on language and poetry, in another law, and so on; each apartment was set aside for books on a single science. I glanced through the catalogue of the works of the ancient Greeks, and asked for those which I required; and I saw books whose very names are as yet unknown to many—works which I had never seen before and have not seen since. I read these books, taking notes of their contents; I came to realize the place each man occupied in his particular science.

So by the time I reached my eighteenth year I had exhausted all these sciences. My memory for learning was at that period of my life better than it is now, but to-day I am more mature; apart from this my knowledge is exactly the same, nothing further having been added to my store since then.

On the Nature of God

THAT THERE IS A NECESSARY BEING. Whatever has being must either have a reason for its being, or have no reason for it. If it has a reason, then it is contingent, equally before it comes into being (if we make this mental hypothesis) and when it is in the state of being—for in the case of a thing whose being is contingent the mere fact of its entering upon being does not remove from it the contingent nature of its being. If on the other hand it has no reason for its being in any way whatsoever, then it is necessary in its being. This rule having been confirmed, I shall now proceed to prove that there is in being a being which has no reason for its being.

Such a being is either contingent or necessary. If it is necessary, then the point we sought to prove is established. If on the other hand it is contingent, that which is contingent cannot enter upon being except for some reason which sways the scales in favour of its being and against its not-being. If the reason is also contingent, there is then a chain of contingents linked one to the other, and there is no being at all; for this being which is the subject of our hypothesis cannot enter into being so long as it is not preceded by an infinite succession of beings, which is absurd. Therefore contingent beings end in a Necessary Being.

OF THE UNICITY OF GOD. It is not possible in any way that the Necessary Being should be two. Demonstration: Let us suppose that there is another necessary being: one must be distinguishable from the other, so that the terms "this" and "that" may be used with reference to them. This distinction must be either essential or accidental. If the distinction between them is accidental, this accidental element cannot but be present in each of them, or in one and not the other. If each of them has an accidental element by which it is distinguished from the other, both of them must be caused; for an accident is what is adjoined to a thing after its essence is realized. If the accidental element is regarded as adhering to its being, and is present in one of the two and not in the other, then the one which has no accidental element is a necessary being and the other is not a necessary being. If, however, the distinction is essential, the element of essentiality is that whereby the essence as such subsists; and if this element of essentiality is different in each and the two are distinguishable by virtue of it, then each of the two must be a compound; and compounds are caused; so that neither of them will be a necessary being. If the element of essentiality belongs to one only, and the other is one in every respect and there is no compounding of any kind in it, then the one which has no element of essentiality is a necessary being, and the other is not a necessary being. Since it is thus established that the Necessary Being cannot be two, but is All Truth, then by virtue of His Essential Reality, in respect of which He is a Truth, He is United and One, and no other shares with Him in that Unity: however the All-Truth attains existence, it is through Himself.

THAT GOD IS WITHOUT CAUSE. A necessary being has no cause whatsoever. Causes are of four kinds: that from which a thing has being, or the active cause; that on account of which a thing has being, or the final and completive cause; that in which a thing has being, or the material cause; and that through which a thing has being, or the formal cause.

The justification for limiting causes to these four varieties is that the reason for a thing is either internal in its subsistence, or a part of its being, or external to it. If it is internal, then it is either that part in which the thing is, potentially and not actually, that is to say its matter; or it is that part in which the thing becomes actually, that is to say its form. If it is external, then it can only be either that from which the thing has being, that is to say the agent, or that on account of which the thing has being, that is to say its purpose and end.

Since it is established that these are the roots and principles of this matter, let us rest on them and clarify the problems which are constructed upon them.

Demonstration that He has no active cause: This is self-evident: for if He had any reason for being, this would be adventitious and that would be a necessary being. Since it is established that He has no active cause, it follows on this line of reasoning that His Quiddity is not other than His Identity, that is to say, other than His Being; neither will He be a subsistence or an accident. There cannot be two, each of which derives its being from the other; nor can He be a necessary being in one respect, and a contingent being in another respect.

Proof that His Quiddity is not other than His Identity, but rather that His Being is unified in His Reality: If His Being were not the same as His Reality, then His Being would be other than His Reality. Every accident is caused, and every thing caused requires a reason. Now this reason is either external to His Quiddity, or is itself His Quiddity: if it is external, then He is not a necessary being, and is not exempt from an active cause; while if the reason is itself the Quiddity, then the reason must necessarily be itself a complete being in order that the being of another may result from it. Quiddity before being has no being; and if it had being before this, it would not require a second being. The question therefore returns to the problem of being. If the Being of the Quiddity is accidental, whence did this Being supervene and adhere? It is therefore established that the Identity of the Necessary Being is His Quiddity, and that He has no active cause; the necessary nature of His Being is like the quiddity of all other things. From this it is evident that the Necessary Being does not resemble any other thing in any respect whatsoever; for with all other things their being is other than their quiddity.

Proof that He is not an accident: An accident is a being in a locus. The locus is precedent to it, and its being is not possible without the locus. But we have stated that a being which is necessary has no reason for its being.

Proof that there cannot be two necessary beings, each deriving its being from the other: Each of them, in as much as it derives its being from the other, would be subsequent to the other, while at the same time by virtue of supplying being to the other, each would be precedent to the other: but one and the same thing cannot be both precedent and subsequent in relation to its being. Moreover, if we assume for the sake of argument that the other is non-existent: would the first then be a necessary being, or not? If it were a necessary being, it would have no connexion with the other: if it were not a necessary being, it would be a contingent being and would require another necessary being. Since the Necessary Being is One, and does not derive Its being from any one, it follows that He is a Necessary Being in every respect; while anything else derives its being from another.

Proof that He cannot be a Necessary Being in one respect and a contingent being in another respect: Such a being, in as much as it is a contingent being, would be connected in being with something else, and so it has a reason; but in as much as it is a necessary being, it would have no connexions with anything else. In that case it would both have being and not have being; and that is absurd.

Demonstration that He has no material and receptive cause: The receptive cause is the cause for the provision of the place in which a thing is received; that is to say, the place prepared for the reception of being, or the perfection of being. Now the Necessary Being is a perfection in pure actuality, and is not impaired by any deficiency; every perfection belongs to Him, derives from Him, and is preceded by His Essence, while every deficiency, even if it be metaphorical, is negated to Him. All perfection and all beauty are of His Being; indeed, these are the vestiges of the perfection of His Being; how then should He derive perfection from any other? Since it is thus established that He has no receptive cause, it follows that He does not possess anything potentially, and that He has no attribute yet to be awaited; on the contrary, His Perfection has been realized in actuality; and He has no material cause. We say "realized in actuality", using this as a common term of expression, meaning that every perfection belonging to any other is non-existent and yet to be awaited, whereas all perfection belonging to Him has being and is present. His Perfect Essence, preceding all relations, is One. From this it is manifest that His Attributes are not an augmentation of His Essence; for if they were an augmentation of His Essence, the Attributes would be potential with reference to the Essence and the Essence would be the reason for the Attributes. In that case the Attributes would be subsequent to a precedent, so that they would be in one respect active and in another receptive; their being active would be other than the aspect of their being receptive; and in consequence they would possess two mutually exclusive aspects. Now this is impossible in the case of anything whatsoever; when a body is in motion, the motivation is from one quarter and the movement from another.

If it were to be stated that His Attributes are not an augmentation of His Essence, but that they entered into the constitution of the Essence, and that the Essence cannot be conceived of as existing without these Attributes, then the Essence would be compound, and the Oneness would be destroyed. It is also evident, as a result of denying the existence of a receptive cause, that it is impossible for Him to change; for the meaning of change is the passing away of one attribute and the establishment of another; and if He were susceptible to change, He would possess potentially an element of passing-away and an element of establishment; and that is absurd. It is clear from this that He has no opposite and no contrary; for opposites are essences which succeed each other in the occupation of a single locus, there being between them the extreme of contrariety. But He is not receptive to accidents, much less to opposites. And if the term "opposite" is used to denote one who disputes with Him in His Rulership, it is clear too on this count that He has no opposite. It is further clear that it is impossible for Him not to be; for since it is established that His Being is necessary, it follows that it is impossible for Him not to be; because everything which exists potentially cannot exist actually, otherwise it would have two aspects. Anything which is receptive to a thing does not cease to be receptive when reception has actually taken place; if this were not so, it would result in the removal of both being and not-being, and that is untenable. This rule applies to every essence and every unified reality, such as angels and human spirits; they are not susceptible to not-being at all, since they are free from corporeal adjunctions.

Demonstration that He has no formal cause: A formal, corporeal cause only exists and is confirmed when a thing is possessed of matter: the matter has a share in the being of the form, in the same way that the form has a part in the disposition of the matter in being in actuality; such a thing is therefore caused. It is further evident as a result of denying this cause to Him, that He is also to be denied all corporeal attributes, such as time, space, direction, and being in one place to the exclusion of all other; in short, whatever is possible in relation to corporeal things is impossible in relation to Him.

Proof that He has no final cause: The final cause is that on account of which a thing has being; and the First Truth has not being for the sake of anything, rather does everything exist on account of the perfection of His Essence, being consequent to His Being and derived from His Being. Moreover the final cause, even it if be posterior in respect of being to all other causes, yet it is mentally prior to them all. It is the final cause which makes the active cause become a cause in actuality, that is to say in respect of its being a final cause.

Since it is established that He is exalted above this last kind of cause too, it is clear that there is no cause to His Attributes. It is also evident that He is Pure Benevolence and True Perfection; the meaning of His Self-Sufficiency likewise becomes manifest, namely that he approves of nothing and disapproves of nothing. For if He approved of anything, that thing would come into being and would continue to be; while if He disapproved of anything, that thing would be converted into not-being and would be annulled. The very divergency of these beings proves the nullity of such a proposition; for a thing which is one in every respect cannot approve of a thing and of its opposite. It is also not necessary for Him to observe the rule of greater expediency or of expediency, as certain Qualitarians have idly pretended; for if His acts of expediency were obligatory to Him, He would not merit gratitude and praise for such acts, since He would merely be fulfilling that which it is His obligation to perform, and He would be to all intents and purposes as one paying a debt; He would therefore deserve nothing at all for such benevolence. In fact His acts proceed on the contrary from Him and for Him, as we shall demonstrate later.

HIS ATTRIBUTES AS INTERPRETED ACCORDING TO THE FOREGOING PRINCIPLES. Since it is established that God is a Necessary Being, that He is One in every respect, that He is exalted above all causes, and that He has no reason of any kind for His Being; since it is further established that His Attributes do not augment His Essence, and that He is qualified by the Attributes of Praise and Perfection; it follows necessarily that we must state that He is Knowing, Living, Willing, Omnipotent, Speaking, Seeing, Hearing, and Possessed of all the other Loveliest Attributes. It is also necessary to recognize that His Attributes are to be classified as negative, positive, and a compound of the two: since His Attributes are of this order, it follows that their multiplicity does not destroy His Unity or contradict the necessary nature of His

Being. Pre-eternity for instance is essentially the negation of not-being in the first place, and the denial of causality and of primality in the second place; similarly the term One means that He is indivisible in every respect, both verbally and actually. When it is stated that He is a Necessary Being, this means that He is a Being without a cause, and that He is the Cause of other than Himself: this is a combination of the negative and the positive. Examples of the positive Attributes are His being Creator, Originator, Shaper, and the entire Attributes of Action. As for the compound of both, this kind is illustrated by His being Willing and Omnipotent, for these Attributes are a compound of Knowledge with the addition of Creativeness.

GOD'S KNOWLEDGE. God has knowledge of His Essence: His Knowledge, His Being Known and His Knowing are one and the same thing. He knows other than Himself, and all objects of knowledge. He knows all things by virtue of one knowledge, and in a single manner. His Knowledge does not change according to whether the thing known has being or not-being.

Proof that God has knowledge of His Essence: We have stated that God is One, and that He is exalted above all causes. The meaning of knowledge is the supervention of an idea divested of all corporeal coverings. Since it is established that He is One, and that He is divested of body, and His Attributes also; and as this idea as just described supervenes upon Him; and since whoever has an abstract idea supervening upon him is possessed of knowledge, and it is immaterial whether it is his essence or other than himself; and as further His Essence is not absent from Himself; it follows from all this that He knows Himself.

Proof that He is Knowledge, Knowing and Known: Knowledge is another term for an abstract idea. Since this idea is abstract, it follows that He is Knowledge; since this abstract idea belongs to Him, is present with Him, and is not veiled from Him, it follows that He is Knowing; and since this abstract idea does not supervene save through Him, it follows that He is Known. The terms employed in each case are different; otherwise it might be said that Knowledge, Knowing and Known are, in relation to His Essence, one. Take your own experience as a parallel. If you know yourself, the object of your knowledge is either yourself or something else; if the object of your knowledge is something other than yourself, then you do not know yourself. But if the object of your knowledge is yourself, then both the one knowing and the thing known are your self. If the image of your self is impressed upon your self, then it is your self which is the knowledge. Now if you look back upon yourself reflectively, you will not find any impression of the idea and quiddity of your self in yourself a second time, so as to give rise within you to a sense that your self is more than one. Therefore since it is established that He has intelligence of His Essence, and since His Intelligence is His Essence and does not augment His Essence, it follows that He is Knowing, Knowledge and Known without any multiplicity attaching to Him through these Attributes; and there is no difference between "one who has knowledge" and "one who has intelligence", since both are terms for describing the negation of matter absolutely.

Proof that He has knowledge of other than Himself: Whoever knows himself, if thereafter he does not know other than himself this is due to some impediment. If the impediment is essential, this implies necessarily that he does not know himself either; while if the impediment is of an external nature, that which is external can be removed. Therefore it is possible—nay, necessary—that He should have knowledge of other than Himself, as you shall learn from this chapter.

Proof that He has knowledge of all objects of knowledge: Since it is established that He is a Necessary Being, that He is One, and that the universe is brought into being from Him and has resulted out of His Being; since it is established further that He has knowledge of His Own Essence, His Knowledge of His Essence being what it is, namely that He is the Origin of all realities and of all things that have being; it follows that nothing in heaven or earth is remote from His Knowledge —on the contrary, all that comes into being does so by reason of Him: He is the causer of all reasons, and He knows that of which He is the Reason, the Giver of being and the Originator.

Proof that He knows all things by virtue of one knowledge, in a manner which changes not according to the change in the thing known: It has been established that His Knowledge does not augment His Essence, and that He is the Origin of all things that have being, while being exalted above accident and changes; it therefore follows that He knows things in a manner unchanging. The objects of knowledge are a consequence of His Knowledge; His Knowledge is not a consequence of the things known, that it should change as they change; for His Knowledge of things is the reason for their having being. Hence it is manifest that Knowledge is itself Omnipotence. He knows all contingent things, even as He knows all things that have being, even though we know them not; for the contingent, in relation to us, is a thing whose being is possible and whose not-being is also possible; but in relation to Him one of the two alternatives is actually known. Therefore His Knowledge of genera, species, things with being, contingent things, manifest and secret things— this Knowledge is a single knowledge.

ACTS EMANATING FROM GOD.   Since you now know that He is a Necessary Being, that He is One, and that He has no Attribute which augments His Essence (for that would imply a succession of various acts, whereas the Act of God is the vestiges of the Perfection of His Essence); this being so, it follows that His First Act is one. For if there had emanated from Him two acts, the emanation would have been in two different manners, for duality in the act implies duality in the agent. He who acts by virtue of his own essence, if his essence is one only one act emanates from it; whereas if he has a duality of essence, he must be a compound; and we have proved the impossibility of this as regards God. It follows necessarily that the first thing to emanate from God was not a body; for every body is compounded of matter and form, and these require either two causes, or a single cause with two aspects; this being so, it is impossible that these two should have emanated from God, it having been established that there is no compounding in God whatsoever. Since the first thing to emanate from God was not a body, it follows that it was an abstract substance, namely, the First Intelligence. This has been confirmed by the true religion, for the Prophet said, "The first thing God created was Intelligence," and again, "The first thing God created was the Pen." The phrase *Thou shalt not find any change in the Way of God* (Koran xxxiii. 62) refers to the perpetuity of the Creation; the phrase *Thou shalt not find any alteration in the Way of God* (Koran xxxv. 41) refers to the perpetuity of the Command. Certainly, the Universe emanated from Him in due succession of order and media. So when we say that this Act emanated from Him through a reason, and that that reason was of Him also, this implies no imperfection in His Activity; on the contrary, totality emanated from Him, through Him, and unto Him. Therefore all things having being emanated from Him according to a known order and known media: that which came later cannot be earlier, and that which came earlier cannot be later, for it is He Who causes things to be earlier and later. Indeed, the first thing having being that emanated from Him was the noblest; thereafter came a descent from the nobler to the lower, until the lowliest of all was reached. First was Intelligence; then Soul; then the Body of Heaven; then the materials of the four Elements with their forms (for their materials are common to all, only their forms differ). Then there is a mounting up from the lowliest to the noblest; the noblest of all ending at a degree parallel to the degree of the Intelligence. Through this process of origination and returning back, God is said to be the Originator and the Returner.

39 AL-GHAZZALI

Avicenna was accused of heresy and atheism both during and after his lifetime. This battle between free speculation and orthodox doctrine ended in favor of the latter with the writings of Islam's outstanding theologian, al-Ghazzali (1058–1111). Losing his father in early life, al-Ghazzali was brought up by a Sufi mystic, but turned to the study of theology and jurisprudence and was appointed professor of theology at Baghdad. He proved spectacularly successful and was soon recognized as the leading authority on theology and law. But fame did not suffice, for al-Ghazzali underwent a spiritual crisis that prevented him from teaching. For two years he lived in complete isolation and for nine years in retreat, until he resolved the crisis and regained peace of mind. During these years he wrote his great Revival of Religious Sciences, *in which he held that the ultimate source of truth is divine revelation, which reason may elucidate but cannot challenge. Hence his emphasis on tradition, and on obedience and devotion to God in daily life. These teachings became accepted doctrine virtually throughout the Moslem world, driving out the secular Aristotelian approach and assuring the orthodoxy and immobility of official Islam to modern times.**

CONCERNING THE PHILOSOPHICAL SECTS AND THE STIGMA OF INFIDELITY WHICH ATTACHES TO THEM ALL. The philosophical systems, in spite of their number and variety, may be reduced to three (1) The Materialists; (2) The Naturalists; (3) The Theists.

(1) *The Materialists.* They reject an intelligent and omnipotent Creator and Disposer of the Universe. In their view the world exists from all eternity and had no author. The animal comes from semen and semen from the animal; so it has always been and will always be; those who maintain this doctrine are atheists.

(2) *The Naturalists.* These devote themselves to the study of nature and of the marvellous phenomena of the animal and vegetable world. Having carefully analysed animal organs with the help of anatomy, struck with the wonders of God's work and with the wisdom therein revealed, they are forced to admit the existence of a wise Creator Who knows the end and purpose of everything. And certainly no one can study anatomy and the wonderful mechanism of living things without being obliged to confess the profound wisdom of Him Who has framed the bodies of animals and especially of man. But carried away by their natural researches they believed that the existence of a being absolutely depended upon the proper equilibrium of its organism. According to them, as the latter perishes and is destroyed, so is the thinking faculty which is bound up with it; and as

* Claud Field, trans., *The Confessions of Al-Ghazzali,* Wisdom of the East Series (London: John Murray Publishers Ltd., 1909), pp. 25-40.

they assert that the restoration of a thing once destroyed to existence is unthinkable, they deny the immortality of the soul. Consequently they deny heaven, hell, resurrection, and judgment. Acknowledging neither a recompense for good deeds nor a punishment for evil ones, they fling off all authority and plunge into sensual pleasures with the avidity of brutes. These also ought to be called atheists, for the true faith depends not only on the acknowledgment of God, but of His Apostle and of the Day of Judgment. And although they acknowledge God and His attributes, they deny a judgment to come.

(3) Next come the *Theists*. Among them should be reckoned Socrates, who was the teacher of Plato as Plato was of Aristotle. This latter drew up for his disciples the rules of logic, organised the sciences, elucidated what was formerly obscure, and expounded what had not been understood. This school refuted the systems of the two others, i.e., the Materialists and Naturalists; but in exposing their mistaken and perverse beliefs, they made use of arguments which they should not. "God suffices to protect the faithful in war" (*Koran,* xxxiii. 25).

Aristotle also contended with success against the theories of Plato, Socrates, and the theists who had preceded him, and separated himself entirely from them; but he could not eliminate from his doctrine the stains of infidelity and heresy which disfigure the teaching of his predecessors. We should therefore consider them all as unbelievers, as well as the so-called Mussulman philosophers, such as Ibn Sina (Avicenna) and Farabi, who have adopted their systems.

Let us, however, acknowledge that among Mussulman philosophers none have better interpreted the doctrine of Aristotle than the latter. What others have handed down as his teaching is full of error, confusion, and obscurity adapted to disconcert the reader. The unintelligible can neither be accepted nor rejected. The philosophy of Aristotle, all serious knowledge of which we owe to the translation of these two learned men, may be divided into three portions: the first contains matter justly chargeable with impiety, the second is tainted with heresy, and the third we are obliged to reject absolutely. We proceed to details:

DIVISIONS OF THE PHILOSOPHIC SCIENCES. These sciences, in relation to the aim we have set before us, may be divided into six sections: (1) Mathematics; (2) Logic; (3) Physics; (4) Metaphysics; (5) Politics; (6) Moral Philosophy.

Mathematics comprises the knowledge of calculation, geometry, and cosmography: it has no connection with the religious sciences, and proves nothing for or against religion; it rests on a foundation of proofs which, once known and understood, cannot be refuted. Mathematics tend, however, to produce two bad results.

The first is this: Whoever studies this science admires the subtlety and clearness of its proofs. His confidence in philosophy increases, and he thinks that all its departments are capable of the same clearness and solidity of proof as mathematics. But when he hears people speak of the unbelief and impiety of mathematicians, of their professed disregard for the Divine Law, which is notorious, it is true that, out of regard for authority, he echoes these accusations, but he says to himself at the same time that, if there was truth in religion, it would not have escaped those who have displayed so much keenness of intellect in the study of mathematics.

Next, when he becomes aware of the unbelief and rejection of religion on the part of these learned men, he concludes that to reject religion is reasonable. How many of such men gone astray I have met whose sole argument was that just mentioned. And supposing one puts to them the following objection: "It does not follow that a man who excels in one branch of knowledge excels in all others, nor that he should be equally versed in jurisprudence, theology, and medicine. It is possible to be entirely ignorant of metaphysics, and yet to be an excellent grammarian. There are past masters in every science who are entirely ignorant of other branches of knowledge. The arguments of the ancient philosophers are rigidly demonstrative in mathematics and only conjectural in religious questions. In order to ascertain this one must proceed to a thorough examination of the matter." Supposing, I say, one makes the above objection to these "apes of unbelief," they find it distasteful. Falling a prey to their passions, to a besotted vanity, and the wish to pass for learned men, they persist in maintaining the pre-eminence of mathematicians in all branches of knowledge. This is a serious evil, and for this reason those who study mathematics should be checked from going too far in their researches. For though far removed as it may be from the things of religion, this study, serving as it does as an introduction to the philosophic systems, casts over religion its malign influence. It is rarely that a man devotes himself to it without robbing himself of his faith and casting off the restraints of religion.

The second evil comes from the sincere but ignorant Mussulman who thinks the best way to defend religion is by rejecting all the exact sciences. Accusing their professors of being astray, he rejects their theories of the eclipses of the sun and moon, and condemns them in the name of religion. These accusations are carried far and wide, they reach the ears of the philosopher who knows that these theories rest on infallible proofs; far from losing confidence in them, he believes, on the contrary, that Islam has ignorance and the denial of scientific proofs for its basis, and his devotion to philosophy increases with his hatred to religion.

It is therefore a great injury to religion to suppose that the defence of Islam involves the condemnation of the exact sciences. The religious law contains nothing which approves them or condemns them, and in their turn they make no attack on religion. The words of the Prophet, "The sun and the moon are two signs of the power of God; they are not eclipsed for the birth or the death of any one; when you see these signs take refuge in prayer and invoke the name of God"—these words, I say, do not in any way condemn the astronomical calculations which define the orbits of these two bodies, their conjunction and opposition according to particular laws. But as for the so-called tradition, "When God reveals Himself in anything, He abases Himself thereto," it is unauthentic, and not found in any trustworthy collection of the traditions.

Such is the bearing and the possible danger of mathematics.

(2) *Logic*. This science, in the same manner, contains nothing for or against religion. Its object is the study of different kinds of proofs and syllogisms, the conditions which should hold between the premises of a proposition, the way to combine them, the rules of a good definition, and the art of formulating it. For knowledge consists of conceptions which spring from a definition or of convictions which arise from proofs. There is therefore nothing censurable in this science, and it is laid under contribution by theologians as well as by philosophers. The only difference is that the latter use a particular set of technical formulæ and that they push their divisions and subdivisions further.

It may be asked, What, then, this has to do with the grave questions of religion, and on what ground opposition should be offered to the methods of logic? The objector, it will be said, can only inspire the logician with an unfavourable opinion of the intelligence and faith of his adversary, since the latter's faith seems to be based upon such objections. But, it must be admitted, logic *is* liable to abuse.

Logicians demand in reasoning certain conditions which lead to absolute certainty, but when they touch on religious questions, they can no longer postulate these conditions, and ought therefore to relax their habitual rigour. It happens, accordingly, that a student who is enamoured of the evidential methods of logic, hearing his teachers accused of irreligion, believes that this irreligion reposes on proofs as strong as those of logic, and immediately, without attempting the study of metaphysics, shares their mistake. This is a serious disadvantage arising from the study of logic.

(3) *Physics.* The object of this science is the study of the bodies which compose the universe: the sky and the stars, and, here below, simple elements such as air, earth, water, fire, and compound bodies—animals, plants and minerals; the reasons of their changes, developments, and intermixture. By the nature of its researches it is closely connected with the study of medicine, the object of which is the human body, its principal and secondary organs, and the law which governs their changes. Religion having no fault to find with medical science cannot justly do so with physical, except on some special matters which we have mentioned in the work entitled *The Destruction of the Philosophers.* Besides these primary questions, there are some subordinate ones depending on them, on which physical science is open to objection. But all physical science rests, as we believe, on the following principle: Nature is entirely subject to God; incapable of acting by itself, it is an instrument in the hand of the Creator; sun, moon, stars, and elements are subject to God and can produce nothing of themselves. In a word, nothing in nature can act spontaneously and apart from God.

(4) *Metaphysics.* This is the fruitful breeding-ground of the errors of philosophers. Here they can no longer satisfy the laws of rigorous argumentation such as logic demands, and this is what explains the disputes which arise between them in the study of metaphysics. The system most closely akin to the system of the Muhammedan doctors is that of Aristotle as expounded to us by Farabi and Avicenna. The sum total of their errors can be reduced to twenty propositions: three of them are irreligious, and the other seventeen heretical. It was in order to combat their system that we wrote the work *Destruction of the Philosophers.* The three propositions in which they are opposed to all the doctrines of Islam are the following:

(a) Bodies do not rise again; spirits alone will be rewarded or punished; future punishments will be therefore spiritual and not physical. They are right in admitting spiritual punishments, for there will be such; but they are wrong in rejecting physical punishments, and contradicting in this manner the assertions of the Divine Law.

(b) "God takes cognisance of universals, not of specials." This is manifestly irreligious. The Koran asserts truly, "Not an atom's weight in heaven or earth can escape His knowledge" (x. 62).

(c) They maintain that the universe exists from all eternity and will never end. None of these propositions have ever been admitted by Moslems.

Besides this, they deny that God has attributes, and maintain that He knows by His essence only and not by means of any attribute accessory to His essence. In this point they approach the doctrine of the Mutazilites, doctrines which we are not obliged to condemn as irreligious. On the contrary, in our work entitled *Criteria of the differences which divide Islam from Atheism,* we have proved the wrongness of those who accuse of irreligion everything which is opposed to their way of looking at things.

(5) *Political Science.* The professors of this confine themselves to drawing

up the rules which regulate temporal matters and the royal power. They have borrowed their theories on this point from the books which God has revealed to His prophets and from the sentences of ancient sages, gathered by tradition.

(6) *Moral Philosophy*. The professors of this occupy themselves with defining the attributes and qualities of the soul, grouping them according to genus and species, and pointing out the way to moderate and control them. They have borrowed this system from the Sufis. These devout men, who are always engaged in invoking the name of God, in combating concupiscence and following the way of God by renouncing the pleasures of this world, have received, while in a state of ecstasy, revelations regarding the qualities of the soul, its defects and its evil inclinations. These revelations they have published, and the philosophers making use of them have introduced them into their own systems in order to embellish and give currency to their falsehoods. In the times of the philosophers, as at every other period, there existed some of these fervent mystics. God does not deprive this world of them, for they are its sustainers, and they draw down to it the blessings of heaven according to the tradition: "It is by them that you obtain rain, it is by them that you receive your subsistence." Such were "the Companions of the Cave," who lived in ancient times, as related by the Koran (xviii.). Now this mixture of moral and philosophic doctrine with the words of the Prophet and those of the Sufis gives rise to two dangers, one for the upholder of those doctrines, the other for their opponent.

The danger for their opponent is serious. A narrow-minded man, finding in their writings moral philosophy mixed with unsupported theories, believes that he ought to entirely reject them and to condemn those who profess them. Having only heard them from their mouth he does not hesitate in his ignorance to declare them false because those who teach them are in error. It is as if some one was to reject the profession of faith made by Christians, "There is only one God and Jesus is His prophet," simply because it proceeds from Christians and without inquiring whether it is the profession of this creed or the denial of Muhammed's prophetic mission which makes Christians infidels. Now, if they are only infidels because of their rejection of our prophet, we are not entitled to reject those of their doctrines which do not wear the stamp of infidelity. In a word, truth does not cease to be true because it is found among them. Such, however, is the tendency of weak minds: they judge the truth according to its professors instead of judging its professors by the standard of the truth. But a liberal spirit will take as its guide this maxim of the Prince of believers, Ali the son of Abu Talib: "Do not seek for the truth by means of men; find first the truth and then you will recognise those who follow it." This is the procedure followed by a wise man. Once in possession of the truth he examines the basis of various doctrines which come before him, and when he has found them true, he accepts them without troubling himself whether the person who teaches them is sincere or a deceiver. Much rather, remembering how gold is buried in the bowels of the earth, he endeavours to disengage the truth from the mass of errors in which it is engulfed. The skilled coin-assayer plunges without hesitation his hand into the purse of the coiner of false money, and, relying on experience, separates good coins from bad. It is the ignorant rustic, and not the experienced assayer, who will ask why we should have anything to do with a false coiner. The unskilled swimmer must be kept away from the seashore, not the expert in diving. The child, not the charmer, must be forbidden to handle serpents.

As a matter of fact, men have such a good opinion of themselves, of their mental superiority and intellectual depth; they believe themselves so skilled in discerning the true from the false, the path of safety from those of error, that they should be forbidden as much as possible the perusal of philosophic writings, for though they sometimes escape the danger just pointed out, they cannot avoid that which we are about to indicate.

Some of the maxims found in my works regarding the mysteries of religion have met with objectors of an inferior rank in science, whose intellectual penetration is insufficient to fathom such depths. They assert that these maxims are borrowed from the ancient philosophers, whereas the truth is that they are the fruit of my own meditations, but as the proverb says, "Sandal follows the impress of sandal." Some of them are found in our books of religious law, but the greater part are derived from the writings of the Sufis.

But even if they were borrowed exclusively from the doctrines of the philosophers, is it right to reject an opinion when it is reasonable in itself, supported by solid proofs, and contradicting neither the Koran nor the traditions? If we adopt this method and reject every truth which has chanced to have been proclaimed by an impostor, how many truths we should have to reject! How many verses of the Koran and traditions of the prophets and Sufi discourses and maxims of sages we must close our ears to because the author of the *Treatise of the Brothers of Purity* has inserted them in his writings in order to further his cause, and in order to lead minds gradually astray in the paths of error! The consequence of this procedure would be that impostors would snatch truths out of our hands in order to embellish their own works. The wise man, at least, should not make common cause with the bigot blinded by ignorance.

Honey does not become impure because it may happen to have been placed in the glass which the surgeon uses for cupping purposes. The impurity of blood is due, not to its contact with this glass, but to a peculiarity inherent in its own nature; this peculiarity, not existing in honey, cannot be communicated to it by its being placed in the cupping glass; it is therefore wrong to regard it as impure. Such is, however, the whimsical way of looking at things found in nearly all men. Every word proceeding from an authority which they approve is accepted by them, even were it false; every word proceeding from one whom they suspect is rejected, even were it true. In every case they judge of the truth according to its professors and not of men according to the truth which they profess, a *ne plus ultra* of error. Such is the peril in which philosophy involves its opponents.

The second danger threatens those who accept the opinions of the philosophers. When, for instance, we read the treatises of the "Brothers of purity" and other works of the same kind, we find in them sentences spoken by the Prophet and quotations from the Sufis. We approve these works; we give them our confidence; and we finish by accepting the errors which they contain, because of the good opinion of them with which they have inspired us at the outset. Thus, by insensible degrees, we are led astray. In view of this danger the reading of philosophic writings so full of vain and delusive utopias should be forbidden, just as the slippery banks of a river are forbidden to one who knows not how to swim. The perusal of these false teachings must be prevented just as one prevents children from touching serpents. A snake-charmer himself will abstain from touching snakes in the presence of his young child, because he knows that the child, believing himself as clever as his father, will not fail to imitate him; and in order to lend more weight to his prohibition the charmer will not touch a serpent under the eyes of his son.

Such should be the conduct of a learned man who is also wise. But the snake-charmer, after having taken the serpent and separated the venom from the antidote, having put the latter on one side and destroyed the venom, ought not to withhold the antidote from those who need it. In the same way the skilled coin-assayer, after having put his hand in the bag of the false coiner, taken out the good coins and thrown away the bad ones, ought not to refuse the good to those who need and ask for it. Such should be the conduct of the learned man. If the patient feels a certain dislike of the antidote because he knows that it is taken from a snake whose body is the receptacle of poison, he should be disabused of his fallacy. If a beggar hesitates to take a piece of gold which he knows comes from the purse of a false coiner, he should be told that his hesitation is a pure mistake which would deprive him of the advantage which he seeks. It should be proved to him that the contact of the good coins with the bad does not injure the former and does not improve the latter. In the same way the contact of truth with falsehood does not change truth into falsehood, any more than it changes falsehood into truth.

Thus much, then, we have to say regarding the inconveniences and dangers which spring from the study of philosophy.

40   IBN KHALDUN

Although philosophy was frowned upon by orthodox Islam, other fields were cultivated by Moslem scholars, including history, in which the outstanding figure was Ibn Khaldun (1332–1406). Born in Tunis, he held various offices in Fez, Granada, Algeria, and Cairo. In his great work Kitab al-Ibar (Universal History) *he was far in advance of his age in treating history as a science and anticipating modern principles of sociology. In the following selection he emphasizes the need for accurate scholarship and analyzes the historical role of Bedouins and the dynamics of empires.**

164

Prolegomena showing the excellence of the science of History, establishing the methods proper to it, and glancing at the errors into which Historians fall, together with some account of their causes.

Know that the science of History is noble in its conception, abounding in instruction, and exalted in its aim. It acquaints us with the characteristics of the ancient peoples, the ways of life followed by the prophets, and the dynasties and government of kings, so that those who wish may draw valuable lessons for their guidance in religious and worldly affairs. The student of History, however, requires numerous sources of information and a great variety of knowledge; he must consider well and examine carefully in order to arrive at the truth and avoid errors and pitfalls. If he rely on bare tradition, without having thoroughly grasped the principles of common experience, the institutes of government, the nature of civilisation, and the circumstances of human society, and without judging what is past and invisible by the light of what is present before his eyes, then he will often be in danger of stumbling and slipping and losing the right road. Many errors committed by historians, commentators, and leading traditionists in their

---

* Reynold A. Nicholson, *Translations of Eastern Poetry and Prose* (Cambridge: Cambridge University Press, 1922), pp. 176-85.

narrative of events have been caused by their reliance on mere tradition, which they have accepted without regard to its (intrinsic) worth, neglecting to refer it to its general principles, judge it by its analogies, and test it by the standard of wisdom, knowledge of the natures of things, and exact historical criticism. Thus they have gone astray from the truth and wandered in the desert of imagination and error. Especially is this the case in computing sums of money and numbers of troops, when such matters occur in their narratives; for here falsehood and exaggeration are to be expected, and one must always refer to general principles and submit to the rules (of probability). For example, Mas'údí and many other historians relate that Moses—on whom be peace!—numbered the armies of the Israelites in the wilderness, after he had reviewed all the men capable of bearing arms who were twenty years old or above that age, and that they amounted to 600,000 or more. Now, in making this statement he forgot to consider whether Egypt and Syria are large enough to support armies of that size, for it is a fact attested by well-known custom and familiar experience that every kingdom keeps for its defence only such a force as it can maintain and furnish with rations and pay. Moreover, it would be impossible for armies so huge to march against each other or fight, because the territory is too limited in extent to allow of it, and because, when drawn up in ranks, they would cover a space twice or three times as far as the eye can reach, if not more. How should these two hosts engage in battle, or one of them gain the victory, when neither wing knows anything of what is happening on the other? The present time bears witness to the truth of my observations: water is not so like to water as the future to the past.

The Persian Empire was much greater than the kingdom of the Israelites, as appears from the conquest of the latter by Nebuchadnezzar, who attacked their country, made himself master of their dominions, and laid waste Jerusalem, the chief seat of their religion and power, although he was only the governor of a Persian province: it is said that he was the satrap of the western frontiers. The Persians ruled over the two 'Iráks, Khurásán, Transoxania, and the lands opening on the Caspian Sea—an empire far more extensive than that of the Israelites; yet their armies never equalled or even approached the number mentioned above. Their army at Kádisíya, the greatest they ever mustered, was 120,000 strong, and each of these was accompanied by a retainer. Saif, by whom this is related, adds that the whole force exceeded 200,000. According to 'Á'isha and Zuhrí, the troops under Rustam who were opposed to Sa'd at Kádisíya were only 60,000 strong, each man having a follower.

Again, if the Israelites had reached this total, vast would have been the extent of their kingdom and wide the range of their power. Provinces and kingdoms are small or great in proportion to the numbers of their soldiery and population, as we shall explain in the chaper concerning empires in the First Book. Now, it is well-known that the territories of the Israelites did not extend, in Syria, beyond al-Urdunn and Palestine, and in the Hijáz, beyond the districts of Yathrib (Medina) and Khaibar.

Furthermore, according to the trustworthy authorities, there were only four fathers (generations) between Moses and Israel. Moses was the son of 'Imrán the son of Yas-hur the son of Káhat or Káhit the son of Láwí or Láwá the son of Jacob or Isrá'ílu 'llah (Israel of God). This is his genealogy as given in the Pentateuch. The length of time separating them is recorded by Mas'údí, who says that when Israel entered Egypt and came to Joseph with his sons, the (twelve) Patriarchs and their children, seventy persons in all, they abode in Egypt under the dominion of the Pharaohs, the kings of the Copts, two hundred and twenty years until they went forth into the wilderness with Moses, on whom be peace. It is incredible that in the course of four generations their offspring should have multiplied so enormously.

165

That being so, the rule for distinguishing the true from the false in history is based on possibility or impossibility; that is to say, we must examine human society, by which I mean civilisation, and discriminate between the characteristics essential to it and inherent in its nature and those which are accidental and unimportant, recognising further those which cannot possibly belong to it. If we do that, we shall have a canon for separating historical fact and truth from error and falsehood by a method of proof that admits of no doubt; and then, if we hear an account of any of the things that happen in civilised society, we shall know how to distinguish what we judge to be worthy of acceptance from what we judge to be spurious, having in our hands an infallible criterion which enables historians to verify whatever they relate.

Such is the purpose of the First Book of the present work. And it would seem that this is an independent science. For it has a subject, namely, human civilisation and society; and problems, namely, to explain in succession the accidental features and essential characters of civilisation. This is the case with every science, the intellectual as well as those founded on authority.

The matter of the following discourse is novel, original, and instructive. I have discovered it by dint of deep thought and research. It appertains not to the science of oratory, which is only concerned with such language as will convince the multitude and be useful for winning them over to an opinion or persuading them to reject the same. Nor, again, does it form part of the science of civil government, *i.e.* the proper regulation of a household or city in accordance with moral and philosophical laws, in order that the people may be led to live in a way that tends to preserve and perpetuate the species. These two sciences may resemble it, but its subject differs from theirs. It appears to be a new invention; and indeed I have not met with a discourse upon it by any one in the world. I do not know whether this is due to their neglect of the topic—and we need not think the worse of them for that—or whether, perhaps, they may have treated it exhaustively in books that have not come down to us. Amongst the races of mankind the sciences are many and the savants numerous, and the knowledge we have lost is greater in amount than all that has reached us. What has become of the sciences of the Persians, whose writings were destroyed by 'Umar (may God be well-pleased with him!) at the time of the conquest? Where are those of Chaldaea, Assyria, and Babylonia, with all that they produced and left behind them? Where are those of the Copts and of peoples yet more ancient? We have received the sciences of but one nation, the Greeks, and that only because Ma'mún took pains to have their books translated from the language in which they were composed. He was enabled to do this by finding plenty of translators and expending large sums on the work. Of the sciences of other peoples we know nothing.

. . . . .

Now we shall set forth in this Book the various features of civilisation as they appear in human society: kingship, acquisition of wealth, the sciences, and the arts. We shall employ demonstrative methods to verify and elucidate the knowledge spread amongst all classes, to refute false opinions, and to remove uncertainties.

Man is distinguished from the other animals by attributes peculiar to himself. Amongst these are

(1) The sciences and arts produced by the faculty of reflection, which distinguishes men from the animals and exalts him above the rest of created beings.

(2) The need for an authority to restrain and a government to coerce him. Of the animals he is the only one that cannot exist without this. As for what is said concerning bees and locusts, even if they have something of the sort, they have it by instinct, not from reflection and consideration.

(3) The labour and industry which supply him with diverse ways and means of obtaining a livelihood, inasmuch as God has made nourishment necessary to him for the maintenance of his life and has directed him to seek it and search after it. *"He gave unto all things their nature: then He directed."*

(4) Civilisation, *i.e.* settling down and dwelling together in a city or in tents for the sake of social intercourse and for the satisfaction of their needs, because men are naturally disposed to help each other to subsist, as we shall explain presently. This civilisation is either nomadic (*badawí*) or *residential* (*hadarí*). The former is found in steppes and mountains, among the pastoral tribes of the desert and the inhabitants of remote sands; the latter in towns, villages, cities, and cultivated tracts, whither men resort for safety and in order to be protected by walls. In all these circumstances it exhibits the phenomena characteristic of a social state. Accordingly, the matter of this Book must be comprised in six chapters:

I. Human society in general, its various divisions, and the part of the earth which it occupies.
II. Nomadic civilisation, with an account of the wild tribes and peoples.
III. Dynasties, the Caliphate, kingship, and the high offices of government.
IV. The settled civilisation of countries and cities.
V. Crafts, means of livelihood, and the various ways of making money.
VI. The sciences, and how they are acquired and learned.

166

The tribes of the desert are kept off from each other by the authority of their chiefs and elders, whom they respect greatly. For the defence of their encampments against a foreign enemy, each tribe has a troop of warriors and knights famous for their prowess; but they would not make a firm resistance and defence unless they were united by kinship and a feeling of solidarity (*'asabíya*). That is what renders them so strong and formidable. *Esprit de corps* and devotion to one's kin is of supreme importance. The affection which God has put in the hearts of His servants towards those of their own flesh and blood is inherent in human nature: it leads them to help and succour one another and inspires their foes with terror. The Koran gives an example in the story of the brothers of Joseph (on whom be peace!), when they said to their father, *"If the wolf devour him, when we are banded together (for his protection), we shall be weaklings indeed,"* *i.e.,* it is inconceivable that violence should be done to any one so long as he has devoted partisans. In those who are not drawn together by the bonds of kinship this feeling towards their comrades is seldom aroused: when dark war-clouds threaten disaster, every man will slip away in alarm to look after his own safety, because he fears to be forsaken by his allies. Such a people cannot live in the desert: they would fall an easy prey to any race that attacked them. Now, if this is clear with regard to those dwelling together, who must needs defend and protect themselves, similarly you will see that it holds good in the case of any enterprise that excites hostility, such as the mission of a prophet or the founding of a kingdom or the propaganda of a sect. An object of this kind is only attained by fighting for it, since opposition is natural to man; and in order to fight with success, there must be a feeling of solidarity as we said just now. Let this principle be your guide in perusing the observations which we are about to make. God aids us to arrive at the truth.

167

On the inability of the Arabs to establish an empire unless they are imbued with religion by a prophet or a saint, or generally inspired by religious enthusiasm.

The reason of this is that, being naturally wild, they are of all peoples the most reluctant to submit to one another owing to the rudeness of their manners, their arrogance, their high spirit, and their jealousy of authority. Seldom, therefore, are they unanimous. But when they follow a prophet or a saint, they are restrained by something within themselves; their pride and jealousy depart from them, submission and concord are no longer difficult. Religion brings them together: it takes away their rudeness and insolence, it removes envy and jealousy from their hearts. If there be among them the prophet or saint who urges them to fulfil the command of God, and requires that they shall abandon their evil ways and cleave to the good, and bids them be of one voice to make the truth prevail, they will become completely united and gain victory and empire. Moreover, no people is so quick to receive the truth and the right. Their natures are uncorrupted by vicious habits and free from base qualities; and as for their savagery, it is conformable and adaptable to good in consequence of its having preserved the original constitution of man (which renders him capable of accepting the true religion), and because it is remote from the bad habits and dispositions which stamp themselves on men's souls. For, according to the Apostolic Tradition already quoted, "Every one is born with a capacity for receiving the truth."

168

Showing that empires, like individuals, have their natural term of life.

You must know that physicians and astrologers declare the natural life of man to be a hundred and twenty years of the kind which astrologers call "the greatest years of the moon"; but it varies in every race according to the conjunctions of the planets, so that sometimes it is more than this and sometimes less. Those born under certain planetary conjunctions live a full century, others fifty years or seventy or eighty; and stargazers believe that all this is indicated by the position of the heavenly bodies. In the Moslem community, as is recorded in Traditions of the Prophet, life runs to sixty or seventy years. The natural life, *i.e.* 120 years, is rarely exceeded: such cases as that of Noah (on whom be peace!), and a few of the people of 'Ád and Thamúd, depend on extraordinary positions in the celestial sphere. The lives of empires, too, vary according to the conjunctions of the planets; but as a rule an empire does not last more than three generations—reckoning a generation as the middle life of an individual, *i.e.* 40 years, a period which marks the end of the body's growth and development: God has said, *"Until, when he reaches his age of strength and attains unto forty years. . . ."* For this reason we said that the length of a generation is the (middle) life of an individual. Our statement is confirmed by what we have already mentioned touching the Divine wisdom which decreed that the Israelites should pass forty years in the wilderness, and the purpose thereof, namely, that the generation then living might decease and another grow up, which had never known the abasement (of slavery). That indicates that forty years, which is the (middle) life on an individual, is the length of a generation.

An empire, as we remarked, seldom outlives three generations. The first maintains its nomadic character, its rude and savage ways of life; inured to hardships, brave, fierce, and sharing renown with each other, the tribesmen preserve their solidarity in full vigour: their swords are kept sharp, their attack is feared, and their neighbours vanquished. With the second generation comes a change. Possessing dominion and affluence, they turn from nomadic to settled life, and from hardship to ease and plenty. The authority, instead of being shared by all, is appropriated by one, while the rest, too spiritless to make an effort to regain it, abandon the glory of ambition for the shame of subjection. Their solidarity is weakened in some degree; yet one may notice that notwithstanding the indignity to which they submit, they retain much of what they have known and witnessed in the former generation—the feelings of fierceness and pride, the desire for honour, and the resolution to defend themselves and repulse their foes. These qualities' they cannot lose entirely, though a part be gone. They hope to become again such men as their fathers were, or they fancy that the old virtues still survive amongst them.

In the third generation the wandering life and rough manners of the desert are forgotten, as though they had never been. At this stage men no longer take delight in glory and patriotism, since all have learned to bow under the might of a sovereign and are so addicted to luxurious pleasures that they have become a burden on the state; for they require protection like the women and young boys. Their national spirit is wholly extinguished; they have no stomach for resistance, defence, or attack. Nevertheless they impose on the people by their (military) appearance and uniform, their horsemanship, and the address with which they manœuvre. It is but a false show: they are in general greater cowards than the most helpless women, and will give way at the first assault. The monarch in those days must needs rely on the bravery of others, enrol many of the clients (freedmen), and recruit soldiers capable, to some extent, of guarding the empire, until God proclaims the hour of its destruction and it falls with everything that it upholds. Thus do empires age and decay in the course of three generations.

Chapter Fourteen

Turco-Mongol invasions

41   Civilization and Nomadism

The great river valley civilizations on the periphery of the Eurasian landmass have from the beginning been subject to periodic invasions by the nomadic peoples of the interior. These invasions played a vital role in Eurasian history, being responsible not only for the rise and fall of empires but also for the diffusion of new techniques and ideas. This analysis by a distinguished American authority on Central Eurasian history emphasizes the interaction between nomadism and civilization and interprets the invasions as a response to the dynamism of civilization.*

Inner Asia, in the past as in the present, has always been a region whose history has been shaped by the spread up to its edges, and intermittently the penetration into it, of the military activities and economic and cultural influences of the great civilized regions to the west, south and east of it. The order of development was as follows:

The improvement of agriculture in the regions of the great river-valley civilizations and the Mediterranean basin, providing enough surplus to feed large cities, created civilizations which had urban superstructures on agrarian bases. When the best farming land was taken up, there was an overflow into secondary land, where the populations had lagged behind the rate of specialization in the more productive areas. In part, these lagging populations were now caught up in the continuing progress of the advanced peoples, but many retreated from their already less favorable land into land which, agriculturally estimated, was even less favorable, and by so doing committed themselves to a new process of speciali-

---

* O. Lattimore, *Studies in Frontier History: Collected Papers 1928-1958* (New York: Oxford University Press, 1962), pp. 503-5.

zation of their own, with less reliance on agriculture and increasing reliance on livestock. This process was one of the origins, though not the sole origin, of pastoral nomadism.

This dual process of the expansion of large, agriculturally supported states, with high urban development, and the formation around their fringes of differently specialized "frontier barbarians" could not go on indefinitely in the same form. The civilized and civilizing peoples encountered problems of magnitude which could not be solved by their pre-industrial technology—the distance to which troops could move and supplies be brought up to them or gathered locally; the speed with which administrative orders could be executed, without dilution or evasion along the chain of command; the costs of moving grain from the provinces to feed cities and fill state granaries. These problems can be summarized in the form of a double question: How high a social, political, and institutional pyramid could be built on how broad a territorial base?

In their search—unconscious of course—for the answers to these questions— the experience of the ancient civilizations can be analyzed under two classifications. Under the first, they either subdivided, or annexed from each other, or conquered each other. This part of the historical experience does not concern us here.

Under the second classification, which concerns Inner Asia, they learned by experiment to discriminate between those territories, resources, and peoples which could be profitably included within their imperial expansion and those which it was better to exclude because military action, administration, and the collection of revenue cost more than they were worth. Inner Asia forms the eastern half of a northern frontier along which all the ancient civilizations found it better to halt, to limit their expansion, and from time to time to fortify—in order not only to "keep out the barbarians" but to keep their own population and responsibilities from spreading beyond control. The western half of this northern frontier is marked by the Greek settlements on the northern shore of the Black Sea and by the Roman fortified *limes* along the Danube and Rhine and between England and Scotland. South of this frontier, from the Atlantic to the Pacific were to be found cities, supported by relatively intensive agriculture (including irrigated agriculture) and the growing of special crops like grapes and olives. In forested Europe there was a mixture of limited, low-yield agriculture, livestock-breeding (especially horned cattle), and forest hunting; north of the Greek wheat-growing colonies on the Black Sea shore there was grazing, giving way still farther north to forest-clearing agriculture and other forest activities; north of the Middle Eastern and Chinese civilizations were the steppes and deserts of Inner Asia, with their northern forest fringes.

This long preamble leads up to the true starting point for analysis of the societies of Inner Asia and their history: not only the frontier between civilization and barbarism, but the barbarian societies themselves, were in large measure created by the growth and the geographical spread of the great ancient civilizations. It is proper to speak of the barbarians as "primitive" only in that remote time when no civilization yet existed, and when the forbears of the civilized peoples were also primitive. From the moment that civilization began to evolve it began also to spread, seeking more land in which to establish the practices of civilization; in taking up more land, it recruited into civilization some of the people who had held that land, and displaced others, and the effect on those who were displaced was that they had diverged from whatever had been their own line of evolution out of the primitive state; they modified their economic practices and experimented with new kinds of specialization, and they also evolved new kinds of social cohesion and political organization, and new ways of fighting. Civilization itself created its own barbarian plague; the barbarian terror that harried the northern frontiers of civilization did not erupt from a distant, dark and bloody ground that had nothing to do with civilization; it was an activity of peoples who were the kind of people they were because their whole evolution had been in contact with, and had been molded by, the advance of civilization.

From archaeology, before written history, from what remains of Greek accounts of the Scyths on the Black Sea, and from the Chinese accounts, which enable us to follow the change from wars in which the Chinese, in chariots, fought against barbarians who were on foot, in the eighth and sixth centuries B.C., to the wars along the line of the future Great Wall at the end of the fourth century B.C. when the Chinese first encountered the mounted archers of a society of true steppe nomads, and, in order to fight them, adopted their costume and imitated their tactics, the record is unbroken, though far from complete. It leads us down through the centuries to 1453, when the Turks took Constantinople; to the end of the Old World's isolation and the eve of the great navigations which discovered the New World and ushered in new modes of history.

By the end of these long centuries of symbiotic development the Inner Asian societies were permeated with Chinese, Indian, Iranian, and Near Eastern influences. All of their practices of production, trade, and war have been evolved through interaction with the fringes of civilization. Nowhere in history can we identify a tribe or a people who appeared abruptly at the gates of civilization in a state of pristine barbarism; a people, that is to say, whose economic, social, and military characteristics had up to that moment never been modified by the influences of civilization.

42   MARCO POLO ON THE MONGOLS

By all odds the most formidable onslaught of the Eurasian nomads upon the centers of civilization was that of the Mongols in the thirteenth century. Within a few decades they conquered the greatest empire in Eurasian history, an empire extending from the Adriatic to the China Seas, and from Muscovy to Indonesia. Soon after the founding of this empire, the famous Venetian merchant Marco Polo visited in 1275 the Mongol capital Cambuluc (Peking), where he entered the service of Kublai Khan. For seventeen years Polo functioned in various capacities, thereby gaining an unequalled firsthand knowledge of the Mongols, or Tartars as he calls them, and of their empire. The following selection presents some of his observations, including his revealing and significant comment concerning the rapid assimilation of the Mongols by their subject peoples—a process foreshadowing the early dissolution that the Mongol empire was to suffer.*

Now that we have begun to speak of the Tartars, I have plenty to tell you on that subject. The Tartar custom is to spend the winter in warm plains, where

* Sir Henry Yule, ed. and trans., *The Book of Ser Marco Polo*, 3rd ed. (New York: Charles Scribner's Sons, 1903), I, 251-52, 256-57, 260-63, 331, 356-58.

they find good pasture for their cattle, whilst in summer they betake themselves to a cool climate among the mountains and valleys, where water is to be found as well as woods and pastures.

Their houses are circular, and are made of wands covered with felts. These are carried along with them whithersoever they go; for the wands are so strongly bound together, and likewise so well combined, that the frame can be made very light. Whenever they erect these huts the door is always to the south. They also have waggons covered with black felt so efficaciously that no rain can get in. These are drawn by oxen and camels, and the women and children travel in them. The women do the buying and selling, and whatever is necessary to provide for the husband and household; for the men all lead the life of gentlemen, troubling themselves about nothing but hunting and hawking, and looking after their goshawks and falcons, unless it be the practice of warlike exercises.

They live on the milk and meat which their herds supply, and on the produce of the chase; and they eat all kinds of flesh, including that of horses and dogs, and Pharaoh's rats, of which last there are great numbers in burrows on those plains. Their drink is mare's milk.

They are very careful not to meddle with each other's wives, and will not do so on any account, holding that to be an evil and abominable thing. The women too are very good and loyal to their husbands, and notable housewives withal. [Ten or twenty of them will dwell together in charming peace and unity, nor shall you ever hear an ill word among them.]

· · · · ·

This is the fashion of their religion. [They say there is a Most High God of Heaven, whom they worship daily with thurible and incense, but they pray to Him only for health of mind and body. But] they have [also] a certain [other] god of theirs called Natigay, and they say he is the god of the Earth, who watches over their children, cattle, and crops. They show him great worship and honour, and every man hath a figure of him in his house, made of felt and cloth; and they also make in the same manner images of his wife and children. The wife they put on the left hand, and the children in front. And when they eat, they take the fat of the meat and grease the god's mouth withal, as well as the mouths of his wife and children. Then they take of the broth and sprinkle it before the door of the house; and that done, they deem that their god and his family have had their share of the dinner.

· · · · ·

All their harness of war is excellent and costly. Their arms are bows and arrows, sword and mace; but above all the bow, for they are capital archers, indeed the best that are known. On their backs they wear armour of cuirbouly, prepared from buffalo and other hides, which is very strong. They are excellent soldiers, and passing valiant in battle. They are also more capable of hardships than other nations; for many a time, if need be, they will go for a month without any supply of food, living only on the milk of their mares and on such game as their bows may win them. Their horses also will subsist entirely on the grass of the plains, so that there is no need to carry store of barley or straw or oats; and they are very docile to their riders. These, in case of need, will abide on horseback the livelong night, armed at all points, while the horse will be continually grazing.

Of all troops in the world these are they which endure the greatest hardship and fatigue, and which cost the least; and they are the best of all for making wide conquests of country. And this you will perceive from what you have heard and shall hear in this book; and (as a fact) there can be no manner of doubt that now they are the masters of the biggest half of the world. Their troops are admirably ordered in the manner that I shall now relate.

You see, when a Tartar prince goes forth to war, he takes with him, say, 100,000 horse. Well, he appoints an officer to every ten men, one to every hundred, one to every thousand, and one to every ten thousand, so that his own orders have to be given to ten persons only, and each of these ten persons has to pass the orders only to other ten, and so on; no one having to give orders to more than ten. And every one in turn is responsible only to the officer immediately over him; and the discipline and order that comes of this method is marvellous, for they are a people very obedient to their chiefs. Further, they call the corps of 100,000 men a *Tuc;* that of 10,000 they call a *Toman;* the thousand they call . . . ; the hundred *Guz;* the ten. . . . And when the army is on the march they have always 200 horsemen, very well mounted, who are sent a distance of two marches in advance to reconnoitre, and these always keep ahead. They have a similar party detached in the rear, and on either flank, so that there is a good look-out kept on all sides against a surprise. When they are going on a distant expedition they take no gear with them except two leather bottles for milk; a little earthenware pot to cook their meat in, and a little tent to shelter them from rain. And in case of great urgency they will ride ten days on end without lighting a fire or taking a meal. On such an occasion they will sustain themselves on the blood of their horses, opening a vein and letting the blood jet into their mouths, drinking till they have had enough, and then staunching it.

They also have milk dried into a kind of paste to carry with them; and when they need food they put this in water, and beat it up till it dissolves, and then drink it. [It is prepared in this way; they boil the milk, and when the rich part floats on the top they skim it into another vessel, and of that they make butter; for the milk will not become solid till this is removed. Then they put the milk in the sun to dry. And when they go on an expedition, every man takes some ten pounds of this dried milk with him. And of a morning he will take a half pound of it and put it in his leather bottle, with as much water as he pleases. So, as he rides along, the milk-paste and the water in the bottle get well churned together into a kind of pap, and that makes his dinner.]

When they come to an engagement with the enemy, they will gain the victory in this fashion. [They never let themselves get into a regular medley, but keep perpetually riding round and shooting into the enemy. And] as they do not count it any shame to run away in battle, they will [sometimes pretend to] do so, and in running away they turn in the saddle and shoot hard and strong at the foe, and in this way make great havoc. Their horses are trained so perfectly that they will double hither and thither, just like a dog, in a way that is quite astonishing. Thus they fight to as good purpose in running away as if they stood and faced the enemy, because of the vast volleys of arrows that they shoot in this way, turning round upon their pursuers, who are fancying that they have won the battle. But when the Tartars see that they have killed and wounded a good many horses and men, they wheel round bodily, and return to the charge in perfect order and with loud cries; and in a very short time the enemy are routed. In truth they are stout and valiant soldiers, and inured to war. And you perceive that it is just when the enemy sees them run, and images that he has gained the battle, that he has in reality lost it; for the Tartars wheel round in a moment when they judge the right time has come. And after this fashion they have won many a fight.

All this that I have been telling you is true of the manners and customs of the genuine Tartars. But I must add also that in these days they are greatly degenerated; for those who are settled in Cathay have taken up the practices of the Idolaters of the country, and have abandoned their own institutions; whilst those who have settled in the Levant have adopted the customs of the Saracens.

. . . . .

Now am I come to that part of our Book in which I shall tell you of the great and wonderful magnificence of the Great Kaan now reigning, by name Cublay Kaan; *Kaan* being a title which signifyeth "The Great Lord of Lords," or Emperor. And of a surety he hath good right to such a title, for all men know for a certain truth that he is the most potent man, as regards forces and lands and treasure, that existeth in the world, or ever hath existed from the time of our First Father Adam until this day.

. . . . .

. . . He is of a good stature, neither tall nor short, but of a middle height. He has a becoming amount of flesh, and is very shapely in all his limbs. His complexion is white and red, the eyes black and fine, the nose well formed and well set on. He has four wives, whom he retains permanently as his legitimate consorts; and the eldest of his sons by those four wives ought by rights to be emperor; —I mean when his father dies. Those four ladies are called empresses, but each is distinguished also by her proper name. And each of them has a special court of her own, very grand and ample; no one of them having fewer than 300 fair and charming damsels. They have also many pages and eunuchs, and a number of other attendants of both sexes; so that each of these ladies has not less than 10,000 persons attached to her court.

When the Emperor desires the society of one of these four consorts, he will sometimes send for the lady to his apartment and sometimes visit her at her own. He has also a great number of concubines, and I will tell you how he obtains them.

You must know that there is a tribe of Tartars called Ungrat, who are noted for their beauty. Now every year an hundred of the most beautiful maidens of this tribe are sent to the Great Kaan, who commits them to the charge of certain elderly ladies dwelling in his palace. And these old ladies make the girls sleep with them, in order to ascertain if they have sweet breath [and do not snore], and are sound in all their limbs. Then such of them as are of approved beauty, and are good and sound in all respects, are appointed to attend on the Emperor by turns. Thus six of these damsels take their turn for three days and nights, and wait on him when he is in his chamber and when he is in his bed, to serve him in any way, and to be entirely at his orders. At the end of the three days and nights they are relieved by other six. And so throughout the year, there are reliefs of maidens by six and six, changing every three days and nights.

Chapter Fifteen

Traditional Byzantine civilization

43   C<small>ONSTANTINOPLE</small>

With the fall of Rome, the West Roman Empire gave way to a collection of barbarian states. The East Roman Empire, by contrast, survived for another millennium and is generally known as the Byzantine Empire. This empire, unlike the West, which declined to agrarian manorialism, was dotted with small towns and boasted a capital, Constantinople, that was the envy of all visitors, who marvelled at its large population, magnificent buildings, dazzling wealth, and commanding location on the Straits separating Europe and Asia. Typical were the reports of the following two visitors: the monk Odo of Deuil, who in 1147 accompanied Louis VII of France on the Second Crusade, and the Jewish traveller Benjamin of Tudela, who was in the capital in 1160.

Odo of Deuil *

Constantinople, the glory of the Greeks, rich in renown and richer still in possessions, is laid out in a triangle shaped like a ship's sail. In its inner angle stand Santa Sophia and Constantine's Palace, in which there is a chapel that is revered for its exceedingly holy relics. Moreover, Constantinople is girt on two sides by the sea; when approaching the city we had the Arm of St. George on the right and on the left a certain estuary, which, after branching from the Arm, flows on for about four miles. In that place the Palace of Blachernae, although having foundations laid on low ground, achieves eminence through excellent construction and elegance and, because of its surroundings on three sides, affords its

---

* Odo of Deuil, *De Profectione Ludovici VII in Orientem*, trans. Virginia G. Berry, No. XLII of the Records of Civilization: Sources and Studies (New York: Columbia University Press, 1948), pp. 63-67.

inhabitants the triple pleasure of looking out upon sea, fields, and city. Its exterior is of almost matchless beauty, but its interior surpasses anything that I can say about it. Throughout it is decorated elaborately with gold and a great variety of colors, and the floor is marble, paved with cunning workmanship; and I do not know whether the exquisite art or the exceedingly valuable stuffs endows it with the more beauty or value. The third side of the city's triangle includes fields, but it is fortified by towers and a double wall which extends for about two miles from the sea to the palace. This wall is not very strong, and it posseses no lofty towers; but the city puts its trust, I think, in the size of its population and the long period of peace which it has enjoyed. Below the walls lies open land, cultivated by plough and hoe, which contains gardens that furnish the citizens all kinds of vegetables. From the outside underground conduits flow in, bringing the city an abundance of sweet water.

The city itself is squalid and fetid and in many places harmed by permanent darkness, for the wealthy overshadow the streets with buildings and leave these dirty, dark places to the poor and to travelers; there murders and robberies and other crimes which love the darkness are committed. Moreover, since people live lawlessly in this city, which has as many lords as rich men and almost as many thieves as poor men, a criminal knows neither fear nor shame, because crime is not punished by law and never entirely comes to light. In every respect she exceeds moderation; for, just as she surpasses other cities in wealth, so, too, does she surpass them in vice. Also, she possesses many churches unequal to Santa Sophia in size but equal to it in beauty, which are to be marveled at for their beauty and their many saintly relics. Those who had the opportunity entered these places, some to see the sights and others to worship faithfully.

Conducted by the emperor, the king also visited the shrines and, after returning, when won over by the urgency of his host's requests, dined with him. That banquet afforded pleasure to ear, mouth, and eye with pomp as marvelous, viands as delicate, and pastimes as pleasant as the guests were illustrious.

Benjamin of Tudela *

. . . one comes to Constantinople, an exceeding great city, and the head of the kingdom of Javanites, or those called Greeks. This is the principal seat of the Emperor Emanuel, whose command twelve Kings obey; for every one whereof there are several palaces at Constantinople, and they have also fortresses and governments, and unto these the whole land is subject. The principal and chiefest is called Apripus, the second Mega Domestikutz, the third Dominot, the fourth Mackducus, the fifth Iknomus Megli, and the rest have names like unto these. The compass of the city of Constantinople containeth eighteen miles, one half of it standeth upon the sea, but the other half on the continent, and it is seated upon two arms of the sea, into one of which the sea flows out of Russia, but into the other from Spain, and it is frequented by many traders from the provinces and countries of Babylon, Senaar, Media, Persia, and all the kingdom of Egypt and land of Canaan, and the kingdoms of Russia, Hungary, and Psanki, Buria, Lombardy, and Spain.

The city itself is excessively populous, unto which merchants resort out of all countries, travelling thither both by sea and land. It hath none to compare with it in the world, except Bagdat, that mighty city of the Ismaelites. Here is the most

* J. Pinkerton, *Voyages and Travels* (London: Longman, Hurst, 1811), pp. 4-6.

famous temple of St. Sophia, and the Patriarch of the Grecians dwelleth here, nor do they agree in doctrine with the Pope of Rome. There are in it also as many altars in number as days in the year; but it hath an exceeding great treasure, almost beyond all estimation, by the offerings and riches, yearly brought from divers countries, islands, castles, forts, and palaces, so that the wealth of no temple in the world can be compared with the riches thereof; and in the midst of the temple there are pillars of gold and silver, huge candlesticks, lanthorns, lamps, and other ornaments of these precious metals, more than any man is able to reckon. Next adjoining to the walls of the temple, there is a place built for the Emperor's diversion, called Hippodromus, where yearly, upon the birthday of Jesus of Nazareth, great spectacles are publicly presented, and there all sorts of men in all manner of habits of the whole world appear before the King and Queen. Lions also, and bears, leopards, and wild asses, are brought forth into the place where these spectacles are to be seen, that they may fight together, and birds also after the same manner: and my opinion is that in no country of the world such princely sports are to be seen.

But this King Emanuel, besides that palace left him by his ancestors, hath built him another upon the sea-shore, which they call Bilbernæ, the pillars and walls whereof he hath overlaid with beaten gold and silver, whereon he hath engraved all the wars made by him and his ancestors; and he hath prepared a throne there for himself of gold and precious stones, and hath adorned it with a golden crown hanging on high by gold chains; the composure whereof is equal with the throne itself, so enriched with precious stones and pearls, that the price thereof no man is able to value; of so great a lustre, that without the assistance of light they shine, and may be seen in the night.

Moreover there are such valuable things in the same place as were incredible if told; and tributes are yearly brought into that palace, wherewith the towers are filled with scarlet and purple garments, and gold; so that the like example of building and riches can no where else be found in the world. And it is affirmed, that the revenue only of this city itself, gathered from the markets, haven, and tribute of merchants, amounted to 20,000 crowns a day. Furthermore, the Grecians themselves, inhabitants of the country, are exceeding rich in gold, and have abundance of precious stones, and are dressed in most sumptuous apparel, their garments being made of crimson intermingled with gold, or embroidered with needle-work, and are all carried upon horses, as if they were the children of Kings. The country itself being very large, abounds with all sorts of fruits, and hath great plenty of corn, flesh, and wine; nor is there a finer spot in the whole world to be found. They are also learned and skilful in the discipline of the Grecians; but giving themselves wholly to pleasure, they eat and drink every one under his own vine and under his own fig-tree. Of all the nations which they call barbarians, they have soldiers to fight with the Soldan, King of the children of Thogarna, who are commonly called Turks, because they themselves, through idleness and luxury, are become quite unfit for the wars, and seem to me more like women than men, through their excessive love of pleasure.

But no Jews dwell within the city, for they are excluded from thence by an arm of the sea of Sophia; they are not so much as permitted to come into the city but by boats, and that for the sake of commerce; and here are about two thousand Jews Rabbanites, besides five hundred Karaites on the other side. There is a wall to separate them from the Rabbanites, that are the disciples of wise men; and among whom Abtalion the Great, and R. Abdias, and Aaron Cuspus, and Joseph Starginus, and Eliakim the governor, have the chief authority. Amongst these some are artificers of silken garments; but there are many merchants, and those too very rich.

No Jew is there permitted to be carried on horse-back, except Solomon the Egyptian, the King's physician, through whose interest the Jews are comforted and eased in their captivity, which they feel to be grievous; for all the Jews are very much hated by the Grecians, without making any difference between the good and evil: but they are worst used by the tanners, who, while they dress their skins, pour out the filthy water into the streets before their doors. They are in general oppressed with a grievous yoke, and are insulted and beaten in the streets, enduring from every hand abundance of injuries. But among the Jews themselves some are rich, as I have said, and good men, and merciful, and observe the commandments, who patiently endure the misery of captivity. The place wherein they dwell is called Pera.

RELIGIOUS DISSENSION   **44**

Behind the facade of imperial grandeur as exemplified by Constantinople, Byzantium from the outset was weakened by recurring religious strife. Outstanding was the Monophysitic controversy of the fifth to the seventh centuries concerning the relationship of the divine and human natures in Christ, and the iconoclasm controversy of the eighth and ninth centuries concerning the worship of images. Religious conflict directly involved the state because of Caesaropapism, the joining of church and state at the top. The emperor considered himself to be the head of the church as well as of the empire and assumed responsibility for defining and preserving the correct doctrine (orthe doxa, or orthodoxy) for his people. As the defenders of orthodoxy the emperors assiduously persecuted heretics such as the Bogomils, who viewed the Christian church and the state as the works of Satan, and who sought to purify themselves by ascetic practices. In the following selection, Anna Comnena proudly describes how her father, Alexius I, tricked the Bogomil leader Basil, and how the heretic remained steadfast in his faith to the end.*

After this, in the course of the years of his reign, a very great cloud of heretics arose, and the nature of their heresy was new and hitherto quite unknown to the church. For two very evil and worthless doctrines which had been known in former times, now coalesced; the impiety, as it might be called, of the Manichæans, which we also call the Paulician heresy, and the shamelessness of the Massalians. This was the doctrine of the Bogomils compounded of the Massalians and the Manichæans. And probably it existed even before my father's time, but in secret; for the sect of the Bogomils is very clever in aping virtue. And you would not find any long-haired worldling belonging to the Bogomils, for their wickedness was hidden under the cloak and cowl. A Bogomil looks gloomy and is covered up to the nose and walks with a stoop and mutters, but within he is an uncontrollable wolf. And this most pernicious race, which was like a snake hiding in a hole, my father lured and brought out to the light by chanting mysterious spells. For now that he had rid himself of much of his anxiety about the East and the West he turned his attention

* Elizabeth A. S. Dawes, trans., *The Alexiad of Princess Anna Comnena* (London: Routledge & Kegan Paul Ltd.; New York: Barnes & Noble, Inc., 1928), pp. 412-18.

to more spiritual matters. For in all things he was superior to other men; in teaching he surpassed those whose profession was teaching; in battles and strategy he excelled those who were admired for their exploits. By this time the fame of the Bogomils had spread everywhere. (For Basil, a monk, was very wily in handling the impiety of the Bogomils; he had twelve disciples whom he called 'apostles,' and also dragged about with him some female disciples, wretched women of loose habits and thoroughly bad, and he disseminated his wickedness everywhere.) This evil attacked many souls like fire, and the Emperor's soul could not brook it, so he began investigating the heresy. He had some of the Bogomils brought to the palace and all proclaimed a certain Basil as the teacher and chief representative of the Bogomilian heresy. Of these, one Diblatius was kept in prison, and as he would not confess when questioned, he was subjected to torture and then informed against the man called Basil, and the disciples he had chosen. Accordingly the Emperor entrusted several men with the search for him. And Satanael's arch-satrap, Basil, was brought to light, in monk's habit, with a withered countenance, clean shaven and tall of stature. The Emperor, wishing to elicit his inmost thoughts by compulsion under the disguise of persuasion, at once invited the man on some righteous pretext. And he even rose from his chair to greet him, and made him sit by him and share his table, and threw out his whole fishing-line and fixed various baits on the hooks for this voracious whale to devour. And he made this monk, who was so many-sided in wickedness, swallow all the poison he offered him by pretending that he wished to become his disciple, and not he only, but probably his brother, the Sebastocrator Isaac, also; he pretended too to value all the words he spoke as if they came from a divine voice and to defer to him in all things, provided only that the villain Basil would effect his soul's salvation. "Most reverend father," he would say (for the Emperor rubbed sweets on the rim of the cup so that this demoniac should vomit forth his black thoughts), "I admire thee for thy virtue, and beseech thee to teach me the new doctrines thy Reverence has introduced, as those of our Churches are practically worthless and do not bring anybody to virtue." But the monk at first put on airs and he, that was really an ass, dragged about the lion's skin with him everywhere and shied at the Emperor's words, and yet was puffed up with his praises, for the Emperor even had him at his table. And in all this the Emperor's cousin [?] the Sebastocrator, aided and abetted him in the play; and finally Basil spued out the dogmas of his heresy. And how was this done? A curtain divided the women's apartments from the room where the two Emperors sat with the wretch who blurted out and openly declared all he had in his soul; whilst a secretary sitting on the inner side of the curtain committed his words to writing. And the nonsense-monger seemed to be the teacher while the Emperor pretended to be the pupil, and the secretary wrote down his doctrines. And that man, stricken of God, spun together all that horrible stuff and did not shun any abominable dogma, but even despised our theology and misrepresented all our ecclesiastical administration. And as for the churches, woe is me! he called our sacred churches the temples of devils, and our consecration of the body and blood of our one and greatest High Priest and Victim he considered and condemned as worthless. And what followed? the Emperor threw off his disguise and drew the curtain aside; and the whole senate was gathered together and the military contingent mustered, and the elders of the church were present too. The episcopal throne of the Queen of Cities was at that time occupied by that most blessed of patriarchs, Lord Nicholas, the Grammarian. Then the execrable doctrines were read out, and proof was impossible to attack. And the defendant did not deny anything, but immediately bared his head and proceeded to counter-demonstrations and professed himself willing to undergo fire, scourging and a thousand deaths. For these erring Bogomils believe that they can bear any suffering without feeling pain, as the angels forsooth will pluck them out of the fire. And although all . . . and reproached him for his impiety, even those whom he had involved in his own ruin, he remained the same Basil, an inflexible and very brave Bogomil. And although he was threatened with burning and other tortures he clung fast to his demon and embraced his Satanael. After he was consigned to prison the Emperor frequently sent for him and frequently exhorted him to forswear his impiety, but all the Emperor's exhortations left him unchanged.

. . . . .

The Emperor had summoned Basil's disciples and fellow-mystics from all over the world, especially the so-called twelve disciples and made trial of their opinions, and found that they were openly Basil's followers. For the evil had gone deep even into very great houses and had affected a very large number. Consequently he condemned those aliens to be burnt, the leader of the chorus and the chorus too. When the Bogomils who had been discovered, were assembled, some clung to their heresy, while others recanted absolutely and resisted their accusers strongly and expressed their abhorrence of the Bogomilian heresy. The Emperor was not inclined to believe them, and to prevent many a Christian being confounded with the Bogomils as being a Bogomil, and a Bogomil escaping as a Christian, he invented a new device for revealing clearly those who were really Christians. Accordingly the next day he took his seat on the imperial throne and many of the senate and the holy Synod were present and a chosen few of the monks who were learned men. Then all the Bogomils accused of heresy were placed together in the centre and the Emperor commanded each to be examined again. Some confessed to being Bogomils and adhered stoutly to their heresy, while others denied it absolutely and called themselves Christians and when accused by others did not yield an inch, so he glowered at them and said, "To-day two pyres shall be lighted and on one of them a cross shall be fixed in the ground itself. Then you shall all be given your choice and those who are ready to die to-day for their Christian faith, can separate themselves from the others and walk to the pyre with the cross, while those who cling to the Bogomilian heresy shall be thrown on the other. For it is better that even Christians should die, than live to be persecuted as Bogomils and offend the consciences of many. Go now and let each one of you choose his station." With this verdict against the Bogomils the Emperor pretended to have closed the matter. They were at once taken and led away and a large crowd had gathered and stood round about them. Then pyres were lighted, 'seven times as large as they were wont to be,' as the hymn-writer says, in the place called Tzycanisterin; the flames rose to the heavens, and the cross stood above the one; each of the condemned was given his choice to walk to which of the two pyres he wished, as all were destined to be burnt. Seeing that there was no escape, the orthodox among them walked to the pyre with the cross, ready really to suffer martyrdom; whereas the godless ones who clung to their abominable heresy turned to the other. And they were all on the point of being thrown on the pyres at the same time and the bystanders all grieved for the Christians who were now to be burnt, and were very wroth against the Emperor, for they were ignorant of his plan. But an order from the Emperor came just in time to prevent the executioners carrying out their duties. Having in this way obtained certain proof of those who were really Bogomils he released the Christians, who had been falsely accused, with many admonitions. The others he recommitted to prison, but had the impious Basil's apostles separated from the rest. And these he sent for daily, and taught some himself, exhorting them earnestly to abandon their hideous religion, and for the others he ordered some picked men of the hierarchy to come every day and teach them the orthodox faith and advise them to relinquish the Bogomilian heresy. And some of them did change for the better and were released from confinement, but others were kept in prison and died in their heresy, but were amply supplied with food and clothing.

However all the members of the holy Synod and the chief monks, as well as the patriarch of that time, Nicholas, decreed that Basil who was the heresiarch and quite unrepentant, deserved to be burnt. The Emperor was of the same opinion and after conversing with him several times and recognizing that the man was mischievous and would not abandon his heresy, he finally had an immense pyre built in the Hippodrome. A very large trench was dug and a quantity of wood, all tall trees piled up together, made the structure look like a mountain. When the pile was lighted, a great crowd slowly collected on the floor and steps of the circus in eager expectation of what was to happen. On the opposite side a cross was fixed and the impious man was given a choice, for if he dreaded the fire and changed his mind, and walked to the cross, then he should be delivered from burning. A number of heretics were there watching their leader Basil. He shewed himself contemptuous of all punishment and threats, and while he was still at a distance from the fire he began to laugh and talk marvels, saying that angels would snatch him from the middle of the fire, and he proceeded to chant these words of David's, 'It shall not come nigh thee; only with thine eyes shalt thou behold.' But when the crowd stood aside and allowed him to have a free view of that terrifying sight, the burning pyre (for even at a good distance he could feel the fire, and saw the flames rising high and as it were thundering and shooting out sparks of fire which rose to the top of the stone obelisk which stands in the centre of the Hippodrome), then the bold fellow seemed to flinch from the fire and be disturbed. For as if wholly desperate, he constantly turned away his eyes and clapped his hands and beat his thigh. And yet in spite of being thus affected by the mere sight he was adamant. For the fire did not soften his iron will, nor did the messages sent by the Emperor subdue him. For either great madness had seized him under the present stress of misfortunes and he had lost his mind and had no power to decide about what was advantageous; or, as seems more likely, the devil that possessed his soul had steeped it in the deepest darkness. So there stood that abominable Basil, unmoved by any threat or fear, and gaped now at the fire and now at the bystanders. And all thought him quite mad for he did not rush to the pyre nor did he draw back, but stood fixed and immovable on the spot he had first taken up. Now many tales were going round and his marvellous talk was bandied about on every tongue, so the executioners were afraid that the demons protecting Basil might perhaps, by God's permission, work some wonderful new miracle, and the wretch be seen snatched unharmed from the middle of the mighty fire and transported to some very frequented place. In that case the second state would be worse than the first, so they decided to make an experiment. For, while he was talking marvels and boasting that he would be seen unharmed in the middle of the fire, they took his cloak and said, "Now let us see whether the fire will touch your garments," and they threw it right into the middle of the pyre. But Basil was so uplifted by the demon that was deluding him that he said, "Look at my cloak floating up to the sky!" Then they 'recognizing the web from the edge,' took him and pushed him, clothes, shoes and all, into the middle of the pyre. And the flames, as if deeply enraged against him, ate the impious man up, without any odour arising or even a fresh appearance of smoke, only one thin smoky line could be seen in the midst of the flames. For even the elements are excited against the impious; whereas, to speak truthfully, they spare those beloved of God, just as once upon a time in Babylon the fire retreated from those young men who were dear to God, and enclosed them like a golden chamber. In this case the men who lifted up the accursed Basil had scarcely placed him on the pyre before the flames seemed to dart forward to snatch hold of him. Then the people looking on clamoured loudly and demanded that all the rest who belonged to Basil's pernicious sect should be thrown into the fire as well, but the Emperor did not allow it but ordered them to be confined in the porches and verandahs of the largest palace. After this the concourse was dismissed. Later, the godless ones were transferred to another very strong prison into which they were cast and after pining away for a long time died in their impiety. This was the last and crowning act of the Emperor's long labours and successes and it was an innovation of startling boldness.

Economic Decline   45

The thousand years of Byzantine history were marked by recurring periods of glory and greatness, as well as of weakness and decline. Yet the fact remains that Byzantium did disappear in the fifteenth century when Constantinople fell to the advancing Turks. And this was at a time when the West was bursting with energy and beginning the overseas expansion that was to lead to global domination. The question naturally arises, then, why the end result in Byzantium was extinction, when in the West it was world hegemony. Many factors were involved, one of the most important being economic, as set forth in the following article by a distinguished American Byzantinist.*

It is now five hundred years since the Byzantine empire was brought to an end by the Ottoman Turks. Scholars today quite justly reject Gibbon's assumption that the Byzantine empire was, throughout its entire existence, in a state of decline. They have come to rank it, instead, as one of the great empires in history. And this for good reasons. It endured for over a thousand years. Down to about the middle of the eleventh century it was the center of civilization in Christendom. It preserved the thought and literature of antiquity; it developed new forms of art; it held back the barbarians. It produced great statesmen, soldiers, and diplomats as well as reformers and renowned scholars. Its missionaries, aided by its diplomats and sometimes by its armies, spread the gospel among the pagan tribes, especially the Slavs, which dwelt along its frontiers and beyond. As a Czech historian has put it, Byzantium "molded the undisciplined tribes of Serbs, Bulgars, Russians, Croats even, and made nations out of them; it gave to them its religion and institutions, taught their princes how to govern, transmitted to them the very principles of civilization— writing and literature." Byzantium was a great power and a great civilizing force.

Yet in a sense Gibbon was right. For the Byzantine empire did not come to an end as the result of a single blow as, for instance the battle of Nineveh of 612 B.C. is said to have brought to an end the mighty Assyrian empire. The empire which Mohammed II destroyed on May 29, 1453, had been wasting away for over three

* Peter Charanis, "Economic Factors in the Decline of the Byzantine Empire," *Journal of Economic History*, XIII (Fall 1953), 412-24.

hundred years, although part of this time, notably during the period of the Comneni, it was not an insignificant force. By the time of the fall of Constantinople, however, the Morea, one or two islands in the Aegean, and Constantinople were all that had been left of its once widely extensive territories. Constantinople itself, which in the tenth century had a population of perhaps one million people, had been reduced to probably not more than 75,000 inhabitants. As a center of commerce it had long been eclipsed by Galata, the Genoese colony on the opposite side of the Golden Horn. The Byzantine emperors became puppets in the hands of the Italian commercial republics, notably Genoa and Venice, served the Ottoman sultans as vassals, or miserably toured the West begging for help in return for which they were ready to sacrifice the religious traditions of their people. What a far cry from the august position of their predecessors of the tenth century who challenged East and West and challenged them not without success! "I shall conquer your lands," wrote Nicephorus Phocas to the Caliph of Bagdad, "and I shall go as far as Mecca. . . . I shall conquer all the Orient and the Occident and I shall spread everywhere the religion of the cross." The same emperor declared to the ambassador of the German emperor, Otto I: "Do you want a greater scandal than that [Otto] should call himself emperor and claim for himself provinces belonging to our empire? Both these things are intolerable; and if both are unsupportable, that especially is not to be borne, nay, not to be heard of that he calls himself emperor." What brought the empire from this pinnacle of power down to the abject position in which we find it in the fourteenth and fifteenth centuries is one of the most interesting problems in history.

In the history of the Byzantine empire, war and religion were the two principal factors that molded the society of the empire and determined its external position. War was the normal state of things throughout its long existence. The external crisis, however, that particularly affected the evolution of its society was that of the seventh century.

The advances of the Saracens and the incursions of the Slavs and Bulgars reduced virtually the whole empire to a frontier province. To cope with this situation the emperors of the seventh century reorganized the provincial administration of the empire, introducing what is known as the *theme* system, the essence of which was the subordination of civil to military authority exercised in each province by the commander of the army corps stationed there. But with the establishment of the *theme* system is connected the establishment of another institution, the system of military estates. These military estates, small in size and granted to individuals in return for military service, became the opening wedge in the formation of a new class of free peasant proprietors. The soldiers themselves constituted the nucleus of this class, but others gradually were added. For while the eldest son of a soldier inherited his father's plot together with the obligation of military service, the rest of the family were free to reclaim and cultivate the land that was vacant. The free peasants, cultivating their own land, paying the taxes, and, if necessary, serving in the army, came to constitute the dominant element in the agrarian society of Byzantium. They became a bulwark of the state, lent to it new vigor, and enabled it eventually to recover its position in the Orient. By the end of the tenth century, Byzantium had become the most powerful state throughout the Christian-Moslem world.

The situation changed in the eleventh century. During the second half of that century the empire suffered a series of military reverses from which it never fully recovered. The most serious of these was the disastrous defeat at Manzikert (1071). The battle of Manzikert decided the fate of Asia Minor and conditioned the subsequent history of the Byzantine empire. But Manzikert was only a battle, and battles had been lost before without the serious consequences that followed Manzikert. What explains the decline that set in after it and that would lead eventually to the disappearance of the empire were the conditions which came to prevail in the social and economic life of the empire in the eleventh century and later. Manzikert itself was the result of these conditions.

The dominant fact in the social and economic life of the empire in the eleventh century is the triumph of the landed military aristocracy and the decline of the soldiery-peasantry which had for centuries served as the bulwark of the state.

From the very beginning of its history the large estate had been a feature of Byzantine society. The complicated and burdensome fiscal administration affected by the reorganization of the empire following the political and economic crisis of the third century worked in such a way as to give impetus to the growth of the large estates. The society revealed by the papyri and the great legislative monuments of the fifth and the sixth centuries is a society dominated by these estates. *Coloni,* reduced to serfs, composed the vast majority of the agrarian population, although the free peasant proprietors did not disappear completely. The development of the soldiery-peasantry in the seventh century lessened the extent of the large estates, but did not eliminate them. By the end of the ninth century they had become larger and more numerous. Those who possessed them occupied important positions in the administration and used these positions to increase their holdings. This they did by absorbing, often through dubious means, the properties of the small peasants. Thus the small, free peasant proprietors began to disappear.

The great emperors of the tenth century realized the dangerous social and political implications of this development and tried to check it. Every major emperor from Romanus Lecapenus to and including Basil II, with the exception of John Tzimeskes, issued more than one novel for this purpose. These emperors sought to preserve the free peasantry because they considered it an essential element for the health of the state. As Romanus Lecapenus put it in one of his novels:

> It is not through hatred and envy of the rich that we take these measures, but for the protection of the small and the safety of the empire as a whole. . . . The extension of the power of the strong . . . will bring about the irreparable loss of the public good, if the present law does not bring a check to it. For it is the many, settled on the land, who provide for the general needs, who pay the taxes and furnish the army with its recruits. Everything falls when the many are wanting.

The strictest among the measures taken for the protection of the free peasantry was that issued by Basil II concerning the *allelengyon,* a measure which required the landed aristocracy to pay the tax arrears of peasants too poor to meet their own obligations. But with the death of Basil (1025) the effort to stop the growth of the large estates came to an end. His law concerning the *allelengyon* was repealed and the other measures, although kept in the books, were not enforced. The fate of the free peasantry was definitely decided.

Meanwhile, a similar fate befell the class of the enrolled soldiers, holders of the military estates. For the aristocracy, which, by one means or another, absorbed the estates of the small peasants, absorbed also those of the soldiers. The protection of the interests of these soldiers had been one of the deepest concerns of the emperors of the tenth century. Wrote Constantine Porphyrogenitus in the novel that he issued for the protection of the estates of the soldiers: "The army is to the state what the head is to the body. . . . He who neglects it neglects the safety of the state. . . . Therefore in promulgating our Constitution [on the military estates], we feel we are working for the welfare of all." But in this as in the case of the small peasants the measures taken by the emperors of the tenth century were of no avail. It proved impossible to stop the aristocracy from absorbing the properties of the small, whether the latter were soldiers or not.

What consummated the depression of the enrolled soldiers, however, was the anti-military policy which some of the emperors of the eleventh century followed in order to reduce the power of the military magnates in the administration of the empire. Those who occupied the high military posts in the empire were also great landholders. Their wealth, plus the powers which they exercised as military commanders, made them extremely dangerous to the central government. This danger, indeed, was one of the principal reasons why Basil II issued the novel concerning the *allelengyon* to which reference has already been made. He had faced two formidable revolts, both headed by members of the powerful aristocracy, and it was only with difficulty that he survived. When, after 987, Basil was reconciled with Bardas Skleros, one of the powerful rebels, the latter advised him that, if he wished to preserve the imperial authority, he should permit no one of the aristocracy to prosper and should exhaust their means by heavy taxes. Hence, the various measures he took, including that of the *allelengyon*, were designed not only to protect the poor peasants but also to crush the aristocracy. But on both the question of land and that of taxation the aristocracy triumphed.

One of the important reasons for the triumph of the aristocracy was the very strong hold that it had upon the military organization of the empire. If it could be shaken from this hold, it would lose in power and influence and would become more amenable to the wishes of the imperial government. And this is precisely what certain emperors of the eleventh century, notably Constantine IX Monomachos (1042–1055), Michael VI (1056–1057), and Constantine X Dukas (1059–1067), tried to do. The means of attack which they employed was to weaken the military organization by reducing the size of the army, thus depriving the aristocracy of its military commands. The great military triumphs of the tenth century, the crushing of the Saracens and the Bulgarians and the pushing of the frontiers to the Euphrates and the Tigris in the east and to the Danube in the Balkans, created a sense of security and the feeling that the maintenance of a powerful army was no longer necessary. With Constantine IX, peace became the keynote of the imperial foreign policy, and there began a systematic elimination of the aristocracy from the army while at the same time the development of a civil bureaucracy was promoted. But the aristocracy fought back, and a new struggle ensued, this time between the aristocracy as a military class and a new party of civil officials who came to dominate the imperial court.

The struggle plunged the empire into a series of civil wars that squandered its resources and manpower at a time when new and formidable enemies were making their appearance, both in the East and in the West. But the most serious result of the imperial policy was the deterioration of the army and the depression of the enrolled soldiers. By the time of Constantine X Dukas the profession of the soldier had lost much of its attraction and so, as a Byzantine historian puts it, "the soldiers put aside their arms and became lawyers or jurists." The same author, writing of the army that took the field in one of the expeditions against the Seljuks, states:

> The army was composed of Macedonians and Bulgarians and Varangians and other barbarians who happened to be about. There were gathered also

those who were in Phrygia [the *theme* Anatolikon]. And what one saw in them [the enrolled soldiers of the *theme* Anatolikon] was something incredible. The renowned champions of the Romans who had reduced into subjection all of the east and the west now numbered only a few and these were bowed down by poverty and ill treatment. They lacked in weapons, swords, and other arms, such as javelins and scythes. . . . They lacked also in cavalry and other equipment, for the emperor had not taken the field for a long time. For this reason they were regarded as useless and unnecessary and their wages and maintenance were reduced.

The enrolled soldiers, depressed and forgotten, became more and more a minor element in the Byzantine army. The bulk of this army, in the eleventh century and later, came to be composed almost entirely of foreign mercenaries—Russians, Turks, Alans, English, Normans, Germans, Patzinaks, Bulgarians, and others. These mercenaries were swayed more by their own interests than by those of the empire.

Meanwhile, the development of two institutions, the *pronoia* and the *exkuseia,* added further to the wealth and power of the landed aristocracy, both lay and ecclesiastic. The *pronoia* was the principal means that the emperors of the second half of the eleventh century, but especially later, adopted to recuperate much of the deserted land, to reconstitute the class of soldiers with landed interests, and to reward many of their partisans. A *pronoia* was granted to an individual for a specific period of years, usually his lifetime, in return for military or other services rendered or to be rendered. It was never hereditary, unless it was specifically declared so by a special measure. It consisted usually of land, but it could be a river or a fishery. Some of the *pronoiae* were very extensive, others less so, but the general effect of all was to increase the power and influence of the aristocracy and to lessen the hold of the central government over the agrarian population. For the holder of a *pronoia* exercised over those who inhabited it important financial and judicial powers which were granted to him along with the land. He was expected to serve in the army and also to furnish troops according to the size of his *pronoia*. But when we first meet with the *pronoia* in the second half of the eleventh century, it was not primarily a military grant; it became so during the reign of Alexius Comnenus and those of his successors. The *pronoia* differed from the old military estate in that it was held by persons high in the social order, whereas the recipients of the latter were peasant soldiers. In a study which I devoted to the aristocracy of Byzantium in the thirteenth century I showed that many of the holders of *pronoiae* belonged to the great families of the empire, families that were related to each other and to the ruling dynasty. The extensive use of the *pronoia* contributed not only to the increase, relatively speaking, of the power and wealth of the aristocracy but also to the development of the appanage system and thus weakened the central administration.

The central administration was weakened also by the development of the *exkuseia*. The term, which derives no doubt from the Latin *excusatio* (*excusare*), refers to the fiscal and judicial immunities that the imperial government often granted, especially to monasteries. It was formerly thought that the *exkuseia* first appeared in the eleventh century, but it is now known to be older than that, and may have developed out of the various privileges granted to the Christian clergy in the fourth century. Its use on a wide scale, however, is associated with the eleventh century and later. As the monastic properties during this period were very extensive, the revenue that the imperial government lost by the grant of *exkuseiae* must have been considerable. At the same time the *exkuseia* contributed to increasing the wealth of members of the lay aristocracy, for the emperors of the second half of the eleventh century and later often rewarded their partisans by granting to them the revenues of monasteries, such grants being then known as *kharistikia*. And monasteries whose revenues were thus granted often enjoyed the privilege of *exkuseia*.

Thus the failure to enforce the measures that had been issued for the protection of the soldiery-peasantry and the various grants of privileges made to the aristocracy had made the large estates, by the eleventh century, the dominant features of the agrarian landscape of Byzantium. These estates were worked by tenant peasants, the *paroikoi* of the Byzantine texts, people who were personally free, but who were tied to certain obligations and corvées that curtailed their movement. Some free peasant proprietors continued to exist, but they had become hardly distinguishable from the *paroikoi*. Besides working for the lord, the *paroikoi* had allotments of their own for which they paid rent and performed various obligations and from which, after the passage of a number of years, they could not be evicted. These allotments were transmissible from father to son. These tenant peasants, weighed down by the heavy burden of taxation and numerous corvées, lost all feeling for the welfare of the state as a whole. It is well known that the peasantry of the interior of Asia Minor offered no resistance to the Seljuk Turks, whose establishment in Asia Minor after Manzikert started the empire on the road to general decline. In the twelfth century the Comneni, by utilizing every resource at their disposal, succeeded in bringing about a partial recovery of the political power of the state, but neither they nor their successors tried to check the economic decay of the agrarian population. In the fourteenth century the deplorable economic conditions of the population were a big factor in the social and political strife that shook the empire and opened the way for the rise of the Ottoman Turks. In the tenth century, as we have pointed out above, Romanus Lecapenus had declared in one of his novels designed to protect the free peasantry that the extension of the power of the strong and the depression of the many would "bring about the irreparable loss of the public good." His prediction had come true. The disappearance of the free peasantry, the increase in the wealth, privileges, and power of the aristocracy, and the consequent depression of the agrarian population constitute, I think, some of the principal factors in the decline of the Byzantine empire.

But the society of the Byzantine empire was not purely agrarian. Included in the empire were a number of cities—Constantinople and Thessalonica immediately come to mind—whose role in the economic life of the empire was by no means insignificant. The penury of the sources makes impossible a detailed analysis of the urban economy of Byzantium, but that it was comparatively highly developed there can be no doubt.

What characterized the urban economy of Byzantium during the great days of the empire was its strict regulation by the state. This regulation consisted of two elements: the strict control over foreign commerce and the organization of the domestic trades and professions into private and public guilds supervised by the government. The object of this regulation was both political and economic: political in that the government sought to assure for itself arms and an ample supply of manufactured goods—in the main, luxuries—not only for the imperial household but also for the use of its diplomacy in the form of presents to barbarian chieftains and other princes; economic in that the government sought to keep the great cities well provisioned with the necessities of life, assure the quality of goods, and prevent exorbitant prices. The urban economy was also an important source of revenue. All imports and exports were subject to a 10 per cent duty, and the professions and trades, besides being liable for certain taxes, also performed various liturgies. The precise amount of this revenue, because of the fragmentary nature of the sources, cannot be determined, but it must have been considerable.

The regulation of urban economy was relaxed beginning with the last quarter of the eleventh century. The significant step in this development was taken in 1082 when Alexius Comnenus granted to the Venetians, in return for their alliance against the Normans of Sicily, various privileges among which the most important was that of trading freely, without the payment of any duty, in virtually all the cities of the empire, including the capital. These privileges, renewed by the emperors of the twelfth century, although not without reluctance, rendered the Venetians virtual masters of the commercial life of the empire. In the thirteenth century, in an effort to lessen the influence of the Venetians, similar privileges were granted to the Genoese (the treaty of Nymphaeum, 1261), but that was the substitution of one exploiter for another. The Italian merchants, whether Genoese or Venetians, became so entrenched in Constantinople that they controlled the economy of that city and determined the price of even the daily necessities. According to the patriarch Athanasius (end of the thirteenth century), the fate of the Romans had completely passed into the hands of the Latins, "who," he complained bitterly to the emperor Andronicus II, "make fun of us and scorn us to the point that, full of overweening conceit, they take the wives of our compatriots as security for the wheat which they deliver to us."

Meanwhile, the guild organization which was such a strong feature of the urban organization of the tenth century had virtually ceased to exist by the end of the thirteenth century. This at least is the impression created by the letters of the patriarch Athanasius which, although not yet published, have been analyzed by two different scholars. The patriarch complained to the emperor that false weights were used, that the wheat was hoarded, was often mixed with chaff or wheat that had rotted, and was sold at exorbitant prices. He urged the emperor to appoint a commissioner to supervise everything that concerned the provisioning of the capital. The emperor (Andronicus II) took cognizance of the complaints and ordered an investigation. He was especially anxious to determine who were those who exercised the trade of baker, how many of them there were, and under what conditions were the ships, which brought the food supplies to Constantinople, sold and bought. Thus, at the end of the thirteenth century it was not officially known who were the bakers in Constantinople and how many of them there were. Nor were they supervised with the view of assuring the quality of and a fair price for their produce. Contract this with what the *Book of the Prefect* says about the bakers as they functioned in the tenth century:

> The bakers shall make their profits according to the amount of grain purchased at the order of the Prefect. They shall purchase the proper amount of grain by the nomisma from their assessor. When they have ground it and leavened it, they shall calculate their profit at a keration and two miliarisia on the nomisma. The keration will be pure profit, while the two miliarisia will go for the support of their workmen, the food of their mill animals, the fuel for the ovens, and the lighting. . . .
>
> Whenever there is an increase or decrease in the supply of grain, the bakers shall go to the Prefect to have the weights of their loaves fixed by the assessor in accordance with the purchase price of grain.

Obviously by the end of the thirteenth century the bakers' guild had completely broken down; there was not even a semblance of governmental control over the baker's trade. And what was true of this trade was probably also true of the others. The only indication of a trade organization in the fourteenth century was that of the mariners of Thessalonica. It has been suggested that this guild was organized by the mariners themselves in order to protect their interests, but more probably it was a continuation of an older organization which became more or less autonomous as the power of the central government declined in the fourteenth century. The guild of the mariners took the leadership in the terrible social upheaval that shook Thessalonica in 1345 and resulted in the slaughter of about one hundred members of the aristocracy.

It has been said that "Byzantium's weakness, which led to her fatal decline in the course of the eleventh century" was "her rigid, defensive attitude toward the outside world . . . embodied in the cultural and economic barriers she raised against all outsiders." The economic barriers spoken of in this statement refer no doubt to the strict controls that Byzantium had exercised over commerce and industry. It is extremely doubtful if this indeed was Byzantium's weakness. The simple observation that the period during which these controls were most rigidly enforced is the period of the greatness of the empire suggests the opposite, and this suggestion is reinforced by the further observation that the period of decline coincides with the breakdown of these controls. The power of a state and as a consequence its ability to maintain its position in the world is commensurate with its financial resources, the principal source of which is taxation. In Byzantium this source, seriously compromised by the disappearance of the free peasantry and the increase in the wealth, privileges, and power of the aristocracy was reduced almost to the vanishing point by the commercial privileges granted to the Italian republics and the consequent loss by Byzantium of control over its urban economy. This was Byzantium's weakness that brought about its decline and final fall.

46   Social Strife

The economic decline described in the preceding reading led in turn to social strife. The poor, oppressed by landowners and tax collectors, rose in revolt repeatedly in both the cities and the countryside. The more the economic decline, the greater the burden on the lower classes and the sharper their discontent and agitation. The nature and extent of the ensuing class conflict is the subject of the following selection.*

The factors which contributed to the collapse of the empire were many. Incompetence in statesmanship; the constant hammerings and almost continuous invasions of the empire by the neighboring peoples, Turks, Slavs, and Latins; the control of the commercial life of the empire by the Italian cities—these were important factors in the downfall of the empire. But still more important, indeed decisive, was the internal strife which characterized the empire throughout the fourteenth century. There was not a single reign in that century that was not disturbed by a revolution. Nor were these revolutions simply for the possession of the throne. The throne was involved, indeed, but behind the struggle for its possession lay deep social and political factors. This is nowhere clearer than in the attempt of John Cantacuzenus to wrest the throne away from John V Palaeologus. Cantacuzenus was supported

* P. Charanis, "Internal Strife in·Byzantium during the Fourteenth Century," *Byzantion*, XV (1940-1941), 208-17.

by the aristocratic classes and relied also on the hesychast monks whose leader, Palamas, he favored; he was bitterly opposed by the lower classes whose leaders fought not only the aristocracy, but showed also anti-monastic feelings. What followed was a series of popular revolts which put most of the cities of the empire in the hands of the people.

The first of these popular uprisings took place in Adrianople, October 27, 1341, after Cantacuzenus had dispatched a letter to that city in which he announced his proclamation to the throne and asked to be recognized emperor. The aristocratic element of Adrianople welcomed the news and declared promptly in favor of Cantacuzenus. Thereupon it called an assembly of the populace where the letter of Cantacuzenus was read and an attempt was made to win popular support for his cause. But instead of approval and support there were murmurs of revolt, and even open denunciations of Cantacuzenus. Those who had dared to speak openly against Cantacuzenus were insulted and whipped, and for the time being all seemed well, but the resentment of the populace smoldered underneath, and when night came it broke out into an open conflagration. This was the work of a certain Branos, a man of low social origins, who earned his living by working with the spade. Branos and a number of other conspirators went from house to house and urged the populace to revolt, promising them not only vengeance against the insolence of the rich, but also seizure of their property. In this way they constituted among the poor a considerable force with which they attacked the wealthy, the friends of Cantacuzenus. In the meantime many of the aristocracy had anticipated the uprising and fled from the city; those who remained were captured and were later sent to Constantinople, while the property of the wealthy in general was plundered and destroyed. A popular regime was established, and it was recognized by the authorities in Constantinople which were still friendly to John V Palaeologus. This regime lasted until the winter of 1345. By then most of the Thracian cities had surrendered to Cantacuzenus and the tide of the war between the two emperors was turning in his favor. A revolt by those of his partisans who were still in the city was partly successful, and the city was finally handed over to him through negotiations.

The example of Adrianople was followed everywhere in the empire. In practically every city there was an uprising of the lower classes which remained loyal to John V Palaeologus against the aristocracy. Here is how Cantacuzenus describes the general situation:

> Later [after the popular revolt in Adrianople] the entire Roman empire was given to a much more savage and grievous strife. The populace everywhere considered its duty to remain loyal to the emperor Palaeologus, while the men of property were either sincerely favorable to the emperor Cantacuzenus or were accused of being so by the poor and the seditious without any proof. Most easy were the attacks against those who had money which the poor sought to seize, and who had refused to act basely like the others. The people were ready to revolt at the slightest pretext and dared the most terrible deeds, for they hated the rich for their bad treatment of them during peace time and now hoped, above all, to seize their property, which was great. The rebels were composed in the main of the most miserable of thieves and brigands, and, compelled by poverty, dared everything. Under the pretext that they were favorably disposed toward the emperor Palaeologus, calling themselves his most faithful subjects, they led the populace to follow their example.
>
> The sedition spread throughout the Roman empire like a malignant and terrible disease, and infected many who before seemed more moderate and just.

For in time of peace both cities and individuals have gentler feelings and are less tempted to commit disgraceful and infamous deeds. This is because they do not have to face conditions of dire necessity. But war which deprives men of their daily wants is a violent schoolmaster and teaches that which seemed before beyond any daring.

And so all the cities in common rebelled against the nobles. Those who were late in entering the struggle, on hearing what had been done before carried themselves to greater excesses, nay, to the perpetration of massacres. The cruelty and reckless audacity of these men were looked upon as courage, while their insensibility to the ties of blood and their lack of kindly feelings as unflinching loyalty for the emperor. The man who was violent against Cantacuzenus and heaped upon him base and bitter insults was considered a faithful subject; while he who was moderate both in words and in deeds and sought to do what was right was immediately suspected. Likewise, the laying of plots and the fabrication of lies and false accusations gave to one the reputation of prudent. The betrayal of one's closest relatives was covered by some fair-sounding name as if it were something good. Thus every form of wickedness made its appearance and there was nothing that the more equitable did not have to endure. For the nobles and the members of the middle class were straightway destroyed, the former either because they had been favorably disposed toward Cantacuzenus or because they did not immediately take up arms against him; the latter, either because they did not coöperate with the rebels or through envy lest they survive. Human nature, always prone to commit injustices in opposition to the laws, seemed then powerless to control its rage.

The strife and conflict which reigned in every city of the empire was greater and more violent in Thessalonica as that city surpassed all others, except Constantinople, both in wealth and population. Thessalonica had always been one of the most populous and wealthiest cities of the Roman empire, and since the seventh century when the great cities of the east were conquered by the Arabs, it ranked second only to Constantinople. Its population in the tenth century has been estimated at 200,000 souls; in the fourteenth century it was still very populous; and despite the disasters of that century its population in 1423 still numbered 40,000. It declined rapidly in the next few years and when it was taken by the Ottomans in 1430 it had no more than 7,000 people, men, women, and children. Most of the inhabitants had doubtless fled or were killed in the defense of the city.

The greatness and prosperity of Thessalonica was due to its commercial activity. Thessalonica was a great international market and its annual fair, held at the time of the feast of St. Demetrius, its patron saint, was famous throughout Europe and the Near East. Merchants of every nationality, Bulgarians, Italians, Spaniards, Portuguese, French, Syrians, Egyptians, and numerous others came to Thessalonica to exchange their goods. These goods were of every kind. Here is how the author of *Timarion* who lived in the twelfth century describes them:

> And if you are anxious to know what it [the fair] contains . . . well, there was every kind of material woven or spun by men or women, all those that come from Boeotia and the Peloponnesus, and all that are brought in trading ships from Italy to Greece. Besides this, Phoenicia furnishes numerous articles, and Egypt, and Syria, and the pillars of Hercules, where the finest coverlets are manufactured. These things the merchants bring direct from their respec-

tive countries to old Macedonia and Thessalonica; but the Empire also contributes to the splendor of the fair, by sending across its products to Constantinople, whence the cargoes are brought by numerous horses and mules.

In the fourteenth century Thessalonica was still a great international market. The
products of every land were found there. And one of the most powerful and turbulent elements of its population were the mariners, some of whom were not only
engaged in the legitimate transportation of commercial goods, but doubtless also in
piracy. The mariners were organized into a guild and exerted considerable influence
in the life of Thessalonica. There was also a numerous middle class which owed its
fortune to commerce and industry. An ecclesiastic of the fourteenth century complains that the people of Thessalonica were more interested in sales and purchases
than in the word of God. They turned the house of God, the church, into a market
place, for they talked business instead of listening to the scriptures. A considerable
portion, probably the majority, of the population of Thessalonica, however, was
engaged in agriculture. Most of the inhabitants, declares Palamas in one of his
sermons, spread into the country in order that they might take care of the harvest
and bring in the crops. The poor were many, whereas some of the aristocracy were
extremely wealthy.

Thessalonica was violently shaken by a popular upheaval which broke out in the
summer of 1342 against Cantacuzenus and his wealthy partisans. The revolt was
headed by a group known as the zealot's because they put the interest of the people
before their own private advantage. This is the definition of zealot given by one of
the writers of the fourteenth century, but the zealots of Thessalonica are represented
by their antagonists as men of low origin, indigent to the last degree, a collection of
riffraff, which included not only the lowest element of Thessalonica, but also
criminals from the islands and barbarians, who incited the people to revolt in order
that they might enrich themselves. This view is not borne out by what is known
of their program; nor is it true that they were drawn entirely from the lower classes.
Their leaders were members of the nobility.

The revolt broke out over the attempt of Synadenus, the governor of Thessalonica
and a partisan of Cantacuzenus, who was supported by the aristocracy, to surrender
the city to Cantacuzenus. The zealots, using as their standard a cross which they
seized from an altar, led the populace against the governor and his aristocratic supporters. Synadenus and about a thousand of the aristocracy fled from the city, while
their property was destroyed and pillaged by the populace which raged for three
days unmolested. They perpetrated every act, remarks Cantacuzenus bitterly, that
"men who are driven on by poverty and carried away by insolence are likely to
commit for the sake of wealth." The zealots seized control of the government and
their regime was recognized by the authorities in Constantinople. John Apocaucus,
the son of the Grand Duke Alexius who was the principal adviser of John V Palaeologus, was sent to Thessalonica as the new governor, but the real authority was
exercised by Michael Palaeologus, the leader of the zealots, who became archon
of the city. Many of the nobles were imprisoned or exiled; their property was confiscated.

.   .   .   .   .

What the character of this regime was is not very easy to determine. The writers
of the period lay stress upon the destructiveness of the revolt, the fury of the populace and the sufferings of their victims, the destruction and pillage of the property
of the rich, but say very little about the kind of government that the zealots estab-

lished. The historian Gregoras has indeed left a description, but this description is negative rather than positive, that is, it tells what the regime of the zealots was not, rather than what it was. Here is the statement of Gregoras:

> The regime of the zealots "recalls no other form of government. It was not an aristocracy such as Lycurgus instituted among the Lacedaemonians to be further developed by them. Nor was it a democracy like the first constitution of the Athenians established by Cleisthenes who raised the number of tribes from four to ten. It was similar neither to the regime decreed by Zaleucus to the Epizephyrian Locrians nor to that established in Sicily by Charondas of Catana. Nor was it mixed constitution formed by the combination of two or three different constitutions, put together in such a way as to give something new, such as was the constitution of the Cypriotes or that of ancient Rome which was established, it is said, by the people after they revolted against the consuls. It was rather a strange ochlocracy brought about and directed by chance. Certain audacious individuals formed themselves into a group of their own, set it up as an authority and persecuted the rest. They led the populace by demagogic appeals to execute their will. They confiscated the property of the rich, while they themselves lived in luxury. No one was allowed to obey any of the leaders from without, while what seemed to them good had the force of law."

This statement, despite its negative and general nature, throws some light on the character of the regime of the zealots. It was a popular regime virtually independent of any outside authority. It introduced new laws while it discarded some old ones. Some connection with Constantinople was maintained, for the latter was represented by an imperial governor, but his powers were only nominal, for even the orders of the emperor were often disregarded. Thessalonica under the zealots was virtually an independent republic.

This republic lasted until 1349, when it was overthrown by a counter revolution. The aristocratic opposition had by no means been crushed, and the triumph of Cantacuzenus everywhere in the empire brought about a conservative reaction in Thessalonica. The imperial governor, Metochites, and members of the nobility entered into a plot, and Andrew Palaeologus, the leader of the zealots and the real governor of the city, was overthrown and expelled. He tried in vain to arouse the populace, but his appeals for loyalty to John V Palaeologus was no longer effective, for the latter had made his peace with Cantacuzenus. The zealots, unable to save the situation by enlisting the support of the populace, turned to Stephen Dushan, the kral of Serbia, for aid, but this only helped to alienate still further the sympathy of the populace, and enabled Cantacuzenus and the nobles to get complete control of the city. The zealots were arrested and sent to Constantinople.

Thessalonica was regarded as the teacher of the other cities in the uprisings of the populace against the aristocracy. The popular revolt which began with the uprising in Adrianople became more intense and widespread after the revolt of the zealots. Every city east of Thessalonica and as far as Constantinople was divided into two factions: the masses who ranged themselves against Cantacuzenus, and the men of property and the garrisons who supported him. The masses prevailed everywhere, took control of the city administrations, imprisoned or cruelly executed the members of the aristocracy and confiscated their property.

The revolt of the lower classes spread also into the country. In the summer of

1342 there was an open revolt of the Thracian peasants inhabiting the villages in the neighborhood of Didymotichon. Thrace had suffered terribly by the civil wars. It was not only ravaged by the opposing armies of the empire; it was continuously devastated by foreign marauding bands, especially Turks and Bulgarians. Most of its inhabitants had fled or were captured to be sold into slavery and those who remained were reduced to great misery. The country took the aspect of a real desert, although it is one of the most fertile regions of the Balkans. The rebellious peasants sought to emulate the populace of the cities. They attacked the wealthy and pillaged their property. They armed themselves as best as they could, advanced against Didymotichon and threatened general destruction unless the city surrendered voluntarily. An attack by the garrison of the city, however, dispersed them, and they did not return to their homes but fled to other villages with their wives and children. Their movable property was seized and their houses destroyed.

GREEK-LATIN FEUD

47

In addition to religious dissension, economic decline, and social strife, the Byzantine Empire was weakened also by its long and bitter feud with the West. This dated back to the fifth century when Byzantine emperors and Roman popes clashed over religious doctrine. The contention continued during the following centuries with the Monophysitic and iconoclastic controversies. In addition to these religious differences, Byzantium and the West drifted apart as language and general cultural differentiation crystallized with the passage of time. Also, there was political rivalry, as Byzantium was loath to accept the loss of the West and to recognize Charlemagne's imperial title. Finally economic rivalry also appeared with the increasing control of eastern Mediterranean trade by Italian merchants. The estrangement became particularly acute during the Crusades, when Westerners regarded the Byzantines as effeminate and untrustworthy, and were in turn viewed as uncouth and dangerous barbarians. These attitudes are reflected in the following selections from Anna Comnena, describing the approach and conduct of the Crusaders, and from Odo of Deuil, expressing his distrust and contempt for the Byzantines despite an agreement that had been reached for pitching camp and obtaining provisions.

Anna Comnena *

Before he had enjoyed even a short rest, he heard a report of the approach of innumerable Frankish armies. Now he dreaded their arrival for he knew their irresistible manner of attack, their unstable and mobile character and all the peculiar natural and concomitant characteristics which the Frank retains throughout; and he also knew that they were always agape for money, and seemed to disregard their truces readily for any reason that cropped up. For he had always heard this reported of them, and found it very true. However, he did not lose heart, but prepared himself in every way so that, when the occasion called, he

---

* Elizabeth A. S. Dawes, trans., *The Alexiad of Princess Anna Comnena* (London: Routledge & Kegan Paul Ltd.; New York: Barnes & Noble, Inc., 1928), pp. 248-52.

would be ready for battle. And indeed the actual facts were far greater and more terrible than rumour made them. For the whole of the West and all the barbarian tribes which dwell between the further side of the Adriatic and the pillars of Heracles, had all migrated in a body and were marching into Asia through the intervening Europe, and were making the journey with all their household. The reason of this upheaval was more or less the following. A certain Frank, Peter by name, nicknamed Cucupeter, had gone to worship at the Holy Sepulchre and after suffering many things at the hands of the Turks and Saracens who were ravaging Asia, he got back to his own country with difficulty. But he was angry at having failed in his object, and wanted to undertake the same journey again. However, he saw that he ought not to make the journey to the Holy Sepulchre alone again, lest worse things befall him, so he worked out a cunning plan. This was to preach in all the Latin countries that 'the voice of God bids me announce to all the Counts in France that they should all leave their homes and set out to worship at the Holy Sepulchre, and to endeavour wholeheartedly with hand and mind to deliver Jerusalem from the hand of the Hagarenes.' And he really succeeded. For after inspiring the souls of all with this quasi-divine command he contrived to assemble the Franks from all sides, one after the other, with arms, horses and all the other paraphernalia of war. And they were all so zealous and eager that every highroad was full of them. And those Frankish soldiers were accompanied by an unarmed host more numerous than the sand or the stars, carrying palms and crosses on their shoulders; women and children, too, came away from their countries. . . .

The incidents of the barbarians' approach followed in the order I have described, and persons of intelligence could feel that they were witnessing a strange occurrence. The arrival of these multitudes did not take place at the same time nor by the same road (for how indeed could such masses starting from different places have crossed the straits of Lombardy all together?). Some first, some next, others after them and thus successively all accomplished the transit, and then marched through the Continent. Each army was preceded, as we said, by an unspeakable number of locusts; and all who saw this more than once recognized them as forerunners of the Frankish armies. When the first of them began crossing the straits of Lombardy sporadically the Emperor summoned certain leaders of the Roman forces, and sent them to the parts of Dyrrachium and Valona with instructions to offer a courteous welcome to the Franks who had crossed, and to collect abundant supplies from all the countries along their route; then to follow and watch them covertly all the time, and if they saw them making any foraging-excursions, they were to come out from under cover and check them by light skirmishing. These captains were accompanied by some men who knew the Latin tongue, so that they might settle any disputes that arose between them.

· · · · ·

. . . the Latin race is always very fond of money, but more especially when it is bent on raiding a country; it then loses its reason and gets beyond control. As they journeyed neither in ranks nor in squadrons, they fell foul of the Turkish ambuscades near the river Dracon and perished miserably. And such a large number of Franks and Normans were the victims of the Ishmaelite sword, that when they piled up the corpses of the slaughtered men which were lying on either side they formed, I say, not a very large hill or mound or a peak, but a high mountain as it were, of very considerable depth and breadth—so great was the pyramid of bones. . . .

Odo of Deuil *

This outcome would have satisfied the messengers if they had not judged one crime in the light of another; for they learned that the emperor had an agreement with the Turks and that the very man who had written to our king that he was going to accompany him in fighting the infidels and had won a recent and renowned victory over them had actually confirmed a twelve-year armistice with them. Also, his treachery was increased and made manifest by the fact that only a great number could get through his realm in safety; for the bishop of Langres and the count of Warenne and certain others, who had sent a few men ahead to Constantinople to provide arms and food for the journey, had suffered a considerable loss of possessions and were mourning their wounded and dead. And this did not happen just once; for from the time when we entered his territory we endured the robberies which his people perpetrated on us because our strength did not equal theirs. Perhaps this condition would have been bearable, and it could have been said that we deserved the evils which we suffered on account of the evils which we had committed, if blasphemy had not been added. For instance, if our priests celebrated mass on Greek altars, the Greeks afterwards purified them with propitiatory offerings and ablutions, as if they had been defiled. All the wealthy people have their own chapels, so adorned with paintings, marble, and lamps that each magnate might justly say, "O Lord, I have cherished the beauty of Thy house," if the light of the true faith shone therein. But, O dreadful thing; we heard of an ill usage of theirs which should be expiated by death; namely, that every time they celebrate the marriage of one of our men, if he has been baptized in the Roman way, they rebaptize him before they make the pact. We know other heresies of theirs, both concerning their treatment of the Eucharist and concerning the procession of the Holy Ghost, but none of these matters would mar our page if not pertinent to our subject. Actually, it was for these reasons that the Greeks had incurred the hatred of our men, for their error had become known even among the lay people. Because of this they were judged not to be Christians, and the Franks considered killing them a matter of no importance and hence could with the more difficulty be restrained from pillage and plundering.

. . . Let no one think that I am taking vengeance on a race of men hateful to me and that because of my hatred I am inventing a Greek whom I have not seen. Whoever has known the Greeks will, if asked, say that when they are afraid they become despicable in their excessive debasement and when they have the upper hand they are arrogant in their severe violence to those subjected to them. However, they toiled most zealously in advising the king to turn his route from Adrianople to St. George of Sestos and there to cross the sea the more swiftly and advantageously. But the king did not wish to undertake something which he had never heard that the Franks had done. Thus, by the same paths, but not with the same omens, he followed the Germans who had preceded us, and when a day's journey from Constantinople met his own messengers, who told him the stories concerning the emperor which we have already related in part. There were those who then advised the king to retreat and to seize the exceedingly rich land with its castles and cities and meanwhile to write to King Roger, who was then vigorously attacking the emperor, and, aided by his fleet, to attack Constantinople itself. But, alas for us, nay, for all St. Peter's subjects, their words did not prevail! . . .

* Odo of Deuil, *De Profectione Ludovici VII in Orientem,* trans. Virginia G. Berry, No. XLII of the Records of Civilization: Sources and Studies (New York: Columbia University Press, 1948), pp. 55, 57, 59.

It was the combination of the circumstances described in the preceding readings that was responsible for the eventual downfall of Byzantium. This occurred in two stages, the first being in 1204 when the leaders of the Fourth Crusade captured Constantinople and established a number of feudal states. These never took root, and in 1261 Constantinople was retaken by the Byzantines, but the restored empire was a small and unviable fragment. The final end came in 1453 with the Turkish conquest, which proved durable, Constantinople becoming the capital of the Ottoman Empire until its demise after World War I. The following selection is a Byzantine view of the Latin sack of Constantinople, the author being the contemporary Greek historian Nicetas Choniates.*

. . . How shall I begin to tell of the deeds wrought by these nefarious men! Alas, the images, which ought to have been adored, were trodden under foot! Alas, the relics of the holy martyrs were thrown into unclean places! Then was seen what one shudders to hear, namely, the divine body and blood of Christ was spilled upon the ground or thrown about. They snatched the precious reliquaries, thrust into their bosoms the ornaments which these contained, and used the broken remnants for pans and drinking cups,—precursors of Anti-christ, authors and heralds of his nefarious deeds which we momentarily expect. Manifestly, indeed, by that race then, just as formerly, Christ was robbed and insulted and His garments were divided by lot; only one thing was lacking, that His side, pierced by a spear, should pour rivers of divine blood on the ground.

Nor can the violation of the Great Church [Santa Sophia] be listened to with equanimity. For the sacred altar, formed of all kinds of precious materials and admired by the whole world, was broken into bits and distributed among the soldiers, as was all the other sacred wealth of so great and infinite splendor.

When the sacred vases and utensils of unsurpassable art and grace and rare material, and the fine silver, wrought with gold, which encircled the screen of the tribunal and the ambo, of admirable workmanship, and the door and many other ornaments, were to be borne away as booty, mules and saddled horses were led to the very sanctuary of the temple. Some of these which were unable to keep their footing on the splendid and slippery pavement, were stabbed when they fell, so that the sacred pavement was polluted with blood and filth.

Nay more, a certain harlot, a sharer in their guilt, a minister of the furies, a servant of the demons, a worker of incantations and poisonings, insulting Christ, sat in the patriarch's seat, singing an obscene song and dancing frequently. Nor, indeed, were these crimes committed and others left undone, on the ground that these were of lesser guilt, the others of greater. But with one consent all the most heinous sins and crimes were committed by all with equal zeal. Could those, who showed so great madness against God Himself, have spared the honorable matrons and maidens or the virgins consecrated to God?

Nothing was more difficult and laborious than to soften by prayers, to render benevolent, these wrathful barbarians, vomiting forth bile at every unpleasing word,

* D. C. Munro, trans., *Translations and Reprints from the Original Sources of European History*, Series I, Vol. III, No. 1, rev. ed. (Philadelphia: University of Pennsylvania Press, 1912), pp. 15-16.

so that nothing failed to inflame their fury. Whoever attempted it was derided as insane and a man of intemperate language. Often they drew their daggers against any one who opposed them at all or hindered their demands.

No one was without a share in the grief. In the alleys, in the streets, in the temples, complaints, weeping, lamentations, grief, the groaning of men, the shrieks of women, wounds, rape, captivity, the separation of those most closely united. Nobles wandered about ignominiously, those of venerable age in tears, the rich in poverty. Thus it was in the streets, on the corners, in the temple, in the dens, for no place remained unassailed or defended the suppliants. All places everywhere were filled full of all kinds of crime. Oh, immortal God, how great the afflictions of the men, how great the distress!

BYZANTINE CHRISTIANITY IN RUSSIA 49

Historians no longer accept Edward Gibbon's verdict on the thousand years of Byzantium's existence as "a uniform tale of weakness and misery." Rather, they now stress the vital historical contributions of Byzantium in shielding the West against eastern invasions, in serving as an economic dynamo for the entire Mediterranean basin, in salvaging and transmitting the intellectual and artistic treasures of antiquity, and in introducing the arts of civilization to the Slavs of Eastern Europe as Rome had done earlier for the Germans to the West. This last contribution is the subject of the following selection from a contemporary source, the Russian Primary Chronicle, *compiled by Kievan monks in the eleventh and twelfth centuries. This reading describes the circumstances in which Prince Vladimir of Kiev, after considering the teachings and practices of Catholicism, Islam, and Judaism, opted for the Christian faith of the Byzantines. His decision was binding also on all his subjects, so the* Chronicle *depicts the mass baptism that followed in the waters of the Dnieper River. After conversion came the building of churches, the organization of an ecclesiastical hierarchy, and the spread of "book learning." The Russians had acquired a new civilization along with their new religion.**

For at this time the Russes were ignorant pagans. The devil rejoiced thereat, for he did not know that his ruin was approaching. He was so eager to destroy the Christian people, yet he was expelled by the true cross even from these very lands. The accursed one thought to himself, "This is my habitation, a land where the apostles have not taught nor the prophets prophesied." He knew not that the Prophet had said, "I will call those my people who are not my people" (*Hosea*, ii, 23). Likewise it is written of the Apostles, "Their message has gone out into all the earth and their words to the end of the world" (*Ps.,* xix, 5).

. . . . .

Vladimir was visited by Bulgars of Mohammedan faith, who said, "Though you are a wise and prudent prince, you have no religion. Adopt our faith, and revere

* S. H. Cross and O. P. Sherbowitz-Wetzor, trans. and eds., *The Russian Primary Chronicle: Laurentian Text* (Cambridge, Mass.: Mediaeval Academy of America, 1953), pp. 96ff.

Mahomet." Vladimir inquired what was the nature of their religion. They replied that they believed in God, and that Mahomet instructed them to practice circumcision, to eat no pork, to drink no wine, and, after death, promised them complete fulfillment of their carnal desires. "Mahomet," they asserted, "will give each man seventy fair women. He may choose one fair one, and upon that woman will Mahomet confer the charms of them all, and she shall be his wife. Mahomet promises that one may then satisfy every desire, but whoever is poor in this world will be no different in the next." They also spoke other false things which out of modesty may not be written down. Vladimir listened to them, for he was fond of women and indulgence, regarding which he heard with pleasure. But circumcision and abstinence from pork and wine were disagreeable to him. "Drinking," said he, "is the joy of the Russes. We cannot exist without that pleasure."

Then came the Germans, asserting that they were come as emissaries of the Pope. They added, "Thus says the Pope: 'Your country is like our country, but your faith is not as ours. For our faith is the light. We worship God, who has made heaven and earth, the stars, the moon, and every creature, while your gods are only wood.' " Vladimir inquired what their teaching was. They replied, "Fasting according to one's strength. But whatever one eats or drinks is all to the glory of God, as our teacher Paul has said." Then Vladimir answered, "Depart hence; our fathers accepted no such principle."

The Jewish Khazars heard of these missions, and came themselves saying, "We have learned that Bulgars and Christians came hither to instruct you in their faiths. The Christians believe in him whom we crucified, but we believe in the one God of Abraham, Isaac, and Jacob." Then Vladimir inquired what their religion was. They replied that its tenets included circumcision, not eating pork or hare, and observing the Sabbath. The Prince then asked where their native land was, and they replied that it was in Jerusalem. When Vladimir inquired where that was, they made answer, "God was angry at our forefathers, and scattered us among the gentiles on account of our sins. Our land was then given to the Christians." The Prince then demanded, "How can you hope to teach others while you yourselves are cast out and scattered abroad by the hand of God? If God loved you and your faith, you would not be thus dispersed in foreign lands. Do you expect us to accept that fate also?"

Then the Greeks sent to Vladimir a scholar, who spoke thus: "We have heard that the Bulgarians came and urged you to adopt their faith, which pollutes heaven and earth. They are accursed above all men, like Sodom and Gomorrah, upon which the Lord let fall burning stones, and which he buried and submerged. The day of destruction likewise awaits these men, on which the Lord will come to judge the earth, and to destroy all those who do evil and abomination. For they moisten their excrement, and pour the water into their mouths, and anoint their beards with it, remembering Mahomet. The women also perform this same abomination, and even worse ones." Vladimir, upon hearing their statements, spat upon the earth, saying, "This is a vile thing."

Then the scholar said, "We have likewise heard how men came from Rome to convert you to their faith. It differs but little from ours, for they commune with wafers, called *oplatki,* which God did not give them, for he ordained that we should commune with bread. For when he had taken bread, the Lord gave it to his disciples, saying, 'This is my body broken for you.' Likewise he took the cup, and said, 'This is my blood of the New Testament.' They do not so act, for they have modified the faith." Then Vladimir remarked that the Jews had come into his presence and had stated that the Germans and the Greeks believed in him whom they crucified. To this the scholar replied, "Of a truth we believe in him. For some of the prophets foretold that God should be incarnate, and others that he should be crucified and buried, but arise on the third day and ascend into heaven. "For the Jews killed the prophets, and still others they persecuted. When their prophecy was fulfilled, our Lord came down to earth, was crucified, arose again, and ascended into heaven. He awaited their repentance for forty-six years, but they did not repent, so that the Lord let loose the Romans upon them. Their cities were destroyed, and they were scattered among the gentiles, under whom they are now in servitude."

Vladimir then inquired why God should have descended to earth and should have endured such pain. The scholar then answered and said, "If you are desirous of hearing the story, I shall tell you from the beginning why God descended to earth." Vladimir replied, "Gladly would I hear it." Whereupon the scholar thus began his narrative: . . .

. . . . .

As he spoke thus, he exhibited to Vladimir a canvas on which was depicted the Judgment Day of the Lord, and showed him, on the right, the righteous going to their bliss in Paradise, and on the left, the sinners on their way to torment. Then Vladimir sighed and said, "Happy are they upon the right, but woe to those upon the left!" The scholar replied, "If you desire to take your place upon the right with the just, then accept baptism! Vladimir took this counsel to heart, saying, "I shall wait yet a little longer," for he wished to inquire about all the faiths. Vladimir then gave the scholar many gifts, and dismissed him with great honor.

Vladimir summoned together his boyars and the city-elders, and said to them, "Behold, the Bulgars came before me urging me to accept their religion. Then came the Germans and praised their own faith; and after them came the Jews. Finally the Greeks appeared, criticizing all other faiths but commending their own, and they spoke at length, telling the history of the whole world from its beginning. Their words were artful, and it was wondrous to listen and pleasant to hear them. They preach the existence of another world. 'Whoever adopts our religion and then dies shall arise and live forever. But whosoever embraces another faith, shall be consumed with fire in the next world.' What is your opinion on this subject, and what do you answer?" The boyars and the elders replied, "You know, oh Prince, that no man condemns his own possessions, but praises them instead. If you desire to make certain, you have servants at your disposal. Send them to inquire about the ritual of each and how he worships God."

Their counsel pleased the prince and all the people, so that they chose good and wise men to the number of ten, and directed them to go first among the Bulgars and inspect their faith. The emissaries went their way, and when they arrived at their destination they beheld the disgraceful actions of the Bulgars and their worship in the mosque; then they returned to their country. Vladimir then instructed them to go likewise among the Germans, and examine their faith, and finally to visit the Greeks. They thus went into Germany, and after viewing the German ceremonial, they proceeded to Tsar'grad, where they appeared before the Emperor. He inquired on what mission they had come, and they reported to him all that had occurred. When the Emperor heard their words, he rejoiced, and did them great honor on that very day.

On the morrow, the Emperor sent a message to the Patriarch to inform him that a Russian delegation had arrived to examine the Greek faith, and directed him to prepare the church and the clergy, and to array himself in his sacerdotal robes, so that the Russes might behold the glory of the God of the Greeks. When the Patriarch received these commands, he bade the clergy assemble, and they performed the customary rites. They burned incense, and the choirs sang hymns. The Emperor accompanied the Russes to the church, and placed them in a wide space, calling their attention to the beauty of the edifice, the chanting, and the pontifical services and the ministry of the deacons, while he explained to them the worship of his God. The Russes were astonished, and in their wonder praised the Greek ceremonial. Then the Emperors Basil and Constantine invited the envoys to their presence, and said, "Go hence to your native country," and dismissed them with valuable presents and great honor.

Thus they returned to their own country, and the Prince called together his boyars and the elders. Vladimir then announced the return of the envoys who had been sent out, and suggested that their report be heard. He thus commanded them to speak out before his retinue. The envoys reported, "When we journeyed among the Bulgars, we beheld how they worship in their temple, called a mosque, while they stand ungirt. The Bulgar bows, sits down, looks hither and thither like one possessed, and there is no happiness among them, but instead only sorrow and a dreadful stench. Their religion is not good. Then we went among the Germans, and saw them performing many ceremonies in their temples; but we beheld no glory there. Then we went to Greece, and the Greeks led us to the edifices where they worship their God, and we knew not whether we were in heaven or on earth. For on earth there is no such splendor or such beauty, and we are at a loss how to describe it. We only know that God dwells there among men, and their service is fairer than the ceremonies of other nations. For we cannot forget that beauty. Every man, after tasting something sweet, is afterward unwilling to accept that which is bitter, and therefore we cannot dwell longer here." Then the boyars spoke and said, "If the Greek faith were evil, it would not have been adopted by your grandmother Olga who was wiser than all other men."

. . . . .

When the Prince arrived at this capital, he directed that the idols should be overthrown, and that some should be cut to pieces and others burned with fire. He thus ordered that Perun should be bound to a horse's tail and dragged down Borichev to the stream. He appointed twelve men to beat the idol with sticks, not because he thought the wood was sensitive, but to affront the demon who had deceived man in this guise, that he might receive chastisement at the hands of men. Great art thou, oh Lord, and marvelous are thy works! Yesterday he was honored of men, but today held in derision. While the idol was being dragged along the stream to the Dnieper, the unbelievers wept over it, for they had not yet received holy baptism. After they had thus dragged the idol along, they cast it into the Dnieper. But Vladimir had given this injunction "If it halts anywhere, then push it out from the bank, until it goes over the falls. Then let it loose." His command was duly obeyed. When the men let the idol go, and it passed through the rapids, the wind cast it out on the bank, which since that time has been called Perun's sandbank, a name that it bears to this very day.

Thereafter Vladimir sent heralds throughout the whole city to proclaim that if any inhabitant, rich or poor, did not betake himself to the river, he would risk the Prince's displeasure. When the people heard these words, they wept for joy, and exclaimed in their enthusiasm, "If this were not good, the Prince and his boyars would not have accepted it." On the morrow, the Prince went forth to the Dnieper with the priests of the Princess and those from Kherson, and a countless multitude assembled. They all went into the water: some stood up to their necks, others to their breasts, and the younger near the bank, some of them holding children in their arms, while the adults waded farther out. The priests stood by and offered prayers. There was joy in heaven and upon earth to behold so many souls saved. But the devil groaned, lamenting, "Woe is me! how am I driven out hence! For I thought to have my dwelling-place here, since the apostolic teachings do not abide in this land. Nor did this people know God, but I rejoiced in the service they rendered unto me. But now I am vanquished by the ignorant, not by apostles and martyrs, and my reign in these regions is at an end."

When the people were baptized, they returned each to his own abode. Vladimir, rejoicing that he and his subjects now knew God himself, looked up to heaven and said, "Oh God, who has created heaven and earth, look down, I beseech thee, on this thy new people, and grant them, oh Lord, to know thee as the true God, even as the other Christian nations have known thee. Confirm in them the true and inalterable faith, and aid me, oh Lord, against the hostile adversary, so that, hoping in thee and in thy might, I may overcome his malice." Having spoken thus, he ordained that wooden churches should be built and established where pagan idols had previously stood. He thus founded the Church of St. Basil on the hill where the idol of Perun and the other images had been set, and where the Prince and the people had offered their sacrifices. He began to found churches and to assign priests throughout the cities, and to invite the people to accept baptism in all the cities and towns.

He took the children of the best families, and sent them for instruction in book-learning. The mothers of these children wept bitterly over them, for they were not yet strong in faith, but mourned as for the dead. When these children were assigned for study, there was fulfilled in the land of Rus' the prophecy which says, "In those days, the deaf shall hear words of Scripture, and the voice of the stammerers shall be made plain" (*Is.*, xxix, 18). . . .

Chapter Sixteen

Traditional Confucian civilization

50   Civil Service Examinations

The millennium between the sixth century, when the Sui dynasty restored imperial unity, and the sixteenth, when the Westerners began their intrusion by sea, was for China an era of unparalleled stability. It was during those centuries that China, after having caught up with the other Eurasian civilizations during the Han period, now forged ahead to become the most populous and wealthiest country in the world. One of China's most significant contributions to modern society was her system of civil service examinations, which served as the basis of her Confucian state structure. These examinations, which were held from 622 to 1905, tremendously impressed the Westerners when they first became familiar with them. Appointment on the basis of merit rather than of family connections—the latter being the norm in the contemporary West, was viewed as a much more efficient and democratic arrangement. Modern scholars have debated the degree to which this system was, in fact, democratic. Disagreement still prevails as to whether it allowed social mobility, or whether the system was dominated by families already holding degrees. As for the content of the examinations, they tested literary style and Confucian orthodoxy, thereby stifling originality and promoting conformity. This generated much protest, and the complaints of the medieval Chinese students, as described below, sound very similar to the complaints of students everywhere today.*

* Reprinted from "Protest Against Conventions and Conventions of Protest," by David S. Nivison, in *The Confucian Persuasion,* edited by Arthur F. Wright (pp. 177-82, 185-94, 198-201), with the permission of the publishers, Stanford University Press. © 1960 by the Board of Trustees of the Leland Stanford Junior University.

Students have often been found to complain about what they are required to learn and how they are held accountable for their lessons. Often their complaints follow a time-worn pattern. But if we look behind the pattern and if the students are serious, we may find that their complaints are both penetrating and important. This has been true even in China, that land of exemplary students, where teachers were respected as nowhere else, and where the emperor himself was the chief examiner.

Let me begin by telling some stories.

I

Shortly before 1060, Ou-yang Hsiu, the early Sung historian, official and man of letters, wrote a short essay, as was often done by Chinese literary men, in the back of a particularly treasured old book from his personal library. The book was an early print, from Ssu-ch'uan, of the collected prose of the ninth-century writer Han Yü. In this essay, Ou-yang Hsiu relates that as a young man, being of a poor family, he had had no books; but, finding this book discarded in the house of a friend, he begged for it and read it with fascination, not fully understanding it but nonetheless aware of its worth. In his own time, regular, so-called "modern" prose (*shih wen*) was preferred over the free style or "ancient" prose (*ku wen*) of Han Yü. "People who were skilled in it," writes Ou-yang Hsiu, "passed the examinations and were the only persons who had any reputation; no one ever talked about the writings of Han Yü." Just at this time, Ou-yang Hsiu himself had attempted the examinations unsuccessfully, and this failure had strengthened his dissatisfaction with the literary standards of his age. "I took my copy of Han Yü," he continues, "and, rereading it, I sighed and said, 'Scholars ought to go no farther than this!' And I marveled that people of the present day were so misguided." Admitting to himself that he must study for the examinations now, to obtain an official position and so be able to support his parents, he nevertheless had resolved that after he had succeeded he would turn back to what he really valued. "Later," Ou-yang Hsiu continues, "learned men throughout the world all turned their attention gradually to the past, and Han Yü's writings eventually became well known. Thirty-odd years have passed since that time, and people now study nothing but Han Yü."

Ou-yang Hsiu clearly feels that his values as a young student were right and the officially sanctioned and conventionally approved ones wrong, and that he has been vindicated, inevitably, by time. Furthermore, he is able to assure himself, his pursuit of learning has been motivated only by the purest interest in learning itself—"It was simply that I was devoted to the past," he says—and not by hope of fame or material advantage. In him, as in other Confucians of his time, conservatism, a love of antiquity, is actually a protest against an ignoble conventionality. But did not Ou-yang Hsiu capitulate? He did study for the examinations, and with conspicuous success. Further, he did this, as he admits, precisely in order to qualify for a salaried official post. The intensity of this conflict, between devotion to higher ideals and the practical necessity of coming to terms with the world, can be seen in the fact that the ultimate Confucian social duty, that of filial piety, had to be invoked to set matters right.

Yet the reasonableness of the appeal can hardly be gainsaid. It is indeed the duty of a Confucian to provide for his parents; and so here is another conflict, now between two values, both of which were Confucian: one social, one intellectual; on the one hand family duty, on the other one's own personal development.

It will be instructive to turn, for a slightly different sort of case, to the early part of the T'ang period, when the modern examination system first became important. The historian Liu Chih-chi in the early eighth century wrote, in an autobiographical essay in his *Shih T'ung* ("General Principles of History"), that when he was a child it had been determined that he should specialize in the third of the Confucian Classics, the *Shang Shu*. But, he writes, "I was always bothered by the difficulty of its language, and . . . although I was frequently beaten, I got nowhere in my study. But when I happened to hear my father teaching my elder brothers the *Spring and Autumn Annals* and the *Commentary of Tso,* I always put aside my books and listened . . . and sighing to myself, I said, 'If only all books were like this, I would no longer be lazy!' " Liu's father was surprised at his son's independence of inclination, and, surprisingly, relented; Liu was allowed to read the *Tso Chuan,* and finished his study of it rather quickly. But now, his father would have him specialize in the *Tso Chuan* alone, going on to read all the existing commentaries to that text. To understand the father's point of view, we need to be aware that an intense study of one or two Classics served a man well in the T'ang examinations: the *chin-shih* and *ming-ching* examinations were probably the two most frequently taken even in Liu's time; and in offering for the first of these, one had to prepare one Classic, and be prepared further to find the questions dealing with commentaries rather than with the text itself. For the latter, one had to prepare somewhat less intensively in two or three Classics.

But although his father's wishes in view of this situation may have been sensible, Liu fought free again. He had wanted to read the *Tso,* not because it was an examination text but because it was history; he now wanted to read more history—not because it would get him somewhere but because it was interesting, and because he thought he had insights into it worth having. Eventually he turned aside from his interests for a few years to learn to write in the poetry and essay forms required in the examinations. He does not indicate that he was bitter about this interruption, but he makes it perfectly plain that it was an interruption in his work.

Both Liu Chih-chi and Ou-yang Hsiu, it is evident, found themselves as young men pursuing conflicting goals. The interest of Ou-yang's and Liu's experience and of their attitudes toward it would be slight, if this experience and these attitudes were unique; but we shall see that, far from being unique, they are so common among Chinese writers of the past thousand years as to seem stereotyped. This surely makes the matter of great interest; for people worry about conflicts, in whatever mode of life they are in; and when people worry, they think.

There exist, I suggest, recognizable conventions of protest against the educational mold into which a student felt himself forced. (1) There is the tendency, perhaps found in any aristocratic social order, to suspect values which are popular and modish of being shallow. Consider the curious feeling often encountered that only a very few people are likely to appreciate a really good painting or book. Surely we see something of this in Ou-yang Hsiu's conviction as a youth that only he saw matters rightly, and that generally accepted literary standards were "misguided." There is much more of this, offered with delicious frankness, in Han Yü himself. And whenever the relative merits of "ancient" and "contemporary" prose come up, no matter how *de rigueur* it may be for a critic to come down on the side of *ku wen,* or in favor of a "devotion to the past," he will usually in doing so manage to think of himself as alone in a Philistine wilderness (for Ou-yang Hsiu's conviction that only he appreciated Han Yü is surely nonsense). (2) But there is another motif which is simply the uncomplicated rebelliousness of a man of original temper when forced to do something distasteful, a motif likely to be found wherever such pressure exists. This was the sort of reaction we found in Liu Chih-chi. Yet, if these two modes of protest are not peculiar to Chinese culture, they certainly arise very naturally in a culture like China's which has been authoritarian—for Liu's independence was a reaction against a strict parental authority—and which has always had the persuasion that there are "superior" men, capable of perceiving values to which ordinary men are obtuse.

These two styles of self-assertion and protest may be seen in the lives and recollections of other writers, even very recent ones; and often we have the impression that specific literary models are playing a role. To cite two modern examples, the contemporary historian Ku Chieh-kang, like Liu Chih-chi, says he wanted, as a boy, to study the *Tso chuan* despite the objections of his parents and his teacher (his *bête noire* was the *Book of Odes,* not the *Shang Shu*), and surprised his mentors with his ability when finally allowed to study it. Hu Shih writes in his autobiography that he happened, while in a neighbor's house, to discover a dilapidated copy of *Shui Hu Chuan,* which he was allowed to keep. This was the beginning of Hu's interest in popular literature, which he championed successfully against the established values of *his* day. I assume that this incident happened; and it may even have had the importance ascribed to it. But the fact that it was worth relating surely owes something to Ou-yang Hsiu.

Wang Yang-ming, in the year 1518, wrote a letter of advice to two young men who were preparing for the examinations:

> Since your home is poverty-stricken and your parents are old, what else can you do but seek emolument and official position? If you seek emolument and official position without studying for the examinations, you will not be able to carry out your duties as men, and will pointlessly find fault with fate. This is hardly right. But if you can firmly fix your aim, in all your pursuits fully express the Tao, and be influenced in thought neither by desire for success nor by fear of failure, then, though you study for the degree, this will be no real hindrance to your learning to become virtuous men.

Wang, like Ou-yang Hsiu, here justifies the pursuit of worldly ends by appeal to the obligation of *filial duty*. There is more, of course, to Wang's attitude than this. He reveals himself highly suspicious of the influence the examinations had on a young man's mind. It may be possible, he reluctantly concedes, for a man to study for the degree of *chü-jen* or *chin-shih* without detriment to his self-development; all too many, however, through "lack of a fixed aim," as Wang puts it, "have come to think exclusively of honor, gain and literary style"; and as a result "they cannot avoid cherishing the desire for small advantages and quick results." A young man must always resist this temptation the examinations present to him to succumb to vulgar values and to let his desires be involved in what he is doing.

· · · · ·

II

We have not been dealing merely with a curious but meaningless set of literary conventions. The civil service examinations have been called the hallmark of the "Confucian state." Preparing for them in order to seek an official career was a basic duty to family and to the world. Their existence as an institution more than anything else signalized the ascendancy of the man of learning and culture in society. Yet, almost from the beginnings of this institution in the later empire, the examinations, and the educational standards they produced, were resented and criticized. Students resented being fettered and constrained. Statesmen found the institution wanting as a means of "nurturing talent" and recruiting the best men for public service. Literary critics and moral philosophers bewailed its influence on the quality of letters and on the state of public and private virtue. This polyphony of protest may be found in every generation. And the surprising fact is that throughout all this we find the examination-education complex, the function and effect of which was to ensure the dominance of the Confucian classical tradition, criticized precisely by appeal to *Confucian* moral, aesthetic, and political values.

This is not a situation we would have expected. Its oddity may help to explain the fact that, for all of the attention scholars have given to the imperial examination system and its ramifications, the long tradition of protest against this system has been almost completely ignored. In what follows I shall attempt to open the matter up. My attempt will of necessity be extremely superficial, for the volume of relevant literature is enormous: in this literature we must include innumerable personal letters and essays, novels (such as *Ju-lin Wai-shih* by Wu Ching-tzu, 1701–54) on the life of the literati, as well as many official and unofficial treatises on public policy. Simply to relate the history of reforms and proposed changes in the system would require volumes. But an analysis of some of the ideals and motivations which perpetually generated this criticism may be more feasible.

. . . . .

. . . In the later T'ang empire, . . . profound (and as yet inadequately understood) social changes were taking place. The great aristocratic families of the north, which had been powerful in an earlier era, were declining or breaking up, and "new men" from outside this closed elite were coming on the scene. The availability of office to members of different social or regional groups was therefore a matter of intense interest, and the question was raised whether the examinations brought into office men who truly deserved it.

A prominent criticism was that the examinations rewarded the man who merely happened to have a good memory, though he might have no grasp of the "essential meaning" of the Classics—their relevance to current moral and political issues. Another persistent issue was the propriety of requiring of the candidate a facility in highly artificial literary forms such as the *fu* ("rhymed prose") and *p'an* ("decision") which could have nothing to do with his performance in office. Yüan Chen in 806, for example, in an essay submitted at the Palace Examination, made a revolutionary proposal that chief emphasis in the examinations be placed on knowledge of contemporary law and history, and that the competition be opened to all ranks of society (he would have abolished the examination on which Han Yü foundered, the placing examination, which required a candidate to prove that his father was neither an artisan, nor a merchant, nor a criminal).

. . . . .

The idea of doing away with the examinations entirely, and of filling the ranks of government servants by recommendation of "virtuous" men from below, was resurrected again and again. It bears witness to an almost incredible extreme of political idealism in Sung and Ming China. The vision was of a perfect society supposed to have existed in antiquity, a government of perfect virtue, in which there would be complete mutual trust and harmony between men of high and low estate. Inferiors would know their station and have no desire to rise beyond their merits, while those above would be motivated only by the purest love of virtue itself. In such a world order, the best man would always be chosen (and those not chosen would have no resentment), for it would always be the best who would come to the attention of the rulers, and the rulers would always be able to recognize the best. Examinations would not only be superfluous in such a state of affairs, they would be incompatible with it, for they would excite a spirit of striving and of selfish competition among the people. This is just what the examinations do; and for many Sung and Ming philosophers this corrupting and disturbing influence exercised upon the mind, preventing men from "fixing their aim" on ultimate moral values instead of short-term gains, is the greatest fault of the system.

The utopian picture of an ancient, prebureaucratic, perfect Confucian society was a basic element underlying and shaping opinion about educational policy and examination practices in the factional politics of the Sung; indeed this utopian conception seems to be central in all reformist and counterreformist thought in that period. Here I cannot take up the details of these policy struggles, save to note that these questions were always important. Examination requirements were changed constantly, and this must have resulted in much anxiety, leading in turn to an intensification of concern over these problems. Basically, the call for ending the examinations and turning back to some earlier and presumably better method of bringing good men into government—easily combined with a Mencius-inspired concern for the reform of local schools—was of a piece with Mencian "well-field" utopianism in economics and land policy. Essentially it was part of an idealistic regret that the "Confucian" bureaucratic state, with its contamination of Legalism and its (real or fancied) attendant moral corruption in official life, had come into existence at all.

Two illustrations will bear this out, both from Sung philosophers of first rank. Ch'eng I (1033–1107), in a long discussion of examinations as conducted in the "three colleges" of the Sung Imperial Academy, expressed the usual regrets: the formal, detailed, legally prescribed literary requirements were not of use in evaluating the moral worth of the students, while the atmosphere of competition turned their minds to a love of "profit," and made them actually forget their parents. The trouble is that the government relies on "detailed regulations" for appraising candidates for the civil service, rather than on whatever ability those in high places may have to recognize "virtue." But are "detailed regulations" really dispensable?

Someone may say, "If the right men are obtained for the highest positions, then all is well. But if not, it is better to have many detailed regulations to guard against wrongdoing, so that there will be a clear course to follow." Such a person fails entirely to realize that the ancient rulers devised laws in the expectation that there would be suitable men to carry them out. I have never heard that they made laws for the case in which capable men could not be found. If the high officials are not good men, and do not understand the principle of education, but merely adhere to the empty letter and the minute details of the law, surely they will not be able by these means to lead men to perfect their talents.

Ch'eng's reply is a standard Confucian rejoinder to quasi-Legalist recipes: the law cannot effect its own implementation; at best it is a guide for the judgment of good men.

But Ch'eng did not proceed very far with these anti-bureaucratic regrets. Another philosopher, Chang Tsai (1020–77), however, was so repelled by the spectacle of vulgar competition for positions that he praised, in contrast, the giving and holding of hereditary offices, which had persisted in the later bureaucratic empire as a not very significant and rather artificial continuation of ancient feudal forms.

> The distinction of hereditary office is the way a ruler gives recognition to those who achieve great things and honors the virtuous, cherishing them and being generous to them, displaying his boundless grace. Their heirs therefore ought to be happy with their duties and be encouraged to achievement . . . excelling in purity and abstaining from the pursuit of profit.

But in these times, Chang complained, "descendants of high dignitaries like to compete with ordinary people, working at the craft of verse-making and selling their wares to the authorities," i.e., sitting for the examinations in the hope of getting appointments, "not realizing that actively seeking for office is wrong."

Chang Tsai's feeling that it is unseemly for a man of quality to engage in the common scramble for advantage is here perhaps reinforced by another persuasion: that the gentleman will not push himself forward. This is the conduct one expects of a social climber; the true "superior man" waits until his prince calls him. But this is not for excess of humility; on the contrary, he may be deeply offended if it be thought that his merits are open to question. An amusing story told of "the philosopher Ch'eng" (either Ch'eng I or his brother Ch'eng Hao, 1032–85) shows how ingrained these attitudes were.

> Hsieh Chi passed through Loyang on his way from Shu to the capital and saw Ch'eng-tzu. The master asked him, "Why have you undertaken this trip?" He answered, "I am about to take the examination for a post in the Bureau of Education." The master did not reply. Chi said, "What do you think of it?" The master said, "Once when I was buying a servant-girl I wanted to test her. Her mother became angry and would not permit it, saying, 'My daughter is not one who may first be tried out.' Today you want to become a teacher of men and want to undergo a test for this purpose! You would certainly be laughed at by that old woman." Chi subsequently did not go.

Dignity is a precious thing indeed! Clearly, a dignified and lofty refusal to compete, a high-minded protest that one is not interested in advancement and will leave this matter to fate, and the cherishing of a picture of society in which the poisonous craving for "profit" is absent, are all attitudes which fit closely together.

In considering the bearing of Neo-Confucian ethical thought upon the examination problem, we cannot neglect the most famous of Sung philosopher-statesmen, Chu Hsi (1130–1200). Chu, describing the idealized ancient practice of recruiting officials by direct recommendation without examinations, says that as a result of it "men's minds were composed and they had no distracting desires. Night and day they were diligent, fearing only lest they be wanting in virtue, and not caring whether rank and salary came their way." Clearly he too shared the common Neo-Confucian nostalgic utopian ideal.

Chu Hsi made the foregoing statement in an essay which in its day was famous —a "Private Opinion on Schools and Examinations," which, the "Monograph on Examinations" in the *Sung Shih* tells us, "was read by the whole world." In it he was bitterly critical of examination standards and practices in his day. He proposed at least a limited use of direct recommendation, and an end to practices of favoritism; in particular he called for fairer geographical distribution when allocating quotas of candidates to be passed. The main part of his proposal, however, would have had the effect of making the examinations very different in content and tone: he would change the subject matter of the examinations through a twelve-year cycle, guaranteeing that the state would have at its disposal men with a wide variety of specialized backgrounds. Examinations in poetry and *fu* would be suppressed. Chu wanted his candidates to think, and to know how to think for themselves; in studying the Classics, they should study not only the classical texts but also the commentaries of different schools of interpreters, and in answering a question should be prepared to cite different opinions, concluding with their own judgment. Chu went on actually to list commentaries he would have examinees required to read; somewhat surprisingly, commentaries by Wang An-shih are included for all the most important Classics, although Chu was in general opposed to Wang's policies. Chu expected much if his proposals were acted upon. If they were adopted, "men's minds would be composed and there would be no spirit of hustling and striving; there would be actual virtuous conduct and none of the corruption of empty words; there would be solid learning and no unusable talent."

Chu in this essay was flailing away at the system, and doing so, at least in part, in terms of his ideal of a perfect social and political order. But this ideal of a perfectly virtuous world was ambiguous. It could be used, not to criticize the edifice of requirements, standards, pressures, or unfair practices which confronted the student, but rather to upbraid the student himself. For one can say that in a perfectly virtuous society the government would not make the mistakes the examination system embodied; but, by the same argument, students would not exhibit the qualities of restless self-seeking and anxiety that these mistakes induced. Chu has a rather often-quoted remark that "it is not that the examinations are a vexation to men, but simply that men vex themselves about the examinations." And he continues,

A scholar of lofty vision and broad understanding, when he reads the books of the sages, will produce writing which reflects what he grasps, and all considerations of gain and loss, advantage and disadvantage, are set aside. Even though he constantly works at preparing for the examinations, he is undisturbed. If Confucius were to come back to life now, he would not avoid the examinations; but surely they would not disturb him.

. . . . .

. . . Chu says that he himself as a young man found examination studies naturally distasteful to him, but argues that this natural disinclination was of no significance. The plain implication in this is that Chu was approached by unhappy students who also found their examination studies distasteful, who felt that the guidance of their own inclinations was valuable, and who found themselves, like Ou-yang Hsiu and Liu Chih-chi, inclined to spend their time on other lines of study and self-improvement. Chu is shown by the *Ch'üan Shu* editors to have dealt with this plaint in various ways. Sometimes he simply pooh-poohs all the fuss about the matter:

> Concerning study for the examinations, there is really nothing very important to be said. When a man of worth devotes himself to it, he will presumably have some energy to spare. If he has understood the true philosophy, then in the course of his daily activities, whatever their degree of importance, he will not need to divide his attention: if he always first understands "this," he will succeed at "that."

In other words, see that you cultivate yourself properly and study the right point of view, and there will be no conflict—you will automatically do well in the examinations. As Han Yü had said, a good man will naturally write well. Chu's friend and rival philosopher Lu Chiu-yüan picked up the same idea when, in 1181, he was guest lecturer at Chu's White Deer Grotto Academy. Cultivate yourself circumspectly, says Lu, instill in yourself a devotion to right, and learn to have no impulses toward selfish expediency. "When one who conducts himself in this way approaches the examination halls, his writing will always express the learning and self-cultivation in which he is constantly engaged and the richness stored up within himself, and he will not offend against the sages."

What if a young man self-importantly and loftily says that he has better things to do with himself than study examination essays? Chu offers the following dash of cold water:

> Not taking the examinations is really only a small matter. But nowadays when someone says he is not going to take the examinations it is treated as something surprising and extraordinary. As I see it, as soon as one devotes one's thought to understanding the Tao, one takes a bit of respite from this sort of thing (i.e., the examinations), and there is obviously nothing of importance in this fact. I don't know why, but [when people begin to understand the Tao] they automatically look down on all sorts of wealth, honor, and attainment . . .

This is less interesting as an example of Chu's attitude than it is as a negative image of a point of view which must have been prevalent among students.

Chu recognizes the common rationalization of students that they must study for the examinations in order to support their parents, and he condemns it. Such an attitude merely indicates that the student's mind is not composed—that he still feels a conflict between studying for the examinations and "real learning." Sometimes, however, Chu admits by implication that there can be such a conflict, and attempts to deal with it or resolve it by some argument or stratagem. On one occasion, a disciple named Huang Ch'ien was ordered by his father to go to the prefectural school and study for the examinations, a course the young student was much disinclined to take. Huang laid his situation before Chu, who replied, "You can study for the examinations in the daytime and read the books you want to at night!" and added that if Huang refused to follow his father's wishes, father and son would become estranged, a situation which, he implies, would be as detrimental to Huang's program of "study" (i.e., self-cultivation) as the examinations course could ever be.

. . . . .

. . . The Ming examinations followed, with some modification, the form of the Sung examinations as revised in 1071 when, as a result of one of the reforms of Wang An-shih, the *ming-ching* examination was abolished and certain features of it incorporated into the *chin-shih* examination. As it ultimately took shape, the Ming examination scheme (for both *chin-shih* and *chü-jen* degrees) consisted of three sittings or tests several days apart. The first test consisted of "essays on the meaning of the Classics" (*ching-i*)—three on the Four Books, and four on texts from other Classics. The second test was given over to *lun* ("essays") and *p'an* ("decisions," a T'ang examination form) and to questions on imperial "instructions"; the third, to *ts'e* ("dissertations") on history and current problems. As far as this description goes, such an examination might be quite comprehensive. Actually, as Ku Yen-wu points out, the only test given any careful attention by the examiners was the first, on the meaning of the Classics and the Four Books. Further, although all candidates had to answer questions on the Four Books, it was possible to get by with specialization on just one other Classic. This was certainly very far from what Chu Hsi had wanted in his "Private Opinion."

But this was not all. Where Chu had wanted candidates to have a knowledge of many different schools of criticism, the Ming system required candidates to prepare themselves in the views of just one school, ironically the school of Chu Hsi himself. After the official publication, in the Yung-lo reign, of the compendium of the opinions of this school, the *Ssu-shu Wu-ching Ta-ch'üan,* even the standard T'ang commentaries were dispensed with. In consequence, less and less came to depend on wide learning or genuine understanding, even of the Classics themselves; more and more it came to be crucially important for the candidate to excel in the style of his essays on the meaning of classical texts in the first test.

. . . . .

. . . the chances were that an examiner would find himself in the situation of passing judgment on a candidate or candidates who knew more philology than he did. Examiners caught in this sort of situation tend to look for a simple and foolproof line of defense into which to retreat. The examiner's recourse in the present case was to limit his inspection once again to mere questions of form: not, now, to the formal correctness of the candidate's essays, but to the form of the individual characters he wrote—to his calligraphy. By the second and third decades of the nineteenth century, it was a ritual perfection in the handling of the brush which was the mark of the candidate most likely to succeed.

Needless to say, this new situation provoked protests appropriate to it. Such an expression of protest is to be found in a bitterly sarcastic essay by Kung Tzu-chen, an intense, brilliant, and erratic scholar-official, philologist, poet, and friend of Wei Yüan and Lin Tse hsü, who attempted the examinations repeatedly before attaining the *chin-shih* degree in 1829, failing, however—as he believed, because of poor handwriting—to pass the palace examination which a successful *chin-shih* normally took. Kung's essay pretends to be a preface to a book he has written on calligraphy. He describes first, with mock reverence, the ritual of the palace examination in which he failed. The examining officers, "in court robes, face the throne and kneel thrice, touching their heads to the floor nine times. All the candidates do likewise, respectfully taking their positions. When the examination is over, the eight examiners then respectfully make a selection of ten papers in which the elevation of characters is according to form and in which even and deflected tones have been properly used, and which exhibit a formal calligraphic style which is especially sparkling and delicate, presenting these for the emperor's perusal. . . ."

Kung describes more examinations—the preliminary examination before the palace examination, and the examination following it, both, again, turning on the candidate's skill in calligraphy. He misses no chance to dwell on the grave and weighty importance of success which turns on so trivial a matter. "Those who place high in all three examinations are appointed to the Han-lin Academy. In our dynasty, the highest officials invariably arise from among members of the Han-lin, and more than half of the assistant ministers at court and of the governors of provinces are chosen in the same way." To be chosen for a clerkship in the Grand Council is likewise a great honor; for "in time of war the function of the Grand Council is to assist the throne in making plans by which victory is decided, while in time of peace it provides advice based on the records of earlier emperors in the issuance of edicts affecting the imperial household." But, "when one is recommended to the Grand Council there is an examination, in which selection is made as before on the basis of calligraphic skill." Kung goes on to explain to us how other important posts are filled, and always with the same final twist.

Finally Kung tips his hand:

> I, Kung Tzu-chen, passed the examination in the Board of Ceremonies; three times I went up for the palace examination and three times I failed. I was not assigned to the Han-lin Academy. I was examined for the Grand Council but was not given a post there. . . . So I have withdrawn to my home and have reproached myself, and have written a book in self-criticism. Its contents consist of twelve sections discussing the principles of selecting a fine brush-tip, five sections on the proper method of grinding the ink and impregnating the brush, . . . one hundred and twenty sections on fine points in the drawing of the dot and in the execution of the sweeping down-stroke, twenty-two sections on the framing of characters, twenty-four sections on the spacing of characters in column, three sections on quality of spirit; and seven sections on natural temper. Having finished the work, I have entitled it *A New Treatise on Gaining Office*, and am entrusting it to my descendants.

Kung dates his "preface" the fourteenth year of Tao-kuang (1834).

Needless to say, Kung's *Treatise* was never written or even seriously contemplated. Kung's bitterness about calligraphy, it should be stressed, was provoked by a situation peculiar to his time. We find a very different attitude in Ku Yen-wu. Ku would have his candidates know how to write characters well, and no nonsense. He cites in this connection, and with evident approval, a practice in court examinations in the Northern Ch'i Dynasty. In those high and far-off times, it seems, if a candidate's writing was sloppy, he was required as a penalty to drink a pint of ink.

The Chinese civil service examinations were not discontinued until 1905. The remainder of the story, however, would be a study in itself, and I lack both the space and the knowledge to enter upon it. But it does seem plain that it would be hasty to ascribe the Chinese state's rejection of the examination system simply to a Westernizing fever, or to say that the Chinese did away with that system merely in order to be rid of a conservative institutional force. Perhaps it will turn out that what the "impact of the West" accomplished was to tip the balance in favor of persuasions which were centuries old, but which had not been strong enough radically to alter the set institutions of a bureaucratic state. The complaint that the examinations failed to nourish talents of practical use to the state was not a new and radical idea in the nineteenth century; on the contrary, it was a familiar criticism in the ninth. . . .

The examination system must certainly be called Confucian. It gave form to the ideal that the ruler should select the best men as his officials, and it provided in most periods a fixed if narrow and difficult avenue to prestige and position for that social group who had a special interest in reading and cherishing the Confucian classical texts. And yet the bitter regrets the Chinese have had about the system must also be called Confucian. The Neo-Confucian utopian ideal, and the "antiformalist" and moral criteria of literary value enunciated by Han Yü in the ninth century and by Ku Yen-wu in the seventeenth are essential parts of the idealistic side of the Confucian tradition which has its roots in Mencius.

When we consider the position of the individual student or candidate, we see that he was pushed in two directions at once. He must do the right thing for his parents and family; the *ipsissima verba* of the Master could be cited in abundance to assure him of this; also it was the duty of a Confucian to take office and "put his Tao into practice" if he could. In the later empire, the only apparent way to perform these duties was to prepare for the examinations and seek official position thereby.

Yet the Confucian also had a duty to cultivate himself and to respect his own dignity. Entry into the competition for office obliged him, it seemed, to place "profit" ahead of "right" in his own personal ordering of values, and at least to seem to be seeking the approbation of persons, whether gossiping townspeople or examining officials, whom he might regard as vulgar or petty-minded. If we read reflectively a novel such as *Ju-lin Wai-shih,* we suspect that the scorn measured out to examiners and examination writing is, so to speak, but the exposed part of an iceberg whose bulk is the pervasive revulsion of independent-minded men against social pressures to conform, to accept the vulgar conventions and values, to chase after the pretty tags of so-called success, to court favor with the "best" families in town. Beneath this disposition was always the conception of the Superior Man, who cannot be moved by mere things.

A Chinese who thought seriously about himself and his society did not live in a placid intellectual world in which all his questions had ready answers. He lived in a world of tensions, both social and intellectual—tensions such as those I have been describing; and if we are to understand his politics, his literature, his philosophy, we must measure these tensions and their effect upon him. We must see him as he was.

CHANGE WITHIN TRADITION

51

*Medieval China, although impressively stable, was far from being static. Despite the common belief that Chinese civilization remained inflexible through the centuries, the fact remains that change was occurring gradually but constantly and decisively. The following selection by an American authority analyzes the precise nature of this "change within tradition" during the Sung period.**

* E. A. Kracke, Jr., "Sung Society: Change Within Tradition," *Journal of Asian Studies,* XIV (August 1955), 479-88. Copyright by the Association for Asian Studies, Inc., reprinted with permission.

When we speak of social change in China we most often have in mind one or the other of two pictures. The first is the change that we see today, when radically new ideas, techniques and forces from foreign countries have shaken the traditional social order, altering the old patterns rapidly and sometimes violently. The second picture is that of the dynastic cycle, a concept that we have inherited from the traditional Chinese historian, sometimes adding a few embellishments of our own. The political fortunes of a ruling house are often reflected (and perhaps affected) by a characteristic cycle in the whole political and economic order of the nation: from successful adjustment and control to maladjustment and chaos. The end of each cycle, if we focus our attention only on these factors, leaves Chinese society much as it was at the end of the cycle before. But this perspective tends to omit qualitative changes that occur in Chinese society on a different plane.

The kind of social change to be considered now differs from both of these. It is the long and continuous process of social development that in China as in our own civilization has accompanied the interplay between the traditional ideas and ways of life and the new concepts, techniques, and patterns of activity that evolve at home or enter from abroad. While at times this process of development moved slowly, and at times even retrogressed in some respects, the Chinese way of life nevertheless underwent through the centuries a cumulative alteration that was essentially irreversible. At times the forces of change so interacted that their gathered momentum was almost revolutionary in its social impact. An outstanding example of such rapid and far-reaching change is supplied by the Sung period, from the tenth century to the thirteenth.

The beginnings of the movement that attained so dramatic a tempo in the Sung period can be traced back, in some respects, through several centuries. Perhaps the first clearly perceptible aspect of the movement is the striking shift in the mass of China's population, from the northern plain country to the valleys of the mountainous south and the southeast coast. This migration had begun in the early centuries of our era, impelled both by economic difficulties and by foreign invaders of the old homeland; but as late as the middle of the eighth century the Yangtse valley and the areas further south still held only some forty to forty-five percent of China's people. By the end of the thirteenth century this area reported no less than eighty-five to ninety percent of the nation's population, and no less than twenty percent were established in the valleys of Fukien and eastern Chekiang along the southeast coast.

The rich new delta lands of the South became the chief suppliers of China's granaries. Some of the economic consequences of this are already well known, and need only be recapitulated here. To feed the armies guarding the northern border, and to provision the capital in the North, the central administration undertook to expand the canal system and subsidiary land communications from the South on a mammoth scale. Aided by the new facilities, private commerce grew rapidly. The Chinese now living along the remote southern coast no doubt found it necessary to import tools and other goods from the older settlements, and exchanged for these the new products native to the semi-tropical land in which they found themselves, as well as products from the South Seas and the countries of the Indian Ocean. Easier contacts by sea with Persia and Arabia encouraged the growth of foreign commerce, soon bringing to the growing coastal cities settlements of Hindu and Arab merchants. The Chinese also, as Mr. Lo points out in the following article in this issue, turned to the sea and assumed a leading place among maritime peoples. Internal commerce among the regions of China, at first confined for the most part to luxury items for the few, now expanded in variety and in its significance for larger groups of the nation.

With the growth of inter-regional trade, money came into its own, for many purposes rapidly superseding the old transactions in kind. By the eleventh century, a system of regulated paper currency was in operation, and the coinage of copper money reached proportions never again approached in Chinese dynastic history. Facilities for the transfer of funds and the provision of credit also developed. The various regions of China were no longer self-sufficient economically, but increasingly specialized in their produce—foods or goods or services—and therefore interdependent. These developments brought into being, by the eleventh century, a Chinese economy apparently far more complex than any of earlier times.

Of the social change that accompanied this economic development we have as yet only a very incomplete picture. But certain of its aspects stand out strikingly in the records. One aspect—perhaps of key significance—is the changing role of the great city. In earlier periods the few outstanding cities had achieved their greatness and economic importance only after designation as national capitals. Their symmetrical and regular plan, centered on the principal imperial palace, gave visible evidence of their origin and purpose. From the tenth century to the thirteenth this was not so. In this later period the cities chosen as capitals had already achieved importance as trade centers at strategic points on the lines of communication.

K'ai-feng, the first Sung capital, exemplified this particularly well. Originally a regional administrative seat at a main transfer point on the arterial canal from the South, its access to southern rice supplies recommended it during the troubled years succeeding the T'ang. The city had grown with its commercial importance, as successive new walls inclosed the suburbs that grew spontaneously beyond the older city gates. Within the sixteen-mile circuit of the outer walls, space was at a premium. The second Sung emperor renounced the planned expansion of his palace because it would have forced the demolition of private dwelling quarters. As a result of this history, although the city lay in the level valley of the Yellow River, it lacked the symmetry that had marked earlier national capitals and would later distinguish Peking (also primarily political in its character).

The later Sung capital of Hang-chou was also an important trade center at the time of its political elevation in 1135. Its population was huge; the numbers within its walls during the later years of the dynasty have been estimated as 900,000, and those in its suburbs as some 600,000 more.

While the capitals of the eleventh to thirteenth centuries had thus grown strongly commercial in character, their supremacy among Chinese cities was challenged by other urban centers still more reliant on business activity. By the year 1100 at least four urban areas far surpassed the capital area in population. We have no exact data on the numbers living within the walls of these cities or in their immediate suburbs, but census reports suggest that each of the urban areas held a million or more people within the borders of its prefecture—a space very roughly comparable to the greater metropolitan areas of London or New York. Such population concentrations would seem to outdistance by far the largest urban agglomerations of that time in Europe, even by the largest estimates of the latter.

During the next two centuries the urban growth continued, and in several instances the prefectural populations apparently doubled, tripled, or quadrupled by 1290. Among the most dramatic increases, three were on the southeast coast (Hang-chou, Su-chou, and Fu-chou), and one (Jao-chou) near the inland trade route from the Yangtse to Canton. The prefecture of Fu-chou in 1290 reported approximately 3,875,000 people, suggesting an urban concentration of impressive proportions.

It was just around this time, soon after the Sung downfall, that Marco Polo visited these places, as an agent of the Mongol conqueror Kubilai. His descriptions of the magnificience of Hang-chou, the capital, and of the trade metropolis Ch'üan-chou, are well known. But he also observed another phenomenon that is suggested by contemporary census figures—the growth and multiplication of smaller cities and towns. In describing the journey from Hang-chou to Fu-chou (less than three hundred miles as the crow flies), he tells of no less than six "large, noble, and beautiful" or "noble and great" cities, and in the stages of his journey between these he notes no less than seven times "always finding cities and villages enough, very beautiful and very great"; on one two-day ride he remarks that these are "so frequent and continuous that you seem as you ride to go through the middle of a single city." Allowing for the colorful exaggerations we must permit to this oldest of China-hands, the regions that Polo saw along the southeast coast must certainly have been advanced in urban development compared with his native Italy—the most urbanized part of Europe in that day. While most of the terrain was mountainous and poorly adapted to farming, the few lands available had been fully exploited. A Sung writer notes that intensive cultivation had transformed once worthless acres to the most fertile in the empire, and while Marco Polo refers occasionally to the livestock he saw (oxen, buffalo, cows, goats, swine, and fowl) and to certain special plant products, he speaks not of fields but of "fine gardens."

But rich as the fields were, they were still too few. The coastal regions still depended for their prosperity on the income from their mines, commerce, manufactures, tea, and sea produce, and beyond the narrow valley floors must have preserved some of the air of an unsettled borderland. On four stages of his journey Polo mentions the "hunting and chase enough of beasts and birds" and refers as many times to the great and fierce "lions" (tigers?) that molest travellers, to such an extent that in one part of the route at least "it is very dangerous to pass through those regions unless people go in great numbers." In an area seeming thus sparsely settled over much of its extent, and developing rapidly in industry and trade, typifying the new trend, it is difficult not to suspect analogies with the frontier of opportunity that played a vital role in the development of our own civilization.

Who were the people that lived in the growing cities of this area? We have no clear picture of them, but there are at least some clues to their character. As in earlier times, there must have been a considerable number of civil and military officials, stationed there for limited terms by the central government, along with a more or less permanent corps of clerks and official underlings. There were the army garrisons usually stationed in all large places. There were no doubt well-to-do scholars without official employment, and poorer scholars who lived on their earnings as teachers, or from such miscellaneous employments as public letter-writing or story-telling. And there were the merchants and artisans, great and small, blending at the lowest economic level with the unskilled laborers. Considering the indicated sizes of the cities, the last three occupations must have constituted the preponderant group of inhabitants in most cases. The composition of the Sung populations cannot have differed too greatly from that observed by Marco Polo only around a decade after the dynasty's fall: in all his comments on the six larger cities he saw between Hang-chou and Fu-chou, and in four of his comments on the places between, he notes that the inhabitants "live by trade and by crafts," and implies mercantile activities indirectly by repeated references to the "abundance of all things for life," which he notes were very cheap. (To other activities he makes very little reference.)

What was true of this area was probably true also, to a more limited degree, of the great cities more widely scattered in other parts of China at this time. All were joined by the same commercial links, and often frequented by the same far-travelling merchants.

Surviving records tell us of the merchants' activities and mode of life chiefly at the capitals, but in these respects too different regions may have presented a rather similar picture.

The merchants, artisans, and providers of services were organized in guilds, which had powers of discipline over their own members, although these organizations had no apparent role in the general administration of the cities. The guild members had to some extent emancipated themselves from the close official supervision that existed during the T'ang. Their business activities were no longer confined within the great walled markets, or limited to the hours in which the government permitted the opening of the market portals. Commerce and manufacture were now carried on in shops scattered throughout the city or beyond the city gates, though establishments of the same trade tended to group together.

Long and persistent governmental efforts to regulate trade and control prices were matched by equally persistent and largely successful evasion on the part of the merchants. Attempts of the state to monopolize certain profitable industries had been costly and only partly successful. But in the Sung the state had learned to apply its taxes more flexibly and to restrict its monopolies to certain key operations of an industry; through such policies the state diverted what was perhaps the lion's share of the profits to its treasuries.

Such state controls may well have retarded significantly the growth of commercial activity and power. At the time, however, there must have been little evidence of this. The more successful merchants accumulated great wealth, and their style of living vied with that of the imperial princes. Sumptuary laws had always, before this, restricted the colors that should be used by each class of society. By 995, however, sumptuary laws were unenforceable, and all were repealed but the ban on a certain shade of deep purple reserved for the imperial house and the highest officials. There is evidence that even this color was taken over by commoners within a few years. We read that the families of great merchants wore pearls and jade. Their carriages thronged the roads, and in the words of a contemporary "rubbed hubs with those of distinguished families." In the T'ang, we are told, even a servant who had served in an aristocratic family scorned a master who haggled in person with a merchant. By the eleventh century, even important officials had discovered the attractions of commerce, and many augmented their income by combining business operations with their official journeys. Merchants were socially accepted in elite circles. Through such connections, or through their wealth, some of them secured government office, and served in positions of some importance.

But the professional trader still found certain barriers to his social advancement. He still lacked the approval of more conservative scholars. His indulgence in luxuries elicited complaints very much like those that had been evoked by a more modest commercial expansion a millennium earlier. His pursuit of money was felt to be unworthy. The officials criticized his disposition to make profits by cornering the market; because this was at the expense of the poor—and no doubt because the official preferred that the state monopolies should garner such profits. The grumbling of the conservatives, however, may have been in itself another indication that power of commerce was recognized as a potential threat to the supremacy of the bureaucrat; in fact, specific complaints of the growing influence that merchants exercised over officials are not lacking.

The new social environment created by the cities surely had its impact on the evolution of Chinese culture. The operation of any but the simplest business naturally required at least a certain minimum of literacy, and the city environment gave better opportunities for even the poorest to gain a smattering of the written character. The successful and ambitious tradesman would naturally hope that education would win for his sons an entree into the bureaucracy. When the new urban reader competed with the older scholar for written texts, a new demand for books was created. In the century after 950 the technique of wood engraving, long used to multiply Buddhist charms and texts, suddenly found new uses, and in a short time the art of printing was applied to practically all the existing varieties of literature.

For the relatively unlettered, a multiplicity of entertainments was also devised, ranging from troops of acrobats and displays of fireworks to puppet shows, shadow plays, and simple theatrical presentations. Through the stories that served as themes for such public performances, some parts of the sophisticated culture could reach the illiterate, and facilitate a sharing of the great tradition with larger groups. Particularly important in this respect was the role of the story-teller: unemployed scholars frequently made their living by recounting some of the dramatic episodes of history to audiences in the market place. Through the prompting-books some of them wrote to aid their confreres, they created the prototypes of the later great fictional themes. At the same time the old themes were presented in the language of the people and transmuted to appeal to a more popular audience, until the content itself reflected their viewpoint and their tastes. It could scarcely be accidental that the Chinese popular novel traces back to this period.

The influence of the new city life also had its impact on society beyond the city walls. The growing importance of a money economy must surely have contributed a significant share to the increasing complications of the farm problem. The crops of different regions were becoming more specialized, leaving the farmer often less self-sufficient, and more vulnerable in years of crop failure. While the farmer probably relied little on the cities for his basic necessities, it seems that travelling merchants from the cities already came to the country fairs to sell such things as salt, and buy for the city market. The glamor of the city had its weakening effect on the old rural patterns of life in other ways, The wealthy peasant, we are told, tended to emulate the merchant's style of living, and we hear repeatedly that the rewards of commerce tempted the poor farmer to abandon the hard and often unrewarding work on his lands, sell his farm implements, and engage in trade.

Finally, we must note the change that came about in the bureaucratic class itself. It was also in this period that new recruitment procedures opened a governmental career to far wider numbers than before. Competitive recruitment examinations were regularly used from the beginning of the eleventh century on a scale far greater than ever before. Improved through the development of elaborate techniques to make the examinations more objective, the new system helped to break the power monopoly once held by a small group of northern aristocratic families. The social origin of the newcomers who replaced them is not entirely clear. The broader distribution of opportunity was certainly made possible by the increase in literacy and the wider availability of books that we have already noted. Several hundred candidates commonly passed the final stage of the triennial examinations, and we are told that for each of these some hundred candidates had attempted the local preliminary tests. The competition was wide indeed. But the fiercest rivalry and the most numerous successful candidates during most of the dynasty came from the southeast coast, where we have seen the rapid pace of urbanization at this time.

How many of these men came from the great cities? How many traced their educational opportunity to families of ultimately mercantile origin? It is still impossible to say. But data from two lists of graduates that have come down to us from the twelfth and thirteenth centuries show that the regions with more and larger urban concentrations tended to supply not only more graduates in proportion to their area, but also more graduates per family, so that they clearly dominated the field. Moreover the largest proportion of apparently new blood tended to appear in the circuits of most rapid population growth, if we may judge from the numbers of graduates counting no officials among their direct paternal forebears. Conspicuous among these regions of growing population were again those containing the great coastal cities and those on the main inland trade routes. We have here, then, a seeming link between the broadening social base of the bureaucracy and the social mobility that probably characterized the great cities in their period of most rapid expansion.

The political importance of this changing character of the bureaucracy is obvious. Its cultural effect, while less tangible and less calculable, was perhaps none the less real. For while the Sung was a time of beginnings for the more popular literary forms, it was also a time of great vigor, and in some ways a time of culmination, in the intellectual activities practiced or patronized by the bureaucrat: the fine arts, the more sophisticated literary forms, and critical scholarship. In government, it was a time of imaginative reform schemes and experiments. It saw great advances in several fields of technology. In all of these realms the contribution made by men of the Southeast was outstanding.

Thus we have evidence that a genuine alteration of Chinese social patterns accompanied the rise of the great city. The influence of the city extended beyond the bourgeois to the farmer and the bureaucrat. Despite the inhibiting pressures of official conservatism, and at times in disregard of laws and decrees, the merchant had expanded his influence and breached many of the barriers that surrounded him when the period of change began.

The limits of his rise are also apparent. If he achieved a place in government, it was by transforming himself into a bureaucrat; as a merchant he still enjoyed no active political role. The professional official remained supreme, and steadfastly unsympathetic toward the development of private economic interests.

The history of Chinese urbanization after the thirteenth century, and the reasons why the movement failed to go further than it did, are beyond the scope of the present topic. As we contemplate the situation of the thirteenth century bourgeois, however, it is difficult to discern any single insuperable barrier to his further social rise. Most of his disadvantages were also faced by some at least of his European confreres during the later Middle Ages or the Renaissance. In the thirteenth century, the Chinese bourgeois had demonstrated by his will and his resourcefulness that under favorable conditions, the traditional Chinese social patterns could be significantly modified through the operation of internal forces.

52 CHINA AS A SEA POWER

One of the most spectacular changes that occurred in medieval China was the growth of naval power and of general maritime activity. The Chinese commonly are thought to have been landlubbers who faced inland toward Central Asia rather than outward over the ocean. This was true by and large through the T'ang period, but it definitely was not so during the late Sung, Yüan, and early Ming. The following article describes the circumstances under which Chinese attention and energy shifted from the interior to the coastal regions, and the resulting emergence of China as the dominant naval power of East Asia.*

One of the topics of Chinese history that deserves greater attention is the nature and direction of the expansion of the Chinese people beyond the geographical confines of China. It is a subject which, for want of more information, is still so cloaked in generalities as to present the misleading impression that the Chinese have always been a landbound people oriented towards the land frontier of the north and northwest. A Western scholar, for example, has written: "China has never been a sea-power because nothing has ever induced her people to be otherwise than landmen, and landmen dependent on agriculture with the same habit and ways of thinking drilled into them through forty centuries." In a recent work we find this statement: "Essentially a land people, the Chinese cannot be considered as having possessed sea-power. . . . The attention of the Chinese through the centuries has been turned inward towards Central Asia rather than outward, and their knowledge of the seas which washed their coast was extremely small."

These quotations represent views that have wide currency. Sea power, according to the dictionary definition of the term, is the possession and application of naval strength for the control and command of the sea. China in the period from Han to T'ang could not qualify as a sea power although fleets were employed to wage coastal wars and to carry out invasions of Korea and Indo-China, for it was towards Mongolia and Turkestan that the diplomatic and strategic attention was focused. Nor could China qualify as a sea power during recent times, for the navies of foreign powers have held sway over her territorial waters. But can we judge the China of the late medieval period by the China of any other time? Can we say, categorically, that the Chinese were always a continentally-minded people and that China was never a sea power? This is a question of some consequence, basic to our understanding of Chinese civilization.

I have spent some time on the study of this subject and I have arrived at certain conclusions which can be summed up in the thesis that, contrary to popular views, China was a naval power during the late Sung, Yüan and early Ming periods and that this seaward expansion was the outcome of acute social and environmental changes.

Although their history abounds with accounts of battles fought on the rivers, lakes and coastal waters, the early Chinese did not regard the navy as anything more than a subordinate adjunct of the army. There were small standing navies maintained by seaboard states during periods of disunity, there were maritime

* Jung-pang Lo, "The Emergence of China as a Sea Power during the Late Sung and Early Yüan Periods," *Journal of Asian Studies*, XIV (August 1955), 489-503. Copyright by the Association for Asian Studies, Inc., reprinted with permission.

fleets mobilized for temporary service in overseas campaigns and under centralized control as in the spacious days of Han, Sui and T'ang, and there were navies composed of river units under provincial command as in the Northern Sung period, but until the creation of the Southern Sung navy, China did not have a national sea-going navy established on a permanent basis.

The shock of their defeat by the Chin invaders in 1127, the capture of the emperor and the fall of the capital at K'ai-feng which drove the Sung court to establish itself at Hangchow, a city exposed to attacks by sea, stirred the Chinese to adopt counter-measures for self-protection. With the cultivated area reduced by enemy occupation and by war, the Chinese had to augment their food supply by intensifying the cultivation of their fields, and the huge network of canals and ditches they dug for transportation and irrigation served them also as means of defense. It gave the Chinese a defensive system which invalidated the superiority of the enemy cavalry. To patrol the waterways of this defensive belt which covered the region between the Huai River and the Yangtze and to guard its eastern and western flanks, the Chinese needed a navy and they succeeded in building a strong and mobile one.

. . . . .

The navy of Southern Sung had the distinction of being the first national navy to be established on a permanent basis and to function as an independent service. It was the first navy to be administered by a special agency of the government, the Imperial Commissioner's Office for the Control and Organization of the Coastal Areas . . . which was established in 1132 with headquarters at Ting-hai, one of the islands of the Chusan group. The fleet steadily grew in strength. In 1130, there were eleven squadrons with three thousand men; in 1174, fifteen squadrons with twenty-one thousand men; and in 1237, the Southern Sung navy had grown to be an effective fighting force of twenty squadrons manned by nearly fifty-two thousand men. . . .

By the first half of the thirteenth century, the Sung navy ranged unchallenged over the East China Sea. As a member of the Privy Council . . . Wu Ch'ien . . . pointed out in a memorial: "The area of control of our navy extends westward to Hsü-p'u, southward to Fukien, northward to Korea and eastward to Japan, an area of over ten thousand *li*. The navy is used for scouting, the navy is used for patrolling, and the navy is used for the defense of strategic points."

But, he went on, the navy was "only strong enough to check the Japanese and the Koreans," and he and other ministers who shared his views urged the further expansion of the navy and its transformation into a weapon of offense. The adoption of a strong naval policy had been advocated by many Sung officials since 1129 when a bold scheme was conceived for the invasion of Korea by naval forces and the use of Korea as an advance base for seaborne attacks on the Chin empire. Others suggested the extension of Chinese naval power into the South China Sea. But, because of insufficient resources and preoccupation with border wars, the Sung court did not heed these proposals. It remained for the Mongols to take the next step of employing the navy as an instrument of aggression.

The alacrity with which the Mongols, a nation of horsemen unacquainted with the sea, took to naval warfare was amazing. As late as the middle of the thirteenth century, they were still using inflated skins and rafts to cross rivers in their war against the Sung. Two decades later, they were conducting large-scale naval wars against Sung China and Japan, against Tongking, Champa and Java, and sending naval units against Quelpart Island and Formosa. How did they accomplish this feat? The answer is that they took over, wholesale, the navies of Korea and Sung China, but added leadership and imbued the men with energy and *élan*. Thus, the Yüan navy was essentially the Sung navy re-vitalized.

. . . . .

After the collapse of Sung resistance, the Yüan court immediately embarked on a gigantic program of shipbuilding. It ordered the construction of fifteen hundred ships in 1279, three thousand ships in 1281, and four thousand ships in 1283. These were to be built in shipyards as far inland as Changsha, as far south as Canton, as far north as Lung-lu (in northeast Hopei), and as far east as the Korean province of Cholla-do. It ordered the authorities of Quelpart Island and the province of Jehol to supply the lumber. It mobilized an army of 17,000 men to fell trees in the mountains of Jehol and to transport the wood to the shipyards. Sung officers, taken as prisoners in the battle of Yai-shan, were assigned to shipyards in China and Korea to assist in shipbuilding, and former Sung troops were integrated into Mongol and Han (Northern Chinese and Jurchen) units and given training in naval warfare.

Although not all the ships that were ordered built were actually constructed, the Yüan government nevertheless had an impressive navy for its overseas campaigns. The invasion of Japan in 1281 was undertaken with forty-four hundred ships, the invasion of Champa and Tongking from 1283 to 1288 with eight hundred ships, and the expedition against Java in 1293 with a thousand ships. In addition, there was a large coastal defense fleet and a maritime transportation fleet to carry tribute, grain, and imported merchandise from South China to the capital in the north. Thus, by wielding their new weapon, the navy, the Mongols extended the naval domination of China from the East to the South China Sea.

The naval program continued into the early Ming period. Like the Yüan navy, the Ming navy grew out of sanguinary wars on the Yangtze. At its maximum strength during the reign of Yung-lo, it consisted of a central fleet of four hundred ships stationed at Nanking, a coastal defense fleet of twenty-eight hundred ships to ward off raids by *wako* from Japan, a maritime transport fleet of three thousand ships, and, the pride of the Ming navy, a fleet of over two hundred and fifty "treasure ships" . . . each with capacity for five hundred men. The possession and application of naval power not only facilitated the reconquest of Annam but also enabled the Chinese to extend their political control beyond the East and South China Seas into the Indian Ocean. The prestige of the Chinese navy was so great that in 1403, when an Annamese fleet invaded the capital of Champa, the appearance of nine Chinese men-of-war was sufficient to compel the Annamese to withdraw.

If the domination of the sea and the employment of naval strength as an instrument of national policy characterizes a sea power, then China during the late Sung, Yüan and early Ming period would qualify. Why was it that China emerged as a sea power at this particular period and not at an earlier or later time? To seek an answer, we must take a broad view of sea power. Mere possession of a navy does not, *ipso facto*, make sea power. Sea power is the culmination and the physical expression of a set of geographical and sociological conditions which Admiral Mahan called the "elements of sea power." The maritime expansion of China from the twelfth to the fifteenth century was the result of a fortuitous combination of these conditions.

Geographical environment is one of the basic determining factors of social development. The long coastline of China, large sections of which, as in Shantung,

Chekiang, Fukien and Kwangtung, are endowed with harbors and timber-clad mountains, and the adjoining seas enclosed by an island fringe, provide the physiographical conditions which favor and promote maritime activities. But the territorial vastness of China and her cohesion with the continent of Eurasia exercise so profound an influence that for long centuries the attention of the Chinese was occupied with internal problems and the defense of their land frontier on the north and northwest, the directions from which danger had historically threatened. During the ancient period, the hub of China was the inland provinces of Shensi and Honan, which became not only the political and strategic, but also the economic, cultural and population center of the country. The diffusion of population was toward the marginal areas around the heartland, and cultural and commercial relations were primarily carried on over caravan routes with countries of the west. The preoccupation with internal affairs and, to a lesser extent, with the affairs of the northwest frontier was again evident during the Ch'ing period.

The prosperity of China's northwestern provinces depended, however, on a number of factors, chief of which were temperate climate, abundant rainfall and fertile soil. During the medieval period, the climate and geology of the entire region underwent a gradual and profound change. The winters became more severe and the atmosphere drier, rainfall diminished in amount but increased in intensity, the streams became shallower and more saline, and erosion ate steadily into the farmlands. The Cheng-kuo Canal and the Pai Canal, which in Han times irrigated two million *mou* of land in the Wei River Valley, site of the capitals of successive dynasties of the past, by the Northern Sung period watered only a hundred thousand *mou,* or five per cent of the former area. As the soil declined in productivity, the struggle to eke out a living began to absorb more and more of the energy of the people.

Coeval with the impoverishment of the Northwest was the prodigious advance of the coastal region of Southeast China as this became the economic center of the nation. In the salubrity of its climate, in the productivity of its soil, and in the potential wealth of its rivers, lakes and mountains, the Southeast far surpasses the Northwest. From the fourth century, when the Northwest was beginning to decline, the progressive peopling of the Southeast and its comparatively peaceful environment led to the extensive development of its resources. The construction of irrigation works was but one example of the efforts of the people of Southeast China to improve the conditions of their already bountiful land. The economy of Southeast China developed to such an extent that by 1119, for example, over seventy per cent of the money and goods . . . sent to the court as tribute came from the lower Yangtze Valley.

For a long time, Chinese rulers, cherishing a sentimental attachment for the ancient centers of China's civilization and motivated by strategic considerations, continued to locate their capitals in Shensi or Honan, and they built an elaborate system of waterways to transport supplies from the Southeast to the civilian population in the capital and to the troops on the northwest frontier. But with the progressive desiccation of the Northwest and the frequent wars, these waterways, like the irrigation canals, suffered from shortage of water, damage and lack of repair. Without a continuous supply of food it was impossible to maintain large garrisons and the weakening of the frontier defenses tempted the border peoples to invade.

On one hand, the absence of effective resistance and the attraction of the riches of China; on the other, their own economic distress and population pressure, the appearance of capable leaders and the consolidation of tribal organization were some of the many forces that agitated the nomads and impelled them to erupt periodically in massive tidal waves. The invasions of border peoples have not only had a profound and far-reaching effect on the history and culture of China but also served as a negative factor in turning the attention of the Chinese people to the sea.

The establishment by foreign conquerors of strong militaristic states in Northwest China sealed off Chinese contact with Central Asia, thus obliging the Chinese to carry on cultural and commercial intercourse abroad by sea. This shift in orientation is illustrated by a spot check in the section on foreign countries in the *Sung hui-yao kao* (*Draft of Sung institutes*). Before the fall of K'ai-feng in 1127, thirty-five per cent of the tribute-with-trade missions came to China by land and sixty-five per cent by sea. After this date all came by sea. The dislodgment of the Chinese from North China also destroyed much of their attachment for Shensi and Honan as sites for their capital. From 1127 on, their capitals were located near the seacoast.

The invasions from outside, coming at times when China was racked by civil strife, aggravated the economic distress and intensified the migration of the people. This happened from the fourth to sixth centuries and, on a greater scale, from the tenth to thirteenth centuries. During these times the slow drift of the population became a swift stream. The magnitude of the unrest may be seen from the fact that the census takers had to divide the population into two classes, "settled" . . . and "transient" . . . and that during the Sung period, as the census of 1080 showed, one-third of the population (mostly from North China) was listed as transient.

Instead of spreading more or less evenly into the southern provinces or, as in the eighth century, streaming into Szechwan, from the tenth to thirteenth centuries the people poured into Southeast China as if they were shoved by a gigantic force from the Northwest. This resulted in an abnormal swelling of the coastal population. The six seaboard provinces, with but a tenth of the area of the nation, had, during the Sung and Ming periods, half of the total population, a proportion higher than any in the pre-Sung or post-Ming periods. But if we examine the Yüan census of 1330, taking into account its imperfections and omissions, we find that two-thirds of the tax-paying population resided in the coastal regions.

With the exception of Kiangsu, the coastal provinces are hilly and cannot support a dense population by agriculture alone. Large numbers of people moved into urban areas to find other means of livelihood and the result was the growth of cities. Hangchow, which boasted a population of nearly two million, was but one of the many teeming cities that rose along the southeastern coast. Urbanization led to the development of commerce and industry which, outgrowing the domestic market, sought to expand abroad. The more venturesome spirits sailed out to sea, some to support themselves by fishing or even by piracy and smuggling in nearby waters, others to trade or to colonize distant lands.

The movement of the people into the cities or out to sea was accelerated not only by civil disturbances but also by natural disasters. According to one investigator, the frequency of floods and droughts increased sharply in the Sung period and reached a peak during the Yüan, with Chekiang and Kiangsu the provinces worst hit.

Thus, as the tilting of a table sends articles on the surface sliding to one side and off the edge, so social turmoil and climatic disturbances caused a shifting of the population to the coastal provinces and out to sea. Governments and rulers felt the impact of social and economic forces and were drawn along by the strong currents of popular feeling to turn their attention to the sea. In the creation of the Southern Sung navy under Kao-tsung (1127–1162), the overseas campaigns of Qubilai Qan, and the naval expeditions sent out by Emperor Yung-lo, the aims and ambition of the rulers and the policies of their governments merely supplemented the tendency of the people.

The contraction of the Sung empire and the disruption of normal economic activities, as a result of the inroads of northern peoples on one hand and the rise of money economy and industry on the other, led to another change in Chinese society. This was the participation of the government in monopolistic enterprises and commerce, a practice which the scholar-official class of China was supposed to regard with disdain. But during the Sung period, not only did foreign trade flourish under private management, not only did officials and members of the court hold shares in shipping and manufacturing companies, but the government itself operated monopolies in domestic trade and various productive enterprises. As a result, half of the government's revenue came in the form of returns from monopolies and excise taxes and as much as twenty per cent of the cash income of the state came from maritime trade, as was true during the first years of Kao-tsung's reign. Even the Emperor declared: "The profits from maritime commerce are very great. If properly managed they can be millions [of strings of cash]. Is it not better than taxing the people?"

Under government patronage, Chinese merchants sailed their ships to Southeast Asia and India and succeeded in wresting from their Moslem rivals the monopoly of the freight and passenger business. The merchants not only contributed funds and imported military supplies but also furnished ships and seamen to the Sung navy. Three hundred and thirty-eight huge merchantmen took part in the war of 1161, notably in the battles on the Yangtze. During the Yüan period, when merchants were in control of the government economy and the government needed funds for its armament program, maritime trade flourished. Shipping magnates such as P'u Shou-keng . . . , a man of Persian ancestry, contributed their services and their ships to help in building the Yüan navy. During the early Ming period, maritime commerce was an exclusive monopoly of the state and the government had a large merchant marine to supplement its combat forces.

Maritime commerce and naval wars spurred the development of technology and the expansion of geographical knowledge. They encouraged the opening of ports and dredging of harbors, they advanced the art of navigation by such means as the mariner's compass and star and sea charts, and they furthered the publication of treatises on tides and currents and maps of foreign countries. Most remarkable was the achievement in naval architecture, for it was by the construction of larger and more seaworthy ships that the Chinese were able to capture the shipping business from the Arabs whose vessels at this time were still flimsy craft lashed together with ropes. The ships of the Chinese, by contrast, were ocean liners boasting staterooms, wineshops, and the service of negro stewards. All were sturdily built, with watertight bulkheads, and the larger ones had lifeboats in tow.

The experience acquired in the construction of merchant vessels was utilized in the building of warships. The cash rewards offered by the Sung court as well as the incentive of war inspired the Chinese, officials and commoners alike, to experiment and to design new types of ships. They turned out paddle-wheel boats, galleys, rams, and many vessels of strange design, some navigable and some not. The "sea hawk", a common type of warship of the Sung period, appears from contemporary description to have been a form of double outrigger. They experimented with square rig and finally evolved the efficient balanced lug sail and, with cotton coming into common use at this time, began to substitute cloth for bamboo mats as sails. Later, when the navy advanced from the thalassic to the oceanic stage, the paddle-wheelers and other experimental craft were abandoned in favor of a few basic types of seagoing ships.

Paralleling the achievement in naval architecture was the development of fire-arms. Incendiary weapons such as flaming arrows, rockets, flame-throwers, and *huo-p'ao,* bombs cast by catapults, made their appearance in the tenth century and were adapted to naval warfare. In the year 1000 a captain of the imperial navy presented to the court some improvements he had made on these weapons, and in 1129 the government decreed that the *huo-p'ao* be made standard equip-ment on all warships. The next development was in explosive weapons, and the best known was the *p'i-li-p'ao* . . . , rudimentary fragmentation bombs. Effective use of the *huo-p'ao* and the *p'i-li-p'ao* enabled the Chinese to win naval victories in 1161. The fire-power of the Sung navy is indicated by the fact that half of the fighting men on the warships were archers, crossbowmen and operators of fire-arms. The Mongols used these weapons in their invasion of Japan in 1274, but in their campaign on the Yangtze against the Sung forces they preferred to use the *hui-hui-p'ao* . . . , giant trebuchets introduced from the Near East.

Already in possession of the *huo-chiang* . . . , a flame-thrower, it was but another step for the Chinese to insert a missile into the tube and let the blast of the charge shoot it out. The result was the *t'u-huo-chiang* . . . , a prototype of the gun. This weapon appeared in the middle of the thirteenth century, and a hundred years later, iron bombards were in general use. By the beginning of the fifteenth century, there were guns forged out of a brass alloy. In 1393, each Ming warship was required to carry four guns with muzzles the size of rice bowls (*wan-k'ou-ch'ung* . . .), twenty guns of smaller caliber, ten bombs, twenty rockets, and a thousand rounds of shot.

A factor which significantly influenced the technological progress and economic development of the Sung, Yüan and early Ming periods was the mental attitude of the people. The jolt of environmental changes loosened the grip of tradition on the men's minds. Not content with classical learning alone, the Chinese of this period displayed a measure of scientific spirit by their inclination to investigate and to experiment, their disposition for noting and sharing their discoveries, and their aptitude for improvisation and invention. Instead of insisting on their own intellectual superiority, they readily accepted the contributions of the Arabs and Hindus in the fields of astronomy, geography and navigation. Instead of opposing foreign trade as unnecessary, they fostered commerce with nations abroad and tried, though unsuccessfully, to import goods needed by and of value to China.

Another manifestation of the broadened outlook of the Chinese of this period was their embarkation on colonial undertakings and voyages of discovery. The spirit of adventure among the Chinese, we are told, is repressed by their attach-ment to the family and the ideals of filial piety. But wars and unrest shattered family ties and, together with economic stress and population pressure, set in motion the first large-scale emigration by sea and the establishment of the first permanent Chinese settlements in Southeast Asia. "The people depended upon the sea and commerce for their livelihood," states the *Gazetteer of Fukien.* "They would leave their parents, wives and children without a thought to dwell among the barbarians."

The stories of adventure and descriptions of foreign lands current in the literature of the times stirred not only the masses but also many men of the scholar-official class. There was, for example, Mo Chi . . . who, as director of the National Academy (*Kuo-tzu chien*) during the reign of Kao-tsung, may be supposed a staunch Confucianist. But when out of office, he would charter ships and sail out to sea both for the thrill of sailing and to satisfy his curiosity. Once he sailed to the "Northern Ocean" (*Pei-yang*) and when his crew became fearful and mutinous, he drew his sword and compelled them to sail on.

The maritime interest of the officials was reflected in the policy of the government. One of the major policy debates in the Southern Sung court took place between those who advocated a counter-offensive to recover North China and those who favored defense to hold and consolidate South China. A counter-offensive would necessitate the employment of land forces, especially cavalry, in which the Southern Sung army was weak. So the policy adopted was that of defense and the physiography of Southeast China dictated the use of naval forces. Chang I . . . , president of the Board of Revenue, in one of three memorials on naval preparedness he submitted in 1131, called the sea and the Yangtze River the new Great Wall of China, the warships the watch-towers, and the firearms the new weapons of defense.

Propaganda was used in support of the naval program. A political pamphlet published in 1131 stated: "Our defenses today are the [Yangtze] River and the sea, so our weakness in mounted troops is no cause for concern. But a navy is of value. . . . To use our navy is to employ our strong weapon to strike at the enemy's weakness." Emperor Hsiao-tsung (1163–1189), converted to the naval program, remarked, "The navy is our strong arm and we cannot afford to neglect it."

As the Yüan inherited the Sung navy so the Ming inherited the Yüan navy. Thus the spirit and tradition of the Sung navy were carried on by the two succeeding dynasties. From a defensive arm the navy developed into an instrument of aggression and political domination, and from the East China Sea the naval power of the Chinese advanced to the South China Sea and into the Indian Ocean.

Broadly speaking, the maritime expansion of China during the late Sung, Yüan and early Ming periods was the cumulative result of changing sociological conditions arising from climatic and geological disturbances, political unrest, and the pressure of alien invaders from the Northwest. The movement of the population to the coastal regions and out to sea, the orientation of the nation towards the Southeast, the interest of the people, even the scholar-official class, in maritime affairs and technological development, and the attention which the government paid to commerce and to the development of a navy, all illustrate the inconstancy of social characteristics commonly attributed to the Chinese and the inconclusiveness of general statements made about them. Social characteristics change under the compelling forces of nature and general statements blur our view of the facts and dynamics of historical change. We cannot discern the zigzags in the course of the historical and cultural development of a people like the Chinese if we remain so close to the ground that we become preoccupied with what Professor Harry Elmer Barnes calls "the episodical aspects of conventional historiography," but we can see them quite clearly if we stand upon an eminence where we can survey the wide sweep of each epoch of Chinese history.

During the medieval period, religion and thought in China were profoundly affected by the impact of Buddhism from India. The diffusion of Buddhism was on a scale comparable to, and as significant as, the diffusion of Christianity from the Middle East through the whole of Europe. Buddhism flourished in China, and, through China, in Korea and Japan, long after it had disappeared in India where it had originated. In this selection, a Chinese scholar analyzes the circumstances of the diffusion of Buddhism, its far reaching repercussions on all aspects of Chinese civilization, and its eventual sinicization and absorption.*

It is my purpose to trace this long process of Indianization through its various stages. Broadly speaking, these stages are:—

1. Mass Borrowing
2. Resistance and Persecution
3. Domestication
4. Appropriation

By mass borrowing I mean not only the simple process of China's taking from India all those things which were either totally absent or weak in the indigenous civilization, but also that mass movement of religious enthusiasm which blindly embraced everything that accompanied the new faith. By resistance and persecution I mean to include those periods of history when the invading culture was openly opposed by Chinese thinkers and persecuted by governmental action. By domestication I mean to include all those tendencies consciously or unconsciously to make the Indian religion, art, thought, and institutions take up more and more Chinese colors, to make them more "at home" in China in order that the Chinese people might feel more at home in them. By appropriation I mean the culminating stage of successful borrowing when the essence, if not the bodily totality, of the borrowed culture was unconsciously "appropriated," recognized by the native population as their own.

In order to appreciate the vast scope of Chinese borrowings from India, it is necessary first to understand the truly striking contrast between the ancient cultures of the two peoples, especially in their religious beliefs and practices. The ancient Chinese people, who built up their civilization in the north temperate zone where the struggle against the forces of nature was severe, had worked out only a very simple and plain religion, consisting of the worship of ancestors, of the natural forces, and of a supreme God or Heaven; the belief in divination; and a vague conception of retribution of good and evil. There was neither Heaven in the sense of a Paradise, nor Hell in the sense of the place of Last Day Judgment. There were practically no mythologies, nor elaborate rituals. It was the religion of a hard-working and plain-thinking people.

* Hu Shih, "The Indianization of China: A Case Study in Cultural Borrowing." Reprinted by permission of the publishers from Harvard Tercentenary Conference of Arts & Sciences, *Independence, Convergence, and Borrowing,* pp. 223-46. Cambridge, Mass.: Harvard University Press, Copyright 1937, 1965, by the President and Fellows of Harvard College.

But, as the race became more mature and more sophisticated, it began to yearn for something more satisfying or at least more tantalizing than the too simple religion of its ancient fathers. Throughout the third and second centuries B.C., there were numerous ambitious quests for strange innovations in religious belief and practice, grandiose imperial quests for the great unknown mystery which the too pragmatic and rational mentality of indigenous China could not possibly satisfy.

Then there came the great religion of the Buddha, together with all the Mahāyāna trimmings of the pre-Buddhist and non-Buddhist religions of India. Never before had China seen a religion so rich in imagery, so beautiful and captivating in ritualism, and so bold in cosmological and metaphysical speculations. Like a poor beggar suddenly halting before a magnificent storehouse of precious stones of dazzling brilliancy and splendor, China was overwhelmed, baffled, and overjoyed. She begged and borrowed freely from this munificent giver. The first borrowings were chiefly from the religious life of India, in which China's indebtedness to India can never be fully told. India gave China, for example, not only one Paradise, but tens of paradises, not only one Hell, but many hells, each varying in severity and horror from the other. The old simple idea of retribution of good and evil was replaced by the idea of transmigration of the soul and the iron law of *karma* which runs through all past, present, and future existences.

These and thousands of other items of belief and practice have poured from India by land and by sea into China, and have been accepted and gradually made into parts of the cultural life of China. The ideas of the world as unreal, of life as painful and empty, of sex as unclean, of the family as an impediment to spiritual attainment, of celibacy and mendicancy as necessary to the Buddhist order, of alms-giving as a supreme form of merit, of love extended to all sentient beings, of vegetarianism, of rigid forms of asceticism, of words and spells as having miraculous power—these are only a few drops in that vast flux of Indian religious and cultural invasion.

The general aspects of the story of the spread of Buddhism in China are comparatively well known. Suffice it to say that, according to our present knowledge, Buddhism had probably come to China long before the year 68 A.D. commonly assigned as the date of its introduction; that probably it had come to China, not as religion officially introduced by an emperor, but only as a form of popular worship and belief gradually taking root among the people—probably among the poorest and the most lowly, to whom the Buddhist missionaries, traders, and travelers had brought the good tidings of mercy and delivery from pain. In all probability, it was from the populace that the prince Liu Ying (died 70), younger brother of the emperor, caught the contagion and was converted to Buddhism. It was also from the popular worship that the Emperor Huan-ti (147–167) elevated the Buddha and made him an object of worship in his palace. The apparently rapid progress made by Buddhism in the Yangtse Valley and on the southern coast towards the end of the second century A.D. seems to indicate that it had had a long period of slow but steady permeation among the people. By the third century, when the men of letters began to admire and defend it, Buddhism had already become a powerful religion, not because of governmental patronage, of which there was very little, but because of its powerful following among the people.

It was as a popular religion of the poor and the lowly that Buddhism first came to stay in China. As such, Mahāyāna Buddhism came *in toto,* and was accepted by the Chinese believers almost *in toto.* It was not for the masses to choose and reject. A great religion of powerful popular appeal came and was accepted. That was all.

Indeed, in their religious enthusiasm, the Chinese people soon came to look to

India as "the Land of the Buddha," and even as "the Western Heaven" from which nothing but the great truths could come. Everything that came from the "Western Heaven" must have a reason and commanded acceptance. Buddhism, or that whole movement of cultural invasion which went by the name of Buddhism, was bodily taken over by China on the high waves of religious fervor and fanaticism.

But the Indianization of a country with an established civilization like China could not long be smooth sailing. Gradually grave doubts began to crop up. Chinese thinkers began to realize that this Indian or Buddhist culture was in many fundamental aspects directly opposed to the best tradition of China. They began to resent the conquest of their ancient civilization by a "barbarian country." Of the truly fundamental differences, a few may be mentioned here.

First, the Buddhist negation of life was contrary to Chinese, especially to Confucianist, ideas. To the Confucianist, the individual life is a sacred inheritance and it is the duty of the individual to make the best of that life—at least not to degrade it or destroy it. One of the most popular texts of Confucianism, "The Book of Filial Piety," says: "The human body, even every hair and every skin of it, is inherited from the parents, and must not be annihilated or degraded." Ancient Chinese thinkers of the fourth century B.C. taught that life is of the highest value. The Buddhist doctrines that life is an illusion and that to live is pain, led to practices which the Chinese in their moments of calmer judgment could not but regard as revolting and inhuman. Throughout the history of Buddhist China, it was common practice for a monk to burn his thumb, his fingers, or even his whole body, as a form of merit in emulation of the supreme sacrifice of the Bodhisattva Bhaishajyarāja, the King of Medicine, one of the deities of Mahāyāna Buddhism. Each of the two great Buddhist Biographical Series devoted one section to biographies of Chinese monks who had burned themselves to death, or otherwise committed suicide, as supreme sacrifices. This section is under the heading "Those who gave up their lives." It contains detailed stories of hundreds of such suicides. A monk would announce his date of self-destruction and, on that day, would tie his whole body in oiled cloth, light the fagot pyre and his own body with a torch in his own hand, and go on mumbling the sacred titles of the Buddhas until he was completely overpowered by the flames. Very often such human sacrifices were witnessed by thousands of pious Buddhists whose plaintive wailings would accompany the slow burning of the pious monk. China seems to have gone completely mad in one of her strange periods of religious fanaticism.

Secondly, the Buddhist monk and nun must renounce all their family relations and must practice celibacy. This was also contrary to Chinese traditions. The whole Confucianist ethics had been one of relationships, of which the family ties, being the most universal and most intimate, were regarded as the most important. Indeed, Mencius once said that of all acts against filial piety the failure to have children was the worst. Celibacy was directly opposed to this traditional emphasis on posterity. The seriousness of this practice became all the more apparent when the number of monks and nuns grew to millions.

Thirdly, the mendicancy of the whole Buddhist order was condemned by Chinese moral and economic thinkers as "parasitic" and as responsible for the poverty and disorder in the country. All the orthodox economic thought of pre-Buddhist China had taught that labor alone was essential to production and that the merchant class were to be discouraged because they were parasites who "were fed without cultivating the fields, and were clothed without their women working in sericulture." And now came the vast host of monks and nuns who not only would not work, but often accumulated immense wealth for their monastic orders through the extravagant almsgiving of the lay patrons. The economic consequences became quite alarming in those times when almost every eighth person in the Empire was a monk, a nun, or a dependent of a monastery.

Fourthly, the whole outlook of Buddhism on life was "other-worldly," pointing to an escape from this world and this life. That too was quite opposed to the moral teachings of classical China. The Buddhist practices all forms of mental control and meditation, and accumulates "merit" by all forms of sutra reading and spell reciting —but for what purpose? The only answer was: For the salvation of the practitioner. Which, of course, was a petty and selfish motive in the eyes of the Chinese thinker. As a Chinese critic of the twelfth century put it: "What we should attend to is precisely that span of life from birth to death. Buddhism completely ignores this life and devotes itself to speculating about what goes before birth and after death. But the earth, the mountains and rivers, which the Buddhists consider as empty and unreal, nevertheless stand out as concrete realities that cannot be conjured away by magic or philosophy."

Fifthly, the whole Indian imaginative power, which knows neither limitation nor discipline, was indeed too much for the Chinese mind. Indigenous China was always factual and rarely bold in imagination. "Extend your knowledge, but leave out those things about which you are in doubt." "Say you know when you really know, and say you don't know when you really don't know—that is knowledge." Such were the wise instructions of Confucius on knowledge. This emphasis on veracity and certainty was one of the most marked traits of ancient Chinese literature, which is strikingly free from mythological and supernatural elements. Confucius once said: "I have devoted whole days without food and whole nights without sleep, to thinking. But it was of no use. It is better to learn [than to think in abstract]." This self-analysis on the part of one of China's greatest sages is of peculiar significance in showing the suspicion with which Chinese thinkers regarded the unbridled exercise of thought and imagination. It must have been very difficult for Chinese readers to swallow down all that huge amount of sacred literature of sheer fancy and imagination. It was probably this native detestation of the unbridled imagination which led the first Chinese leaders of anti-Buddhist persecution in the fifth century to declare that the entire Buddhist tradition was a myth and a lie.

These and many other fundamental differences between indigenous China and the Indianized China were largely responsible for the numerous religious controversies and for the four major anti-Buddhist persecutions of 446, 574, 845, and 955. It is significant to note that all edicts for the persecution of Buddhism emphasized the fact that Buddhism was an alien religion introduced from a foreign barbarian country, and that it was a national disaster and humiliation for the Middle Kingdom to be thus "barbarized." Han Yü (768–824), probably the intellectual father of the great persecution of 845, coined these concise slogans: "Restore their people to humanity! Burn their books! And convert their buildings to human residences!" The first slogan literally reads "Man their men!" meaning that all those who embraced this alien religion were not to be considered as "men." Thus in the edict of persecution of 845, after enumerating the temples and monasteries demolished, the millions of acres of monastic land confiscated, and the vast numbers of monks and nuns forced to return to lay life, the Emperor said: "Henceforth all affairs of monks and nuns shall be dealt with by the Bureau of Foreign Affairs." That is to say, all who are converted by a foreign religion are no longer considered as Chinese subjects.

These were expressions of a nationalistic consciousness behind which was the only partially articulate recognition that this great religion introduced from the

"Western Heaven" contained many ideas and practices which had undermined the moral, social, and economic traditions of the Chinese nation.

But none of these nation-wide persecutions ever lasted more than a few years and none succeeded in eradicating or even diminishing the tremendous influence of the Indian religion in the country. When a persecuting Emperor died, his successor invariably adopted a more lenient policy, and in the course of the years the once persecuted religion flourished again in all its former splendor and grandeur.

It is a significant historical fact, however, that while no more governmental persecution of Buddhism was undertaken after the tenth century, the religion of Buddhism gradually weakened, withered, dwindled in its power and influence, and finally died a slow but natural death. Why? Where drastic persecution had failed, the more subtle processes of domestication and appropriation were meeting with greater and greater successes. Buddhism in its domesticated form was gradually and unconsciously "appropriated" by the Chinese people.

Domestication is a common phenomenon in all cultural borrowings. A folksong or a folk story introduced from a distant province is soon revised by nobody knows whom, and, while the main theme—the motif—is always retained, most of the details (names, scenery, fashion, dress, footwear, hair-dress, et cetera) are retouched with "local color." And, after a period of successive domestications, it becomes quite difficult to recognize its distant or even alien origin.

Almost every phase or element of Buddhism has undergone some degree of domestication during these twenty-odd centuries. Look at the faces of the deities in a Buddhist temple in China today and trace each to its earliest Indian originals, and you will realize how the process of domestication has worked. The most striking examples are the various stages of transformation of the god Avalokiteśvara, who was long ago "unsexed" and became the Goddess of Mercy, often represented as a beautiful woman with tiny bound feet. Maitreya has now become the big-bellied, good-natured, heartily laughing Chinese monk that greets you as you enter any Buddhist monastery in China. Indeed, all faces of the Buddhist deities have been Sinicized—through a long but unconscious process of domestication. Even in those cases, as in the case of the sixteen or 500 Arhats, where the sculptor or molder consciously tries to create "foreign" types, the resultant creations are invariably more Chinese than Indian.

Music, painting, architecture, and the other fine arts which came from India together with the Buddhist religion were also subject to processes of domestication. The reciting and sing-songing of Sanskrit texts have become entirely Sinicized; and Indian melodies have been made vehicles of Chinese songs in which their Indian origins are often forgotten. In painting, as in sculpture, the domestication went so far that later Buddhist paintings are essentially Chinese and differ radically from the early Buddhist art and also from the later artistic development in India herself.

The most difficult phase of domestication, naturally, lay in the sphere of the religious, moral, and philosophical teachings of Buddhism. Being in most cases basically opposed to ancient Chinese tradition and contrary to the intellectual habits of the Chinese people, these teachings could not be easily digested. Sufficiently abstruse in themselves, they became unintelligible in the translations, of which, as we know, very few were made by really competent scholars well versed in the languages and in the subject matter.

The most natural step in early attempts to understand this alien religion was to interpret it in terms of concepts which came nearest to the foreign ideas and which were most familiar to the native mind. Buddhism came to China at a time when the philosophical ideas of Lao-Tze and Chuang-Tze were being revived and having a general vogue among the intellectuals who had tired of the Neo-Confucianists of the Han Dynasty. The philosophical naturalism and nihilism of this Taoist school had certain affinities with a number of ideas of philosophical Buddhism, and it soon became a fashion to translate Buddhist terminology into words bodily taken from the sayings of these Taoist thinkers. Such borrowed terms are never exact; *Nirvāna,* for example was not *wu-wei,* and an *arhat* was not a *shien jen.* But that was the best that could be done in the early stages of intellectual and philosophical borrowings. These Taoistic interpretations furnished the bridge of cultural transmission and made the new ideas of India more easily acceptable to the Chinese intelligentsia. It was the first stage of domestication.

As the work of translation proceeded in later centuries, the Buddhists insisted on the importance of not using existing philosophical terms of the historic schools of ancient Chinese thought. They preferred the method of exact transcription of the original sound, such as *bodhi* (wisdom), *prajñā-pāramitā* (the path of attainment through philosophic understanding), *nirvāna, yoga, dhyāna, samādhi* and so forth. But the Chinese readers continued to "interpret" and understand them in the light of what had been most familiar and intelligible to them. And it was the naturalistic and nihilistic background of ancient Taoistic philosophy that made it possible for the philosophical thought of such Mahāyāna schools as the Madhymaka to be understood by the Chinese intellectuals.

Wherever such a favorable background was lacking, understanding and acceptance became well-nigh impossible, despite great native leadership and imperial patronage. Hsüan Chuang (596–664), the great Chinese pilgrim, went to India at the height of Vijñānavāda thought, and, after spending fifteen years studying it, brought back a vast amount of Vijñānavāda literature and devoted the remainder of his life to translating it into Chinese. This school had developed a most abstruse system of what may be termed introspective psychology which analysed consciousness into over 500 states of mind and their corresponding faculties and objects. Such hairsplitting differentiation simply could not be done in the Chinese language. In spite of the great personal leadership of Hsüan Chuang and some of his immediate disciples, the vast amount of Vijñānavāda literature remained a sealed book and exerted practically no influence on the intellectual life of China. The study of the psychological and logical treatises of this school was revived during the recent decades in Japan and later in China because the introduction of modern European psychology and logic had furnished new materials and a new set of terms for comparison and for interpretation. This is another illustration of the fact that borrowing in the field of speculative thought can only be done under such favorable conditions as to make it possible to interpret the unfamiliar in terms of the familiar.

The failure of the Vijñānavāda system in China also shows the negative phase of cultural domestication. What we cannot digest, we discard. Discarding means the elimination of all those elements which the native culture cannot assimilate or which the native population regard as non-essential. The never-ending importation of new sutras and treatises from Buddhist India throughout many centuries began to trouble the Chinese intellectuals. As early as the fourth century, Chinese Buddhists began to ask the question: What after all is the essence of this great system of the Buddha? Gradually they formulated their answer: The essence of Buddhism is Meditation and Insight. All else can be discarded. Gradually it was recognized that these two phases might be conveniently combined in the one term *yoga* or *dhyāna,* which means meditation but which also implies and relies on philosophical insight. From 400 on, there was a clear tendency among Chinese Buddhists to grasp the idea and practice of *dhyāna* or *yoga* as the essence and consummation of Buddhism.

Simultaneously, there arose the movement to give special prominence to the Amitābha or Pure Land Sect. This sect laid special stress on Faith. Faith in the existence of the Pure Land presided over by the Amita Buddha of infinite longevity and infinite enlightenment, and constant reminding oneself of his faith by daily repeating the formula "Nama Amitābha!"—these alone are sufficient to insure final attainment and salvation. This form of Buddhism, because of its extreme simplicity, has had the greatest appeal to all classes, and has survived all other more sophisticated sects.

All these tendencies were towards simplification or filtration. But a more radical voice arose in the fifth century in the person of the learned monk Tao Sheng, who taught the revolutionary idea of "Sudden Enlightenment" as against all forms of "gradual attainment." He had been trained in the nihilistic philosophy of Lao-tze and Chuang-tze and, paraphrasing the latter, he declared: "The word is the symbol for the idea; and when the idea is grasped, the symbol may be discarded." In these words we hear the first declaration of Chinese Zennism revolting against the terrible burden of the hairsplitting verbalism and pedantry of Indian scholasticism. And "sudden enlightenment" was to be the weapon of this revolt. Grasp the idea and throw away the wordy symbols!

For even *dhyāna* or *yoga* includes a tediously long series of arduous and minute practices of gradual attainment, beginning with the simple form of breath control, passing through all intermediate stages of rigid mental and emotional control, and finally ending in the attainment of perfect tranquillity and ease together with the acquisition of magical powers. Even this was too scholastic for the Chinese mind.

From the seventh century on, there arose the Southern Schools of Chinese Zennism, which was built on the central idea of Sudden Enlightenment and discarded all the scholastic verbalism, the slavish ritualism, and even the minute practices of meditation. "Buddhahood is within you. Worship not the Buddha, for the Buddha means the Enlightened One, and Enlightenment is within you. Abide not by the Law, for the Law simply means Righteousness, and Righteousness is within you. And abide not by the *Sangha* (the brotherhood of monks), for the brotherhood simply means purity in life, and purity is within you." Thus spoke Hui-neng (died 713), the founder of Southern Zennism.

By the eighth and ninth centuries, the Zennists were becoming truly iconoclastic. They frankly said: "There is neither Buddhahood to attain, nor the Truth to obtain." "Wherefore do ye busy yourselves without cease? Go home and take a rest. Try to be an *ordinary man,* who eats, drinks, sleeps, and moves his bowels. What more do you seek?"

And they developed a pedagogic technique of their own, the essence of which consisted of urging the novice to seek his own awakening or enlightenment through his own thinking and living. No other salvation was possible.

The whole Zen movement from 700 to 1100 was a revolt against Buddhist verbalism and scholasticism, but it was also a movement to Sinicize Buddhism by sweeping away all its scholastic verbiage and giving special prominence to the idea of salvation through one's own intellectual liberation and insight.

True, this process of discarding and expurgation left very little of Buddhism in the net outcome. But we must admit as a historical truth that 400 years of Zennist expurgation had really domesticated the Buddhist religion and made it intelligible and attractive to the Chinese mind. By the eleventh century, Zennist Buddhism was more a philosophy than a religion. But that was exactly what it should be. For was not original Buddhism more a philosophy than a religion? Unconsciously and unwittingly the Chinese Buddhists, throughout a long period of a thousand years, had succeeded in shearing Mahāyāna Buddhism of all its extraneous verbiage and in remaking it into a philosophy, a method, and a technique. Unconsciously, they had made their Buddhism nearer to primitive Buddhism than any Hīnāyāna or Mahāyāna sects had ever been. And incidentally, they had thereby so domesticated Buddhism as to make it easily understood and appreciated by the Chinese intelligentsia.

By the eleventh century, this process of domestication was complete, and it remained for the Chinese intelligentsia to appropriate this domesticated Buddhism as an integral part of Chinese cultural life.

No cultural borrowing is permanent until the borrowed culture is "appropriated" by the native people as their own and its alien origin is completely forgotten. In the case of Buddhism, all those elements which have not been so appropriated by the Chinese people remain to this day as the unassimilated elements of a foreign culture. The work of Indianization of Chinese thought and institutions has come about through those phases of Buddhism and Indian culture in general which have been so thoroughly domesticated and assimilated as to be unconsciously regarded by the Chinese people as their own.

Chinese borrowings from the culture of India were made in two main instalments. The first portion of the borrowings came as a result of the period of mass conversion to Buddhism. The religion of Mahāyāna Buddhism which contains numerous elements of the pre-Buddhist Hindu religions, became firmly established as a great popular religion in China. Many of the cultural elements that came with the Buddhist faith, as I have pointed out, were things which the traditional culture of ancient China never possessed. They filled what may be called a cultural (at least religious) vacuum and were eagerly accepted by the believing masses. It was this portion of the borrowed culture that was the first to be appropriated by the Chinese.

The second portion consisted of more subtle elements of the Indian culture— the philosophy of the world and of life, the moral and social standards, the intellectual habits—things to which the believing masses were indifferent, and which had much resistance to encounter from the age-long cultural make-up of the Chinese people. It was these elements which had required much intermediate work of shifting, discarding, distilling, and reinterpreting, before some of them were sufficiently domesticated to be unconsciously appropriated into the Chinese culture.

Historically, the first period of appropriation coincided with the rise of the religion of Taoism, and the second appropriation coincided with the revival of the secular Confucianist philosophy.

Taoism as a popular religion (as distinct from Taoism as a philosophy) rose in the centuries following the gradual spread of Buddhism in China. "Tao" means "a way." There were many "ways" toward the end of the second century A.D. After the third century, one form of Taoism, with its charity organizations, its practices of healing by praying and of confession of sins, and its polytheistic worships, gradually acquired a large following, not only among the people, but also among the upper classes. Beginning as a consolidated form of the earlier "Sinitic" religion of the Chinese people, Taoism received a great impetus from its impact with the imported religious system of Buddhism. There seemed to be a strong desire on the part of the Taoists to supersede and kill this foreign rival by imitating every feature of it. They accepted the heavens and hells from the Indian religion, gave them Chinese names, and assigned to them Chinese gods to preside over them. A Taoist canon was consciously forged after the model of the Buddhist sutras. Buddhist rituals were freely adopted into the Taoist worship. Orders of priests and priestesses were established after the fashion of the Buddhist orders of monks and nuns. The Taoists had also a form of meditation which was undoubtedly a modification of the Yoga practice of India. The ideas of *karma* and transmigration of the soul throughout the existences were also appropriated by the Taoists and made the central idea in their conception of retribution of good and evil. The idea of transmigration was only modified by the Taoist belief that the individual could attain personal and physical immortality, and thereby escape transmigration, by contemplation, medical aid, and accumulation of merit.

Since the fifth century, there had been many attempts of the Taoists to oust Buddhism as an alien religion and to establish Taoism as its sole native substitute. Taoist influence was behind practically all the governmental persecutions of Buddhism.

While Taoism was intended to be a rival and substitute for Buddhism, it was too much an imitation—indeed a crude imitation—of that foreign religion to differentiate itself from it and to command real respect and adherence from the intellectual class. Moreover, its whole outlook on life was just as other-worldly as the Buddhist's. The Taoist ideal was also to flee from this life and this world and seek individual salvation. It was as selfish and anti-social as the Buddhist. It was for this reason that, in the Confucianist attacks on the medieval religions, Taoism and Buddhism were always mentioned together as the joint object of attack. By too much appropriation of an ill-digested alien religion, Taoism had alienated the sympathy of the more nationalistic critics in the country.

The revival of the secular Confucianist philosophy in the eleventh and twelfth centuries was professedly anti-Buddhistic. Its object was to revive and re-interpret the moral and political philosophy of the school of Confucius and Mencius as a substitute for the individualistic, anti-social, and other-worldly philosophies of the Buddhist and Zennist schools which had prevailed throughout the medieval period. The object was to revive a purely secular Chinese philosophy to take the place of the religious and non-Chinese thought of the previous age.

A statesman of the eleventh century had pointed out that, during the whole Buddhist period of about a thousand years, the best minds of the nation flocked to Buddhist schools of thought and belief merely because the Confucianist teachings were too simple and insipid to attract them. The problem in the revival of Confucianist thought, therefore, was how to re-interpret the Confucianist classics so as to make them sufficiently interesting and attractive to the best minds of the nation.

As if by a miracle, the Confucianist philosophers of the eleventh century suddenly discovered that the old classical writings of Confucius and his school could be made as interesting and attractive as the Buddhist and Zennist teachings. They discovered, to their great delight, that all the philosophical problems of the universe, of life, of the mind, of knowledge, and of religious reverence, which had engaged the speculative philosophers of Buddhism for centuries, were to be found in the ancient classical writings and only required a little re-interpretation to bring forth the hidden meanings of those long-neglected works of the ancient sages. So they set themselves to work at this re-interpretation.

These philosophers succeeded in working out a "rational philosophy of Neo-Confucianism" which had a cosmology, a theory or theories of the nature and method of knowledge, and a moral and political philosophy. This new secular philosophy also laid great stress on the perfection of the individual which was to be achieved through extension of knowledge, purification of the will, and rectification of the mind. The extension of knowledge was to be achieved by going to the things and investigating the reasons thereof. And the rectification of the mind and purification of the will depended upon the cultivation of the attitude of reverence.

But, these Confucianists proudly pointed out, the perfection of the individual was not the end in itself, as it was with the medieval religions. The perfection of the individual was only a step leading to the social ends of successfully ordering the affairs of the family, the state, and the world. All intellectual and moral training leads to the rectification of the individual life from which shall radiate all its social and political activities. It was this social end which differentiated the secular Confucianism from the other-worldly religious system of old.

And all this new philosophy was found in the old neglected writings of Classical Confucianism. The new interpretation seemed so natural, so reasonable, and so satisfactory, that it was really inconceivable how such precious teachings could have been allowed to lie unnoticed for all those centuries.

The historical fact was that all this re-interpretation had been the result of one thousand years of Buddhistic philosophizing and training. Especially the four hundred years of Zennist Buddhism had given the Chinese philosopher a new insight, a new set of intellectual habits, and a new source of reference material. It was as if the naked eye had been aided by a new eyeglass which enabled him to see things which he had been unable to see before. And the eyeglass was, unfortunately, colored. He now saw things through this eyeglass colored by centuries of Buddhist and Zennist training. He now re-interpreted all he saw in that new light. He was unconsciously appropriating what he had honestly disowned and revolted against.

The Rationalist philosophers made a great success of their Confucianist revival and of their re-interpretation of the Confucianist philosophy, which had now become sufficiently interesting to attract the best minds of the nation, who from that time on no longer flocked to the doors of the Zennist monasteries. And when the first-rate minds of the nation ceased to be recruited into Buddhism, that great Indian religion gradually faded into nonentity and died almost an unmourned death.

But what was the real nature of this secular substitute for the Indian religion? Was it a real repudiation of the Buddhist religion, as it claimed to be?

In reality, the Confucianist revival since the eleventh century has been only a *secularization* of the Indian religion. By secularizing it, the Chinese philosophers had actually *universalized* it, so that what had once ruled the life of the members of the Buddhist order was now extending its control over the whole non-Buddhist population through the teachings of the philosophers.

Prior to the Rational philosophers, Indianization was more or less confined to those who actually fled the world; but after the secularization of Buddhist ideals by the Rational philosophers, the rules of life of an other-worldly religion were seriously applied to secular life. The age of Rational Philosophy presents to us, not the human and common-sense atmosphere which one finds in the writings of Confucius and Mencius, but an austere and icy atmosphere of the medieval monastery. Indianization was universalized by being unconsciously appropriated by the philosophers and extended by them to regions never before seriously invaded by the Indian religion.

Let us first examine into this philosophy itself to see how much it differs from the medieval religions. This new philosophy has been formulated as consisting of two main paths: "To increase learning, one must extend one's knowledge to the utmost. For moral cultivation, one must resort to the attitude of reverence." (Cheng Yi, 1033–1107.) The first road is intellectualistic; the second, moral and religious. "Reverence" to the ancients simply meant taking things seriously. But to the Rational philosophers it has acquired a religious connotation. To be reverent now means to act in accordance with the Divine Reason. Now, what is this Divine Reason? The answer is: It is the opposite of human desire. And how can one know the

Divine Reason? The answer is: The best way is through sitting in quiet meditation.

Even the other path, that of extension of knowledge, was not free from the religious impress of medieval China. To Chu Hsi (1130–1200), extension of knowledge was to be achieved through piecemeal investigation into the reasons of things—which was a strictly intellectualistic and scientific attitude. But, in the absence of the necessary equipment and of the experimental procedure, this was a difficult path, too difficult for the soft-minded majority of the philosophers, who soon gave it up in despair and declared that true knowledge must come from within one's own mind and the approach must be through quiet meditation and introspection.

But it is in the peculiar exaltation of Divine Reason and suppression of human desire that we see the best evidence of the deepening of the influence of the Indian religion through its secularization. When asked whether a widow of a very destitute family might not be justified in remarrying, Cheng Yi, the philosopher, calmly replied: "No. Death by starvation is a very small matter. But violation of chastity is a very important thing." This famous saying was included by Chu Hsi in his "Text Book for Elementary Schools" which became the standard reading in all China for seven hundred years.

Now, this prohibition of the remarriage of widows had never been the practice of pre-Buddhist China. In the first century A.D., when the sister of the first Emperor of the Eastern Han Dynasty became a widow, the Emperor offered to make a new match for her and asked her to choose her ideal husband from among his ministers. She expressed her preference for Minister Sung Hung. The Emperor invited the Minister for a chat and approached the subject by saying: "What do you think of the proverb that 'Wealth changes friends and high position changes wives'?" The Minister answered: "That proverb is not so good as the other one which says, 'A friend of poverty should never be forgotten, and the wife who has shared the coarsest meals with me should never be deserted.'" Upon hearing this, the Emperor shouted across the screen which shielded his widowed sister, "Sister, I am afraid my match-making has failed." What a human tale this was! And how different it was from the austere puritanism of the philosopher of a thousand years afterwards who cold-bloodedly laid down the principle that death by starvation was preferable to the remarriage of a destitute widow!

What had happened during these thousand years to bring about such a tremendous difference in the Chinese outlook on life? Nothing but the gradual deepening and intensifying of the Indianization of Chinese thought, life, and institutions. Buddhism was fading away, but its cultural content had been domesticated and appropriated by the secular thinkers and had penetrated into Chinese life and institutions far beyond the confines of the monasteries and nunneries of Buddhism. . . .

Chapter Seventeen

Revolutionary Western civilization

TECHNOLOGY IN THE MEDIEVAL WEST **54**

In most of medieval Eurasia, traditional civilizations flourished that carried on many of the basic institutions and practises of the preceding classical civilizations. China, for example, did undergo "change within tradition," as noted in Reading 51, yet its civilization remained fundamentally Confucian within an agrarian-based bureaucratic imperial structure. In the sprawling Moslem world, the indigenous Greco-Roman, Iranian, Semitic, and Egyptian traditions were not obliterated, but rather fused into the syncretic civilization of Islam. Likewise the East Roman Empire continued without interruption for a full millennium as the Byzantine Empire, so that its inhabitants referred to themselves until modern times as Romaioi, *or Romans. The one exception to this general pattern was in the West where the classical civilization was disrupted to an unprecedented degree by prolonged invasions and turmoil. Only in the West, therefore, was the ground sufficiently cleared for the emergence of a revolutionary new civilization. One of the features of this new civilization was a unique labor-saving power technology and productive new agricultural methods, as described in the following account by a noted American medievalist.**

The Dark Ages doubtless deserve their name: political disintegration, economic depression, the debasement of religion and the collapse of literature surely made the barbarian kingdoms in some ways unimaginably dismal. Yet because many aspects of civilization were in decay we should not assume too quickly that everything was back-sliding. Even an apparent coarsening may indicate merely a shift of interest:

* L. White, Jr., "Technology and Invention in the Middle Ages," *Speculum,* XV (April 1940), 149-56.

in modern painting we recognize that Van Gogh's technical methods were not those of David; so, when we contrast a Hellenistic carved gem with a Merovingian enamel, our judgment should be cautious. Few will dispute that the Irish illumination and the Scandinavian jewelry of the seventh and eighth centuries stand among the supreme arts of all time; yet they are far from classical canons of taste, being rooted in an ancient, and quite separate, tradition of Northern art. So in the history of technology we must be discriminating. Changing tastes and conditions may lead to the degeneration of one technique while the technology of the age as a whole is advancing. The technology of torture, for example, which achieved such hair-raising perfection during the Renaissance, is now happily in eclipse: viewed historically, our modern American 'third degree' is barbaric only in its simplicity.

Indeed, a dark age may stimulate rather than hinder technology. Economic catastrophe in the United States during the past decade has done nothing to halt invention—quite the contrary; and it is a commonplace that war encourages technological advance. Confusion and depression, which bring havoc in so many areas of life, may have just the opposite effect on technics. And the chances of this are particularly good in a period of general migration, when peoples of diverse backgrounds and inheritances are mixing.

There is, in fact, no proof that any important skills of the Graeco-Roman world were lost during the Dark Ages even in the unenlightened West, much less in the flourishing Byzantine and Saracenic Orient. To be sure, the diminished wealth and power of the Germanic kings made engineering on the old Roman scale infrequent; yet the full technology of antiquity was available when required: the 276-ton monolith which crowns the tomb of Theodoric the Ostrogoth was brought to Ravenna from Istria; while more than two centuries later Charlemagne transported not only sizable columns but even a great equestrian statue of Zeno from Ravenna across the Alps to Aachen. Incidentally, we should do well to remember that the northern peoples from remote times were capable of managing great weights, as witness Stonehenge and the dolmens.

In military machines especially we might expect the barbarians to fall below the ancient standard; but at the siege of Paris in 886 we discover the Vikings, who presumably would be as untouched by Roman methods as any western people, using elaborate and powerful artillery; while the city itself was defended with catapults. However, the Dark Ages do not seem to have improved on ancient artillery: the Roman level was not surpassed until the twelfth century when the trebuchet, worked by counterweights, began to drive the less efficient tension and torsion engines from the field.

If the political and economic decay of the Dark Ages affected any technique adversely, it was that of road-building. Yet even here the case is not clear. For northern climates at least, the technical excellence of Roman roads has been exaggerated. They had massive foundations, which sometimes survive to the present day; but the surface, consisting of slabs of masonry cemented together, made no provision for contraction or expansion. Heat made the slabs buckle and crack; water seeped under them and froze, separating them from the foundation. Repairs were difficult and expensive: no modern road-builder would consider imitating Roman methods. It was the Middle Ages which developed the cheaper and more efficient method of laying cubes of stone in a loose bed of earth or sand which permitted expansion and made repairs easy: a type of paving still common.

Indeed, the technical skill of classical times was not simply maintained: it was considerably improved. Our view of history has been too top-lofty. We have been dazzled by aspects of civilization which are in every age the property of an élite, and in which the common man, with rare exceptions, has had little part. The so-called 'higher' realms of culture might decay, government might fall into anarchy, and trade be reduced to a trickle, but through it all, in the face of turmoil and hard times, the peasant and artisan carried on, and even improved their lot. In technology, at least, the Dark Ages mark a steady and uninterrupted advance over the Roman Empire. Evidence is accumulating to show that a serf in the turbulent and insecure tenth century enjoyed a standard of living considerably higher than that of a proletarian in the reign of Augustus.

The basic occupation was, of course, agriculture. We have passed through at least two agricultural revolutions: that which began with 'Turnip' Townshend and Jethro Tull in the early eighteenth century, and another, equally important, in the Dark Ages.

The problem of the development and diffusion of the northern wheeled plow, equipped with colter, horizontal share and moldboard, is too thorny to be discussed here. Experts seem generally agreed: (1) that the new plow greatly increased production by making possible the tillage of rich, heavy, badly-drained river-bottom soils; (2) that it saved labor by making cross-plowing superfluous, and thus produced the typical northern strip-system of land division, as distinct from the older block-system dictated by the cross-plowing necessary with the lighter Mediterranean plow; (3) most important of all, that the heavy plow needed such power that peasants pooled their oxen and plowed together, thus laying the basis for the mediaeval coöperative agricultural community, the manor. But whatever may be the date and origin of the fully developed heavy plow, its effects were supplemented and greatly enhanced in the later eighth century by the invention of the three-field system, an improved rotation of crops and fallow which greatly increased the efficiency of agricultural labor. For example, by switching 600 acres from the two-field to the three-field system, a community of peasants could plant 100 acres more in crops each year with 100 acres less of plowing. Since fallow land was plowed twice to keep down the weeds, the old plan required three acres of plowing for every acre in crops, whereas the new plan required only two acres of plowing for every productive acre.

In a society overwhelmingly agrarian, the result of such an innovation could be nothing less than revolutionary. Pirenne is only the most recent of many historians to speculate as to why the reign of Charlemagne witnessed the shift of the center of European civilization, the change of the focus of history, from the Mediterranean to the plains of Northern Europe. The findings of agricultural history, it seems, have never been applied to this central problem in the study of the growth of the northern races. Since the spring sowing, which was the chief novelty of the three-field system, was unprofitable in the south because of the scarcity of summer rains, the three-field system did not spread below the Alps and the Loire. For obvious reasons of climate the agricultural revolution of the eight century was confined to Northern Europe. It would appear, therefore, that it was this more efficient and productive use of land and labor which gave to the northern plains an economic advantage over the Mediterranean shores, and which, from Charlemagne's time onward, enabled the Northern Europeans in short order to surpass both in prosperity and in culture the peoples of an older inheritance.

In ways less immediately significant the Dark Ages likewise made ingenuous improvements. One of the most important of these was a contribution to practical mechanics. There are two basic forms of motion: reciprocal and rotary. The normal device for connecting these—a device without which our machine civilization is inconceivable—is the crank. The crank is an invention second in importance only to the wheel itself; yet the crank was unknown to the Greeks and the Romans. It appears, even in rudimentary form, only after the Invasions: first, perhaps, in hand-querns, then on rotary grindstones. The later Middle Ages developed its application to all sorts of machinery.

Clearly there are nuggets in this stream for anyone to find. Perhaps the most successful amateur student of early mediaeval technology was the Commandant Lefebvre des Noëttes, who after his retirement from active service in the French cavalry, devoted himself to his hobby, the history of horses. He died in 1936 having made discoveries which must greatly modify our judgment of the Carolingian period. From his investigations Lefebvre des Noëttes concluded that the use of animal power in antiquity was unbelievably inefficient. The ancients did not use nailed shoes on their animals, and broken hooves often rendered beasts useless. Besides, they knew only the yoke-system of harness. While this was adequate for oxen, it was most unsatisfactory for the more rapid horse. The yoke rested on the withers of a team. From each end of the yoke ran two flexible straps: one a girth behind the forelegs, the other circling the horse's neck. As soon as the horse began to pull, the flexible front strap pressed on his windpipe, and the harder he pulled the closer he came to strangulation. Moreover the ancient harness was mechanically defective: the yoke was too high to permit the horse to exert his full force in pulling by flinging his body-weight into the task. Finally, the ancients were unable to harness one animal in front of another. Thus all great weights had to be drawn by gangs of slaves; since animal power was not technically available in sufficient quantities.

According to Lefebvre des Noëttes this condition remained unchanged until the later ninth or early tenth century when, almost simultaneously, three major inventions appear: the modern horse-collar, the tandem harness, and the horse-shoe. The modern harness, consisting of a rigid horse-collar resting on the shoulders of the beast, permitted him to breathe freely. This was connected to the load by lateral traces which enabled the horse to throw his whole body into pulling. It has been shown experimentally that this new apparatus so greatly increased the effective animal power that a team which can pull only about one thousand pounds with the antique yoke can pull three or four times that weight when equipped with the new harness. Equally important was the extension of the traces so that tandem harnessing was possible, thus providing an indefinite amount of animal power for the transport of great weights. Finally, the introduction of the nailed horseshoe improved traction and greatly increased the endurance of the newly available animal power. Taken together these three inventions suddenly gave Europe a new supply of non-human power, at no increase of expense or labor. They did for the eleventh and twelfth centuries what the steam-engine did for the nineteenth. Lefebvre des Noëttes has therefore offered an unexpected and plausible solution for the most puzzling problem of the Middle Ages: the sudden upswing of European vitality after the year 1000.

However, Lefebvre des Noëttes failed to point out the relation between this access of energy and the contemporary agricultural revolution. He noted that the new harness made the horse available for agricultural labor: the first picture of a horse so engaged is found in the Bayeux Tapestry. But while the horse is a rapid and efficient power-engine, it burns an expensive fuel—grain—as compared with the slower, but cheaper, hay-burning ox. Under the two-field system the peasant's margin of production was insufficient to support a work-horse; under the three-field system the horse gradually displaced the ox as the normal plow and draft animal of the northern plains. By the later Middle Ages there is a clear correlation on the one hand between the horse and the three-field system and on the other between the ox and the two-field system. The contrast is essentially one between the standards of living and of labor-productivity of the northern and the southern peasantry: the ox saves food; the horse saves man-hours. The new agriculture, therefore, enabled the north to exploit the new power more effectively than the Mediterranean regions could, and thereby the northerners increased their prosperity still further.

Naturally Lefebvre des Noëttes made mistakes: only when his work receives the recognition it deserves will these be rectified. His use of the monuments is not impeccable; his almost exclusive concern with pictures led him to neglect the texts, particularly Pliny's assertion that at times Italian peasants (presumably in the Po valley) plowed with several yokes of oxen; and he overlooks the complex question of the eight-ox plow-team as a basis for land division in pre-Carolingian times. Moreover an etymologist has recently shown that the word for 'horse-collar' in the Teutonic and Slavic tongues (English: hames) is derived from Central-Asiatic sources, implying a diffusion of the modern harness westward from the nomadic steppe-culture. Doubtless criticism will eventually show that Lefebvre des Noëttes' three inventions developed rather more slowly than he thought. But that they grew and spread during the Dark Ages, and that they profoundly affected European society, seems already proved.

These discoveries regarding the utilization of animal power illustrate the novel results which may be expected from the study of mediaeval technology. No less profitable is Marc Block's brilliant and thoroughly documented investigation of the origin and spread of the water-driven mill. His conclusion that, while it was invented in the first century before Christ, it did not become common until after the collapse of the Empire, confirms Lefebvre des Noëttes' contention that the technological position of the Dark Ages has been misunderstood.

The development of the windmill has not been so carefully sought out. Windmills are found in tenth-century Persia, but rotating on a vertical rather than on a horizontal axis. The first authenticated windmill in Europe turns up in Normandy *ca* 1180. Twelve years later Jocelin of Brakelond mentions one near St. Edmundsbury and gives no indication that he considers it unusual. Within a generation this power-engine had become a typical part of the landscape on the plains of northwestern Europe. In such a region it was a great boon; for the fall of rivers was so gradual that expensive dams and mill-ponds often had to be constructed to run water-driven mills; likewise these mill-ponds must often have flooded good agricultural land which the windmill freed for production. The spread of the windmill into the more mountainous southern regions, which were better equipped with rapid streams, was slow. The first Italian reference to a windmill seems to be Dante's description (*ante* 1321) of Satan threshing his arms like 'un molin che il vento gira' (*Inferno,* XXXIV, 6). This southward and eastward diffusion, together with the horizontal axis of the western mill, probably indicates that the windmill was not an importation from Islam.

The cumulative effect of the newly available animal, water, and wind power upon the culture of Europe has not been carefully studied. But from the twelfth and even from the eleventh, century there was a rapid replacement of human by non-human energy wherever great quantities of power were needed or where the required motion was so simple and monotonous that a man could be replaced by a mechanism. The chief glory of the later Middle Ages was not its cathedrals or its epics or its scholasticism: it was the building for the first time in history of a complex civilization which rested not on the backs of sweating slaves or coolies but primarily on non-human power.

The study of mediaeval technology is therefore far more than an aspect of economic history: it reveals a chapter in the conquest of freedom. More than that, it is a part of the history of religion. The humanitarian technology which our modern world has inherited from the Middle Ages was not rooted in economic necessity; for this 'necessity' is inherent in every society, yet has found inventive expression only in the Occident, nurtured in the activist or voluntarist tradition of Western theology. It is ideas which make necessity conscious. The labor-saving power-machines of the later Middle Ages were produced by the implicit theological assumption of the infinite worth of even the most degraded human personality, by an instinctive repugnance towards subjecting any man to a monotonous drudgery which seems less than human in that it requires the exercise neither of intelligence nor of choice. It has often been remarked that the Latin Middle Ages first discovered the dignity and spiritual value of labor—that to labor is to pray. But the Middle Ages went further: they gradually and very slowly began to explore the practical implications of an essentially Christian paradox: that just as the Heavenly Jerusalem contains no temple, so the goal of labor is to end labor.

55   RISE OF COMMERCE AND OF TOWNS

*Technological progress meant increased productivity, which left a growing surplus available for trading purposes. Hence the rise of commerce and of commercial centers, or towns. The following contemporary description of late twelfth-century London reflects the diverse and vigorous life of that city, albeit in rhetorical prose.**

Among the noble and celebrated cities of the world that of London, the capital of the kingdom of the English, is one which extends its glory farther than all the others and sends its wealth and merchandise more widely into distant lands. Higher than all the rest does it lift its head. It is happy in the healthiness of its air; in its observance of Christian practice; in the strength of its fortifications; in its natural situation; in the honour of its citizens; and in the modesty of its matrons. It is cheerful in its sports, and the fruitful mother of noble men. Let us look into these things in turn.

If the mildness of the climate of this place softens the character of its inhabitants, it does not make them corrupt in following Venus, but rather prevents them from being fierce and bestial, making them liberal and kind.

. . . As regards the practice of Christian worship, there are in London and its suburbs thirteen greater conventual churches and, besides these, one hundred and twenty-six lesser parish churches.

It has on the east the Palatine castle, very great and strong: the keep and walls rise from very deep foundations and are fixed with a mortar tempered by the blood of animals. On the west there are two castles very strongly fortified, and from these there runs a high and massive wall with seven double gates and with towers along the north at regular intervals. London was once also walled and

* D. C. Douglas and G. W. Greenway, eds., *English Historical Documents 1042-1189* (New York: Oxford Univerity Press; London: Eyre & Spottiswoode, 1953), pp. 956-61.

turreted on the south, but the mighty Thames, so full of fish, has with the sea's ebb and flow washed against, loosened, and thrown down those walls in the course of time. Upstream to the west there is the royal palace which is conspicuous above the river, a building incomparable in its ramparts and bulwarks. It is about two miles from the city and joined thereto by a populous suburb.

Everywhere outside the houses of those living in the suburbs, and adjacent to them, are the spacious and beautiful gardens of the citizens, and these are planted with trees. Also there are on the north side pastures and pleasant meadow lands through which flow streams wherein the turning of mill-wheels makes a cheerful sound. Very near lies a great forest with woodland pastures in which there are the lairs of wild animals: stags, fallow deer, wild boars and bulls. The tilled lands of the city are not of barren gravel, but fat Asian plains that yield luxuriant crops and fill the tillers' barns with the sheaves of Ceres.

There are also outside London on the north side excellent suburban wells with sweet, wholesome and clear water that flows rippling over the bright stones. Among these are Holywell, Clerkenwell and St. Clement's Well, which are all famous. These are frequented by great numbers and much visited by the students from the schools and by the young men of the city, when they go out for fresh air on summer evenings.

. . . . .

Immediately outside one of the gates there is a field which is smooth both in fact and in name. On every sixth day of the week, unless it be a major feast-day, there takes place there a famous exhibition of fine horses for sale. Earls, barons and knights, who are in the town, and many citizens come out to see or to buy. It is pleasant to see the high-stepping palfreys with their gleaming coats, as they go through their paces, putting down their feet alternately on one side together. Next, one can see the horses suitable for esquires, moving faster though less smoothly, lifting and setting down, as it were, the opposite fore and hind feet: here are colts of fine breed, but not yet accustomed to the bit, stepping high with jaunty tread; there are the sumpter-horses, powerful and spirited; and after them there are the war-horses, costly, elegant of form, noble of stature, with ears quickly tremulous, necks raised and large haunches. . . .

By themselves in another part of the field stand the goods of the countryfolk: implements of husbandry, swine with long flanks, cows with full udders, oxen of immense size, and woolly sheep. There also stand the mares fit for plough, some big with foal, and others with brisk young colts closely following them.

To this city from every nation under heaven merchants delight to bring their trade by sea. The Arabian sends gold; the Sabaean spice and incense. The Scythian brings arms, and from the rich, fat lands of Babylon comes oil of palms. The Nile sends precious stones; the men of Norway and Russia, furs and sables; nor is China absent with purple silk. The Gauls come with their wines.

London, as historians have shown, is a much older city than Rome, for though it derives from the same Trojan ancestors, it was founded by Brutus before Rome was founded by Romulus and Remus. Wherefore they still have the same laws from their common origin. This city is like Rome divided into wards; it has annual sheriffs instead of consuls; it has its senatorial order and lower magistrates; it has drains and aqueducts in its streets; it has its appointed places for the hearing of cases deliberative, demonstrative and judicial; it has its several courts, and its separate assemblies on appointed days.

I do not think there is a city with a better record for church-going, doing honour to God's ordinances, keeping feast-days, giving alms and hospitality to strangers, confirming betrothals, contracting marriages, celebrating weddings, providing feasts, entertaining guests, and also, it may be added, in care for funerals and for the burial of the dead. The only plagues of London are the immoderate drinking of fools and the frequency of fires.

To this it may be added that almost all the bishops, abbots and magnates of England are in a sense citizens and freemen of London, having their own splendid town-houses. In them they live, and spend largely, when they are summoned to great councils by the king or by their metropolitan, or drawn thither by their private affairs.

. . . . .

On feast-days throughout the summer the young men indulge in the sports of archery, running, jumping, wrestling, slinging the stone, hurling the javelin beyond a mark and fighting with sword and buckler. Cytherea leads the dance of maidens, and until the moon rises, the earth is shaken with flying feet.

In winter on almost every feast-day before dinner either foaming boars, armed with lightning tusks, fight for their lives "to save their bacon," or stout bulls with butting horns, or huge bears do battle with the hounds let loose upon them. When the great marsh that washes the north wall of the city is frozen over, swarms of young men issue forth to play games on the ice. Some, gaining speed in their run, with feet set well apart, slide sideways over a vast expanse of ice. Others make seats out of a large lump of ice, and whilst one sits thereon, others with linked hands run before and drag him along behind them. So swift is their sliding motion that sometimes their feet slip, and they all fall on their faces. Others, more skilled at winter sports, put on their feet the shin-bones of animals, binding them firmly round their ankles, and, holding poles shod with iron in their hands, which they strike from time to time against the ice, they are propelled swift as a bird in flight or a bolt shot from an engine of war. Sometimes, by mutual consent, two of them run against each other in this way from a great distance, and, lifting their poles, each tilts against the other. Either one or both fall, not without some bodily injury, for, as they fall, they are carried along a great way beyond each other by the impetus of their run, and wherever the ice comes in contact with their heads, it scrapes of the skin utterly. Often a leg or an arm is broken, if the victim falls with it underneath him; but theirs is an age greedy of glory, youth yearns for victory, and exercises itself in mock combats in order to carry itself more bravely in real battles.

56   Role of Western Cities

Commerce and cities and merchants were not peculiar to the West. They were to be found also in the other Eurasian civilizations, and often on a larger scale, as noted by Marco Polo in thirteenth-century China. Yet commerce and cities and merchants played a revolutionary role in transforming Western society, in contrast to China where they were encapsulated and immobilized within the bureaucratic imperial struc-

ture. The nature and historical significance of this fundamental difference is analyzed in the following selection.*

Every sedentary society has built cities, for even in a subsistence economy essential functions of exchange and of organization (both functions dealing with minds and ideas as much as with goods or with institutions) are most conveniently performed in a central location on behalf of a wider countryside. The industrial revolution has emphasized the economic advantages of concentration and centrality. But is it true to say that change, revolutionary change, has found an advantage in urbanization; in concentration and in numbers? The city has instigated or led most of the great changes in Western society, and has been the center of its violent and non-violent revolutions. In western Europe the city has been the base of an independent entrepreneur group which has successfully challenged and broken the authority of the traditional order. In China, while cities with the same universal economic functions arose, they tended until recently to have the opposite effect on the pattern of change. China has consistently reasserted itself as a single political unit, but it is otherwise the appropriate qualitative and quantitative counterpart of Europe, and provides a reasonable basis for comparison. China and Europe have been the two great poles of world civilization, and an examination of the different roles which their cities played may help to elucidate other differences between them.

. . . . .

The cities of western Europe have been, at least since the high middle ages, centers of intellectual ferment; of economic change; and thus, in time, of opposition to the central authority. They became rebels in nearly every aspect of their institutional life. It was trade (and to a somewhat lesser extent specialized manufacturing) which made them strong enough to maintain their challenge to the established order. Their spirit of ferment was the spirit of a new group, urban merchant-manufacturers, which could operate from a base large and rich enough to establish increasingly its own rules. This setting tended to ensure that the universities, which grew up in cities originally for convenience and centrality, would frequently nourish skepticism, heresy, and freedom of enquiry. Even where they did not overtly do so, the concentration of literacy and learning in the cities was a stimulus to dissent.

Most of the cities which rose out of the cultural and social chaos following the destruction of Roman unity and preceding the development of a new national unity grew in answer to new conditions, for northwest Europe was ideally situated for trade. Most of them were in their origins much older than this, and had begun as administrative, military, or ecclesiastical centers. But a score of major rivers, navigable and free from floods, silting, or ice throughout the year in this mild maritime climate, led across the great European plain to the open sea; the peninsular, indented nature of the coast critically heightened mobility. The invitation which this presented to inter-European trade furthered the ascendancy of the commercial function. The shift of commerce and associated urbanism from the Mediterranean to northwest Europe seems to have begun before the Age of the Discoveries, notably in the Hansa towns and in Flanders. This may be in part a

* R. Murphey, "The City as a Center of Change: Western Europe and China," pp. 349-62. Reproduced by permission from the *Annals* of the Association of American Geographers, Volume 44, 1954.

reflection of the mobility inherent in the lands around the Baltic and North Seas, once they had learned from the Mediterranean the lessons of commerce and absorbed the civilizing influences of this earlier developed area. In any case, these northern cities came to be dominated by trader-manufacturers. Trade was a heady diet, and enabled urban merchants to command cities which had originally been administrative creations. While the cities did not alone destroy feudalism, they owed much of their prosperity and independence to its decline: freer trade, wider exchange, and failing power of the landed mobility. And their very growth as rival power bases accelerated the collapse of the old feudal order.

As the growth of national unity progressed, under the institutional and emotional leadership of monarchy, an alliance of convenience between king and city arose which met the crown's demands for funds and the city's demand for representation. Urban merchants had the money to support the king in his foreign wars and in his struggle with the divisive domestic ambitions of the nobility and the church. In return the city received an increasing voice in the affairs of state, through representation in parliaments, and indirectly through the making of policy in which the throne was obliged to follow. But while this alliance of revenue in exchange for concessions was one of mutual interest, its ultimate result was the strengthening of the urban commercial sector until it overthrew or emasculated the monarchy, and with it the traditional order as a whole. Having helped the king to power over the nobility, the city achieved a *modus vivendi* with him which left it in control of the affairs vital to it. As a current reminder of the development of urban independence, "the city" of London retains its originally hard-won privilege of excluding the reigning monarch, who is also excluded from the House of Commons, in part the city's creation and in part its weapon. To a certain extent the king, and even the nobility, were willing to go along with the process of economic change instigated by the city since they profited from it as the principal source of wealth in which they were often investors as well as tax collectors. But the new values which the city emphasized, and their institutional expression, were in direct conflict with the traditional society based on land; the city repeatedly bred overt revolutionary movements designed to establish its new order as the national way of life.

As centers of trade, the cities were free of the land and of its social and political limitations embodied in the institutions of post-Roman society. They developed their own law which was in differing degrees independent of the traditional, rural law. Their institutions were self-made, and they were not beholden to the traditional system which they challenged. The companies and corporations which the merchants organized went far beyond the scope of guilds in their successful attempt to order most of the social and economic fabric (instead of being limited to a trade-union function, as the guilds of China predominantly were). Traditional guilds were overlaid with new merchant organizations, or were clothed with new functions and powers, although some of the older guilds remained as conservative or retarding influences. The economic institutions which arose concurrently were also new-made sources of strength: banking, letters of credit, private property, interest, speculation and investment, representing needs and ideas which were almost wholly foreign to the traditional society of the countryside, and which were the accompaniment of an ever-widening trade. For the invitation to commercial expansion overseas was as strong in Europe's geography as the earlier invitation to trade among the lands surrounding the Baltic, Mediterranean, and North Seas. A leading agent of this process was necessarily the city, where trade flowed through break-in-bulk points such as the mouths of the Rhine or the English ports facing the Channel. Merchant corporations for overseas trade became the strongest and most progressive, or revolutionary, of the city's agents. Interestingly, the original charter of the British East India Company stated that "gentlemen" (by which was meant the landed gentry) "shall be excluded" from membership.

The city was the natural center of political change as it had been of economic change. The growth of modern Europe may be regarded as the steady progress of a new class of urban traders and manufacturers toward a position of control in a society and economy which their own enterprise had largely created. It was they who had realized the potential of Europe's location for world trade, and they who had developed and applied the technological and economic tools which made Europe the center of the world. The destruction of the old pattern was implicit in this process, and also implicit was the revolutionary expression, by the cities, of their claim to political power. . . .

. . . The first great modern revolution, in seventeenth century England, was the work of a city-country alliance, but London was mainly Puritan, and the outcome might be regarded as the victory of urban merchants and their country confreres over the traditional authoritarian alliance of cavalier and peasant based on the land. Two centuries later Manchester and Birmingham had joined London in the final stages of the contest between urban "radicalism" and country "conservatism," epitomized in the struggle over the Corn Laws, the Reform Bills, free trade, and the Manchester School. By this time cotton textiles had well supplanted woolen textiles as the chief manufacturing industry; since it came relatively late it was not greatly hampered by guild restrictions, as wool had been; it established itself in Manchester, which as a then unincorporated town lacked formalized controls. It may irritate many readers as a loose generalization, but still seems worth stating for argument, that representative government and the industrial revolution, perhaps modern Europe's two most significant products, were created by the city. The Low Countries provide as good an illustration of this as does England.

In France the picture was less clear since urban merchant-manufacturers were less prominent in the national economy. Even so, it was Paris which created and carried the revolution. Paris used peasant distress and rebellion, but was never dethroned by it. One may say that Paris later destroyed Charles X and Louis Philippe. . . . In eastern Europe it is difficult to draw distinctions between city and country, or to find an independent urban-based group living on trade and challenging the existing order. Nevertheless even in twentieth century Russia, while the Soviet revolution was in part carried by peasant groups, leadership remained in the urban intellectual group which had instigated the change.

. . . . . .

In China, while the peasant and the countryside were in some respects like the West, the city's role was fundamentally different. Chinese cities were administrative centers. With few exceptions this function dominated their lives whatever their other bases in trade or manufacturing. Their remarkably consistent, uniform plan, square or rectangular walls surrounding a great cross with gates at each of the four arms, suggests their common administrative creation and their continued expression of this function.

. . . . .

. . . In China most cities or towns of 5,000 or more had well-defined commercial or manufacturing districts, and special areas for each important enterprise: banking, metal goods, food markets, textiles, woodwork, and so on. This pattern remains in most contemporary Chinese cities. But the cities were not decisive centers of change in a commercialized economy. They served as imperial or provincial capitals, seats for garrison troops, and residences for governors, viceroys, and the ubiquitous cloud of officials and quasi-officials with their "service-providers." Their business was administration, and exploitation, of the countryside. Marco Polo, in describing the magnificence of Peking, accounts for it as follows:

> . . . and this happens because everyone from everywhere brings there for the lord who lives there and for his court and for the city which is so great and for the ladies and barons and knights of whom there are so many and for the great abundance of the multitude of the people of the armies of the lord, which stay round about as well for the court as for the city, and of other people who come there by reason of the court which the great lord holds there, and for one and for another . . . and because the city is in too good a position and in the middle of many provinces.

Here is a clear picture of a city based on administration from a central location, where trade flows in largely in response to the existing structure of officials, troops, court, hangers-on, and the host of people necessary to support them, from secretaries and servants to bakers and dancers. Six hundred years later at the end of the nineteenth century European travellers in China reported the same phenomenon, on a smaller regional scale: large cities whose sole function appeared to be administration, or important trading cities at key locations which were nevertheless dominated by officials and the magistrate's *yamen* (office). . . .

The trade process appears to have lacked the dynamic quality by means of which Europe's cities rose to power. Pre-eighteenth century China had a trade as great as or greater than pre-eighteenth century Europe, but Europe's subsequent commercial expansion left China far behind. Why this happened, and why China never produced the revolutionary economic and political changes which remade Europe into an arbiter for the rest of the world is a vital question. An analysis of the city's role may help to suggest some relevant factors. Why was the Chinese city not a European-style center of change?

China is geographically isolated by a formidable assemblage of barriers. To landward lies the greatest mountain mass in the world, with its extensions from the Pamir Knot, reinforced on the south by rainforests and spectacular river gorges, on the north by the barren wastes of Siberia, and on the west and northwest by a vast sweep of desert. Seaward a coast deficient in harbours faces a huge and until recently commercially underdeveloped ocean, by European standards. Chinese trade with Japan was at several periods considerable, and with southeast Asia even larger, but it did not approach eighteenth or nineteenth century European levels. It tended to be characterized by luxury goods, strategic goods (such as copper for coinage), or specialties such as Chinese porcelain. With these exceptions, especially the highly developed and diversified trade between southeast coastal China, and southeast Asia, China did not greatly extend herself commercially, and was for the most part content to send specialized goods, like silk, to the rest of the world through middlemen intermediaries: the Arabs by sea and the Turkish peoples of central Asia by land. Significantly, the largest concerted Chinese attempt in foreign trade was an imperial government project (the famous Ming expeditions of the fifteenth century), which lasted only some 30 years and apparently found no solid base in the Chinese economy or in its merchant group.

Internally, trade moved largely on the great river systems, running fortunately east and west, but there was no such close interconnection between these river basins as in Europe, by sea or across plains. Physically China is built on a grander scale, but the landscape presents no such invitation to exchange as has sparked the development of Europe. Europe is multi-peninsular, each peninsula tending toward economic distinctiveness and political independence, but joined by cheap sea and river routes. This plethora of complementary areas and their transport links magnified the basis and the means of exchange. Although its early trade development was not larger than China's, by the middle of the eighteenth century commercial expansion overseas had joined and accelerated commercialization at home, and Europe stood in a class by itself. The cities of western Europe were both the creators and inheritors of this development. But in China the cities remained centers of the unitary national state and of the traditional order rather than its attackers, epitomes of the status quo. As direct links in the official hierarchy, they were the props of the empire. The universities were urban, for convenience as in Europe, but they stimulated no dissent. Their accepted function was to train scholars who could staff the imperial civil service, and they fed their graduates into the imperial examination system. This, and the better economic and social position of scholars generally in China than in Europe, encouraged the universities and the literati to support the status quo; European intellectuals may have taken a vow of poverty, but they remained a dissident or discontented group.

Physically, China lacked Europe's outstanding advantages for trade, and on the other hand presented a base for highly productive agriculture, through irrigation. Wittvogel's revealing work on the organic connection between the need for mass organized water control and the growth of a monolithic bureaucratic state in China lends insight into the origins and pattern of the institutional structure. With China's environmental advantages, water control made agriculture the massive core of the economy, and at the same time left the bureaucracy in a position of ramified command. It was not possible for urban merchants to win independence from this system. They had less economic leverage than the rising European merchants because, with the preponderant position of agriculture, they never occupied proportionately as large a place in the economy.

The state of course did its part to prevent the development of a rival group, and by taxation, requisition, and monopoly ensured that the merchants would be kept relatively impotent. This was a job which European states and monarchs, though equally determined, failed to accomplish; their merchants were in a stronger position, and the state was weaker: it was merely *primus inter pares*. Land hunger in China, as a reflection of a population too large for the available arable land (increasingly serious during the past 200 years, but even in Han times worse than in most other parts of the world, including Europe), also acted to restrict commercial development, since it meant high land rents. Capital could almost always be invested with greater profit and safety in land, or in rural loans, than in productive or capital-generating enterprises outside the agrarian sphere.

Where extra-agricultural opportunities for investment did exist, the individual entrepreneur was at the mercy of the bureaucratic state. Many of the major trade goods were government monopolies. Elsewhere the essentially Western concepts of private property and due process of law, in a word, of the entrepreneur, were lacking in a society dominated by agriculture and officials. Extortion, forced levies, confiscation, and simple financial failure as the result of arbitrary government policies were the daily risk of the merchant. Some individuals did indeed become very rich, for example the famous *hong* merchants of Canton, but their wealth came necessarily through official connection: by possession of gentry status, by office holding or official favour, or by trading as part of a government monopoly (such as foreign trade under the Canton system and at most other periods was). Even so their gains were never secure. The greatest and richest of the *hong* merchants died in poverty, having lost official favour. While this also happened to many of the pre-eighteenth century European capitalists, it did not prevent the survival and growth of individual capitalist families or firms or of a moneyed group. The famous Ch'ing dynasty billionaire Ho Shen, said to have been worth the equivalent of nearly a billion and a half U. S. dollars, was not a merchant at all, but a favourite minister of the emperor Ch'ien Lung, which demonstrates the real source of wealth in traditional China. Yet he too died in poverty and disgrace (by suicide in place of a suspended death sentence in 1799) at the hands of Ch'ien Lung's successor.

In China merchant-capitalists did not use their money to establish their independence, as did the merchants of London or Antwerp, or to stimulate the growth of a new economic pattern. Unfortunately for the Chinese merchants, the imperial revenue was at most periods derived largely from the land tax and from the government trade monopolies. Agriculture was proportionately more productive than in Europe, and revenue from trade less necessary. Peking thus did not need the merchants as the king had needed them in Europe to finance the ascendancy of the national state, to pay for its wars with rival states, or to meet its normal bills. No concessions were necessary; the merchants could be squeezed dry, and were, with no harm to the state. The commanding position of the bureaucracy, and the fact of the bureaucratic state, are perhaps explainable by a similar process of default. Merchants were necessary or useful to perform essential (and, to the state, profitable) commercial functions; they were tolerated, but kept under strict control, and this was simpler and cheaper than for the state to manage all commercial dealings itself.

But the merchants were also identified with the state as well as being stifled by it. Their numbers were recruited largely from the gentry class, who had the capital and the official connections essential to commercial success. Gentry merchants worked willingly with gentry officials in the management of the state monopolies, including foreign trade. Outside the monopolies, the same partnership operated, as a matter of mutual interest. In addition, most gentry members, whether or not they were engaged in trade, also performed other semi-official functions, comparable in some degree to the British landed gentry. These "services" represented a considerable part of their income; they were not likely to attack the system which nourished them. In a more general sense, the tradition of revolt in this hierarchical society did not include the re-ordering of social or economic groups, but concentrated on the removal of bad government. Individual or group improvement was not to be won by destroying the fabric, but by making optimum use of one's position within it.

Finally, China had maintained since Han times and with few breaks a remarkable degree of unity and a central power which no single European state achieved until quite late in its modern development. In China even towns of the *chen* (market town) rank (population c. 3000–5000) were seats of garrison troops, whatever their prominence in trade. In Europe in the course of the crown's contest with the nobles, and of the international rivalries which also developed among the plethora of separate national states, urban merchants found an opportunity which contrasted sharply with the rooted monolithic nature of the Chinese state.

The cities of China were consequently microcosms of the empire, not deviants. . . .

. . . The city has been a center of change in western Europe, while it has been the reverse in traditional China, despite the broad similarity in urban economic functions in both areas. Urban character and urban roles may be useful indicators of the nature and dynamics of the diverse entities of society.

RELIGION AND THE EXPANSION OF EUROPE   57

The new civilization taking form in Western Europe was unique also because of the militancy of its Christian religion, which asserted itself as a universal faith. Thus, missionary effort has characterized the church from the days of the apostles to modern times. When the technological and economic developments described in the preceding readings led to an increase in the number and power of the Western Europeans, they promptly took the offensive against the enemies of the faith. One manifestation was the series of crusades to reconquer the Holy Land. These were precipitated by the famous speech delivered by Pope Urban II in 1095, one of several versions of which is given below. Another manifestation of the aggressive dynamism of Western Christendom was the drive of the German crusading orders into northeast Europe at the expense of the heathen Slavs. The following account by the monk Helmold (born ca. 1125) describes the manner in which Count Adolph of Holstein conquered the pagan lands, built fortresses, and planted colonies. This crusading tradition of the Western Europeans is of particular significance for world history because their later expansion overseas was in part a continuation of their earlier crusades, as suggested by the red crosses on the sails of Columbus' ships.

Pope Urban II *

. . . Since, oh sons of God, you have promised the Lord more earnestly than heretofore to maintain peace in your midst and faithfully to sustain the laws of the church, there remains for you, newly fortified by the correction of the Lord, to show the strength of your integrity in a certain other duty, which is not less your concern than the Lord's. For you must carry succor to your brethren dwelling in the East, and needing your aid, which they have so often demanded. For the Turks, a Persian people, have attacked them, as many of you know, and have advanced into the territory of Romania as far as that part of the Mediterranean which is called the Arm of St. George; and occupying more and more the lands of those Christians, have already seven times conquered them in battle, have killed and captured many, have destroyed the churches and devastated the kingdom of God. If you permit them to remain for a time unmolested, they will extend their sway more widely over many faithful servants of the Lord.

Wherefore, I pray and exhort, nay not I, but the Lord prays and exhorts you, as heralds of Christ, by frequent exhortation, to urge men of all ranks, knights and foot-soldiers, rich and poor, to hasten to exterminate this vile race from the lands of our brethren, and to bear timely aid to the worshippers of Christ. I speak to those who are present, I proclaim it to the absent, but Christ commands. More-

* D. C. Munro, trans., *Translations and Reprints from the Original Sources of European History*, Series I, Vol. I, No. 2, rev. ed. (Philadelphia: University of Pennsylvania Press, 1902), pp. 2-3.

over, the sins of those who set out thither, if they lose their lives on the journey, by land or sea, or in fighting against the heathen, shall be remitted in that hour; this I grant to all who go, through the power of God vested in me.

Oh, what a disgrace if a race so despised, degenerate, and slave of the demons, should thus conquer a people fortified with faith in omnipotent God and resplendent with the name of Christ! Oh, how many reproaches will be heaped upon you by the Lord Himself if you do not aid those who like yourselves are counted of the Christian faith! Let those who have formerly been accustomed to contend wickedly in private warfare against the faithful, fight against the infidel and bring to a victorious end the war which ought long since to have been begun. Let those who have hitherto been robbers now become soldiers of Christ. Let those who have formerly contended against their brothers and relatives now fight as they ought against the barbarians. Let those who have formerly been mercenaries at low wages, now gain eternal rewards. Let those who have been striving to the detriment both of body and soul, now labor for a two-fold reward. What shall I add? On this side will be the sorrowful and poor, on the other the joyful and the rich; here the enemies of the Lord, there His friends. Let not those who are going delay their journey, but having arranged their affairs and collected the money necessary for their expenses, when the winter ends and the spring comes, let them with alacrity start on their journey under the guidance of the Lord.

Helmold *

. . . In those days a variety of idolatrous cults and superstitious aberrations grew strong again throughout all Slavia.

Besides the groves and the household gods in which the country and towns abound, the first and foremost deities are Prove, the god of the land of Oldenburg; Siva, the goddess of the Polabi; Redigast, the god of the land of the Abodrites. To these gods are dedicated priests, sacrificial libations, and a variety of religious rites. When the priest declares, according to the decision of the lot, what solemnities are to be celebrated in honor of the gods, the men, women, and children come together and offer to their deities sacrifices of oxen and sheep, often, also, of Christians with whose blood they say their gods are delighted. . . .

. . . Besides, there has been inborn in the Slavic race a cruelty that knows no satiety, a restlessness that harries the countries lying about them by land and sea. It is hard to tell how many kinds of death they have inflicted on the followers of Christ. They have even torn out the bowels of some and wound them about a stake and have affixed others to crosses in ridicule of the sign of our redemption. . . .

Since the illustrious Caesar Lothar and his very worthy consort Richenza were most devoutly solicitous for the divine service, the priest of Christ, Vicelin, went to him while he was tarrying at Bardowiek and suggested to him that he should provide for the Slavic race some means of salvation in keeping with the power that had been bestowed on him by Heaven. Vicelin, moreover, made known to him that there is in the province of Wagria a mountain adapted for the erection of a royal castle for the protection of the land. . . . The emperor attended to the prudent counsel of the priest and sent competent men to determine the fitness of the mountain. On being assured by the reports of the messengers, he crossed

* Helmold, *The Chronicle of the Slavs,* trans. F. J. Tschan (New York: Columbia University Press, 1935), pp. 158-61, 168-69.

the river and went into the land of the Slavs to the place appointed. He ordered all the Nordalbingian people to come together for the building of the castle. In obedience to the emperor, the princes of the Slavs also were present, taking part in the business, but with great sadness, for they discerned that the structure was being erected for their oppression. One prince of the Slavs, therefore, said to another:

> Do you see this strong and commanding structure? Behold, I foretell to you that this castle will prove a yoke for the whole land; for going out hence, they will first break upon Plön and afterward Oldenburg and Lübeck; then they will cross the River Trave and subdue Ratzeburg and all the land of the Polabi. And the country of the Abodrites will not escape their hands.

The castle was finished and secured with a numerous soldiery and called Segeberg. In charge of the castle the Caesar put Hermann, one of his henchmen. Not content with these arrangements, he ordered the establishment of a new church at the foot of the mountain and set aside, for the maintenance of divine worship and for the support of the brethren to be congregated there, six or more villages, confirming the grant by charters according to usage. Furthermore, he committed the stewardship of that basilica to the lord Vicelin, that he might be the more disposed to push forward the erection of dwellings and bring together clerics. He also made a like arrangement about the church of Lübeck, warning Pribislav, if he would hold his favor, to be with all diligence mindful of the priest there, or whomsoever acted in his stead. His purpose was, as he himself publicly declared, to subject the whole Slavic race to the divine religion and to make a great bishop of the minister of Christ.

. . . . .

. . . As the land was without inhabitants, he sent messengers into all parts, namely, to Flanders and Holland, to Utrecht, Westphalia, and Frisia, proclaiming that whosoever were in straits for lack of fields should come with their families and receive a very good land,—a spacious land, rich in crops, abounding in fish and flesh and exceeding good pasturage. To the Holzatians and Sturmarians he said:

> Have you not subjugated the land of the Slavs and bought it with the blood of your brothers and fathers? Why, then, are you the last to enter into possession of it? Be the first to go over into a delectable land and inhabit it and partake of its delights, for the best of it is due you who have wrested it from the hands of the enemy.

An innumerable multitude of different peoples rose up at this call and they came with their families and their goods into the land of Wagria to Count Adolph that they might possess the country which he had promised them. First of all the Holzatians received abodes in the safest places to the west in the region of Segeberg along the River Trave, also the Bornhöved open and everything extending from the River Schwale as far as Agrimesov and the Plöner-See. The Westphalians settled in the region of Dargune, the Hollanders around Eutin, and the Frisians around Süssel. The country about Plön, however, was still uninhabited. Oldenburg and Lütjenburg and the rest of the lands bordering on the sea he gave to the Slavs to live in, and they became tributary to him.

NON-EURASIAN
WORLD TO 1500

Chapter Eighteen

Africa

THE NATURE OF AFRICAN HISTORY   58

*Archaeologists and research scholars are now uncovering the errors in widely-held assumptions that the African Negro is incapable of progress and that his history is one of stagnation and savagery before the advent of the white man in the fifteenth century. Findings clearly demonstrate that the African Negro had reached a high level of political and cultural development before the appearance of the Europeans, and even of the Arabs before them. In fact, the more advanced indigenous Negro cultures were in many respects comparable to those of Europe until the past few centuries when the Europeans bounded ahead with their scientific, technological, and economic revolutions. "Allowing for the difference between the Moslem and the Christian intellectual climates," writes an English scholar, "a citizen of 14th century Timbuktu would have found himself reasonably at home in 14th century Oxford. In the 16th century he still would have found many points in common between the two university cities. By the 19th century the gulf had grown very deep." * The important point here is that the gulf had grown deep not only between the Europeans and the Africans, but also between the Europeans and all the other people of the world. For the Europeans were the mavericks—the deviants—while the Africans, together with the rest of humanity, represented the norm in continuing along the traditional channels. In the following selection, this new approach to African history is expounded, and its implications are analyzed.***

. . . just because various African peoples have known nothing of the industrial revolution in its later, urban, phases; have remembered orally and not literally;

* T. Hodgkin, "Islam in West Africa," *Africa South,* II (April-June, 1958), 98.
** Basil Davidson, "The Fact of African History: An Introduction," *Africa South,* II (January-March, 1958), 44-49. Reprinted by permission of Curtis Brown, Ltd.

fought without chariots; and refrained from sailing across the seas that lapped their shores, there is no ground for saying that they are not inherently as capable as anyone else. . . . But the fact remains that these African peculiarities are often used to buttress the general European belief that all was savage chaos before the Europeans came, and to suggest that the reason for this savage chaos lay not in a certain set of objective circumstances, but in African incapacity to emerge from them. "Their thinking," a South African publicist wrote lately, "was not concerned with objective validity and was pre-occupied by the mystic powers of persons and things. This centuries-long stagnation cannot be attributed to their isolation from the main stream of civilization"; the implication, of course, being that it must be attributed to an African inability to evolve and progress.

So it is a matter of quite unusual interest and importance that the last few years should have raised the whole subject of African history—pre-European history—to a new and academically respectable status. Many scholars are producing many new facts about it. Far from being unconcerned with "objective validity" or hypnotized by the "mystic powers of persons and things," Africans, it would appear, were engaged in a great many "civilized activities," of one kind and another, for many centuries before European settlement, or even before European discovery. At a time when European mariners had yet to reach the Indian Ocean, or even the Bight of Benin, the kings and counsellors of Central Africa were eating from Chinese porcelain, and when Mr. Strijdom's forebears drove their ox carts into the old Transvaal, they encountered men and women who were not at the beginning of a long period of civilized development, but, through times of painful dissolution, were perilously near the end of one. In this tide of new information, and of reassessment of old information, the study of humanity in Tropical and Southern Africa has really begun: even if it is still in its infancy, its findings are a long way beyond the point where any but the obsessively bigoted will care to ignore them. . . .

Africans south of the Sahara were in fact evolving and progressing towards destinations recognizably the same as Europeans (or Asians)—at a time long before Europeans first came across them.

A gap in social and technical development may always have existed, no doubt, between those who lived close to the cradles of ancient civilization and those who lived far from them. There is no more sense in sentimentalizing about the misery and barbarism of much of the African past than there is in pretending that European history does not tell the same kind of story. The important point is the width of the gap at any one time. If, as people are fond of saying, the gap was *always* immensely wide, then something might well be missing from the African make-up. But if the gap, though wide to-day, had once been relatively narrow, then history will draw quite other conclusions. Now the main consequence of a good deal of recent research into Southern and Central and East African history—over the past thousand years or so—is precisely to suggest that the gap was once a relatively narrow one, and not always to Europe's advantage either.

Writing in 1067, the mediaevel Arab scholar El Bekri described the court of the king of Ghana such as the Arabs knew it from their penetration and eventual conquest of that country. "When he gives audience to his people," wrote El Bekri, "to listen to their complaints and set them to rights, he sits in a pavillion around which stand his horses caparisoned in cloth of gold; behind him stand ten pages holding shields and gold-mounted swords; on his right hand are the sons of the princes of his empire, splendidly clad and with gold plaited into their hair. . . ." A barbaric king and a barbaric kingdom? But were they more barbaric or less civilized than the king and kingdom that William of Normandy had conquered the year before? Were they not, conceivably, less barbaric and more civilized?

When the Portuguese adventurers first rounded the Cape of Good Hope they were certainly as much concerned with "the mystic powers of persons and things" as the most superstitious native of any part of Africa. Their ignorance of the Eastern world was no smaller than East Africa's ignorance of Europe and was quite possibly greater. They were astonished to find the harbours of the East Coast—of what are now Mozambique and Tanganyika and Kenya—the goal and shelter of long-range ocean shipping; and when they sailed for India it was with pilots whose navigational equipment was, in some ways, better than their own. The superiority of the society of Lisbon over the society of Kilwa and Mombasa was not, in those days, by any means obvious. The one certain superiority of those Europeans was in cruelty and aggressiveness.

Yet three hundred and fifty years later, in the hey-day of Victorian rediscovery, the gap had grown immensely wide—so wide, indeed, that it became easy for Europeans to wonder (as many still do) whether Negroes did not after all belong to an inferior species. There is little mystery about the reasons for this widening of the gap: while Europe, freeing itself from mediaeval limits, plunged into commercialism and industrialism and won its great technical superiority over the rest of the world, much of Africa lay fettered in the oversea slave trade. The one went forward, the other went back, and the gap, narrow enough in 1500, grew into a gulf.

Historians and archaeologists are now building new bridges of explanation across that gulf. . . .

What appears to emerge from the present state of knowledge is nothing like a state of savage chaos, but, on the contrary, the long-enduring growth and development of an African Metal Age—beginning over two thousand years ago and producing, for example, the Monomotapa culture of what were Rhodesia and Mozambique in the 15th century—that went through many phases and vicissitudes, but showed remarkable flexibility of invention and resource. It is certain that there developed down the East Coast, sometime after the discovery of the trading use of the monsoon winds in the first century A.D., a flourishing and stable African trade with Arabia, Persia, India, Indonesia and China. It is probable that while the Arabs became the intermediaries and chief carriers in this trade, they were no more the originators of it in Africa than they were in India or China. They established trading posts as far south as Sofala, at points where African kingdoms already existed or subsequently grew. Behind these coastal kingdoms, in the hinterland of Africa, there was meanwhile developing a network of Metal Age polities whose growth was increasingly stimulated by the coastal and oversea demand for gold, ivory and iron. These African goods were exchanged by Africans —through Arab and Indian intermediaries—for Indian textiles, Indonesian beads, and Chinese porcelain. Only when the Portuguese arrived to monopolize this trade, and rapidly destroy it, did these coastal and inland civilizations enter their decline. The hand of the European guided, as it came about, not away from chaos, but towards it.

And what continually surprises, in reviewing the evidence so far available, is the *coherence* of these African cultures. Already it is possible to glimpse connexions, whether by cultural drift, migration, or trade, between the early kingdoms of Uganda, for example, and those of Rhodesia; between Zimbabwe and the coastal cities as far north as Gedi, sixty miles beyond Mombasa; between the wooden cities of West Africa and the stone cities of Monomotapa. All these links between

African societies of the past, whether immediate or remote, have the same kind of coherence and suggestions of common origin, native origin, as those which gave the Indo-European tribes their historical affinity as they spread across the northern world. We are clearly in the presence of a large segment of the human story: of another contribution to the proof of that unity-in-diversity which scientists otherwise ascribed to all branches of *homo sapiens*.

59   MALI EMPIRE IN THE SUDAN

*Westerners commonly refer to their appearance in Africa as the "Opening of Africa." But the fact is that Africa had been "opened" to the outside world many centuries earlier. This was particularly true after the conversion of large regions of Africa to Islam, which drew those regions into the far-flung Moslem world. Thus in 1324 Mansa Kankan Musa, the famous ruler of the great Sudanese Mali empire, left his capital on the Upper Nile for a pilgrimage to Mecca. His camel trains, servants, and wives, and the vast supplies of gold that he distributed lavishly, all created such an impression that the event was long remembered, as indicated in the following account by Allah al Omari, a Cairo resident. Omari also provides illuminating information concerning Mali, making clear the high level of development of that empire.**

TRAVELING THROUGH CAIRO. During my first journey to Cairo and sojourn there I heard talk of the arrival of the Sultan Musa [*Mansa* Musa, emperor of Mali] and I found the Cairenes very glad to talk of the large expenditures of those people. I questioned the Emir Abu'l 'Abbas Ahmed ben Abi'l Haki, el Mehmendar, who spoke of the sultan's noble appearance, dignity and trustworthiness. "When I went out to greet him in the name of the glorious Sultan el Malik en Nasir [of Egypt]," he told me, "he gave me the warmest of welcomes and treated me with the most careful politeness. But he would talk to me only through an interpreter [that is, his spokesman or linguist] although he could speak perfect Arabic. He carried his imperial treasure in many pieces of gold, worked or otherwise.

"I suggested that he should go up to the palace and meet the Sultan [of Egypt]. But he refused, saying 'I came for the pilgrimage, and for nothing else, and I do not wish to mix up my pilgrimage with anything else.' He argued about this. However, I well understood that the meeting was repugnant to him because he was loath to kiss the ground [before the Sultan] or to kiss his hand. I went on insisting and he went on making excuses. But imperial protocol obliged me to present him; and I did not leave him until he had agreed. When he came into the Sultan's presence we asked him to kiss the ground. But he refused and continued to refuse, saying: 'However can this be?' Then a wise man of his suite whispered several words to him that I could not understand. 'Very well,' he thereupon declared, 'I will prostrate myself before Allah who created me and brought me into the world.' Having done so he moved toward the Sultan. The

* From *The African Past,* ed. Basil Davidson, pp. 75-79, by permission of Atlantic-Little, Brown and Co. Copyright © 1964 by Basil Davidson.

latter rose for a moment to welcome him and asked him to sit beside him: then they had a long conversation. After Sultan Musa had left the palace the Sultan of Cairo sent him gifts of clothing for himself, his courtiers and all those who were with him; saddled and bridled horses for himself and his chief officers . . .

"When the time of pilgrimage arrived, [the Sultan of Egypt] sent him a large quantity of drachmas, baggage camels and choice riding camels with saddles and harness. [The Sultan of Egypt] caused abundant quantities of foodstuffs to be bought for his suite and his followers, established posting-stations for the feeding of the animals, and gave to the emirs of the pilgrimage a written order to look after and respect [the Emperor of Mali]. When the latter returned it was I who went to greet him and settle him into his quarters . . ."

"This man," el Mehmendar also told me, "spread upon Cairo the flood of his generosity: there was no person, officer of the [Cairo] court or holder of any office of the [Cairo] sultanate who did not receive a sum in gold from him. The people of Cairo earned incalculable sums from him, whether by buying and selling or by gifts. So much gold was current in Cairo that it ruined the value of money." . . .

Let me add [continues Omari] that gold in Egypt had enjoyed a high rate of exchange up to the moment of their arrival. The gold *mitqal* that year had not fallen below twenty-five drachmas. But from that day [of their arrival] onward, its value dwindled; the exchange was ruined, and even now it has not recovered. The *mitqal* scarcely touches twenty-two drachmas. That is how it has been for twelve years from that time, because of the great amounts of gold they brought to Egypt and spent there.

THE EMPIRE OF MALI. The king of this country is known to the people of Egypt as the king of Tekrur [roughly, inland Senegal]; but he himself becomes indignant when he is called thus, since Tekrur is only one of the countries of his empire. The title he prefers is that of lord of Mali, the largest of his states; it is the name by which he is most known. He is the most important of the Muslim Negro kings; his land is the largest, his army the most numerous; he is the king who is the most powerful, the richest, the most fortunate, the most feared by his enemies and the most able to do good to those around him.

His kingdom consists of the lands of Gana, Zagun, Tirakka, Tekrur, Bambugu, Zarquatabana, Darmura, Zaga, Kabora, Baraguri, Gao-gao. The inhabitants of Gao-gao are of the tribes of Yarten. The region of Mali is that where the residence of the king is situated [in] the town of Niane, and all the other regions are dependent on it; it has the official name of Mali because it is the capital of this kingdom which also includes towns, villages and centers of population to the number of fourteen.

The honorable and truthful Sheikh Abu Sa'id Otman ed Dukkali, who has lived in the town of Niane for thirty-five years and traveled throughout the kingdom, has told me that this is square in shape, being four months [of travel] in length and at least as much in breadth . . .

The sultan of this country has sway over the land of the "desert of native gold," whence they bring him gold every year. The inhabitants of that land are savage pagans whom the sultan would subject to him if he wished. But the sovereigns of this kingdom have learned by experience that whenever one of them has conquered one of these gold towns, established Islam there and sounded the call to prayer, the harvest of gold dwindles and falls to nothing, meanwhile it grows and expands in neighboring pagan countries. When experience had confirmed them in this observation, they left the gold country in the hands of its pagan inhabitants, and contented themselves with assuring their obedience and paying tribute.

RECEPTION AT COURT.   The sultan of this kingdom presides in his palace on a great balcony called *bembe* where he has a great seat of ebony that is like a throne fit for a large and tall person: on either side it is flanked by elephant tusks turned towards each other. His arms stand near him, being all of gold, saber, lance, quiver, bow and arrows. He wears wide trousers made of about twenty pieces [of stuff] of a kind which he alone may wear. Behind him there stand about a score of Turkish or other pages which are bought for him in Cairo: one of them, at his left, holds a silk umbrella surmounted by a dome and a bird of gold: the bird has the figure of a falcon. His officers are seated in a circle about him, in two rows, one to the right and one to the left; beyond them sit the chief commanders of his cavalry. In front of him there is a person who never leaves him and who is his executioner; also another who serves as intermediary [that is, official spokesman] between the sovereign and his subjects, and who is named the herald. In front of them again, there are drummers. Others dance before their sovereign, who enjoys this, and make him laugh. Two banners are spread behind him. Before him they keep two saddled and bridled horses in case he should wish to ride.

THE IMPORTANCE OF HORSES.   Arab horses are brought for sale to the kings of this country, who spend considerable sums in this way. Their army numbers one hundred thousand men of whom there are about ten thousand horse-mounted cavalry: the others are infantry having neither horses nor any other mounts. They have camels in this country but do not know the art of riding them with a saddle . . .

The officers of this king, his soldiers and his guard receive gifts of land and presents. Some among the greatest of them receive as much as fifty thousand *mitqals* of gold a year, besides which the king provides them with horses and clothing. He is much concerned with giving them fine garments and making his cities into capitals.

ROYAL BUREAUCRACY.   It is one of their customs that whenever someone charged with a certain task of important affair reports to the king, the latter questions him on everything that has happened from the time of his departure to the time of his return, and in great detail. Legal cases and appeals also go up to the sovereign who examines them himself. Generally he writes nothing; but gives his orders, most of the time, orally. He has *qadis,* secretaries, offices.

60   PYGMIES OF THE CONGO

Very different from the advanced culture of the Mali Empire is the Paleolithic culture of the Pygmies of the Ituri forest in the Congo. These are a people who are exclusively food gatherers, who do not know how to make fire, and who have no rulers, courts, armies, or bureaucrats as in the case of Mali. Their retardation may be ex-

plained in part by the difficult rain-forest environment. But at least equally important is their isolation from the centers of civilization in Eurasia. Whereas the culture of Mali had been much stimulated by contact with the Islamic world, the Pygmies by contrast were completely isolated except for their relations with their Negro neighbors who provided them with plantains and tools in return for the honey and meat that the Pygmies collected in the forests. With Patrick Putnam, who lived with the Pygmies for nearly two decades, we catch a glimpse of their way of life.*

The Ituri forest is rolling country, so densely covered with trees that the relief of the landscape is invisible except from the air. It is a primary rain forest; that is, in most of the region it rains every day or every other day, averaging about one half of the days, from four to six in the afternoon—some 180 days a year. . . .

This forest is inhabited by two kinds of people, Negroes and pygmies, who maintain an almost symbiotic relationship, based on trade. A Negro village may own approximately 100 square miles of forest territory. In this territory are the Negro village and the pygmy village. The former is permanent, in a clearing; the latter is temporary, under the forest trees. In maintaining their relationship, it is the pygmies' job to take in honey and meat, while the Negroes' obligation is to give them plantains. In addition, the pygmies may bring in a certain amount of wild baselli fruit in season, or roofing leaves, or rattan and fibers for net making; in return they may acquire ax blades, knives, and arrowheads from the Negroes.

There is no strict process of barter involved, and no accounting kept, other than through general observation. If the pygmies are stingy, their Negroes will hold back their bananas. If the Negroes are stingy, the pygmies will leave the territory and go to live with other pygmies serving other Negro hosts.

This relationship is interfamilial, between a pygmy family and a Negro family. It is a matter of close personal relations, inherited, on both sides, from father to son. These alliances may change from time to time, but when they do there are usually hard feelings; if a man's pygmy leaves him to serve another host it is a kind of divorce. In the old days, a frequent cause of inter-village warfare among the Negroes was the luring away of each other's pygmies.

Before the Belgians stopped inter-village and intertribal warfare, the most important single duty of the pygmy was to act as scout and intelligence agent in the forest. As soon as he became aware of a raiding party crossing the boundary of his host's territory he would hotfoot it to the village to give warning. This eternal vigilance on the part of the pygmy was probably of more value to his hosts than the meat that he brought in. Now that the need of this has ceased he is fulfilling only half of his contract; the Negro, who still provides plantains and manufactured objects, is still fulfilling all of his. Still both are satisfied. . . .

BASIC TOOLS. The keynote to the simple and specialized pygmy technology is the fact that they do not have to make any of their basic tools, but instead obtain effective iron cutting tools from their Negro hosts. This eliminates much work and the need for much skills in toolmaking, and provides them with more efficient instruments than they could possibly make for themselves at a food-gathering level of technology.

* From "The Pygmies of the Ituri Forest," in *A Reader in General Anthropology,* ed. Carleton S. Coon, pp. 322-34. Copyright 1948 by Holt, Rinehart & Winston, Inc. Reprinted by permission of Holt, Rinehart & Winston, Inc.

When a pygmy needs an ax he will beg one from his Negro host. Perhaps the Negro will give him a whole ax, haft and all. The blade is a triangular piece of iron, made locally by Negro smiths, and set in a solid wooden handle, adzed out of a larger piece of wood. The handle has a hole which has been burned through it from side to side with a hot iron. Through this hole goes the narrow end of the ax. This is essentially a Neolithic type of hafting.

Perhaps the Negro will give him only the ax head, without a haft. In this case the pygmy will cut down a thin sapling, or a tree branch, just the right thickness, and use it bark and all. He splits this with his knife, at one end. Then he wraps the split and the blade which he has thrust through it with twine or rattan. The pygmy will use the Negro-hafted ax on the ground, but if he is climbing a tree and needs an ax while up there, he will take along one of his own hafting by preference, because it is lighter. . . .

FIRE. The pygmies do not know how to make fire, nor do many of the Negroes with whom they are associated. Throughout all this countryside people keep fires going, and when one fire dies out the people will borrow it from each other. While on the march the pygmies carry glowing embers with them; they can keep a brand lighted for ten miles during a rainstorm. They do this by wrapping the burning ends in green leaves, and swinging it up and down; every two or three minutes they uncover it a bit and blow on it. At night these brands serve as torches. The Negroes have special wood which they use for torches but the pygmies do not. Their firewood is always fallen wood, and therefore always somewhat rotten and punky. . . .

Hunting is the principal occupation of the pygmies; it is their principal reason for being able to maintain their relationship with their Negro hosts. Although between themselves the pygmies have little division of labor, in another sense they are all specialists in hunting, and the division of labor is between them and the Negroes. In this sense the pygmies form an ethnic caste, a genetically and occupationally segregated segment of a larger economic entity.

This does not mean that the Negro does no hunting. However, the pygmy spends all of his time hunting, the Negro only a portion of his. The pygmy depends largely on his ability to move noiselessly and swiftly about the forest, and to climb trees. The Negro depends on his greater patience and mechanical ingenuity, for he hunts largely by means of elaborate traps, deadfalls, pits, weighted spears dangled over elephant paths, and other deadly devices. The pygmy could never be induced to dig a pit; it is too much work, takes too long, and takes too much concentration and persistence. Nor do they ever use traps. . . .

BOW AND ARROW HUNTING. In bow and arrow hunting, the pygmy relies not on his endurance but on his ability to move through the forest silently; that is his greatest skill and greatest asset. He can track an antelope to a thicket where it has lain down to sleep, and shoot it from five yards' distance before it wakes up. He shoots machine-gun style; he will pump five arrows in rapid sequence in the antelope's direction, and probably but one will hit him. The pygmy can do just as well by leaping on the animal barehanded, and either strangle it or kill it with a knife, and he often does this.

In his quiver the pygmy usually carries two kinds of arrows, the first with iron tips, which he generally uses on the larger, antelope-size, animals, and wooden-tipped ones which are poisoned, and which he uses for monkeys. He rarely shoots a monkey with an iron-tipped arrow, through fear of losing it. Each man makes his own poison as well as his own darts. The plants from which the poison is made are well known, and there is neither ritual nor mystery attached to the process. The vital plant is a strophanthus; they will mix other plants with it, but they know which one does the trick.

The strophanthus poison is a heart stimulant. Its action is not immediate. The monkey runs along a bit, grows weaker, and urinates. The pygmies watch for this, for the moment of urinating is the fatal one. If the monkey is out on a limb where there are no other branches, he will fall off; if he is within reach of a lateral branch or one rising upward, he will clutch it, and the hunter will be obliged to climb the tree if he wants the monkey. . . .

GOVERNMENT.   There are no chiefs, councils, or any other formal governing bodies in a pygmy camp. In making any decisions concerning the whole camp, two factors are involved. The first of these is respect for older people.

A pygmy will always, in addressing a man of an older age group in any formal situation, call him "senior"; he will listen respectfully to an older man and will always obey any reasonable orders he may give. If a younger man shows disrespect, the other members of the camp will gang up on him and berate him. This respect for age, and for the opinions of wise old men, is the basis of pygmy government.

Secondly, while the opinions of most of the old men are respected, every man in the camp is entitled to state his own views on any subject. Thus, during the evening talking time, the pygmies will discuss whether to move camp, where to move it, and why; or whether to go nut hunting, and where to hunt. The discussion has no leader and may go on for several evenings. Finally the men who are shouting out different opinions will come to an agreement and the decision will be acted upon.

In general it is the older and more experienced men who make the decision, but as some of the old men are considered eccentrics and freaks, little attention is paid to them. Rather, it is an oligarchy of the more respected among the old men, a body with no formal membership or specific composition. In their decisions the pungent remarks of the women also have a considerable influence.

Chapter Nineteen

Americas and Australia

61   Aztec Civilization of Mexico

In Australia, all the aborigines were still at the food-gathering stage when the Europeans arrived in the late eighteenth century. This is a prime example of the effect of complete and prolonged geographic isolation, this island continent being the home of archaic plants such as the eucalyptus, archaic animals such as the monotremes and marsupials, and archaic humans—the aborigines. The paleolithic culture of these aborigines is described in Reading 5, "Culture of the Food Gatherers."

In the Americas, by contrast, there was great diversity in the levels of development attained by the various Indian peoples. Most advanced were the Aztecs and Mayas of Mesoamerica and the Incas of Peru. The nature of the Aztec civilization is described below by Bernal Díaz, a conquistador who accompanied Cortez in the conquest of Mexico. Bernal Díaz was a gifted and objective observer, describing with color and accuracy the religion and institutions of the Aztecs, their palaces, temples, and markets, and the character of their leader Montezuma.*

When it was announced to Cortes that Motecusuma himself was approaching, he alighted from his horse and advanced to meet him. Many compliments were now passed on both sides. Motecusuma bid Cortes welcome, who, through Marina, said, in return, he hoped his majesty was in good health. If I still remember rightly, Cortes, who had Marina next to him, wished to concede the place of honor to the monarch, who, however, would not accept of it, but conceded it to Cortes, who now brought forth a necklace of precious stones, of the most beauti-

---

* J. I. Lockhart, trans., *The Memoirs of the Conquistador Bernal Díaz de Castillo* (London: J. Hatchard, 1844), I, 220-23, 228-41.

ful colours and shapes, strung upon gold wire, and perfumed with musk, which he hung about the neck of Motecusuma. Our commander was then going to embrace him, but the grandees by whom he was surrounded held back his arms, as they considered it improper. Our general then desired Marina to tell the monarch how exceedingly he congratulated himself upon his good fortune of having seen such a powerful monarch face to face, and of the honour he had done us by coming out to meet us himself. To all this Motecusuma answered in very appropriate terms, and ordered his two nephews, the princes of Tetzuco and Cohohuacan, to conduct us to our quarters. He himself returned to the city, accompanied by his two other relatives, the princes of Cuitlahuac and Tlacupa, with the other grandees of his numerous suite. As they passed by, we perceived how all those who composed his majesty's retinue held their heads bent forward, no one daring to lift up his eyes in his presence; and altogether what deep veneration was paid him.

The road before us now became less crowded, and yet who would have been able to count the vast numbers of men, women, and children who filled the streets, crowded the balconies, and the canoes in the canals, merely to gaze upon us? . . .

We were quartered in a large building where there was room enough for us all, and which had been occupied by Axayacatl, father of Motecusuma, during his life-time. Here the latter had likewise a secret room full of treasures, and where the gold he had inherited from his father was hid, which he had never touched up to this moment. Near this building there were temples and Mexican idols, and this place had been purposely selected for us because we were termed teules, or were thought to be such, and that we might dwell among the latter as among our equals. The apartments and halls were very spacious, and those set apart for our general were furnished with carpets. There were separate beds for each of us, which could not have been better fitted up for a gentleman of the first rank. Every place was swept clean, and the walls had been newly plastered and decorated.

When we had arrived in the great court-yard adjoining this palace, Motecusuma came up to Cortes, and, taking him by the hand, conducted him himself into the apartments where he was to lodge, which had been beautifully decorated after the fashion of the country. He then hung about his neck a chaste necklace of gold, most curiously worked with figures all representing crabs. The Mexican grandees were greatly astonished at all these uncommon favours which their monarch bestowed upon our general.

Cortes returned the monarch many thanks for so much kindness, and the latter took leave of him with these words: "Malinche, you and your brothers must now do as if you were at home, and take some rest after the fatigues of the journey," then returned to his own palace, which was close at hand.

We allotted the apartments according to the several companies, placed our cannon in an advantageous position, and made such arrangements that our cavalry, as well as the infantry, might be ready at a moment's notice. We then sat down to a plentiful repast, which had been previously spread out for us, and made a sumptuous meal.

This our bold and memorable entry into the large city of Temixtitlan, Mexico took place on the 8th of November, 1519. Praise be to the Lord Jesus Christ for all this. . . .

The mighty Motecusuma may have been about this time in the fortieth year of his age. He was tall of stature, of slender make, and rather thin, but the symmetry of his body was beautiful. His complexion was not very brown, merely approaching to that of the inhabitants in general. The hair of his head was not very long, excepting where it hung thickly down over his ears, which were quite hidden by it. His black beard, though thin, looked handsome. His countenance was rather of an elongated form, but cheerful; and his fine eyes had the expression of love or severity, at the proper moments. He was particularly clean in his person, and took a bath every evening. Besides a number of concubines, who were all daughters of persons of rank and quality, he had two lawful wives of royal extraction, whom, however, he visited secretly without any one daring to observe it, save his most confidential servants. He was perfectly innocent of any unnatural crimes. The dress he had on one day was not worn again until four days had elapsed. In the halls adjoining his own private apartments there was always a guard of 2000 men of quality, in waiting: with whom, however, he never held any conversation unless to give them orders or to receive some intelligence from them. Whenever for this purpose they entered his apartment, they had first to take off their rich costumes and put on meaner garments, though these were always neat and clean; and were only allowed to enter into his presence barefooted, with eyes cast down. No person durst look at him full in the face, and during the three prostrations which they were obliged to make before they could approach him, they pronounced these words: "Lord! my Lord! sublime Lord!" Everything that was communicated to him was to be said in few words, the eyes of the speaker being constantly cast down, and on leaving the monarch's presence he walked backwards out of the room. I also remarked that even princes and other great personages who come to Mexico respecting law-suits, or on other business from the interior of the country, always took off their shoes and changed their whole dress for one of a meaner appearance when they entered his palace. Neither were they allowed to enter the palace straightway, but had to show themselves for a considerable time outside the doors; as it would have been considered want of respect to the monarch if this had been omitted.

Above 300 kinds of dishes were served up for Motecusuma's dinner from his kitchen, underneath which were placed pans of porcelain filled with fire, to keep them warm. Three hundred dishes of various kinds were served up for him alone, and above 1000 for the persons in waiting. He sometimes, but very seldom, accompanied by the chief officers of his household, ordered the dinner himself, and desired that the best dishes and various kinds of birds should be called over to him. We were told that the flesh of young children as a very dainty bit, were also set before him sometimes by way of a relish. Whether there was any truth in this we could not possibly discover; on account of the great variety of dishes, consisting in fowls, turkeys, pheasants, partridges, quails, tame and wild geese, venison, musk swine, pigeons, hares, rabbits, and of numerous other birds and beasts; besides which there were various other kinds of provisions, indeed it would have been no easy task to call them all over by name.

. . . . .

I had almost forgotten to mention, that during dinner-time, two other young women of great beauty brought the monarch small cakes, as white as snow, made of eggs and other very nourishing ingredients, on plates covered with clean napkins; also a kind of long-shaped bread, likewise made of very substantial things, and some pachol, which is a kind of wafer-cake. They then presented him with three beautifully painted and gilt tubes, which were filled with liquid amber, and a herb called by the Indians tabaco. After the dinner had been cleared away and the singing and dancing done, one of these tubes was lighted, and the monarch took

340

the smoke into his mouth, and after he had done this a short time, he fell asleep.

About this time a celebrated cazique, whom we called Tapia, was Motecusuma's chief steward: he kept an account of the whole of Motecusuma's revenue, in large books of paper which the Mexicans call *Amatl*. A whole house was filled with such large books of accounts.

Motecusuma had also two arsenals filled with arms of every description, of which many were ornamented with gold and precious stones. These arms consisted in shields of different sizes, sabres, and a species of broadsword, which is wielded with both hands, the edge furnished with flint stones, so extremely sharp that they cut much better than our Spanish swords: further, lances of greater length than ours, with spikes at their end, full one fathom in length, likewise furnished with several sharp flint stones. The pikes are so very sharp and hard that they will pierce the strongest shield, and cut like a razor; so that the Mexicans even shave themselves with these stones. Then there were excellent bows and arrows, pikes with single and double points, and the proper thongs to throw them with; slings with round stones purposely made for them; also a species of large shield, so ingeniously constructed that it could be rolled up when not wanted: they are only unrolled on the field of battle, and completely cover the whole body from the head to the feet. Further, we saw here a great variety of cuirasses made of quilted cotton, which were outwardly adorned with soft feathers of different colours, and looked like uniforms. . . .

I will now, however, turn to another subject, and rather acquaint my readers with the skilful arts practised among the Mexicans: among which I will first mention the sculptors, and the gold and silversmiths, who were clever in working and smelting gold, and would have astonished the most celebrated of our Spanish goldsmiths: the number of these was very great, and the most skilful lived at a place called Ezcapuzalco, about four miles from Mexico. After these came the very skilful masters in cutting and polishing precious stones, and the calchihuis, which resemble the emerald. Then follow the great masters in painting, and decorators in feathers, and the wonderful sculptors. Even at this day there are living in Mexico three Indian artists, named Marcos de Aguino, Juan de la Cruz, and El Crespello, who have severally reached to such great proficiency in the art of painting and sculpture, that they may be compared to an Apelles, or our contemporaries Michael Angelo and Berruguete. . . .

The powerful Motecusuma had also a number of dancers and clowns: some danced in stilts, tumbled, and performed a variety of other antics for the monarch's entertainment: a whole quarter of the city was inhabited by these performers, and their only occupation consisted in such like performances. Last, Motecusuma had in his service great numbers of stone-cutters, masons, and carpenters, who were solely employed in the royal palaces. Above all, I must not forget to mention here his gardens for the culture of flowers, trees, and vegetables, of which there were various kinds. In these gardens were also numerous baths, wells, basins, and ponds full of limpid water, which regularly ebbed and flowed. All this was enlivened by endless varieties of small birds, which sang among the trees. Also the plantations of medical plants and vegetables are well worthy of our notice: these were kept in proper order by a large body of gardeners. All the baths, wells, ponds, and buildings were substantially constructed of stonework, as also the theatres where the singers and dancers performed. There were upon the whole so many remarkable things for my observation in these gardens and throughout the whole town, that I can scarcely find words to express the astonishment I felt at the pomp and splendour of the Mexican monarch. . . .

We had already been four days in the city of Mexico, and neither our commander nor any of us had, during that time, left our quarters, excepting to visit the gardens and buildings adjoining the palace. Cortes now, therefore, determined to view the city, and visit the great market, and the chief temple of Huitzilopochtli. . . . The moment we arrived in this immense market, we were perfectly astonished at the vast numbers of people, the profusion of merchandise which was there exposed for sale, and at the good police and order that reigned throughout. The grandees who accompanied us drew our attention to the smallest circumstance, and gave us full explanation of all we saw. Every species of merchandise had a separate spot for its sale. We first of all visited those divisions of the market appropriated for the sale of gold and silver wares, of jewels, of cloths interwomen with feathers, and of other manufactured goods; besides slaves of both sexes. This slave market was upon as great a scale as the Portuguese market for negro slaves at Guinea. To prevent these from running away, they were fastened with halters about their neck, though some were allowed to walk at large. Next to these came the dealers in coarser wares—cotton, twisted, thread, and cacao. In short, every species of goods which New Spain produces were here to be found; and everything put me in mind of my native town Medino del Campo during fair time, where every merchandise has a separate street assigned for its sale. In one place were sold the stuffs manufactured of nequen; ropes, and sandals; in another place, the sweet maguey root, ready cooked, and various other things made from this plant. In another division of the market were exposed the skins of tigers, lions, jackals, otters, red deer, wild cats, and of other beasts of prey, some of which were tanned. In another place were sold beans and sage, with other herbs and vegetables. A particular market was assigned for the merchants in fowls, turkeys, ducks, rabbits, hares, deer, and dogs; also for fruit-sellers, pastry-cooks, and tripe-sellers. Not far from these were exposed all manner of earthenware, from the large earthen cauldron to the smallest pitchers. Then came the dealers in honey and honey-cakes, and other sweetmeats. Next to these, the timber-merchants, furniture-dealers, with their stores of tables, benches, cradles, and all sorts of wooden implements, all separately arranged. What can I further add? If I am to note everything down, I must also mention human excrements, which were exposed for sale in canoes lying in the canals near this square, and is used for the tanning of leather; for, according to the assurances of the Mexicans, it it impossible to tan well without it. I can easily imagine that many of my readers will laugh at this; however, what I have stated is a fact, and, as further proof of this, I must acquaint the reader that along every road accommodations were built of reeds, straw, or grass, by which those who made use of them were hidden from the view of the passers-by, so that great care was taken that none of the last mentioned treasures should be lost. But why should I so minutely detail every article exposed for sale in this great market? If I had to enumerate everything singly, I should not so easily get to the end. And yet I have not mentioned the paper, which in this country is called amatl; the tubes filled with liquid amber and tobacco; the various sweet-scented salves, and similar things; nor the various seeds which were exposed for sale in the porticoes of this market, nor the medicinal herbs.

In this market-place there were also courts of justice, to which three judges and several constables were appointed, who inspected the goods exposed for sale. I had almost forgotten to mention the salt, and those who made the flint knives; also the fish, and a species of bread made of a kind of mud or slime collected from the surface of this lake, and eaten in that form, and has a similar taste to our cheese. Further, instruments of brass, copper, and tin; cups, and painted pitchers of wood; indeed, I wish I had completed the enumeration of all this profusion of merchandize. The variety was so great that it would occupy more space than I can well spare to note them down in; besides which, the market was so crowded with people, and the thronging so excessive in the porticoes, that it was quite impossible to see all in one day. . . .

On quitting the market, we entered the spacious yards which surrounded the chief temple. These appeared to encompass more ground than the market-place at Salamanca, and were surrounded by a double wall, constructed of stone and lime: these yards were paved with large white flag-stones, extremely smooth; and where these were wanting, a kind of brown plaster had been used instead, and all was kept so very clean that there was not the smallest particle of dust or straw to be seen anywhere.

Before we mounted the steps of the great temple, Motecusuma, who was sacrificing on the top to his idols, sent six papas and two of his principal officers to conduct Cortes up the steps. There were 114 steps to the summit. . . . Indeed, this infernal temple, from its great height, commanded a view of the whole surrounding neighbourhood. From this place we could likewise see the three causeways which led into Mexico,—that from Iztapalapan, by which we had entered the city four days ago; that from Tlacupa, along which we took our flight eight months after, when we were beaten out of the city by the new monarch Cuitlahuatzin; the third was that of Tepeaquilla. We also observed the aqueduct which ran from Chapultepec, and provided the whole town with sweet water. We could also distinctly see the bridges across the openings, by which these causeways were intersected, and through which the waters of the lake ebbed and flowed. The lake itself was crowded with canoes, which were bringing provisions, manufactures, and other merchandize to the city. From here we also discovered that the only communication of the houses in this city, and of all the other towns built in the lake, was by means of drawbridges or canoes. In all these towns the beautiful white plastered temples rose above the smaller ones, like so many towers and castles in our Spanish towns, and this, it may be imagined, was a splendid sight.

After we had sufficiently gazed upon this magnificent picture, we again turned our eyes toward the great market, and beheld the vast numbers of buyers and sellers who thronged there. The bustle and noise occasioned by this multitude of human beings was so great that it could be heard at a distance of more than four miles. Some of our men, who had been at Constantinople and Rome, and travelled through the whole of Italy, said that they never had seen a marketplace of such large dimensions, or which was so well regulated, or so crowded with people as this one at Mexico.

On this occasion Cortes said to father Olmedo, who had accompanied us: "I have just been thinking that we should take this opportunity, and apply to Montecusuma for permission to build a church here."

To which father Olmedo replied, that it would, no doubt, be an excellent thing if the monarch would grant this; but that it would be acting overhasty to make a proposition of that nature to him now, whose consent would not easily be gained at any time.

Cortes then turned to Motecusuma, and said to him, by means of our interpretress, Doña Marina: "Your majesty is, indeed, a great monarch, and you merit to be still greater! It has been a real delight to us to view all your cities. I have now one favour to beg of you, that you would allow us to see your gods and teules."

To which Motecusuma answered, that he must first consult the chief papas, to whom he then addressed a few words. Upon this, we were led into a kind of small tower, with one room, in which we saw two basements resembling altars, decked with coverings of extreme beauty. On each of these basements stood a gigantic, fat-looking figure, of which the one on the right hand represented the god of war Huitzilopochtli. This idol had a very broad face, with distorted and furious-looking eyes, and was covered all over with jewels, gold, and pearls, which were stuck to it by means of a species of paste, which, in this country, is prepared from a certain root. Large serpents, likewise, covered with gold and precious stones, wound round the body of this monster, which held in one hand a bow, and in the other a bunch of arrows. Another small idol which stood by its side, representing its page, carried this monster's short spear, and its golden shield studded with precious stones. Around Huitzilopochtli's neck were figures representing human faces and hearts made of gold and silver, and decorated with blue stones. In front of him stood several perfuming pans with copal, the incense of the country; also the hearts of three Indians, who had that day been slaughtered, were now consuming before him as a burnt-offering. Every wall of this chapel and the whole floor had become almost black with human blood, and the stench was abominable.

. . . . .

Respecting the abominable human sacrifices of these people, the following was communicated to us: The breast of the unhappy victim destined to be sacrificed was ripped open with a knife made of sharp flint; the throbbing heart was then torn out, and immediately offered to the idol-god in whose honour the sacrifice had been instituted. After this, the head, arms, and legs were cut off and eaten at their banquets, with the exception of the head, which was saved, and hung to a beam appropriated for that purpose. No other part of the body was eaten, but the remainder was thrown to the beasts which were kept in those abominable dens, in which there were also vipers and other poisonous serpents, and, among the latter in particular, a species at the end of whose tail there was a kind of rattle. This last mentioned serpent, which is the most dangerous, was kept in a cabin of a diversified form, in which a quantity of feathers had been strewed: here it laid its eggs, and it was fed with the flesh of dogs and of human beings who had been sacrificed. We were positively told that, after we had been beaten out of the city of Mexico, and had lost 850 of our men, these horrible beasts were fed for many successive days with the bodies of our unfortunate countrymen. Indeed, when all the tigers and lions roared together, with the howlings of the jackals and foxes, and hissing of the serpents, it was quite fearful, and you could not suppose otherwise than that you were in hell.

. . . . .

Our commander here said smilingly, to Motecusuma: "I cannot imagine that such a powerful and wise monarch as you are, should not have yourself discovered by this time that these idols are not divinities, but evil spirits, called devils. In order that you may be convinced of this, and that your papas may satisfy themselves of this truth, allow me to erect a cross on the summit of this temple; and, in the chapel, where stand your Huitzilopochtli and Tetzcatlipuca, give us a small space that I may place there the image of the holy Virgin; then you will see what terror will seize these idols by which you have been so long deluded."

Motecusuma knew what the image of the Virgin Mary was, yet he was very much displeased with Cortes' offer, and replied, in presence of two papas, whose anger was not less conspicuous, "Malinche, could I have conjectured that you would have used such reviling language as you have just done, I would certainly not have shown you my gods. In our eyes these are good divinities: they preserve our lives, give us nourishment, water, and good harvests, healthy and growing weather, and victory whenever we pray to them for it. Therefore we offer up our prayers to them, and make them sacrifices. I earnestly beg of you not to say another word to insult the profound veneration in which we hold these gods."

As soon as Cortes heard these words and perceived the great excitement under which they were pronounced, he said nothing in return, but merely remarked to the monarch with a cheerful smile: "It is time for us both to depart hence." To which Motecusuma answered, that he would not detain him any longer, but he himself was now obliged to stay some time to atone to his gods by prayer and sacrifice for having committed *gratlatlacol,* by allowing us to ascend the great temple, and thereby occasioning the affronts which we had offered them.

INDIAN AGRICULTURISTS OF VIRGINIA 62

At the next level below that of the great civilizations of Mesoamerica and Peru were the farming cultures of the eastern United States and most of South America, except for the Argentine plains. Typical of this group were the Indians of Virginia, described below by Captain John Smith, founder of Jamestown in 1607. *

Of their planted Fruits in Virginia, and how they use them. . . . The greatest labour they take is in planting their corn, for the country naturally is overgrown with wood. To prepare the ground, they bruise the bark of the trees near the root, then do they scorch the roots with fire that they grow no more. The next year with a crooked piece of wood they beat up the weeds by the roots, and in that mould they plant their corn. Their manner is this. They make a hole in the earth with a stick, and into it they put four grains of wheat and two of beans. These holes they make four feet one from another. Their women and children do continually keep it weeding, and when it is grown middle high, they hill it about like a hop-yard.

In April they begin to plant, but their chief plantation is in May, and so they continue till the midst of June. What they plant in April they reap in August, for May in September, for June in October. Every stalk of their corn commonly beareth two ears, some three, seldom any four, many but one, and some none. Every ear ordinarily hath between two hundred and five hundred grains. The stalk being green hath a sweet juice in it, somewhat like a sugar cane, which is the cause that when they gather their corn green, they suck the stalks: for as we gather green peas, so do they their corn being green, which excelleth their old.

* Captain John Smith, "The General History of Virginia, New England, and the Summer Isles," in J. Pinkerton, *Voyages and Travels* (London, 1812), XIII, 32-43.

They plant also peas they call assentamens, which are the same they call in Italy fagioli. Their beans are the same the Turks call garnanses; but these they much esteem for dainties.

Their corn they roast in the ear green, and bruising it in a mortar of wood with a polt, lap it in rolls in the leaves of their corn, and so boil it for a dainty. They also reserve that corn late planted that will not ripe, by roasting it in hot ashes, the heat thereof drying it. In winter they esteem it being boiled with beans for a rare dish, they call pausarowmena. . . .

In May also amongst their corn they plant pumpions, and a fruit like unto a muskmelon, but less and worse, which they call macocks. These increase exceedingly, and ripen in the beginning of July, and continue until September. They plant also maracocks, a wild fruit like a lemon, which also increase infinitely. They begin to ripen in September, and continue till the end of October. When all their fruits be gathered, little else they plant, and this is done by their women and children; neither doth this long suffice them, for near three parts of the year they only observe times and seasons, and live of what the country naturally affordeth from hand to mouth, &c. . . .

Of the natural Inhabitants of Virginia. The land is not populous, for the men be few; their far greater number is of women and children. Within sixty miles of James Town, there are about some five thousand people, but of able men fit for their wars scarce fifteen hundred. To nourish so many together they have yet no means, because they make so small a benefit of their land, be it never so fertile. . . . Each household knoweth their own lands and gardens, and most live of their own labour. For their apparel, they are sometime covered with the skins of wild beasts, which in winter are dressed with the hair, but in summer without. . . .

Their buildings and habitations are for the most part by the rivers, or not far distant from some fresh spring; their houses are built like our arbours, of small young springs bowed and tied, and so close covered with mats, or the barks of trees very handsomely, that notwithstanding either wind, rain, or weather, they are as warm as stoves, but very smoky, yet at the top of the house there is a hole made for the smoke to go into right over the fire.

Against the fire they lie on little hurdles of reeds covered with a mat, borne from the ground a foot and more by a hurdle of wood, on these round about the house they lie heads and points one by the other against the fire, some covered with mats, some with skins, and some stark naked lie on the ground, from six to twenty in a house. Their houses are in the midst of their fields or gardens, which are small plots of ground, some twenty acres, some forty, some one hundred, some two hundred, some more, some less. In some places from two to fifty of those houses together, or but a little separated by groves of trees. Near their habitations is little small wood or old trees on the ground by reason of their burning of them for fire, so that a man may gallop a horse amongst these woods any way, but where the creeks or rivers shall hinder. . . .

Their fire they kindle presently by chafing a dry pointed stick in a hole of a little square piece of wood, that firing itself, will to fire moss, leaves, or any such like dry thing that will quickly burn. In March and April they live much upon their fishing wires, and feed on fish, turkies, and squirrels. In May and June they plant their fields, and live most of acorns, walnuts, and fish. But to amend their diet, some disperse themselves in small companies, and live upon fish, beasts, crabs, oysters, land-tortoises, strawberries, mulberries, and such like. In June, July, and August, they feed upon the roots of tocknough berries, fish, and green wheat. It is strange to see how their bodies alter with their diet, even as the deer and wild beasts they seem fat and lean, strong and weak. Powhatan, their great king, and some others, that are provident, roast their fish and flesh upon hurdles as before is expressed, and keep it till scarce times. . . .

In their hunting and fishing they take extreme pains, yet in being their ordinary exercise from their infancy, they esteem it a pleasure, and are very proud to be expert therein; and by their continual ranging and travel, they know all the advantages and places most frequented with deer, beasts, fish, fowl, roots, and berries. At their huntings they leave their habitations, and reduce themselves into companies, as the Tartars do, and go to the most desert places with their families, where they spend their time in hunting and fowling up towards the mountains, by the heads of their rivers, where there is plenty of game; for betwixt the rivers the grounds are so narrow, that little cometh here which they devour not: it is a marvel they can so directly pass these deserts, some three or four days journey, without habitation. Their hunting-houses are like unto arbours covered with mats; these their women bear after them, with corn, acorns, mortars, and all bag and baggage they use. When they come to the place of exercise, every man doth his best to shew his dexterity, for by their excelling in those qualities they get their wives. Forty yards will they shoot level, or very near the mark, and one hundred and twenty is their best at random. At their huntings in the deserts they are commonly two or three hundred together. Having found the deer, they environ them with many fires, and betwixt the fires they place themselves, and some take their stands in the midst. The deer being thus frightened by the fires and their voices, they chase them so long within that circle, that many times they kill six, eight, ten, or fifteen at a hunting. They use also to drive them into some narrow point of land, when they find that advantage, and so force them into the river, where, with their boats, they have ambuscadoes to kill them. . . .

Of Their Religion. There is yet in Virginia no place discovered to be so savage in which they have not a religion, deer, and bow and arrows. All things that are able to do them hurt beyond their prevention, they adore with their kind of divine worship; as the fire, water, lightning, thunder, our ordnance, pieces, horses, &c. But their chief god they worship is the devil. Him they call Okee, and serve him more of fear than love. They say they have conference with him, and fashion themselves as near to his shape as they can imagine. In their temples they have his image evil favouredly carved, and then painted and adorned with chains of copper, and beads, and covered with a skin in such manner as the deformities may well suit with such a god. By him is commonly the sepulchre of their kings. Their bodies are first bowelled, then dried upon hurdles till they be very dry, and so about the most of their joints and neck they hang bracelets, or chains of copper, pearl, and such like, as they use to wear, their inwards they stuff with copper beads, hatchets, and such trash. Then lap they them very carefully in white skins, and so roll them in mats for their winding sheets. And in the tomb which is an arch made of mats, they lay them orderly. What remaineth of this kind of wealth their kings have, they set at their feet in baskets. These temples and bodies are kept by their priests.

For their ordinary burials they dig a deep hole in the earth with sharp stakes, and the corpse being lapped in skins and mats with their jewels, they lay them upon sticks in the ground, and so cover them with earth. The burial ended, the women, being painted all their faces with black coal and oil, do sit twenty-four hours in the houses mourning and lamenting by turns, with such yelling and howling, as many express their great passions. . . .

Upon the top of certain red sandy hills in the woods, there are three great houses filled with images of their kings and devils, and tombs of their predecessors. Those houses are near sixty feet in length, built harbour-wise, after their building. This place they count so holy as that but the priests and kings dare come into them; nor the savages dare not go up the river in boats by it, but they solemnly cast some piece of copper, white beads, or pocones into the river, for fear their Okee should be offended and revenged of them.

. . . . .

Of the Manner of the Virginians' Government. Although the country people be very barbarous, yet have they amongst them such government as that their magistrates for good commanding, and their people for due subjection and obeying, excel many places that would be counted very civil. The form of their commonwealth is a monarchical government, one as emperor, ruleth over many kings or governors. Their chief ruler is called Powhatan; but his proper name is Wahunsonacock. Some countries he hath which have been his ancestors, and came unto him by inheritance, as the country called Powhatan, Arrohateck, Appamatuck, Pamaunkee, Youghtanund, and Mattapanient. All the rest of his territories expressed in the map, they report, have been his several conquests. In all his ancient inheritances he hath houses built after their manner, like arbours, some thirty, some forty yards long, and at every house provision for his entertainment, according to the time. At Werowcomoco, on the north side of the river Pamaunkee, was his residence, when I was delivered him prisoner, some fourteen miles from James Town, where, for the most part, he was resident; but at last he took so little pleasure in our near neighbourhood, that he retired himself to Orapakes, in the desert betwixt Chickahamanta and Youghtanund. He is of personage a tall-well-proportion man, with a sour look, his head somewhat grey, his beard so thin that it seemeth none at all, his age near sixty, of a very able and hardy body to endure any labour; about his person ordinarily attendeth a guard of forty or fifty of the tallest men his country doth afford. . . .

A mile from Orapakes, in a thicket of wood, he hath a house, in which he keepeth his kind of treasure, as skins, copper, pearl, and beads, which he storeth up against the time of his death and burial. Here also is his store of red paint, for ointment, bows and arrows, targets and clubs. This house is fifty or sixty yards in length, frequented only by priests. At the four corners of this house stand four images as sentinels, one of a dragon, another a bear, the third like a leopard, and the fourth like a giant-like man, all made evil favouredly, according to their best workmanship.

. . . . .

He nor any of his people understand any letters, whereby to write or read, only the laws whereby he ruleth is custom. Yet, when he listeth, his will is a law, and must be obeyed; not only as a king, but as half a god, they esteem him.

348

The most retarded of the American Indians were the food gatherers of Canada, western United States, and the Argentine plains. The Mormon pioneer Major Howard Egan has left a vivid and detailed account of how the Indians of the Southwest adapted to their arid environment.*

INDIAN CRICKET DRIVE.   I was on a three days' horseback trip in the wilderness, and had for a companion the Indian called "Egan Jack," a trusty, intelligent buck of about thirty years of age. We were on a prospecting or exploring trip to the Northwest of Deep Creek, or Ibapah as the Indians called it. At one place, as we came out of a canyon onto the bench land, we saw quite a number of Indians that were quite busy, some digging trenches and some gathering arms full of the tall wheat grass that grew on the flat in the bottom of the canyon, I asked Jack what they were doing. He said, "Catching crickets for bread." "Well, we will go and see how they do it." We went, and saw that they had dug quite a number of trenches about a foot wide and a foot deep and about thirty or forty feet long, and around like a new moon with the horns uphill.

They had been a number of days at the work, but were now ready for their cricket drive, having five or six of the trenches strung across the bench, the end of each trench joined, or was very close to the end of another. They covered these with a thin layer of stiff wheat grass straw . . . but I thought they were making a mistake, for the crickets could crawl over the ditch on it, but I must wait and see.

As it was getting the hottest time of the day, and therefore the best time for the drive, they were soon ready, . . . Well, there was a few crickets scattered all around, but were more of them above the trenches and near the foothills. . . .

These trenches ran in a north and south direction, the land sloping to the west. The Indians, men, women and children, divided into two parties, one going to the north end and the other to the south end, all carrying a bunch of grass in each hand. They went single file towards the foothills, and making the distance between the parties wider than the length of the trenches. When they had gone what they thought far enough, as judged by the scarcity of grass left by the black insects, the party closed in and, walking back and forth swinging their grass bunches they gradually worked down toward the trenches.

We followed them on horseback and I noticed that there were but very few crickets left behind. As they went down, the line of crickets grew thicker and thicker till the ground ahead of the drivers was as black as coal with the excited, tumbling mass of crickets.

A cricket when disturbed can jump about one foot down hill at a jump and but half that distance up hill, but will never jump up hill if it has any show to avoid it. Well, as we neared the trenches I noticed the Indians were going down slower. Jack said this was to give the crickets time to crawl through the grass into the trenches.

When all had been driven in the Indians set fire to the grass they had in their hands and scattered it along on top of that they had over the trenches, causing a big blaze and smoke, which soon left the crickets powerless to crawl out, if any were left alive when the grass had all burned up, which did not take many minutes.

---

* Egan, Major Howard R., *Pioneering the West, 1846 to 1878* (Salt Lake City: Skelton Publishing Co., 1917), pp. 230-47.

I rode along the line and in some places the trenches were over half full of the dead and legless crickets. I went down below the trenches and I venture to say there were not one out of a thousand crickets that passed those trenches.

They are a scary and excitable, but a clumsy insect, that hardly ever when excited land on their feet, but roll over, then turn their head down hill and jump again. If not molested they seldom ever jump, but travel by crawling. Now the bucks and children had done their part and were sitting around in groups. The squaws were busy gathering up the game.

. . . . .

Having seen enough there we rode on across a narrow valley, and in the foothills came to a large camp of Indians, the chief of whom I was well acquainted with, and we decided to stay all night with them, . . . We were also getting hungry. We had no provisions of our own, except a couple of rabbits I had killed on the way.

They treated us fine and we had a good time telling and hearing the news. Jack took one of the rabbits and put it to roast on the fire, the other he gave to the chief. When the rabbit was done to his liking, Jack asked the chief if he had any bread; he nodded and called in a low voice the name of his squaw, who came into the tent at once. When told to bring some bread she went out, but returned immediately with a cake of black bread about two inches thick and ten inches in diameter, which she handed to me. I thought it looked too black for pine nut bread, for the latter has a yellow cast and this was decidedly black. Holding the bread in one hand and pointing to it with the other, I asked her if there was pine nuts in it. "Yes," she said unconcernedly. "Is there crickets in it?" "Yes, yes," smilingly. "Sure."

. . . . .

A RABBIT DRIVE. One afternoon, while visiting the Indians, I heard them talking of rabbits and, asking them what it was all about, the chief said a rabbit hunt. I said I would like to go along to see how they done it. He seemed pleased at me taking so much interest and said, "Good! Come tomorrow before noon, as we want to start the drive about noon and it is quite a distance to the place. You had better come on horseback."

About the middle of the forenoon next day I was at their camp. Most of the hunters had already started. Going about three or four miles, we came to the place selected for the drive—a piece of sage and rabbit brush land about a mile in diameter. The party I was with stopped, when we saw a fire about a half mile to our right and soon another about the same distance to the left, and then we could see the smoke rising a mile ahead of us. My party soon had their torches at work and the drive was on.

Working all around the circle and towards the center was a continuous ring of fire and smoke, which was gradually closing in and the rabbits were being crowded together thicker and thicker. Each Indian, squaw and papoose had a stick about four feet long, the only weapon they carried. A small boy or girl was just as good as a man, and oh, the fun of it—all laughing and hollering and making as much noise as possible. The rabbits got so dazed by the fire, smoke and tumult that they simply could not run. They would jump a few jumps and sit up trying to see a way out. I saw dozens of them stop within reach of the sticks and many of them were picked up that had not been hit. When a rabbit was seen to pass out of the human ring, someone would follow him in the smoke and put his body in one of the piles of rabbits they had made as they proceeded towards the center, for they could not carry much of the game and do their work at the same time.

. . . . .

MOUNTAIN RAT, FOOD FOR INDIANS. On one of my days out I came across an old Indian going home with his day's catch of rats. He had a large sheet iron camp kettle nearly filled with them. They had all been caught the night before by dead falls, as we call them, which consists of two sticks about three and a half or four inches long fastened together at their centers by a string that will allow them to spread apart about four or five inches in the shape of the letter "H." One of these, with any convenient flat rock heavy enough to smash and kill a rat, is one dead fall. This Indian had over a hundred of the triggers that he hadn't used, but said he had set the most of them.

His plan was to go up one side of the canyon, setting the traps wherever he saw the sign of rats, and the same down the other side. The next day, taking the same route, gathering the catch and resetting the traps. The rats the Indian had were six to eight inches long, two and a half inches wide and half an inch thick. They were packed as close as he could pack them in the kettle and were quite heavy for the old man to pack to camp, so I carried them for him. At his camp was where I first saw the squaws making rabbit skin robes. This is how it was done:

They had a lot of twine, that had been made of some fiberous bark or grass, and a pile of rabbit skins that had been dried and then rubbed pliable. But it must have been done with care, for a rabbit skin is very tender. These squaws were not making a new robe, but patching up and making an old one larger. The robes are of length to reach from the neck to about the middle of the thighs, say about three or four feet long, and wide enough to reach around the body at the shoulders.

One of the squaws was twisting the strips of skin around a twine that was stretched to two stakes, placed a little past the length of the robe, and as she proceeded the other was following her up and tying that fur rope thus made and laid alongside the previous one close together at about every four inches. They worked back and fourth in this fashion till the skins were all used up. There was a strip about two feet wide of new robe attached to the old one. I examined it and found that the tie strings were placed in a straight line across the robe, with the ends of the ties left to attach more robe or to be used to tie the robe together as wanted.

When hung around the neck the person so clothed can stand in a hard rain or snow storm and not one drop of wet will pass through the robe. They are wind and rain proof and almost cold proof. There is no right or wrong side, as both sides are just the same—one solid piece of fur that will stand the wear of years, used as a mattress or bed covering or wind brake. In fact, they never completely wear out.

When the fur at any place gets worn off it is replaced with a few strands of new. This makes an old robe look striped and of different colors. The squaws while at work seemed as happy as a party of white women at a quilting and were talking and laughing just as fast. . . .

PINE-NUT HARVEST. Jack and I were taking a scouting trip high up in the Shell Creek range of mountains, when we came across an Indian who, with his squaw and children, were busily engaged gathering pine-nuts. The man had a long pole with a strong hook fastened to one end. He would reach up in the tree to the pine cones, hook the crook around the branch on which they hung and pull branch and all down, the squaw and children carrying them to a place and piling them up in a heap. When they had collected as many as they wanted that day, the buck had finished his part of the work and could pass the rest of the time sleeping or hunting squirrels just as he pleased.

The squaws and children gathered a little dry brush, which was thrown loosely over the pile of cones and set fire to. The cones are thickly covered all over with pitch, for this reason they make a hot fire, the squaw watching and stirring it up as needed to keep the nuts from burning, as all she wants is to burn the pitch off. When this is done she rakes them back from the fire as a man would do when drawing charcoal.

When the pitch was all burned off the burs, or cones, the squaw spreads a blanket down close to the pile, then taking up one cone at a time, would press them end ways between her hands, which opens the leaves, under which there were two nuts to every leaf. Then shaking the cone over the blanket the nuts would all fall out as clean as you please.

We stayed with them to see the finish, which was not so very long. When the nuts had all been cleaned from the cones they were put in a large basket that would hold over two bushels and was nearly full, the squaw carrying that on her back to a place where they were to be cached and left till wanted. These caches were placed all through the pine-nut grove to save carrying them too far and save time, for the harvest does not last long, for a heavy frost will cause the cones to open and the nuts drop to the ground, where the squirrels and coyotes feast on them.

. . . . .

HUNTING FOR WATER.   In traveling through Go-Shute [Go-siute—Ed.] Valley (later called Flower Lake Valley), we were getting very thirsty, having been traveling five or six hours from the last water hole and it being a dry, hot and sultry day I and the horses needed water. The nearest I knew of was about twelve miles distance and that not in the direction of our travel, and our one canteen being empty, I thought we would have to change our course to get water. I asked Jack, "How far to water this way," pointing the way I wanted to go. He said, "I do not know, maybe no water." "Well, are you thirsty?" "Yes." "Well then, think fast and locate water or Indian no better than white man."

We were about the middle of the valley, facing south-easterly, and were among the sand-dunes, which spread a few miles in width and many miles in length through the valley. We had not gone far after this talk when Jack said, "Wait," and pointing to some rat or gopher holes in the side of the sand-dunes, said, "They must have water, I see." Dismounting, he picked a place between the dunes and with his hands scraped off the loose sand to a depth of about six or eight inches to water. He then made the hole nearly a foot deeper and a foot wide, which quickly filled to the water level. Waiting for it to settle, we then tasted it and found it to be a little brackish, but still nice and cool and quite drinkable. Having drank what we wanted, filling the canteen, we let the horses have their turn. They got some, but soon caved the sand in and made the water so riley they would drink no more.

. . . . .

MAKING FIRE WITH A STICK.   On one of my trips with a comrade we camped for the night just before sundown and soon found out that we had no matches that were dry enough to light a fire with. That did not put us out much and we did not worry a bit, for we could soon make fire with our pistols, but just before we were ready to do it an Indian came up and squat down close to the little pile of wood we had collected.

Then the thought struck me that I would see if an Indian was always prepared to make a fire, so I said to him, "Make a good fire and I will give you something to eat." He jumped up and said, "Give me white fire stick." (Matches.) I told him, "No, they are all wet and no account, and Indian no good either if he could not make fire." He gave a grunt and proceeded to get busy.

He took a stick about eighteen inches long and the thickness of an arrow out of the quiver he carried his arrows in and another flat stick about six inches long, one-half inch thick and three-quarters to one inch wide, there being four or five counter-sunk holes in the flat piece about one-fourth inch deep. After rubbing some dry cedar bark with his hands till it was very fine, he placed the flat stick on the ground and one end of the long stick which was at one end a little smaller, and putting the largest end in one of the counter-sunk holes, placed his hands together around the top of the stick, which he made to turn around back and forth very fast. As he worked his hands this way, at the same time pressing down all he could, it caused his hands to work down on the stick and he had to place them at the top very often. In about twelve or fifteen minutes he had a few tiny sparks of fire he had made with the sticks, burning the fine ground bark.

After that it was easy, but when the fire was lighted Mr. Indian was in a very sweaty condition. . . .

Chapter Twenty

Epilogue:
the world on the eve
of Europe's expansion

64   Dawn of a New World Era

The fifteenth century witnessed the beginning of a new era in world history. Hitherto, this history had been essentially, though not exclusively, regional in scope. It is true that a Eurasian ecumene had gradually evolved, incipient during classical times and full-fledged during the medieval period. Yet relations between Eurasia and Africa remained restricted and tenuous because of formidable geographic barriers, both within Africa and between Africa and the outside world. And as for Australia and the Americas, their isolation had been complete since the distant period when immigrants had been able to cross over to these regions from Eurasia because of the lowered sea levels during the Ice Ages.

This traditional regional pattern of world relationships changed suddenly and dramatically when the Europeans expanded overseas in all directions, establishing for the first time direct contact among all continents. The nature and significance of this transition from regional to global history is the subject of this interpretative essay by the well-known historian Arnold J. Toynbee.*

. . . since about A.D. 1500 (to reckon in terms of our Western parochial era), mankind has been gathered into a single world-wide society. From the dawn of history to about that date, the earthly home of man had been divided into many isolated mansions; since about A.D. 1500, the human race has been brought under one roof. This has been accomplished, under God, by human action, and here we come to the really sensational point. The agent of this revolutionary change in the affairs of men might have been any one of the divers parochial societies that were

* A. J. Toynbee, *Civilization on Trial* (New York: Oxford University Press, 1948), pp. 64-71.

on the map when the revolution was put in hand, but the particular parochial society that has actually done the deed is the one that, of all of them, was the most unlikely candidate.

In an effort to jump clear of my native Western standing-ground and to look at this question from a less eccentric point of view, I have asked myself who was the most centrally placed and most intelligent observer that I could think of among notable non-Westerners who were alive at the moment when a few ships' companies of Western mariners embarked on the enterprise of unifying the world, and I have found my man in the Emperor Babur. Babur was a descendant, in the fifth generation, of Tamerlane, the Transoxanian conqueror who made the last attempt to unify the world by land operations from a continental centre. Within Babur's lifetime—A.D. 1483–1530—Columbus reached America by sea from Spain and da Gama India from Portugal. Babur started his career as prince of Farghana in the upper valley of the Jaxartes: a small country which had been the centre of the [ecumene] since the second century B.C. Babur invaded India overland twenty-one years after da Gama had arrived there by sea. Last but not least, Babur was a man-of-letters whose brilliant autobiography in his Turkish mother-tongue reveals a spirit of outstanding intelligence and perceptiveness.

What was Babur's horizon? To the east of Farghana it included both India and China, and to the west it extended to Babur's own distant kinsmen, the Ottoman Turks. Babur took lessons from the 'Osmanlis in military technique, and he admired them for their piety and prowess in extending the bounds of Islam. He refers to them as 'the Ghāzis of Rum': the happy warriors who had succeeded, where the primitive Muslim Arabs had signally failed, in conquering for Islam the homeland of Eastern Orthodox Christendom. I could not recollect any mention of Western Christendom in Babur's memoirs, and I have found none in the exhaustive geographical index of Mrs. Beveridge's magnificent English translation. Of course Babur was aware of the existence of the Franks, for he was a cultivated man and he knew his Islamic history. If he had had occasion to allude to them, he would probably have described them as ferocious but frustrated infidels living in a remote corner of the world at the extreme western tip of one of the many peninsulas of the Continent of Asia. About four hundred years before his time, he would have gone on to relate, these barbarians had made a demonic attempt to break out of their cramped and uninviting corner into the broader and richer domains of Rum and Dar-al-Islam. It had been a critical moment for the destinies of civilization, but the uncouth aggressors had been foiled by the genius of Saladin, and their military reverses had been capped by a crushing moral defeat when the Christians of Rum, faced with a choice between two alternative future masters, chose the side of the angels by opting for 'the Prophet's turban' in preference to 'the Pope's tiara,' and accepted the boon of an Ottoman Peace.

The arrival of Frankish ships in India in A.D. 1498, twenty-one years before Babur's own first descent upon India in A.D. 1519, seems to have escaped Babur's attention—unless his silence is to be explained not by ignorance of the event, but by a feeling that the wandering of these water-gypsies were unworthy of a historian's notice. So this allegedly intelligent Transoxanian man-of-letters and man-of-action was blind to the portent of the Portuguese circumnavigation of Africa? He failed to perceive that these ocean-faring Franks had turned the flank of Islam and taken her in the rear? Yes, I believe Babur would have been utterly astonished if he had been told that the empire which he was founding in India was soon to pass from his descendants to Frankish successors. He had no inkling of the change that was to come over the face of the world between his generation and ours. But this,

I submit, is not a reflection on Babur's intelligence; it is one more indication of the queerness of the major event in the history of the world in our time.

Since A.D. 1500 the map of the [ecumene] has indeed been transformed out of all recognition. Down to that date it was composed of a belt of civilizations girdling the Old World from the Japanese Isles on the north-east to the British Isles on the north-west: Japan, China, Indo-China, Indonesia, India, Dar-al-Islam, the Orthodox Christendom of Rum, and another Christendom in the West. Though this belt sagged down, in the middle, from the North Temperate Zone to the Equator and thus ran through a fairly wide range of climates and physical environments, the social structure and cultural character of these societies was singularly uniform. Each of them consisted of a mass of peasants, living and working under much the same conditions as their forefathers on the morrow of the invention of agriculture some six to eight thousand years back, and a small minority of rulers enjoying a monopoly of power, surplus wealth, leisure, knowledge, and skill which in turn enhanced their power. There had been one or two earlier generations of civilizations of the same type in the Old World. In A.D. 1500 some of these were still remembered, while others (since brought to light by modern Western archaeologists) had been forgotten. There were two of the same type in existence at this date in the New World, unknown to those of the Old World and barely known even to each other. The living civilizations of the Old World were in touch with each other, though not so closely as to be, or feel themselves to be, members of a single society.

Their contact, such as it was, down to A.D. 1500, had been established and maintained along two different lines of communication. There was a maritime line which will be familiar to latter-day Westerners as the Peninsular and Oriental Steamship Company's route to Kobe from Tilbury. In A.D. 1500, and indeed as recently as the time of a great-uncle of mine (a vivid memory of my childhood) who commanded one of the Honourable East India Company's passenger sailing ships and retired from the sea before the cutting of the Suez Canal without ever having served on board a steamer, this waterway through a chain of inland seas was broken by a portage between the Mediterranean and the Red Sea, with an alternative portage between the Mediterranean and the Persian Gulf. In the Mediterranean and Japanese sections of this maritime route, traffic had frequently been lively, and, from about 120 B.C. onwards, an infectious wave of maritime enterprise, set in motion by Greek mariners from Alexandria who found their way to Ceylon, had travelled on eastwards through Indonesia till it had carried Polynesian canoes to Easter Island. Yet, adventurous and romantic as these pre-Western seafarers were, the water-route that they opened up never came to be of more than secondary importance as a line of communication between the civilizations. The main line was provided by the chain of steppes and deserts that cut across the belt of civilizations from the Sahara to Mongolia.

For human purposes, the Steppe was an inland sea which, in virtue of happening to be dry, was of higher conductivity for human intercourse than the salt-water sea ever was before the close of the fifteenth century of the Christian era. This waterless sea had its dry-shod ships and its quayless ports. The steppe-galleons were camels, the steppe-galleys horses, and the steppe-ports 'caravan cities'—ports of call on oasis-islands and termini on the coasts where the sand-waves of 'the Desert' broke upon 'the Sown': Petra and Palmyra, Damascus and Ur, Tamerlane's Samarkand and the Chinese emporia at the gates of the Great Wall. Steppe-traversing horses, not ocean-traversing sailing ships, were the sovereign means of locomotion by which the separate civilizations of the world as it was before A.D. 1500 were linked together—to the slight extent to which they did maintain contact with each other.

In that world, as you see, Babur's Farghana was the central point, and the Turks were, in Babur's day, the central family of nations. A Turco-centric history of the world has been published in our lifetime by the latest in the series of the great Ottoman Turkish Westernizers, President Mustafa Kemal Atatürk. It was a brilliant device for restoring the *morale* of his fellow-countrymen, but it was a still more brilliant feat of genuine historical intuition; for, from the fourth century of the Christian era, when they pushed the last of their Indo-European-speaking predecessors off the Steppe, down to the seventeenth century, which witnessed the collapse of the Ottoman, the Safawi, and the Timurid Turkish dynasties in their respective domains of Rum, Iran, and India, the Turkish-speaking peoples really were the keystone of the Asiatic arch from which the pre-da Gaman belt of civilizations hung suspended. During those twelve hundred years, the overland link between the separate civilizations was commanded by Turkish steppe-power, and, from their central position in this pre-da Gaman world, the Turks rode out, conquering and to conquer, east and west and south and north: to Manchuria and Algeria, to the Ukraine and the Deccan.

But now we come to the great revolution: a technological revolution by which the West made its fortune, got the better of all the other living civilizations, and forcibly united them into a single society of literally world-wide range. The revolutionary Western invention was the substitution of the Ocean for the Steppe as the principal medium of world-communication. This use of the Ocean, first by sailing ships and then by steamships, enabled the West to unify the whole inhabited and habitable world, including the Americas. Babur's Farghana had been the central point of a world united by horse-traffic over the Steppe; but in Babur's lifetime the centre of the world made a sudden big jump. From the heart of the Continent it jumped to its extreme western verge, and, after hovering round Seville and Lisbon, it settled for a time in Elizabeth's England. In our own lifetime we have seen this volatile world-centre flit again from London to New York, but this shift to a still more eccentric position on the far side of the 'herring pond' is a local movement, not comparable in magnitude to the jump, in Babur's day, from the steppe-ports of Central Asia to the ocean-ports of the Atlantic. That huge jump was caused by a sudden revolution in the means of locomotion. The steppe-ports were put out of action when the ocean-going sailing-ship superseded the camel and the horse; and now that, under our eyes, the ocean-going steamship is being superseded by the aeroplane we may ask ourselves whether the centre of the world is not likely to jump again—and this time as sensationally as in the sixteenth century—under the impetus of a technological revolution that is at least as radical as the sixteenth-century substitution of da Gama's caravel for Babur's *tipuchaq*. . . .

INDEX

Index

C

Change within Tradition, 283
Ch'ao Ts'o, 177
Charanis, Peter, 251, 258
Charlemagne, Life and Times of, 188
Childe, V. Gordon, 16, 43
China as a Sea Power, 290
Christianity and the Roman Empire, 149
Chronicle of the Slavs, Helmold, 324
Cicero on Verres, 143
"City as a Center of Change: Western
    Europe and China," Murphey,
    317
Civilization:
    man's earliest, 51
    nature of, 43
    nomadism, 238
Civilization on Trial, Toynbee, 354
Civil Service Examinations, Confucian,
    272
Classical World, Expanding Horizons of
    the, 115
Commerce and Towns, Rise of, 314
Confessions of Al-Ghazzali, Field, 226
Confucianism, 169
Constantinople, 244, 266
Coon, Carlton S., 335
Cooper, A., 123
"Cooperative Ricefield Cultivation
    among the Siang Dyaks of Cen-
    tral Borneo," Provine, 95
Cross, S. H., 267
Culture Diffusion, 16
Cuneiform Tablets, 52

D

Davidson, Basil, 329, 332
Dawes, Elizabeth A. S., 247, 263
de Bary, W. T., 172

*De Profectione Ludovici VII in Orien-
    tem,* Berry, 244, 265
Douglas, D. C., 314

E

"Early Germans," Howland, 183
"Early Neolithic Village in Greece,"
    Rodden, 27
"Economic Basis of the Athenian De-
    mocracy," Jones, 126
"Economic Factors in the Decline of the
    Byzantine Empire," Charanis,
    251
Egan, Major Howard R., 349
Eginhard, 188
"Emergence of China as a Sea Power
    during the Late Sung and Early
    Yüan Periods," Lo, 290
*English Historical Documents, 1042–
    1189,* Douglas and Greenway,
    314
Epics, Indian and Greek, 102
Erman, A., 97
Essence of Chinese Civilization, Li, 176
*The Evolution of Culture; The Develop-
    ment of Civilization to the Fall
    of Rome,* White, 34

F

"Fact of African History: An Introduc-
    tion," Davidson, 329
"Fall of Lo-Yang," Waley, 178
Field, Claud, 226
Food Gatherers, Culture of the, 19
"Forgotten Empire of Antiquity," Pig-
    gott, 90

G

"General History of Virginia, New England, and the Summer Isles," 345
Gilgamesh, the Epic of, 59
Giles, Lionel, 169, 170
Gillen, F. J., 19
Gracchi, the, 136
Greenway, G. W., 314
Greenwood, L. H. G., 143

H

Hammurabi's Code, 67
Han Empire, 176
Helmold, 324
Histories of Polybius, Shuckburgh, 115
History of Thucydides, Jowett, 119
Hitti, Philip K., 214
Hodgkin, T., 329
Hodgson, M. G. S., 9
Howland, A. C., 183
Hsiung-nu, 176
Hu Shih, 298

I

Ibn Khaldun, 232
India:
    Chinese view of, seventh century A.D., 160
    Greek view of, fourth century B.C., 158
    traditional civilization of, 154
Indian Agriculturists of Virginia, 345
"Indian and Greek Epics," Antoine, 102
"Indian Culture Today," Kirpal, 154

Indian Food Gatherers of the Southwest, 349
"Indianization of China: A Case Study in Cultural Borrowing," Hu Shih, 298
India's Forgotten Civilization, 90
"Internal Strife in Byzantium during the Fourteenth Century," Charanis, 258
"In the Centre of the Map," Hodgson, 9
"Islam in West Africa," Hodgkin, 329

J

Johns, C. H. W., 67
Jones, A. M. H., 126
Jowett, Benjamin, 119

K

Kautilya's Arthashastra, Shamasastry, 163
Kirpal, P., 154
Koran, 210
Kracke, E. A., Jr., 283
Kramer, S. N., 51

L

Land, Labour and Diet in Northern Rhodesia, Richards, 32
Lattimore, O., 238
Legalism, 172
Li, Dun J., 176
Life of the Emperor Karl the Great, Eginhard, 188

W

Waley, A., 178
Ward, William A., 85
Western Cities, Role of, 316
White, Horace, 136
White, L., Jr., 309
White, L. A., 32
Wiser, W. H., and C. V., 99

Wollaston, Arthur N., 210
World History: Origins and Nature, 3
Wright, F. A., 187

Y

Yule, Sir Henry, 205, 240